GALILEO
Man of Science

GALILEO

Man of Science

EDITED BY *Ernan McMullin*

The Scholar's Bookshelf

Princeton Junction, New Jersey

Published by The Scholar's Bookshelf
51 Everett Drive, P.O. Box 179
Princeton Junction, N.J. 08550

First Scholar's Bookshelf printing, 1988

ISBN 0-945726-02-3
ISBN 0-945726-03-1 (pbk.)

Publisher's Note: This edition omits
nearly one hundred pages of appendixes
from the original publication.

Printed in the United States of America

THE AUTHORS

Silvio A. Bedini is Assistant Director of the Museum of History and Technology of the Smithsonian Institution, and author of *Ridgefield in review* (New Haven, 1958); *Early American scientific instruments and their makers* (Washington, 1964); *The Borghesi astronomical clock* (U.S. National Museum Bulletin No. 240, 1964); "The scent of time", *Trans. Amer. Phil. Soc.*, 1963; "Mechanical universe", *Trans. Amer. Phil. Soc.*, 1966.

Carl B. Boyer is Professor of Mathematics at Brooklyn College, and author of *The concepts of the calculus* (New York, 1939); *History of analytic geometry* (New York, 1956); *The rainbow: from myth to mathematics* (New York, 1959), and many articles on the history of mathematics.

Ernst Cassirer (1874–1945) was Professor of Philosophy at the University of Hamburg, and later taught at Oxford, Göteburg and Yale. He wrote *Das Erkenntnisproblem in der Philosophie und Wissenschaft der Neuen Zeit* (4 vols., 1906–1950); *Philosophie der Symbolischen Formen* (3 vols., 1923–1929), and many other books.

Eric Cochrane is Professor of History at the University of Chicago, and author of *Tradition and enlightenment in the Tuscan academies* (Chicago, 1961); "French literature and the Italian tradition in 18th century Tuscany", *Journ. Hist. Ideas*, 1962; "Machiavelli, 1940–1960", *Journ. Mod. Hist.*, 1961; "The end of the Renaissance in Florence", *Bibliothèque d'Humanisme et Renaissance*, 1965; and other essays.

I. Bernard Cohen is Professor of the History of Science at Harvard University and author of *Benjamin Franklin's experiments* (1941); *Franklin and Newton* (1956, 1966); *Birth of a new physics* (1960), and co-editor with Alexandre Koyré of a critical edition of Newton's *Principia*, forthcoming.

MICHAEL J. CROWE is an Assistant Professor of the History of Science at the University of Notre Dame, and author of *A history of vector analysis: the evolution of the idea of a vectorial system* (Notre Dame, 1967).

STILLMAN DRAKE is Professor of the History of Science at the University of Toronto, and translator into English of most of Galileo's major works, as well as author of fifteen essays, "Galileo Gleanings", in various journals.

DOMINIQUE DUBARLE, O.P. is Professor of the Philosophy of Science at the Institut Catholique of Paris, and author of *Humanisme scientifique et raison chrétienne* (Paris, 1953); *La civilization et l'atome* (Paris, 1963); *Approches d'une theologie de la science* (Paris, 1967), and many essays.

ARON GURWITSCH is Professor of Philosophy at the New School of Social Research, and author of *La théorie du champ de la conscience* (Paris, 1957); transl. as *The field of consciousness* (Pittsburgh, 1964); *Studies in phenomenology and psychology* (Evanston, 1966); and many articles on phenomenology.

A. RUPERT HALL is Professor of the History of Science and Technology at Imperial College (London), and author of *The Scientific Revolution* (London, 1954); *From Galileo to Newton* (London, 1963); and co-author with M. B. Hall of *Unpublished scientific papers of Isaac Newton* (London, 1962); *Correspondence of Henry Oldenburg* (London, vol. 1, 1965).

MARIE BOAS HALL is Reader in the History of Science and Technology at Imperial College, and author of *Robert Boyle and 17th century chemistry* (New York, 1958); *The scientific renaissance* (London, 1962), and the joint works with A. R. Hall listed above.

WILLY R. HARTNER is Professor of the History of Science at the Goethe-Universität of Frankfurt, and author of numerous essays in history of science.

ALEXANDRE KOYRÉ (1892–1964) was Director of Studies at the École Pratique des Hautes Études (Paris) and later member of the Institute for Advanced Studies at Princeton. He translated Copernicus' *De revolutionibus* (Paris, 1934), and wrote *Études Galiléennes* (Paris, 1939); *From the closed world to the infinite universe* (Baltimore, 1957); *La révolution astronomique* (Paris, 1961); *Introduction à la lecture de Platon* (Paris, 1962); *Newtonian studies* (New York, 1966), and many other works.

ERNAN MCMULLIN is Professor of Philosophy at the University of Notre Dame, editor of *The concept of matter* (Notre Dame, 1963) and author of "Galileo Galilei", *Colliers' Encyclopedia*, 1962; "Medieval and modern science: continuity or discontinuity?", *Intern. Phil. Quarterly*, 1965.

THOMAS MCTIGHE is Professor of Philosophy at Georgetown University, and author of "The meaning of the couple: *complicatio-explicatio* in Nicholas of Cusa" (*Proc. Amer. Cath. Phil. Assoc.*, 1958); "Nicholas of Cusa and Leibniz' principle of indiscernibility" (*Modern Schoolman*, 1964); "Scotus, Plato and the ontology of the bare *X*" (*Monist*, 1965); "Nicholas of Cusa as a forerunner of modern science" (*Actes du Xe Congrès Intern. Hist. Sciences*, 1964).

SERGE MOSCOVICI is Professor of the History of Science at the École Pratique des Hautes Études (Paris), and author of *L'expérience du mouvement* (Paris, 1967); "Recherches de Giovanni Battista Baliani sur le choc des corps élastiques", *Actes II Symp. Intern. Hist. Sciences, Firenze*, 1961; "Sur l'importance des rapports entre expérience et théorie en 17e siècle: la loi de Baliani", *Riv. Storia Scienza,* 1960; "Remarques sur le dialogue de Galilée: *De la force de la percussion*", *Revue Hist. Sciences,* 1963; "À propos d'une controverse entre Torricelli et Baliani" in *Mélanges A. Koyré* (Paris, 1964).

LEONARDO OLSCHKI (1885–1961) was Professor of Romance Languages at the University of Heidelberg, and later Research Associate in Oriental Languages at the University of California at Berkeley. He wrote *Die Literatur der Technik und der Angewandten Wissenschaften vom Mittelalter bis zur Renaissance in Italien,* 1922; *Galilei und sein Zeit* (Halle, 1927); *Giordano Bruno* (Halle, 1927); *Marco Polo's precursors* (New York, 1944); *The genius of Italy* (New York, 1949); and many other works.

ANGIOLO PROCISSI is Professor at the Istituto Matematico dell'Universita degli Studi at Firenze, and editor of *Anteriori Galileo,* vol. 1 of *La collezione galileiana della Biblioteca Nazionale di Firenze* (Rome, 1959).

VASCO RONCHI is Director of the Istituto Nazionale d'Ottica at Firenze, President of the Union Internationale d'Histoire et Philosophie des Sciences, and author of 18 books and more than 600 papers on pure and applied optics and the history of optics.

THOMAS B. SETTLE is Assistant Professor of History at the Polytechnic Institute of Brooklyn, and author of "An experiment in the history of science", *Science,* 1961.

EDWARD STRONG is Professor of Philosophy at the University of California at Berkeley, and author of *Procedures and metaphysics* (Berkeley, 1936); "Newton's mathematical way", *Journ. Hist. Ideas,* 1951; "William Whewell and J. S. Mill", *Journ. Hist. Ideas,* 1955; "Newtonian explications of natural philosophy", *Journ. Hist. Ideas,* 1957; "Hypotheses non fingo" in *Men and moments in the history of science* (Seattle, 1959); "Galileo on measurement" in *Homage to Galileo,* ed. by M. Kaplan (Cambridge, Mass. 1965).

PAUL TANNERY (1843–1904) was Director of Manufacture for the Manufacture des Tabacs de France. He wrote hundreds of articles in history of science (comprising seventeen volumes in the collected edition), and edited the standard modern editions of Descartes, Fermat and Diophantus.

JAMES A. WEISHEIPL, O.P. is Associate Professor of the History of Medieval Science at the Institute of Medieval Studies at the University of Toronto, editor of *The dignity of science* (Washington, 1961), and author of *Nature and gravitation* (River Forest, 1955); *The development of physical theory in the Middle Ages* (London, 1959); "The place of John Dumbleton in the Merton school", *Isis,* 1959; "*The Problemata Determinata XLII* ascribed to Albertus Magnus", *Mediev. Studies,* 1960.

PREFACE

The year 1964 may be best remembered for its centenaries—Michelangelo, Shakespeare, Galileo, and a host of lesser lights, were recalled in solemn convocation in that year. Scholars scurried by jet to Florence and Rome and Stratford and other lesser places, and penciled last-minute reasons why the world should remember someone who was born or who died in a '64. The reflections of a centenary speaker often tell us more about himself and the values of his age than they do about the person whose centenary is being celebrated. If that person is someone whose achievement is as complex and whose call on men's emotions as insistent as is Galileo's, it is likely that each new centenary will bring a new balance in the evaluation of the past, one that reflects the present at least as much as it does that past. And even the most superficial study of the multitude of Galileo centenary addresses from 1842, 1864, 1942, and now 1964 bears this out in striking fashion. The earlier addresses are for the most part eulogies; they come to honor their man, not to dissect him. They tend to take Galileo's contribution to science for granted and emphasize rather his conflict with the Church and his role in defining and symbolizing a new freedom for human inquiry.

In 1942, and even more so in 1964, the focus shifted in a most interesting way. The newspaper pieces were still routine evocations of the famous trial. But the many congresses in 1964—in Florence, Rome, Los Angeles, Rochester, Notre Dame—had other business: nearly all of the papers had to do in some way with Galileo as a scientist. There was still almost as much controversy and irreducible disagreement as there was in the old days. But now the disagreement centered around a different set of issues. And, hopefully, its resolution seems to be proceeding along less emotive lines.

Most of the essays in this volume took shape as papers delivered at the Galileo Quatercentenary Congress held at the University of Notre Dame, April 9–11, 1964. There were some special reasons for holding the Congress at Notre Dame: not only was the University beginning the celebration of the centenary of its own College of Science, but it seemed appropriate that a Catholic university should take the initiative in honoring a man whose fidelity to his Church had been so cruelly tested. After the Congress, a number of Galileo scholars (Silvio Bedini, I. Bernard Cohen, Serge Moscovici, Angiolo Procissi, Thomas Settle, Edward Strong) were asked to contribute to the centenary volume in order to fill out some aspects of Galileo's scientific achievement that had not been covered at the Congress. In addition, representative essays (none of them available in English) from four great Galileo scholars now dead (Ernst Cassirer, Alexandre Koyré, Leonardo Olschki, Paul Tannery) were included as a tribute to the generation of historians of science to which we owe more than we sometimes realize.

Thanks are due to a great many people for the part they played in bringing this volume to completion. First, to the University of Notre Dame and especially to its President, Reverend Theodore Hesburgh, C.S.C., and his Assistant, Dr. George Shuster, a special assurance of gratitude for their support of the Galileo Quatercentenary Congress and of this commemorative volume. Without a generous subsidy from the University neither project could have been carried through. Second, to the committee in charge of the Centennial of Notre Dame's College of Science, and especially its chairman, Dr. Milton Burton, and the Dean of the College, Dr. Frederick Rossini, for their support in designating this volume as a special memento to alumni and friends of the College of Science, symbolizing, hopefully, something of what the College of Science of the University of Notre Dame aspires to. Third, to the many who helped freely with their advice in planning the Congress and the commemorative volume, notably Professors Stillman Drake and I. B. Cohen. Fourth, to those who collaborated in the notable Book Exhibit connected with the Congress, and especially Dr. Michael Crowe, whose catalog will be found as an appendix See to this volume. Fifth, to the many who cooperated in the immense and below tedious task of producing the *Bibliografia Galileiana, 1940–1964*. Sixth, to the Office of Science Information Service of the National Science Foundation whose financial support made possible the printing of the *Bibliografia* as an appendix to this book. Seventh, to Mrs. Patricia Poulin, who took care of all the typing involved. Eight, to James Kowalski, who compiled the Index of Names. Lastly, to those whose support helped the editor face what at times seemed a life work.

E. McMULLIN

December 1967

Publisher's Note: In order to publish an affordable reprint edition, we have omitted nearly one hundred pages of the Appendixes that appeared in the original edition. An asterisk after the footnotes indicates that full bibliographical information can be found in the *Bibliographia Galileiana, 1940–1964* of the first edition.

CONTENTS

Part I

*Introduction
to Galileo*

I ⚙ Introduction: Galileo, man of science

ERNAN MCMULLIN

This book honors a great man who was born just four centuries ago, a man whose achievement has touched on almost all fields of human effort. Galileo was a powerful, passionate figure, a man who dominated every room and every discussion he entered. His excitement over the new world he saw opening up, and his blistering intolerance of those who would not see it as he did, break through in every page of his writings. These are infectious qualities, especially when joined with the gaiety and enormous vitality of a man who treasured every moment of life. As we read his letters we can hardly help falling into step behind his banners; we laugh with him, lock swords with his enemies, rejoice at his triumphs. His is no clean-cut world of concept and theorem, but a brawling world where Venetian senators and Medici princes and Renaissance cardinals and Aristotelian pedants clash and scheme. No place for a scientist, one might say. But the sort of place in which someone who has set himself to tearing down an age-old system of thought and replacing it with a new is likely to feel at home.

Galileo loved the fray. Not for him the laborious hours of observation of a Tycho; not for him the endless calculations and curve-fittings of a Kepler. He was a man with a vision of the way the universe had to be, and a talent for communicating that vision to others. None knew better than he that, whereas theorems have to be proved, people have to be persuaded. To someone as strongly convinced of his own rightness as Galileo was, proof is at best secondary. But when someone has a message as novel and as far-reaching as he had, the ability to persuade others of its worth is altogether vital. Most of his professional life was spent not in observing, not in calculating, not in proving, but simply in persuading. He had to convince reluctant hearers that what he had to say about Nature made far more sense than anything that had ever been said before. His historic role was to change a world view, and this demanded talents of a far more diverse order than would be required by the simple establishment of a new theory. His works are thus characterized by a vigor and an immediacy that set them apart in the annals of scientific writing. They are exuberant, brash, speculative, and wheedling by turn. Galileo had somehow to validate an entire new approach to physical knowledge. It is true that none of the constituents of this method were strictly new, but his way of deploying them turned out almost immediately to have a power that set off the new science sharply from the old.

This was the man, then, who was a legend almost in his own lifetime and who has never since ceased to light up men's imaginations. His life, his work, his death were all of a piece; there was the sort of symbolic unity about his career that sets up an immediate resonance in anyone who shares even a part of the vision that animated it. Defects in character, failures in accomplishment are overlooked; what one sees is a vast energy directed singlemindedly to the changing of history. This is the stuff of which heroes and villains and legends innumerable are made. There have been few educated people in the Western world in recent centuries for whom Galileo has not been a symbol of something or other. Such symbols are necessary for most of us, as guides in the complexities of living. But symbols come after a time to have a historical life of their own; they become opaque, and the historical events and personages from which they took their origin are more and more obscured by them. Much of the voluminous writing on Galileo—5,890 titles are listed in the *Bibliografia Galileiana*—has *used* Galileo to make a point about something or other: the nature of science, the relationship between medieval and modern thought, the tension between faith and reason, the dangers of authoritarianism, and so forth. In all this deluge of interpretation the historical Galileo has been at times almost lost from sight. Only in the past century did his scientific works and correspondence become scrutinized as worthy of attention in their own right; only in recent decades has the outline of his scientific achievement begun to emerge with some degree of clarity and objectivity.

Yet there is still a surprising amount of controversy swirling around him. This is what makes him such a fascinating figure. And there is enough haze in the historical record to make it likely that he will always remain an enigma. Historians, philosophers, scientists, novelists, playwrights can scarcely avoid seeing something of their own shadows as they peer through the haze. That a book of essays on the accomplishment of a man born four centuries ago should exhibit the divergences of interpretation that this one, for instance, does is in itself perhaps Galileo's most impressive claim to the modern reader's interest. A similar book on Boyle or on Huygens or on Gilbert or even on Descartes or Bacon would involve nowhere near the same diversity of view.

In this introductory essay we shall try to introduce the reader to the intellectual history of Galileo, to that complex of ideas and argument that leads us to title him "a man of science", perhaps even "the man of science". A general review of this kind will, it is hoped, provide a background for the more specific topics to be treated in the other essays below. Much of what is reported in this introduction scarcely needs to be said to the Galileo scholars who may pick up the book. But to other readers, whose knowledge of Galileo may be shadowy, a general outline of what makes him our "man of science" will be of some service.

The originality of Galileo's mechanics

The first historians of seventeenth-century science, the French Encyclopedists, were inclined to see the "new science" as making a clean break with the past. They knew little of Renaissance and less of medieval thought; as sons of the Enlightenment they favored unambiguous distinctions between their own age and the obviously unenlightened ones preceding it. In their view, Galileo's work marked the watershed between old and new; Galileo was portrayed by them as the pioneer of a new spirit, the father of the "new sciences" that the title of his greatest work proudly proclaimed. So great did the chasm between scholasticism and the thought of their own day appear to these writers that Galileo's science had to be conceived as virtually without antecedent, a violent creative break with all that had gone before. An additional reason for their emphasis on his originality was their unanimous adoption of him as protomartyr and patron of the popular cause of intellectual freedom. There was little of the heroic about the other seventeenth-century pioneers of science: the disgraced Lord Chancellor, the careful courtier, the psychotic Keeper of the Mint. If a patron saint were to be found for the autonomous new empirical way of thought, it had to be Galileo.

It is always easier to write in terms of discontinuity; continuity requires more documentation.[1] The requisite documentation took a long time to appear in this instance. Not until the early part of the present century was attention turned to the natural philosophers of the late medieval and Renaissance periods. Almost at once the facile assertions of two centuries began to crumble. The "revolt of the medievalists", as it has been called, was under way. Scores of forgotten *Commentaries* on the *Physics* of Aristotle were unearthed; manuscripts by unknown fourteenth- and fifteenth-century mathematicians and philosophers were edited for the first time. Duhem's great multi-volume *Système du monde*, the first volume of which was published in 1907, was the most notable fruit of the new scholarship. And it immediately stood the conventional Galilean historiography right on its head.

Duhem traced the renaissance of mechanics and statics in Western Europe in the thirteenth century and resurrected two regular "schools" of physics at the universities of Oxford and Paris in the fourteenth and early fifteenth centuries. According to him, the nominalist natural philosophers of this period constructed a mechanics that became increasingly non-Aristotelian in its leading principles. It was mathematical in method and gradually developed a motion of *"impetus"* that foreshadowed seventeenth-century ideas of momentum and inertia, besides providing the "odd-number rule" relating spaces traversed to time-intervals taken, in uniformly accelerated motion. To make things worse, when applied to free fall this rule is mathematically equivalent to the $S \propto t^2$ law which generations of historians of science were wont to describe as the chief contribution to mechanics of Galileo's *Discorsi*. If Duhem were right, it would seem that the major transitions to "modern" science occurred in the fourteenth century rather than in the seventeenth. Galileo's role would then have been to rescue the nominalist mechanics from the relative neglect into which it had fallen, due to the misguided classicism, both neo-Platonist and Aristotelian, of the Renaissance and to carry this mechanics through to its first coherent general formulation.

Much of the Galileo scholarship of the last half-century has been a response of one sort or another to Duhem's challenge.[2] Marshall Clagett's massive *Science of mechanics in the Middle Ages* (1959*) brought together a great number of the medieval sources on which Duhem had rested his case. Koyré turned his attention to Galileo's immediate predecessors in Italy—Tartaglia and Benedetti—and discovered significant analogies, as well as striking dissimilarities, between their work and his.[3] Anneliese Maier, in a series of major studies, analyzed the "nominalist" theories of mechanics and argued that they are philosophically so far removed from the mechanics of Galileo's *Discorsi* that Duhem's case is simply invalid. Perhaps the most important development in recent years has been a considerable clarification of Galileo's *own* intellectual growth between his earliest essay on mechanics, the *De motu* of 1592 (his "Pisan dynamics"), the sketches toward a new theory of mechanics made during the fruitful middle years 1597–1610 at Padua (the "Paduan mechanics"), the astronomical researches of 1609–1612 that initiated twenty years of effort in the defense and propagation of the Copernican world view, and finally the last period of summation (1633–1637), when he returned to his earlier mechanical concerns and published the great *Discorsi* of 1638. There are still many lacunae, especially in the account of the crucial Paduan period. He wrote virtually nothing for publication during that period, and many of the letters he wrote were not preserved. Nevertheless, it is now possible to reach at least some agreement on the issues surrounding Duhem's challenge to the originality of Galileo's achievement in mechanics.

A favorite way of estimating this originality has been to take the *De motu* to represent Galileo's inheritance from the past, and the distance between it and the *Discorsi* to be Galileo's personal contribution. Since the *De motu* is the sort of thing that could conceivably have been written by one of the Paris or Oxford physicists who flourished two centuries before Galileo's time, and since the *Discorsi* contains the germ of Newtonian mechanics both in its results and its methods, this mode of approach suggests that the transition from "medieval" to "modern" science was accomplished almost single-handedly by Galileo in the almost fifty years that separated his two writings on mechanics. There is much of truth in this claim, but it has to be rather carefully qualified.

Medieval background

Two rather different ways of accounting for projectile motion, a problem that Aristotelian mechanics had been so singularly unable to handle, were worked out during the later medieval period.[4] Early critics of Aristotle's theory of forced motion, such as John Philoponus (sixth century) and Francis of Marchia (fourteenth century), had suggested that the mover impresses a quality on the thrown body and that this quality (often called a *virtus impressa*) accounts causally for the continuance in motion of the projectile after it leaves the original mover. The *virtus* was thought to decay of itself, so that the natural downward motion of the body could then re-assert itself. Buridan (fifteenth century) and other Paris physicists following him spoke, on the other hand, of a quality which did not of itself tend to decay, an *"impetus"* which caused the thrown body to continue in motion, and which was gradually reduced only because of the resistances that all bodies must meet as they move. Both Francis' *virtus impressa* and Buridan's *impetus* were thought of as effects produced in the projectile by the mover; both become causes of motion in their own right.[5] But they differ from each other in three important respects: (1) *Impetus* would make a body continue forever in its imparted motion were it not to be interfered with; *virtus impressa* quickly dies out on its own. (2) *Impetus* is thought to play a part both in natural and in forced motion, indeed Buridan makes it account for the acceleration of natural fall; *virtus impressa* is introduced only to explain forced motion. (3) The magnitude of the *impetus* is said to depend on the "quantity of matter" and the speed of the moved body; no such quantification is suggested for the other.[6]

It was customary in the fourteenth century to draw a quite sharp distinction between discussions of the causes of motion and discussions of their effects, a distinction analogous to the later one between dynamics and kinematics. In kinematics, attention was focused on the problem of natural motion. Aristotle had bequeathed a rather ambiguous legacy in this domain too. He suggested that the speed of free fall is proportional to the weight of the body and inversely proportional to the resistance of the medium: $V \propto F/R$.[7] But he also held that motion is accelerated: it will quicken as the body gets nearer its natural place. Thus V is variable with time and we cannot set $V = \text{constant} \times F/R$, as the Aristotelian text might otherwise lead us to do. The point of the F/R law is to compare the speeds of two bodies of different weights, or in different media. It appears to be assumed that the F/R ratio is to be calculated for "corresponding" points in the paths of the two bodies, although how these would be determined (the lapse of a given time-interval after a common start for the two motions? the traversal of a given space by both bodies?) is not clear. Some of the earliest commentators on Aristotle (Alexander, for instance) expressed his notion of acceleration by saying that bodies move more swiftly in proportion to the distance they have fallen, suggesting the $V \propto d$ law that came to be assumed by many physicists of the later medieval period.[8] If these two proportionalities are combined, we have $V \propto d. F/R$, although no one appears to have put the two together in this way.

During the medieval period, the F/R kinematic law came in for much discussion; a host of critics, from Philoponus down to Benedetti, showed that many of its implications were unacceptable. Modifications were suggested, of which the $V \propto (F - R)$ "law" of Avempace and the $V \propto \log (F/R)$ "law" of Bradwardine are the most celebrated.[9] The basis for these suggested modifications was in all cases a kind of common-sense recourse to what "obviously happens" when bodies fall. But oddly enough no attempt was made to relate the F/R type of analysis (which could easily be taken to imply that the velocity of fall of a given body is a constant for a given medium, depending only on the weight of the body and the resistance of the medium) with the universally conceded assertion that the speed of falling bodies tends to increase indefinitely. It is almost as though the connection between the kinematics of speed and the kinematics of acceleration was overlooked.

One reason for this may have been that the relevant factors governing the kinematics of acceleration were unknown, and even more seriously, no clearly defined notion of acceleration itself was available. Thus, when someone wished to discuss the velocity of falling bodies, it was simplest to fall back on the hypothesis that it depended on F and R alone, and leave out of account the question of how it varied in time, since no way of handling this could be visualized. Yet this tended to leave the whole notion of acceleration unanalyzed, a serious *lacuna*, given that natural motion was known to be accelerated.[10] What happened in consequence was that a purely speculative mathematical investigation of accelerated motion was undertaken by the Merton school, leading to the formulation of the celebrated mean-speed theorem for uniformly accelerated motion, and later on in Paris to the odd-number rule relating the increments of distance to units of time elapsed.[11] This "speculative kinematics", as one might call it, was entirely divorced from any consideration of what actually happened in free fall, since no empirical way of measuring acceleration was available. In particular, it was not claimed that the acceleration of natural motion was uniform, so that the ingenious mathematical theorems that had been derived for uniform acceleration were never applied to the actual motion of falling bodies.

One thus finds in such later medieval writers as Oresme and Albert of Saxony a curious hybrid theory of free fall, whose kinematics is derived from the F/R law of Bradwardine and whose dynamics is based on the notion of a causal *impetus* that increases regularly with the velocity of fall. In discussions of the role of *impetus* in such motions, it was usually assumed, without proof, that the velocity of fall increases uniformly, either with the distance fallen (Albert) or, less commonly, with the time elapsed (Oresme). But this claim was not associated with the Mertonian analysis of uniform acceleration; the conceptual gulf between the dynamics of impetus and the arithmetical and geometrical *calculationes* was apparently too great to encourage analogies between the "uniform difform" motion of one and the uniformly increasing velocity of the other. In particular, no one seemed to be interested in deriving the $S \propto d$ or $S \propto t$ "laws" of the *impetus* theorists from the familiar (though complicated) mathematics of the mean speed rule.

The *De motu* of 1592

Now we can return to Galileo and explore a little more objectively the relations between his successive mechanical theories and the theories that had preceded them. The kinematics of the natural motion of fall in his Pisan *De motu* was novel in one way at least: he rejected the almost unanimous voice of earlier natural philosophers and held that falling motion is accelerated only in its initial stages; it then settles down to a uniform speed, which depends only on the relative densities of body and medium.[12] He was led to this view by his reliance on analogies with Archimedean hydrostatics, the science with which he felt most at home during those first years at Pisa. We have seen that there was an unresolved tension in the kinematic theories deriving from Aristotle: on the one hand, the F/R type of analysis suggested that the speed of fall ought to be constant, whereas it was also supposed, on different grounds, that falling motion is inherently accelerated. Galileo eliminated this tension by carrying the F/R type of analysis to its logical conclusion in term of relative densities, and by simply rejecting the supposition of a natural acceleration.

The advantage of this was that it provided a neat Archimedean arithmetic for deriving theorems about the speed of falling bodies. The disadvantage was that it simply did not square with observation, which seemed to show beyond question that falling motion *is* accelerated. Galileo solved this difficulty by supposing a gradually decreasing acceleration in the early stages of motion; as it decreases, the body takes on a uniform and characteristic velocity. But how was he to explain this in causal terms? Here he resorted to an ingenious and novel modification of the older *virtus impressa* dynamics. In this dynamics, an active quality transmitted by the mover was regarded as causally responsible for the continuance of projectile motion. Galileo postulated a similar quality in free fall also, but taken to be acting *against* the downward force of the weight. It is communicated to the body by whatever agency had held it back from falling before the movement of fall commenced. Thus the hand which holds a stone for a moment before dropping it is taken to impart an upward *virtus impressa* that lingers on and prevents the body from attaining its "natural" uniform downward velocity right away. The *virtus* is assumed to be a quickly decaying one;[13] Galileo thought that bodies attained their characteristic uniform velocity of fall rather speedily. The *impetus* notion of Buridan would clearly not have served Galileo's purpose here; had the upward impressed *virtus* been nondecaying, the falling motion would have been uniform, even from the beginning, and the theory would have been even more clearly in contradiction with the simple facts of experience.

On the other hand, the *impetus* concept would have served Galileo better than did *virtus impressa* in his discussion of inclined planes in the *De motu*. He argued that the motion of a body on a horizontal plane from which all resistances had been removed could be neither natural nor forced, and hence could be initiated by any force however small.[14] He could not go on to regard this motion as perpetual, however, because a continuing cause for the motion would be needed, and neither the original mover nor the temporary *virtus impressa* communicated by the mover to the body would suffice for this purpose. Hence the conclusion he draws from this example of a motion "neither natural nor forced" is much less interesting than the one drawn from such examples by earlier physicists of the *impetus* school, i.e., that the motion is in principle perpetual.

Transition to the *Discorsi*

This first effort of the young scientist, working with the meager materials given him by his brief training at Pisa,[15] already showed some originality in the ingenious way familiar components were put to use. But the theory was flatly inconsistent with observation, as he himself ruefully recognized and tried to account for.[16] After his move to Padua, he must have kept on re-working his mechanics to try to make it more consistent. Over the next eighteen years, a new and very different mechanics gradually took shape in his mind. We shall never be able to reconstruct the sequence of steps that led him to the *Discorsi;* he could probably not even have done so himself, although there is much he could have told us about the reading and experimenting of those years. Historians of science have tended to read their own philosophy of science into the methodology that guided those crucial and creative years; the temptation to do so is great, since the evidence available in scattered remarks in letters or in the *Dialogo* and *Discorsi* is scant and very ambiguous. Summarizing, one may say that the inspiration leading Galileo to the new mechanics has been sought in four different quarters: in his reading, in experiment, in conceptual re-formulation, in Copernicanism.

First, in his reading. Clagett, Moody, and many other historians of medi-eval science have pointed out that a teacher of natural philosophy in a uni-versity with the great tradition in that field that Padua possessed would have had to be conversant with the major variations on Aristotelian dy-namics worked by the earlier theorists of *virtus impressa* and *impetus*, besides knowing the complicated mathematics of the *calculationes* de-riving from the Merton school. It might well have occurred to Galileo in his reading of Benedetti or of Albert of Saxony that the discrepancies with observation over which he had worried in the *De motu*[17] could be elimi-nated by the introduction of an *impetus* that would provide for a con-tinuing acceleration in free fall; it would not be too difficult to abandon the central thesis of the *De motu*, the constancy of the velocity of free fall, since he had been entirely unable to find direct evidence in its support. Further, it seems most unlikely that in his reading he would not have come across the Merton mean-speed rule, which was a commonplace in sixteenth-century textbooks of natural philosophy.[18] From this, the "squared-time" law governing uniform acceleration had been derived by Oresme. Galileo mentions this law in a letter of 1604, and (incorrectly) asserts it to be derivable from the (incorrect) principle, sometimes enun-ciated, as we have seen, by writers of the *impetus* school, that velocity is proportional to distance fallen. It can scarcely be regarded as coincidental that Galileo should incorrectly conjoin two principles that had been sim-ilarly conjoined by writers of the *impetus* school.[19] He describes his postu-lated velocity-distance proportionality as "a principle completely indubit-able, which I could pose as an axiom", a proposition "very natural and evident"; it seems more likely that he had come on it in his reading than that it could have had an empirical basis in trials with inclined planes.

But such trials there almost certainly were. And that brings us to those who would emphasize the part played by observation, and even experi-ment, in arriving at the mechanics of the *Discorsi*.[20] Galileo describes ex-periments "repeated in full hundred times" demonstrating the squared-time law of fall for inclined planes, and notes that "where mathematical demonstrations are applied to natural phenomena . . . the principles once established by well-chosen experiments become the foundation of the en-tire superstructure".[21] In the *De motu*, as we have seen, the topic of in-clined planes had already been treated in some detail. Galileo discusses there the relationship between the speed of descent of a ball on a friction-less inclined plane and the angle of inclination of the plane. Using an in-genious geometrical analysis, he claims to prove that "the speeds of the same body moving on different inclinations are to each other inversely as the lengths of the oblique paths, if these entail equal vertical descents".[22]

But then he wistfully and honestly adds that "it happens that the ratios we have set down are not observed". How did he know this? It sounds as though he may have empirically tested his theorem, at least in some rough way.[23] Might he have hit on the squared-time law in doing this? It is not impossible, though, admittedly, not very likely. The fact that Galileo was no empiricist in matters of proof, and frequently asserted physical principles without seeing any necessity of testing them experimentally, need not lead us to conclude that *none* of his results were first hit on experimentally. It is true that he would never have simply set out to discover the empirical relations between two parameters, in order to proclaim the result as a law of physics.[24] This conception of scientific inquiry would not come until two centuries later, and would have been wholly foreign to Galileo's mentality. But on the other hand, it is not unthinkable that he might have seen in the inclined plane,[25] with whose vagaries he was already familiar, a way of deciding whether the Mertonian analysis of uniformly accelerated motion actually *did* apply to the motion of fall or not.

But it was clearly not enough just to read, or to observe rolling motion. Here we come to a third group of historians, led by Koyré, who stress the conceptual nature of the revolution worked by Galileo, in his life-long effort to reformulate the science of mechanics. He had to rely on the resources of dynamic and kinematic models drawn from ordinary experience, and conveyed by such loose concepts as *velocità, impeto, momento, virtù, accelerazione*. Much of the conviction with which he presents his central insights ultimately derives from a controlled metaphorical extension and clarification of the way in which we describe our everyday experiences of motion: "When one holds a stone in his hand, does he do anything but give it a force impelling it upwards equal to the power of gravity drawing it downwards? And do you not continuously impress this force upon the stone as long as you hold it in your hand?"[26] There is an implicit ontology of motion in our ordinary use of such terms as 'force' and 'resistance', but it is a very vague one. The early history of mechanics was largely a progressive sharpening of this usage, in the context of "thought-experiments" (which are simply devices for exploring the implications of one's postulations), like that used by Galileo to show that on a horizontal frictionless plane there could be no cause either of retardation or acceleration, and so the motion would be perpetual. What is sought here is logical consistency, as the conceptual network is drawn tighter and tighter, and the consideration most often relied on is some form of the principle of sufficient reason: "there is no reason why two bodies dropped *in vacuo* would fall faster if tied together than if let fall separately", and the like.

What is involved in conceptual reformation of this sort? What are its sources? Koyré liked to describe it as "Platonic"; others have called it "*a priori*"; Burtt saw in it a progression of some sort from a prior metaphysical starting point. None of these is quite adequate, although each has a valid point to make. It ought to be emphasized that the transition to the

Discorsi differed in two important respects from a "standard" piece of
scientific research of the kind we are familiar with today. Methodological
inferences from it to "standard" methodology cannot, therefore, easily be
made. It was not a matter of replacing one physical theory with another,
and justifying the second by proving a hypothetico-deductive advantage
over the first. It was a matter rather of groping toward a new way of approaching the world, a philosophy of nature in which experience would be
handled symbolically in a new way. The choice between the Aristotelian
and the Galilean philosophies of nature, or the mechanics associated with
them, was not one that could be mediated in terms of more or less successful predictions. The issue was much more fundamental than that: it
concerned the categories in which a stable knowledge of the world could
best be expressed. If Aristotle was right in stressing the superiority of the
qualitative mode of description, it would not matter if the Galilean quantization produced better predictions; when a similar situation had arisen in
medieval astronomy, the far more predictively successful "mathematical"
astronomy of Ptolemy had been set aside as of no philosophical relevance,
and the qualitatively more consistent "physical" astronomy of Aristotle
was thought to tell what "really" went on in the cosmos. The validation of Galilean mechanics had first and foremost to be a validation of the
natural philosophy in which this mechanics was embedded.[27] Only later
could scientists go on to the much simpler task of validating one specific
physical theory against another, within a mutually accepted natural philosophy. Basic disagreements in natural philosophy rarely arise today
among scientists (though instances of them are still not altogether unknown); three centuries of pragmatic success have quieted most doubts
about the propriety of the Galilean combination of quantization, idealization and experiment. Thus what passes as "scientific method" today does
not have to take account of the first and primary hurdle that the *Discorsi*
had to face.

A further difference between Galileo's task in mechanics and that of the
"standard" scientist was that advances in mechanics have, of necessity, a
much more "conceptual" character than do those in other parts of natural
science. This is even more true if dynamical issues be left aside and one
concentrates on kinematics alone, as Galileo did. In such a case, the scientist is not seeking for a new hypothetical model, strictly speaking, but
rather for a set of concepts in terms of which motion can be adequately
described. It is true that his choice of a set of descriptive concepts is not
without theoretical commitment, but at the first level, at least, the criteria
of evaluation of a new kinematics will be the completeness and consistency
of the description afforded and the aesthetic appeal of the new concept
structure itself. Theoretical advance in the domain of mechanics has much
of the conceptual about it—one thinks immediately of Newton's "Laws"
and Einstein's relativity theories; in both of these cases, it was a matter of
interdefining a set of kinematic and dynamic parameters in a consistent

and operationally satisfactory way. What is required in cases such as these is not new experimental results so much as a better mode of conceptualization of the familiar, although it is not easy to get agreement as to what constitutes a "better" mode. The conventional boundary between the scientific and the philosophic modes of analysis and validation is hard to draw in this domain; how is one to classify Newton's *General scholium* or Einstein's discussion of simultaneity?

Galileo's reformulation of some of the leading concepts of mechanics (*acceleration* and *impetus* notably) cannot properly be described as a "*a priori*" since it rested on a wide experiential basis. But it is true that, like Newton and later Einstein, his main effort in mechanics would be to rethink what he already obscurely knew. We ought to be wary, however, of labeling his methodology "Platonic" simply on this account. The tight conceptual reworking of familiar experience that we find in the *Discorsi* is far more characteristic of Aristotle's *Physics* than it is of the *Timaeus*. It is true that Galileo's analysis is radically mathematicist in intent, which allies him with Plato rather than Aristotle. It is also true that his mode of demonstration is frequently that of the Platonic dialogue; his way of eliciting concessions from Simplicio in the *Dialogo* is obviously in the tradition of the *Meno*, not of the *Posterior Analytics*. But this is the rhetoric of persuasion; it does not necessarily reveal the structure of validation that moved Galileo himself. In the last analysis, his way of relating mechanics and experience is neither Platonic nor Aristotelian, though it has clear affinities with both of these great intellectual traditions.[28]

There is no reason, either, to suppose that Galileo's mechanics derives from a prior metaphysical starting point, prior in the sense of being adopted in advance of the mechanics. As we have seen, it incorporates an implicit philosophy of nature, one which would have at least as far-reaching an effect on philosophy as the mechanics would on science. But the philosophy of nature did not really precede the mechanics; it came with it. Even though Galileo undoubtedly had from the beginning some leanings of an Archimedean sort to a mathematicist reconstruction of experience, it was in all likelihood the success of the mechanics of the *Discorsi*, by contrast with that of the *De motu*, in accounting for the phenomena of motion that led him to espouse a new approach to Nature with such conviction.

When he wrote in 1623 that the Book of Nature is written in the language of mathematics, this sentiment was assuredly neither the metaphysical starting point from which he had been led to the construction of a mathematicist mechanics, nor was it on the other hand simply a major inference from such a mechanics. Rather does it seem to have been the case during those fruitful days of reading and reflection and (probably) experimentation in Padua that metaphysics and mechanics mutually influenced each other so that one could not properly draw the arrow of inference in either direction exclusively. It is just as wrong to claim that Galileo developed his mechanics wholly without philosophical preconception as it is to suppose that there was available to him a ready-made metaphysical standpoint from which the methodology and philosophy of nature implicit in his mechanics could have been logically derived in advance.

To attribute the major part in the creative effort that led to the *Discorsi* to a single factor is, in the last analysis, unhelpful. We can be sure of one thing. All three of the factors discussed above: the influence of precursors, the generalizations based on experiment, the "armchair" conceptual reformulations, had at least *some* part in the transition to the mechanics of the *Discorsi*. In addition, some writers (notably two of the essayists below, Paul Tannery and A. R. Hall) have emphasized the special role played by Copernicanism in this transition. But before we come to examine this controverted issue, it will be necessary to trace in some detail the complex argument of the sections of the *Discorsi* that deal with the law of falling bodies.

The Paduan mechanics

We shall, for reasons to be given later, take the last section of the First Day and the whole of the Third Day of the *Discorsi* to define Galileo's "Paduan" mechanics. This mechanics is concerned with a single issue: the formulation of a law of falling bodies. The First Day sets the stage, conceptually, for the triumphant geometry of the Third. Galileo begins with bodies of the same density, but of different sizes, and shows, partly by alluding to observation ("I, who have made the test . . .") and partly by an ingenious logical analysis of the consequences of physically joining bodies that they must fall almost together. This was not a new result. But then he goes on to the case where the bodies are of different density, and his reply makes a crucial advance, in several respects, over what had been said before. He shows first that Aristotle's claim that speed is inversely proportional to density leads to logically contradictory consequences, since a body can fall in one medium, and rise in another. This disposes of the basis of Aristotle's argument that motion could not take place *in vacuo*, a step that was an indispensable logical preliminary to Galileo's own account. Then he notes that bodies of very different density fall at quite different speeds in dense media, but at almost the same speed in air. "Having observed this, I came to the conclusion that in a medium totally devoid of resistance, all bodies would fall with the same speed." Galileo was apparently guided to this result by a reflection on the observational data readily available to him, meager as they were:

> Our problem is to find out what happens to bodies of different weight moving in a medium devoid of resistance, so that the only difference in speed is that which arises from inequality of weight. Since no medium, except one entirely free from air and other bodies, be it ever so tenuous and yielding, can furnish our senses with the evidence we are looking for, and since such

a medium is not available, we shall observe what happens in the rarest and least resistant media as compared with what happens in denser and more resistant media. Because if we find as a fact that the variation of speed among bodies of different specific gravities is less and less according as the medium becomes more and more yielding, and if finally in a medium of extreme tenuity, though not a perfect vacuum, we find that in spite of great diversity of specific gravity, the difference in speed is very small and almost inappreciable, then we are justified in believing it highly probable that in a vacuum all bodies would fall with the same speed.[29]

The stages of this argument are worth noting. (1) In order to find out what effect weight has on the speed of fall, one ought to eliminate variations in other parameters, notably the density of the medium. (2) It is best to consider a medium of zero density (i.e., a vacuum) and thus eliminate the effect of the medium entirely from the analysis. (3) No such medium exists, so that since observational evidence is required, we must turn to the closest approximation to *in vacuo* fall that we can find in Nature. (4) When we do this, it appears that as the density of the medium decreases, the differences in the speed of fall of bodies of different density also decrease until they are almost inappreciable. (5) This warrants the "highly probable" extrapolation that all bodies fall at the same speed *in vacuo*, so that weight and density turn out, quite unexpectedly, to have no direct effect on speed of fall.

The consequences of this type of reasoning are very far-reaching for natural science. The notion of *nature* itself is about to be altered by it.[30] The medium is considered as an "interference"; if one is to isolate the effect of weight on fall, it apparently can be done only by conceptually eliminating the medium entirely, even though this forces one to consider a situation that admittedly does not exist in Nature, and which can be reached only on the basis of extrapolation.[31] This runs directly contrary to the entire Aristotelian tradition, within which the "natural" is what normally happens in the normal context. Since there is normally a resistant medium present, one could never arrive at any insight into nature by considering a motion that *de facto* does not occur in nature.

Furthermore, there could be no direct empirical evidence in favor of one's conclusion here, since it is reached only by logical extrapolation to a nonexistent situation. Galileo's predecessors at Paris had considered what would happen if the resistances to motion were eliminated. But it would never have occurred to them to think of the resultant of such an idealization as *natural* motion. This is, however, just what Galileo was claiming: to know what is "natural", one has to prescind from the inevitable disturbances that occur in all actual motion. What is "natural" is thus what is isolatable as a "pure" case of a concept, on the basis of a careful extrapolation from observational evidence.

It is at this point that Galileo came closest to the Platonic tradition; one is reminded, in particular, of Nicholas of Cusa who supposed that Nature is best revealed in quantitative metaphor based on ratios. But apart from the fact that Nicholas' work was virtually unknown in Galileo's day, the Platonic and the Galilean notions of idealization differed fundamentally. There was no suggestion in Plato's works of an extrapolation of a progressive and controllable sort whose relation to the empirical order would be precise. The leap from image to Form is, in Plato's view, not itself of a purely rational kind; there is the unpredictable flickering of shadow about the projection of Form in the world of sense,[32] so that science does not lie at the end of any successive approximation. Besides, it would have seemed perverse to Plato to seek a science of *motion*. Motion is, in fact, the antithesis of science; it is that which blocks scientific inquiry in the natural order. It is indeed by changing that things fall away from the perfect intelligibility of Form, so that change itself has no intrinsic structure which would allow the mind to grasp it. There was not, nor could there have been, a Platonic science of mechanics.

Nor had the neo-Platonists showed any interest in the mechanical theories of their day. When Nicholas of Cusa sought a quantitative mode of understanding nature, he sought it, characteristically, in statics and especially in the results of weighing, not in the equally mathematical *calculationes* of Merton or the F/R analyses of Paris. It is misleading, therefore, to see Galileo's mode of idealization in the *Discorsi* as a logical extension of Platonism. Even though it did rely on mathematics, and even though it did concede that the concepts of science are only imperfectly represented in the actual order of observation, the *Discorsi* is a mechanics, and its extrapolation to the "pure concept" of *in vacuo* motion is presented as logically coercive. In both of these respects it is quite remote from the *Timaeus*, and from the medieval tradition inspired by Plato.

The result of this particular piece of reasoning was almost as far-reaching in its consequences as was the methodology adopted. Because weight and density are shown to have of themselves no effect on free fall, a purely kinematic treatment of fall in terms of distance, time, velocity and acceleration is now for the first time proved to be legitimate. It had never been clear, as we have seen, how the Mertonian kinematic geometry was supposed to apply to real fall, since it was unable to take account of the nongeometric parameters of weight and density. Yet these parameters were supposed to determine the natural motion of fall, according to the F/R mode of analysis. By showing that the acceleration of fall does not depend on weight, and that the F/R factors have to be allowed for only when determining the effects of different media on fall, Galileo justified the geometrical approach to kinematics; the new mechanics he proceeds to sketch rests entirely on this assumption. He handles free fall and projectile motion in an elegant series of theorems that never mention weight, density, nor of course mass. He ends the Third Day by comparing his own axiomatic treatment of mechanics to Euclid's of geometry, and his enthusiasm soars as he reflects on "the numerous and wonderful results" that this union of mathematics and physics is bound to produce.[33]

Since the section of the First Day that we have been discussing provides

the basis for the new Galilean science, it is worth inquiring into the sort of warrant on which it rests. The author cites observations on falling bodies of different materials, both in air and in water. But his language in this section is more often that of the "thought-experiment":

> Imagine lead to be ten thousand times as heavy as air while ebony is only one thousand times as heavy . . . The lead will in air lose in speed one part in ten thousand; the ebony, one part in a thousand . . . Is it not clear, then, that a lead ball allowed to fall from a tower two hundred cubits high will outstrip an ebony ball by less than four inches? . . . Lead is twelve times as heavy as water; ivory twice as heavy. Their speeds, which when entirely un- hindered are equal, will be diminished in water, that of lead by one part in twelve, that of ivory by half . . . Employing this principle we shall, I believe, find a much closer agreement of experiment with our computation than with that of Aristotle.[34]

One wonders, with Koyré, how he could possibly have come by these numbers in any experimental way. When he says that "a ball of ivory weighs 20 ounces; an equal volume of water weighs 17 ounces; hence the speed of ivory in air bears to its speed in water the approximate ratio of 20:3",[35] the "hence" here must be understood simply as the "hence" of mathematical inference. The conclusion is surely not an empirical claim.

In general, the numbers assigned to various ratios of speeds and densities in the First Day must be understood as illustrations of the proof he is elaborating, and not as results actually obtained and here presented as part of the warrant for the theory. At the end of the section, Galileo notes the difficulties in the way of measuring the times of direct fall, and pro- poses instead to test, by means of a pendulum experiment, the principle that the times of descent are independent of weight or density. This experi- ment was almost certainly carried out as described, and the proportionality between l and t^2 was apparently discovered in the process.[36] Nevertheless, it seems safe to say that the strength of the argument of the First Day in Galileo's own mind lies in its succeeding, where all previous efforts had failed, in reducing to a consistent order a wide range of data, many of them supplied by imagination on the basis of an analogy with familiar everyday observations.

With this principle as starting point, Galileo is able to build a quasi- axiomatic mechanics using purely geometrical methods. The main results he announces are the two basic Galilean "laws of motion": the squared- time law of natural downward motion, and the parabolic law of projectile motion. Instead of the traditional F/R analysis, he eliminates both the F and R factors and in this way for the first time shows how the mathematics of the *calculatio* is to be applied to real motion. He goes on to try to com- pute what the effect of a resisting medium would be, but the simple hydro- static analogies he uses, which seem to equate the resistance of medium with its upward thrust, are seriously inaccurate, and he is forced[37] to pos- tulate that the resistance of the medium increases very sharply as the velocity of the body's fall increases. Rather ironically, this leads him back to the same law of fall that he had defended in the *De motu* forty years before:

> Under the circumstances which occur in Nature, the acceleration of any body falling from rest reaches an end. The resistance of the medium finally reduces its speed to a constant value which is thereafter maintained.[38]

This value depends only on the difference between densities of body and medium. So we are back, "in the circumstances which occur in Nature" at least, to the *De motu* dynamics.

One can see how far he is here from the conceptual framework of the *De motu*, however, despite the coincidence in the form of "law" arrived at. In the *De motu*, the initial acceleration of the motion is a temporary effect due to residual *virtus impressa;* the natural motion is the uniform downward one ultimately attained, in which the resistance of the medium plays a central and readily determinable part. In the *Discorsi*, the initially accelerated state is the nearest approximation to "natural" motion; once the effect of the resistance becomes considerable, the uniform resultant motion is no longer natural. Instead of being a "natural" factor in explaining fall, the effect of the medium is now treated as a disturbance only, something that interferes with the exact mathematical form of "natural" motion. The "natural" fall of the *Discorsi* is fall that never occurs in Nature, strictly speaking; in Nature, a medium is always present so that downward motion is necessarily impeded, "mixed".[39]

Even though Galileo does suggest a mathematical measure for such motion, the fact that he simply retains for this purpose the old $(F - R)$ type of law that he had adopted in the *De motu* reminds us once again that, unlike the earlier natural philosophers of Merton and Paris, he was really not much concerned with the "circumstances of Nature". He says elsewhere that because of the inequalities of shape and surface "rugosity", the effects of resistance on downward motion in the long run "do not submit to fixed laws and exact description".[40] Perhaps he had tried to verify his density-difference law of fall, and had to find a reason for the failure that would almost certainly have resulted. The transition from the *De motu* to the "Paduan" mechanics can clearly be seen, then, to hinge around the interpretation of the idealization involved in the conceptual analysis of *in vacuo* motion. Such analyses had been understood by Buridan and Benedetti and the young Galileo simply as useful devices for clarifying concepts. But now the product of the idealization defines "science" itself, because it tells what is actually happening behind the forbiddingly complex appearances in which the mathematically exact structures of the real are cloaked.

If the above analysis is correct, the two major theorems in the mechanics of the First and Third Days are those which state the nondependence of *in vacuo* fall on weight, and the squared-time law of fall. Both of these were certainly known before Galileo left Padua, and as we have seen, a good deal can be said of the factors that are likely to have played a role in their discovery. Was Copernicanism one of them? There has been no mention so far here of the mechanical ideas that bear directly on the Copernican hypothesis; the "Paduan" mechanics of the First and Third Days can be defined, it would seem, without any explicit reference to them. But is this really the case? In the next section, we shall try to answer this currently controverted question.

Copernicanism and the origins of the *Discorsi*

Galileo is known to have been interested in the heliocentric world view early in his career at Padua. He would have realized that the major difficulty facing it was the flagrant contradiction between it and some of the central tenets of Aristotle's physics. Not only had Aristotle provided a physical argument for the earth's being at the center of the universe, but one could also use his principles to show that objects on the surface of the earth would tend to fly off were the earth to move in any way. And it was impossible to classify the earth's alleged motion as either natural or forced, following the familiar Aristotelian dichotomy. If natural, it ought to be downward, since the earth could not be supposed to share in the circular motion proper to the incorruptible heavenly bodies; if forced, it could not be eternal, and the motion would die away.

To enforce the Copernican hypothesis, then, there was no alternative but to put forward a completely different mechanics, one in which motions could be superposed, and a commonly shared motion would produce no perceptible effects, a mechanics in which unresisted motion, no matter what its origin, would tend to continue indefinitely, one in which the elements would not be thought each to have its own proper "natural" motion. In other words, what was needed was something like the mechanics of the *Discorsi*. It seems plausible, therefore, to suppose that one of the major factors in the evolution of Galileo's views on mechanics during his Paduan years was the desire to find a mechanics to support Copernican astronomy.

But an opposite point of view is argued by Willy Hartner in his essay in this volume. It is not at all clear, he argues, that Galileo *was* a Copernican in any confirmed sense until he had begun the series of astronomical discoveries that immediately preceded his departure from Padua in 1610. In his letters and in his lectures up to 1606, the indications seem, if anything, contra-Copernican.[41] Tannery on the contrary maintains that the mechanics of the *Discorsi* was constructed specifically in defense of Copernicanism and that Galileo arrived at what Tannery regards as its two main principles (inertia and independent superposition of motions[42]) more or less by way of logical inference from a previously adopted Copernican standpoint.

In favor of Tannery's view is the remarkable interdependence of the two sides of Galileo's life effort in science, his mechanics and his astronomy. What an odd coincidence it would be if they were in fact, carried on independently! There is reason to suppose that the mechanics of the *Discorsi* was relatively complete by the time Galileo left Padua. There are scattered references in his correspondence suggesting this,[43] and the *De motu locali*, written in Latin, which forms the basis of the section on mechanics of the *Discorsi*, is attributed to a "Paduan professor", a device to indicate (so it is argued) the period from which this section comes.[44] Since this mechanics contains the essentials for a defense of Copernicanism, why should one suppose that the interrelation between the two only occurred to Galileo later on when the great debate leading up to the *Dialogo* commenced? Above all, there is Sagredo's comment at the beginning of the Fourth Day, after Salviati has shown how projectile motion is to be analyzed into two components, the horizontal component of which is to be visualized as a uniform motion on a frictionless plane:

> One cannot deny that the argument is new, subtle and conclusive, resting as it does upon this hypothesis, namely, that the horizontal motion remains uniform, that the vertical motion continues to be accelerated downwards in proportion to the square of the time, and that such motions and velocities as these combine without altering, disturbing or hindering each other, so that as the motion proceeds, the path of the projectile does not change into a different curve.[45]

Judging by this passage, it seems clear that by the time Galileo edited the *Discorsi* for publication he was well aware that the entire structure of his analysis of projectile motion in the Fourth Day depends on the principles of inertia and of superposition of motions; he also seems to have realized, to some extent at least, how far-reaching these principles were.[46] Was it not more likely that they had been arrived at on Copernican grounds (Copernicus himself had been groping toward them, and an adequate defense of Copernicanism fairly obviously demanded them), than that they should have been hit on first in terrestrial mechanics? Whatever of the principle of inertia, there was very little hint of the principle of superposition of motions in earlier mechanics; it was very difficult to break away from the first Aristotelian conviction that the imposition of one motion alters the other. If the principles derive primarily from a reflection on the implicit mechanics of Copernicanism and if they are as basic to the *Discorsi* as Galileo himself seems to suggest above, then Tannery's thesis that the mechanics of the *Discorsi* was the outcome of Galileo's early interest in Copernicanism appears well founded. Against this is, first, Hartner's case: there were frequent occasions between 1597 and 1606 when Galileo did not defend a Copernican point of view, even though a favorable opportunity for doing so presented itself. To claim that Copernicanism played the major role in shaping the mechanics he was engaged on in this period appears, therefore, somewhat implausible. Sec-

ond, it seems much more natural to situate Galileo's treatment of downward motion and specifically his squared-time law within the definite historical tradition stretching back to the schools of Paris and Oxford, rather
than to attribute it to a new and complex analysis of the mechanical pre-
requisites of the Copernican position. Third, the principles of inertia and
of relativity of motion play a surprisingly small role in the actual text of
the *Discorsi*.[47] Since the Third Day is carefully laid out in deductive
fashion, with considerable emphasis given to what Galileo thought to be
its axiomatic starting points, it cannot be overlooked that the inertial principle appeared in the first edition only in one casual scholium, a reference
that might easily have been added in 1633, when Galileo began to rework
the *De motu locali* in the light of twenty years of reflection on the Copernican problematic of the *Dialogo*.

Indeed, if one examines what we called above the "Paduan mechanics"
(the First and Third Days), it is hard to see any direct logical connection
between its analysis of *in vacuo* fall and Copernican issues. There does
not seem to be any positive reason for supposing that a Copernican conviction must have played a leading role in the original drafting of this
material, which centers after all on the question of *accelerated*, not uniform, motion.[48] On the other hand, the problem of resolving projectile
motion into analyzable components, which is the topic of the Fourth Day,
is directly relevant to the two major mechanical difficulties the Copernican hypothesis faced: the constant continuance of the earth's motion and
the nonobservability of dynamic effects of the earth's motion. Or to put
this the other way round, the two principles necessary for the solution of
these difficulties will also automatically provide a way of analyzing projectile motion.

It seems best, then, to separate the Fourth Day from the "Paduan mechanics" of fall and to suppose that it dates from Galileo's Florentine
period. There does not appear to be any direct evidence for the assumption
that it was formulated before Galileo left Padua in 1610. The fact that the
De motu locali around which the Third and Fourth Days are built is attributed to a "Paduan professor" does not necessarily imply that the
treatise was completed in Padua, and that all Galileo had to do in the year
or more he spent (1633–1634) on the redaction of the *Discorsi* in Siena
and Florence was to add some peripheral dialogue.[49] A few months before
Galileo's attention was drawn away from mechanics by his astronomical
discoveries in 1609 he wrote that he had completed his analysis of the
strength of beams and that he had just commenced the study of some questions concerning projectiles.[50] A year later, as he was preparing to leave
for Florence, he noted that there were some pieces of work he wished to
complete, notably three books on an entirely new science of motion.[51]
It seems likely that the analysis of projectile motion then initiated was
actually carried through only much later.[52]

How much later? The central result of the Fourth Day was the parabolic law of projectile motion. At the time the *Dialogo* was written, Galileo had not yet reached this theorem. In a well-known passage in the *Dialogo*, he argues that a falling body will follow a semi-circular trajectory ending at the center of the earth.[53] In arriving at this result, as we shall see in more detail in a moment, he assumes a principle of independent superposition of motions, but incorrectly takes the inertial motion to be circular. Furthermore, he is not able to give a proper demonstration of his result; he relies on a rather vague argument from "indivisibles", about whose validity he rightly shows himself to be uneasy.[54] The *Dialogo* was completed in January 1630. Two years later, Cavalieri published the correct law of projectile motion in his *Lo specchio ustorio* (Bologna 1632). Galileo was extremely upset about this, as a letter to Cesare Marsili shows:

> I cannot hide from your most excellent Lordship that the information scarcely pleased me, seeing that the first fruits of more than forty years' study, of which I had revealed a large part in close confidence to the said Father, were to be taken away from me, and I was to be deprived of that glory that I desired so ardently and that I was promising myself after such long efforts; for really my first intention, that which incited me to meditate upon motion, had been to find that line, and though I succeeded in demonstrating it, I know how much trouble I had in arriving at that conclusion.[55]

When *had* he demonstrated it? Some time between 1630 and 1632? Were it not for the fact that Cavalieri had freely conceded Galileo's priority in the discovery and even contritely offered to withdraw his book, one would wonder whether Galileo had indeed been the first to analyze correctly the implications for the analysis of projectile motion of the inertial ideas underlying Copernican astronomy. The discussions of the *Dialogo* clearly set the stage for the analysis of projectile motion, but a very notable clarification was still necessary before the geometrical precision of the Fourth Day of the *Discorsi* could be attained. It was here that the originality of the *Discorsi* most clearly showed itself; it was here that Galileo's predecessors of Paris and Oxford were most clearly superseded.

Suppose the telescope had not come to Galileo's notice in 1609; after all, it very easily might not have done. Would the Fourth Day have been written? Without his astronomical evidence for Copernicanism, would Galileo ever have gone over to unqualified support of the new astronomy? And without a strong Copernican conviction, would he have forged the mechanical principles that formed the basis of the Fourth Day? It is true, as we have seen, that these principles—the principle of inertia, at least—had antecedents that were independent of Copernicanism, and were already foreshadowed in the early *De motu*. Yet it seems doubtful that Galileo would have been able to "find that line", the hope of whose discovery, as he says, first "incited him to meditate upon motion", were it not for twenty years of arduous shaping of the Copernican argument of the *Dialogo*.

It would appear, then, that Galileo's efforts in mechanics ought to be divided into four periods, not two. There is first the Pisan dynamics of the *De motu* (1589–1592); then there is the Paduan mechanics incorporated in the account of *in vacuo* fall in the First and Third Days of the *Discorsi* (1592–1610); then comes the mechanics of the *Dialogo*, the implicit mechanics of Copernicanism that Galileo gradually elaborated over the period 1616–1632; finally there is the mechanics of projectile motion of the brief but crucial Fourth Day of the *Discorsi*, in which the resolution of composite motions is first successfully worked out (1630–1637). The last two periods together could properly be called Galileo's "Florentine mechanics" of inertial and composite motion. The periods are, of course, not sharply delimited; they have the dynamic continuity given them by a powerful and never-resting mind.

One of them we have still not seen in any detail. In order to clarify further the problem of the interrelation of mechanical and astronomical considerations in Galileo's thinking, let us turn to the Copernican argument of the *Dialogo*.

The mechanics of the *Dialogo*

The *Dialogo*, on the face of it, is concerned with the defense of an astronomical system. But it is really a polemical work of physics, as it had to be to accomplish its end. It was brought home to Galileo during the debates which followed the series of startling astronomical discoveries he announced in 1610–1613 that no one had any difficulty in accepting the Copernican theory as a mathematical device for astronomical computations. The distinction between a computational and a physical astronomy had been a familiar one from Ptolemy's time onward; it was a commonplace in medieval thought. Ptolemy's complex apparatus of epicycles obviously gave a far better account of the apparent planetary positions than did Aristotle's mathematically unworkable system of spheres. But it seemed equally obvious that to know what was "really" going on in the skies, one had to turn to the physics of Aristotle, which provided a generalized causal accounting for all movements, celestial and terrestrial. Ptolemy had not attempted to do this, and the physical artificiality of the eccentrics and epicycles of later Ptolemaic astronomy discouraged any hope that this astronomy could become the basis of, or even be harmonized with, a system of physics.

When Bellarmine urged on Galileo in 1616 the acceptance of the same computational status for Copernican astronomy that the Ptolemaic system had traditionally been assigned, he did what anyone familiar with the history of astronomy up to that time would be likely to have done. To find out what was really moving in the cosmos and why it moved, and what it meant for it to "move" in the first place, one turned to physics, not to mathematical astronomy. The circles on circles of the astronomer had not been taken by Ptolemy or his followers as physical fact; on what grounds could Copernicus claim a more privileged status for the far less physically plausible circles of *his* system?

So to physics Galileo would have to turn if he wished Copernicanism to be taken more seriously than Osiander or Bellarmine had taken it. He had two reasons for confidence in this ambitious enterprise of replacing Aristotelian cosmology with a combination of new astronomy and new physics. One was that his first researches in mechanics and hydrostatics had already provided compelling reason to question some of the most fundamental theses of Aristotle's physics; the other was that the new telescopic discoveries clearly refuted some equally fundamental principles of the Aristotelian astronomy. It was now a matter of organizing and developing these two critiques into a single crushing polemic against Aristotelian cosmology. And this is what he did in the slow and sickness-ridden years between 1616 and 1632, when the *Dialogo* was finally ready.

Aristotle constructed his theory of motion around two dichotomies: celestial versus terrestrial motion, natural versus impressed motion. Galileo set out to refute the first of these and to redefine the second. From the fact that the "natural" motion of celestial bodies seems to be circular and stable, while that of terrestrial bodies is rectilinear and temporary, Aristotle inferred that two quite different sorts of essence are involved and thus that basically different sciences are required for the two, in only one of which is the stability of mathematical description appropriate. This conclusion shaped the entire later development of Aristotelian mechanics. The First Day of the *Dialogo* is devoted to an exhaustive and careful review of the new astronomical findings; Galileo shows that they tell conclusively against the traditional celestial-terrestrial dichotomy. The heavens are clearly not immutable: new stars appear, the sun rotates and shows a pattern of changing spots, there are clear analogies between the lunar surface and that of earth, the planets are dark just as earth is, and so on. The cumulative argument is overwhelming; from now on, there can be only one mechanics, for earth and sky alike.

The discussions of the lengthy Second Day concentrate on the Aristotelian theories of natural and violent motion. Galileo shows that the traditional distinction is itself logically inconsistent and that the associated theories of natural and especially of projectile motion are at odds with the data of experience. In this way he discredits the major arguments against Copernicanism which had almost all been derived from these theories.

But in order once and for all to refute these arguments, some of which were intuitively quite persuasive, it was necessary for Galileo to formulate, implicitly at least, a mechanics of his own in which the consequences of the earth's rotation could be clearly analyzed. Three interrelated principles govern his treatment of this problem, as we have seen: the principles of superposition of motions, of relativity of motions, and of inertia. These principles define what we can legitimately call the "mechanics of the *Dialogo*". They rest on plausible analyses of mechanical concepts drawn

from everyday experience, with a frequent use of idealization (and its cor-
relative, thought-experiment) in order to isolate, and thus define, the
concepts more exactly.

The first two of the principles rely on a more direct recourse to experience than does the third. Galileo suggests experiments in support of
them, but does not think it necessary to rely on these, so great is his
confidence in the coercive character of the analysis he gives.[56] He shows
that if a stone is dropped from a moving carriage, the stone *must* share in
the motion of its carrier, and so will have two mutually perpendicular
"motions" superimposed. There is no reason, he argues, why these should
interfere with each other; their resultant can be computed, therefore, by
calculating the effect of each separately. Otherwise the motion of fall
would have to act against the original *impeto*, but this is not possible since
they are at right angles, and there is thus no retarding or helping component.[57]

The imposition of a uniform motion is thus equivalent to a change in
frame of reference. A stone dropped from a moving mast is, from the view
point of someone on shore, equivalent to a projectile thrown with the
velocity of the ship, even though someone on the ship will see the stone
falling downward. This means a uniform translation of the frame of reference can never be detectable to someone moving with the frame of reference: a superimposed uniform motion has no effect on what is going on,
from the point of view of one who shares the motion. Galileo gives a
cogent series of examples to make his conceptual point and establishes
with some degree of assurance what has come to be known as the principle
of "Galilean relativity".

This solves the major Aristotelian (and commonsense) argument
against Copernicanism: if the earth moves, why do we not notice the motion? And Galileo's answer is: as long as the motion is uniform, it will be
imperceptible to us, since all objects on the earth's surface, including us,
share in the movement. Only changes of *impeto*—and these require some
special causal agency—are perceptible:

> With respect to the earth, the tower and ourselves, all of which keep moving
> with the diurnal motion along with the [falling] stone, the diurnal move-
> ment is as if it did not exist; it remains insensible, imperceptible, and without
> any effect whatever. All that remains observable is the motion we lack; the
> drop [of the stone] to the base of the tower . . . [There is thus] a non-
> operative quality of motion among the things which share it in common.[58]

But there is an ambiguity about the "uniform" motions of which Galileo speaks. Are they rectilinear or circular or both? He asserts above that
the rotation of the earth can produce no perceptible results on its surface;
it is, he assumes, a movement with constant *impeto*, and this is apparently
enough to qualify it as the sort of "uniform" motion to which his relativity
principle applies. But this raises an obvious difficulty. Since millwheels, for

instance, can throw off objects set on their upper surface, why not the earth? Galileo tries to show (by an ingenious but altogether fallacious application of infinitesimals) that this does not happen because event the smallest *gravità* will, he argues, bend the path of surface objects enough to hold them on the earth. This is, of course, incorrect, as an analysis of the radial tension in a slingshot cord might have shown. But more important, invoking *gravità* suggests that in the case of circular motion the relativity principle alone does not suffice to prove that the motion is not perceptible from the "inside". It would seem, then, that the principle of relativity applies only where *rectilinear* uniform motions are concerned. Galileo is never definite on this point, however, because he can never quite clarify the relation between *impeto*, and the causal agencies of *gravità* and *forza*.[59] This will await Newton's Second Law. But to see this same ambiguity as it effects an even more basic issue, let us turn next to the third of the principles which define the mechanics of the *Dialogo*, the principle of inertia.

The principle of inertia

As we have already seen, Galileo's principle of inertia derives very probably from a dual source: the paradoxes of "neither-natural-nor-forced" motion of fifteenth-century dynamics and the exigencies of the Copernican thesis that the earth is in perpetual rotation. Since 1939, when Koyré argued[60] that Galileo never really succeeded in formulating the inertial principle correctly, and that the familiar label 'Galilean' for the inertial frames of modern physics is thus a misnomer, there has been a complicated and sometimes heated debate concerning the priorities to be accorded to Galileo, Descartes, Newton and others in this matter. Let us note from the beginning that there are two ways in which one might try to define the term 'inertial motion': (1) as a motion which began as "forced" but continues indefinitely, once all impeding factors are removed, (2) as a motion "under no forces", i.e., for whose stable continuance neither extrinsic not intrinsic causes need be postulated.

The first of these motions had already been discussed by the theorists of *impetus*, and their analysis had sufficed to show that a rotating earth would not need a continuing extrinsic cause for its movement; the intrinsic *impeto* would suffice.[61] Galileo spoke in much the same terms of an *impeto* that in the case of a thrown ball, for instance, "is received from the arm", and "is conserved in the ball and continues to urge it on".[62] Metaphors of this sort abound in the text of the *Dialogo*, calling into question the frequently-made claim that Galileo's *impeto* is cut off by an ontological abyss from the *impetus* of the Paris theorists. Galilean *impeto* (it is asserted) is no more than a measure of motion and has lost the Parisian connotation of force or cause. For the modern reader who grasps the full implications of Galileo's ideas on inertia this may well be so, but it is apparent—and not surprising—that Galileo did not have our insights into the matter. The traditional language he uses to describe *impeto* implies over and over that it is a quality communicated from mover to moved, playing a definite causal role in the continuation of motion, after the analogy of a force. Since he is little concerned about dynamic problems of cause, he nowhere troubles to examine the question of the causality of *impeto*, so we have to take his language at its face value.

On a few occasions it is true that he appears to treat *impeto* as no more than the measure of the velocity of a projectile. But as Drake points out, these contexts are rather special ones.[63] It is also true that the logic of his whole treatment of change of motion (acceleration) suggests that a definite resistance (either from intrinsic *gravità* or extrinsic impediment) would be required to slow down any motion once initiated, so that there would be no need to ask why a motion continues, only why it changes. There is undoubtedly a tension in the *Dialogo* between the metaphor of the *impeto* that causally explains the continuance of projectile motion and an argument-structure that suggests that the *continuance*, as such, of the motion needs no explanation. The latter thesis is sufficiently definite to allow one to recognize in the *Dialogo* the essence of Newton's First Law, though of course without the Second Law its full potentialities could not be tapped.

But, if instead of stressing perpetuity as the defining characteristic of inertial motion, one stresses its being "under no forces", the contribution of the *Dialogo* becomes less clear-cut:

> A moving body has neither a resistance nor a propensity to motion which does not approach toward or depart from the center, and in consequence no cause for diminution in the property impressed on it . . . There exist two distinct causes. Of these, heaviness (*gravità*) pertains only to the drawing of the movable body to the center and impressed force only to its being let around the center, so no occasion remains for any impediment.[64]

A new dichotomy between motion under *gravità* and impressed motion has replaced the Aristotelian dichotomy between natural and "violent" motion. According to Galileo, the movement of a body can be altered only by *gravità* or by some external agent. Consequently, if neither of these operate, the motion will be perpetual. But when *does* the *gravità* of the body operate? Since Galileo refuses rather categorically to speculate about the "how" of *gravità*,[65] he is in difficulties about the "when" also. In the passage quoted above, he assumes that *gravità* does not affect a body's motion, provided the body remains at the same distance from the center (of the earth). But does this lead to rectilinear motion or to circular motion? The analysis of movement on an inclined plane leads him to think of horizontal motion on a smooth plane as the clearest example of inertial motion. But this immediately leads to a difficulty, one which is clearly expressed by Simplicio in the *Discorsi:*

> We suppose the horizontal plane which slopes neither up nor down, to be represented by a straight line as if each point on this line were equally distant

from the center, which is not the case. For as one starts from the mid-point, he departs farther and farther from the center (of the earth) and is therefore constantly going uphill. Whence it follows that motion cannot remain uniform through any distance whatever.[66]

Those are two quite different answers one might make to this, one correct, the other incorrect. Oddly enough, Galileo makes the correct one in the *Dialogo* and the incorrect one in the *Discorsi*, even though the context of the discussion in the two works would lead one to expect the contrary. In the *Discorsi*, he incorrectly takes the disturbance due to *gravità* on such a horizontal plane to be such a small effect that it can be disregarded by a permissible idealization, akin to the idealization by which the plane itself is taken as smooth.[67] In the *Dialogo*, on the other hand, he argues that the effect of *gravità* is to bend motion that would otherwise be rectilinear into circular form. Instead of assuming the body to be moving on a plane, he turns to slingshot projectile motion:

> The circular motion of the projector impresses an *impeto* upon the projectile to move, when they separate, along the straight line tangent to the circle of motion at the point of separation . . . *The projectile would continue to move along that line if it were not inclined downward by its own weight, from which fact the line of motion derives its curvature.*[68]

This passage exhibits a relatively exact understanding of the principle of inertia. Inertial motion "under no forces" is seen to be rectilinear; once *gravità* is taken into account, however, the path becomes curved. When a body moves in a circular path around the center of the earth, even though it gets no nearer to or further from the center, according to the principle above, *gravità* is still responsible for the curvature of the path, i.e., for altering the direction of the body's motion, though not its velocity or distance from the center. In a valid sense then, *gravità* is being assumed to operate in such a motion. Even though it may be a perpetual circular motion, its "actual" perpetuity is not equivalent to the "theoretical" perpetuity of the slingshot's motion on the tangent. The latter motion is dependent on no agency whatever, whether extrinsic or intrinsic, for its form, whereas the former depends on the *gravità* of the body, and the position of the center of the earth. Galileo thus has implicitly distinguished between the two possible criteria for inertial motion mentioned earlier: perpetuity after the initial projection ceases, and absence of any causal agencies affecting the motion. Both the circular motion of a body around the center of the earth and the rectilinear motion of a body let go from a sling (if the effect of weight be left aside) satisfy the first criterion, the one that the old "neither-natural-nor-forced" approach of the *De motu* and the reliance on inclined plane analysis had led him to emphasize first. Only the rectilinear component of unresisted projectile motion satisfies the second, however. The motion of a body on a smooth horizontal plane satisfies neither.

It is curious that in the *Discorsi*, where the correct inertial principle is

implicit in the analysis of the Fourth Day, his attempts to formulate it
explicitly should still be so defective:

> Any velocity once imparted to a moving body will be rigidly maintained as
> long as the external causes of acceleration or retardation are removed, a
> condition found only on horizontal planes. In the case of planes which slope
> downwards, there is already present a cause of acceleration, while on planes
> sloping upward, there is retardation. From this it follows that motion along
> a horizontal plane is perpetual.[69]

Of course, this does *not* follow, and for reasons Galileo had already
pointed out. Admittedly this passage occurs in the Third Day, and its
wording may be a holdover from the earlier Paduan reworking of the
ideas of the *De motu*. What is more interesting about the passage is that
Galileo no longer classifies circular motion as inertial; only on planes can
the external causes of change of motion be removed.

  In the formulation found in the Fourth Day, Galileo does not seem to
realize that his inertial motion might not need a plane under it to keep it
up. The horizontal component of projectile motion is *already* an abstraction; one abstracts from *gravità* in order to define this component, i.e.,
one considers the body apart from its weight factor. A plane to hold it up
is, therefore, unnecessary. But he goes out of his way to say that the
moving body "is imagined to be a heavy one", even while in inertial motion. If the plane is taken to be limited, he notes furthermore, the body
will start falling once it passes over the edge of the plane. It is thus the
solid plane that, in this view, keeps inertial motion from turning into projectile motion. This is, of course, incorrect. For once, Galileo's technique
of idealization has failed him. He does not see that his own analysis ought
to force him to abstract from weight when considering the inertial component of projectile motion by itself. He ought to "idealize" to a weight-
less particle, and it is an inconsistency on his part not to do so; it is not just
a matter of his not yet fully grasping the nature of *gravità*. Koyré is thus
right in holding that Galileo in the explicit formulations of the principle of
inertia found in the Fourth Day of the *Discorsi* never properly abstracts
from *gravità*.

  But Koyré's wider claim that Galileo never really gets to the principle
of inertia at all has to be rejected for the two reasons we have just seen.
First, the formulation cited above from the *Dialogo does* satisfactorily abstract from *gravità*. Second, though the explicit formulations of the principle in the *Discorsi* happen to be defective, the correct form of the principle is implicit throughout the Fourth Day; the horizontal component is
defined as the part of the motion into which *gravità* does not enter. One
feels that Galileo's imagination was bound by the rocking plane that had
first given him the idea of inertial motion in the *De motu* forty years
before. Otherwise he would surely formulate the inertial principle correctly in the *Discorsi*, since it is *used* correctly there, as well as in the
"tidal" argument of the *Dialogo* (see below).

To sum up, then, three commonly made claims about Galileo and the principle of inertia seem worth disputing. One is that he at no time formulated it adequately. He was not so consistent about it as Descartes, but he *did* formulate it and use it correctly. The second is that Galileo moved from an imperfect understanding of inertia in the *Dialogo* to a clear formulation of it in the *Discorsi*. It is true that the rectilinear character of inertial motion is established in the *Discorsi*, but it is in the *Dialogo* that the *inertial* character of the motion receives its clearest formulation. Finally, the contrast often drawn on ontological grounds between Galileo's understanding of inertia and Buridan's of *impetus* is not sound. Galilean mechanics implicitly contain the beginnings of a radically new ontology of motion and causality. But Galileo was concerned to put first things first; because he had voluntarily confined himself to kinematic issues, it was unnecessary for him to reshape the causal metaphors of *impeto* that he had inherited from his teachers. He was still groping in a tangle of such terms as *'momento'*, *'velocità'*, *'forza'*, *'motù'*, *'virtù'* for the clue he needed to convert his kinematics into a dynamics. The ontological consequences of the new notion of *impeto* will not be clearly realized until Newton's *Principia* makes them explicit.

A matter of demonstration

In evaluating Galileo's contributions as a "man of science" we have dwelt primarily on his work in mechanics. But it would be odd if we were to finish this review without so much as a glance at the problem which dominated his intellectual effort during most of his later life. From 1610 to 1630, Galileo sought a way of demonstrating the truth of the Copernican claim that the earth is really in motion. There can be little doubt that he would himself have assessed the success or failure of his life's effort as a scientist largely by his success or failure in this demonstration. He took on a formidable undertaking here: the "realist" interpretation of Copernicanism, which made the motion of the earth a reality and not just a computational convenience, ran contrary to three powerful forces: the commonsense belief in the obvious stability of the earth on which we stand; the emphasis on the geocentric thesis by the orthodox Aristotelian natural philosophers of the day; the feeling on the part of many theologians that the heliocentric doctrine challenged Christian faith in the inspiration of Scripture.

Galileo's task was further complicated by the fact that he set himself what turned out to be an unrealizable goal of *demonstrating* the earth's motion, not just of showing it to be by far the most plausible hypothesis. To "save the appearances" is not enough:

> However well the astronomer might be satisfied merely as a calculator, there would be no satisfaction and peace for the astronomer as a scientist . . . (Copernicus) very well understood that although the celestial appearances might be saved by means of assumptions essentially false in nature, it would

be very much better if he could derive them from true suppositions . . . One of the arrangements must be true and the other false. Hence it is not possible within the limits of human learning that the reasons adopted by the right side should be anything less than clearly conclusive, and those opposed to them vain and ineffective.[70]

There were several reasons for his thinking that nothing less than a strict demonstration would suffice. His Aristotelian opponents believed natural philosophy to be a demonstrative science; this had been a central point in the methodology of Aristotle's *Posterior analytics*. If a purported scientific thesis were to be acceptable to the Aristotelian, it would have to be either an evident first principle (which the movement of the earth quite clearly was not), or else demonstrable from such principles. Aristotle's own geocentric thesis was thought to be satisfactorily demonstrated. An opponent who came along with a critique of the Aristotelian proof, no matter how cogent, would not get a hearing for his own thesis, if it were presented simply as a plausible hypothesis. The only way in which Galileo could have contested this requirement would have been to construct a theory of science in which the older ideal of demonstration would have been shown to be impossible of realization and a new view of scientific theory as necessarily hypothetical would have been defended.

But Galileo was far from wanting to do this. Indeed, in his theory of science, he was a thoroughgoing Aristotelian, a point that historians have until recently often overlooked.[71] His frequent use of hypothesis and what we would today call the hypothetico-deductive method of verification[72] must not mislead us into supposing that he thought science to be hypothetical or provisional in any way. For him hypothesis was only a stage along the way to science proper; it served as an aid where intuition could not divine the principles unaided. This is clearly seen in the Third Day. At the beginning of his discussion of fall, "the Author makes a single assumption" that the speed of descent of a body on an inclined plane depends only on the height of the plane. Then he describes an ingenious pendulum experiment by means of which he "hopes to increase the probability to an extent which shall be little short of a rigid demonstration". After his account of the experiment, he concludes: "Let us then for the present take this as a postulate, the absolute truth of which will be established when we find that the inferences from it correspond to and agree perfectly with experiment." [73]

Quite often, of course, Galileo has Salviati guide Simplicio to a realization that he "already knows, though perhaps without realizing it" [74] the very principle that is being sought. This Platonic twist ought not mislead us into thinking that Galileo is content with the hypothetical status that Plato assigns to physics. Galileo's dialogue proceeds from a totally different ontology; it is Platonic only in technique, not in intention, since it is meant to lead to a physical principle capable of being grasped with clarity and certainty. Galileo believes with Aristotle that implicit in our common experience of such basic natural realities as motion is a set of principles which can be disengaged by patient analysis. The entire treatment of inertial motion in the *Dialogo*, where Salviati over and over shows himself to "see" the truth without the need for experimental test, illustrates this conviction. Galileo thus found himself forced to seek a demonstrative proof for the earth's motion, though there are occasional indications in his writings that he was not wholly at ease about the propriety of this requirement.[75]

There was a second, less obvious, reason why Galileo could not have remained content with an argument that was less than demonstrative. In his *Letter to the Grand Duchess Christina*, he hesitated between two quite different views of the relation between the Bible and natural science. One series of arguments leads quite cogently (as we would now say) to the conclusion that the language used in the Bible is necessarily the common language of the time of writing, and thus that apparent scientific implications of turns of phrase such as 'the sun standing still' must be discounted. In this view, the incidental references to physical phenomena in the Bible are simply irrelevant to problems of natural science; the indirect conveying of scientific truth by the choice of the wording in which natural events are described was wholly foreign to the purposes of the Scriptural writers.

But Galileo also makes use of other arguments that lead to a totally different hermeneutics, the traditional hermeneutics of Augustine, according to whom the scientist must provide a "conclusive demonstration" of the truth of his claim before the theologian needs to ask whether an apparently conflicting passage in Scripture ought to be given a nonliteral interpretation. Galileo writes:

> I should judge that the authority of the Bible was designed to persuade men of those articles and propositions which, surpassing all human reasoning, could not be made credible by science, or by any other means than through the Holy Spirit directly. Yet even in those propositions which are not matters of faith, this authority ought to be preferred over that of all human writings which are supported only by bare assertions or probable arguments, and not set forth in a demonstrative way. This I hold to be necessary and proper to the same extent that divine wisdom surpasses all human judgement and conjecture.[76]

The Augustinian thesis was clear-cut: the insights of Revelation so far surpass ordinary human knowledge that a literal interpretation of any given Biblical passage (assuming that there are no internal stylistic grounds to suspect that metaphor or allegory is being employed) carries more weight than any human "conjecture". Only if there is a *demonstrated* human truth which conflicts with the passage as literally interpreted are we entitled to question whether the passage ought to be interpreted literally or not. To put it briefly: the lightest probability from Scripture outweighs any human conclusion, save one that is provable with certainty.

That Galileo realized the burden he was laying on himself by conceding the Augustinian view seems perfectly clear. Phrases such as 'truly demonstrated physical conclusions', 'demonstrated truths', 'points which admit of direct demonstration or unquestionable reasoning', 'manifest experience and necessary demonstrations', 'rigorous demonstration',[77] are dotted throughout the *Letter*, wherever Galileo discusses the requisites a scientific thesis must satisfy before one can properly claim that a conflicting phrase in Scripture ought be nonliterally taken. It would be extraordinary, given his redoubtable logical acumen, if he did not notice the flat contradiction between the two hermeneutical views his *Letter* defends.

The most likely explanation of the inconsistency would seem to be that the principle to which Galileo himself, with his exceptional sensitivity to matters of meaning and language, leaned was the first one above. Realizing, however, that it went contrary to the near-unanimous tradition on this issue, he compromised by juxtaposing with it the traditional view, confident in the belief that he could in any event provide the necessary demonstration of the earth's motion. Since he was already committed, as we have seen, to holding that a hypothesis did not become "science" until it was rigorously demonstrated, it may not have seemed so great a concession to him as it would to us to admit the demand voiced by Bellarmine, in the name of traditional Augustinian hermeneutics, that a strict *demonstration* be given of the earth's motion before the Scriptural passages implying the motion of the sun could be assumed to have a nonliteral import.

Nevertheless, this concession would ultimately leave Galileo in an untenable position. Instead of concentrating on the powerful reduction arguments in support of the heliocentric theory, Galileo chose to focus his attention on an ingenious but wholly unconvincing attempt to provide a strict demonstration of the earth's motion through an analysis of tidal motions. Indeed, his first choice of title for the *Dialogo* had been *On the ebb and flow of tides*, and the entire Fourth Day, the climax of the carefully constructed rhetoric of the *Dialogo*, is concerned with the unfortunate tidal argument. This made it all too easy for opponents to reject the *Dialogo* entirely; Galileo made everything hinge on an eventual *demonstration* of the earth's motion, one that even to the less scientifically endowed reader quite obviously did not come off.

Had he satisfied himself with the high degree of probability that (as we shall see in a moment) his reduction arguments undoubtedly possessed, had he defended a theory of science in which the Aristotelian ideal of rigorous demonstration was admitted to be impossible of attainment in physics, had he defended in more forthright fashion the hermeneutical view that the Biblical turns of phrase carry no weight whatever in matters of scientific analysis, so that the theologian has no right to demand a conclusive demonstration before he will concede any probability whatever to the scientific theory on the other side, Galileo would have had a cogent case. But this is to ask him to drive even further ahead of the philosophy and theology of his day than he already did, which is scarcely a reasonable wish. Had he done so would his *Dialogo* have fared any better than it did at the hands of the Church authorities?

This is not easy to answer. Urban had permitted Galileo to treat Copernicanism "hypothetically", but what he almost certainly meant by that was "as a computational fiction", the sense in which 'hypothesis' had ordinarily been taken in this context. He had, it would seem, no intention of allowing the new doctrine to be taken "hypothetically" in the modern sense of that term, i.e., as a likely account of the way things actually are, for whose truth definite evidence could be adduced.[78] Such an approach had been excluded by the misguided Index Decree of 1616, and there seems to be little reason to suppose that Urban was willing to have this decree rescinded. Since Copernicanism had been rejected in the decree as "false and altogether contrary to Holy Scripture", to present it as the most probable (or even *a* probable) theory would have contravened orthodoxy just as much as its presentation in allegedly demonstrative form.

Nevertheless, there was so much unclarity at the time about the whole notion of probability that there might well have been a considerable psychological difference between the reception afforded a dialogue in which the motion of the earth was affirmed as the most solidly supported theoretical likelihood, and one in which it was affirmed as demonstrated beyond any shadow of doubt. The latter sort of claim not only ran counter to the declared theological orthodoxy of the day, but also to the sharpening (though still rather vague) scientific awareness of the inevitably hypothetical character of physical theory generally. Most scientists among Galileo's readers were persuaded that the Copernican view had been adequately validated by the arguments of the *Dialogo*, but it is doubtful if they were any more impressed by their strictly *demonstrative* character than the theologians were.

The movement of the earth

To what extent *did* Galileo "prove" the motion of the earth, if the word 'prove' be taken in the sense in which it would be used in contemporary science? He certainly destroyed Ptolemaic astronomy, and conclusively refuted the counter arguments brought against the Copernican position. But what of his own positive case? Is it not curious that the *Dialogo* confines itself to *two* chief world systems, leaving out of account the Tychonic system? This latter was a far more serious rival to Copernicanism than was the Ptolemaic view, once the discoveries of 1610–1612 had been made. To refute Tycho, Galileo had to produce something special in the way of an argument, because the Tychonic and Copernican systems were mathematically equivalent to each other. They could be adjusted to the astronomical data equally well, so no ordinary "saving of the appearances" type of analysis could separate them.

A further difficulty arose from Galileo's own inertial mechanics. Against the Aristotelian objection that the motion ought to produce perceptible effects, he argued with great force that a generally shared motion is not perceptible to someone inside the moving system. But if this be so, how can one possibly prove the motion of the earth? Surely he is trying to have it both ways? Even more seriously, how can one even *define* motion once his principle of relativity be admitted, since it makes one inertial frame of reference as good as another? Aristotle's universe had a definable center in relation to which a purported motion could be determined to be "real" or not. But Galileo is not at all sure that the universe has a center and is pretty certain that the term 'motionless' is meaningless in its regard.[79] He wants to argue that the earth goes round the sun, but in no way wants to commit himself to proving that the sun is in some absolute sense "at rest".[80]

To this last difficulty, Galileo has the beginnings of an entirely new answer. Accelerated motions are non-inertial, and so can in principle be detected from within. Uniform inertial motions can be detected as such only from without. Since any body we choose as reference base could be an inertial system moving uniformly relative to other inertial systems, the only "rest" frame that one can fall back on is the system of the "fixed" stars, taken as a whole, with their relative motions, if any, averaged out. This will then be a "privileged" inertial frame since there is no other extrinsic frame relative to which it could be in uniform motion. If one wishes to think of it being "at rest", there is no harm in this, provided one is more careful than usual in defining rest. There are, of course, only hints of this new inertial definition in the *Dialogo*, but quite enough to let us see where Galileo's argument is leading.

The arguments one can bring for the earth's motion are, Galileo tells us, of two kinds. "Some pertain to terrestrial events without relation to the stars, and others are drawn from the appearances and observations of celestial things." [81] Only the first kind can be demonstrative; the models used in the second kind can never be shown to be unique. Yet *can* there be any strictly terrestrial or physical arguments? He commences his inquiry by saying: "Whatever motion comes to be attributed to the earth must necessarily remain imperceptible to us and as if non-existent so long as we look only at terrestrial objects." [82] This seems to rule out physical arguments. So for the moment he turns quite optimistically to the other kind of argument:

> [If the earth have a motion, it must] display itself very generally in all other visible bodies and objects which, being separate from the earth, do not take part in this movement. So the true method of investigating whether any motion can be attributed to the earth, and if so what it may be, is to observe and consider whether bodies separated from the earth exhibit some appearance of motion which belongs equally to all. For a motion which is perceived only, for example, in the moon and which does not affect Venus or Jupiter or the other stars, cannot in any way be the earth's or anything but the moon's.[83]

Nevertheless, his enthusiasm is a tempered one since he regards proofs of this sort as "merely plausible reasons. For I understand very well that one single experiment or conclusive proof to the contrary would suffice to overthrow both these and a great many other probable arguments." [84]

What validity does this sort of argument, now called a "reduction" argument, since it reduces the number of motions in a system, actually have? Does it rely on nothing more than an appeal to Occam's razor, or to some aesthetic principle of mathematical simplicity? If this is all, could not a scientist quite properly say that this has nothing to do with the "truth" of the matter, the "reality" of the motion, since real motions are not necessarily simple or aesthetically pleasing? Cannot the conventionalist or positivist maintain that there is nothing more to such decisions than convenience in computation, and that no frame of reference is ontologically sufficiently privileged to make it meaningful to assert that the earth really moves around the sun?

The answer is no. A reduction argument is *not* simply a kinematic or descriptive argument, as is often supposed. It is, in fact, a dynamic argument of a particularly cogent sort. One may refuse to "reduce" motions. But one has still to account for them dynamically; one has to provide a dynamics for one's "unreduced" system, and this may not be so easy. Take, for example, the apparent motions of the planets as seen from earth. Ptolemy accounted for them in terms of a double motion: each planet revolves in a smaller circle whose center is carried round on a larger circle. So each planet has two periods, one for its epicycle and one for its deferent circle. It was discovered that for every single planet one of these periods is exactly a year. How can we account for this? Can we leave it just as an extraordinary coincidence? Ptolemy was forced to do this. But the scientific mind is uneasy with unexplained "coincidences" of this sort and seeks a reason *why* one of the two periods of each planet is the same. A theory in which this alleged "coincidence" is rationally explained is to be preferred over one in which it remains as an unexplained brute fact.

Carrying this further, when a scientist notes that two or more bodies share a motion of this sort, two alternative hypotheses immediately suggest themselves. They may form a dynamic system of some sort so that the motions have a common cause. There may in other words be a "bond" of some sort between them which imposes a single motion on all of them. Or else the motion may be simply that of the observer himself. If it is the latter, it should be shared by *all* the bodies he sees, as a periodic component superimposed on their own "proper" motions. And "proper" motions are to be understood as motions whose dynamical and inertial laws can be specified.

Galileo finds two sets of motions, looking out from the vantage point of earth, that call out for reduction. One is the circular movement of the stars around the earth in the period of exactly one day; the stars on the ecliptic move fastest, those near the poles move slowly. The other is a component which can be separated off in the complex movement of the planets and has a period of one year. Are these to be attributed to the earth or not? The case for the diurnal rotation of the earth is much the stronger of the two. It is shared by *all* celestial bodies, although in the case of the planets it has to be separated off as a periodic component, whereas it is the only perceptible motion of the stars. Galileo gives seven reasons why the diurnal motion ought to be attributed to the earth. The basic one is that a dynamic explanation of the motion of the entire system of stars is almost impossible to conceive of: "If the heavens are fluid (as may much more reasonably be believed) so that each star roves around in it by itself, what law will regulate their motion so that as seen from the earth they shall appear as if made into a single sphere?" [85]

This is a very strong argument. The Copernican can provide not only a correct description of the "appearances", but also an inertial explanation of why the rotation of the earth continues. This single mechanical explanation is all that is needed for the entire range of "appearances", whereas the anti-Copernican cannot even begin to provide a dynamics to govern the complex motions of the stars. How do they form a single system, first of all? At distances so vast, and given their size, what could hold them together in such a rigid array? To maintain this array, some have to move much faster than others; even worse, over the centuries, it had been noticed that constellations gradually sink or rise, thus having to change their velocities and yet keep in perfect time. What an enormous force would be needed to move these great bodies, known to be far larger than the earth! How can the earth remain at rest, apparently untouched by the immense forces acting everywhere else in the universe? The periods of the planets increase as one goes outward from the sun. The stars are even more distant. If the cause for all these rotations is the same, one would expect by analogy that the period of the stars would be far slower than that of Saturn, and not shorter even than that of the moon. And so on.

One notes a common theme here. The anti-Copernican is challenged to find a *theory* to account for the appearances. It is conceded that he can *describe* them correctly. But this is not yet science. He will have to introduce all sorts of odd and incredible *ad hoc* forces to make his universe come out right. And thus he will be unable to construct an adequate dynamics of motion. This argument is cogent, and suffices to "prove" the diurnal motion of the earth in the only sense of 'prove' appropriate to the context. Even though Galileo does not yet have a dynamics of his own (so that the completion of the argument must await Newton's *Principia*), he has a sufficiently clear grasp of the causalities of motion to be able to decide what constitutes an adequate explanation and what does not. Ptolemaic astronomy wholly lacked a dynamics. Aristotelian astronomy had a dynamics of sorts, involving some sort of contact between spheres. But this dynamics had never really worked, and in any event had been in ruins since the *nova* of 1572 had shattered the solid spheres that formed the mechanical basis for the Aristotelian celestial dynamics.

The other motion of the earth posed Galileo a much less easy task. It is not shared by all other celestial bodies, so far as one can tell; it is a periodic component in planetary motion only. Simplicio is quick to point out that a parallax ought to be observed in all stellar positions if the earth really follows an enormous orbit around the sun. Salviati is forced to reply that the parallax is below the level of observation because of the great distance of the stars. A motion of translation is harder to prove than one of rotation, because the "perceptible effect" of the former on other bodies drops off with their distance, and, if the distances are not known (and Galileo could estimate them only very roughly), it may look as though the argument is somehow being rigged. Nevertheless, Galileo is able at least to dispose of the major objections to the enormous stellar distances postulated by the Copernican view.

He can then go on to show, on the basis of copious astronomical evidence, that the center of rotation of the planets must be the sun. Simplicio objects that the evidence drawn from the relative brightnesses of the planets at different times tells against this thesis. The Copernican model would make Mars, for instance, seven or eight times farther from the earth at some times than it is at other times. This ought to cause a brightness variation of sixty times, whereas in fact the observed variation is no more than a factor of four or five. Galileo deals with this objection in detail, noting admiringly that Copernicus was aware of it and yet was able "to make reason conquer sense" so thoroughly that the awkward apparent refutation was simply ignored.[86] He shows that brightness is difficult to estimate because of distortion at the eye. Using the telescope, however, something Copernicus could not fall back on, he is able to compute relative brightnesses, and they come out exactly as the Copernican model demands.

There is more than a suggestion in Galileo's argument at this point that his proof that the data on planetary brightnesses are satisfied by the Copernican model counts positively in favor of Copernicanism, and not just against the counter-arguments brought by Simplicio. Actually, as Derek Price has shown, this is not the case, since the Ptolemaic model must be made to give the same relative proportions between the maximum and the minimum distances of each planet from the earth, as the Copernican model does.[87] Admittedly this was never clear in Ptolemaic astronomy, since it was understood that the "appearances" to be saved were the angular positions of the planets only, and not their varying relative brightnesses (presumably a measure of their varying radial distances from the earth).

Galileo is, however, able to bring a powerful reduction argument against his Ptolemaic opponents. How can they possibly account for the fact that one of the two periods assigned each planet is exactly one year? What sort of dynamic explanation can be given for this? Only if the planets are united in a single dynamic system do the data become intelligible. But how can one decide whether the sun is at the center of rotation of all the planets including the earth, or whether the sun carrying the planets does not re-

volve around a central earth? In other words, how can one separate the
Copernican and the *Tychonic* models? Galileo does not mention this problem, although it must have been uppermost in the minds of many of his
scientific readers.

Admittedly, Tycho's own model, which denied also the diurnal rotation
of the earth, could easily be attacked. But what if a modified Tychonic
model be proposed, with an earth that rotates but does not revolve? Galileo himself alludes to such a view.[88] Here the Copernican thesis was at its
weakest, because the reduction argument worked much less well. Tycho
did see a single dynamic system in the sun and planets as they swung
around the earth. He did not have any unexplained coincidences of period
to cope with as the Ptolemaeans did in this context. Galileo's only resource
is to press him further as to what sort of dynamics he could provide for
such an ill-balanced system, where the heavier masses rotate rapidly around
a light one, even though their own center of rotation is not that light one.
It would obviously be difficult to find a dynamic explanation for such a
system. But not necessarily impossible, the "semi-Tychonic" might retort.
And since Galileo does not yet have his own theory of gravitational attraction to support his own choice of center of rotation, he does not have
a compelling reply.

There was one final reduction-type argument on which Galileo depended. It concerned the complicated motions of the sunspots, about
which he had amassed a great deal of data over the years. As the sun rotates
on its axis, the spots slowly move across its face, the track being more and
more curved the nearer the spot is to the sun's poles of rotation. If the
earth had two movements, one of rotation and one of revolution, these
must have a quite complicated effect on the way in which the sunspot
tracks will be observed by us. He works out in detail what this effect
would be and exclaims triumphantly when in fact it is found to be present.
To get an equivalent effect with the earth at rest, would involve attributing four independent motions to the sun:

> two around its own center, on two different axes, one of which would com-
> plete its rotation in a year, and the other in less than a month. To my mind
> such an assumption seems very difficult, almost impossible; this arises from
> having to attribute to the same solar body two other movements about the
> earth on different axes, tracing out the ecliptic in a year with one of these,
> and with the other forming spirals or circles, one a day.[89]

Galileo is *not* saying (as some modern commentators have supposed)
that the observed appearances could not be saved except by having the
earth in motion. He knows perfectly well that motions can be described
in *any* frame of reference; even though we have here an extremely complicated system where two spheres are rotating and one is revolving
around the other, the observed movement of spots on one of them can be
described from whatever vantage point we choose. A purely *kinematic*

reduction argument is impossible in such contexts: it is never possible to show that the data cannot even be correctly *described* from any frame of reference within the system. But to prove this would take us too far afield at this stage.[90]

Galileo is not, therefore, relying on any such claim as a reading of the text will show. He is saying once again that a *dynamics* for the imputed quadruple motion of the sun is not, and is never likely to be, available, whereas a simple dynamic analysis is known for the Copernican alternative. The anti-Copernican will have to explain why, for example, two of the motions he imputes to the sun have exactly the same period of a year; he can call on inertial ideas perhaps to explain the continuance of the dual rotatory motion.[91] But above all, Galileo is relying in this instance on a hypothetico-deductive type of validation. He has a hypothesis, with strong evidence in its support from elsewhere. Now he applies it to a completely new domain of phenomena. And its predictions are verified down to the last detail. To say that another model *might* be found to do this is pretty unconvincing to a scientist in such a case.[92]

Finally, we come to the famous Fourth Day of the *Dialogo*, the "demonstration" on which Galileo rested his hopes. Attempts have been made in modern times, most recently by Harold Burstyn,[93] to attribute some sort of probative force to this argument, but they have not been notably successful. Galileo tried to show that the tides could be explained by two major factors: the character of the individual sea basin or sea coast (depth, length, period of natural oscillation, etc.) and the double movement of the earth.[94] The first factor accounts for the notably different tidal phenomena in different places. The second factor is supposed to account for the periodic character of the tides.[95] Now the tides were known from antiquity to have a triple period. The basic period of ebb and flow is a little over twelve hours, so that there are two tides (in most places) approximately every day. Each month the size of the tides varies, and there is also a biennial size effect occurring at the solstices and equinoxes. The first two of these effects had been associated with the moon's motion long before Galileo's day; the third was associated with the position of the sun.

Galileo rejected the attraction of the moon as a partial explanation, calling it a "vain fantasy". But how could he hold for perceptible effects of the earth's motion on water when he had rejected them in the case of air and all other phenomena on the earth's surface? Had he not attributed a circular inertia to stones on towers and ships? In the Fourth Day, he correctly takes the motion of a point on the surface of the earth to be doubly accelerated, corresponding to the two motions of the earth, neither of which is truly inertial. Had he conceded this in the Second Day, he would have seen that the rotation of the earth *could* throw off bodies on its surface along a tangent, were it to be rapid enough; he would also have realized that to concede this would not damage his main case, which was that the earth's motions, being approximately inertial, would not cause gross *differential* (i.e., two perceptible) effects among the bodies on the earth's surface.

Now it is perfectly correct that the dual motion of the earth *does* have an effect on the tides, a "tide of reaction" on the side of the earth away from the *sun*. But this diurnal tide is not identical with the tide on the side of the earth away from the *moon*. Their periods are different. It is not enough to show that Galileo is perceptive in his remarks about the effect of local peculiarities on tides and that he is correct in arguing that the earth's non-inertial motions affect the seas.[96] One would have to show either that he separates off this latter effect and gives direct evidence of its presence, or else show that this effect was entirely responsible for the periodic character of the tides. Galileo attempted to do the latter, but naturally was unable to do so, since his motion effect is not a principal cause of the tidal periods. By excluding lunar and solar attractions, a move with which we could well sympathize, he thus made it difficult for his theory even to get a hearing, since the connection of the time of the semi-diurnal tide with the moon's position was far too well established to allow it to be set aside.

One last note should be added to our account of the Galilean argument for the motion of the earth. Is it true, as has so often been asserted, that in the light of contemporary relativistic principles the Galilean claim that the "earth really moves around the sun" no longer makes sense and that the Copernican and Ptolemaic (or more correctly Tychonic) models can now be taken as equivalent? As this story is sometimes told, there is a real note of pathos about the way Galileo's herculean efforts have all come to naught in the trackless space-time of general relativity.

The assertion is simply erroneous. Relativity theory, in one sense, is misnamed. It does not "make all motion relative" in some sense that excludes inertial systems entirely. It does not argue for a "relativity" of accelerations, as V. A. Fok, the Russian physicist who has written more on this topic of "Einstein and Galileo" than anyone else has, has reminded us.[97] But instead of launching into a technical account of the issue, let us content ourselves with a very simple Galilean dialogue in which we ask our supposed "relativist" what would someone in a spaceship launched outward from earth see as he receded from the solar system? Would he see the planets revolving around the sun or not? Even though he would share in the earth's dual motions at the moment of impact, from then onward inertial principles take over. Unless he were to ascribe to the spaceship a spiral orbit which would have to be corrected for, he will see the earth in an elliptical orbit around the center of gravity of the solar system. He *could*, of course, imagine an orbit for the spaceship which, when corrected for, would make the sun go in an ellipse about the earth. But this brings us back to a reduction argument once again: in such a case, he will have to introduce all sorts of special forces and will find a general theory of dynamics correspondingly hard to formulate.

Concluding unscientific postscript

We have tried in this chapter to present the main outlines of the system of thought and argument that has led men for three centuries to regard Galileo as a great man of science. We have said little of those wider human issues which give Galileo's life and achievement a unique significance in the story of human effort. These are perhaps best left to the playwright, to the political philosopher, to the historical novelist. There are large gaps in the historical record, more than enough room for the creative imagination of poet or moralist to make his own point. Of course, his point will be primarily about man and only secondarily about Galileo. And so the differences may be difficult to adjudicate. When a de Santillana or a Koestler evokes with consummate literary skill the intrigues and battles and weaknesses and conquests of long ago, one leaves the scene saddened, exalted, angry, aghast, jubilant. But in this essay, and in the book it introduces, we have tried to stay in the realm of ideas that make their way independently of the human qualities and human histories of their inventors, ideas today called "scientific" whose warrant is not a moral or a political one. Yet by voluntarily restricting ourselves in this way to a less colorful arena we would never want to lose sight of the fact that Galileo's magnificent effort to move the earth has always had and will always have an even greater power to move men.

NOTES

1. See my essay, "Medieval and modern science: continuity or discontinuity", *Intern. Philos. Quarterly*, 5, 1965, 103–129.

2. See the essay by J. A. Weisheipl below. For a quite different estimate of the Duhem thesis, see E. A. Moody, "Galileo, and his precursors" in *Galileo reappraised*, ed. by C. L. Golino, Los Angeles, 1966, pp. 23–43. See also E. J. Dijksterhuis, *The mechanization of the world-picture*, Oxford, 1961, pp. 175–184, 333–358.

3. His essay on Benedetti will be found below.

4. See Moody, *op. cit.* Clagett finds traces of both in earlier Arabic writers, Avicenna and Abu 'l-Barakat (*op. cit.*, pp. 510–514).

5. It should not be thought that the terms '*virtus impressa*' and '*impetus*' were consistently and carefully used in these two different senses. The same author will freely move from one term to the other; *impetus* will often be described in the Paris school as a *virtus impressa*. It might be more correct to distinguish the two notions by special labels such as 'temporary' *virtus* and 'nondecaying' *virtus*.

6. A further difference of a more elusive sort comes from Buridan's close identification of *impetus* with the actual movement of the body. In free fall, "because the movement becomes swifter, therefore the *impetus* also becomes greater and stronger" (*De Coelo*, quoted in Clagett, *op. cit.*, p. 551). Though

impetus is still thought of as a sort of in-dwelling force or cause, it is no longer such a difficult step (especially with the assistance of the nominalist critique of the metaphysics of causes and qualities) to identify it simply with the movement which is its measure; *virtus impressa*, which is not linked in this way with the observed motion, would not lend itself to any such reduction.

7. It must be emphasized that Aristotle did not possess the concepts of velocity or acceleration, so that expressing his theory in modern terms risks anachronism. Their use can be justified only insofar as they are taken without the precision given them in later mechanics.

8. Clagett, *op. cit.*, pp. 545, 555.

9. Once again, we must remember that the use of modern mathematical notation is permissible here only if one keeps in mind that the original expression of the "laws" was a vague verbal one. The $V \propto \log (F/R)$ translation of Bradwardine's complicated language says much more than the original did.

10. As early as Strato (third century B.C.), this claim was based on the fact that a stone dropped from a height makes a greater impact than one dropped from a short distance.

11. First formulated, so far as we know, by Oresme in his discussion of the "latitude of qualities". See Clagett, *op. cit.*, chs. 5 and 6, and "Some novel trends in the science of the fourteenth century," in *Art, science and history in the Renaissance*, ed. by Charles S. Singleton, Baltimore, 1968.

12. In making the velocity depend on relative densities in the way he did, he may have been influenced by Benedetti. (See the essay by A. Koyré below.) But Galileo's theory differed basically from that of Benedetti, who utilized a permanent *impetus*, not a temporary *virtus*, and who held free fall to be continually accelerating, with *impetus* as a causal factor acting downward, not upward as Galileo had it. Koyré (*Études Galiléennes, 1*, pp. 58–60) emphasizes how unusual Galileo's denial of the accelerated character of natural motion was, and yet how much more consistent it was with the notion of *virtus impressa*.

13. Galileo's teacher at Pisa, Buanamici, defended the view that the *virtus* communicated by a mover tends of itself to decay. It is quite possible that Galileo did not encounter Buridan's notion of nondecaying *impetus* until he went to Padua.

14. *De motu*, pp. 66–68. Galileo notes that since a plane can touch a sphere at only one point, a body will be moving "up" once it leaves that point. Hence his analysis does not apply to bodies on the surface of the earth. (Another reason, he says, that it does not apply is that it is impossible in practice to eliminate all resistances on a plane.) This leads him to transfer his "neither-natural-nor-forced" analysis to circular motion around the center of the universe.

15. The *De motu* does not testify to much direct acquaintance with medieval sources. Aristotle and Simplicius are quoted often; Borri and Pereira are referred to now and then. It seems likely that Galileo was relying heavily on the enormous compilation of texts by Buanamici.

16. See the essay by T. Settle below.

17. *Ibid.*

18. "I think it can hardly be doubted that Galileo obtained both the (mean-speed) theorem and the essentials of its proof from the medieval Paris-Oxford tradition, although the exact sources he used are not known." M. Clagett, *The science of mechanics in the Middle Ages*, 1959,* p. 346.

19. I. B. Cohen has shown how anyone using the Mertonian mode of analysis would very easily jump to the velocity-distance proportionality, because of an implicit confusion in this analysis between what we would call today space integrals and time integrals ("Galileo's rejection . . .", 1956*).

20. One might mention Drake, Settle and L. Geymonat. (See the latter's *Galileo Galilei*, New York, 1965, p. 185.)

21. *Discorsi*, pp. 179, 178.

22. *De motu*, p. 68.

23. One might also note that in *Le meccaniche*, a manuscript on machines probably written early in his Paduan stay, he analyzes the screw in terms of the inclined plane, and arrives at a substantially correct law relating the forces necessary to move bodies up frictionless planes of different inclinations. (See *Le meccaniche*, pp. 169–177.)

24. One recalls Mach's famous attempt to cast him as a proto-Machian who "investigated and established, wholly without preconceived opinions, the actual facts of falling" (*Science of mechanics*, McCormack transl., London, 1893, p. 140.) It is safe to say that no historian or philosopher today would feel easy with *this* interpretation of what happened in Padua!

25. And also the pendulum. He is particularly emphatic in the *Discorsi* in presenting an ingenious pendulum experiment in support of the basic assumption that the speed of a body on the inclined plane depends only on the perpendicular distance fallen. This is first presented as "plausible", then: "I hope by experiment to increase the probability to an extent which shall be little short of a rigid demonstration . . . This experiment leaves no room for doubt as to the truth of our supposition" (pp. 170–1). It is hard to discount such statements as these entirely, even though we know that in other contexts Galileo felt so sure of the accuracy of his conceptual analysis that he felt this sort of recourse to experiment to be unnecessary.

26. *Discorsi*, p. 166.

27. This must, however, be qualified in one important respect. It was precisely with Galileo that the mode of validation of a philosophy of nature began to shift in a highly significant way. Before his time, the criteria of a philosophy of nature were to be found in its harmony with a metaphysics and a theory of knowledge. The methodology prescribed for natural science in the *Posterior analytics* and in the myriad medieval commentaries on this work was not derived from a study of the actual methodological exigencies of the natural sciences of the day. Rather was it an ideal based on a theory of what human knowing *ought* to be able to attain in a world of essences connatural with it. The shift that most clearly defines the "Scientific Revolution" as a "revolution" is the implicit shift in the validation of a proposed methodology for science away from a metaphysics to a relatively pragmatic norm based on the descriptive and

predictive adequacy of the natural science inspired by the methodology. It is a shift from "downward seepage" to "upward seepage" in the vital second-level domain of validating modes of validation. This shift is still only in its earliest stages with Galileo, and will not be complete until Newton, or even, to be exact, until our own century. See my essay: "Empiricism and the Scientific Revolution", in *Art, science, and history in the Renaissance, supra.*

28. See my "Empiricism and the Scientific Revolution", *op. cit.*

29. *Discorsi*, p. 72.

30. See the essay by A. Gurwitsch below.

31. See the essay by A. R. Hall below.

32. See T. McTighe's article below.

33. *Discorsi*, p. 243.

34. *Discorsi*, pp. 75–76. The "principle" he speaks of seems to be that $V_1/V_2 = (d_1 - d_0)/(d_2 - d_0)$ where d_0 is the density of the medium. This is equivalent to the classical $F - R$ law, going back to Avempace, enunciated in Galileo's earlier *De motu*. See below.

35. *Discorsi*, p. 77.

36. There is some analogy between this law, and the squared-time law of free fall, but the l in the two cases is different, and the theoretical relation between the two is not worked out in the *Discorsi*. From references in Galileo's correspondence we can be fairly sure that the pendulum law was known empirically long before it could be "demonstrated", i.e., derived theoretically. This may well be one instance where Galileo hit on an important mechanical "law" as the result, not of theorizing, but of a series of experiments whose outcome was not known in advance.

37. *Discorsi*, p. 50.

38. *Discorsi*, p. 94. He supposes this terminal velocity to be very rapidly attained, even in air. No matter from what height a cannonball be dropped he says, it could not, because of air resistance, attain the speed it would from a gun muzzle.

39. Although Galileo uses the phrase 'natural motion' in both the *Dialogo* and the *Discorsi*, it is not clear what he means by it in his own mechanics. In an *ad hominem* passage of the *Dialogo* (pp. 131 135), he argues that rectilinear motion cannot be natural. In the *Discorsi*, however, natural motion appears to be motion due to *gravità* alone. If the motion be in a resisting medium, would it still be "natural"? He conceives of resistance as an extrinsic force, alien to the scientific consideration of fall. Yet he speaks of *resisted* motion as the only sort that occurs "in Nature". And he usually associates 'natural' with 'accelerated', which once again would suggest that motion in a resisting medium, being ultimately non-accelerated, would not count as "natural". But one can see that the term has lost most of its significance for him; we are more than half-way to Newton's *Principia*, where the distinction between "natural" and "non-natural" motions vanishes altogether.

40. *Discorsi*, p. 252.

41. "The greatest physicist of his time, in the decisive years in which he was laying the foundations of a new dynamics, proved a loyal Aristotelian in the field of astronomy." Hartner, p. 186, this volume.

42. "The principle that the effect of a force does not depend on the prior state of motion of the body acted upon"; see Tannery, p. 174, this volume.

43. See A. R. Hall, "Galileo and the science of motion", *Brit. Journ. Hist. Soc.*, 2, 1964, 185–199.

44. See E. J. Dijksterhuis, *op. cit.*, p. 343.

45. *Discorsi*, p. 250.

46. However, one might question Geymonat's assertion (based on the passage quoted above) that Galileo clearly recognized the inertial principle "as the point of departure for his principle of relativity" and that he attributed "a decisive importance to the connection" between the two principles, this being the "truly notable advance" of the *Discorsi* over the *Dialogo* (*op. cit.*, pp. 176–177). There do not seem to be adequate grounds in the text for these claims; as we shall see in a moment, it is doubtful whether there *is* a "notable advance" in regard to the inertial and relativity principles between the *Dialogo* and the *Discorsi*.

47. The inertial principle appears explicitly in only a few passages: a scholium to Proposition XXIII of the Third Day, a scholium added (in the second ed.) to corollary II of Proposition II, a cross-reference at the beginning of the Fourth Day, and finally the brief passage from the Fourth Day quoted above.

48. The brief section on uniform motion at the beginning of the Third Day might well have incorporated a reference to inertial ideas, but in fact it did not.

49. Since the first part of the *De motu locali* had almost certainly been completed in Padua, it is natural that the remainder of it (the technical section of the Fourth Day) would have been given the same literary form, no matter when it was written. It is also worth noting that Galileo was anxious to claim priority for his discovery of the parabolic law of projectile motion (see below). Inserting it in a treatise by a "Paduan professor", most of which clearly dated back more than twenty years, would have been a convenient literary device for reinforcing his claim.

50. Letter to Antonio de'Medici, February 11, 1609.

51. Letter to Belisario Vinta, May 7, 1610.

52. Antonio Favaro asserts that much remained to be done on the substance of the *Discorsi* as late as 1633 (Preface to the Crew–de Salvio translation).

53. *Dialogo*, pp. 165–167. See Drake's useful footnote to this passage.

54. "I think it very probable . . . If the line described by a falling body is not this, it is very near to it." *Dialogo*, pp. 165, 167.

55. Letter of September 11, 1632, translated in R. Dugas, *Mechanics in the seventeenth century*, 1958*, p. 75. It is significant that Galileo should regard the parabolic law, rather than the law of free fall, as the primary result of his "meditations on mechanics".

56. "Without experiment, I am sure that the effect (dropping a stone from the mast of a moving ship) will happen as I tell you, because it must happen that way; and I might add that you yourself also know that it cannot happen otherwise . . . But I am so handy at picking people's brains that I shall make you confess this in spite of yourself." *Dialogo*, p. 145.

57. This point is left implicit in the *Dialogo*, but can be immediately inferred from the arguments used there.

58. *Dialogo*, p. 171.

59. The same ambiguity can be seen in the word 'motion', as Galileo uses it: "Two motions come under our consideration: a motion of projection . . . following the tangent, and another of downward tendency . . . along the radius to the center" (*Dialogo*, p. 196). But these are "motions" in very different senses: in one, there is zero acceleration and a finite velocity along the tangent, while in the other, zero velocity and a finite acceleration along the radius. So 'motion' is radically equivocal here. Had Galileo had the mathematical techniques needed to untangle this particular knot, he might have realized that a body can be accelerated even when its velocity is zero, and this might have led him to see how *gravità* can bring about results even when the distance of the body from the center of force does not alter. See the next section.

60. In his *Galilée et la loi d'inertie*, Paris, 1939.

61. E. A. Moody challenges A. Maier's contention that Buridan did not really maintain the perpetuity of such motions. See his "Galileo, and his precursors", p. 32.

62. *Dialogo*, p. 156. For Galileo's causal notion of *impeto*, see Moscovici, p. 447 below.

63. *Dialogo*, p. 24.

64. *Dialogo*, p. 149.

65. *Dialogo*, p. 234.

66. *Discorsi*, pp. 250–251.

67. "I grant that these conclusions proved in the abstract will be different when applied in the concrete, so that neither will the horizontal motion be uniform . . . nor the path of the projectile a parabola. But on the other hand I ask you not to begrudge our Author what other eminent men have assumed, even if not strictly true . . . Archimedes in his Mechanics . . . takes for granted that the beam of a balance . . . is a straight line, every point of which is equidistant from the center (of the earth) . . . When we wish to apply our proven conclusions to distances which, though finite, are very large, it is necessary for us to infer on the basis of demonstrated truth, what correction is to be made for the fact that our distance from the center of the earth is not really infinite, but merely very great in comparison with the small dimensions of the apparatus" (*Discorsi*, pp. 251–252). This does *not* answer Simplicio's objection.

68. *Dialogo*, p. 193. Italics mine.

69. *Discorsi*, p. 215.

70. *Dialogo*, pp. 341, 356.

71. This is documented in my "Empiricism and the Scientific Revolution", *supra*. See also A. C. Crombie, "Galileo's conception of scientific truth", 1955*; R. Blake *et al.*, *Theories of scientific method*, 1960*, chap. 1; E. Grant, "Late medieval thought . . .", 1962*; and T. McTighe's essay below.

72. A particularly good example of this is the lengthy discussion of the nature of the lunar surface in the First Day of the *Dialogo*. He assumes to be similar to that of the earth, and then tests numerous consequences that would follow from this.

73. *Discorsi*, pp. 169, 170, 172. On the basis of this and similar passages, Crombie sums up: "In all this an Aristotelian type of intuition was paramount. Intellectual intuition, abstraction and mathematical analysis reached hypothetical possibilities; experiment was necessary to eliminate false hypotheses among these and to identify and verify the true one. Galileo could not have stated more explicitly his conviction that an hypothesis verified in this manner was an absolute truth, a verified intuitive insight into the details of the real structure of the physical world", *op. cit.*, p. 137.

74. *Dialogo*, p. 12. See also the passage cited in note 56.

75. Around 1616, in a comment on Bellarmine's letter to Foscarini, before Galileo had begun work in earnest on the Copernican problem, he wrote: "If these men (the Copernicans) are only ninety percent right, then they are defeated; but when nearly everything the philosophers and astronomers say on the other side is proved to be quite false . . . the (Copernican) side should not be deprecated or called paradoxical simply because it cannot be completely proved. . . . It is true that to prove that the appearances may be saved with the motion of the earth . . . is not the same as to prove this theory true in nature; but it is equally true, or even more so, that the commonly accepted system cannot give reasons for those appearances. That system is undoubtedly false, just as . . . this one may be true. And no greater truth may or should be sought in a theory than that it corresponds with all the particular appearances" (Drake, *Discoveries and opinions of Galileo*, 1957*, p. 169).

The positivism of this last remark is so much at variance with the methodology of the *Dialogo* and the *Discorsi* that it ought not be taken too seriously. Yet it is worth noting that there is a tension in Galileo's writings between two rather different conceptions of "science": according to one, science rests on principles seen to be implicit in ordinary experience and is this sense "necessary"; according to the other, science is reached through hypotheses whose implications have been sufficiently explored experimentally to convince us that alternative hypotheses can be ignored. The latter view of science is empiricist, the former rationalist; the latter easily leads to the positivistic notion of scientific truth implicit in Galileo's remark about the "appearances".

76. Drake, *Discoveries and opinions of Galileo*, p. 182.

77. *Op. cit.*, pp. 194, 206, 208, 209, 197.

78. No record was made of the fateful interviews between Urban and Galileo in 1624, but the instructions noted down by the censor of the *Dialogo* describe the topic as "the mathematical consideration of the Copernican position concerning the motion of the earth, so as to prove that except for the revelation of God and Holy Writ, it would be possible to save the appearances with that doctrine . . . The absolute truth should never be conceded to that position, only the hypothetical" (Transl. in G. de Santillana, *The crime of Galileo*, 1955*, p. 317).

79. The most he will say is that "since all the planetary orbs move around the sun as center, it seems most reasonable for the state of rest to belong to the sun rather than to the earth" (*Dialogo*, p. 326). "If any center may be assigned to the universe, we shall rather find the sun to be placed there" (p. 33).

80. In one remarkable passage (*Dialogo*, p. 453), he says that "the annual move-

ment of the earth in its orbit along the ecliptic is not uniform and that its irregularity derives from the moon and has its periods monthly". He appears to have in mind that the point that describes the smooth circular orbit around the sun is not the center of the earth but the center of the earth-moon system. Would he have said that the earth and sun form a dynamic system of the same kind? Even though he repudiates attraction as an "occult quality", and "idle imagining" (*Dialogo*, p. 445), he does (not very consistently) speak of "the force which moves the earth and moon around the sun"; he supposes it to weaken with distance (p. 453) and suggests that it is analogous with whatever it is "that moves earthly things downward" (p. 234). This comes close to making *gravità* a mutual force between all bodies, as Newton later would, in which case the sun too will be in motion around the common center of the earth-sun system. However, Galileo never does say anything explicitly about the effects of the planets on the sun.

81. *Dialogo*, p. 125.

82. *Op. cit.*, p. 114.

83. *Op. cit.*, p. 114.

84. *Op. cit.*, p. 122.

85. *Op. cit.*, p. 120.

86. His enthusiasm for Copernicus in this instance is not altogether easy to reconcile with his intolerance of those of his own opponents who seem to do exactly what Copernicus did, ignore awkward facts. Indeed, he himself often insists on the epistemological primacy of the test of experience, a "single experiment" being enough, he exclaims, to overthrow even the most probable hypothesis (*op. cit.*, p. 122). This illustrates once again the futility of trying to find a single unambiguous epistemology of science in his work. He is at the great epistemological crossroads in the history of science; almost any view can be documented by an appeal to carefully chosen passages in his work. But the truth is that he does *not* have a worked-out consistent theory of evidence. But there is the beginnings of one showing, still hesitantly, not so much in what he *says* about science as in what he *does* as a scientist. See my "Empiricism and the Scientific Revolution", *supra*.

87. If it did not, it would not arrive at the Copernican (i.e., the correct) latitudes and longitudes for the planets either. "Contra-Copernicus", in *Critical problems in the history of science*, 1962*, pp. 197–218.

88. *Op. cit.*, p. 444.

89. *Op. cit.*, p. 355.

90. An exhaustive technical proof of this has been given by Dr. Cecil Mast of the University of Notre Dame in a recent paper, as yet unpublished.

91. Though he will have some trouble with the varying angular momenta.

92. It may be worth noting that although there would have been no reason to predict such effects from a Ptolemaic model, a Tychonic model could, it would appear, predict them correctly. It would not, of course, *explain* them. But neither would it be in the position of the Ptolemaic model, to which the dual rotations of the sun would simply have to be added as new and unpredictable facts.

93. "Galileo's attempt to prove that the earth moves", 1962*. See the detailed bibliography given by Burstyn. Drake has shown that Galileo may have formulated his tidal theory as early as 1597, and that it may thus have had a considerable influence in strengthening his support of Copernicanism even prior to the astronomical discoveries of 1610. ("Galileo gleanings X: Origin and fate of Galileo's theory of the tides", 1961*.)

94. Galileo asserts as one of the two "conclusions" of his tidal analysis: "When we confer upon the globe the [diurnal and annual] movements just assigned to it, the seas are necessarily subjected to an ebb and flow agreeing in all respects with what is to be observed in them" (*Dialogo*, p. 417). Not only does he claim that the major tidal effects can be deduced from the postulate of the earth's dual motions, but since he wishes to *demonstrate* these motions, he also has to hold that the major tidal effects must follow from them "necessarily, in such a way that it would be impossible for them to take place in any other manner. For such is the property of things that are natural and true" (p. 424).

95. "It has already been decided that the monthly and annual periodic alterations of the tides *could derive from no other cause* than from the varying ratios between the annual motion (of the earth) and the additions to it and subtractions from it of the diurnal rotation" (*Dialogo*, p. 453; italics mine). But the best-known of the tidal periodicities, the semi-diurnal one with a total period of a little over twelve hours, did not lend itself so readily to his argument. From the earth's dual motions he thought he could infer a single diurnal tide, which is, he claims, masked by oscillation effects due to the local features of tidal basins. The semi-diurnal periodicity, he boldly suggests, may well be peculiar to the Mediterranean; its six-hour period of ebb, he is convinced, is "no more proper or natural" to it than any other short time-interval (pp. 432–434). In effect, then, he is forced to deny any kind of universal significance to the semi-diurnal periodicity, and to postulate a diurnal periodicity so heavily masked as to be unobservable. Whereas he attempts to connect the earth's postulated dual motions *directly* with the monthly and annual tidal periodicities, he makes these motions responsible only for the *fact* of short-period tides, not for any regular periodicity observed in them (something he questions).

96. Burstyn argues: "To our modern view, Galileo's proof is a partial success. Though the primary cause of the tides is not what Galileo thought it to be, his theory demands that the earth rotate on its axis and revolve in orbit around the sun, and these are the conditions demanded by a correct theory of the tides. Hence Galileo offered good evidence for the motion of the earth around the sun" (*op. cit.*, p. 181). There appears to be a formal fallacy here. The motions of the earth are not the only "conditions demanded by a correct theory of the tides", as Burstyn himself concedes when he says that the *primary* cause (condition) is not, in fact, what Galileo thought it to be. Hence, one could *not* infer a correct theory of the tides from the dual motions of the earth, even though one *could* infer the motions of the earth from a complete tidal theory (which incidentally we still do not have).

97. See the entries under his name in the *Bibliografia Galileiana, 1940–1964*.

2 ❋ Galileo:
A biographical sketch

STILLMAN DRAKE

It is presumed that those who are attracted to the present volume are already acquainted with the life and achievements of Galileo. Nevertheless, it may be useful to have at hand a sketch of his career in which some commonly repeated but erroneous or doubtful statements have been corrected, and to which some material that is not widely known has been added. An attempt has therefore been made to provide such an account of Galileo's life and character.

Galileo was born at, or more probably near, Pisa on February 15, 1564 (according to the Julian calendar). His father, Vincenzio Galilei, was a Florentine by birth and a professional musician. His mother, Giulia Ammanati, was a woman of good intelligence and education, but selfish and difficult. Vincenzio was able to earn but a meager livelihood as a performer and teacher of music, though a number of his compositions were published. He was also the author of two respectable books dealing with music theory, and one spirited reply to his former teacher, the celebrated theorist Gioseffo Zarlino, who had sharply disagreed with some of Vincenzio's published opinions. With respect to Galileo's early background, it is worth mentioning that Vincenzio ridiculed reliance on authority alone, experimented with the monochord in order to interpret and reconstruct the ancient tonal systems, and displayed a good knowledge of and respect for mathematics.

Galileo's early education was with the monks at Vallombroso, where it appears that he seriously considered entering upon the monastic life. His father, however, intervened and removed him from the monastery on the pretext that the boy's eyes required medical attention. In 1581 he was enrolled at the University of Pisa, in the school of medicine. His family having returned to Florence to live, Galileo resided at Pisa with the family of his mother's niece. At the university he gained the reputation of a rebel against the Galenist and Aristotelian authorities in medicine and philosophy. It was while he was a student at Pisa that Galileo observed the isochronism of the pendulum. Tradition has it that this came about through his observation that a heavy hanging lamp in the cathedral preserved the same period of swing as its arc diminished after having been drawn far back in order to be lighted. The fixture now in that place, known as "Galileo's lamp", was in fact not installed until 1587. Moreover the present lamp, though now electrified, was originally designed in such a manner that it would not have been withdrawn for lighting, since the subsequent swing back to center would have extinguished the flame. These facts contradict the name bestowed on the lamp by modern guides, but they scarcely support those writers who wish to classify the tradition as a myth—"as if", wrote Professor Antonio Favaro, "there was no lamp there previously; or as if its predecessor swung according to a different law of physics". In any event, experiments with the pendulum formed an early and important part of Galileo's insights into the law of falling bodies, and later afforded him an invaluable means of improving the methods of timing for astronomical observations.

Galileo's first formal training in mathematics came in 1583, not at the university but under the tutelage of Ostilio Ricci, a friend of his father's who was tutor to the pages of the Tuscan court. Ricci's mathematical interests were oriented toward practical applications, to judge by his surviving manuscripts; he was associated with the Academy of Design at Florence, and it is likely that Galileo's preference for applied rather than pure mathematics had its origin in Ricci's teaching. Galileo's father did not encourage his mathematical studies at first, probably because of the superior prestige and pay of the medical profession and because the most distinguished of Galileo's ancestors had been a physician. Ricci, however, interceded with Vincenzio on this point, and Galileo turned to mathematics in earnest, leaving the university without a degree in 1584 after his failure to obtain a scholarship from the Grand Duke. He returned to Florence, where he continued his mathematical researches and composed his first scientific paper, *La bilancetta*, reconstructing the process by which Archimedes had detected the goldsmith's fraud in making the crown of Hiero and describing an ingenious and useful hydrostatic balance. He also developed some new theorems concerning the centers of gravity of certain solids about this time, concerning which he corresponded with the illustrious Jesuit mathematician Christopher Clavius at Rome, and with his friend and future patron, the Marquis Guidobaldo del Monte. He gave some lessons at Florence and at Siena, and then in 1587 he set out for Rome in the company of a scion of the wealthy Ricasoli family, with some idea of seeking his fortune in the Near East. Ricasoli, however, was afflicted with some mental disorder, and after the short-lived excursion he became the subject of protracted judicial proceedings to set aside his will and reclaim his impulsive gifts; Galileo's deposition in this lawsuit is still extant.

In 1588, Galileo attempted unsuccessfully to gain the post of mathematician at the University of Bologna, with recommendations from those who had been impressed by his theorems on centers of gravity. The chair at Bologna was awarded to Giovanni Magini, who remained an antagonist of Galileo's, but in 1589 Galileo succeeded in getting the chair of mathematics at the University of Pisa on the recommendation of Guidobaldo. There he commenced the writing of a treatise, *On motion*, in opposition to Aristotle, which was clearly intended for publication but was not in fact published. Its central thesis is the destruction of Aristotle's two rules, that the speed of descent is proportional to weight and that it is inversely proportional to the density of the medium. Galileo attempted unsuccessfully to substitute for this a "hydrostatic" theory of fall, in which different speeds of descent would be accounted for in terms of a buoyancy principle. It is likely that he was led to this theory by his studies of specific gravity, though many of his conclusions resemble those published by Giovanni Battista Benedetti at Turin in 1585, and most scholars suppose him to have borrowed them without acknowledgment from that source. Several important results were obtained by Galileo, notably a fruitful demonstration of the conditions of equilibrium on inclined planes, but because of his failure to recognize at this time the importance of gravitational acceleration, he was unable to reconcile his conclusions about motion on such planes with the observed facts. His failure to complete and publish the treatise on motion suggests that he was dissatisfied with it on account of this conflict.

Vincenzio Viviani, Galileo's "last pupil", who lived with him in his final years and doubtless had the story from his own lips, first described the celebrated (and much questioned) dropping of weights from the Leaning Tower during Galileo's professorship there. According to Viviani, weights of the same substance but different sizes were dropped, and came to earth simultaneously, thus contradicting Aristotle. He says further that the entire student body was present. The story has been challenged on several grounds, but principally because the descent is not strictly simultaneous in air, and because the university records show no trace of such an event, nor is it mentioned in contemporary letters. The controversy is aggravated by the habit of modern writers of referring to the event as an "experiment". In all probability it did occur, but it was certainly not an experiment; it was a demonstration. Galileo had already arrived at the conclusion that the descent should be simultaneous from his (incorrect) buoyancy theory of fall. The Aristotelians had a totally different view of the relative speeds, and the demonstration was adequate to contradict that view, whether or not the impact of the weights was strictly simultaneous. But Galileo was by no means the first to contend that the different weights would fall together, nor was he the first to conduct a test of the conclusion, if indeed he did so. The proposition had been published by Benedetti in 1553, and the test had been made and published by the Flemish engineer Simon Stevin in 1586. Galileo, in later years, remarked that his attention had first been called to the fallacy of Aristotle by a hailstorm in his youth, in which very large and very small hailstones reached the ground together; had Aristotle been right, this would have necessitated either their origin at very different heights or their departure at times related to their sizes, either of which Galileo considered improbable.

At Pisa, Galileo was not only in conflict with many of the other professors, but he also gained the enmity of an important person, probably Giovanni de'Medici, by pointing out the fallacy in an engineering proposal of his. Most likely this was a device for the use of floating cranes in the dredging of the Bay of Leghorn, based on the idea that the flatness of a surface adds buoyancy over and above that gained from the density of the material used. In any case, various disputes seem to have made him despair of advancement at Pisa, while his father's death increased his financial responsibilities, and in 1592 he resigned his post. Later in that year, again with the assistance of Guidobaldo, he was able to secure the chair of mathematics at the University of Padua, where he remained until 1610.

At Padua the intellectual climate was vastly more to Galileo's taste than at Pisa. One of his close friends was Fra Paolo Sarpi, an astute student of mathematics and science until the theological troubles between Venice and Rome later came to monopolize his attention. Another was Giovanni Vincenzio Pinelli, whose home at Padua was the meeting place of distinguished scholars of all nations, and whose library was filled with treasures. A still more intimate friend was Giovanfrancesco Sagredo, a Venetian nobleman and talented amateur of science. Galileo maintained a large establishment at Padua, in which boarding students and their servants were housed, and in which a workshop was maintained for the manufacture of instruments. In addition to his assigned lectures, which included elementary astronomy and mathematics, Galileo gave private lessons in mechanics, military architecture, and other special instruction requested by his pupils.

In 1593, Galileo composed an outline of his lectures on mechanics, which he revised from time to time, bringing it to its final form about 1600. Dealing with the inclined plane in this treatise, he stressed the fact that a body on a horizontal plane may be moved by any minimal force, contrary to the belief of Pappus. He had given a proof of this in his earlier treatise *On motion*, and it led him to his first idea of inertia, in opposition not only to Aristotle but to the medieval writers who had explained projectile motion in terms of an impressed force called "impetus". Galileo was the first to perceive that motion and rest were states of a body to which the body was indifferent.

About the year 1602, he devised a thermoscope by warming the air in a glass bulb provided with a long thin neck, and then inverting it in water; the height of the water in the neck thereafter gave an indication of the temperature of the surrounding air. He had also noted the utility of the pendulum for time measurement, and adapted this to the purposes of medicine by devising a *pulsilogium*. This consisted of a board to which a pendulum was attached, in such a manner that the string could be stopped at any desired length by pressing the thumb against it. The swing of the bob was synchronized with the patient's pulse in this way, and markings on the board against which the thumb was pressed indicated whether the pulse was sluggish, normal, or feverish. Both these devices were taken up and improved by Sanctorio Sanctorius, another professor at Padua, who did much to make medicine more of a science.

In 1604, a conspicuous nova appeared which aroused much interest, partly from superstitious awe and partly because of the significant studies that had been made by Tycho Brahe of the nova of 1572. Galileo delivered three public lectures concerning this phenomenon, which aroused such interest that no hall at Padua would accommodate the audiences. The lectures are lost, but an idea of their content may be drawn from a satirical dialogue, published in the rustic dialect of Padua, in which Galileo is known to have had a hand. He poked fun at the Aristotelians as well as the astrologers, and probably used the nova to refute the idea that the heavens are unchangeable. A booklet on this nova was published by Baldessar Capra, a young student at Padua, who mentioned in it that the discovery was not made by Galileo but by him and his teacher, Simon Mayr, and reproached Galileo for not having duly credited them in his lectures.

Galileo did not reply in print at the time, but in 1607 he took occasion to do so in connection with another matter. About 1597, Galileo had devised an instrument of great utility to engineers, probably on the basis of work by his patron Guidobaldo. It was a proportional compass, known today as a sector, containing various scales which enabled the user to solve a wide variety of problems dealing with map-making, construction of geometrically similar figures, computation of roots, and the calculation of densities. Galileo wrote a handbook for users of the instrument, which was manufactured for sale by a craftsman retained by Galileo, and in 1606 he had this booklet privately printed in Italian. On Mayr's instigation, Capra obtained one of the instruments and a copy of the book with the aid of his father, who was acquainted with Galileo. They then composed a Latin treatise on the construction and use of the instrument, drawing heavily on Galileo's book. Capra claimed the invention for Mayr, and accused Galileo of having wrongfully appropriated it. Galileo brought the matter before the authorities, demonstrated his priority and the incompetence of Capra to explain many propositions in the book he had published, and had the publication suppressed and its ostensible author censured. Mayr, who was doubtless the true author, had returned to Germany, but his plagiarisms from Galileo were not yet finished. Galileo published an account of the proceedings in 1607, in a book called *Defence against the calumnies and impostures of Baldessar Capra*, in which he also replied to the criticisms that had been leveled against him in Capra's earlier book concerning the 1604 nova.

By 1609, Galileo had arrived at many new and valuable propositions concerning mechanics and the strength of materials, and was about to publish them when a series of events focused his attention anew on astronomy. In the autumn of 1608, a Dutch spectacle-maker had applied for a patent on a device consisting of two lenses, which was capable of magnifying distant objects. From contemporary reports, this must have consisted of two convex lenses, since it inverted the image. Rumors of this interesting invention reached Italy soon afterward, Galileo's friend Fra Paolo Sarpi at Venice being one of the first to hear of it. Sarpi sought more information, and in the early part of July, 1609, its existence was confirmed by a former pupil of Galileo's, named Jacques Badovere (or Giovanni Badoer), in a letter sent probably to Sarpi. Galileo was visiting Venice at the time, and hastened back to Padua, where a visiting foreigner had already shown one of the instruments. Probably with the assistance of descriptions by friends who had seen it, he set to work at once to construct such an instrument himself. He first experimented with a convex objective and concave eyepiece fixed in a metal tube, and thus obtained an erect image. He quickly improved this instrument so that it would magnify about nine times, and returned to Venice late in August with a telescope which was vastly superior to any that had been previously reported. This he demonstrated to several senators and other Venetian dignitaries, showing that by means of it ships could be detected from the Tower of St. Mark long before they were visible to trained naked-eye observers. He then presented the device to the Venetian government, receiving in return an increase in salary and a lifetime appointment. But Galileo had not intended to commit himself to remain for life in the Venetian Republic. He had been negotiating for some time to obtain appointment by the Grand Duke of Florence, his friend and former pupil Cosimo II de'Medici, and lost no time paying a visit to Florence with one of his telescopes to renew his efforts along that line.

Upon his return to Padua, Galileo worked hard to improve the telescope still further, and early in January, 1610, he was in possession of a thirty-power instrument which enabled him to make a number of startling astronomical discoveries. Apart from the mountainous character of the moon's surface and the detection of innumerable fixed stars never previously seen, he observed four satellites of Jupiter and commenced to plot their movements. In March, 1610, he published these discoveries in a book called *Sidereus nuncius* (*Starry messenger*), which caused a sensation throughout Europe. He christened the newly discovered satellites the "Medicean stars", and again visited Tuscany, this time with the hoped-for result, an appointment as Chief Mathematician and Philosopher to the Grand Duke, and Chief Mathematician of the University of Pisa without obligation to reside in that city. In the summer of 1610, he left Padua permanently for Florence.

During his residence in Padua, Galileo had taken a Venetian mistress named Marina Gamba, by whom he had two daughters and a son. She remained in Padua with the infant son, Vincenzio, while Galileo's mother at Florence took temporary custody of the daughters. Galileo's relations with Marina Gamba remained amicable, and when Vincenzio was old enough for the trip, he also was sent to Florence. Galileo's mother, however, was a very difficult woman, and in order to solve his family problems, Galileo managed to have the two girls admitted to a convent near Arcetri, though they were not yet of full age for this move. The elder daughter took the name Maria Celeste, and was a source of much comfort to her father throughout her brief life. The younger daughter tended to be peevish and frail in health. Of the son, little is heard until many years later; it is frequently said that he was a problem to his father, but this appears to be largely a confusion with Galileo's nephew who bore the same name (Vincenzio Galilei) and who was sent to live in Italy while his father (Galileo's brother Michelangelo) remained at Munich. Michelangelo Galilei was a professional musician, like his father, but lacked the sense of responsibility characteristic of his more famous relatives. Instead of assisting in the financial problems of the family, or contributing to the dowries of his sisters, he left Galileo to meet these obligations and frequently asked for financial and other assistance himself.

Shortly after his arrival at Florence, Galileo observed the phases of Venus (which had been too close to the sun for observation earlier in the year) and described the unusual shape of Saturn. Galileo's telescope did not resolve the rings, which he took to be two small stationary satellites close to the planet. These new discoveries he announced in cryptic form, as anagrams, pending their formal publication after full confirmation. Galileo's experience with Capra and Mayr seems to have converted him from an open-handed man, who prior to 1607 freely gave out his ideas and his writings, into an unduly suspicious man who thereafter guarded his discoveries jealously.

Johannes Kepler, to whom Galileo had transmitted the *Sidereus nuncius* and then made one of his telescopes available through the Tuscan Ambassador to the Emperor by whom Kepler was employed, fully confirmed Galileo's discoveries and beseeched him to reveal these new phenomena, which Galileo did in letters published by Kepler in his *Dioptrice* of 1611. Meanwhile considerable opposition to Galileo's claimed discoveries had developed. Many astronomers were unwilling to admit them, and even some who had had the opportunity to use Galileo's telescope were unable to see the things he had observed. Some books appeared attacking Galileo's claims, to which he did not reply in print. He preferred to journey to Rome and show his discoveries personally to the influential Jesuit astronomers with whom he was in correspondence. Illness detained him for some time, but he finally arrived at Rome in April, 1611. There he was feted by important church dignitaries, won the support of the Jesuit astronomers, and was made a member of the Lincean Academy, the first true scientific society, organized in 1603 by Marquis (later Prince) Federico Cesi.

While Galileo was establishing the highest reputation away from home, various adversaries of his at Florence did a good deal to undermine him there. Probably his original detractors were courtiers who did not want him to upset their influence on the young Grand Duke, and professors at Pisa who resented the special appointment given to him there. At any rate, there is evidence that his new post had already become uncomfortable by the summer of 1611. Shortly after his return, in June, he took part in a philosophical disputation in which the nature of ice and the causes of bodies floating in water were discussed; Galileo took the Archimedean position in opposition to Aristotle. This led to open controversy, in which a certain Ludovico delle Colombe boasted that he would defeat Galileo by experimental demonstrations. The debate was not actually held, and Galileo appears to have been asked by the Grand Duke to refrain from such oral debates and to confine his remarks to written treatises. Toward the end of September, the same subject was debated at the Grand Duke's own table, two cardinals being present; one of these, Maffeo Barberini, later to become Pope Urban VIII, took Galileo's side. Galileo then set down his entire position in writing, and it was published in 1612; the first edition being speedily exhausted, a second appeared in the same year. In his book, *Bodies in water*, Galileo set forth in Italian his scientific arguments, complete with descriptions of corroboratory experiments which might easily be performed by anyone. Galileo remarked in later years that ignorance had been his best teacher, as the ignorance of his opponents had led him to search for evident demonstrations which he would not otherwise have considered necessary.

Late in 1612, a German Jesuit, Christopher Scheiner, wrote a series of letters to a distinguished amateur of science, Mark Welser of Augsburg, describing sunspots and setting forth the erroneous theory that they were tiny planets revolving erratically about the sun. Welser published these letters, concealing the author's name under the pseudonym Apelles, and sent them to Galileo for his comment. Galileo replied in three letters, published in 1613 under the auspices of the Lincean Academy. He stated that he had observed sunspots sometime before, and had shown them to friends while at Rome in 1611, but hesitated to come forth with a theory concerning them until he was sure of his ground. It was his opinion, however, that they were generated and dissolved on the very surface of the sun, which rotated on its axis in approximately a month. These views were stoutly opposed by the Aristotelians, who held the heavens to be perfect and not subject to generation and decay. Galileo, on the other hand, saw in the sunspots and the lunar mountains conclusive evidence for holding that heavenly bodies were of material similar to that of the earth, and moreover he declared himself unequivocally in his *Letters on sunspots* to favor the Copernican theory.

Toward the end of 1613, Galileo's former pupil Benedetto Castelli, who had secured the chair of mathematics at the University of Pisa, was present at a discussion of Galileo's astronomical views at the table of the Grand Duke. In this discussion a professor of philosophy remarked that the earth could not be in motion, as this was contrary to the Bible. Castelli, who was a Benedictine monk, argued the point, and wrote to Galileo of the affair. Galileo replied with a long letter setting forth his opinion as to the relations of science and religion in such matters. This letter was circulated among the professors at Pisa.

About a year later, a young Dominican named Tommaso Caccini denounced from the pulpit at Florence the views of Galileo and of scientists generally. An elderly Dominican, Nicolò Lorini, visited Pisa shortly afterward and expressed his regret at the intemperance of that sermon. Castelli obligingly showed him Galileo's letter, of which Lorini took a copy back to Florence. Having read it, he proceeded to notify the Roman Inquisition that the views of the Galileists should be reviewed as possibly heretical, forwarding a copy of the letter. When Galileo learned of this, he took steps to place a correct copy in the hands of church authorities who were friendly toward him, but inquiries conducted at Pisa on behalf of the Inquisition made him aware that a prohibition of the Copernican theory was more than a possibility. He proceeded to rework and improve the text of his letter to Castelli, addressing an extended version of it to the Grand Duchess Christina.

Galileo's *Bodies in water* had been the subject of at least four published attacks, one by Colombe and three by university professors. Galileo had prepared extensive replies to their arguments, but in view of the battle that was brewing around him on other and more serious topics, he turned these over to Castelli, who published replies to Colombe and one professor in 1615. This *Risposta*, without name of author but with an introduction signed by Castelli, was in fact almost entirely from Galileo's pen.

During the summer of 1615, Galileo was seriously ill, but late in the year he journeyed once more to Rome, against the advice of his Roman friends and of the Tuscan Ambassador, in the hope of clearing his own name and also preventing action against the teaching of Copernicanism. In this he not only failed, but in all probability it was his public debating there which brought the matter to a head. A special commission appointed by Pope Paul V pronounced the twin affirmations of the stability of the sun and motion of the earth to be rash and contrary to Scripture. Galileo was enjoined by Cardinal Bellarmine, on express order of the Pope, to abstain from holding or defending these views any longer, and early in March 1616, a decree was issued against books which attempted to reconcile them with Scripture and suspending the *De revolutionibus* of Copernicus "pending correction". The Pope had ordered that if Galileo was recalcitrant to Bellarmine's injunction, then the Holy Office was to issue a formal injunction forbidding him even to teach the condemned views orally or in writing, under penalty of imprisonment. It appears probable that this stronger language was in fact employed toward him by another official present at the interview, though its use was improper, since it does not seem that he had, in fact, been recalcitrant.[1] Rumors that Galileo had been forced to abjure circulated throughout Italy, and before he left Rome he applied to Bellarmine for documentary evidence that nothing of the sort had happened, which the Cardinal supplied in his own handwriting.

Upon his return to Florence in mid-1616, Galileo entered a period of scientific inaction. He turned his attention primarily to the practical problem of the determination of longitudes at sea, which he tried to calculate on the basis of observations of the satellites of Jupiter. Negotiations with the Spanish government to conduct tests of his scheme and for its sale if successful were carried on, but came to naught. Meanwhile, he refrained from publishing anything further for a time. Toward the end of 1618, however, while he lay ill, three comets appeared in rapid succession, the last being unusually bright and of long duration. These comets were the subject of much discussion and of many pamphlets. The event offered Galileo a pretext for re-entering the field of astronomical debate without treading on forbidden ground. He took the precaution of having his views on comets set forth by a pupil, Mario Guiducci, who was then Consul of the Florentine Academy, but he made it clear that he had little regard for the opinions expressed by an anonymous Jesuit writer at Rome, who followed the theories of Tycho Brahe. The Jesuit, Horatio Grassi, was much incensed and replied with a direct attack on Galileo himself, ignoring Guiducci, but concealing his own identity under a pen name. Galileo in turn replied in detail in 1623 with a great polemic, *The assayer*, in which he undermined the principal assumption of his opponent and illustrated, by vivid examples, the role played by scientific doubt in the acquisition of true knowledge.

Galileo's *Assayer* is a book of interest and importance in several respects. In 1614, Simon Mayr had published in Germany a book called *Mundus jovialis*, in which he declared on the very title page that he had discovered the satellites of Jupiter in 1609, and in which he gave a long and rather implausible account of the circumstances. The date of his first claimed observation, computed according to the Julian calendar in use in Germany, was precisely that of Galileo's second published observation in the *Sidereus nuncius* of 1610, as Galileo pointed out in the opening pages of *The assayer*. Galileo also mentioned a number of other incidents concerning his previous books, and among them he recounted the many writers who had claimed credit for the discovery of sunspots. Christopher Scheiner, who was unaware of any book on that subject other than Galileo's and his own, took great offense at this passage, with serious consequences in later years. It should also be mentioned that *The assayer,* which is of relatively small scientific importance and has not been widely read outside Italy, is usually portrayed as a book in which Galileo was wholly wrong and his Jesuit opponent right concerning the nature of comets. This view, which at one time I accepted on superficial evidence, is not tenable. Galileo's purpose in the book is not to set forth a theory of comets, but to show that his opponent's fundamental assumption might be completely erroneous, and that his entire argument would fall to the ground if comets were masses of lighted vapor rather than solid bodies. While this book was in the press, Galileo's old friend, Maffeo Cardinal Barberini, succeeded to the papal chair, with the result that many of his other friends received appointments to important Church posts. *The assayer* was dedicated to the new Pope and found great favor with him.

In 1624, Galileo went once more to Rome. There he paid homage to Pope Urban VIII and sought permission to publish his long-promised book on the system of the world. In several long audiences, the new Pope granted him permission to discuss the rival theories "hypothetically" and impartially, but refused to revoke the earlier decree or to countenance "physical" arguments (as opposed to mathematical reasoning) in favor of Copernicus. Galileo returned to Florence and commenced work on a book which he believed was in compliance with these instructions. The *Dialogue concerning the two chief world systems* proceeded slowly, with many interruptions, but was finally completed in 1630. Galileo then returned to Rome with the manuscript, intending to have it licensed for publication there and have it printed by the Lincean Academy, as had been done with two of his previous books. It soon became apparent, however, that it would not be easy to secure the license, and Galileo had to return without it. There ensued many arguments and delays, during which Prince Cesi, the sole financial support of the Academy, died suddenly. Castelli, then at Rome, advised Galileo to have the book published at Florence instead, and after various negotiations the book was reviewed and approved by the Church authorities there. It was finally published at Florence in March, 1632, and was widely acclaimed.

At Rome, however, Galileo's foes busied themselves to secure the Pope's displeasure with the book. Among these the leader was unquestionably Christopher Scheiner, who was now still further incensed against Galileo over a lengthy discussion of sunspots in the *Dialogue,* in which Galileo not only again asserted the priority of his observations, but gave a long and reasoned argument for the motion of the earth based upon the seasonal variations in sunspot paths. Scheiner was convinced that Galileo

had learned of those variations from a book he had published in 1630, with
the title *Rosa ursina*, though in fact Galileo's *Dialogue* was almost through
the press before he ever saw a copy of Scheiner's book, in addition to
which he could scarcely have introduced important new material after the
securing of the *imprimatur*. At any rate, Scheiner and his friends were
successful in getting Galileo into serious trouble, for a search of the Inquisition records disclosed an unsigned memorandum to the effect that Galileo had been ordered not to teach Copernicanism in any way, orally or in
writing. When this was found, the Pope felt that he had been tricked into
the granting of permission for Galileo to discuss this topic, and then into
permitting the licensing of the book. Accordingly, he ordered Galileo to
come to Rome to be tried by the Inquisition.

Galileo, who was seriously ill and was nearly seventy years of age, asked
for protection from the Grand Duke, but to no avail. In the spring of
1633, he faced trial at Rome. It was his contention that the book had been
properly licensed and that in it he did not hold or defend the Copernican
view, but merely discussed it impartially in conjunction with that of Ptolemy. When asked to recount the circumstances of Bellarmine's injunction
of 1616, he produced the Cardinal's certificate that he had merely been
apprised of the general decree, which had been published. Asked whether
he had also been enjoined not to discuss Copernicanism in any way, he
replied that he did not recollect any such order. The trial then dragged on
for a long time. Galileo's authentic certificate from Bellarmine, the existence of which could not have been known to the inquisitioners, was a powerful document as against their own unsigned memorandum in the files. In
the end, Galileo was induced to confess that he had gone too far in his
book, but he did not admit any wrongdoing; rather, he said, the fault was
one of the vanity every man has for his own arguments. Even this degree
of confession was extracted from him only by extrajudicial dealings, and
probably with the promise of a light penalty. When he then faced the
judges and was sentenced to life imprisonment, the shock nearly killed
him. The sentence was, however, speedily softened to allow him to return
first to Siena, where he was in the custody of his old pupil and friend
Ascanio Piccolomini, then Archbishop of Siena, and ultimately to Arcetri,
near Florence, to his own villa. There he remained under the surveillance
of officers of the Inquisition, but without formal imprisonment.

One of the most distressing circumstances of his condemnation was that
Galileo's works, published and unpublished, were forbidden. It will be
recalled that before his astronomical observations with the newly devised
telescope made him world-famous, Galileo had been about to publish a
great work on mechanics and strength of materials. During his stay with
the Archbishop of Siena, despite his great age, he turned again to this
project of a quarter-century earlier, and proceeded to write in dialogue
form, with the same interlocutors as those of the ill-fated book which had
brought about his condemnation, a treatise on *Two new sciences* which is

unquestionably the cornerstone of modern physics. A manuscript of this great work was taken out of Italy to France and was ultimately published, in 1638, by the Elzevirs at Leyden. No reprisals were carried out against Galileo, who pointed out in a preface to the book that arrangements for its publication had been made without his knowledge or consent by friends abroad, to whom it had been entrusted in confidence merely for its scientific interest. In the *Two new sciences*, Galileo gave to the world not only the true laws of accelerated motion and of falling bodies, but fundamental theorems concerning projectile motion and important applications of mathematics to a variety of other physical problems.

In Galileo's last years he was afflicted with total blindness, which overtook him about the time of publication of his last book. He continued, however, in a vast scientific correspondence with the assistance of his son and of two young men, both to become scientifically illustrious in their own right, Vincenzio Viviani and Evangelista Torricelli. To his son he dictated a method of applying the pendulum to clocks. Early in 1642, being almost seventy-eight years of age, he died at Arcetri. The implacable hostility of Urban VIII, who had even made difficulties about his request to go into Florence for medical treatment at the time his sight was failing, prevented his honorable burial with a suitable monument to his greatness, "lest any word of it reflect upon the Holy Office". He was interred in the Church of Santa Croce, at Florence, but nearly a century elapsed before his remains were moved to their present magnificent tomb, opposite that of Michelangelo near the entrance to the church.

Galileo was of average stature, heavy-set, quick to anger and as quickly restored to good humor. His natural talents, his wit and his brilliant conversation won him an illustrious list of friends among dignitaries of the court, the Church and the universities, as well as among artists, musicians and craftsmen. At the same time he made a formidable number of bitter opponents by his biting sarcasm against those so unfortunate as to offer vulnerable arguments against his scientific views. Galileo had in his nature a curious mixture of prudent caution and uncompromising defiance. The former trait is apparent in his long hesitation to embrace unequivocally the Copernican theory, the latter in his fearless appearance at Rome in 1615–1616 when his own reputation as well as the fate of his scientific convictions was at stake, and when his best-informed advisers warned him against the probable consequences of an open fight. His reluctance to take a firm position on the Copernican theory long before 1613, at least sixteen years after it had won his scientific preference, is often ascribed solely to his fear of public ridicule. That was certainly one of his reasons, as it had earlier been for Copernicus himself, but it was almost equally certainly not his sole motivation. The study of Galileo's entire scientific career indicates that he thoroughly understood, as indeed he preached, the overwhelming importance of reserving final judgment until mathematical certainty could be reached. It is likely that he was a long time in overcoming in his own mind all the formidable objections to the earth's motion as a physical fact even after he had arrived at a position generally favoring Copernicus as against Ptolemy and Brahe. It is noteworthy that most of his serious errors in scientific matters are to be found only in his unpublished manuscripts and not in his printed books. Had he been as much inclined to rush into print with his novel ideas as were most men of his time (and many of ours), his prodigious influence upon scholars of the first rank in his own day and for decades thereafter would doubtless have been greatly weakened. On the whole, it appears that problems and contradictions often held him back from publication and urged him to persevere in researches that were ultimately fruitful. Perhaps it is to this facet of his character that we owe the loss of several papers he is known to have composed (on mathematical indivisibles and continuity, for example, and on light and color) which would be of great interest to historians of science as well as to his own biographers.

When he was a young man, he suffered an accident which probably led to his lifelong bouts with almost crippling arthritis or rheumatism. On a summer day, in search of relief from the heat, he and a number of companions took shelter in a cave where they lay down without clothing. The air of the cave was cool but noxious; several who fell asleep became very ill, and some of them died. Galileo was also afflicted in later life with a severe double hernia, for which he was obliged to wear an iron truss that made it excessively difficult and painful for him to travel any long distance.

Galileo's talents were extremely varied. Apart from his scientific and literary abilities, he was a skilled musician, delighting especially in the lute, and so proficient in drawing that he seriously considered becoming a professional artist. Ludovico Cardi di Cigoli, his good friend, remarked that all his knowledge of perspective had been learned from Galileo; other artists consulted him, and many evidences of his familiarity with and liking for painting are to be found in his letters and essays.

Of all his personal characteristics, however, the most striking is his extraordinary skill as an observer. Nothing seems to have escaped his attention, and the popular appeal of his books is attributable partly to the apt use of countless illustrations drawn from the experience, or potential experience, of anyone willing to repeat his observations. The appearance of distant clouds and mountains, of various lights at night, of rainbow colors in sunlit hair, of reflections in heated air; the sounds of nature and of music; the behavior of filings on a vibrating plate, and so on almost without end—when we read continual references to such phenomena, we are no longer astonished that Galileo, when he was confronted by countless fixed stars seen through his thirty-power telescope, immediately noted the linear arrangement of three near Jupiter, and on the following night knew that either they had moved or that Jupiter was going the wrong way, which led him to his most startling astronomical discovery. We are less astonished than we should otherwise be by his noticing the isochronism of the pendulum and by his early recognition of its relation to the true law of falling bodies, or by his utilization of the inclined plane to facilitate the observation of motions too fast in nature to permit precise measurement.

It is probably to Galileo's inherent capacity to *observe* that modern science owes its inception; for despite his extraordinary capacity for reasoning, he turned away from excessive speculation about the causes of things in the tradition of philosophers. His desire was to see precisely what things happen and how they happen, rather than to explain why they happen so.

NOTE

1. A full reconstruction of this famous and much-debated interview will be found in Appendix I to my translation of L. Geymonat's *Galileo Galilei*, New York, 1965.

3 | ✺ The significance of Galileo's thought for the history of science

A. RUPERT HALL

Exactly what Galileo did we cannot know. Only in a few cases and in limited respects can we even discern Galileo's direct influence upon his immediate contemporaries, apart from the small group of men who were his friends and supporters. As early as the next generation—with men like Wallis, Huygens and Newton, who were born while Galileo still lived or very soon thereafter—the exact impact of Galileo's writings becomes shadowy. Already he has become part of the hinterland, the climate of opinion, or the shaping tradition.

Inevitably we must form Galileo in our own image, as we reconstruct every piece of history in our own image, believing, with our greater depth of insight and our wider range of fact, that our vision is a closer approximation to the reality than that of our predecessors. As regards Galileo, there can hardly be any doubt that a few years after the quatercentenary of his birth Galileo seems a far more potent figure in the history of science than he did in 1864 or in 1764—though his great stature was always assured. There are a number of reasons for this. Obviously the publication of the mass of Galileana by Antonio Favaro, and his sustained emphasis on Galileo had a stirring effect; the growth of the history of science as a professional discipline, and especially the perception that the origins of modern science presented a crucial historiographical problem, confirmed Galileo's significance as a pivotal figure, the giant in an epoch of decision. But not less important have been the changes in our own attitudes to science and its evolution, because these have impelled us not only to redouble the light cast upon Galileo's tomb, but to shift its line and balance.

Earlier estimates of Galileo's contribution

If we could return to the second centenary of Galileo's birth, for instance, we should find him regarded as a revered pioneer. As such, he was assigned a double role; never since has Galileo quite escaped this schizoid personality. On the one hand, he was the observant successor to Copernicus, the astronomer who had first turned the newly discovered telescope to the heavens and at least destroyed the old cosmology, if he did not thereby establish the new. On the other hand, Galileo deserved credit for first setting out, obscurely and imperfectly indeed, the laws of motion that Newton was to enunciate for all time; and for deriving from these correct principles a few of their more obvious mathematical consequences. Possibly Newton himself, never excessively generous to his predecessors, regarded the great Italian in such a light; at any rate this was in crude summary the view of Montucla in his great *Histoire des mathématiques* which is, rather, a history of all the physical sciences. Montucla recognized with perhaps excessive clarity that:

> The name of Galileo is no less celebrated in mechanics, than in astronomy. However brilliant the discoveries with which he enriched the latter, they would not have assured him so remarkable an esteem in the eyes of posterity. . . . Less genius was required to turn the telescope to the heavens and to perceive the phenomena whose discovery is credited to him, than to unravel the laws of nature in the fall of heavy bodies, the kind of curve they describe in descending obliquely, and the solution of other problems in mechanics which he treated with much good sense.[1]

And as Montucla goes on to say, while there were those hot enough on Galileo's track to dispute his priorities in celestial observation, there were none near enough to challenge his pre-eminence in mechanics.

To this William Whewell could add, nearly a century later, that if in mechanics Galileo was more profound, it was in astronomy that he made the most noise. For Whewell, as for Montucla, Galileo is still defined by his relation to others: as the follower of Copernicus and the forerunner of Newton. Nevertheless, Whewell paid Galileo a rather splendid compliment:

> If we were to compare Descartes with Galileo, we might say, that of the mechanical truths which were easily attainable in the beginning of the seventeenth century, Galileo took hold of as many, and Descartes of as few, as was well possible for a man of genius.[2]

Perhaps it is not altogether surprising that such historians as Montucla, whose heart was in mathematics, and Whewell whose concern was induction, failed to emphasize further the general intellectual pre-eminence of Galileo in the development of science; for Galileo's thought is indeed signalized neither by exceptional mathematical penetration, nor by frequent induction from experiments.[3] In any case many, Whewell among them, preferred another candidate for the role of general legislator of modern science: Francis Bacon. It would be absurd and improper for me, at this time, to try to pull down Bacon (for whom in any case I have the greatest respect) in order to elevate Galileo; yet these two great men are inevitably seated at opposite ends of a seesaw.[4] Faith in induction swings the beam one way; faith in the hypothetico-deductive method swings it the other. The English were so long inductivists—right through the seventeenth century and long after—that they rated Bacon *the* philosopher of modern science. William Wotton wrote:

My Lord Bacon was the first Great Man who took much pains to convince the World that they had hitherto been in a wrong Path, and that Nature herself, rather than her Secretaries, was to be addressed to by those who were desirous to know much of her Mind.[5]

In this view Galileo *could* only be one of the pioneers who had foreshadowed the true inductive science of Newton.

The unity of Galileo's work

With all respect to Bacon, we no longer hold such a view nowadays; the first step toward our modern sense of Galileo's historical significance is recognition of the importance of conceptualization. I shall not attempt to be precise here; it is enough to say that the modern trend in the historiography of ideas took shape in the last decades of the nineteenth century. And with interest in scientific concepts comes, almost forced upon one, recognition of the truth that Galileo's work is a unity. Certainly his activity as an observer is very different from anything else he did;[6] but his mind as an astronomer was one with his mind as a philosopher. Paul Tannery first stressed this point, in 1901; it was the decision of the mature Galileo, he wrote, to make a *tabula rasa* of Aristotelian dynamics before revealing his own.[7] Tannery maintained—and he was perfectly right— that just as the only science of motion consistent with the heliocentric system was Galileo's new one, which alone could "save" the new astronomy from the traditional mechanical objections, so also Copernicus alone provided a universe in which Galileo's science of motion made sense. Galileo's mechanics would not only have been useless in an Aristotelian universe; it would have been actively negated by the privileged position of the earth.[8]

In fact, therefore, defense of Copernicus and preparation for Newton were one and the same thing; indeed in another way this is obvious, since Newton synthesized and resolved the whole crisis in physical science.[9] It was a profound underestimation of the true significance of Galileo's role in human thought ever to suppose that the conjunction of his work in astronomy and his work in mechanics was coincidental. The two are not simply biographically united: they are historical and logical counterparts, two aspects of a single course of intellectual development. And now we begin to see those famous telescopic discoveries in an altogether different light, grand though they were. Galileo's credit for extending the range of the human eye may properly be described as fortuitous. It was initiated and always guided by his powerful personal ambitions. It led to a brilliant, brief space of practical work and exploration; but Galileo did not continue, in later life, either the optical improvement of the telescope or the extension of its use.[10] Instead he devoted himself, from the time of his return to Florence, to a more useful task: the marshaling of the full weight of evidence in favor of the Copernican theory and the revelation of the character of the opposing side—shallow, blind and inconsistent.

Everyone knows that the new telescopic disclosures were but a small fraction of the evidence that Galileo deployed. In his greatest work of polemic and most complete statement on the subject, they do not even figure very largely, for the *Dialogo* of 1632 added nothing on these points to what he had already said. An unalerted reader might well be astonished to find the inductive element in the *Dialogo* so slight; if he looks to Galileo for an astronomical observation proving the motion of the earth he will not find it. Instead the *Dialogo* is devoted for the most part to such topics as the rationality of cosmology, the reflectivity of the moon, the properties of moving bodies and the distinction of appearance from reality. We discover Galileo persuading the reader, arguing with him, trying first this device, then that, in order to help him to see familiar facts in a new light—not to see new facts that no one has discovered before. For Galileo is a Socratic philosopher and Simplicio sometimes his Meno, an unwitting possessor of the truth.[11] Within every Ptolemy there is a Copernicus crying to get out; it is Galileo's duty to assist him to escape from his mental prison.

I will not labor the point. We are well enough aware of Galileo's immense importance as an opponent of scholastic science with its outworn traditions, and its adhesion to literal authority which he mocked in the character of Simplicio. We know how Galileo picked out for all to see the illogicalities, inconsistencies and impossibilities in the doctrines of Aristotle and Ptolemy. We watch amazed as the author who was too timid to avow his Copernicanism in 1597, and who (as the statutes required) taught dignified falsehood in class throughout his term at Padua, launches a total attack on dogma. Above all, we know Galileo as the most eloquent advocate of the new cosmology, and much more than this as a fabricator of a new attitude to nature and to knowledge in which this cosmology made sense; in which, moreover, the scientific revolution as a whole made sense. We understand that Galileo is the chief architect of an intellectual revolution—M. Alexandre Koyré has taught this far more effectively than I could do.

Whether or not this was a situation to which arguments from induction were in principle irrelevant, *de facto* in the early seventeenth century Galileo had to endeavor to sway the conviction of his readers because the battering-ram of induction was not accessible to him. There was no proof for either side: there was only the choice between *this* way of regarding things which belonged to antiquity, and *that* which belonged to Galileo and modern science. The very depth of vision that enabled Galileo to refute the anti-Copernicans denied him the possibility of ever proving his own case.[12] Whewell might have regarded this as evidence of the weakness of noninductive argument, just as Koestler (recently) has urged that absence of proof ought to have persuaded Galileo to hold his tongue. Most of us, on the contrary, feel that it is this double triumph of reason—cosmological and mechanical—which is Galileo's glory: that to have forced the world to look straight at the issues is precisely his significance. Those who proved the earth's motion by demonstration—Bessel and Foucault—long after the Copernican issue was decided, did what was necessary but dull.

Galileo's method of science

Hence we may be inclined to believe that Galileo's thought has a more general lesson for us, that it is indicative of the universal process of conceptual change in science and assures us that all theoretical decision-taking is a matter of choice between unprovables according to the pattern of one's outlook. For my own part, though I am not eager to enter on controversy here, I believe we should exaggerate neither Galileo's idealism, nor the virtues of idealism in general. Galileo wrote the *Dialogo* as he did because he could do no other; I find it difficult to imagine that if Galileo could have relied on the manifestations of stellar parallax he would not have done so. Book IV of the *Dialogo* reminds us that Galileo did search for—and think he had found—a positive demonstration of the motion of the earth. Accordingly, we should be cautious in supposing that it is part of Galileo's significance to teach that science consists *wholly* of the development of ideas, nor is it a necessary deduction from the character of his thought that the scientific revolution was *exclusively* a transformation of concepts.

Galileo's ideas on procedure, method and epistemology were, I am sure, confused and inconsistent. As with Newton, as with most practicing scientists phrasing their intuitions rather according to the exigencies of the moment than according to an articulate philosophy, Galileo saw green grass on both sides of the fence. Accordingly he has been claimed as an adherent of the empirical as well as of the idealist school. Those who see him as the pioneer exponent of the hypothetico-deductive method can point to the inclined-plane experiment and other passages in which Galileo seems scrupulous in submitting his developing theories to experimental verification. Those who do so are making a major historical as well as philosophical claim for Galileo, since they are asserting that (1) the hypothetico-deductive method is the method of modern science, and (2) this is the method of which Galileo was the first to make effective use.[13] If any version of this claim *were* capable of being fully upheld, one would need to go no further to demonstrate Galileo's importance in the evolution of science. The man who picked up and turned the golden key to Pandora's box needs no other claim to fame.

Such a view of Galileo has been subjected to hardly less criticism than the more dubious view that he was an inductive philosopher.[14] Although Galileo's thought ranged very widely in science, the number of instances of his offering a precise piece of experiment in support of his notions is small indeed. Even the positive assertions of experimental verification made by Galileo have been doubted.[15] The inclined-plane experiment, in particular, has been both criticized and defended; against M. Koyré's argument that the experiment could not play the clear, decisive role of proof demanded of it by Galileo—which his successors failed to confirm —it has been urged that the experiment can be done as a perfectly satisfactory laboratory demonstration, giving just as good consistency in results as Galileo claimed for it.[16] However that may be, Galileo's case for the law of fall in the *Discorsi* of 1638 rests wholly on reason; this is the law that *must be*. The experiment is adduced to prove the applicability of the theory, not its truth, in response to the demand of the empiricist, Simplicio. It is to "illustrate the conclusions reached" which Salviati says "is the custom, and properly so, in those sciences where mathematical demonstrations are applied to natural phenomena".[17]

Moreover, it seems that sufficient-reason considerations and mathematical arguments were of greater effect in winning support for the law of falling bodies than any experiments: we have good reason to believe that Mersenne or Huygens or Wallis or Newton would have distrusted, just as much as Galileo did, any law of motion that was founded only on empiricism, and not on a probable contemplation of the nature of things. For Galileo is above all aware that the senses must be educated and assisted to perceive realities. Thus one could *know* the true nature of the moon without the telescope: that instrument simply makes reality easier to discover. It is the Aristotelian Simplicio who is made to object "So you have not made a hundred tests, nor even one?" when Salviati *knows* the truth intellectually; it is Simplicio again who alleges that Copernicus upsets the "criterion of science" which says,

in agreement with philosophers of every school, that the senses and experience should be our guide in philosophizing. But in the Copernican position, the senses much deceive us when they visually show us, at close range and in a perfectly clear medium, the straight perpendicular descent of very heavy bodies.[18]

And it is Salviati who remarks admiringly on Copernicus' rectitude in believing that obvious empirical objections to his astronomy would be removed. A Platonist, a Copernican, a mechanical philosopher could not possibly be a naive empiricist; and it was hardly more possible for him to be, systematically, a follower of the hypothetico-deductive logic.

Frankly, I do not think that this weakness of Galileo as an experimental scientist matters much. If one should ask: "What did Galileo do for positive knowledge?" it is quite enough to point to his work with the telescope. As an experimental scientist the best you can say for him is that he was a pioneer; we know very well that our modern traditions of laboratory science derive from other and later sources. Now, as I indicated before, a claim for Galileo that he was a pioneer of something is a weak claim; it is his function in transforming science which is transcendent, and to which I now return.

Idealization

We may further resolve this function under the four headings of idealization, geometrization, mechanization and unification. Traditional learning allowed its imagination to run free from heaven to hell; yet it was also extremely literal and pettifogging, the creature of plausible example and an easy victim to doubtful counterinstance. The intellectual macrocosm was, so to speak, interlocked with the material microcosm. Galileo, on the other hand, acted on the belief that in a given area of discussion some issues are significant, others irrelevant. One need not—one cannot—keep one's eye on the total complexity of nature all the time. (It is interesting to contrast this simplicist, brutal view of the relations between things, associated with mechanism, with the Renaissance magical conception of nature, teaching that seemingly trivial acts such as reciting certain words may have the most stupendous consequences.)

Idealization is the reduction of each problem to its basic, essential form. It is the idea of the mass-point. It is the treatment of the earth's surface as a plane, and of perpendiculars to it as parallel. It is the famous distinction between primary and secondary qualities made by Galileo in the *Saggiatore*. It is the confidence with which Galileo ignores friction, resistance, and the non-Euclidean character of all physical things. It is the assurance with which Galileo denies that color is other than subjective;[19] which causes him to assert that the air could only cool down meteors as it does porridge;[20] which renders him skeptical of the complications introduced by professional astronomers—whether the observational complications due to Tycho Brahe or the theoretical ones madly proposed by Kepler—so that all his life Galileo held to his faith in perfect circular motion. It is the Platonism of Galileo's conviction that the pendulum is perfectly isochronous, that projectiles move in parabolas and chains hang in them. It is the delightful simplicity of his theory of structures.

It is not only the case that idealization enabled Galileo to reach many results that were essentially correct, but that he could not have reached any results without it. He could have had no mathematical theory of projectiles, of pendulums or of structures except a simple one; he could not have written the *Dialogo* or the *Discorsi* had he accepted Kepler's ellipses. The extraordinary thing is that Galileo's idealization was so sound and so fruitful. In this it set a pattern for what was to happen when other branches of sciences, reaching maturity, assumed their modern form: all required some idealization, a pattern of idealization that would work satisfactorily until amended and filled out. What is unusual with Galileo and the science of motion is the low significance of induction (as compared, say, with chemistry, electricity, or natural history) and the high content of mathematics. I do not know whether this makes Galileo's task harder than Darwin's—comparison is pointless; but it *does* suggest that Galileo's is not the only model.

Geometrization and mechanization

Geometrization is closely allied to idealization: once again I need scarcely do more than refer you to the writings of M. Koyré. Of course we know now that the simple attempt to make a calculus of motion was far from original with Galileo: we know how far the Middle Ages had anticipated his theorems.[21] However, even at this level I believe Galileo had much greater significance for the seventeenth century (and all time pre-Duhem) than some recent work might lead one to suppose. Whether the medieval and Renaissance investigators of motion were forgotten or misunderstood, I do not know: but I have not heard that Galileo's large claims in this respect were ever in his lifetime rebutted with charges of plagiarism.

And he was surely a popular target. Descartes, Beeckman and others failed precisely where Galileo succeeded, though their inheritance from the past was as competent as his. Neither they nor their successors doubted that the credit was entirely Galileo's. It is a curious story. We must say that Galileo comes at the end of a long tradition of investigation in mechanics, upon which he obviously drew, "Merton Rule" and all; yet, paradoxically enough, his significance as a writer on mechanics for posterity is as great as though that tradition had never existed. There is no doubt at all that Galileo first correctly defined acceleration for modern physics, and introduced into it the law of fall. And it is almost equally certain that no others at that time would ultimately have succeeded in the absence of Galileo; everyone else of whom we know seems to have been on quite the wrong track.

It is still more interesting to consider Galileo's status as the founder of modern mathematical physics—which is a larger version of Koyré's "geometrization of space". At the outset it must be allowed that Galileo had a kind of blindness in detail—I have touched on it—the idealist's blindness toward the true mathematical intricacy of nature. He could have learned something of that from the astronomers, but the means for such a synthesis did not yet exist. What we admire in Galileo's removal of physics from the polarized, spherical coordinates of the Aristotelian cosmos to an unbounded space of Euclidean coordinates is a move of surpassing simplicity. Too simple indeed; so simple that of course even Galileo could not quite complete it, as we shall see later.

Mathematical physics has many roots. The chief of them, the longest, and the most continuous, is in astronomy: for astronomy was the first branch of science to be rendered numerical. We know that Galileo's relation to mathematical astronomy was ambiguous, and I shall explore this further. The next in importance if not in age is Archimedes' science of statics; Archimedes, whom Galileo regarded as his grand master, and whose methods he sought to emulate. Then there are other branches of "applied mathematics"—optics, music, geography, not to mention the dubious or the useful mathematical arts.

Before Galileo, all the mathematical sciences (if we except the black ones) were colored by superficiality; they described, but sometimes only in a fictional voice ("saving the appearances"), and they did not go to the heart of things. Here was the natural philosopher's province. It was the natural philosopher who told how the heavenly spheres are put together; who determined the nature of light, and knew its strange significance; who was the authority on matter and change, and the manifold phenomena of things. At best the mathematician was concerned with a few accidental properties; at worst he was a mere numerical drudge. Fourteenth-century scholastics were indeed far more mathematical than Aristotle, yet even so they left numerical analysis highly artificial (because it was arbitrary) and narrowly limited. I do not say that the mathematical physics of the seventeenth century stemmed wholly from Galileo; we must give due weight to the medieval background and to Galileo's direct predecessors and contemporaries—Tartaglia, Cardan, Benedetti, Stevin, Snel, Descartes and many more too numerous to recite. Nevertheless, there are good reasons for singling out Galileo's influence and example as the decisive ones.

In the first place, he expressed his metaphysical confidence in the mathematical form of knowledge decisively and clearly, separating it (by the way) from the dubious kind of "mathematics" beloved by such as Bruno and Fludd.[22] Galileo's is hard-headed mathematics, even if it is figuratively described as "the language of the book of nature". The passages in the *Saggiatore*, the *Dialogo*, the *Discorsi* and elsewhere are quite familiar; allow me merely to remind you of Galileo's awareness of the process of successive approximation by which Euclidean idealism can be adjusted to the irregularities and imperfections of the physical world.[23] The potential complexity of mathematical science is in principle unlimited, Galileo knows, though he prefers with Plato (and Kepler) to regard nature as possessing the beauties of economy and simplicity.

Secondly, by making successful analyses of particular phenomena, Galileo showed how the mathematical physicist could solve problems and add to knowledge. Mathematics was not necessarily either mystic or arbitrary: it could be intellectually useful—especially with regard to motion, but in other ways too. Further, it is through such analyses of the vacuum, of sound, and so on, of the kind Galileo attempts in the *Discorsi*, that the mathematical philosopher is enabled to penetrate to the heart of physical reality. Indeed, for Galileo there is no physical reality outside the scope of mathematical analysis; and so, thirdly, he proves that a mathematical science can be constructed in a formal way so as to leave no room for wordy "natural philosophy".

Archimedes had done this long before for statics. Galileo's was only the second attempt and the second success. The author of the Third Day of the *Discorsi* must yield to Archimedes in point of sheer originality of aim, but he wins on the generality, scope and importance of his subject. Is not this formality of treatment, with its internal logical rigor, a very significant advance on Galileo's part beyond the level of his medieval precursors? For this formality is the essence of modern mathematical physics, to the extent that it becomes impossible to express equations in physical terms or even in adequate forms of words; a result that could not possibly follow from the medieval attempt to express philosophical concepts in numerical form.

Finally, by mathematizing motion Galileo carried mathematics to the heart of physics. Presumably no one ever doubted that the central questions of physics involve problems of motion (in the most general sense), for Aristotle had made this plain. But with Aristotle movement is undefinable, nonnumerical, precisely because it is universally causative. It was Galileo's genius—once more, with prior hints—to reduce this Protean dynamism of things to order, by separating causes from modes, among other things. I do not need to develop this argument at length because one has only to survey the reactions of Galileo's contemporaries to discover their sense of the universal, transforming import of his achievement. At the time, I think, it certainly seemed no simple matter of falling stones and flying cannon-balls. Everyone realized that philosophy was at stake.

Nor need I dwell on the obvious point that this mathematical success of Galileo's was of even greater interest to those who ascribed all the dynamism of nature to the motion of its minute component parts. The mechanical philosophy was held and, with some restraint, taught by Galileo himself. It was the seventeenth-century flowering of mechanism that made Galilean mathematical physics—that is, the science of the motions of physical bodies—the fundamental science. But equally, without mathematics mechanism would have remained empty speculation, much as it had been in antiquity. To marry together these essential complementary attitudes to nature—the mechanical and the mathematical—was the deeper, less obvious aspect of the Newtonian synthesis, prepared by Galileo. Perhaps Galileo nowhere explicitly envisages a physics that is both particulate and mathematical; but it would be a hardened skeptic who could read him without the sense that this was what he was driving at, even if he was not fully conscious of his direction. The rapid conceptual development of nonmathematical mechanism in mid-century through the work of Descartes, Gassendi and Boyle did not wholly obscure the connection which Galileo had begun and Mersenne confirmed; which Huygens was to extend and Newton to perfect.

The unification of science

There remains Galileo's role in the unification of science, and I have already given away the secret. The mathematization of nature itself entails a certain unity in the world-view; it is imposed by the opinion that there is no knowledge more fundamental than that of the mathematical physicist. I have already attributed such an opinion to Galileo.

It would be elementary to contrast this with the categorization of the Aristotelian cosmos. To break down these categories, one must be a Copernican; to be a Copernican, one must be a Galilean. That is why the important issue of philosophical and scientific controversy during the early seventeenth century was: is it true or false that the earth moves? Not: are the appearances more consistent with the motion or fixity of the earth? It is imaginable that the Copernician issue might have been left as a specialist problem for astronomers, on the ground that it was an insoluble problem. Certainly, however, if this had happened, the history of science would have been quite different, because the unification of ideas effected by Galileo on the foundation of Copernicanism would have been absent and (correspondingly) the mechanical philosophy would have been emasculated or destroyed. Hence there could have been no Newton.

There is no doubt, then, that philosophically Galileo was highly successful in inculcating belief in a single physics, with mechanics, astronomy, chemistry and so on as its specialized departments. But from a scientific point of view, this single fabric was full of holes and patches: what Galileo sometimes seemed to take for granted was indeed still an aspiration, not to be fulfilled until long after the seventeenth century closed. As everyone now knows, Galileo succeeded, or nearly succeeded, in removing the physical objections to the motion of the earth; he did not succeed in reconciling the true—I mean the Newtonian—laws of motion with the Copernican planetary system. Hence Galileo's reticence or doubt about the exact construction of that system as he conceived it; hence his silence concerning Kepler's laws, and his skepticism regarding computational astronomy.

There was bound to be some discontinuity when the attempt was made to fit circular orbits into Euclidean space: Galileo's attempt to resolve the strain by identifying the straight line with the arc of circle of near-infinite radius could not succeed. Of course this was an idealization: the idealization (as Galileo pointed out) that permitted Archimedes' theory of the balance to take a practicable shape. Its function for Galileo was that it enabled him to pull mechanics and astronomy together in a kind of synthesis, inadequate and premature as it must seem to post-Newtonian eyes. Given that inertial motion in very large circles is possible, as in the horizontal or concentric component of motion of a falling body, then the motion of the planets requires no explanation, and earthbound bodies become free of centrifugal acceleration.[24] Or, to put it another way, Galileo is able to eschew the concept of nonimpulsive mechanical forces, though of course he recognized the esoteric ones, such as gravity and magnetism, which had so far defied rational explanation.[25] In fact, pursuing simplicity so ardently, Galileo comes near to saying that the science of motion is kinematics and nothing more.[26]

I do not produce these difficulties to belittle Galileo. We are not here concerned with some oversight or mistake but with a conception (erroneous, it is true) so essential to Galileo's achievement that he could have taken no step forward without it, unless indeed he had avoided it by himself writing the *Principia*. The point to which I mean to draw attention is the way in which this crucial feature of Galileo's thought lies at the root of seventeenth-century research into mechanics: it concerns the establishment of the precise laws of motion, the concept of force, the investigation into centripetal acceleration, the dynamics of orbits and, inevitably, the theory of gravitation itself. It is hardly too much to say that Newton had to write the *Principia* because Descartes had corrected Galileo's notion of inertia. All this discovery unfolded and was bound to unfold from the critical consideration of Galileo's attempt to reconcile physics and astronomy through his form of a general concept of inertia. That is indeed a measure of intellectual fertility! Just as one can properly say of Kepler that his discovery of the three laws of planetary motion sprang from his peculiar combination of qualities—an extraordinary ability in mathematical astronomy combined with an extravagantly Platonic imagination—so one can say of Galileo that only the man who could systematize and unify even at the cost of blending the straight line into the circle could have succeeded in creating the appropriate platform on which further research could be built. Like Newton's gravity, Lavoisier's combustion, Rutherford's atom, Galileo's mechanics was wrong in a way that made it triumphantly right.

Conclusion

To sum up: I suppose we may express the historical significance of a scientist metaphorically by saying that it consists in the strength or the deflection which he has given to a line or several lines of scientific activity. We are not to judge this in terms of good or ill; it either happened or did not happen. Galileo, I believe, strengthened many nascent lines of modern science, and deflected them in appropriate directions. Among them I would single out: his handling of the Copernican crux, beyond all praise adroit and creative; his development of mathematical physics with mechanics as its basis, setting the pattern which classical physics was to follow; and his assertion of the unity of knowledge. These were magnificent and necessary accomplishments.

There are on the other hand some matters of which I have said little, where I think the credit sometimes given to Galileo may be excessive: I do not think he had a decisive formative influence upon the later evolution of experimental science, or that he had much to do with making science useful and sociologically functional, or that he effectively liberated scientific thought from shackles of dogma. As that is a perverse skepticism, perhaps a word of explanation may be added: it was not until very much later that science was confident enough to depart from the protection of orthodoxy, wherever it was practiced. Perhaps, as a last word, the warmest admirer of Galileo may allow that other minds have made even more profound or enduring contributions to thought about nature: Aristotle, Archimedes, Newton, for example. But one thing can be said of Galileo beyond all doubt: surely of all the great intellects in our race, none is more fascinating; none is a richer, more varied, more human being; none wider, more entertaining, or more astonishing in the play of his mind. Anyone who knows anything of Galileo—even the fairy tales that scholars have tried so hard to dispel—knows him not as a disembodied mind alone, or a name, but as a man who lived long, passionately, and effectively.

NOTES

1. Jean Etienne Montucla, *Histoire des mathématiques*, Paris, 1758, vol. 2, p. 260.
2. William Whewell, *History of the inductive sciences*, London, 1837, vol. 2, p. 51.
3. I mean to deny neither that Galileo was a competent, indeed a gifted mathematician, nor that he made some inductions; but his capacities in either respect (taken alone) would not have given him his present stature.
4. Compare the first few pages of M. Alexandre Koyré's admirable *Études galiléennes*, 1939*. I believe M. Koyré would later have agreed that in order to emphasize the crucial importance of the intellectualist approach to nature, it is not necessary to denounce the empiricist.
5. William Wotton, *Reflections upon ancient and modern learning*, 3rd edn., London, 1705, p. 348.
6. As everyone knows, although he taught the elements of the subject expected of a teacher of mathematics, Galileo never was a professional astronomer in the ordinary sense, like, say, Magini, or Clavius or Kepler. In fact, he profoundly distrusted positional astronomy, whose results conflicted seriously with his own world-view. Galileo's qualitative astronomy, and his use of it in philosophical argument, were his own inventions.

7. Paul Tannery, "Galilée et les principes de la dynamique", p. 394. (This essay will be found in its entirety later in this volume.)

8. Obviously, many limited problems in mechanics, including some with which Galileo was greatly concerned (including descent on inclined planes and the law of fall) could be and had been discussed within the Aristotelian frame of things. But this frame could not have tolerated Galileo's great discussions of inertia and the relativity of motion, nor his corresponding insistence on the unity and universality of mechanics. It was the Copernican problem that here gave him his breadth of vision.

9. I have suggested elsewhere that Galileo and Newton were much more alike in their combined defense of heliocentricity and rational mechanics than is usually supposed: see my *From Galileo to Newton*, 1963*, p. 306.

10. This generalization requires qualification in detail. Galileo continued to seek for a perfect *ephemeris* of Jupiter's satellites with the hope of solving the problem of longitudes. For his late technical interest in astronomy, see, for example, *Opere, 17*, p. 212 (letter of November 5, 1637). Nevertheless, nothing came of all this.

11. See, for example, Drake's translation of the *Dialogo: Two chief systems of the world*, 1953*, pp. 81, 322–327.

12. Nevertheless, Galileo deceived himself into thinking that his theory of the tides substantiated Copernicus. One can only remark of this that his error (repeated much later by John Wallis) was systematic as well as particular. It flew in the face of his own relativistic principles.

13. For a full treatment, see Richard Braithwaite, *Scientific explanation*, 1953*. It may be quite properly urged that the "Galileo" or "Newton" of a philosophical thesis is not necessarily to be identified with the historical figure of the same name; yet it can hardly be doubted that the analysis derives some strength from the measure of its historical accuracy.

14. Fortunately one hardly encounters any longer the statement that Galileo derived his law of acceleration from a long series of experiments on the inclined plane!

15. I am grateful to Mr. David Lindberg for a study of instances in the *Discourse on floating bodies* where Galileo seems to base unjustifiable statements of fact upon points of theory which he regarded with confidence. In a well-known case, it is agreed that Galileo could not (in any serious sense) have derived the design of his first telescope, unaided, from an adequate theory previously known to him, though this is what he claimed.

16. See Alexandre Koyré, "An experiment in measurement", 1953*; Thomas Settle, "An experiment in the history of science", 1961*. However, it remains true: (1) there were causes of experimental error that Galileo could not have evaluated; (2) it is not independently demonstrated that the experimental results are applicable to free fall; and (3) Galileo relies on assertion—not data.

17. *Discorsi*, p. 171.

18. *Dialogo*, pp. 145, 248.

19. The first association of color—or rather of whiteness and blackness—with absorption of heat is in a very amusing letter from Benedetto Castelli to Galileo of June 27, 1637 (*Opere, 17*, pp. 121–122). Castelli seems to deduce the idea

that black absorbs more heat than white on the basis of some unspecified notions of Galileo concerning the nature of heat, and reports a validating experiment whose result he calls "an astonishing thing".

20. The "Babylonian" passage is justly one of the most celebrated in Galileo's writings (cf. Stillman Drake, *Discoveries and opinions of Galileo*, 1957*, p. 272), yet one must admit that its logic is false.

21. Cf. Marshall Clagett, *The science of mechanics in the Middle Ages*, 1959*, esp. pp. 331–367.

22. Cf. Frances A. Yates, *Giordano Bruno and the Hermetic tradition*, London, 1964.

23. *Dialogo*, pp. 203–208. When it is said above that Galileo had insufficient awareness of the intricacy of physics, I meant that he did not perceive how profoundly and how invariably such adjustments must be made.

24. It is significant that Galileo nowhere makes it clear—except in his theory of projectiles—that the component of motion "parallel" to the surface is actually a straight line, even though he knew that bodies "fly off at a tangent" from a rotating wheel.

25. Among other things, this follows from the previous point. For Galileo could not conceive of a body being accelerated from a point (e.g. the center of its previous rotation) without a physical impulse acting upon it.

26. Although Galileo is to define "naturally accelerated motion" in the *Discorsi*, in the *Dialogo* he seems to infer in two strange passages (pp. 19, 32) that "only circular motion can naturally suit bodies which are integral parts of the universe" (e.g. the planets) and such circular motion can obviously be no other than uniform. Rectilinear movements are accordingly "violent" or such as are "assigned by nature to its bodies (and their parts) whenever these are found outside their proper places . . ." If these statements of Salviati are to be taken as reflecting Galileo's thoughts at some time in his life, then clearly for him (as for Aristotle) there are no natural forces, properly speaking. However, it is clear that this double dichotomy of circular/rectilinear, celestial/terrestrial effectively violates Galileo's endeavor toward a unified physics, and later (e.g. p. 165) he seeks to get around it.

Part II

Background

4 · Galileo and his precursors

JAMES A. WEISHEIPL

Galileo is not the only genius whose quatercentenary we celebrated in 1964. Galileo was born at Pisa on February 15, 1564, prospered intellectually at Padua, and died in his villa near Florence seventy-eight years later. But William Shakespeare too was born that same year at Stratford-on-Avon, possibly in April, prodigiously produced his plays in London, and died in his home at Stratford fifty-two years later. Galileo and Shakespeare are not so far apart as we might imagine at first. Although Galileo staged no plays, he wrote dialogues of undoubted literary merit. Although Shakespeare discovered no new sciences, he revealed the cosmos in lines of unquestioned philosophical perfection. Shakespeare trod the wooden stage of the Globe Theatre, while Galileo played the virtuoso on that wider stage of which Shakespeare spoke in *As you like it* (Act 2, Scene 7): "All's the world's a stage, and all the men and women merely players. They have their exits and their entrances." While Shakespeare found "Tongues in trees, books in the running brooks, sermons in stones and good in everything", Galileo found "philosophy written in that vast book, the universe, written in the mathematical language of triangles, circles and other geometrical figures, without which it is humanly impossible to comprehend a single word".[1] Galileo, in his unique performance on the stage of life, often shared the sentiments of Shakespeare's great characters: the introspective melancholy, the clear-sighted objectivity of Hamlet, the zest for reality and life of the Duke in *As you like it*. But there is a decided difference between Shakespeare and Galileo in retrospect. Shakespeare never occasioned an epidemic of *precursoritis* among historians. But Galileo has not ceased to afflict historians since 1906 with infectious precursoritis in mild, chronic and acute forms.

Before the work of Pierre Duhem in 1906, historians thought of Galileo as an intellectual Melchisedech, "without father, without mother, without genealogy".[2] Even today youthful readers still read this myth in outdated textbooks. Duhem changed that. After him an entirely new field of historical investigation opened up, and scholars brought to light a mountainous mass of material hitherto unsuspected. Scholars, disagreeing with one another, began to discover precursors of Galileo everywhere or else nowhere. Today, almost half a century after the death of Pierre Duhem, there is some confusion, consternation and uncertainty about the precursors of Galileo.

In general, historians of science promote and dispute among themselves five precursorships for Galileo. Actually there are more, but five is sufficient for one essay: (1) the scholastic theory of impetus; (2) the nominalist theory of Ockham; (3) the Paduan method of composition and resolution; (4) the Mertonian mathematics of kinematics and dynamics; (5) the influence of the Platonic and Archimedean traditions. This last has already been discussed at length in several other essays in this book. We may have a better understanding of Galileo after a glance at his "precursors".

The scholastic doctrine of impetus and the Galilean principle of inertia

Shakespeare starts one of his more sonorous sonnets with the words:

> Let me not to the marriage of true minds
> admit impediments. Love is not love
> which alters when it alteration finds . . .
> O, no! It is an ever-fixed mark . . .

Galileo sought to remove impediments to the motion of two bodies. He found impediments in Aristotelian final causes, in a love for natural place, that alters when it alteration finds, as in projectile motion. He sought an ever-fixed mark, the principle of inertia.

The principle of inertia is undoubtedly, as Whitehead called it, "the first article of the creed of science". In its classical formulaton by Newton, it runs: "every body continues in its state of rest or of uniform motion in a straight line, unless it is compelled to change that state by forces impressed upon it". This principle, envisaged by Galileo in the *Discorsi*, and enunciated by Beeckman, Descartes and others as the first law of nature, states that motion and rest are equally privileged states, not needing any cause to explain their continuation—no efficient cause, no final cause, no medium. Only a change of state needs explanation.

The case of a moving body is of particular interest for both Aristotle and Duhem. Aristotle found no difficulty in explaining what he called "natural motions", i.e., invariable, spontaneous motions, such as the free fall of heavy bodies, and the self-motion of living bodies. In living bodies, the soul or vital principle allows the animal to move itself by means of its parts; all living things (according to Aristotle) are true self-movers, efficient causes of their own motion. Nonliving things, not being able to move themselves, have within themselves, however, a spontaneous source for natural motions; this intrinsic source for Aristotle is *"physis"*, or nature as form. Natural motions are defined as those which arise from such an intrinsic source, from *physis*. *Physis* is not, therefore, an efficient cause of self-motion; it is not a *movens* or *motor conjunctus*, accompanying the body, as some historians have imagined. It is simply a source, a beginning, an *arché* of spontaneous, natural activity, whether this activity be locomotion, alteration or growth. When forced to determine the efficient cause of natural activity in *Physics* VIII, Aristotle simply explains that it is the original generator of the body. The original generator endowed the body with all it needs to do what comes naturally.

The real problem for Aristotle was to explain compulsory or "violent" motions in nature. Since violent motions are forced upon a body from without, their source cannot reside in the body itself. Aristotle, therefore, suggested—an advance over Plato—that the medium in which the body is moving must be held to possess, in such a case, the power to exert continuous extrinsic force upon the body. When a boy throws a stone, he is the real cause, the culprit in Aristotle's view. The continuation of the forced motion toward a window is made possible only by the continued exertions of the air upon the stone. The boy, of course, would be the real efficient cause of the atmospheric perturbations as well as of the initial projection. It is important to realize why Aristotle suggested this theory, so contrary to common sense. It was not that everything in motion needs to be moved by another, as some believe. It was simply that all forced or nonnatural motions must be imposed from without (*ab alio*), and indeed continuously, simply because they *are* forced.

Pierre Duhem began his investigations with Leonardo da Vinci and Albert of Saxony. He soon discovered that there had been a lively discussion of projectile motion among Parisian masters in arts early in the fourteenth century. This discussion involved the rejection of Aristotle's view, as well as a new explanation of continued violent motion in terms of an alien, soon-to-be-lost force (*vis*) impressed upon the projectile itself by the thrower. This force would make continued exertion by an external medium unnecessary. Jean Buridan, intellectual leader of the Paris masters, went so far as to suggest that in the absence of any resistance, the impressed force would continue forever. Since celestial bodies, in Aristotelian theory, are not subject to external resisting forces, Buridan saw no reason why God could not have given them *impetus impressi* in the beginning and thereby dispense with angelic movers of the spheres. Duhem published the third volume of his *Études*, subtitled *Les précurseurs parisiens de Galilée* in 1913; there for the first time, Jean Buridan and his followers were credited with anticipating the principle of inertia.

Duhem was aware that the sixth-century Christian scholar, John Philoponus of Alexandria, had likewise rejected Aristotle's suggestion and developed a theory of an "incorporeal motive power" impressed on the moving body. But the Latin scholastics did not know Philoponus' Greek commentary, and Simplicius, whose work was translated, did not bother to present the Alexandrian's position clearly. Professor Pines suggests that Avicenna may have transmitted the theory of Philoponus to the West. But the Latin version of Avicenna's paraphrase, the *Sufficientia*, covers only the first four books, and the single vague reference in Book II, ch. 8, can still be understood in the orthodox Aristotelian sense. Every attempt thus far to connect the scholastic theory of impetus with John Philoponus has failed to convince.

Konstanty Michalski, and later Anneliese Maier,[3] have shown that Buridan, the secular master in arts, was anticipated by the Franciscan theologian, Francis de Marchia, who expounded the impetus theory clearly in his discussion of instrumental causality of the sacraments in the academic year 1319–1320 at Paris. Historians have been endeavoring to determine, if possible, whether there was any earlier philosophical source for the theory put forward in Marchia's theological commentary on the *Sentences;* they are also anxious to determine whether—and, if so, how—Buridan learned of the theologian's theory. But these are minor details not affecting the real issue.

Fundamentally, the scholastic theory of impetus was not an overthrow of Aristotle, although it constituted a rejection on the grounds of implausibility of a particular view proposed by Aristotle. Corrections of this kind were made from the very moment Aristotle's work arrived in the Latin Christian West and never ceased. With regard to the theory of impetus, Francis de Marchia and Jean Buridan were most careful to point out that this *"impetus"* or *"virtus derelicta a motore"* is an "accidental and extrinsic force", an alien and violent imposition, which will gradually be overcome by the innate, natural forces of the body. Therefore, *impetus* remains extrinsic and *ab alio*, while it affects the moving body. Instead of overthrowing the Aristotelian distinction between natural and violent motions, the theory of impetus strengthened it by eliminating a most improbable hypothesis. Later scholastics, like Laurence Londorius, first Rector of St. Andrew's, Agostino Nipho, Tommaso de Vio, and Alexander Piccolómini, presented the impetus theory as the true doctrine of Aristotle. Eminent Thomists, such as John Capreolus and Domingo de Soto, claimed it as the "opinion of St. Thomas". When the scholastics corrected Aristotle, they generally considered the correction to be the "true" mind of the Philosopher.

Not all scholastics, however, explained the theory of impetus with the

same ability, accuracy and precision, just as not all modern historians understand scholastic principles with equal ability, accuracy and precision.
The best scholastic minds did not, in fact, explain the projectile as a self-
mover—some modern histories notwithstanding. They did not explain *impetus* as a *motor conjunctus*, a mover accompanying the body. And they
did not think that *impetus* eliminated causal explanations of motion as a
process. As far back as 1940, Anneliese Maier clearly showed that the
scholastic theory of impetus had nothing whatever in common with the
principle of inertia. Ten years ago I myself reached the same conclusion
quite independently, working from another direction. Although the word
'*impeto*' in early classical physics is undoubtedly derived from the Latin
'*impetus*' in late scholastic philosophy, the conceptual significance of the
two is radically different. To put the matter simply, Galileo's *impeto* or
momento is a characteristic quantity associated with every moving body
(later to be defined as the product of mass and velocity), whereas Buridan's *impetus* is an instrumental cause of projectile motion, an alien quality by means of which an agent carries out his intent.

Recently Professor E. J. Dijksterhuis has acknowledged the "ontological" difference between the *impetus* of the scholastics and the *impeto* of
classical physics. But he insists that "phenomenologically" there is not the
slightest difference between the two.[4] In this and in other "phenomenological" comparisons, Dijksterhuis reaches agreement or disagreement by
describing ideas, principles and theories of antiquity in modern mathematical notation and by eliminating their historical, philosophical and ontological significance, as Miss Maier has pointed out. Such a "phenomenological" comparison leaves much to be desired. Some historians, such as Fr.
Jean Abelé, go even further than Dijksterhuis. Others, like Herbert But-
terfield and René Dugas, are content to repeat Duhem's original claim.

The question is not whether Galileo shared and taught the views of
medieval critics of Aristotle. Of this there can be no doubt. Galileo's *De
motu*, written when he was between twenty-five and twenty-eight years
of age, is no more than a reflection of fourteenth-century views and arguments, less profound and perceptive perhaps than the work of Buridan,
but recognizably medieval nonetheless. The question, however, is whether
the scholastic theory of *impetus* inspired the new Galileo and the principle
of inertia. Alexandre Koyré, who has himself helped to throw light on
the long continuous tradition from Buridan to Benedetti, Bruno and Galileo, summarizes the present position as follows:

> The conclusion drawn therefrom by Duhem is a delusion: a well-prepared
> revolution is nevertheless a revolution . . . the science born from (Galileo's)
> efforts and discoveries does not follow the inspiration of the "Parisian pre-
> cursors of Galileo"; it places itself at once on a quite different level.[5]

Miss Maier goes so far as to say that not only did the scholastics not perceive the principle of inertia, but that they could not have perceived it,

precisely because of their erroneous doctrine of "*Omne quod movetur ab alio movetur*". This last point is another matter. But as far as the scholastic doctrine of impetus is concerned, at least, the foremost scholars of today believe the time has come to apply Ockham's razor to Duhem's theory.

Ockham as a precursor

In Act II, Scene 2, old Polonius asks of Hamlet, "What do you read?" to which Hamlet replies, "Words. Words. Words." This brings to mind William of Ockham.

A surprising number of historians consider Ockham to be the real "father of modern science" and the most significant precursor of Galileo. This early fourteenth-century English Oxford Franciscan initiated a new intellectual movement, known to historians as late scholastic nominalism; it was to have considerable influence on later theological speculation. For Ockham, only individual substances and individual qualities are real; everything else is a word, a term, a *nomen*, needing logical analysis. Consequently the problem of projectile motion and the theory of impetus were meaningless to Ockham, and he rejected the theory of impetus proposed by Francis de Marchia. Words such as 'motion', 'time', 'cause' and 'quantity' signify nothing other than individual substances and qualities under different circumstances. The term 'quantity', for example, signifies that the parts of matter are not all together; not-being-all-together is a negation, an *ens rationis*, which clearly cannot be a positive reality in things. It is surprising, therefore, that historians should consider Ockham the "father of modern science", where quantitative characteristics play such a fundamental role.

Other scholars see Ockham as the forerunner of modern linguistic analysis. Some regard him as the promoter, if not the founder, of the sort of empiricism that is characteristic of modern science, since he admitted the reality of concrete individuals only. Yet the empiricists of early modern science rejected the Aristotelian concept of substance; nor would they have wished to reduce the notion of quantitative measure to a mere verbalism. Still other historians describe Ockham's identification of quantity with substance as a simple Cartesian insight, i.e. the recognition that the essence of matter is extension. But Ockham's relating of quantity to matter was far more subtle than that of Descartes. In Ockham's view, a material substance may or may not be extended in space. If its parts are extended, i.e. not-all-together, we say that it is quantified. But this so-called "quantity", according to Ockham, is variable, as is proved by condensation and rarefaction. In fact, the parts of matter can be so condensed as to eliminate extension altogether, as occurs in the Holy Eucharist. I have pointed out elsewhere the vast difference between Ockham's conception of "quantity" and the conception of Descartes and Galileo.[6]

The most interesting case presented for Ockham as a forerunner of Galileo and modern physics is suggested by Professor Dijksterhuis and Sir

Edmund Whittaker. In their view, Ockham eliminated the concept of motion as an absolute reality, a process to be maintained; moreover, he rejected the fundamental principle of medieval physics, namely that "everything that is moved must be moved by another"; therefore Ockham in effect anticipated the modern principle of inertia. Sir Edmund Whittaker, in a recent critique of Aquinas' first proof for God's existence, said:

> The first proof, or the proof from motion, is open to the objection, first brought against it by Duns Scotus and William of Ockham, that the principle *omne quod movetur ab alio movetur*, on which the whole argument depends, is irreconcilable with sound dynamical science, and is therefore false.[7]

Sir Edmund takes this fundamental law of Aristotelian physics to mean that whatever is actually in motion must be preserved in motion by a distinct mover (*movens*) in continuous contact. This is the common understanding of the principle by modern historians. A more elaborate modern paraphrase of "*omne quod movetur ab alio movetur*" is expressed by Miss Maier when she says:

> Every movement requires a particular mover bound to it and generating it directly, and every normal, successive motion taking place requires a resistance which opposes the moving force and which is overcome by that force, since without resistance there would be no *motus*, but *mutatio*, i.e. an instantaneous change of place.[8]

This indeed is what Ockham and Scotus took the principle to mean, and they rejected it, for rather different reasons. Ockham rejected the principle because 'motion' is only a word; it does not signify a distinct reality needing preservation. Scotus rejected the principle "*Omne quod movetur ab alio movetur*", partly because it is not self-evident that everything in motion must be moved by another, and also because some things in the universe, e.g., the human will, living things, water becoming cool, move themselves and do not need to be moved by any other natural cause. Scotus thus rejected the universality of the principle in order to safeguard the existence of self-motion in the universe. Scotus merely rejected the universality of the Aristotelian principle, but Ockham, studying at Oxford one generation after Scotus had departed, rejected the principle itself as meaningless.

Ockham, however, was not the first scholastic to reject the principle "*omne quod movetur ab alio movetur*", in the sense in which it has been understood by modern historians and by most scholastics. My own researches have shown that it was also rejected in no uncertain terms by Thomas Aquinas, Albertus Magnus, and even by the great Aristotelian, Siger of Brabant. To summarize these researches, three points can be made. First, the commonly accepted interpretation of the "fundamental law of medieval physics" is not Aristotle's, Aquinas', Albert's or Siger's interpretation. There is no doubt in my mind now that this interpretation was imposed upon Aristotle's text by Averroes. I do not say that it is

original with Averroes, but only that the Latin West received this interpretation from Averroes, not from Aristotle. Second, the requirement
that all motion should meet with resistance, a requirement clearly expressed by Miss Maier's paraphrase, derives likewise not from Aristotle,
but from Averroes. Aristotle never said that motion in a vacuum would
have to be instantaneous, and that it is therefore impossible. But this is
what Averroes thought Aristotle meant. Ernest Moody's famous study,
"Galileo and Avempace" (1951*), clearly shows that Avempace and
Aquinas were justified in rejecting Averroes' doctrine of resistance.
Third, and most important, even rejection of the Averroist "*omne quod
movetur ab alio movetur*" does not necessarily lead to the principle of
inertia; in fact, it does not even prepare the way for it. Certain scholastics
of the thirteenth and fourteenth centuries did in fact reject the Averroist
principle, but they were far, very far, from discovering the principle of
inertia. This required the genius of Galileo, who was well acquainted with
the Paduan Averroists of his day.

The School of Padua

Galileo might very well have expressed the sentiments of Lucentio in
The taming of the shrew, Act 1, Scene 1:

> . . . For the great desire I had
> To see fair Padua, nursery of arts,
> I am arriv'd for fruitful Lombardy,
> The pleasant garden of great Italy, . . .
> Here let us breathe and haply institute
> A course of learning and ingenious studies.
> Pisa, renowned for grave citizens,
> Give me my being and my father first . . .
>   . . . I have Pisa left
> And am to Padua come, as he that leaves
> A shallow plash to plunge him in the deep, . . .

Galileo's conscious concern with scientific method, demonstration and
the problem of knowledge was carefully studied over fifty years ago by
Ernst Cassirer. In 1906, Cassirer noted that Galileo's description of his
own *metodo resolutivo* and *metodo compositivo* is very similar to that of
Giacomo Zabarella, the Italian Averroist who "summed up the collective
wisdom of the Paduan school". According to Galileo, when one has ascertained a fact or conclusion by means of the senses, experiments and observations, one employs the method of resolution to discover "some proposition before demonstrated" or "some principle known *per se*". When some
such proposition has been discovered, one assumes this proposition to be
true and by the compositive or syllogistic method deduces the consequences that must follow.

Cassirer's comparison of Zabarella and Galileo has been taken up by

A. C. Crombie and by J. H. Randall. Crombie has studied the significance of the resolutive and compositive method in the writings of Robert Grosseteste; he claims that medieval discussions of scientific method prepared the way for Galileo's scientific methodology. Randall has described the views on scientific method in Padua immediately prior to Galileo's arrival at that university:

> The originality of Zabarella and of the whole development of which he is the culmination is to set off a "scientific experience" from mere ordinary observation. . . . Scientific method proceeds from the rigorous analysis of a few selected instances or illustrations to a general principle, and then goes from the principle back to the systematic and ordered body of facts, to the science itself formally expressed. Zabarella calls this the combination of the resolutive and compositive methods; and such were precisely the procedure and the terms of Galileo.[9]

The methods of resolution and composition, of course, are purely Aristotelian. The whole of the *Posterior analytics* explains the method of resolution or analysis, while composition or synthesis is nothing but the syllogistic presentation evaluated in the *Prior analytics*. Randall, therefore, concludes that Galileo belonged to the Aristotelian tradition characteristic of the school of Padua. Randall's thesis has "won wide acceptance" among historians.

Neal Gilbert, at one time a supporter of Randall's thesis, has recently expressed "a dissenting opinion with regard to its crucial point, namely, the presumed debt of Galileo to Zabarella".[10] Dr. Gilbert offers three reasons for his dissenting view. First, Galileo's expressed opposition to the "Aristotelians" and their method would seem to include Zabarella: "The methodology of the Aristotelians relied exclusively on the syllogism, but Galileo specifically insists that the syllogism has no value in scientific discovery." Second, Galileo never acknowledged a debt to Zabarella; nor as far as we know did he even possess a copy of Zabarella's work. Third, Galileo tells us in the *De motu* that his method is "that which my mathematicians taught me", and not that of "certain philosophers" who take too much for granted. Gilbert, therefore, believes that Galileo was not indebted to Zabarella and the Aristotelian method, but to Archimedes and the geometrical method.

No one, I think, would doubt Galileo's indebtedness to Euclid, Archimedes and Pappus in mathematics. Mathematical reasoning, however, is not an alternative to the logical reasoning described in Aristotle's works in logic. In any discussion of scientific demonstration, the crucial point is the middle term; the entire force of the demonstration depends on the middle term. According to Aristotle, mathematical middle terms cannot produce true, proper and adequate explanations or demonstrations of natural phenomena. Of this view Galileo was well aware, as is evidenced in the Second Day of the *Dialogo*. Yet his own conviction was that *only* a mathematical middle term can produce a true, proper and adequate explanation of natural phenomena. He insisted that "trying to deal with physical problems without geometry is attempting the impossible". "Without [mathematical language], it is humanly impossible to comprehend a single word." The real difference between Galileo and Aristotle lies here. Galileo insisted on the primary and exclusive competence of mathematical language in the explanation of nature. Aristotle did not and would not concede this. Koyré is undoubtedly correct when he says:

> It is the right of mathematical science, of the mathematical explanation of Nature, in opposition to the non-mathematical one of common sense and of Aristotelian physics, much more than the opposition between two astronomical systems, that forms the real subject of the *Dialogue*.[11]

The insistence on mathematical explanations of nature, so fundamental in Galileo's world-view, was not entirely original. One need not jump all the way to Plato for an antecedent. The ground for the new physics of Galileo was in this respect, at least, prepared at Oxford.

Bradwardine and the Merton School

In *Henry IV* Part II (Act 3, Scene 2) two justices, colleagues and cousins, discuss their family. The first justice asks: "I dare say my cousin William is become a good scholar. He is at Oxford still, is he not?" Second Justice: "Indeed, sir, to my cost."

Thomas Bradwardine, Oxford master, mathematician, theologian, and later Archbishop of Canterbury, is a worthy candidate for precursorship. His piety and theological renown have been immortalized by Chaucer in the *Nun's priest's tale*. Bradwardine not only led a full academic life in early fourteenth-century Oxford and London, but his minor revolution in scientific thought is not altogether unworthy of being compared with the scientific revolution of three centuries later. Considering the age in which he lived, there can be little doubt that Bradwardine was a mathematical genius, who, in the words of Anneliese Maier, "would have wanted to write the *Principia mathematica philosophiae naturalis* of his century".[12] It was he who introduced mathematics into scholastic philosophy, initiated the two new sciences of kinematics and dynamics, and made the initial move toward uniting celestial and terrestrial motions under a single mathematics. In a burst of enthusiasm reminiscent of Robert Grosseteste, Roger Bacon or Galileo, Bradwardine declared:

> It is [mathematics] which reveals every genuine truth, for it knows every hidden secret, and bears the key to every subtlety of letters; whoever, then, has the effrontery to study physics while neglecting mathematics, should know from the start that he will never make his entry through the portals of wisdom.[13]

To modern ears all of this may seem commonplace, for we have been brought up to understand scientific words in a certain way, and to assume the importance of mathematics in understanding the physical universe. But all beginnings, as an old German proverb has it, are difficult.

Modern historians often refer to Bradwardine as the "founder of the Merton school" of mechanics, somewhat as Duhem described Buridan as the founder of a new school of scientific thought. The title is justifiably given Bradwardine in that he inaugurated a new approach which was immediately exploited by his colleagues and successors, as Miss Maier has shown. His importance in the development of physical theory rests largely on his influential *Treatise on the proportion of velocities in moving bodies*, composed in 1328, when he was a student of theology at Oxford. The treatise has been thoroughly analyzed by Anneliese Maier, Marshall Clagett, Eduard Dijksterhuis and others. Its purpose was to propose a mathematical law that would be valid for all changes of velocity, a universal law of motion that would suffer no exception. Bradwardine was concerned about the case where the moving force is less than the resistance, where of course no motion should result. His formula was equivalently in our terms an exponential function; if the power of the ratio of force to resistance be raised, one obtains a double, triple or any desired velocity. If F/R produces velocity v, $(F/R)^n$ will produce a velocity nv. This formula was claimed to be valid for all cases; thus the awkward problems of zero velocity were eliminated.

It would be interesting to dwell on this ingenious formula, and on the later Mertonian developments like the "theorem of mean speed", their formulation of principles of kinematics and dynamics, their invention of an ingenious calculus, using letters as variables, their analysis of mathematical functions and coordinate systems, their attempts to specify the notions of uniform velocity, uniform acceleration, velocity at an instant, the infinitesimal, force, all of which were to become part of the common heritage bequeathed to Galileo. But what is important here is their general mathematization of physical concepts and their attempt to carry this mathematization even further. This is already evident in Bradwardine's own work. The concept of motion itself would furnish a typical and fundamental example. According to Aristotle, motion is a process, a becoming. It is defined as the actualization of a thing in potentiality, precisely as it is in potentiality for further motion. Motion as such is in this view not a quantity; only quantities *accidental* to motion can be measured, e.g., distance, time, size and weight. This Aristotelian concept of motion as a process is useless to the mathematician. Bradwardine and the Mertonians conceived motion simply as a velocity, a ratio of distance to time, an intensive "quality" which can be increased and decreased according to determinable proportions. Today Bradwardine's concept of motion is taken for granted. But it required real genius to leap to it from an Aristotelian springboard, one which had little spring. The same could be said for the mathematical concept of mass, achieved one generation later by another Mertonian.

Not content with a mathematical function for rectilinear terrestrial velocities, Bradwardine wished to discover a single kinematics, if not a dynamics, for both terrestrial and celestial motion. The seldom-noticed final chapter of Bradwardine's treatise was devoted to the special problem of rotational motion; his hope was to establish that celestial and terrestrial velocities are commensurable, something that Aristotle had claimed to be impossible. After much labor, he concluded: since the velocity of any motion consists in a body's traversal of given fixed spaces (real or imaginary) in a given time, it seems reasonable to say that "the velocity of a rotating sphere is measured by the velocity of the most swiftly moving point of the sphere", i.e., by the linear distance the fastest-moving point would traverse, if it were to go off in a straight line. In practice, this would mean that the velocity of a celestial body would be determined by the distance it would cover in a given time, if it were considered to be moving in a straight line. By thus imagining a circle as stretched out into a straight line, Bradwardine gave some meaning to the commensurability of terrestrial and celestial motions. This elementary feat of imagination had been rejected as impossible by Aristotle, since he held the line and circle to be incommensurate species. Bradwardine would indeed have wanted to write the *Principia mathematica* of his century. But history had to await the colossal efforts of Galileo and Newton.

Archimedes and Galileo

Cassius says of Julius Caesar: "Why man, he doth bestride the narrow world like a Colossus." (Act I, Scene 2.) The metaphor could be applied even more appropriately to Archimedes, who sought a fulcrum for a lever to move the world. Galileo found in the work of Archimedes, and in the Platonic tradition generally, a lever to move his world. Archimedes geometrized space, bodies and motions, in notable contrast to the qualitative differentiations of places, natures and natural motions defended by Aristotle. Koyré has presented, I think, overwhelming evidence of Galileo's debt to Archimedes, the theoretician of mechanics, as well as to Plato, the philosopher of mathematical objectivity. Some of the writings of Archimedes were translated in the thirteenth century by the Dominican Archbishop of Corinth, William of Moerbeke; however, they attracted little attention at that time. The complete works of Archimedes were published almost half a century before the young Galileo wrote his *De motu*, and Galileo freely acknowledges his indebtedness to Archimedes, the "*philosophus platonicus*": "I would answer that I cover myself with the protecting wings of the superhuman Archimedes, whose name I never mention without a feeling of awe." [14] We must keep in mind, however, that Archimedes' own achievement had extended only to statics. The Oxford "calculators", it is true, did establish a terrestrial dynamics and kinematics. But Galileo was concerned with a much wider philosophy—one that would comprise the whole universe, terrestrial and celestial, in the unity first grasped by Copernicus. Archimedes can in truth be called a precursor of Galileo, but not apart from the Oxford calculators and Copernicus. Without them, he is only a ray of light, but with them he becomes a star in Galileo's galaxy of thought.

NOTES

1. *Saggiatore*, Drake translation, 1957*, p. 238.

2. *Hebrews*, 7, 3.

3. "Ergebnisse der Spätscholastischen Naturphilosophie", *Scholastik*, *35*, 1960, 161–187; translated in *Philosophy today*, *5*, 1961, 92–107. This article and the other works by Miss Maier listed in the *Bibliografia Galileiana, 1940–1964*, are the principal sources for this section of the present paper.

4. "The origins of classical mechanics from Aristotle to Newton", 1959*.

5. "Galileo and Plato", *Roots of scientific thought*, 1957*, p. 153.

6. In "Matter in fourteenth-century science", *The concept of matter*, ed. by E. McMullin, Notre Dame, 1963, pp. 319–341.

7. *Space and spirit*, London, 1947, p. 41.

8. *Op. cit.*, p. 97. I have given elsewhere a detailed account of the various ways in which the *Omne quod movetur* principle was understood by different medieval philosophers. See "The principle *Omne quod movetur ab alio movetur* in medieval physics", *Isis*, *56*, 1965, 26–45. The findings of this study are summarized below.

9. "The development of scientific method in the school of Padua", 1940*, p. 199.

10. "Galileo and the school of Padua", 1963*.

11. *Op. cit.*, p. 166.

12. *Die Vorlaufer Galileis im 14 Jahrhundert*, 1949*, p. 86n.

13. *Tractatus de continuo*, Amplon ms. (Erfurt), q. 385, 31*v*. See my "Dumbleton and the Merton school" (*Isis*, *50*, 1959, 439–454), for a fuller discussion.

14. *On motion*, Drabkin transl., 1960*, p. 67.

5 ⊛ Giambattista Benedetti, critic of Aristotle

ALEXANDRE KOYRÉ

Giambattista Benedetti [1] is certainly the most interesting Italian physicist of the sixteenth century; he is also the one whose historical role was the most important. His influence on the young Galileo, who followed him step by step in his treatise *De motu*, is undeniable and profound. Benedetti, doubtless, did not break through the boundaries that separated medieval and Renaissance science from modern science; to have done this is the distinctive merit of Galileo. But he pushed the mathematization of science much further than did Tartaglia, his master and immediate predecessor. Moreover, in conscious opposition to the determinedly empirical and qualitative physics of Aristotle, he tried to build, on the basis of Archimedes' statics, a physics which (in his own phrase) would be a "mathematical philosophy" of nature.

His attempt did not succeed, nor could it have, since (unlike Galileo) he was never able to free himself from the confused idea of *impetus* as the cause of motion; on the contrary, he based his dynamics on this notion. He succeeded nonetheless—and this is no small claim to fame—in demonstrating mathematically the nonexistence of the *quies media* and the paradoxical continuity of back-and-forth movement. He also proved, in opposition

NOTE: This article originally appeared in the *Mélanges Gilson*, 1959*. It has been translated by Brian Dibble and Ernan McMullin.

to a venerable tradition, that two bodies of the same "nature" or "homogeneity" (that is, specific gravity) fall at the same speed, whatever be the individual weight of each. Here again, it is to Galileo that the credit goes for extending Benedetti's proposition to all bodies, without distinction of "natures"; while it may not be true that it is the first step that counts, it certainly facilitates the second!

The speed of fall in a dense medium

In the preface (a letter-dedication to Gabriel de Guzman) of his work *Resolutio omnium Euclidis problematum* . . . (Venice, 1553), showing at twenty-three the first manifestations of his brilliant talent for geometry, Benedetti explains to his illustrious correspondent that the doctrine of Aristotle, according to which heavy bodies fall faster than light ones in proportion to their weights, needs to be corrected on two essential points. First, it is not *weight* as such, but the *excess* of the weight of the moving body over that of the surrounding medium that determines the speed of fall; next, it is the specific gravity rather than the weight of the body that counts. But we shall let Benedetti speak for himself. It is interesting to follow the young geometer as he gropes his way painfully along the path to the great discovery, interesting too to contrast the early awkwardness with the perfect clarity and precision with which he treats these same problems twenty years later.[2]

Like Tartaglia in his *Nova scientia* (1537), Benedetti concerns himself only with the motion of "homogeneous" bodies of similar shape. "The proportion of one body to another [provided they are homogeneous and of similar shape] is the same as that of one *virtus* to another." But this proportion will not tell us the ratio of their speeds in free fall. To find this latter in his aim:

> I assume, therefore, that the proportion of the speeds of similar bodies of different homogeneities, moving in the same medium and across the same space is that which is found between their excesses (particularly that of their weights or lightnesses) with regard to the medium, provided that the bodies be of similar shape. The reverse is likewise true: the proportion found between the above-mentioned excesses, with regard to the medium, is the same as that between the motions. This is demonstrated in the following manner: Take a uniform medium BFG (water, for example), into which are placed two [spherical] bodies of different homogeneities, that is, of different kinds (fig. 5-1). Let body DEC be of lead and AUI of wood, and each of them be heavier than a body of the same size made of water; let these latter spherical bodies of water be M and N. Place the center of the earth at S. Let the terminus *ad quem* of the motion be HOXK, and the terminus *a quo* the line AMD. . . . Let both of these be circles around the center of the earth. Then if one extends the lines SO and SX to their *terminus a quo*, the lines cut off by them will be equal. . . . Let us assume, in addition, that the center of the body AUI is located at the point of intersection of the line SO extended to the line AMD, and [the center of] the body DEC on the intersection of SX

with *AMD*. Next, let the aqueous body equal in size to the body *AUI* be *M*, and [the body] *N* be equal in size to the body *DEC*. Finally, let the body *DEC* be eight times heavier than the body *N*, and the body *AUI* twice as heavy as the body *M*.

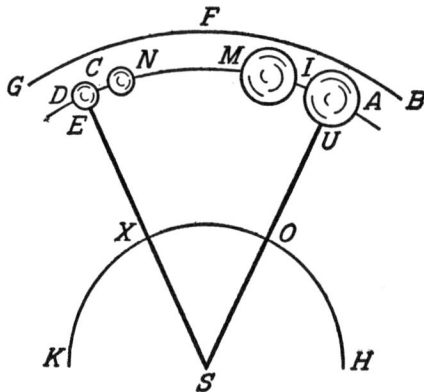

Figure 5–1

I claim, then, that the proportion of the motion of the body *DEC* to that of the body *AUI* . . . is the same as that found between the excess weights of the bodies *DEC* and *AUI* with regard to the bodies *N* and *M*; that is, that the time in which the body *AUI* is moved will be seven times that in which the body *DEC* is moved. For it is clear, by proposition 3 of Archimedes' *De insidentibus*, that, if the bodies *AUI* and *DEC* were of the same weight as the bodies *M* and *N*, they would not move at all, neither up nor down; and by proposition 7, that bodies heavier than the medium move toward the bottom. Consequently, the bodies *AUI* and *CED* will move toward the bottom, and the resistance of the liquid (that is, the water) to [the motion of] the body *AUI* will be proportionately halved, and that of *DEC* divided by eight. It follows that the time in which the center of the body *DEC* will traverse the given space will be in a seven-fold proportion to [seven times longer than] the time taken by the center of the body *AUI*. (I speak of natural movement, because nature everywhere moves by the shortest lines, that is, straight lines, at least if nothing interferes.) This is why (as one can deduce from Archimedes' book mentioned above) the proportion of motion to motion is not the same as the proportion of the gravities of *AUI* and *DEC*; it is given by the proportion between the [ratio of the] gravity of *AUI* to *M* and that of *DEC* to *N*. The inverse of this proposition is sufficiently clear.

I say, therefore, that if there were two bodies of the same shape and kind, whether they are equal or unequal [in size], they will move through a given space in the same medium in equal times. This proposition is evident since, if they moved in different times they would have to be either of different kinds or else moving in different media . . . which is contrary to the hypothesis.

To show this more clearly, let *G* and *O* be two similar and homogeneous (spherical) bodies (fig. 5–2), and let *AC* be the uniform medium. The lines *BDE*, *PIQ* and *RMUT* are terminal and equidistant circular lines having *S* for a center. The line *PIQ* passes through the terminus *a quo*, and the line *RMUT* through the terminus *ad quem* of the motion. I now show that the bodies *G* and *O* move across the given space in the given medium in equal times.

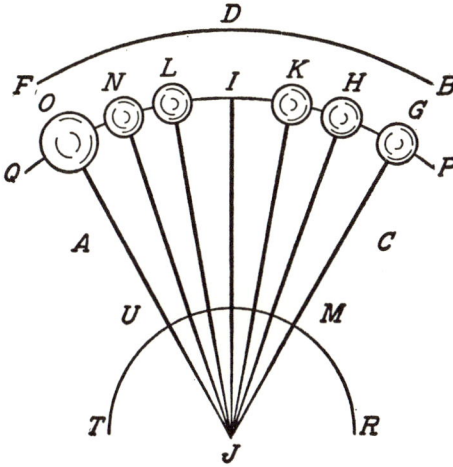

Figure 5-2

Let the body *O*, for example, be, in quantity [volume], four times the body *G*. It is clear from what has been said above that it will also be four times as heavy as *G* (because, if it were equal in size and weight, there would not be any doubt that these bodies would move in equal times). Then, I imagine the body *O* to be divided into four equal parts, similar in their spherical shape to the original whole. Let these be *H*, *K*, *L*, and *N*, whose centers I place on the line *PQ* in such a way that the distance between *L* and *K* is the same as the distance between *L* and *N*. Next I divide the line *KL* into two equal parts at the point *I*. According to common knowledge and also according to Archimedes, the centers of gravity of the bodies *H*, *K*, *L*, and *N* will be at this point. Moreover, it is obvious that each of the bodies *H*, *K*, *L*, and *N* will move from the line *PIQ* to the line *RMUT* in the same time as the body *G*. . . . If, therefore, the bodies *H*, *K*, *L*, and *N* are released at the same instant, they will move equally, that is, in the same time, and the line passing through their centers of gravity will always be equidistant from the line *RMUT*.

Finally, if one imagines that the line joining the center of body *O* and the point *I* be divided into two equal parts . . . then this point of division will be the center of gravity of the bodies *H*, *K*, *L*, and *N* and the body *O*. If, then, this line, moved by the force of the above-mentioned bodies, were released from the line *PQ*, or [from a line] equidistant from it, the body *O*, moving with natural movement, will traverse in a given time a space equal to that passed through by the bodies *H*, *K*, *L*, and *N*. The reason is that the line *OI*, having been equidistant from *RMUT* at the beginning of the movement, will always remain equidistant from it. The space traversed is the same as that passed through by the body *G*.

Beginning from this, I am therefore able to demonstrate a part of the above-mentioned supposition: namely, that if one has two bodies of the same shape but of different homogeneities and unequal corporeities, each heavier than the medium they move in, and the smaller of a heavier kind of substance than the larger, but the larger heavier overall than the smaller, then the supposition made above would be verified. For example, take two bodies M and N of the same shape but of different homogeneities; further, let them be unequal [in size], because, if they were equal, there would be no doubt. Of the two bodies, let M be the larger, but let the substance of body N be heavier than the substance of body M. Let the body M, nevertheless, be heavier overall than the body N, and let each of them be heavier than the medium in which it moves. I say that our supposition will then be verified. Suppose the first body to be AUI [returning to fig. 5–1]; let it be equal and similar in shape to the body M, but of the substance of body N. Then, for the bodies AUI and M, the supposition is perfectly obvious. But according to the demonstration already given, the body N will move in the same time as the body AUI. For this reason, the proposition is still true.

From which, it appears that the faster movement is not caused by excess of the heaviness or the lightness of the faster body, by comparison with that of the slower (the bodies being of similar shapes), but, rather by the specific difference between the bodies in comparison with the heaviness and lightness [of the medium]. This does not conform to Aristotle's doctrine, nor to that of any of his commentators whom I have had the occasion to read, or with whom I have been able to converse.[3]

Benedetti is inclined to stress the originality of his thought[4] and the authenticity of his discoveries; we have no reason to suspect him of a lack of veracity. And indeed, his theory has no precise parallels among the ancient, medieval or modern commentators on Aristotle's *Physics*. It remains nonetheless true that there were analogies to his doctrine in earlier writings, namely, in those that made the speed of a moving body depend not on the geometrical relation of the force to the resistance ($V=P/R$), but on the excess of the force over the resistance ($V=P-R$). These analogies are close enough to allow us to see in his doctrine (essentially, the substitution of an Archimedean schema for an Aristotelian one) not an historical accident, but the issue of a long tradition.

Benedetti's theory of impetus

Thirty years after the publication of the *Resolutio omnium problematum*, Benedetti brought out a collection of articles, letters and short treatises, *Diversarum speculationum mathematicarum et physicarum liber*.[5] Here, in the section on physics, there is an onslaught on Aristotle's physics, a subject about which Benedetti was not far from professing Ramus' famous assertion ("everything Aristotle said is false"). This section also contains the best account he ever gave of the dynamics of *impetus*, of which he proclaimed himself a resolute partisan. At the outset, like all his predecessors, he directs his critique against the Aristotelian theory of projectile motion, but more radical than most of them, he considers the entire theory to be worthless:

Aristotle, at the end of *Physics*, VIII, suggests that a body moved violently, and separated from its moving force, continues to move because, for a time, it is moved by the air or by the water that follows it. But this cannot be the case, because the air which enters the place left by the body in order to prevent a void, not only does not push the body, but rather holds it back. Indeed, the air is in violent fashion pushed aside by the body; the air at the back is separated from that at the front. It resists the body. The more the air at the front is condensed, the more it is rarefied at the rear. This rarefaction is brought about by violence, which prevents the body from continuing at the same speed with which it was originally propelled, since every agent suffers a loss in acting. This is why, although the air is carried along by the body, the body itself is held back by the air. For the rarefaction of the air is not natural, but violent; and for this reason, the air resists it and drags the moving body toward itself, because nature will not allow a void to develop [between the moving body and the air]. Also, since they are always in contact and the moving body cannot separate itself from the air, its speed will be slowed by it.[6]

Thus, it is not the reaction of the medium that explains the continuing motion of a projectile. On the contrary, this reaction cannot but hinder it. As for the motion itself, whether it be violent or natural, it is always explained by a moving force inherent in the moving body. In fact:

the speed of a body separated from its first mover derives from a certain natural impression, a certain "impetuosity" received by the body. . . . For every heavy body, whether moved naturally or violently, receives in itself an *impetus*, an impressed motion of such a sort that it continues to move by itself for a certain time when separated from its moving force. Then, when a body moves with natural motion, its speed increases constantly; here the *impetus* (or *impressio*) in the body constantly increases because it remains united to the moving power. From this, it follows, for instance, that, after having started a wheel rolling with the hand, if one removes one's hand, the wheel does not stop immediately, but continues to turn for a certain time.[7]

What is this *impetus*, this moving force, the cause of the motion immanent in the moving body? It is difficult to say. It is a sort of quality, power or force that impresses itself on the moving body; better, it impregnates the body because of the latter's association with the mover possessing the quality, i.e., because it participates in the actual motion of the mover. It is also a kind of *habitus* that the moving body acquires; the longer it is subject to the action of the moving force,[8] the more it acquires. Thus, for example, if a stone is thrown farther by a sling than by hand, it is because it makes numerous revolutions in the sling, so that the "impression" it receives is greater:

The real reason why a heavy body is thrown farther by a sling than by hand is this: the motion produces a greater impression of *impetus* on the body if the latter is revolved in a sling than if it is thrown by hand. The body freed from the sling and guided by nature, will follow a path along a line continuous with its final movement of rotation. It is clear that the sling is able to impress the greater *impetus* on a body, because in the course of numerous revolutions the body receives a continually greater *impetus*. But the hand, when it whirls the body around, is not the center of its movement (despite what Aristotle says); the chord is not the radius.[9]

He wishes to say that the circularity of the motion (the feature on which Aristotle had relied for his explanation) has nothing to do with the matter. Moreover, the circular motion produces an *impetus* which moves the body *in a straight line*. As a matter of fact:

> As nearly as possible, the hand describes a circle. This circular motion forces the projectile to adopt a circular motion, whereas, by its natural inclination, it wants to continue along a straight line as soon as it has received an *impetus*. One can see this in the figure (fig. 5–3), where E is the body and AB is the straight line, tangent to the circle AAAA at the moment when the body is released.[10]

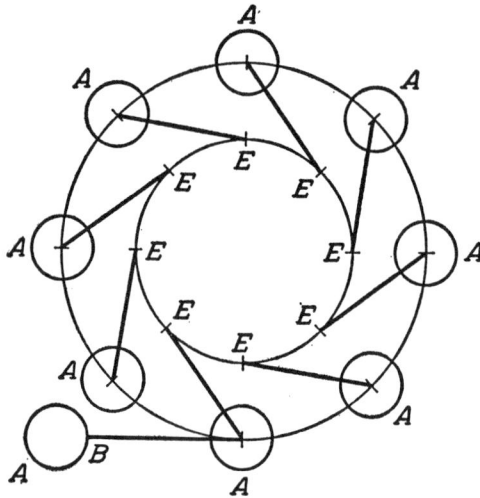

Figure 5–3

Thus, when it is set free, the body follows the straight line which is tangent to the circumference described by the hand or sling; it is thus that it conforms with its "natural inclination", that is, with the nature that is proper to the *impetus* that has been given to it by the circular motion. But it will not follow a rectilinear motion for long:

> This *impetus impressus* continually wanes, and, little by little, the heaviness gains influence, which, mixing with the impression made by the force, does not long allow the line AB to remain straight. It quickly becomes curved, because the body in question is being moved by two forces, one of which is the impressed violence and the other is nature. This is contrary to Tartaglia's opinion which denies that any body can simultaneously move with natural and violent motions.[11]

Benedetti's explanation, though conforming closely enough to the tradition, may well seem confused to us. This should not surprise us very much: the notion of *impetus* is basically a very confused one. In the last analysis, it does no more than translate into "scientific" terms a concept based on daily experience, on a datum of common sense. What, indeed, is the *impetus*, the *forza*, the *virtus motiva*, except a condensation, so to speak, of muscular effort and of *élan?* It accords well with the "facts" (real and alleged) that form the experiential base of medieval dynamics, especially with the "fact" of the initial acceleration of a projectile—does it not take time for the *impetus* to gain influence over the moving body? Besides, everyone knows that it is necessary to "pick up speed" before jumping over an obstacle; the wagon, when pushed, starts off slowly and progressively gains speed; and everyone knows—even children playing ball—that to hit the target hard, one puts it some distance away in order to let the ball pick up speed.[12]

Impetus, impression, quality or moving power; all these are things that pass from the mover to the moved. Having entered into the moving body (i.e., having "impregnated" or "impressed" it), they affect its behavior. They can interfere with other qualities or powers, even natural ones; different acquisitions of *impetus* may interfere with one another, and indeed exist together only with difficulty. Thus the *impetus* of violent motion hinders the action of natural heaviness; it restrains heavy bodies from moving downward. In other words, it makes them lighter.

Nevertheless, it should be noted that Benedetti's conception of *impetus* is somewhat more precise than that of his medieval predecessors. In addition, he insists much more strongly than they on the linear character of *impetus*, rejecting, it seems, the notion of a rotary *impetus*, although, on the other hand, he reproaches Aristotle for having erred in his classification of motions as violent and natural. Aristotle did not understand (he says) that only circular motion is truly natural. Rectilinear motion never is entirely natural; not even the falling of heavy bodies and the rising of light ones fully qualifies:

> The upward or downward rectilinear movement of natural bodies is not natural, *primo* and *per se*, because natural motion is perpetual or, more accurately, is incapable of ceasing, and cannot therefore be other than circular. Any part joined to its whole cannot have a natural motion other than that proper to the whole. But if one such part were thrown off and separated from its whole, and allowed to move freely, it would move spontaneously and by the shortest path to the place assigned by nature to its whole. This latter motion is not *primo* and *per se* natural to the body, since it has its origin in a cause contrary to its nature; that is, it arises from the fact that it is outside of its [proper] place, [in another] which it finds to be contrary to its nature. Consequently, such a motion is partially and not wholly natural. Now, proper and natural motion is that which derives from the nature of a given body, which is not the case in straight-line motion. *Ergo* . . .[13]

This reasoning ought to have led Benedetti, it would seem, to affirm the privileged character of circular motion as well as motion of rotation, by comparison with motion in a straight line. But as a matter of fact, as we have seen, he asserts exactly the contrary: the circular motion of the sling or the hand impresses on the projectile an *impetus* in a straight line:

> The more the speed of gyratory motion makes the *impetus* of the slingshot increase, the more the hand feels pulled by the body via the cord attached to it. The greater the *impetus* of the motion impressed on the body, the stronger is the inclination of the body to move in a straight line; the greater too is the force with which it drags, as it attempts to take on this motion. . . . All heavy bodies that move, whether by nature or by violence, naturally desire to move in a straight line. We can see this clearly when we whirl the arm for throwing stones with a sling; the cords acquire more weight and pull the hand all the more strongly as the sling turns faster and the motion becomes more rapid; this results from the natural appetite rooted in the stone which pushes it in a straight line.[14]

And it is not only movement in a circular orbit that begets a rectilinear *impetus* (and, therefore, a centrifugal force); the same is also true of rotary motion. For rotary motion is nothing more than an ensemble of motions of revolution of each part of the body about the axis of the body as a whole. They all possess a linear *impetus*, which explains why such a motion does not continue as one would expect it to do. Rotary motion is not, therefore, a natural motion but a set of motions that are doubly violent, as it were:

> It is in rectilinear rather than in rotary motion that each of the small parts of the millstone would be carried along by its own *impetus*, if it were free; during rotary motion, each of these partial *impetus* is a type of violent motion, and, consequently, must decay. Imagine a horizontal wheel, as perfectly round as possible, resting on a single point. Let us give it a rotary spin with all the force we can muster, then leave it. Why will not its rotary motion be perpetual? There are four reasons. First, because such a motion is not natural to the wheel. The second is that the wheel, although resting on a single mathematical point, necessarily requires a second point of support on top to keep it horizontal, and this support would have to be supplied by some bodily mechanism; the result would be a certain friction that would give rise to resistance. The third is that the air surrounding the wheel continually restrains it; and, in this manner, resists the motion.
>
> Here is the fourth reason. Consider each of the bodily parts which moves by the *impetus* that has been impressed on it by an extrinsic moving force; each part has a natural inclination to rectilinear, not to curved, motion. If one piece on the circumference of the above-mentioned wheel were to be detached, it would indubitably move for a time through the air in a straight line. We can understand this by the example of the slings that hurl stones. In them, the *impetus* of the motion that has been impressed on the projectile describes, by a sort of natural propensity, a rectilinear path. It seems reasonable to admit that the thrown stone begins a rectilinear path, following a line

tangent to the circle it just described, meeting it at the point where the stone left it.

For the same reason, the larger the wheel, the greater is the *impetus* received by the different parts on the circumference of the wheel. And it will often happen that, when we want to stop it, it will involve much effort and difficulty. In effect, the larger the diameter of the circle, the less curved is the circumference of the circle, and the less, therefore, is the rectilinear *impetus* weakened by the deviation imposed on it by the circular trajectory. Therefore, the motion of the parts on the circumference approaches more and more in this case a motion conforming to the inclination given them by nature, an inclination to follow a straight line, and it becomes all the more difficult to counteract it.

Rotary motion is necessarily violent

Benedetti again takes up the study of these problems (the relation between circular and rectilinear motion, the noncontinuance of rotary motion) in a letter to Paul Capra of Novara, Duke of Savoy, in which he uses his theory to explain the fact that a spinning-top maintains a vertical posture while it is rapidly spinning, and then falls when it stops spinning. Of course, he accepts the traditional explanations of this fact (that the *impetus* of the different parts being incompatible, mutually impede one another's action; that a body becomes lighter in motion). But he completes and clarifies this by his conception of the violent character of rotary motion:

> You ask in your letters if the circular motion of a millstone, once begun, would not last forever in the case where the stone rests, on a mathematical point, as it were, and where the stone is perfectly round and smooth. I answer that such a motion could not be perpetual and that it could not even last very long. First of all, it is slowed by the air that sets up a resistance on the outer edge of the millstone. In addition, however, it is slowed by the resistance of the parts of the moving body. Once set in motion, these parts have an *impetus* which naturally tends to move them in a straight line; but since they are joined together and follow one another, they suffer violence as they are moved in a circle. It is only by force that, in such a motion, they remain joined together. The more rapid their motion becomes, the more the natural inclination in them to move in a straight line increases, and the more contrary to their nature it becomes to oblige them to move in a circle. In order, therefore, that they should retain their natural union with one another despite their own tendency to move in a straight line once motion begins, they have to resist one another all the more, and each will drag back the one in front of it all the more strongly as the rotary motion becomes faster.

> Because of the inclination of the parts of round bodies to rectilinear motion, it follows that a spinning-top, which turns on itself with great violence, remains nearly steady for a time on its iron point, not inclined more towards one side than another relative to the center of the earth. The reason is that in such a motion, each of its parts does not tend absolutely and uniquely toward the center of the earth, but rather it tends to move perpendicularly to

the line of rotation in such a way that the body as a whole must necessarily remain upright. And if I say that these parts do not automatically tend towards the center of the earth, I do not mean to imply that they are entirely lacking in such an inclination, the sort of inclination which the body itself as a whole possesses towards this point. It is true, however, that the faster it moves, the less it tends there; in other words, the body becomes lighter. This is well illustrated by the example of an arrow coming from a bow or any other machine: the faster its violent motion, the stronger its inclination to fly straight, that is, the less it tends towards the center of the earth. In other words, it becomes lighter.[15] To see this more clearly, imagine that a spinning-top is cut into a great number of parts as it spins very rapidly. You would find that they do not immediately fall towards the center of the earth, but move straight towards the horizon, so to speak. This, so far as I know, has never previously been noted concerning spinning-tops.[16] And the example of such a top clearly shows to what degree the peripatetics were confused about violent motion, which they supposed to be caused by the reaction of the air . . . whereas, in fact, the medium plays quite another role, namely that of resisting the motion.

Aristotle's errors concerning motion of fall

In Aristotelian physics, the medium plays a double role; it is both resistance and moving force. The physics of *impetus* denies motive power to the medium. Benedetti adds that even its retarding action had been poorly understood and badly evaluated by Aristotle. Aristotle in no way realized (he asserts) the role of mathematics in the science of physics. He nearly always ended in error; for it is only by building on the "unshakeable foundations" of mathematical philosophy—in effect, by beginning from Archimedes and being inspired by Plato—that one can substitute for Aristotle's physics a better physics founded on the truths that the human intellect sees directly.

Benedetti is fully conscious of the importance of his endeavor. He assumes a heroic pose on occasion:

> Surely, the greatness and authority of Aristotle is such that it is difficult and dangerous to write anything contrary to what he has taught; dangerous for me particularly, to whom his wisdom has always seemed admirable. Nonetheless, driven by a concern for truth, the love of which, if he were living, would fire him as well . . . I do not hesitate to say, in the common interest, in what way the unshakeable foundation of mathematical philosophy forces me to diverge from him.

> Since we have assumed the burden of proving that Aristotle was mistaken about natural motions, we should begin by setting forth some basic truths, truths that the intellect can grasp immediately.[17] In the first place, any two heavy or light bodies of equal volume and similar shape, but made of different materials, will, in their local movements, keep the proportion of their weight or lightness in the same media. From nature this is quite obvious, as soon as we recall that greater speed or slowness (so long as the medium remains uniform and at rest) must result from one or more of the following

four reasons: (1) greater or lesser heaviness or lightness; (2) difference in form; (3) the position of the form in relation to a line extending from the circumference to the center of the earth; and, finally, (4) difference in size of the moving bodies. It is clear, therefore, that if one does not change the form in quality or in quantity, nor the position of this form, the motion will be proportional to the moving power, which in this case is the heaviness or lightness. Now what I have said about the quality, the size and the position of the figure, I say also with regard to the resistance of the medium. For dissimilarity or inequality of figures, or their occupying different positions, modifies the motion of bodies in a nonnegligible way, since the smaller form more easily divides the continuity of the medium than does the larger, just as the pointed does it more quickly than the rounded. Similarly, the body that moves with its point in front will move more rapidly than one which does not. Therefore, every time that two bodies meet the same resistance, their motions will be proportional to their moving powers; conversely, every time that two bodies have one and the same heaviness or lightness, and meet different resistances, their motions will take on the inverse proportion of these resistances. . . . And if a body be compared with another of the same heaviness or lightness which is meeting more resistance, the former will be the quicker of the two in the proportion that its surface engenders less resistance than does that of the other body. . . . Thus, for example, if the ratio of the surface of the larger body to that of the smaller were 4/3, the speed of the smaller would be greater than that of the larger body as the quaternary number is greater than the ternary.[18]

An Aristotelian could, and indeed should, admit all this. But, adds Benedetti, taking up the theory he had elaborated twenty years earlier, there is still something else to be said:

The natural motion of a heavy body in different media is proportional to the weight of the body in the same media. Thus, for example, if the total weight of a given body be represented by AI, and the body be placed in a medium less dense than itself (if it were placed in a denser medium it would not be heavy, but light, as Archimedes has shown), the medium would cancel out a part of the weight (EI, say,) so that only the part AE of the weight would come into play. Now if the body were placed in another denser medium (one less dense than the body itself), the medium would cancel out a part (UI, say,) of the weight, leaving the part AU still free to act.

Figure 5–4

In such a case, the proportion between the speeds with which the body will fall in the two media will be as AE to AU. This conforms more closely to reason than to say that the speeds would be as UI to EI, since the speeds proportion themselves only to the moving forces, when the figures are the same in quality, quantity, and position. This is clearly in agreement with what we have written above: to say that the proportion of the speeds in the same medium of two heterogeneous bodies (similar in shape, size, etc.) is equal to the proportion of the weights themselves is the same thing as saying that the speeds of one and the same body in different media are in the proportion of the different weights of the body in these media.[19]

From his point of view, Benedetti is, of course, entirely correct. If the speeds are proportional to the moving forces, and if one part of the moving force (of the weight) is neutralized by the action of the medium, it is only the remaining part that counts, and in media more and more dense, the speed of the body will diminish following a progression that is arithmetical and not geometrical, as Aristotle wanted to make it. But Benedetti's reasoning, founded on Archimedes' hydrostatics, begins from a starting-point altogether different from Aristotle's. According to the latter, the weight of a body is one of its constant and absolute properties, not relative as Benedetti and some of the "ancients" made it. Aristotle would thus assume that the weight acts as a whole in the various media, with their different resistances. Benedetti thinks that Aristotle's physics betrays that its author "knows neither the cause of the heaviness nor the lightness of bodies, which consists in the density or rarity of a heavy or light body, and the lesser or greater densities of the media".[20] Density and rarity are the absolute properties. Weight (i.e. heaviness and lightness) is no more than a resultant. In themselves, all bodies are "heavy", and the "light" are so only in comparison with the medium in which they are found.[21]

Wood is heavy in air and light in water, just as iron is heavy in water and light in mercury. To keep us from falling into an easy error, Benedetti warns us that "the proportions of the weights of the same body in different media do not follow the proportions of the densities of the media. It necessarily follows that the speeds of fall will not have the same proportions either. In particular, the speeds of . . . bodies of the same material or same shape but of different sizes, will follow, in their natural motions in the same medium, a proportion very different from that which Aristotle asserts." For example, if two bodies are "of equal weight, the smaller of the two will move faster", because the resistance of the medium to it will be less. In brief, according to Benedetti, Aristotle never understood motion at all, whether natural or violent. Concerning the former, for example, "Aristotle ought never to have declared that a body moves faster as it approaches its destination, but, rather, that a body moves swifter the farther it moves from its starting point." [22]

Does this last point constitute a genuine disagreement? Does not a body, as it gets farther from its starting point automatically approach its destination? One might well think so. Thus, Tartaglia, who based his dynamics on an analysis of the starting points of bodies in their natural and violent motions, writes: "If a uniformly heavy body moves with natural motion, the farther it gets from its starting point, or the nearer it gets to its destination, the faster it goes." [23] It may be added that Benedetti himself by no means neglects to consider the natural destination of the motion of heavy bodies. In fact, just after the criticism of Aristotle just cited, he writes:

In natural rectilinear motions, the impression, the "impetuosity" received, continually increases because the moving body has in itself its cause of motion, that is, *the inclination to return to the place assigned to it by nature.* . . . For the impression increases in proportion as the motion continues, the body continually receiving a new *impetus.* In fact, it contains in itself the cause of its motion, which is the inclination to regain the natural place from which it was displaced by violence.

Thus, it is clear that the *cause* of falling motion is for Benedetti exactly the same as it was for Aristotle, i.e., the natural tendency of a body to return to its natural place. But the mechanism by virtue of which the movement and its acceleration are realized is taken over by Benedetti from the dynamics of *impetus.* Consecutive acquisitions of *impetus,* continually produced by the moving cause in the course of the motion, as secondary causes push (or carry) the body toward its destination. Now these acquisitions of *impetus* are produced in proportion as the body gets farther from its starting point. Doubtless it will at the same time be approaching its destination. But, even though Tartaglia asserted the contrary, mathematically the two are not at all the same thing.[24]

Aristotle's mistaken doctrine of *quies media*

Aristotle did not understand violent motion very well either. He did not see the essentially violent character of upward motion. This motion is in no way an effect of substantial lightness, something nonexistent *in rerum natura;* it is, rather, an extrusion by the medium of a body less dense than itself. Nor did he grasp the continuity of back-and-forth motion, and the nonexistence of a moment of rest (*quies media*) between going and coming. Nor the possibility of rectilinear motion being infinite in time. Concerning back-and-forth motion:

Aristotle says [25] that it is impossible that something move over and back on a straight line, without coming to rest at the extremes. On the contrary, I claim that this is possible. To examine this question, imagine the circle *UAN* moving continuously in either direction, right or left, around the center *O.* Let us now suppose that *B* is a point somewhere outside the circle. From *B,* let us draw two straight lines, *BU* and *BN,* tangent to the circle at *U* and *N.* Between these two lines, imagine another line which could be *UN* or *CD* or *EF* or *GH.* From any point *A* on the circumference of the circle draw a line to *B.* Imagine this line *AB* to be fixed at *B,* yet able to follow *A* in its rotation around *O.* Now, this line will coincide sometimes with *BU,* sometimes with *BN;* sometimes it will move from *BU* towards *BN,* and then again from *BN* towards *BU,* as happens with the forward and retrograde motions of the planets. Consequently, the circle *UAN* will be like the epicycle, and *B* like the center of the earth. Therefore, it is clear that when *BA* coincides with *BU* or *BN,* it will not be motionless because it turns back in an instant; *BN* and *BU* touch the circle at one point only. It is also clear that *BA* always cuts the line *UN* (or *CD* or *EF* or *GH*) at some point *T.* Now imagine that someone moves with the point *T* on any one of these lines. It is clear that he will never be at rest, even at the extremes. Therefore, Aristotle's opinion is not correct.[26]

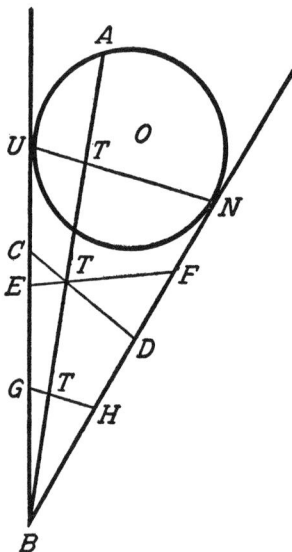

Figure 5–5

Can a continuous motion be infinitely prolonged on a finite straight line? Suppose that I is the point of intersection of the lines RX and OA (see fig. 5–6). The line OA turns about the fixed point A. It is clear that the distance between X and C (the point of intersection of OA and XT) can be increased to infinity, and that I can approach R indefinitely closely, but can never reach it. Its motion will slow down progressively but will never come to an end.[27] Aristotle's first mistake, it is plain, was to have excluded geometrical reasoning from physics, rather than constructing it on the "unshakeable foundation of mathematical philosophy".

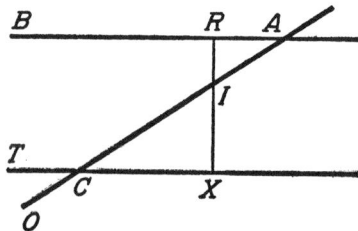

Figure 5–6

Aristotle's unwarranted rejection of the void:

But we have not yet exhausted the list of Aristotle's errors in physics. Now we arrive at the gravest: the denial of the void. Benedetti asserts without qualification that the Aristotelian demonstration of the nonexistence of the void is worthless.[28] The impossibility of the void is shown (as everyone knows) by a *reductio ad absurdum* argument. In a void, there would be no resistance so that motion would occur with infinite speed. In Benedetti's view, this is altogether false. If the speed is proportional to the relative weight of the body, that is, its absolute weight *diminished by* and not *divided by* the resistance of the medium, it follows immediately that the speed does not increase indefinitely; as the resistance diminishes, the speed still remains finite. "To see this more easily, imagine an infinity of bodily media, one rarer than the next in whatever proportion we please, beginning with unity, and let us also imagine a body Q, denser than the first medium." The speed of this body in the first medium will obviously be finite. Now, if we place it in the different media that we have imagined, its speed will undoubtedly increase, but it will always have an upper limit. Thus motion in a void is perfectly possible.[29]

But what will its speed be? Aristotle thought that if motion in a vacuum had been possible, the relation of the speeds of the different bodies would be the same as they would be in a plenum. Benedetti retorts that this is completely erroneous:

> Because in a plenum the proportion of the external resistances subtracts from the proportion of the weights, and what remains determines the proportion of the speeds. This will be zero, if the proportion of the resistances is equal to the proportion of the weights. Because of this, the proportion of the speeds in a void will differ from that [of the same bodies] in a plenum. That is, the speeds of different bodies (i.e. bodies composed of different kinds of material) will be proportional to their absolute specific weights, that is, to their densities. Bodies made of the same material will have the same natural speed

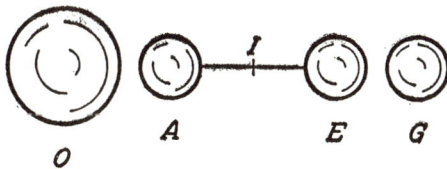

Figure 5-7

in a void. [This is proved as follows:] Let there be two homogeneous bodies, O and G, and let G be half the size of O. Also, let there be two homogeneous bodies in addition to the first, A and E, of which each is equal to G. Suppose these two bodies to be placed at the ends of a line, of which I is the midpoint. It is clear that the point I will bear the same weight as the center of O [considering AE as though it were the beam of a balance]. By virtue of the bodies A and E, I will move in the void with the same speed as would the center of O. But if these bodies A and E were detached from this line, this would not change their speed. Each of them thus moves at the same speed as G. Therefore, G moves at the same speed as O.[30]

Benedetti's rejection of Aristotelian finitism:

Motion in the void, the simultaneous fall of homogeneous weights: we are already far from Aristotle's physics. But the "unshakeable foundations of mathematical philosophy", the Archimedean model of science never far from Benedetti's mind, does not allow him to stop at this point. Aristotle's mistake (he goes on) was not just to deny the possibility of a void in the world. It lay rather in making a false image of the world and in adapting his physics to it. His false world-view [31] was based on a finitist presupposition, and gave rise to an unduly limited notion of natural place. "There is no body in the world or out of the world (no matter what Aristotle may say) that does not have its place." Extraterrestrial places? Why not? Would there be "any drawback whatever about there being an infinite body outside the world"? Doubtless, Aristotle would deny such a possibility. But his reasons are no more evident than those he gives us for the impossibility of a plurality of worlds, the unalterability of the heavens, and many other things. It all comes back to one central defect: Aristotle simply did not understand mathematics. And for Benedetti, the clearest manifestation of this lack of understanding lay in Aristotle's denial of the reality of the infinite:

> He claims (but without proving it and without even giving any reason) that the infinite parts of the continuum are not actual [*in actu*], but only in potency. Yet this cannot be conceded to him, because if the entire real continuum is actual, all of its parts must be actual too, because it is stupid to think that things that are actual could be made up of things that exist only in potency. Nor should it be claimed that the continuity of these parts makes them exist only in potency, and not at all in actuality. Suppose for example, we divide a continuous line AU into equal parts at E. There can be no doubt that, before the division, the half AE (even though joined to the other half, EU) is as actual as is the whole line AU, although it is not distinguished from it by the senses. And I maintain the same is true of a half of AE, i.e., of one-fourth of the line, the same of an eighth, of a thousandth, and so on.

The infinite multiplicity is no less real than is the finite. The infinite found in nature is actual and not just potential. And the actual infinite can be understood fully as well as the potential.

The lack of comprehension of mathematics for which Benedetti so often reproaches Aristotle is, therefore, a clue to something far more serious, namely anti-infinitism. This is at the root of all his errors, especially of those which concern the structure of thought itself. Conversely, it was Benedetti's rejection of finitism that, in the last analysis, led him to oppose the Aristotelian doctrine and tradition, and gave him his place among those who have led mankind from the closed world of the ancients to the infinite universe of the moderns.

NOTES

1. Giambattista Benedetti was born at Venice in 1530. Although of a patrician family (as he never fails to mention on the flyleaves of his books), in 1567 he became "mathematician of the Duke of Savoy" and lived in Savoy until his death in 1590. See the work of R. Bordiga on Benedetti in the *Atti Istituto Veneto*, 1925/6; my *Études galiléennes*, 1939*; and Raffaele Giacomelli, *Galileo Galilei giovane e il suo De motu*, 1949*.

2. This preface was republished by Benedetti under the title *Demonstratio proportionum motuum localium contra Aristotelem* (Venice, 1554), and reprinted by G. Libri in his *Histoire des sciences mathématiques en Italie* (Paris, 1840, vol. 3, n. 25). As this small volume of Benedetti's is extremely rare, I will follow Libri's reprint. Despite its importance, this work of Benedetti does not seem to have drawn the attention of his contemporaries; one does not find any part of it quoted, at least not to my knowledge. It was the object of an impudent plagiarism by Jean Taisnier, who reproduced both the text and the drawings in his *Opusculum . . . de natura magnetis . . . item de motu continuo . . .* (Cologne, 1562). Despite Benedetti's vehement protest in his *De gnomonum umbrarumque solarium usu* (Turin, 1574), it is Taisnier (and not Benedetti) that Stevin names as the first to assert that bodies of the same specific gravity fall at the same rate. See Simon Stevin, "Appendice de la statique", *Oeuvres mathématiques*, Leyden, 1634, p. 501.

3. Libri edn., pp. 258–259.

4. Perhaps too much, at times. He feels it necessary to remind us, for example, that even though he had been a student of Tartaglia, he had studied with him only the first four books of Euclid.

5. Turin, 1585. I cannot here dwell on this interesting work in the detail it deserves. He provides, for example, a way of reckoning the diagonals of a quadrilateral inscribed in a circle (fifteen years before Viète); a study of the equilibrium of solutions in communicating vessels, with the theory of an hydraulic press (nearly twenty years before the publication of Stevinus' *Wisconstighe Gedachtnissen*), as well as an excellent account of Copernicus' system of the world. I must confine myself to treating his dynamics.

6. Benedetti, *op. cit.*, p. 184.

7. *Ibid.*, pp. 184, 286.

8. Benedetti's reasoning may seem to us absurd; however, if, with the partisans of the *impetus*, one conceives the moving force to be like a quality, a *qualitas motiva*, analogous, for example, to heat, the apparent absurdity disappears. It is clear that a body becomes hotter (becomes more impregnated with heat) the longer it remains near the fire. This was the way the young Galileo would later reason in his *De motu*. Much later, Gassendi, in his *De motu impresso a motore translato* (Paris, 1652), explained the continuance of motion in the moving body by the latter's growing more "accustomed" to the motion. Borelli rightly protests against this in his *Theoretica planetarum medicearum . . .*, Florence, 1664, p. 57.

9. Benedetti, *op. cit.*, p. 160.

10. *Ibid.*, p. 160. Cited by P. Duhem, *Études sur Léonard de Vinci*, 1913*, vol. 3, p. 216.

11. Benedetti alludes to the theory, elaborated by Tartaglia in his *Nova scientia* (Venice, 1537), according to which a blending or mixing of violent motion with natural motion is strictly impossible; cf. *Nova scientia*, bk. I, prop. 5.

12. Artillerymen and harquebusiers of the Middle Ages and of the Renaissance (and not a few of later times) believed that a shell accelerated at the beginning of its flight; they were not entirely wrong about this, since the gas-pressure built up by the explosion of the powder does not immediately cease once the shell emerges from the mouth of the cannon. But it is not from this fact that the belief originally came. It was firmly established well before the invention of firearms; from antiquity, everyone believed in the initial acceleration of an arrow.

13. Benedetti, *op. cit.*, p. 184. The theory of heaviness developed here by Benedetti is that of Copernicus.

14. *Ibid.*, pp. 160, 287.

15. Benedetti's reasoning is a good example of the conceptual confusion that reigned in pre-Galilean dynamics with regard to weight. That a top would become lighter on account of its rapid spinning seems to us too great an absurdity to be admitted by anyone. However, in affirming it, Benedetti was, in fact, drawing a correct conclusion from the commonly admitted doctrine of the incompatibility—relative or absolute—of natural and violent *impetus*. From this doctrine, it would follow that a body in horizontal motion would be lighter than the same body at rest.

16. Benedetti is right; the rectilinearity of the *impetus* of circular motion had never been taught before him.

17. Note the Platonic profession of faith.

18. Benedetti, *op. cit.*, p. 168.

19. *Ibid.*, p. 168.

20. *Ibid.*, p. 185.

21. It is interesting to note that this doctrine is found much earlier in Marco Trevisano's unpublished treatise *De macrocosmo*. See G. Boas, "A fourteenth century cosmology", *Proc. Amer. Philos. Soc.*, *98*, 1954, 50ff.; M. Clagett, *The science of mechanics in the middle ages*, 1958*, p. 97.

22. *De caelo*, chap. 8.

23. See Nicolo Tartaglia, *Nova scientia*, bk. I, props. 2 and 3.

24. Benedetti's conception of the mechanism of acceleration is the same as that of Nicole Oresme; see Duhem, *Études sur Léonard de Vinci*, vol. 3, pp. 358ff; *Le système du monde*, 1958*, vol. 8, pp. 299ff. The emphasis on starting-point instead of arrival is found as early as Strato of Lampsacus and John Philoponos. In the Middle Ages, one finds it in Giles of Rome and Walter Burleigh. See *Le système du monde*, vol. 8, pp. 266ff.; Anneliese Maier, *An der Grenze von Scholastik und Naturwissenschaft*, 1952*, pp. 195ff.; Clagett, *The science of mechanics . . .*, pp. 525ff. Tartaglia's whole dynamics is, in fact, founded on the principle of the acceleration of natural motions and the slowing of violent

motions, beginning from the point of departure. The proportionality of the acceleration of the motion of fall to the distance covered was first admitted by Galileo, and then rejected by him as impossible; see my *Études galiléennes*, vol. 2.

25. *Physics*, bk. VIII, chap. 8.

26. Benedetti, *op. cit.*, p. 183. Several medieval authors rejected *quies media*, e.g., François de Meyronnes and Jean Buridan. See Duhem, *Système du monde*, vol. 8, pp. 272ff.

27. According to Oresme, a motion over a finite distance can be infinitely extended on the condition that the spaces traversed in successive equal times be diminished by half. See Maier, *op. cit.*, pp. 214ff.; Clagett, *op. cit.*, pp. 528ff.

28. Benedetti, *op. cit.*, p. 172.

29. The possibility of movement in a vacuum had already been affirmed by John Philoponos, using an argument similar to Benedetti's.

30. It is amusing to discover that the same "experiment" led Leonardo da Vinci to a conclusion directly opposite to that of Benedetti. According to da Vinci, two bodies *A* and *B* tied together will fall twice as fast as either of them would, if let fall separately.

31. Benedetti was partial to the world-view of Copernicus; this may be why he insisted so strongly (as we saw above) on the natural character of circular motion.

6 ❀ The Florentine background of Galileo's work

ERIC COCHRANE

Galileo and his compatriots

For the historian bent upon discovering the relationships and connections among the single events of the past, Galileo is not a particularly comforting personage to deal with. True, he was no *solitario*, as Croce points out,[1] for he was succeeded by several generations of disciples. But the search for near or distant predecessors, and hence for an explanation of his accomplishment in terms of what preceded it, has been considerably less fruitful than the search for descendants. The attempt to make Galileo a continuer of Aristotelian philosophy has had to overlook his emphatic opposition to the Aristotelians of his day;[2] the attempt to make him a Platonist has had to ignore his very un-Platonic concept of the relation between mathematics and physics; and the attempt to see him as a restorer or an heir of the nominalist philosophers of the fourteenth century or of the Italian humanists of the fifteenth has been limited so far to putting together parallel passages, which may well have a logical connection, but which do not necessarily have an historical one. If what is new in Galileo can be traced to the inspiration of Archimedes, it is not clear why the many other readers of the same books from the Middle Ages on did not receive the same inspiration. If instead it is to be understood as a sudden meeting of practical and theoretical science, then it must still be shown why Galileo, rather than some other philosopher of the same or earlier ages, first thought to look seriously at what the lens-makers were up to. It may be, of course, that Galileo was wholly original, that he really was, as he claimed to be, the first to tear down the whole splendid palace to its foundations rather than just patching it up like everyone else,[3] and that he really was, as he appears to the historian, a kind of phoenix completely unmarked by the ashes from which he rises.

There is no reason to suppose, of course, that a study of sixteenth-century Florence will provide a background for Galileo's work any more successfully than a study of fourteenth-century Paris or fifteenth-century Padua. Not much is known, for one thing, of just what went on in Pisa and Florence at the time,[4] and very little can be found out about Galileo's youth either from the scanty remnants of his early writings or from the correspondence of those who may have known him. He may, indeed, have had very little to do with his compatriots. It was at Padua, after all, not at Pisa, that he spent his most formative years; and it was in the Lincei at Rome rather than among the Alterati at Florence where he found the most sympathetic group of kindred spirits. In the quietness of his comfortable town house up on the Costa San Giorgio, or in the tranquillity of his small villa high above the Arno near Bellosguardo, Galileo led a life of relative isolation, shunning the repeated attempts of the Florentine Academy to bring him down into the city, corresponding with foreigners more often than he conversed with Florentines, and giving all his time to what in modern university jargon is called "research and writing".

Yet there is much about Galileo's work and about the environment in which much of it was accomplished that suggests a somewhat closer bond between the two than has so far been apparent, particularly to those historians who have concentrated largely on the former. It was in Florence, first of all, that Galileo found many of his most enthusiastic and most faithful followers, where the admiration of "the chief ornament of our country" most rapidly turned into a cult,[5] where the Academy of the Cimento consciously elaborated his scientific methods, or at least a more decidedly empirical version of them, in physics and astronomy, where Francesco Redi applied Galilean principles to medicine and biology, where Lorenzo Magalotti meditated upon the theological consequences of Galilean cosmology, and where the Academy of the Crusca at last brought out the first edition of his *Opera omnia*.[6]

The environment, secondly, was not one that Galileo or anyone else could easily ignore. Florence was still, at the end of the sixteenth century, a fairly exciting place to live and work in.[7] Florentines were so flattered by the deference paid them all over Italy in matters of correct language and good literary style, and they were so convinced of the inestimable value of their current debates and investigations, that they were seldom discouraged by some of the more disquieting signs of the times. They were apparently oblivious, for instance, to the loss of their former supremacy in most other fields to Rome, Paris, and Leyden, to the somewhat

less than uplifting standards of court life set by Bianca Capello and her
worthless favorites,[8] to the constant drain of the grand dukes' foreign
ventures on their capital reserves, to the gradual waning of the economic
prosperity so laboriously restored by Cosimo I, and to the gradual increase
in the frequency of periodic famines and in the number of unemployed.
Florence was also a city of incomparable beauty, particularly now that
Vasari and Ammannati had filled it with splendid palaces and surrounded it
with stately villas;[9] and it was one in which elegance and refinement had
neither degenerated into pompousness and extravagance nor lost contact
with plebeian coarseness and businesslike restraint. Who could resist the
gay night life provided by the Bertucce, the Porco, the Sant'Andrea, and
the other saloons and gambling joints where young noblemen dissipated
their time, talents and money, to the distress of their elders?[10] And, above
all, who could resist the charm of a summer evening, when the slamming
saracinesi in front of the shops of the wool merchants and the tolling of
the Angelus from Giotto's tower sent clouds of pigeons into the air, and
when weavers and dyers, bricklayers and silk-stockinged young gentlemen gathered, after a busy day, on the marble steps of the cathedral or on
the gracious news Santa Trinità Bridge over the Arno for an hour or so of
chatter, tall tales, and wry observations in the last glimmer of twilight?
Certainly not Galileo, who recalled such moments with great affection.[11]
The very nature of Florence and the Florentines at the turn of the seventeenth century, indeed, makes it at least improbable that Galileo, alone of
all his fellow citizens, could have remained completely aloof from the life
of the city he belonged to by birth and by choice.

The waning of the older disciplines

Not all aspects of late, or post-Renaissance Florentine culture, to be
sure, were particularly conducive to the emergence of a creative mind.
Most Florentine men of letters, first of all, had become so satisfied with
themselves and with their times that they no longer could even conceive
of the possibility of progress, or constructive change. Yet certainly the
endless back-patting in which they all indulged, certainly the disposition
of even so perspicacious a critic as Lionardo Salviati to pour extravagant
praises on even the most insipid of his colleagues' academic speeches [12]
(and on his own for that matter), certainly the increasingly general assumption among linguists and legislators that the perfect locutions and the
economic prosperity of more or less historical "golden ages" could be
recaptured, but never surpassed—certainly all these are indications not so
much of achievement as of complacency. In a number of disciplines, secondly, the spirit of independent inquiry seems to have given way to a
tendency to elevate one particular author to a position of superhuman
infallibility—Petrarch in poetry, Aristotle in literary criticism, Tacitus in
political philosophy. And when the poets, critics and political philosophers discovered the delights of snuggling up in the bosom of certainty,

they could hardly complain when the Congregation of the Index and the nail-chewing Archbishop Alessandro de'Medici encouraged them to stop reading anything else—to refer to Machiavelli and Savonarola merely as "a certain writer" and "a Dominican friar",[13] and to remove from their "must read" shelves almost the entire literary and philosophical heritage of the early and high Renaissance. One critic, indeed, was so pliant that he had the nerve to call Salviati's expurgated version of Boccaccio's *Decameron* a restoration of the original text;[14] and another was so unaware that Petrarch had written anything but the *Canzoniere* that he had the audacity to call the description of Laura's eyes perfectly Aristotelian.[15] Indeed, the scramble for authority had the even more deleterious effect of sealing off the authors so apotheosized from the hearts of those who read their works. Thus a certain Lorenzo Giacomini could translate the whole of the *Nicomachean ethics* into Italian without being the least bit affected by it—the same text, that is, that had inspired its Latin translator, Leonardo Bruni, to work out a radically new vision of man in society a century and a half earlier.[16] Hence neither Giacomini nor most of his contemporaries could have understood how the reading of Archimedes might have inspired a young mathematician in their midst to investigate for himself the problem of the relative weight of Hiero's golden crown.[17]

Yet even these negative qualities of Florentine culture during Galileo's youth may have had some positive effect—at least in facilitating later on a favorable reception for his innovations. For one thing, many of the subjects that formerly had absorbed the attention of Florentines—and, as some historians think, distracted them from the sciences—were rapidly being exhausted. Theology, for instance, had been turned over to the "experts", and political affairs had been turned over to the princes; and both were now banned by statute from the sessions of the academies. Religion, similarly, had been shut up in convents; religious oratory had been walled off from practical piety by inflexible rules of propriety and rhetoric;[18] and the ordinary layman, which included the vast majority of Florentine literati as well as peasants and artisans, was left with little but miracles, indulgences, and the sort of tinselly votive offerings that poured into the private chapel of Galileo's friend, Lodovico Cigoli, after the Virgin cured him of the fever.[19] Ethics, similarly, had been reduced to the level of Lorenzo Giacomini's violent tirades against "this world";[20] political philosophy had been transformed into mere power calculations (usually based on pretty flimsy data),[21] history had dwindled into little more than a convenient grab bag of moral examples; and commerce and manufacturing, upon which, after all, the economy of the country rested, had now gone out of fashion—to the point, indeed, where one of the most adventurous businessmen of the time insisted that his very competent memoranda on economic policy were the work of a mere amateur, only momentarily distracted from the higher pursuits of letters and poetry.[22] Even the *novella*, and its dramatic counterpart, the comedy, which had flourished for some fifty years, had by now exhausted all possible attempts to rework the plot of Machiavelli's *Mandragola*, still the undisputed classic of the genre; and it is perhaps just as well that Galileo left in draft form his own clumsy stabs at getting the wrong people into the right beds, because Anton Francesco Grazzini, better known as 'Il Lasca', had already raked over the purely physical act of love until there was nothing funny left in it.[23] The old fields, in other words, no longer provided much to talk about; and, for the lack of anything better, the Florentine academicians ended up filling their sessions with purely humorous denunciations of their officers and even, on one occasion, delivering an oration "on how to excuse oneself for not having found a subject".[24]

At the same time, Florentines were not particularly attached to any one system of metaphysics, cosmology, or logic that might have predisposed them in advance against that of Galileo. They had learned a good bit about such subjects, it is true, from the lecture notes Benedetto Varchi brought back from Padua in the '40's and from Pier Vettori's editions and commentaries of several works of Aristotle in the '50's and '60's; and they freely followed contemporary fashions by sprinkling their treatises and orations (to the point of absurdity, in fact) with Aristotelian terminology. But in general they tended to think of such matters as the business of university professors rather than of gentlemen; and they found nothing particularly shocking about the radically new approach to these problems with which an "obscure mathematics teacher" from Fermo, as Leonardo Olschki has called Ostilio Ricci, was infecting their sons, young Galileo included, in that perfectly gentlemanly institution, the Fine Arts Academy.[25]

Nor, for that matter, were Florentines particularly susceptible to influence from what was to become the center of opposition to Galileo in Tuscany, the University of Pisa. For in spite of the considerable sums the first grand dukes had invested in robbing the faculties of all the other universities in Italy,[26] and in spite of the four years that all young Florentines of good family were expected to spend there in their teens, the University of Pisa still remained rather isolated from the cultural life of the capital. The students, for one thing, seem to have taken the university somewhat less than seriously. They chuckled at the syllogism-slinging that their teachers engaged in publicly for their supposed edification; they laughed at the pompous mannerisms which, as Galileo himself pointed out, forced professors to abstain from ordinary sins and take up extraordinary ones;[27] and they saw nothing wrong with cutting classes for the sake of parties, brawls, meetings of the Pisan chapters of the Alterati and the Crusca, or the rough-and-tumble "Game of the Bridge", in which students joined with city thugs to push each other into the Arno.[28]

The alumni, moreover, were hardly more respectful. Unlike Galileo, most of them threw away their lecture notes as soon as they had passed their examinations; and their contacts with the university thereafter were usually limited to those few of their teachers who, being Florentine or at least Tuscan, could speak decently the only language they recognized as legitimate,[29] and who could be relied upon not to bore audiences in Florence that had already at graduation had quite enough of classroom *demonstrationes* and *conclusiones*.[30] The Florentine literati stood little danger, then, of being infected by the sort of heresy-calling that made Andrea Cesalpino's life miserable in 1590, or by the kind of intellectual conformity and interdepartmental bickering that Galileo complained of on the eve of his departure for Padua. Since most of them affected a rather Ciceronian aloofness toward learning in general anyway, even when they were at their busiest with books and ink, and since few of them could figure out any better purpose for their poems and dissertations than that of filling up leisure time or of bringing glory to their families and their princes, they had no *a priori* reason, as had the professionals in the pulpits, the schools, and the theological commissions, for rejecting whatever new questions might be posed or whatever new approaches might be suggested.

Cracks in the cosmos: from Varchi to Cesalpino

Such new questions, indeed, and such new approaches actually did come up from time to time, well before they were reproposed in a systematic fashion by Galileo. Ever since it had first been introduced among them, for instance, Aristotelian philosophy, and above all the tendency to refer all questions to the authority of Aristotle that Galileo ridiculed in the *Dialogo*,[31] had never fully satisfied the Florentine literati. Even Lodovico Boccadiferro of Bologna, who had taught Benedetto Varchi most of his metaphysics, did not hesitate to snipe at Aristotle in small details;[32] and there had been enough dispute among the Paduan professors in the '40's about just which Aristotle or which authoritative commentary to follow to leave their Florentine admirers a bit confused, or at least disposed to "pass on to more pleasant matters" when confronted, for instance, with Galen's assurance that the heart was hot and with Avicenna's assertion that it was cold.[33] The confusion was such, at times, that they even permitted themselves some rather unorthodox suggestions, without, of course, ever realizing the full consequences of what they tossed out in passing. Thus Varchi, while constantly telling his listeners to look into Averroes and Alexander for whatever definite answers they could not find in Aristotle, admitted at times that the heat of the sun might be the product of fire, that Vesalius' anatomical observations might be more valid than Galen's pronouncements, that mathematics might be the measure of physical reality rather than just a way of keeping idle Egyptian priests out of trouble or teaching Florentine painters how to draw triangles, and that mere artisans, those scorned members of the irredeemable rabble, might know more about some sciences than the scientists themselves.[34]

Such admissions occur even more frequently in the works of another ardent Aristotelian of the next generation, Andrea Cesalpino, professor of medicine at Pisa for twenty-seven years until he was called to Rome as personal physician to Pope Clement VIII in 1591.[35] Cesalpino was basically a conservative, and no one really thinks any longer that his occasional intuitions concerning the circular motion of the blood can possibly qualify him as a forerunner of Harvey.[36] Indeed, he became even more conservative in his later years, even more disposed to "concentrate on understanding the founders of the sciences without bothering much about subsequent writers", even more anxious to patch up the least crack in Peripatetic doctrine, and even less inclined to follow the example of his teacher and predecessor, Realdo Colombo, who had discovered the so-called "smaller circulation". But Cesalpino was not just a teacher of academic medicine. He was also a practicing physician, and, still more important, the curator of the university's well-endowed botanical garden. Once outside the classroom, and once absorbed by more practical matters, Cesalpino soon came to realize that Hippocratic medicine was more useful than Galenic medicine, not so much because it was more consonant with Aristotelian principles, but above all because it put together (and his words here sound strikingly like what Vasco Ronchi and Lodovico Geymonat have said about Galileo) what previously had been kept apart—experiment, that is, and reason. It was just such a separation, indeed, that still stifled botany and medicine in his own time:

> Among the pharmacists [he complained in 1583] there are very few who complement their professional activities by studying philosophy, without which little good can be accomplished; and among the philosophers there are very few who ever have looked into the particular phenomena that concern the pharmacist, even though in them is to be found the very nerve of philosophy.[37]

He also found that the ancient authorities to whom he turned for help in the immense task of sorting out the new plants in the garden were not wholly satisfactory, even though they were still far more complete, particularly in recent critical editions, than anything written since. Theophrastus, for instance, was admirably comprehensive in scope, but full of errors in detail; and Dioscorides was generally accurate but of very little use, since his classification, based on curative effects alone, prevented the discovery of similar medical qualities in plants of the same species. Moreover, the immense number of new specimens that Cesalpino had run across himself while trying to corroborate the authorities, and the even greater number sent back from India by the learned Florentine merchant Filippo Sassetti or from Spain and America by agents of the Grand Duke, were rapidly making all ancient authors relatively obsolete. "This science", he confessed in some bewilderment, "seems not only to have come back to life, but to have grown to such an extent that it is obviously far more flourishing today than it has ever been in the past." [38]

When he got down to particulars, then, Cesalpino forgot all about the authorities he praised in his prefaces and was willing to consider seriously a number of opinions, even regarding the composition of the heavens, that were really irreconcilable with the systems he hoped to save. The "Quarrel" between the ancients and the moderns, which Hans Baron shows to have been worked out in favor of the latter in letters, art, and political theory by the Quattrocento humanists, was here decided in favor of modern botanists by one of the most fervent advocates of the ancient masters, just as Galileo was soon to decide it in favor of modern physicists and astronomers.[39] Cesalpino realized that unless botany and metallurgy were to remain merely book learning or merely a mass of undigested and uncertain lore, there was nothing to do but to start from scratch, and to rearrange both the old and the new data according to completely different criteria— according, that is, to observable exterior structure. And he ended up by asserting the autonomy of botany from metaphysics as well as from medicine and by providing it with a system of classification that was to remain definitive until Tournefort figured out a better one at the end of the following century.

The contribution of the antiquarians

A very similar change in attitudes can be observed in another field that had even less apparent connection with physics and astronomy than did botany and metallurgy, that is, antiquarianism, a field that had grown in popularity all over Italy as history itself withered away. Antiquarianism was by its very nature dedicated exclusively to the consideration of the concrete and the individual, which it deliberately abstained from putting together as part of a general historical thesis.[40] Antiquarianism could (and often did) end up in little more than the mad scramble for *anticaglia* that Galileo ridiculed as the little passion of curious dilettantes.[41] But it could also take the form of a completely dispassionate search for the truth—as it did in the case of Girolamo Mei, who even left Florence so that his inquiries into the distant past of his native city would remain completely untouched by his own lingering patriotism or by his friends' anxious cultivation of their family trees. Through his teacher, the eminent Hellenist Pier Vettori, Mei inherited the whole Renaissance tradition of critical philology, from Valla, Biondo, and Poliziano on. But he surpassed his predecessors, and most of his contemporaries as well, by ripping down the last compartment of infallibility left by the humanists in ancient literature, namely, the chronicle of events contained in the narratives of the Greek and Roman historians; and he came up with internal evidence of deliberate as well as of unconscious falsification even in Tacitus, whom all the political scientists of the day accepted as perfectly accurate.

For Mei, the study of the past was not an end in itself: it was endowed with the far more noble purpose of promoting justice and truthfulness in an age which had sacrificed both to partisanship. Hence he could not let initial doubt lead him to skepticism, as it did in the notable case of Francesco Patrizi. Just as Galileo was to insist that his precise mathematical calculations actually did correspond to physical reality, so Mei had no hesitation in embracing as actual fact what the rigorous application of Vettori's critical methods assured him to have happened in the past. Florence actually *was*, he proclaimed, founded by the Lombards, whatever all other historians and Cosimo I himself may have said to the contrary; and Greek music actually *was* what he thought he had discovered in certain manuscript notations in the Vatican library, no matter what Gioseffo Zarlino said it ought to have been according to philosophical principles.

That such similar changes should have taken place in two such widely separated and, at the time, such marginal fields—that an offshoot of natural science and an offshoot of historiography should both have been beset by a breakdown of the old authorities and by a demand that the old theories be revised in accordance with the specific data they were meant to describe—all this is not so surprising as it may seem. Nor, for that matter, is it wholly improbable that Galileo, self-conscious specialist though he was, may have been affected by these changes. Cesalpino, for instance, may never have budged from Pisa before 1591, and he probably knew Galileo, if at all, only as a freshman in the back of a large lecture hall. But Cesalpino taught medicine, after all, which is what Galileo first went to Pisa to study,[42] and he was always respectfully excepted from the irreverent jibes at the university by its student-critics. He may never have met Mei either, but he also had been subjected in his youth to the rigorous philological training of Mei's teacher, Pier Vettori, whose methods are often so similar to his own; and it may have been Vettori's experimental garden at San Casciano that first aroused Cesalpino's interest in botany, as it was Vettori's desire to pad his scholarly footnotes that sent Filippo Sassetti scurrying about India for remnants of classical antiquity.[43]

Cesalpino only vaguely recalled, in later years, having met Sassetti as a student; but he, like everyone in Florence, read all the letters Sassetti sent back from Goa and made special requests for seeds, geographical data, and astronomical observations through their common friend and, as it happens, one of Galileo's later correspondents, the learned librarian Baccio Valori, whose son Filippo became a close companion of his own son Giovan Battista during Valori's term as high commissioner for Pisa.[44] Mei, similarly, may never have met Galileo either; but he knew Valori very well,[45] and it was largely the letters he had circulated in the famous Camerata of Giovanni de' Bardi that converted Galileo's father, Vincenzo, the musical mentor of the Camerata, from polyphony to accompanied monody (thus starting, by the way, one of the most important revolutions in the history of music).[46] It is hardly likely that the son, who knew a good bit of music himself, would have been unaware of what was certainly discussed in his father's house. The tightly knit Florentine world of letters, then, with its academies, its weekend house-parties, and its chains of correspondence, kept in close contact with even its most distant members; and it provided a clearinghouse for all the new ideas of new information that each of them separately might come up with.

Philosophy and literary criticism

Meanwhile several of the fields in which Florentines had been most interested in during the '70's were running into serious difficulties by the end of the century—difficulties from which the only possible escape may have been that taken by Galileo. In systematic philosophy, first of all, Aristotelianism could reign undisturbed among the professionals at Pisa, and Francesco Buonamici could introduce all the heterodox opinions he wanted without ever fearing that, torn out of context, they might endanger his system as a whole. But among the amateurs at Florence, the increasingly obvious irreconcilability of certain Aristotelian doctrines with what everyone thought to be the philosophical corollaries of Christianity—or with what everyone knew to be actual fact—led to a frantic scurrying through just about every other ancient philosopher in the hope of patching up the whole shaky structure.

The most obvious philosopher to turn to, of course, was Plato, whom the Pisan professors might admit only on the express command of the Grand Duke,[47] but whom Francesco Vieri had good hopes of reviving, partially for the benefit of his own depleted pocketbook, through the re-establishment of something like Ficino's famous Academy in Florence.[48] Indeed, the outlook for Plato seemed more than promising in the early '90's, particularly after the arrival of Jacopo Mazzoni, who had just finished reconciling him with Aristotle, Averroes and Pico (and almost everyone else except Copernicus and Lucretius), and after the election of Clement VIII,[49] who began his pontificate by inviting the most pugnacious Platonist of the age to a lucrative chair in Rome. But the outlook quickly changed. Vieri evidently forgot that the Platonism *he* had learned from his father and from Francesco da Diacceto had turned away from Ficino's project to bolster Christianity with Plato and Plotinus and that it admitted a number of theses which even the most tolerant or superficial of eclectics could not easily reconcile with Aristotelian physics.[50] He first tried, in the 1580's, to make Plato fit Aristotle. He then tried, in the 1590's, to make Aristotle fit Plato.[51] And he ended up by abstracting both so far from the actual flesh-and-blood Greek writers edited by Pier Vettori that he brought as much discredit on Plato as the use of syllogisms in inappropriate contexts had already brought on Aristotle.

In its Florentine form, Platonism contributed even less to Galileo's vision of the universe than did Pisan Aristotelianism; for it admitted the study of numbers and of matter only as a way of rising above both to the contemplation of God.[52] But it did make that vision more possible by breaking down the whole vast attempt to put together a workable cosmology based on the authority of ancient writers. And when the Holy Office put Patrizi's *Nova philosophia* irrevocably on the Index in 1594,[53] it may well have suggested to Galileo, as similar incidents certainly did to his disciples, that he look for a more reliable support to Christian doctrine in a science fundamentally different from the traditional versions of a *Philosophia christiana*.

In literary criticism, secondly, a subject that absorbed most of the attention of the Florentine academies during Galileo's student days, the first cracks in the magnificent system built carefully over a half century began to appear at just the moment when the last objections to it seemed to have vanished.[54] So thoroughly, indeed, had Pier Vettori's Latin commentary and Filippo Sassetti's critical revision of Alessandro Piccolomini's Italian translation established the authority of Aristotle's *Poetics*, so methodically had the Academy of the Alterati eliminated Horace and Cicero and Plato as possible competitors, and so voluminously had Lionardo Salviati, and with him the whole Academy of the Crusca, applied the principles he discovered in Aristotle to the classics of Italian literature,[55] that when the young Galileo tried his hand at the same questions all his friends were talking about (in his notes on Ariosto and his commentary on Tasso) he had only to take over the ready-made principles Salviati had already worked out for him and to accept without hesitation the final judgment of the Crusca—namely, that Dante and Ariosto fitted the principles perfectly, and that Tasso did not.

Unfortunately this approach to literature ran into a few snags that occasionally troubled even its staunchest defenders. It proceeded, first of all, from the top down, from literature as a whole to prose and poetry, to lyric and epic, etc., and it obliged the critics above all to find the right slot for each piece under consideration. They finally managed to squeeze the *Decameron* into one slot, the *Orlando* into another, and the *Gerusalemme* into some three or four in succession. But there was one form of poetry that could not be overlooked in the late sixteenth century and that turned out to be as ill-accommodated to Aristotelian poetics as the Medicean planets were to be to Ptolemaic cosmography: the madrigal; and Galileo's wealthy, talented young friend Giovan Battista Strozzi, an accomplished madrigalist in his own right, finally admitted what Sassetti had already suspected, that in this case, at any rate, it would be better to work from the bottom up and figure out the categories to fit the phenomena.[56]

Secondly, the Aristotelianism of the Florentines so emphasized structure at the expense of language, and logical relationships at the expense of intuitive ones, that it threatened to become completely isolated from the actual writing of poetry, which was, after all, its principal *raison d'être*. As treatises on *ars historica* were drowning out history itself all over Italy at the time,[57] so literary criticism, in Florence at least, was suffocating creative literature in part, perhaps, because of the reluctance of would-be poets to subject themselves to the kind of systematic tearing apart that the critics administered so mercilessly to Tasso and Guarini. What happened in botany, physics, and for that matter music, did not happen, to be sure, in poetics; for the successors to Salviati chose to ignore the revolutionary implications of Strozzi's suggestions about the madrigal and to shun the task of thinking up a new critical system to replace the one Salviati had perfected in all but tiny details. What did happen, though, was that they simply forgot about critical principles altogether— and, given the poverty of Galileo's own literary judgments, Bernard Weinberg may have more than simply chronological reasons for ending his monumental history of criticism in 1600. They welcomed Tasso with open arms when he visited Florence in 1590, and they turned from the critics back to the poets in order to learn how to write themselves, just as Galileo advised them to do.[58]

The survival of humanism

With the breakdown of the principle of argument from authority in some fields, with the exhaustion of the arguments themselves in others, and, in still others, with the abandonment of traditional theoretical frameworks in favor of the single, the peculiar, and the concrete, it is not so surprising that certain of the attitudes commonly associated with earlier Renaissance humanism should have begun to appear once again in the late sixteenth century. After Girolamo Mei had refused to consider Pliny or any other ancient writer as a perfect philosopher or an impeccable astronomer and had classified him instead simply as a "well-informed, diligent, and scholarly man" like so many of his friends, after Cesalpino had put all the ancient scientists back into a chronological perspective in order to discover a pattern of development from one to the other, and after Galileo's father had poured ridicule on "all those who try to prove any conclusion by referring solely to the authority of someone else", it was fairly easy for Galileo himself to bring Aristotle down to the level of an ordinary, fallible human being, without ever having read Petrarch's *De ignorantia*.[59]

After death at long last put an end to Vasari's domination of Tuscan painting,[60] after the failure of its pupils to produce anything but shadowy imitations of the great mannerists put an end to the brilliant expectations of the Fine Arts Academy, after the Grand Duke Ferdinand put an end to his brother's attempt to impose his own *"petite manière"* on court artists by turning over all commissions to a competent administrator, it was not too difficult for Galileo [61] and for his good friend Lodovico Cigoli, who as a poet and a musician as well as an artist and a member of the Crusca was fully *au courant* of the literary discussions of his fellow citizens, to turn for inspiration to the Bolognese neoclassicists and to aesthetic principles very close to the those of Alberti and Leonardo. Even the stifling complacency of the Florentine literati occasionally broke down, although in a way more like the quiet resignation of the seventeenth century than like the anxious dissatisfaction of the fifteenth that Galileo himself seems to echo. For a few of them had already begun to realize that a great age had passed away and to confess, well before Galileo set out to remedy the deficiency, that their former position of cultural leadership had been appropriated by the nations beyond the Alps.[62] Given the closeness of Galileo to some of the leaders of Florentine intellectual life, these similarities in judgment may be more than just coincidental.

It is in the form, however, more than in the content of his work that Galileo most nearly reflects Florentine culture in the late sixteenth century. Throughout the seventeenth century, after all, he was applauded as much as a stylist as he was as a philosopher; and to judge from the stream of articles on the subject in current Italian periodicals, he is so still today. His use of the vernacular, first of all, may have shocked Kepler and many non-Tuscan Italian philosophers of the time; but to Florentines, Galileo was simply obeying the prescriptions of the Florentine Academy about the extension of the Florentine language, as it was called, into all realms of human knowledge, and he was accepting the results of the painstaking labors of Lionardo Salviati,[63] who had finally rid the language of the numerous irregularities of vocabulary and orthography still observable in the correspondence even of learned men. In adopting a vigorous, colloquial, at times a bit plebeian, and, from a modern point of view, rather local form of the vernacular, he was taking sides in the battle between the "Florentinists" and the "Italianists" that had raged ever since the days of Castiglione and Machiavelli, and he was echoing the warning of his senior contemporary, Bernardo Davanzati, against any attempt to separate the written from the spoken language.[64] Even if he had known of them, to be sure, Galileo would probably not have sympathized with the purely technical nature of Davanzati's experiments with language, which sought to do no more than prove the superiority of Tuscan to French by reducing, in translation, the laconic prose of Tacitus to even fewer words than were contained in the Latin original. But he might have been more impressed with the potential utility of these experiments had he seen their application in Davanzati's planting and harvest manual, which is as clear and concise as a modern income tax form.[65] Just at the moment, in fact, in which Galileo was upbraiding Tasso for obscurity and excessive verbiage, Davanzati was leading a campaign, with the help of Tacitus himself, the favorite author of the Alterati, against the bloated, hyperbolic "sea of eloquence" that was threatening to engulf Tuscan prose.[66] And even if his own crisp, precise, "anti-baroque" style [67] is not directly indebted to the Florentine Tacitists of his youth, at least its reception as a model for Tuscan writers thereafter owes something to the personal triumph of their chief apologist, Davanzati, whose reputation remained undiminished for two centuries thereafter.

Galileo's use of the dialogue and the epistle as a means of exposition, finally, need not be attributed to the example of Plato. Indeed, the introduction of real historical personages, each with his own personality and each with a perfectly valid point of view, carrying on a perfectly credible

conversation within a perfectly possible length of time in a real place
where they all might easily have met, is far less reminiscent of Plato than
it is of Leonardo Bruni or Lorenzo Valla. So, for that matter, are the di-
gressions, the anecdotes, the pleasantries, the amenities, the backtracking,
the careful shunning of technical jargon, and the insistence that the gentlemanly confrontation of various opinions is more important than the
ultimate victory of any one of them.

The humanists had adopted the epistle and the dialogue not merely for
literary, but above all for rhetorical purposes [68]—for the purpose, that is, of
affecting the wills as well as the minds of a large, educated, but nonprofes-
sional audience. Both forms had died out toward the middle of the sixteenth century, or rather both had yielded to such forms as the discourse
and the oration, which were more in keeping with the isolated and disengaged élite that had taken the place of the educated representatives of
Renaissance society. Yet even Benedetto Varchi had preserved some elements of the obsolescent forms in his effort to communicate the latest
theories in medicine and metaphysics to his sensitive, but unacademic,
friends; Flaminio Nobili had preserved others in the Latin conversations
he recorded among his companions on Plato and Aristotle;[69] and Francesco Vieri had preserved still others in recognizing the relevance of philosophy to all "gentle souls", whether they understood Latin or not.[70]
Indeed, a few Florentine writers had come still closer to what the humanists had done before and what Galileo was to do later: Filippo Sassetti, for
instance, in insisting that the original elaboration, not just the popularization, of the sciences should take place in a living language, and Pierfran-
cesco Giambullari, who turned a traditional commentary on Dante's Inferno into a discussion of recent geographical discoveries, the same
framework that Galileo was later to use for his theorems on spheres and
cones.[71]

Thus Florentine culture of the late sixteenth century passed on to Galileo, at least in fragments, the forms of discourse that had been more current a century earlier than they were in his own times. It may even have
given him the inspiration to apply those forms to a new subject, natural
philosophy, one which the humanists had generally left to the professors.
And still more important, it may also have given him the sense of belonging to a large community of intelligent, widely read, and broadly educated gentlemen, rather than to a closed caste of highly trained specialists
—a sense that seems to be reflected not only in his choice of a language and
a style most decidedly not those of his professional colleagues, but in his
recognition of the Florentine Academy as a perfectly competent forum
for the discussion of his work.

None of the possible connections between Galileo and the cultural
community in which he lived, to be sure, is anything but hypothetical,
given the absence of conclusive evidence in those of his writings that have
survived. Even if they were something more than merely fortuitous,

moreover, none of the striking similarities between single ideas and attitudes in Galileo and in his immediate predecessors would in any way diminish the originality of his achievement. But the city he eventually converted may well have also lent him some assistance—by transmitting to him, that is, the many aspects of Renaissance humanism present in his work, by breaking down ways of reasoning that were to prove incompatible with his own, by exhausting the discussion of certain questions that otherwise might have distracted him from the ones he was to pose, and by providing him with a sympathetic audience already familiar in other contexts with the approach he was to apply to the study of the physical world. Galileo may still elude the historian, then; he may still resist being reduced to the normal, the average, the typical. But in the light of what his compatriots had been doing for the three or four decades before he focused his telescope on the satellites of Jupiter, Galileo is perhaps somewhat less of a phoenix.

NOTES

1. Benedetto Croce, *Storia dell'età barocca in Italia*, 2nd edn., Bari, 1946, p. 64.

2. I refer here to the well-known theses of Galvano Della Volpe, J. H. Randall, Antonio Banfi, Ernst Cassirer, Anneliese Maier, Giuseppe Saitta, Giovanni Gentile, Alexandre Koyré, Lodovico Geymonat, Marshall Clagett, Eugenio Garin, Vasco Ronchi, Giorgio de Santillana, Adriano Carugo, *et al.* (and not necessarily in that order), which need not be cited here explicitly. I cite specific passages from the *Opere* only where the reader might find it helpful to look them up.

3. *Opere*, 7, p. 82.

4. The most complete account of the political, and to some extent cultural and economic, affairs of the period is still Books III–V of Riguccio Galluzzi's *Istoria del Granducato di Toscana sotto il governo della Casa Medici*, Florence, 1781, and Livorno (2nd edn.), 1821. Other more recent monographs on single aspects or persons will be mentioned in the notes that follow.

5. The expression is from Carlo Roberto Dati's manifesto of Galilean philosophy, the *Esortazione allo studio della geometria*, published in his *Prose*, ed. by Ettore Allodoli, Lanciano, 1913, pp. 63–79. Since I am presently engaged in writing about post-Galilean Galileanism in Italy, the reader will pardon my not bolstering these comments with the usual barrage of quotations and titles.

6. Florence, 1718. The plans for the publication venture go back to 1655–1668, when the Grand Duke Ferdinand II ordered the assembly of the surviving letters and papers. The diplomatic correspondence on the question has been published by Anna Maria Crinò in *Physis*, 1960*. The preparatory work for the 1718 edition dates from as early as 1691: see my *Tradition and enlightenment in the Tuscan academies*, Chicago and Rome, 1961*, p. 113, as well, of course, as the relevant entries in the *Bibliografia galileiana* of Carli, Favaro, and Boffito.

7. Again I omit bibliographical and documentary notes, all of which will be found instead in a paper I have just finished called "The end of the Renaissance in Florence", *Bibliothèque d'humanisme et renaissance*, 27, 1965, 7–30.

8. The reader may correct the false impression of court life of the time created by the lurid stories circulated ever since, by looking into the accurate, but still amusing account by Fabrizio Winspeare, *Isabella Orsini e la corte medicea del suo tempo*, Florence, 1961.

9. The building was still going on when Galileo returned to Florence, and in accordance with the same tastes, as shown in Niccolò Arrighetti's description of the new palace of Galileo's good friend Filippo Salviati in *Delle lodi del sig. F. S.*, Florence, 1614, p. 12.

10. The inns are mentioned by Galileo in "Contro il portar la toga", *Scritti letterari*, ed. by A. Chiari, Florence, 1943, pp. 287–288. Numerous edicts of the period repeat the warning of the *Bando* of May 18, 1579: "Having heard in many parts and from truthful and upright persons of the improprieties and enormous blasphemies, the thieveries and other kinds of misbehavior that derive from the holding of games of chance and all sorts of gambling, besides the crooked dealing, trickery, and falsehood committed in order to steal or win at the games . . . to the harm and ruin of many, and especially of the young nobility. . . ." Except for the last phrase, the wording sounds strikingly familiar to a Chicagoan of 1964. Filippo Sassetti felt impelled to write all the way from India to warn his sister against letting her nephew get involved in the dangerous night life of the city: e.g., letter of February 10, 1584, in *Lettere di F. S.*, ed. by Ettore Marcucci, Florence, 1855, pp. 275–276.

11. Sonnet I: "Per via Mozza raccolte in be' drappelli . . . " in *Scritti letterari*, p. 13.

12. Salviati to Lorenzo Giacomini, January 16, 1588, in Salviati, *Lettere edite e inedite*, ed. by P. Ferrato, Rimini, 1875, no. 66, referring to Giacomini's *Oratione de le lodi di Francesco Medici*, delivered in the Accademia Fiorentina and published by Sermartelli in Florence in 1587.

13. Such terms are used most notably by Scipione Ammirato in his *Discorsi sopra Cornelio Tacito*, first published in 1594 and several times thereafter, and by Serafino Razzi, himself a barely disguised follower of Savonarola, in his *La vita della . . . madre suor Caterina de'Ricci*, Lucca, 1594. (St. Catherine was particularly devoted to Savonarola as the reformer of her convent of S. Vincenzo of Prato.) In general, see Rodolfo de Mattei, *Dal machiavellismo all'antimachiavellismo europeo del Cinquecento*, Rome, 1956.

14. Francesco Cambi in his *Delle lodi del cavaliere Lionardo Salviati*, republished in *Prose fiorentine*, vol. 3, part I, n. 5 (pp. 55–65 of the Venetian edition of 1751, which I use for all but part III). The *Decameron* had been put on the Tridentine Index, *donec corrigatur*, and not until a special commission appointed by the Grand Duke had done an extensive revision was at least some of it taken off again. See Peter M. Brown, "I veri promotori della 'Rassettatura' del *Decameron*", *Giornale storico della letteratura italiana*, 134, 1957, 314–332.

15. Francesco de'Vieri ("Verino secondo"), *Lezione . . . delle idee e delle bellezze*, Florence, 1581, in the Introduction. The only Quattrocento Florentine authors of whom I have found any but the briefest mention in the litera-

ture of this period are Ficino and Pico, both for reasons that will become clear later on in this paper. The only reference to anything by Petrarch other than the *Canzoniere* I have run across is Giovan Battista Strozzi's mention of a passage in the *Familiares*—which he then uses for the sole purpose of supporting Castelvetro's thesis that rhyme was invented by the Sicilians: *Sopra i madrigali* (1584), printed in his *Orazioni et altre prose*, Rome, 1635.

16. On Giacomini's translation, which was never published, see D. Moreni in the Preface to the 1821 edition of Giacomini's *Della nobiltà delle lettere e delle armi*, Florence, 1821 (composed in 1576). Giacomini *might* have found something of interest in Bruni's version (which he evidently paid no attention to), since he was responsible for the extensive business affairs of his family (although no one would know anything about them from his many extant writings).

17. The *Bilancetta*, as Antonio Favaro has shown, was written in 1586.

18. This seems to be Galileo's judgment as well, in his reference to the then famous preacher Francesco Panigarola, in *Scritti letterari*, p. 117.

19. Filippo Baldinucci, *Notizie de'professori del disegno da Cimabue in qua*. I use the edition of Florence, 1845–1847, here cited at vol. 3, p. 237.

20. Particularly in *Esortatione alla vita cristiana e confermatione della fede*, Florence, 1571, but also in many others of his numerous dissertations of this sort.

21. Most notably by Lionardo Salviati in his *Discorso intorno alla ribellione di Fiandra*, 1577 (published by Luigi Manzoni in *Prose inedite*, Bologna, 1873) which provided Philip II with infallible rules, deduced from infallible principles, for smashing the Flemish rebels. But this tendency is widespread in all Italian political thought of the time, from Giovanni Botero to the adopted Florentine Scipione Ammirato, on whom there is a considerable bibliography —e.g. Rodolfo de Mattei, "Il pensiero politico di S. A.", *Studi salentini*, *3*, 1957, and Alberto Alberti, 'Politica e ragion di stato nell'opera di S. A.", *Atti R. Accademia di s. l. e a. di Torino, Classe di storia, morale* . . . , *66*, 1930–1931, 598–626.

22. Filippo Sassetti, namely (about whom more will be said in the following pages), in "Sul commercio tra la Toscana e le nazioni levantine", ed. by F. L. Polidori in *Archivio storico italiano*, 1853, Appendix 9, pp. 169–184.

23. Published in *Scritti letterari*, pp. 30–44. On the contemporary Florentine novel and comedy, see Luigi Russo, "Novellistica e dialoghistica nella Firenze del '500", Part 2, *Belfagor*, *16*, 1961, 261–283.

24. Vincenzo Pitti's "Orazion sopra lo scusarsi del non trovare soggetto" is recorded in the manuscript *Diario di Bastiano de' Rossi* (an eighteenth-century copy) preserved in the present halls of the Accademia della Crusca in Florence: MS A.2, March 8, 1588/1589. The *Prose fiorentine* are full of academic *accuse*.

25. L. Olschki, *Galilei und seine Zeit*, Halle, 1927, pp. 141ff. Varchi presented his lectures to the Accademia Fiorentina under the title of *Lezioni su Dante*, which I read in vol. 2 of his *Opere*, Trieste, 1859, pp. 284ff.

26. The policy inaugurated by Cosimo I was continued in Galileo's time by Ferdinand I, who hired Jacopo Mazzoni from Cesena and brought in Girolamo Mercuriale, later a friend and correspondent of Galileo's, for salaries of some 1,000 scudi a year—which contrasts favorably with the 400 scudi paid to the Tuscan Cesalpino and the mere 60 paid to Galileo. Cesalpino's career is a good

example of the kind of backbiting this policy provoked: see Ugo Viviani, *Vita e opera di A. Cesalpino*, Arezzo, 1922, p. 107, and numerous particulars in the still standard *Historia Academiae Pisanae* of Angelo Fabroni, Pisa, 1791–1795.

27. Compare Galileo's "Capitolo contro il portar la toga" in *Scritti letterari*, pp. 287–288, with Filippo Sassetti's frequent ironic comments on "filosofiche astrattezze" and "certe cause un po' universalotte" in his letters from Pisa to his employer Lorenzo Giacomini in the 1570's: *Lettere*, pp. 25, 27, *et al.*

28. Bernardo Davanzati gives a good description of the president of the Pisan branch of the Alterati leading one of the teams in the "game" in *Opere*, ed. by Enrico Bindi, Florence, 1852, vol. 2, pp. 476ff.

29. There were a couple of exceptions, of course. Jacopo Mazzoni of Cesena, for instance, was elected to the Accademia della Crusca (which also, according to Salvino Salvini in *Fasti consolari dell'Accademia Fiorentina*, Florence, 1717, p. 279, had a branch in Pisa; and Salvini's volume, based upon the most painstaking researches, is still one of the best sources for the history of Florentine culture at the time). But the linguistic division between the Latin-speaking university and the Florentine-speaking student body was reflected even in the *Canti carnascialeschi del Rinascimento*, ed. by Charles Singleton, Bari, 1936, e.g., in Girolamo Amelonghi's *La gigantea*, p. 383: "Abbián la lingua greca e latina / per gran pratica a mente; / ma l'è più dolce assai la fiorentina . . . " It was this taste for the "Florentine" language, common to most of Italy at the time, that seems to have given rise to the (according to Favaro, unfounded) supposition that Galileo's students at Padua brought pressure on him to lecture in the vernacular (since as a genuine Florentine he could speak it better than any of them).

30. The Florentine professor Francesco de'Vieri, whose father, after all, had been an intimate associate of the Florentine literary world and who had taught philosophy to Varchi, carefully disguised his lectures on Platonism before the Accademia Fiorentina in 1580 as a commentary on Petrarch. He was apparently embarrassed about even bringing up the subject: note the opening lines of his *Lezione . . . della idee et delle bellezze*.

31. E.g. *Opere*, 7, pp. 134, 138, *et al.*

32. See Umberto Pirotti, "Benedetto Varchi e l'aristotelismo del Rinascimento", *Convivium*, *31*, 1963, 280–311. The following paragraph is much indebted to this excellent essay.

33. Varchi, *Opere*, vol. 3, p. 290. On Padua, I follow Bruno Nardi, "La fine dell'averroismo", now in his *Saggi sull'aristotelismo padovano dal secolo XIV al XVI*, Florence, 1950, pp. 113 155, but similar observations are made by J H Randall in "The development of scientific method in the school of Padua", 1940*.

34. *Opere*, vol. 2, p. 286.

35. The following remarks on this little-known figure are based on a study of the huge quantity of letters and other writings gathered together by Viviani in the *Vita e opera di A. C.* cited above in n. 26, even though the text is full of errors.

36. Marie Boas Hall, *The scientific renaissance*, 1961*, pp. 274–275, which apparently refutes the somewhat overly patriotic theses of Giovanni Arcieri in *The circulation of the blood and Andrea Cesalpino of Arezzo*, New York, 1945.

37. To Alfonso de'Tornabuoni, September 14, 1583, in Viviani, *op. cit.*, p. 83.

38. Cesalpino in the Introduction to his *De plantis*, Florence, 1583.

39. Hans Baron, "The *Querelle* of ancients and moderns as a problem for renaissance scholarship", *Journal of the history of ideas*, 20, 1959, 3–22.

40. Even the historian Jacopo Nardi confessed much the same thing in 1552: "Ma noi rimirando più basso . . ."—in *Vita d'Antonio Giacomini*, Lucca, 1818, pp. 15–16. On the spread of antiquarianism at the time, note the remarks of Carlo Dionisotti in *Rivista Storica Italiana*, 71, 1963, 890ff.

41. Galileo in *Scritti letterari*, p. 96. In general, see H. J. Erasmus, *The origins of Rome in historiography from Petrarch to Perizonius*, Assen, 1962. Most of the remarks in this paragraph are based on a study of the letters of Mei to Pier Vettori and Vincenzo Borghini printed in part III, vol. 2 of *Prose fiorentine* (in the edition of Venice, 1735). On Mei himself, I follow the long Introduction of Claude Palisca to his *Letters on ancient and modern music to Vincenzo Galilei and Giovanni Bardi*, 1960*, rather than Fabio Fano's *La camerata fiorentina*, Milan, 1934.

42. Galileo's story about the Peripatetic physician in the *Dialogo* (*Opere*, 7, p. 134) may be a reference to him.

43. Cesalpino to Vettori, December 12, 1560, in Viviani, *op. cit.*, pp. 173–174; Sassetti to Vettori, January 27, 1585, *Lettere*, p. 277, reporting that "relics of every ancient custom may well be found scattered throughout the Orient".

44. See Angelo Maria Bandini, *Memorie per servire alla vita del senator Pier Vettori*, Livorno, 1756. Vettori even wrote a small treatise, *Trattato . . . delle lodi e della coltivazione degli ulivi* ("on the cultivation of olives"), which probably circulated only in manuscript, since the earliest edition I have found is that of 1722 (2nd edn., Florence, 1762).

45. In fact, he addressed his important, if slim, *Discorso sopra la musica antica*, Venice, 1602, to him.

46. See Palisca, "Vincenzo Galilei", in *Die Musik in Geschichte und Gegenwart*, 4, 1955, 1265–1270. The lay reader should be warned that Palisca's chronology of Renaissance music is not exactly the same as that presented in the somewhat more comprehensive survey of Edward E. Lowinsky, "Music in the culture of the Renaissance", *Journal of the history of ideas*, 15, 1954, 509–553.

47. A special decree of Francis I in 1576 gave Vieri permission to offer a non-scheduled course on Plato, without extra pay, of course, and the permission was transferred to Jacopo Mazzoni in 1588. See Paul Oskar Kristeller in *Studies in Renaissance thought and letters*, Rome, 1956, pp. 291–292, and Eugenio Garin in his *La filosofia*, Milan, 1947, vol. 2, chap. 2. Notwithstanding Kristeller's and Garin's rather favorable impression of late Cinquecento Florentine Platonism, I tend, after reading (*ahimè!*) just about all of his works, to agree with Vieri's probably not altogether sincere portrait of himself in 1568 as "di mediocre ingegno, di manco sapere, et occupatissimo nella cura di tanta mia famiglia . . ." *Discorsi . . . del soggetto, del numero . . . degl'habiti dell'animo*, Florence, 1568, Preface.

48. Vieri to Valori, February 7, 1590, Viviani, *op. cit.*, p. 170.

49. *De triplice hominum vita, activa, nempe, contemplativa, & religiosa methodi tres . . . in quibus omnes Platonis et Aristotelis, multis verò aliorum Grae-*

corum, Arabum & Latinorum . . . discordiae componuntur, Cesena, 1577. Mazzoni, of course, tried it again, even more thoroughly, in his *In universam Platonis et Aristotelis philosophiam praeludia* . . . , Venice, 1597, even though, as Bruno Nardi observes, the argument had fairly well run itself aground elsewhere in Italy (*Saggi di aristotelismo padovano*, p. 363).

50. See for instance Francesco Cattani da Diacceto, *I tre libri d'amore*, Venice, 1561.

51. Particularly in *Vere conclusioni di Platone conformi alla dottrina christiana et a quella d'Aristotile*, Florence, 1590. He mentions the project in a letter to Baccio Valori (to whom the book is dedicated) of a "great table of 2000 Peripatetic distinctions and a collection of 200 conclusions in which Aristotle is in conformity with Plato and which he [Aristotle] took from Plato, even though he hid the fact . . . ", in Viviani, *op. cit.*, p. 171.

52. Vieri's definition of philosophy "per la quale l'huomo si fa simile a Dio . . . " in 1568 in the *Discorsi* (n. 47, above) is substantially the same as that given in his letter to Valori (n. 48, above); and it backs up Antonio Favaro's well-known theses concerning Galileo's supposed Platonism.

53. On this whole affair, see Tullio Gregory, "L'*Apologia* e le *Declarationes* di Francesco Patrizi", in *Medioevo e rinascimento: Studi in onore di Bruno Nardi*, Milan, 1955, pp. 385ff., and Luigi Firpo, "Filosofia italiana e Controriforma", *Rivista di filosofia*, *41*, 1950, 150ff.

54. Most of the critical writings of the authors mentioned in this paragraph are examined one by one in Bernard Weinberg's monumental *History of literary criticism in the Italian Renaissance*, Chicago, 1961; and those presented to the Alterati are discussed in his "Argomenti di discussione letteraria nell'Accademia degli Alterati (1570–1600)", *Giornale storico della letteratura italiana*, *131*, 1954, 175–194, and "Accademia degli Alterati: literary taste from 1570–1600", *Italica*, *31*, 1954, 207–214, with all relevant bibliography. On Sassetti in particular, see Mario Rossi, *Un letterato e mercante fiorentino del secolo XVI: F. S.*, Città di Castello, 1899.

55. Much of the relevant literature is mentioned in Mario Sansone, "Le polemiche antitassesche della Crusca", in *Torquato Tasso*, Milan, 1957, pp. 527–574.

56. Sassetti to Strozzi, November 19, 1574, in *Lettere*, p. 67. This Strozzi is not to be confused with G.B.S. the Elder (1505–1571), even more famous for his madrigals, nor with a nephew of the same name, who edited his orations—see A. S. Barbi, *Un accademico mecenato e poeta*, *G. B. S.*, Florence, 1900. See his discourse on the madrigal, cited above at n. 15 (p. 188). Strozzi's other orations are good examples of the attempt to reduce everything to Aristotelian categories.

57. See Giorgio Spini, "I trattatisti dell'arte storica nella Controriforma italiana" in *Contributi alla storia del Concilio di Trento e della Controriforma*, Florence, 1948, pp. 109–136.

58. Among Galileo's numerous comments to this effect, see his letter to G. B. Strozzi of January 5, 1601, *Opere*, *11*, p. 83 (the approach is directly contrary to what Weinberg describes as that of Castelvetro). That Galileo's tastes in poetry remained much the same right to the end is attested by Carlo Roberto Dati in *Prose*, p. 64. It seems to me after a superficial examination (I am not prepared to

defend such a thesis yet) that Galileo's literary principles, poor as they are in comparison to those of Salviati and Sassetti, and reduced as they are to the repetition of such words as *vago, alto,* and *chiaro,* dominated the critical thought of his successors throughout the seventeenth century—a century in which flourished such poets of lasting excellence as Chiabrera and Redi.

59. Mei to Borghini, February 2, 1566, *Prose fiorentine,* part III, vol. 2, p. 36; Cesalpino in the Introduction to the *Praxis universae artis medicae* (1603), Tarvissi, 1606; Vincenzo Galilei in the introduction to his *Dialogo della musica antica et moderna,* 1581; reprinted in Rome, 1934. Cf. *Opere,* 7, pp. 153, 157.

60. It was Baldinucci's opinion that art in Tuscany suffered from the longevity not of Michelangelo but of Vasari. I follow here Walter Friedlaender, *Mannerism and anti-mannerism in Italian painting,* New York, 1957, as well as Baldinucci's life of Cigoli, in which he finds, needless to say, the first concrete example of the kind of artistic theory he himself, with Bellori, was promoting later on in the century. Friedlaender's chronology, of course, is not wholly unprecedented, for it is similar, except for his positive evaluation of "Mannerism" and for his hesitation to include Vasari in the same category as Bronzino and Pontormo, to that of Luigi Lanzi in *Storia pittorica della Italia,* Milan, 1823, vol. 2, pp. 204ff.

61. Erwin Panofsky, *Galileo as a critic of the arts,* 1954*.

62. Hints in Bernardo Davanzati's sketch for a chronology of great ages in *Le opere,* ed. by Enrico Bindi, Florence, 1852, vol. 2, p. 594; in Francesco Bonciani's warning (1575) of the stifling effects of the Index in "Sopra il comporre delle novelle", *Prose fiorentine,* part II, vol. 1, n. 6, in the complaints of the physician Andrea Pasquali four years later in a letter to Cosimo I published by Antonio Panella in *Rivista storica degli archivi toscani,* 1, 1929, 22, and in the strains of an inferiority complex in Paolo Mini's *Difesa di Firenze e de'Fiorentini,* Lyon, 1577, and *Discorso della nobiltà di Firenze e de'Fiorentini,* Florence, 1593. Cf. Galileo in *Opere,* 7, pp. 29–31.

63. Principally in the *Degli avvertimenti della lingua sopra il Decamerone,* Venice, 1584, and Florence, 1586. Salviati, it will be remembered, was the chief "corrector" of Boccaccio. Cf. Galileo on Tuscan as "completely adequate to treat and to explain the concepts of all branches of learning", *Opere,* 5, p. 189.

64. Davanzati to Baccio Valori, May 20, 1599, in the Preface to his translation of Tacitus (*Opere,* vol. 1, p. lxxi). I am admittedly oversimplifying here, for there was a considerable gradation of opinion even among Florentines, running from Davanzati ("every city has its own language; let it use it") to the Academy of the Crusca ("the proper written *and* spoken language is that of the Trecento modified by Giovanni Della Casa and Salviati"). See in general, among many works on the subject, Robert A. Hall, *The Italian "Questione della lingua": An interpretative essay,* Chapel Hill, 1942.

65. *Della toscana coltivazione: Delle viti e delli arbori* (1579), in *Opere,* vol. 2, pp. 487ff. See Ferdinando Vegas, "B. D.", in *Letteratura italiana: I minori,* Milano, 1961, vol. 2, pp. 1327–1337.

66. Note particularly Galileo's comments in *Scritti letterari,* p. 103, and Francesco Bonciani's harsh criticism of Salviati's "mare d'eloquenza" in his *Sulla maniera di fare le orazioni funerali,* ed. by D. Moreni, Florence, 1824, pp.

51–52. The same standards of brevity and clarity are upheld by Giovan Battista Strozzi (e.g., *Orazioni et altre prose*, pp. 178ff.), and by most other Florentine writers thereafter. The effect of Tacitus on prose style in other parts of Europe at the time is noted by Morris W. Croll, "Juste Lipse et le mouvement anti-cicéronien à la fin du XVIe siècle et au début du XVIIe siècle", *Revue du seizième siècle*, 2, 1914, 200–242.

67. The expression is that of Enrico Falqui, whose article "G. G. e la prosa scientifica del Seicento", *Letteratura italiana: I minori*, vol. 2, pp. 1523–1571, sums up most recent literature on the subject.

68. See Hanna H. Gray, "Renaissance humanism: The pursuit of eloquence", *Journal of the history of ideas*, 24, 1963, 497–514.

69. Note especially the remarks on p. 358 of his *De vera ac falsa voluptate* (published together with his *De hominis felicitate* and other works, Lucca, 1563).

70. *Discorsi del soggetto* . . . , in the Preface.

71. Sassetti to Pier Vettori, January 27, 1585, *Lettere*, p. 283. Giambullari, *De sito, forma & misura dello Inferno di Dante*, Florence, 1544. Galileo probably did not know this address to the Accademia Fiorentina, however, since he cites only Antonio Manetti and Alessandro Vellutello in his two *Lezioni* to the same academy *Circa la figura, sito e grandezza dell'Inferno di Dante* of 1588. But the occasion and the purpose are much the same.

7 ❋ Galileo's literary formation

LEONARDO OLSCHKI

In the period between Machiavelli and Manzoni, Galileo is the master of Italian prose as well as the creator of its classic style; to discover the roots of subsequent Italian prose one must seek them in Galileo's writings. That perfection of prose as an art form should be achieved in the field of natural science is a unique, almost paradoxical phenomenon in the history of world literature because, while science and prose ordinarily developed separately, significant advancements in both areas are nevertheless evident in the works of Galileo. His writings not only put an end to a basically erroneous method of scientific thought, but also rejected strained style in artistic language. Conventionality in content and expression gave way to the adventure of creative thought, and a personal confrontation between nature and man. The beauty of Galileo's prose lies in the harmonious rela-

NOTE: This is a translation and adaptation of "Galileis literarische Bildung", a chapter in *Galilei und seine Zeit*, Halle, 1927, pp. 167–197. The book was the third in a series of three volumes, *Geschichte der neusprachlichen wissenschaftlichen Literatur*, the first of which (1919) dealt with the period up to Leonardo, the second (1922) the sixteenth century, and the third Galileo. Olschki's prose is exceptionally ornate, so that putting it into readable English required extensive modification of the original German style. However, the sense of the original has been retained as faithfully as possible. The translation is by Thomas Green, S.J., and Maria Charlesworth, edited by Ernan McMullin.

tionships of objective knowledge and subjective realization, of mathematics and literature, of abstraction and reality. The interplay of these factors explains the complexity and intrinsic difficulties of his writings. In this essay, we shall examine the formative elements of his style, its development from instinct to consciousness, and finally to mature art.

Galileo's literary accomplishment

Galileo, like all the other molders of Italian prose, was a humanist. In his scientific research, he linked empirical knowledge with a rediscovered and thoroughly comprehended blend of Platonic thought and Archimedean method, to their mutual refinement and enrichment. Similarly, he combined in a literary way the norms of national prose with the vital natural forms of his mother tongue, again to their mutual advantage and enrichment. Before Galileo's time, Italian prose had never attained so uniform a harmony in tone and structure. One would search in vain in the rich variety of Renaissance literature to find such a perfect balance between artistic will and natural inclination, between respect for established canons and driving originality, of the sort that pictorial art from Masaccio to Michelangelo manifests in such diverse and delicate nuances. In Boccaccio, the literary design, determined by Latin rhythm and syntax, stifled the natural evolution of a living style of speech. The resulting tension between artistic language-formation and ordinary language-usage, which had been confirmed and emphasized by the literary and cultural predominance of humanism, survived for centuries until resolved by Galileo.

This act of liberation for which he was acclaimed by his contemporaries, although not itself an explicitly literary accomplishment, was nevertheless his greatest contribution to literary history. The extent of this achievement becomes clear when one notes the stylistic inconsistency of those of his predecessors who, like Machiavelli and Bruno, oscillated between realistic and artistic expression; they were often driven by the demands of the latter to employ a style alien to reality, a compromise which in turn affected both their thinking and their power of imagination.[1] Even the most original thinkers of the Renaissance saw the objects of their contemplation from a double perspective: from their own standpoint and from that of antiquity. As these two points of view did not always coincide, inner tensions resulted which not only reflected on their style, but also gave rise to varied interpretations of their assertions. Just as during the Quattrocento the predominance of Latin as the artistic language prevented the rise of any other language, so also in the following centuries the notion of Boccaccio's style as an unattainable ideal led to the "academizing" of all literary expression. The direct, unaffected naturalness of Cellini has scarcely anything in common with the verbose and empty bombast of other writers of his time. Even scientific literature, as several examples attest, was wavering between these two extremes.

The idea that a writer of prose must have something to say was still unfamiliar to the authors of that day, so that they continued to view prose in terms of fixed, constantly recurring and academically enforced concepts. Thus, without real necessity, language changed over the years from a bare skeleton for thought into a brilliantly colorful theatrical dress. Fiction, history and moral philosophy were all equally an excuse for rhetorical exercise, so that there was no room for personal style or individual opinion. Throughout the full range of his accomplishments, however, Galileo adapted this art-language to his own difficult, compact and multi-leveled world of thought. He infused literary prose with positive and personal content, and transformed it into a language both monumental and practical, both literary and scientific, a language at once expressive and highly polished. He effected this not only by a new and concrete richness of content, but also by adhering to definitive norms of style. Sometimes these agreed with academic prescriptions, but they were subject to a conscious modification arising from a new and personal interpretation of their purpose. What made this possible was his lifelong interest in literary matters—a concern which went hand in hand with his researches in natural science and whose fruits matured just as slowly as did the results of his scientific work. Galileo was as intent to express the latter in a precise, purposeful formulation as to bring together science and literary style in a richly articulated formal relationship; he thereby satisfied his aesthetic sense as well as his desire for scientific clarity. Although these qualities were not unknown to his contemporaries, it was from him that they received form and purpose. By bringing out the distinctiveness of his educational background and the general direction of his criticism, the story of his literary formation will reveal the process whereby his artistic and scientific ideals—in short, his taste—were gradually refined.

His literary background

Disregarding the conventional, elementary literary instruction which every boy of good family received in Galileo's day,[2] we will direct our attention especially to his humanistic education, which laid the foundation for his later literary and critical activity. The writings and interests of his father, who showed great concern for Galileo's education, reveal the humanistic milieu in which the boy was reared. Viviani tells of Galileo's thorough and profound knowledge of Latin poetry, his favorites being Virgil, Ovid, Horace and Seneca, a large part of whose poetry he knew by heart.[3] This predilection is not remarkable, however, for it betokens simply an ordinary humanistic education rather than a personal preference; but taken as such, it is an indication of the principal area of his literary interests. The few quotations from, and allusions to, these authors' works appearing in Galileo's writings [4] show that he, unlike contemporary thinkers such as Bruno and Campanella, liked them not because of their philosophical content but solely for their poetic quality. The fact that Lucretius is never mentioned confirms the impression that Galileo held poetry and science to be fields distinct from one another. As he separated poetic attitudes and language from philosophical concepts, each to prosper or languish in its own proper sphere, he brought to completion the slow development of what we would call today the "aesthetic approach" to ancient poetry.

In the Middle Ages, this aesthetic approach was less significant than that of the moralizing allegory, and in the Renaissance it was less influential than were mystical and philosophical interpretations drawn from antiquity. Galileo's aversion to allegory and mysticism, and his striving for clarity and exactitude in scientific and philosophical questions, resulted in his seeing the art of poetry in its purity. He sought in it no hidden reality; for him, it was not a source of secrets or revelations. The aesthetic consciousness that led him to break with the traditional canons of judging poetry that had influenced all the humanistic thinkers, manifested itself in his categorical condemnations of complex poetry, in his criticism of any intentional combining of ethical and aesthetic goals, or of mystical and sensual motifs, in a single work of art:

> Poetic fables and fiction should be taken allegorically only when no slightest shadow of strain can be detected in such an interpretation; otherwise they will seem weak, forced, irrelevant and absurd. It is like a work of art in which perspective is emphasized and which, if viewed from the wrong angle, will appear ridiculous and distorted.[5]

Before Galileo, no one had recognized so clearly nor expressed so precisely the absolute and symbolic value of art. This was Galileo's yardstick in appraising all poetry. The feeling for limits which led him to circumscribe the provinces of knowledge and their respective purposes, to separate rigorously science from theology, to isolate the phenomena and to grasp the problems of each discipline separately—this feeling was also at work for him in the spheres of literature and of aesthetics in general. The aesthetic value of poetic art, for Galileo, is characterized by the victory over philosophically or philologically oriented humanism, for he considered poetry to be a self-contained creation in the endless yet bounded world of artistic imagination. Galileo's classical understanding of art was, therefore, different from that of both the humanist and the classicist. The former regarded ancient poetry as a model for imitation, while the latter saw in it didactic beauty in the highest sense. At the height of the Baroque period, classical poetry was, for the greatest thinkers, a world of beauty freed from all intermediaries, a world in which the spirit submitted only to its own laws.[6]

Galileo arrived at his views in the more mature years of his young manhood, but his active life prevented these feelings from degenerating into a purely sensual aesthetic. His classical sense made him not a poet but a critic, especially in the context of Latin poetry, the knowledge of which he shared with all educated men of his time. No less noteworthy is his

attitude toward the Greek world, one which makes understandable both
his later choice of reading material and his personal assimilation of certain decisive ideas. Some of his papers are testimony even today of his
youthful preoccupation with the Greeks; on one side they contain notes
for his early treatise, *De motu*, and on the other, are the young scientist's
translation exercises, corrected by an unknown hand.[7] This remarkable
coincidence, however, does not give a real clue to the time of his interest
in the Greeks, although we can conclude that the technical-scientific and
philological-humanistic aspects of his formation went on simultaneously,
at least insofar as the latter extended to the usually more remote field of
Greek thought. Galileo did not allow his knowledge of Greek to remain
unused, for in 1604 he began a verse translation in Italian of the *Batracho-
myomachia* about which, unfortunately, we possess no further information.[8] While this undertaking shows his particular fondness for light verse,
his general attitude toward Greek poetry is the same as that toward Latin.
The extent of his concern with its formal peculiarities, in contrast to that
of Bruno, is shown by a striking characterization of Pindar's poetry in a
letter on a scientific topic written shortly before his death.[9] It reveals
Galileo's continuing interest in Greek poetry in his old age, despite the
fact that his remark reflects no more than a standard attitude, and that he
makes but few allusions elsewhere to the other great poets of Greece.

Galileo's relationship to classical poetry was more intense than that of
any other mathematician or natural philosopher of the Renaissance. It
was not of the objective, or expository type, but rather of a sensual nature, that of a dilettante of good taste. His interest nevertheless became
livelier whenever the art-forms of a style offered an appealing theory and
dialectic. Of all the ancient authors, for Galileo as for all humanists,
Plato was the master and the model of every combination of beauty and
truth. There is no trace in Galileo's writings of the usual custom of playing Plato against Aristotle, or of the dialectical reconciliation of the two
which was so often attempted, even in his day. Nor did he ever use specific Platonic ideas in order to verify his own; he never, for example,
adopted any of the Platonic maxims as a starting point for his own deductions. Since he always spoke of Plato with words of esteem, however,
commenting on Plato's thoughts with respectful criticism,[10] we realize
that his relationship to Plato was more emotional than scientific and scholarly; it rested on a feeling of spiritual kinship rather than on any consciousness of a similarity of view. His general intellectual orientation was
Platonic, but he was more attracted by Plato's literary characteristics than
by his philosophical theories. The fruit of his intensive study of the Platonic dialogues can be seen in the structure and organization of his own
dialogues.

For the most part, Galileo's literary training can be inferred only indirectly from his specifically critical writings and from his attempts at poetry. The humanistic custom was to quote and interweave poetical passages

into scientific and scholarly contexts, but he was careful not to allow such considerations of form to outweigh the demands of realism. His classical education, his readings in poetry and literature, were his very element, and not a mere treasure chest of rhetorical or aesthetic riches. His world was one of cheerful outlook, linguistic music and absolute integrity of expression, and in it he fashioned his own sense of form. In doing this, he chose the features which answered to his own everyday need for beauty. One would never gather from his writings that he knew Petrarch's poems from memory, nor ever suspect that he owed the clarity of his own works to his complete knowledge of his favorite poet, Ariosto.[11] This last statement will appear less strange if we realize that his literary activities were for him both linguistic training and intellectual pleasure, a lifelong engagement for his vivid imagination as well as for his sense of criticism. To his literary interests we owe his early philological writings, whose aesthetic canons suggested that perfection of literary form should be blended with scientific objectivity. From these writings, we can discover something of his literary formation and in particular, of the development of his critical standards in the field of Italian poetry.

Galileo and Dante

Shortly before he assumed the position of lecturer in mathematics at Pisa, and therefore long before his originality as a scientist and author had clearly manifested itself, Galileo was invited by the Florentine Academy to solve once and for all an argument about the topography of the Dantean hell, a problem with which the interpreters of the *Divina commedia* had long struggled without success. He had to appear solemnly in the role of judge before the entire Academy and its guests; this would suggest that even at the age of twenty-four he was already a member of this institution, whose concern was "the cultivation and enrichment of the vernacular".[12] So that his linguistic talents and literary interests must already have been acknowledged among those who were concerned professionally with the diffusion of knowledge and the refinement of language. Since the executive board of the Academy specifically entrusted this young scholar with the Dantean problem,[13] the choice must have been made in view of the conjunction of literary and mathematical interests which distinguished him even at so youthful an age. One can see that these academicians, who are usually blamed for the decline of Italian poetry, were not lacking in knowledge of human character, and that Galileo's expression of gratitude at the end of his lectures is not mere rhetoric.[14] More than thirty years later, he was chosen as their chairman "in recognition of his admirable services to Florentine letters".[15] On this occasion, the younger Michelangelo Buonarotti delivered the address.[16]

The question which Galileo was called upon to elucidate lay on the border between literature and science; problems in this area were the essential concern of the Florentine Academy, especially in connection with the *Lectura Dantis*.[17] In the Baroque period, the *Divina commedia* came to be used to instruct people in matters of language rather than to quicken them in their faith.[18] As long as the work was read as a work of piety, meant for edification, no one had bothered about the exact topography of the nether world; the gradation of sins and penances seemed obvious and complete enough. It is an indication of an awakening newly rational approach both to the world and to literature that Brunelleschi's friend, Antonio Manetti, undertook in the 1570's to define the geographical position of hell according to the dimensional indications given in the *Commedia*. Manetti's question, despite diligent study, remained a controverted one.[19] Manetti himself was a member of the circle of Toscanelli, the man whose geographical calculations encouraged Columbus to undertake his great adventure. His topography for Dante's hell was later adopted by Cristoforo Landino in his great commentary on the *Commedia*. But it was then vehemently attacked and substantially amended by another widely read commentator, Allesandro Vellutello.[20] At this point, the Academy commissioned Galileo to use his literary background, as well as his knowledge of mathematics, to defend the older interpretation of Dante's topographical data against the newer. The dignity and expertise with which he executed the difficult task attested to his mastery both of the poem and of the various mathematical devices employed. Unlike other academic speeches of the day, Galileo's avoided all rhetoric. After a few words of introduction, he turns directly to the subject at hand and, following a strict topical order, first analyzes Dante's text, and then discusses interpretations of the major commentators.[21] He apologizes for having to speak as a mathematician and thus offend the delicate ears of the Academicians with strange-sounding technical terms. In his arguments, the sonorous *terzarima* of the poem does indeed alternate with long mathematical calculations. The dark scenery of hell's crater is organized into a geometrically ordered structure with the help of the Archimedean theory of conic sections; the structure of the spheres is arrived at by means of architectural statics, and their proportions are established according to Albrecht Dürer's rules! The versatility of the young scientist's training was revealed here in an economy of words that was to be characteristic of him: spatial imagination and mathematical precision conditioning each other, just as they had done in Dante's own vision.

Dante's work had so determining an influence on Italian culture that, to those surrounding Galileo, his intimate knowledge of the poem must have seemed completely natural. The content and structure of his lectures are a clear indication of his desire for measurable forms, clear outlines and exact proportions, even in the realm of imagination. Neither the fine arts nor the poetry of his time paid much attention to such aesthetic ideals as these, reminiscent as they were of classicism. But the *"esprit géometrique"*, which was beginning to conquer French literature, was becoming the critical standard of comprehension and judgment in Italy too. It was the heritage of a great era whose ideals were still normative, even though the creative artist sensed their influence on him just as little as the average man is aware of the three-dimensional limitations of his daily activities.

Galileo and Ariosto

Galileo's Dante lectures move in too peripheral an area and too much within the confines of an academic framework, however, to reveal his own aesthetic consciousness in any definitive way. But his persistent and devoted concern with his favorite poet, Ariosto, shows clearly that in his critical attitude toward poetry he was an heir to older views, just as in science he was the inheritor of earlier experimental results. The words of his son, his friends and his disciples,[22] as well as his own occasional expression of sincere admiration,[23] prove that for him Ariosto's *Orlando furioso* was the book of books, the work in which poetic imagination, linguistic perfection and artistic vision had best been combined. The diligent critical work which he continued for years on the margin of his copy of the poem,[24] and his passionate dissection of Tasso's *Gerusalemme liberata*, which he thought much inferior to Ariosto's work, show that his literary pursuits were not just an idle diversion from his usual activities. These critical notes are an indispensable aid to us in our attempts to understand his personality and the historical context and influence of his works. They illuminate for us the union in him of scientist and poet, and give us some hints of the literary background of his own style.

The marginal notes to the text of *Orlando furioso* are chiefly metric and stylistic corrections. Besides modifying individual words, he also changed entire verses and parts of stanzas. His emendations were not irrelevant, pedantic ones; rather, they testified to a quiet dialogue with the poet, whose own self-tormenting, never-finished polishing was consistently carried forward by Galileo himself, drawing upon his rich command of the Florentine tongue. From the marginal notes and still more from his critique of Tasso, one can infer the Galilean aesthetic, much as one can gather the norms of classical taste in France at this same time from a study of Malherbes' comments on Desportes. Galileo's critical notes and emendations show a remarkable similarity of taste between the Italian scientist and the French poet. In both cases, an effort was made to retain uniform verse-music, unbroken by dissonance. Through the rearrangement and substitution of words, Galileo tried to achieve caesural regularity as well as to avoid the dissonant juxtaposition of similar consonants; he sharply attacked every hiatus and cacophony. In this way, he carried on Ariosto's own struggle for euphony of verse and strophic harmony, but brought to it a more consistent understanding of verse melody. He strove to eliminate harshness and rhythmic inconsistency in order to achieve a more harmonious sound. When replacing uneven expressions of this sort, he substituted more specific and apter terms for general ones, replaced archaic expressions with generally comprehensible turns of phrase, rearranged obscure passages through syntactical corrections, as well as taking into account the demands of rhythm and of stylistic uniformity.

It would be a mistake to see in this purely stylistic concern, this strong feeling for metrical and phonetic refinement, no more than a transfer of mathematical demands to the domain of poetry. We need only recall that there were many others of the day who shared Galileo's insistence upon strict stylistic norms over wide areas of artistic creation, even at a time when these smooth forms were being dissolved by the exaggerated metaphors of Baroque art and poetry. From the way in which he frequently toned down obscene passages in Ariosto's epic, it is clear that his critical standards derived solely from his aesthetic consciousness.[25] To interpret his toning-down as prudery or as a concern for moral principles would be erroneous; Galileo manifested no such concern in his own poetry, where gross improprieties may be found, nor does he find fault with the coarse speech of the innkeeper on the whorelike perfidy of the women in the twenty-eighth canto of *Orlando*. This apparent inconsistency disappears if one reflects that the innkeeper episode illustrates the crudity of the narrator in the poem, and thus has a definite role to play. On the other hand, the occasional indelicacies and titillating allusions, which delighted Ariosto's gay and spirited poetic muse, quite frequently can be attributed to poetic levity only. Considered from the standpoint of aesthetic reason, which for Galileo created all the norms of style and expression, those of the allusions that were not justified by the context seemed to strike a dissonant note, and he emended them by his corrections.

Galileo's revisions, therefore, must not be confused with the attempts of some of his contemporaries to banish from art every supposedly offensive remark.[26] While he, like many other critics of his time, spoke out for decorum in painting, he did so solely in defense of the artistic unity of pictorial composition, not in the penitential tone of a Bartolomeo Ammannati who, in the name of a pious Counter-Reformation morality, fought against even the most ingenuous representation of nudity in art.[27] Like Pietro Arentino before him (whom one can scarcely accuse of prudery or moral affectation), Galileo found fault with the nude figures in Michelangelo's "Last Judgment" because they seemed to him unsuited to the purpose of the painting.[28] The classical realism that Galileo harked back to was not characterized by nude figures for their own sake; indeed, it showed itself rather by a critique of the appropriateness of such figures when there was no special reason for them. This was the major criterion underlying Galileo's critiques of Ariosto and Michelangelo; it was clearly the first demand of his aesthetic consciousness. It led him to seek an interior and exterior unity of representation, whether the art in question was poetic, pictorial or plastic. In each of these, unity is achieved by seeing that each part is both necessary and sufficient for its purpose, as well as being true to nature and to the artistic purpose of the work.

This is the fundamental demand of classical taste, whether it be realized in the *Orlando furioso* or in Racine's tragedies, in Molière's comedies or in Goethe's *Iphigenie*. It forms the artistic dimension of the "esprit géometrique", fusing science and literature, making the areas of research and imagination in Galileo's writings appear as one. It presupposes a Platonic "ideal reality" as the ruling element both in the events of nature and in the vision of the artist. From such a standpoint, concessions to the reader, lyrical voices, and the like, appear as mere ornamentation, rhetorical exaggeration, meretricious costume. In this pure world, everything which is not immediately useful is dissonant and superfluous; it may be ingenious but is never truly meaningful. This sort of superfluity is illustrated, for example, by the antitheses and stilted metaphors of the pretentious romantic poetry, in Galileo's day already labeled as "conceits" (*concetti*).

Galileo and Tasso

While one may enjoy the full flowering of the classical ideal of style in the *Orlando furioso*, one can only deplore the way in which this ideal is betrayed by the sentimentality of Tasso's *Gerusalemme liberata*. Tasso merged history and fable, sensuality and piety, the epic and the lyric, observation and evaluation, play and pathos. The reader marvels at the poet's serenity, his pensive play, his plastic virtuosity—and yet his apparent lack of human sympathy. When Tasso peopled his immense stage with fantastic symbols of the human and the all-too-human, it seemed as though he did so from a great distance. His laments were those of a man whose soul-rending tensions appeared to him a troublesome obtrusion on his pure poetic enjoyment. Thus the frequent comparison of the epics of Ariosto and Tasso was not merely an idle quarrel of pedants; it was a serious attempt to arrive at an understanding of art-forms which sprang from generically related but mutually contradictory artistic experiences and purposes.[29] Ariosto's constructive genius and Tasso's decorative talents are obviously expressions of quite diverse artistic approaches. Characteristically, Galileo opted for the former without hesitation and found in Tasso's work by contrast a shallowness and confusion of poetic form.

The marginal notes to *Gerusalemme liberata* which Galileo jotted down over several years culminated in an essay which was highly critical of Tasso's poetry.[30] It sounds an echo for us of a bitter and widely publicized dispute which raged for decades in the academic and literary circles of Galileo's day. In our age of eclectic artistic enjoyment, his judgments may sometimes seem to us spiteful and unjust; his comparison of the two epics may strike us as petty. Tasso himself, however, had in a sense brought this on himself by publicizing his rivalry with Ariosto, and by calling for a judgment in his own favor from the most famous literateurs and grammarians of his time. The essential distinction between Galileo and the other critics is that Galileo alludes neither to the structure nor to the content of the epic, nor to the poet's intent. He discusses only questions of style and of the psychological development of character, or, as he himself put it: "the meaning and the expression" [31] of individual episodes. Considerations of linguistic form also provoke him to criticism and correction on occasion, but they played a much smaller part than the others. Their diminished role seems to indicate that Galileo found less fault with Tasso's verse melody than with Ariosto's. What did, however, provoke his violent anger and sharpest ridicule were the disproportions in Tasso's work, the gewgaws, the wordplays and antitheses, the "troubled images", [32] the padding, as well as the vagueness and opaqueness of the descriptions and character portrayals. The consistency of his criticism shows that he employed very definite standards of judgment. The fault he finds with the poet's "paltriness" in the invention and formation of episodes and heroes seems more than justified. In his desire to create the heroic, Christian and national epic of Italy, Tasso so much esteemed Homer and Virgil, Lucan and Trissino, Apollonius and Ariosto, that he would never stray far from them, the models for him of epic greatness. At the same time, he borrowed tone and fashionable idiom from the courtly lyrics of his own time, and drew the historical scenario and the content of his epic fantasies from the chronicles of William of Tyre and others.

This heterogeneous blend of poetic elements wounded Galileo's sense of harmony and propriety. [33] Just as he admired the psychological consistency of character and language in all of Ariosto's heroes, particularly the unobtrusive description of the slow progress of Orlando's mental deterioration, [34] so also was he distressed by Tasso's inconsistencies and inaccuracies, which he never wearied of attacking. The oppressive seriousness which pervades the entire epic provoked Galileo's ridicule, and caused him to display an ironic wit which makes his criticism still delightful reading today. His critique makes it clear not only that he considered the *Orlando furioso* to be an embodiment of his own artistic ideals, but also that he felt a close affinity of mind with Ariosto himself. Their affinity manifests itself in a joyous contemplation of the world, in an attitude which made of poetic jests an implicit affirmation. From such an attitude came that intimacy of style which had so charmed Ariosto's contemporaries. [35]

Galileo as a comic writer

Galileo's sense of humor showed itself in his writings by his frequent recourse to irony and light bantering. It also determined his predilection for the light verse which the cruder muse of his age cultivated in comedies and pasquinades of all kinds. His favorite among the lampooners was that Florentine master of Renaissance satire, Francesco Berni, whose poems he had committed to memory and often quoted to add a humorous touch to a conversation. [36] What attracted him to this moody and whimsical eccentric was Berni's satirical reversal of the poetic phraseology of the cold, affected imitators of Petrarch, as well as his lively ridicule of priests and monks in anecdotes that echo an ancient Florentine tradition. In his crusade against platitude and in his defense of himself from clerical criticism, Galileo found in Berni a kindred spirit.[37] The latter's poems were so widely known that after his death a large number of them could be gathered from popular tradition and committed to print. They exhibited the critical, satirical spirit of contemporary Florence, and found numerous imitators who gave rise to a distinctive literary fashion.[38] Galileo also took delight in their form: a lofty Dantean *terzarima* ironically superimposed upon language and theme that were far from lofty. Their distinctive quality was their parody-by-contrast and their paradoxical juxtaposition of serious and trifling themes, of courage and cunning. The themes are presented in concise narrations and in abrupt bursts of emotion, and are sometimes cautious, sometimes frank. Berni, who paid with his life for his honest and courageous satire, was still in Galileo's time the most popular poet in Florence and throughout Italy.[39]

Shortly after his summons to Pisa in 1589, Galileo wrote a poem in Berni's style, a satirical attack on the ordinance which required all university professors to wear their academic gown, not only in the classroom but also on the street.[40] Written in authentic popular speech, the poem is a comic mixture of elegiac woe and blunt language, fused in the solemn tone of the *terzarima*. A young professor, earning the meager salary of sixty florins a year, with deductions for any unexcused absences from his lectures, is commanded to display his costly academic robes at all times, for the sake of academic dignity.[41] But what of the intimate adventures of youth? Must they be abandoned? Is he to sacrifice his youth for the sake of his robes? And how is he to behave when he goes to the market, dressed in his finery, to buy his humble food, and his tattered everyday clothing shows under his velvet gown? Besides, since people judge from externals, it will be damaging to the reputation of a professor to be seen in the streets alone while his more ambitious colleagues trail a crowd of students after them. The neophyte can scarcely avoid being disturbed by such thoughts. But if he is self-made, a scholar who has worked his way up from a modest family background, he will already know something of the hypocrisy of human conventions. He will sigh for the time when men went naked, when there was no clothing to make a distinction between the great and the lowly, when a man's worth was determined by his own accomplishments. How different the state of affairs in his own day! This harking back to a lost innocence reflects in conscious parody the longing for the golden age which set the mood for the pastoral themes of the courtly poetry of Galileo's day, particularly the elegy and the drama.[42]

Sharp attacks on priests were a part of the satirical tradition of Florence, a part with which Galileo was not unsympathetic. The realization that he would himself sooner or later have to face head-on clerical opposition may well have been of earlier origin than his academic appointment. The long clerical cassock provoked all sorts of taunting innuendo. Lorenzo de'Medici had already used the long robes to symbolize clerical trickery, those robes "under which they get ready to kick even before one sees their leg".[43] Galileo annotated a well-known stanza where Ariosto gave an allegory of deceit, with the words: "the habit worn by priests and monks".[44] The moral reform of the clergy effected by the Counter-Reformation had not put an end to these satirical attacks; there are still echoes in Galileo's writings of the tone employed a half-century before by that master of satire, the canon of the Cathedral of Florence, Francesco Berni.

The same feeling for the genuine and the joyous which led Galileo to prefer this direction of literature also gave him an understanding of, and a love for, the often coarse verse of the people, and for the vernacular with all its expressive liberty and crudity. During his stay in Padua and throughout his later life, he took great delight in the wild humor of Ruzzante, a poet who displayed the natural impudence of the sons of Bergamo and Padua as well as employing their rustic, unpolished mode of expression.[45] Galileo greatly enjoyed this kind of verse because of the unspoiled common sense which survived in it. At a time when literary refinement had, to his mind, become altogether excessive, he felt he could rely on this common sense in his own struggle against unreason. It was in this genre of writing that Galileo found literary devices that had already been put to telling effect in mocking every sort of pedantry and narrow-mindedness. He chose among them those that would be most effective in winning his reader over to his own teaching. There was no malicious intent in this; his use of satirical devices testifies rather to his stubborn rejection of the conventions of scholarship as well as to his own distinctive literary formation. His fondness for humor was united with an unbending dedication to scientific truth; this unusual combination showed itself in the devastating but witty polemics by which he defended his theories.

For the Florentine, whose language had been adopted as the literary language of Italy, literature written in the local dialect was a rich comic resource. Their own simple artistic instinct led the writers of comedies, as well as those who acted in them, to introduce characters speaking in the common idiom, as a sure way to comic success. Galileo put his knowledge of Ruzzante's comic dialogue to use when in collaboration with a friend and student, he composed a dialogue in Paduan dialect about the *nova* which appeared in 1604.[46] His intention was to educate the general public about the striking astronomical event (which had evoked an almost apocalyptic mood among the masses), as well as to ridicule those with whose explanations of the event he disagreed. The appearance of various comets and two "new stars" around this time had given rise to a copious pamphlet literature, to which Galileo's dialogue is similar in tone and style. Two shepherds present in their rustic idiom the contrasting theories advanced by Galileo and by certain of his colleagues in Padua to explain the phenomenon. They make clear the apparently already well-known breach between Galileo and his Aristotelian opponents, their disagreement not

only on specific points of astronomical theory but also on the entire approach to natural science. Galileo had already expounded his views on the
nova in public lectures at Padua.[47] His opponents attacked him in pamphlets, insisting that the mathematical approach was inappropriate to
problems of the nature of the heavenly bodies. Only philosophy could
solve these problems.[48] The two shepherds instruct one another about
stars and parallaxes in general, and about the position, constitution and
light intensity of the new star in particular. Galileo has them ask whether
it is sublunar in origin or one of the fixed stars, and through them considers the implications of each of these possibilities, just as Antonio Francesco Doni, half a century earlier, had had two Florentine rascals discuss
the then current problems of astronomy in their common speech.[49]

The point of this dialogue is not, however, to instruct the uneducated,
as it might first seem. Its humor lies in its ironical context, the presenting
of the lofty theories of astronomy in peasant garb, and the caricaturing of
Galileo's own lectures as well as the writings of his adversaries in recog-
nizable yet cleverly distorted form. The ironic contrast between speech
and topic is heightened by the inclusion of curses and coarse turns of
speech, after the fashion of Ruzzante, though these expressions no longer
retained their literal meaning in this sort of context by Galileo's day. Galileo's motive was clearly to provide a stylistic spice for the educated
reader, as well as satisfying his own taste for such humor. Whenever he
gave free play to his native wit in any of his scientific works, the humor
was refined by careful literary techniques, so that it fitted well with the
intellectual character proper to the work. His inclination toward crude
folk humor and to vernacular idioms shows on occasion even in his polished works.[50] These passages reveal to us how deeply ingrained humor
and irony were in his disposition; they do so even more effectively than
does an unfinished draft he left for a comic play.[51] This draft shows Galileo's familiarity with contemporary literary comedy; quite schematic in
structure, it was a hodgepodge of complicated intrigues, disguises and
recognitions, frozen into the inflexible categories of motivation and characterization peculiar to Roman comedy, and alien to anything in the real
world. The conventional character of his projected comedy can be clearly
seen in that he had not got as far as writing any actual dialogue for it;
perhaps the difficulty in doing this was what deterred him from proceed
ing with the play.

The craftsman of language

The effort that Galileo put into the literary dimension of his work
shows that it was not for him a mere ornamental addition to the reporting
of his research; his dedication to literature helped him to achieve the
sharpness of form and the mastery of language he knew to be essential to
his scientific program. At a time when mathematicians, scientists and philosophers were already almost unable to converse with one another, he

was the first to break through the barriers of compartmentalized scholarship, and thus to discover a unity between action, thought and beauty that had been hidden from all others. His formation both as a scientist and as a writer proceeded directly from the technological as well as the intellectual culture of his day; he mastered the full sweep of this culture and brought it to a new perfection. The tension between nature and culture was resolved in him by a harmonious integration of truth and beauty on the levels both of thought and of imagination. For him, beauty was the artistic form of perceived truth, and truth the ideal form of the perceptible. Protected from the exaggerations of emotion and imagination by his habits of introspection and by his geometrical training, he strove to conform thought to reality; while by conforming expression to thought, he gave to the latter its appropriate and therefore its artistic form.

For him, poetry and science were the domains of realization. Since problems of content and of form seemed to him one and the same, he did not reduce his knowledge to formulas but expressed it in words also. What was important to him was visualization, whether technological or scientific, scholarly or artistic. Geometric deductions were not enough. The word, as the material in which speech is artistically structured and given visual embodiment, attained significance as the vehicle of an awareness at once both scientific and artistic.

This may help us to grasp the deeper significance of his untiring literary activity. Only in a work of literary quality could he bring to bear the precision of linguistic structure that he had learned to value in Ariosto. The vocabulary utilized in the mathematical literature of his day was a meager one, while philosophy, on the other hand, lacked the precision and the sense of style he so greatly desired. He and the generation he taught must have greatly disliked the rhetoric of Bruno, Campanella and Benedetti. We can see why he was attracted to Plato and why he detested the tasteless and unclear language of the Aristotelians of his time, as well as the empty pathos of the rhetoricians and their wearisome reliance on *verba ampullata*.[52] His emphasis on language, the care he himself took to weigh each word and polish each sentence, explain the dislike he felt for discussions where the issue was a purely verbal one, and his oft-expressed criticism for the then common practice of basing teaching and argument "on the comparison of texts and the explanation of word meanings".[53]

For Galileo, therefore, the touchstone of intellect was the written word rather than the spoken repartee, as celebrated and practiced by Bruno and taught in the schools. "The pen", he wrote, "is the only means of distinguishing coherent speech from mere babbling." And again: "Writing is the most appropriate tool for distinguishing truth from falsity and genuine principles from merely apparent ones; oral discussion, since it is so easily swayed by vanity, excitement or caprice, will not serve."[54] He never tired of admonishing his adversaries on this score,[55] and he demanded that a scholar have the right to "revise and restyle his writings once, twice, a hundred times".[56]

From the beginning of his career as a teacher and a scientist, Galileo did, however, take part in private academic discussions, and even initiated them on occasion with a certain importunity, particularly at the Florentine court and in clerical circles in Rome. In these instances, he overcame his distrust of the value of oral argument in the hope of reaching circles of influence not attainable in any other way. The slow and hesitating revision of his major written works, the materials for which he had accumulated quite early in his career, and the care with which he edited his polemical writings, go to prove how sensitive he was to the niceties of literary form. Indeed, his constant revisions of language may well have occupied him more than did his strictly scientific concerns. References in letters and in his critical commentaries on the writings of his opponents give eloquent evidence of his conscientiousness in literary matters, a trait which led him to wring from the words he read their last drop of meaning and to impress upon the words he wrote all the content they could sustain without violence. Most of his scientific research is now obsolete; the language he so laboriously constructed for his discussions of motion is now of historical interest only, since the introduction of analytical mechanics. Yet his style has lost none of its immediacy and its power. Even today, when Aristotle and Ptolemy are no longer important adversaries, the reader is still captivated by the freshness and the tempo of his narrative. The quest for meaning gripped his intellect and channeled his emotions, and drove him to make the most of the available materials of written and spoken language. Because he succeeded so well in this, it may be said that language attained with him a peak of versatility and expressiveness. His literary mastery is illustrated by his artistic distribution of accent, tension and tone in the presentation of intrinsically brittle and unpromising material. Even with such material, he was able to realize the ideals of style of which he had become so conscious through his criticisms of literary works.

Galileo very distinctly drew and consistently observed a borderline between poetic truth and scientific truth. When he called the difference between the two to the attention of the unhappy representative of the dialectic of the schools, Orazio Grassi, whom he lampoons so mercilessly in the *Saggiatore*, he was really addressing himself to all thinkers and poets who were not sufficiently aware of this distinction: "Philosophy, unlike the *Iliad* and the *Orlando furioso*, is not a book or a conceit of the human imagination in which it is completely irrelevant whether the contents are true." Philosophy is written down in that gigantic "book" which we have always before our eyes, the universe. But one can only understand it if one has learned the language and letters in which it is written.[57] This ability to draw a careful boundary between poetic and scientific truth appears as a sort of intellectual discipline in all of Galileo's writings. This discipline was the instinctive safeguard of his versatile literary and scholarly talents, protecting them from the eclectic and speculative exaggerations to which his contemporaries were so prone. It sprang from his yearning for a spiritual freedom characterized by clarity and order; to

Galileo, even as a young man, such a freedom seemed to bespeak greater independence than did the deceitful freedom of the speculative and poetic imagination. Harnessed by the severe criteria Galileo demanded of scientific writing, the intellect could finally provide a slow, searching way to the light.

A comparison of the differing functions of poetry in the writings of Bruno and of Galileo discloses some interesting points. Their literary formation was roughly the same, and in their partiality for Virgil, Ariosto and Berni, at least, their poetical inclinations were alike. In Galileo's work, however, poetry stays in the background; it never becomes an integral part of his objective exposition, nor does it even work as a ferment in the development of the exposition. In philosophy, Bruno and Galileo both defended pre-Socratic opinions against current teaching, and yet with a fundamental difference. In Bruno's work, dialectical proof never went far beyond the level of faith. Whereas in Galileo's case, the criteria for the adoption of pre-Socratic views were the empirical proofs furnished by experimental science.

The resemblances between Galileo and Bruno derive from the late Renaissance culture which they shared. Their differences were due to temperament, milieu and education; they reveal themselves especially in individual turns of phrase. During Galileo's youth, the universities were torn by the struggle between the humanistic and the Thomistic traditions. Though he took sides against the latter, Galileo was free from the antiquarianism which characterized humanism both in philosophy and in poetry. He did not wage war on behalf of humanism against the Thomistic universe; rather, he represented a new sort of "classical" spirit informing a few favored men and communities, a new way of reaching nature in human symbols, reminiscent of the revolution that had already taken place in the fine arts in Leonardo's age. In this sense, Galileo stood on the threshold of a new era and a new culture which took upon itself the burden of geometrical laws in order to be freer and more genuine.

NOTES

1. See L. Olschki, *Geschichte, op. cit.*, vol. 1, pp. 303ff.
2. See the standard biographies by Favaro (vol. 1, chap. 1) and Wohlwill (pp. 42ff).
3. *Opere, 19*, p. 627.
4. See Indici dei Nomi, *Opere, 20*.
5. *Considerazioni al Tasso, Opere, 9*, pp. 129–130.
6. During the Renaissance, poets like Virgil, Lucretius and Seneca were called upon as authorities in natural philosophy. One of Galileo's bitterest opponents, Orazio Grassi, S.J., was willing to enlist poets on his side in his *Libra astronomica* (1619) where he argues against Galileo that motion is a cause of heating. He

felt that one could rely on poets, "whose authority ought to be taken seriously because they are well-versed in the affairs of nature"; in fact, he called Ovid, Lucan, Statius and Virgil to his aid. Upon reading the book, Galileo wrote angrily on the margin of his copy: "This whole discourse is idle. Galileo did not argue that [Grassi's] view was not shared by poets and others. What he said was that it was false, and that this can be shown by experience." (*Opere, 6,* p. 163.)

7. It is a schoolboyish interlinear translation of the *Parainesis pros dēmonikon* of Isocrates. A few lines from it are given in *Opere, 9,* p. 283. From the same period we have several aphorisms and quotations from an Italian translation of Plutarch's *Moralia* (*ibid.,* p. 285). See the *Avvertimento* of the editor (*ibid.,* pp. 275ff.).

8. See Galileo's notes in his copy of *Aesop's Fables* (*Opere, 20,* p. 585).

9. "Pindar, the prince of lyricists, rises to lofty heights because he departs from his original task of eulogizing his heroes and devotes only one-tenth or even one-twentieth of his verse to them; he fills his verses with the most varied things, ultimately tying them with the very thinnest of threads to the original subject." Letter to Prince Leopold of Tuscany, 1640, *Opere, 8,* p. 492.

10. Mainly in the *Dialogo* (*Opere, 7,* pp. 44ff., 53), and in the *Discorsi* (*Opere, 8,* pp. 283ff.).

11. Viviani, *Racconto istorico, Opere, 19,* p. 627; Gherardini, *Vita, ibid.,* p. 645.

12. Letter from Mario Guiducci, 1620, *Opere, 6,* p. 186.

13. *Lezione prima, Opere, 9,* p. 32.

14. Galileo says he is "indebted to them in many respects"; *ibid.,* p. 57.

15. Letter of his predecessor, Iacopo Giraldi, January 21, 1621, *Opere, 13,* p. 55f.

16. *Opere, 15,* p. 445. Buonarotti was a nephew of the great artist, a friend of Galileo and author of a play (*La fiera e la tancia*), chaotic but interesting, which mirrored the morals of his time.

17. *Geschichte, op. cit.,* vol. 2, pp. 143–144; 178ff.

18. Michele Barbi, *Della fortuna di Dante nel secolo XVI,* Pisa, 1890.

19. A. Manetti, *Dialogo circa al sito, forma et misure dello Inferno di Dante,* Florence, 1506 (Reprint by N. Zingarelli, Citta di Castello, 1897). The bibliography of the controversy is in C. A. Scartazzini, *Dantologia,* Milan, 1906, pp. 388ff.

20. *Comento di Christoforo Landino Fiorentino sopra la Comedia di Dante Alighieri,* Florence, 1481; *La Comedia di Dante Alighieri con la nuova esposizione di Allessandro Vellutello,* Venice, 1544.

21. *Due lezioni all'accademia fiorentina circa la figura, sito e grandezza dell' inferno di Dante, Opere, 9,* pp. 32–57. There is a critical evaluation of this piece in O. Gigli, *Studi sulla divina Commedia di Galileo Galilei,* Florence, 1855, and N. Vaccalluzzo, *Galileo letterato e poeta,* Catania, 1896, pp. 92ff. The clumsy verses at the beginning of the first lecture (*Opere, 9,* p. 31) are the final portion of a stanza; they are the translation of vv. 125ff. of the sixth book of the *Aeneid,* probably by Galileo.

22. *Opere, 19,* pp. 596, 627, 645.

23. *Il saggiatore, Opere, 6,* pp. 317 ("a great poet"), 330 ("the keenest of poets"), 338 ("inferior to none").

24. *Postille all'Ariosto, Opere, 9,* pp. 151–194.

25. Canto VII, str. 29, vv. 7–8 (*Opere, 9,* p. 157); Canto XX, str. 10, v. 8 (*ibid.,* p. 171).

26. See Julius Schlosser, *Die Kunstliteratur,* Vienna, 1922, p. 378, and the references found there.

27. "In considering the decorum proper to painting, one must take care above all that the arrangement and proportioning of the subjects do not give rise, contrary to the purpose of the representation, to offensive and unbecoming poses." Galileo, *Considerazioni al Tasso, Opere, 9,* p. 94.

28. *Ibid.,* and Schlosser, *op. cit.,* p. 381.

29. The history of this dispute is given in A. Solerti, *Vita di Torquato Tasso,* Turin, 1895, vol. 1, chaps. 20ff. Also T. Spoerri, *Renaissance und Barock bei Ariosto und Tasso,* Berne, 1922.

30. *Considerazioni al Tasso, Opere, 9,* pp. 61–148.

31. "La sentenza e la locuzione", *ibid.,* p. 76.

32. "Torbide immaginazioni", *ibid.,* p. 143.

33. See, for example, *ibid.,* pp. 63f., 75f.

34. *Postille all'Ariosto, Opere, 9,* p. 193.

35. See Benedetto Croce, *Ariosto, Shakespeare, Corneille* (translated by Julius Schlosser), Vienna, 1922, esp. chaps. 4 and 5. Also Giulio Bertoni, *Lodovico Ariosto,* Rome, 1925.

36. See the comments by Viviani and Gherardini, *Opere, 19,* pp. 627, 644.

37. As early as 1615, his friend Sagredo suggested to him that the reading of Berni's and Ruzzante's works would help him "rise above the storms of adversity and the pain of sickness". See *Opere, 12,* p. 156.

38. See the description of this poetry in A. Gaspary, *Geschichte der italienischen Literatur,* Strasbourg, 1885–1888, vol. 2, pp. 514ff., and the many published collections of satirical poems, e.g. the three volumes: *Il libre dell'opere burlesche di M. Francesco Berni, M. Giovanni della Casa . . . ,* Utrecht, 1726.

39. Bruno also liked this kind of poetry very much. See *Galilei und seine Zeit,* p. 65.

40. *Capitolo contro il portar la toga, Opere, 9,* pp. 213ff.

41. On these duties see A. Favaro, *Galileo Galilei e lo studio di Padova,* Florence, 1883, vol. 1, p. 43. Concerning the deductions, see *Opere, 19,* pp. 37ff.

42. See Tasso's *Aminta* and Guarini's *Pastor Fido.*

43. *Facezie e motti dei secoli XV e XVI,* Bologna, 1874, p. 75, n. 104.

44. *Postille all'Ariosto, Opere, 9,* p. 164.

45. *Geschichte, op. cit.,* vol. 2, pp. 151ff. See also A. Favaro, "Scampoli galileiani", *Att. Mem. R. Accad. Scien. Lett. Arti Padova, 2,* 1886, pp. 14ff. On Ruzzante, see the two-volume work by A. Mortier (Paris, 1926), which contains a translation and analysis of his comedies.

46. See the *Dialogo de Cecco de Ronchitti da Bruzene in perpuosito de la stella nuova,* Padua, 1605 (*Opere, 2,* pp. 309–334). This is the pseudonym of

P. Girolemo Spinelli, O.S.B. The occasion and contents of the dialogue are noted in E. Wohlwill, *Galileo Galilei*, vol. 1, pp. 212–223. The popular literature on the "new star" is discussed in *Geschichte, op. cit.*, vol. 2, pp. 249ff. An example of this literature, *Canzone per le stelle medicee* (written by Andrea Salvadori, and revised by Galileo) is given in *Opere, 9*, pp. 238ff.

47. See the notes thereto, *Opere, 2*, 275ff.

48. See response by Baldassare Capra, *ibid.*, pp. 285ff.

49. *Geschichte, op. cit.*, vol. 2, pp. 137ff.

50. *Opere, 9*, p. 229.

51. *Ibid.*, pp. 194, 229.

52. *De Motu, Opere, 1*, p. 398.

53. See marginal note by Galileo on Castelli's criticism of Giorgio Corresio's work on floating objects, *Opere, 4*, p. 248, n. 4. Castelli's own criticism of the quarrel of the literary critics is wholly according to the mind of his teacher.

54. See *Frammenti attenenti al trattato delle cose che stanno sù l'acqua* (*Opere, 4*, p. 30) and the treatise itself (*ibid.*, p. 65).

55. See also letter to Matteo Carosio, May 21, 1610, *Opere, 10*, p. 358; letter to Vincenzo Giugni, June 25, 1610, *ibid.*, p. 380.

56. *Difesa . . . contro B. Capra, Opere, 2*, p. 521.

57. *Il saggiatore, Opere, 6*, p. 232.

Part III

Galileo's contributions to science

8 · Galileo and the principles of dynamics

PAUL TANNERY

The title of Galileo's last work, which was printed by the Elzevirs at Leyden in 1638, made no empty boast. He called it: *Discourses and mathematical demonstrations regarding two new sciences,* and indeed from this book the sciences of the strength of materials and of dynamics may be said to have taken their origin. For the latter, in particular, Galileo's "mathematical demonstrations" provided the model to be imitated; they showed that one could proceed in mechanics just as the ancients had done in geometry, by deducing from a small number of carefully chosen axioms or postulates an indefinitely long chain of consequences, many of them unexpected.

Nevertheless, Galileo's mode of exposition differs on one essential point from the one that would later become standard. The problem that he treated, and fully resolved was, in modern terms, that of a material point acted upon by a force of constant intensity and direction. Nowadays it would be assumed that the solution of this problem would require as starting-point two basic dynamic principles, the principle of inertia, and the

NOTE: This article first appeared as: "Galilée et les principes de la dynamique" in the *Revue générale des sciences pures et appliquées*, 1901, 330–338. It is included in Tannery's *Mémoires scientifiques*, Paris, 1926, vol. 6, pp. 387–413. The translation is by Ernan McMullin.

principle that the effect of an impressed force is not dependent upon the prior state of movement of the body. Galileo did, in fact, maintain both of these, though not, of course, in the terms we now use to state them. Yet the sequence of thought in the Latin treatise, *De motu locali*, which constituted the Third and the Fourth Days of the *Discorsi* and summarized Galileo's views on dynamics, was altogether different. The notion of a "material point" is nowhere to be found there; while the distinction between mass and weight would not come until later with Newton. Galileo spoke in general fashion of a *"mobile"*, though he did in fact represent it geometrically as a point. But what is more significant is that he quite deliberately chose not to speak of forces (or of weights); because of this, his postulates took on a quite special character.

The starting-point

First, he defines uniform motion and deduces its properties. Then he passes on to uniformly accelerated motion, as being the next simplest type, and notes in a preamble that this must be regarded as the natural motion of freely falling bodies. In support of this assumption, he adduces some *a priori* considerations which are not very fully developed; he claims that they are confirmed by the same observations that attest to the validity of the predictions made by the theory. He summarizes his position as follows:

> Since Nature employs, in the descent of heavy bodies, a certain manner of acceleration, we will discover the theory of these effects if the definition which we are about to give of accelerated motion does in fact correspond with the essence of this motion. Nature makes use in all her works of the simplest and easiest means. When I notice that a stone falling from rest acquires successive increments of velocity, why should I not hold that these increments must occur according to the formula which is simplest and which suggests itself before all others?

Galileo then puts forward, as the only explicit postulate necessary for his proof, that the speed of a falling body will be the same for all inclinations of the plane on which it moves, provided the vertical height of fall be the same. From the definition of uniformly accelerated motion, he deduces that the velocity depends on the square of the time of fall, and goes on to develop a theory both of free fall and of fall on inclined planes. He shows that the speed acquired by a falling body will suffice to allow it to ascend again to the same height.

When he arrives at the movement of projectiles, he states the guiding principles of his treatment:

> I conceive of a body launched on a horizontal plane, and by an effort of thought I assume all impediment to be removed. It is clear from what has already been said that its movement on the plane will be uniform and perpetual if the plane extends indefinitely. But if we conceive the plane as limited

and also inclined, the body (which I take to be endowed with gravity) will arrive at the end of the plane and will continue forward, having in addition to the former uniform and nondecaying motion, that of the descent proper to its gravity. So that the resultant is a motion composed of a horizontal uniform motion and a motion of vertical descent, uniformly accelerated.

The writing of the *De motu locali*

Despite the late date of its publication in the *Discorsi*, the treatise *De motu locali* had certainly been conceived in the early years of the century, at the time when Galileo first arrived at the main results that it contains.[1] Notes from this period, edited in the National Edition of his works (vol. 8), indicate that its formulation was already quite advanced. A problem, however, that is likely to remain insoluble is that of determining how the first draft came later to be successively developed or transformed. In particular, one would like to know whether the mode of exposition outlined in the citations above represents, in fact, Galileo's final thought, the definitive stage of a long development, or whether it already belonged to the very first conception of the treatise, or whether it dates from some intermediate period.

I am inclined to the second of these alternatives, even though it may appear less likely from certain points of view. It will, however, first be necessary to unravel, as far as possible, another enigma, namely that of the motives which led Galileo to defer publication for thirty years of those discoveries which would later allow him to claim, with justifiable pride, to have created a new science.

The first reason for the delay was, of course, the discovery of the telescope; the fame it brought to Galileo was immediate, and far beyond what he could have expected on the basis of his earlier researches. Here he was, no longer young, engaged in all sorts of new occupations, and at the same time defending his discoveries against detractors. He was busy overthrowing the Aristotelians, and already had committed himself to a fateful advocacy of Copernicanism. The years of semiretirement that followed these first battles would have given (so one would have thought) the opportunity to complete the work of which he had dreamt for so long. Its publication would have greatly strengthened his position. Nor would it have involved him in any risk, since all polemic against Aristotle had been carefully avoided in the first sketch of the *De motu locali*. Its method was strictly mathematical, and the new ideas introduced in it are held to a strict minimum. Had it been carried to a successful conclusion, Galileo could not but have been in a stronger position to engage upon his defense of Copernicus.

Yet by an apparent tactical error, of a sort one would not expect from a mature and experienced man, he decided instead to work on the *Dialogo*, in which the Aristotelian position would be rendered untenable and Copernicanism would be defended, and to wait patiently for years for what seemed like a favorable opportunity to publish it. The risky gamble failed. The *Discorsi* appeared six years later as a continuation of the controversial *Dialogo;* the dialogue form was retained, and the central characters were the same. It was thus conceived and executed after the *Dialogo.* Yet this appears to be true only of the first two Days, those concerned with the resistance of materials. The Second Day ends abruptly, and the next two Days are occupied (without any preliminary explanation) by the formal treatise, *De motu locali*, enlivened only occasionally by snatches of dialogue. The structure of this section is quite perfunctory from a literary point of view.

It seems clear that Galileo was taken by surprise by the turn of events; wishing to save, as best he could, the most precious of his scientific treasures, he adopted at the last moment a mode of publication for the *De motu locali* for which it had in no way been designed. The haste in which the adaptation had to be carried through evidently made any thoroughgoing revision of the earlier format impossible.

Let us now recall what Galileo said, in the preamble cited above, about the movement of projectiles. His formulation of the principle of inertia could well have been based on what he had already developed at length elsewhere. One could, in fact, easily derive it from the postulate concerning movement on inclined planes and from the sequence of theorems that followed. But it is very unlikely that this is what Galileo wanted to suggest. Either the *De motu locali* had originally contained arguments which were then omitted in the *Discorsi* version (because they had already appeared in essence in the *Dialogo*), or—a little more likely—the treatise had been from the start planned to follow after a polemic against the dynamics of Aristotle, or lastly (and most probable of all) there is question of a simple cross-reference to the *Dialogo*, added at the last moment.

At any rate, this is the heart of the problem facing us; only by resolving it can we understand the apparent tactical error mentioned a moment ago. Paradoxically, the man who did more than anyone else at that critical time to introduce new truths with the least contamination of error, had not himself the temperament of an innovator. He put off publication of a dynamical theory, and when he did begin to formulate one in the *De motu locali*, he originally imposed a quite artificial mold upon the exposition, one which required him on the one hand to exert extraordinary efforts to avoid formal contradiction with the *Physics* of Aristotle, and on the other to camouflage the two fundamental principles of the new dynamics in a mathematical formulation, the mode of presentation that would be least likely to attract the attention of his scholastic opponents. But having accomplished this difficult task, he realized, before the last touches had been put on the treatise, that his precautions had been in vain. For his astronomical discoveries had now forced the issue in an altogether different quarter, and he was already the object of violent and growing attack from the Aristotelian camp. From then on he would be too near the storm center of controversy for anyone to miss the latent opposition between his new mathematical theory of movement and the theory of Aristotle.

Galileo was no innovator by temperament; he was not one to push for the immediate adoption of a new view, leaving aside all personal considerations. Yet he *did* have the temperament of a polemicist. He never drew back from the battle once it was joined; when he believed his own person to be touched, he fought with tenacity, not to say ferocity. Attacked in the name of Aristotle, he would henceforward aim directly at Aristotle. He would adopt the bold but logical strategy that he had previously decided against, of destroying the Aristotelian dynamics utterly, before expounding his own. But to do this, he had first to defend the Copernican hypothesis, because the two principles on which his system rested implicitly required a Copernican basis. This, it seems to me, gives the best explanation of the course followed by Galileo in the last twenty-five years of his life.

Aristotelianism and the new dynamics

The claim of a logical and historical relation between Galileo's twin principles (inertia and the nondependence of the effect of impressed force on the prior state of motion) and the Copernican hypothesis clearly needs to be justified before we go any farther. The point is centrally important in its own right, all the more because it is so often obscured in contemporary expositions of dynamics.

It may be noted, first of all, that the explicit or implicit admission of these two principles provided a sort of touchstone of Copernicanism in the early seventeenth century, before Galileo's works had appeared. Questions of priority are tedious and unprofitable in this regard. Nowadays, it has become customary to attribute the first principle to Kepler and the second to Galileo. But this can scarcely be justified, since both principles are contained, more or less equally clearly, in Kepler's *Astronomia nova* of 1609, long before the appearance of the *Dialogo*. Yet from the beginning of the century, and before his major discoveries in dynamics, Galileo was himself a Copernican, so that problems of relative priority or even of mutual interaction between himself and Kepler are virtually insoluble. And in any event, such questions are of little interest here. We have two thinkers whose own originality leaves its impress upon everything they do. Besides, the main thing in science is not so much to formulate principles as to make use of them in constructing a theory. And on this last score, there can scarcely be any debate: the honors go to Galileo.

What is more interesting is to ask how *anyone* of that period could have come to adopt principles so flagrantly in disagreement with the dominant views of the day. Are we, for example, to make of Galileo (as is too often done) a scientist who proceeded solely on the basis of experience, who grounded every theory on observations alone? Later on, we shall see that this view is just as erroneous as the related thesis that the principles of dynamics are directly established on the basis of experience. Or are we to rally in support of the conjecture that the principle of inertia was formulated in the sixteenth century by a return to the ideas of Democritus and a corresponding revolt against the tyranny of Aristotle? It may suffice to note that not a single one of the fragments that remain to us of Democritus' work suggests in any way the notion of inertia, and that the only information we have about his views on mechanics derives from the polemics of Aristotle against him. Yet neither Galileo nor Kepler were the dedicated enemies of Aristotle that Bacon was; it was not their wont to support a view just because Aristotle opposed it. Their motivation on this issue was a much more decisive one.

To understand this motive, it will be useful to ask first what dynamical principles were being taught in the name of Aristotle in the early seventeenth century. An answer to this question will allow us to appreciate all the more fully the progress made by Galileo. Aristotle divided motions into two kinds, natural and violent. The nature of every being includes a principle of movement and rest which is "natural" to that being. A "violent" motion is one which is brought about in an "accidental" fashion by an outside force. Natural motions differ from one kind of body to another. The celestial substance is arranged in spheres moving uniformly. (Aristotle had supposed these spheres to be concentric with the earth, following Eudoxus, but this view was gradually abandoned in favor of the epicycles of Hipparchus and Ptolemy.)

These uniform revolutions thus have a cause which is permanent, internal and constant.[2] If the action of this cause were to cease, the motion would immediately stop. The causal action is, besides, not mechanical in character. The First Mover is the object of desire on the part of lower beings; to resemble him as far as is possible for the mutable to resemble the immutable is the incentive proper to the nature of the celestial bodies. The "mover" itself neither acts nor is acted upon. The natural movements of the four sublunary elements are vertical, and either directed downward (water and earth) or upward (air and fire). The cause of their movement is, as before, permanent and internal, but is no longer regarded as constant. Aristotle was aware that falling or rising bodies tend to accelerate, but he attributed this to a variation in the cause, supposing that it increased as the body approached its natural place. The measure of the cause he also took to be the velocity at each instant, since this velocity is the direct effect of the continuing cause.

In the case of violent movement, on the other hand, the external action which determines it is not taken to impress upon the moved body a force which will tend to prolong the motion. If the motion does, in fact, continue after the action of the cause has ceased, i.e., if the thrown stone does not return to its normal downward motion immediately on leaving the hand, it is only because the action of the medium (which has been disturbed by the motion) is substituted for that of the former cause, and suffices for a time to keep the "violent" type of motion going. Whatever this continuation of movement, it is clear at least that Aristotle supposed "violent" action to produce at each instant a velocity which had no tendency to continue in the absence of the cause. From this point of view, external (violent) action and internal (natural) action are fully alike.

It follows from this that Aristotle had no concept corresponding to *force* in the modern sense. He denied, as explicitly as he could, the notion of inertia; he did not believe that a movement could be previously acquired. And these are the fundamental concepts of our mechanics. No agreement is possible between his doctrine and ours on this question of "instantaneous forces". Indeed, this very phrase is a sort of survival from scholastic terminology; it clashes so strongly with the rest of contemporary usage, that it will doubtless be discarded eventually.

Since Aristotle did not have the concept of force, he had of course no word corresponding to it either. The term, 'potency' (*dunamis*), has in his technical language a special meaning. It signifies *possibility*, and it is thus that his celebrated definition of motion ("the actualization of the potential insofar as it is potential") must be understood.[3] If, therefore, Aristotle uses the term 'potency' to designate a force (a weight, for example, in a static condition or in a simple machine), it must be emphasized that he means by this only a possibility of movement (though admittedly one capable of being measured). And there is no reason to believe that any other physicist of antiquity understood the term any differently.

This lack of an appropriate term delayed the formulation of an adequate concept of force. The seventeenth-century scientists hesitated between the pair of terms for potency ('*dunamis*' and '*potentia*') and the pair for effort or impressed action ('*bia*' and '*vis*'). Ultimately the Italian '*forza*' found favor, but '*dunamis*' provided the adjective for mechanical situations involving forces, while '*vis*' became standard in Latin treatises. In the *De motu locali*, Galileo made use of the notion of force, but in the *Dialogo* he does not seem to feel any need for it, and follows the language of Aristotle except for the occasional employment of a vague expression, '*virtus*'. In a few passages of the *Discorsi*, on the other hand, he uses '*forza*', sometimes of potency, sometimes of violent action. It is difficult to be sure whether he intended any precise sense to be given to these terms, which in the usage of the time were quite ambiguous.

In evaluating the dynamical system of Aristotle, one must leave aside the prejudices that derive from contemporary education; one may then appreciate the state of mind of an independent thinker of the early seventeenth century. From this point of view, it is clear that Aristotle's system is much more faithful to the world of direct observation than is our modern view. Indeed, the major criticism that one is ultimately led to bring against him is that he stays *too* close to a level of observation that we would now characterize as macroscopic, and that he does not press on to a sufficiently exact experimental analysis. There is, however, one notable exception where this fidelity to observation is not maintained; his claim that the medium is the active agency in continuing projectile motion is obviously not derived from experience in any way. It is a theoretical postulate, linked with his rejection of the vacuum. The attribution of this role to the medium was not novel; Plato had earlier done the same. It was in fact, an Eleatic doctrine, broadly speaking, accepted by all save Democritus. That this view is in no way absurd is illustrated by its revival in an article concerning the ether in the *Revue scientifique* around 1875. The hypothesis put forward was that ponderable matter is absolutely inert, and that the continuation of the motion it acquires, as well as the attractions and repulsions between its particles, is due to the action upon it of the medium in which it is immersed. The advantage of such an hypothesis would be that it eliminates problems of friction in the ether.

Aristotle's system was undoubtedly insufficient to constitute an adequate dynamics, because it lacks the wherewithal for a mathematical formulation. This might not have been altogether impossible to remedy, despite Aristotle's basic distinction between two types of body, celestial and terrestrial, on the basis of their motion. Yet this distinction *did* fundamentally militate against the sort of mathematical abstraction that serves to establish postulates of universal validity. And it led to a serious logical flaw: the role of the medium must be allowed to be altogether different in violent motion (where it conserves the motion) and in natural motion (where it does not intervene). Nevertheless, in spite of all these lacunae and incoherences, at the time Galileo came along there was as yet nothing that would justify the total rejection of Aristotle's mechanics.

Galileo and the experimental method

How then was Galileo led to believe that this destruction was absolutely necessary? Can one accept the traditional view that would make him from the beginning of his career the champion, against Aristotle, of the "experimental method"? That he had a genius for observation is certain. His precocious discovery of the isochronism of the pendulum would suffice to assure us of this. But this discovery had no relevance one way or another to Aristotelianism. Galileo continued to describe it as an experimental fact and never attempted to explain it theoretically, nor did he come to realize that the duration of the oscillations was not altogether independent of the amplitude of the arc. The invention of the pendulum is thus one of those frequent instances in the history of science where a practical need and a rough-and-ready observation sufficed; there was no question of "scientific method", in the elaborate sense often given this phrase nowadays.

As for the celebrated experiment from the Leaning Tower, its purpose was simply to show that one pound of lead falls at the same rate as does two pounds. And Aristotle had never said anything different, as many classical medieval treatises (such as Jordanus Nemorarius' *De gravi et levi*) had stressed. If there was an Aristotelian at Pisa who had twisted the text of Aristotle to derive a consequence quite evidently absurd *a priori*, and if Galileo contrived an experiment to disprove this consequence, it could be at most only an accidental circumstance illustrating the decay of scholasticism. Aristotle and his school never refused to appeal to experience; their problem was rather that they did not know how to make observations that would be precise and conclusive, which is really where the whole trouble lies. In this respect, Galileo is certainly one of the masters of modern science, because it was he who first showed by his own successful practice how complicated one's precautions must be and how much ingenuity one must expend if useful results are to be obtained. But he did this only later in his career (for example, in the *Discourse on bodies in water* of 1612), and invariably in order to justify a theory arrived at *a priori*, not to constitute one *a posteriori*.

We do, in fact, possess some youthful unpublished works of Galileo's on motion and on weight that date back to his time at Pisa. From these, it is possible to conclude that although he may have had a more independent spirit than did his colleagues, his ideas were not much more accurate than theirs. He alleged as facts of experience errors whose very formulation invited criticism; for instance, that at the beginning of free fall the rate of fall is more rapid than it is a little later, and that the acceleration of the fall does not begin until after this first slowing-up. In these early essays, there is only one important idea, one to which Galileo always remained faithful: it is that the Aristotelian theory of weight, in particular, the sharp distinction between heavy and light bodies, is incompatible with the principle of Archimedes and the confirmed consequences of this principle. It was the mathematical spirit of Archimedes, then, that provided Galileo's basic inspiration; he studied the great Syracusan's work intensively, and acknowledged its influence on his own writings.

Another ancient writer on mechanics whose effect on scientific thinking during the Renaissance was very considerable was Heron of Alexandria. The preface to his *Pneumatics* was the major source (far more than Lucretius' work *De rerum natura*) of the view that matter is formed of small corpuscles separated by empty space. This view had come to be accepted even by many Aristotelians, and did not give rise to the same hesitations as did the still-suspect doctrine of Epicurus. But Galileo does not seem to have been affected much by these thinkers; he was not especially interested in the problem itself, even though he did opt for the "corpuscularian" view in his discussion of heat in the *Saggiatore*. It was characteristic of his special genius that despite a speculative ability of a very high order, he avoided and indeed ignored in his attempts to find a solid basis for physics any problem that did not seem to him capable of direct solution.

Copernicanism and the principles of dynamics

We are thus led to the conclusion that it is equally improbable that the two leading principles of Galileo's dynamics were conceived *a priori* (to replace a system judged to be insufficient) or that they were established *a posteriori* (following experimental procedures). Their origin, however, becomes quite clear if one compares the Copernican hypothesis with the theses of Aristotle. They were, it appears, engines of war designed to defend the Copernican view. Indeed, they were so closely related to it logically that Copernicus himself had begun to grasp them. Even though he did not formulate them explicitly, it is to him that they must ultimately be traced.

Aristotle gave an explanation—a theological one, which complicated matters—of the diurnal motion of the sphere of the "fixed" stars. This explanation was rejected by Copernicus, who attributed the movement entirely to the earth. But such a movement could be regarded neither as natural nor as violent, in Aristotle's senses of these terms. Its perpetuity could be conceived only as a fact, having no other explanation than its prior existence. But this is the principle of inertia.

The case was equally clear for the other principle. Ever since antiquity, the frequently discussed hypothesis of the rotation of the earth had given rise to the natural objection first formulated clearly by Ptolemy: would not such a rotation have a disturbing effect on all motions taking place on the earth's surface? To counter this objection, it was necessary to hold that movement, once communicated to bodies, remains with them when they are released and is thus (in the situation on the earth's surface) imperceptible because shared by all. Whether Galileo understood the principle of the independence of previously acquired motion in this precise sense or not, it is certainly this principle that underlies his assertion in the *Dialogo* that everything happens on the surface of the earth just as though there were no rotation.

He makes only one exception to this, albeit an unfortunate one. He attempts to explain ocean tides by invoking the earth's rotation. (This was one of the two indirect dynamic arguments in favor of Copernicanism adduced by him in the *Dialogo*.) Yet even in ancient times, it had been realized that the period of the tides is primarily linked with the positions of the moon. Another less obvious error occurs when he is calculating the time taken by a heavy body to fall from the sphere of the moon to the earth. He wrongly assumes that its path will be vertical, not realizing that there is a deviation to the east. The exact formulation of this principle had to wait for Newton's *Principia*.

Inertia and the rotation of the earth

Even today, there is no more solid observational evidence in support of the principle of inertia than that of the constancy of the earth's daily rotation. A point that is often overlooked in our teaching of mechanics is that the principle of inertia contains an implicit definition of time. A rotational motion which is free of external and internal forces, or else subject to forces that exactly counterbalance, serves as an operational measure of time. Of course, it will not be possible to give a rigorous demonstration that the body *is* in free motion, though a strong probability can be established. By analogy, one can then go on to regard as free (or as subject to counterbalancing forces) any body in rectilinear uniform motion. This suffices to provide a sort of negative definition of force, one which is in reasonable accord with the everyday static conception (Aristotle's *dunamis*). The adequacy of this analogy can now be shown: using some more or less disguised postulates (involving idealized concepts like *mass-point* and *rigid body*) as well as the principle of inertia, one can prove the uniformity of rotation of a rigid solid about one of its principal axes. This closes the circle. One never really leaves the circle; one begins from an hypothesis and finds it again at the end.

Even the celebrated Foucault experiment does not prove the rotation of the earth unless one admits the absolute character of a frame of reference permanently oriented with respect to the "fixed" stars—and this is ultimately equivalent to the Copernican hypothesis itself. This hypothesis thus provides the indispensable substructure for the entire system of classical dynamics, just as Newton's hypothesis of universal gravitation (since it entails the key "law" of equality of action and reaction) provides the equally indispensable superstructure.

Galileo's second principle (that of the independence of previously acquired motion) was the beginning of a positive definition of the notion of force, because it helped to clarify the definition of acceleration, thus providing a measure-ratio for force in terms of its effect on the motion of a given body. The other constituent of the Newtonian definition of force is *mass*, but this could not be reached until a third dynamical principle (that of the noninterdependence of the effects of forces) had been enunciated. The third is rather like the second, but Galileo never reached it. He used a special postulate when discussing the inclined plane, in order to avoid the question of the decomposition of forces, and he altogether left aside problems like that of the motion of a system of opposing weights.

We cannot know with any assurance how he would have handled problems involving the action of multiple forces. The crucial concept of mass was not, in fact, constituted until the time of Newton. Some foreshadowing of it may be noted in the much older idea that had often been discussed (by Galileo among others) of the variability of weight with distance from the center of the earth. But no experimental way of confirming this variability had been thought of, nor did it seem conceivable that a common measure of the motions of celestial and sublunary bodies might be found.

The effect of a force does not depend
on the prior state of motion

Concentrating for a moment on the second principle, we have seen that Galileo got it slightly wrong in the *Dialogo*, holding that it was true of acquired movements of rotation (at least around the center of the earth) as well as for straight-line motion. In the *De motu locali*, however, he formulated it rigorously, and limited it to straight-line motion alone. But he did not propose any experimental verification for it in the case where the previous movement and the accelerating force are not directed along the same line. The observations he made with the inclined plane in support of the "time-squared" law (which had been arrived at *a priori*) illustrate only the special case where the prior movement and the acceleration are in the same line (which is reducible to the case of simple fall). No matter what precautions are taken with the inclined plane to diminish friction and sharpen the measurements, it is clear that what is actually verified is only that the time-squared law holds where the distance of fall is so small that frictional and other disturbances can safely be neglected. Galileo was not, of course, claiming any more for the experiment than this. But under these restrictions, it is clear that observation alone could not seriously be said to justify either the rule itself or the principle from which it derives. If the experiment be tried with greater distances of fall, the most that would be shown (assuming the time-squared law to be valid) would be the size of the effects due to resistance and to variation in gravity.

Those of Galileo's contemporaries who criticized his theory had no more decisive a claim upon experience than he had. Baliani gave a different formula, according to which the distances fallen during equal and consecutive intervals of time increased in proportion to the natural numbers, and very probably he had done some experimentation in support of this. But there were really not enough accurate observational data available to make possible a decision between the different proposals.

Two objections (both of which he had foreseen) were especially raised against Galileo's theory. The first of these emphasized that the action of the medium could never be entirely eliminated, and so the theory could never be rigorous. This was Descartes' criticism, in particular. As it happened, he had himself—through a singular fault of reasoning—just missed deducing the time-squared law in 1619; his later rejection of the void and advocacy of a "subtle matter" made him suspicious of Galileo's procedure.[4] The criticism here was not of the principle itself—this was not denied—but of the genuineness of its alleged empirical confirmation. Yet it was precisely his neglect of the effect of the medium that constituted Galileo's stroke of genius, since it was this that made a mathematically expressed theory possible.

The second objection derived from the difficulty many physicists felt about a movement that began gradually from a null initial velocity. With the habits of thought inherited from the Aristotelian tradition, it seemed as though weight ought to produce instantaneously, at the beginning of the motion, a finite velocity. Baliani's formula did not give rise to this difficulty, which was a strong consideration in its favor. In the polemics that followed, Galileo's main critic was Gassendi; Fermat, however, supported him. Descartes admitted Galileo's formula as an approximation for small distances of fall, but could not allow the idea of a null initial velocity.

Later developments

As the eighteenth century passed, the entire approach to the principles of dynamics gradually changed. Physics came to be an independent science, exclusively founded (so it was thought) upon experience. Its decisive successes gave confidence in what were claimed to be its methods, and these methods in turn took on a universal scope. It gradually came to be asserted that the principles of dynamics had been reached on the basis of an induction from facts observable on the earth's surface. Even if there was some difficulty in establishing them directly by means of precise observations, at least their immediate consequences could be verified. These latter were thus regarded as natural laws which had been discovered and established by a simple generalizing from experience; from them, it was only one step back to the principles that were their theoretical presupposition.

This view of scientific method was reinforced by the use of a very ingenious piece of apparatus, Atwood's machine, in the classroom teaching of mechanics. By using counterweights, the speed of fall was slowed as much as desired, and a direct verification was given of Galileo's relation between speed, time and distance. By varying the weights, one could even verify the third dynamical principle mentioned above (the mutual independence of the effects of forces), for a very special case, it was true, yet one sufficiently general to allow the rigorous formulation of the concept of mass as a consequence. The cumulative effect of this sort of laboratory demonstration, as well as the increasing glorification of the all-powerful "experimental method", led scientists of the nineteenth century to an uncritical acceptance of this new account of the principles of dynamics. So oblivious, indeed, did they become to historical truth that Galileo was transformed by them into an experimenter who had discovered the laws of free fall by means of his inclined-plane experiments.

A reaction had to occur, and it occurred when physics had once more to fall back on the resources of mathematics in order to maintain its own forward progress. Thus it lost something of the apparent independence it had come to claim. In order to develop in analytic fashion the theoretical concepts in which the physicists had clothed their observations, the mathematicians were forced to criticize them first, and thus came to recognize more precisely the limits that had to be set to the experimental conclusions. In this way, the rights of *a priori* speculation were emphatically vindicated, rights that all of a sudden came to be dramatically extended in the domain of mathematics itself by the creation of the purely postulational non-Euclidean geometries.

The *a priori* impossibility of verifying the principles of dynamics by direct experimentation was established by Henri Poincaré at the Congress of Philosophy in 1900. The case is similar to that of the Euclidean postulate of parallels, but different conclusions must be drawn, from the point of view of the teacher especially. The postulate of parallels was admitted from the very beginnings of science; it had only to be formulated and proposed. But the principles of dynamics had to be *discovered*, and this discovery was preceded by two thousand years of speculations concerning movement and force. Thus they have to be *justified*.

But to justify them, I know of no better way than to return to the sequence of history. It was not by the making of observations on the earth's surface that these principles were discovered; it was not from physics that they proceeded. Instead, they were constructed in order to explain celestial phenomena, along the lines (in the case of the first two, at least) of the Copernican hypothesis. The celestial bodies are still the only ones that can be properly represented by the mass-points or the rigid bodies of traditional mechanics. And it is only from the further progress of astronomy that one can expect any new development of the fundamental concepts of mechanics, notably with reference to the role of the medium both in propagating force and in resisting motion.

The exposition of the laws of fall by means of Atwood's machine must, then, be abandoned. These alleged "laws" are, in fact, mathematical theorems, and they ought not be presented as something different. The important thing in *physics* would be to do something that is in fact never done —to teach what the limits of these theorems are, what corrections have to be applied to them for given heights of fall, and so on. Even more important would be to show how science is really made, how discoveries come about. At the very least, one should not falsify matters by spending time on the detailed study of an apparatus for simple demonstration, when the data it provides are illusory from the scientific point of view. The time would be better spent on real instruments of research.

In discussing the fall of bodies, Galileo's experimental verifications could be mentioned by the teacher. But it would be essential to explain their true import. Although they are absolutely insufficient to establish the unlimited range and precision of the mechanical formulae, they do at least show that these latter are sufficiently in conformity with one range of facts to allow them to be employed theoretically on a wider scale, provided all the appropriate reservations are made.

NOTES

1. [See Drabkin's edition (1960*) of the earlier *De motu* of Galileo's youth, and the masterly new edition (1958*) of the *Discorsi* by A. Carugo and L. Geymonat for much additional material on this point. (Translator's note)]

2. The word 'cause' is used here in the contemporary sense. Aristotle made the unmoving First Mover the "cause" of the motion, whereas he supposed the "principle" of the motion to be internal to each celestial being. The same would be true for sublunary bodies, except that here the motion of the celestial bodies would be an additional secondary cause. But I do not think it worthwhile to dwell on these metaphysical subtleties.

3. The Greek term '*kinesis*' was applied to change in general; this is why when they spoke of movement, they would qualify it (as Galileo still did) as "local" movement. In modern usage, 'change' is the general term, while 'movement' is ordinarily used only for change of place. Aristotle's definition of change is of interest only at the most general level; it becomes a tautology when applied to movement.

4. See the Adam and Tannery edition of the *Correspondance de Descartes*, Paris, 1897, vol. 1, p. 75. [Tannery has several other discussions of the relations between Galileo and Descartes in these volumes of the *Correspondance*; vol. 1, pp. 282–290; vol. 2, pp. 402–405; vol. 5, p. 553. (Editor's note)]

9 ☀ Galileo's contribution to astronomy

WILLY HARTNER

I am writing about Galileo Galilei as an astronomer, about his contributions to that branch of science which since the remotest antiquity, for preponderantly irrational reasons, has possessed man's interest and stimulated his imagination to a higher degree than has any of the diverse other branches of the tree of science, despite its limited practical applicability. In so doing, it is certainly not my aim to enumerate the many discoveries by which he contributed to the removal of age-old prejudices, and cleared the way to a new and supposedly unbiased approach to science in general, and to astronomy in particular. The facts that constitute Galileo's glory are too well-known to be brought to your attention once again. Following my personal taste, therefore, may I start out on an appreciation of significant details rather than on a comprehensive report; the many details to be taken into consideration would prevent me from composing a panegyric, even if I wanted to.

Introduction

Although I am convinced that the psychoanalytic method is the surest way to obscure the understanding of historical connections, I believe that some consideration of psychological factors is indispensable in so complex a case as the present. For we can hardly do justice to Galileo and to his work without taking into account the many conflicting currents in his reasoning, from which sprang his griefs and preoccupations, as well as his joys; they were the cause of his humiliations no less than of his triumphs.

Galileo's powerful and extraordinarily sensitive personality could not possibly be met with indifference by his contemporaries. In point of fact, apart from major political figures, there are not many great men in history who exercised such a magic spell on their adherents and disciples, and simultaneously incurred the most acrimonious hatred on the part of those who, whether for personal or other reasons, had become their opponents. And during the three-and-a-half centuries that have elapsed since the conflict reached its first climax (on March 5, 1966, it was 350 years since the decree banning Copernicanism was published by the Holy Office) the controversy has continued, though centered more perhaps about his person than about his work. As far as his actual work is concerned, aside from differences of opinion concerning a series of questions of secondary importance, the evaluation of his actual contribution to scientific progress seems no longer subject to change.

It is not simply the progress of science, however, that the modern historian of science wishes to estimate. We have fortunately abandoned that childish attitude, commonly called positivistic, which measured the scientist and his work with a simple yardstick, counting only those of his achievements which actually served to promote scientific progress, and which are still of interest and importance to the most recent science. Such worshipers of progress will remember Galileo (if at all) as the discoverer of the law of falling bodies, of the satellites of Jupiter, of the phases of Venus and of the sunspots. (For the latter discovery, they can give him no more credit than the Chinese, who knew about sunspots a thousand years before him and never doubted—as he did, for good reasons— whether they really belonged to the sun.) For them, Kepler will be of importance only on account of his three laws and one equation. All the rest of the thousands of pages written by the two men and printed in the impressive standard editions of their works, will be disposed of as irrelevant.

For most of us, I trust, the problems that claim our special interest are of a different kind. We are anxious to find out to what antecedents a scientist was particularly indebted, what sort of milieu he lived in, what were the main external and internal obstacles or inhibitions he had to overcome, in what respect and to what degree he was a revolutionary or a traditionalist, and why. By overstressing the importance of categories, however indispensable they may be to logical reasoning, we run the risk of going hopelessly astray. Our neat pairs of exhaustive logical opposites are invaluable for mathematics and science, but they are not necessarily applicable to the affairs of man. In labeling an individual according to logical distinctions, no matter how well-chosen, we will hardly ever hit more than 50 percent of the truth.

Galileo as a revolutionary

To ask whether Galileo was a revolutionary or a traditionalist seems to make even less sense in his case than this sort of question usually does. If I had to answer in a nutshell, I should say that because of his deep roots in religious, philosophical and scientific traditions, it was with regret that he saw himself driven to become a radical; his radicalism was always attenuated by a quite surprising degree of conservatism. It is not hard to find other historical instances of such a mixture of apparently contradictory attitudes. Take Max Planck, for instance (I know this from one of his close collaborators), who regretted so much his responsibility for the overthrow of classical physics, of which he had always been a most ardent admirer. Neither Galileo nor Planck was a revolutionary by birth or by conviction, though both had good reason to be proud of the revolutions they had caused, and though both greatly enjoyed the fame they had gained by their discoveries. An impartial appreciation of Galileo's motives must, however, take into account a rather disagreeable trait by which the nobility of his character was perceptibly impaired and obscured. I am thinking of a certain pettiness, which became evident time and again, and which apparently sprang from a kind of juvenile vanity, hard to reconcile with the unquestioned greatness of his genius. Thus whenever an important discovery was made by someone else, it grieved him not to have made it himself; he often wasted time and energy in trying to prove that he had at least *thought* of it before anyone else had.[1] Even the most benevolent of his biographers have not really succeeded in giving a plausible explanation (let alone an excuse) for this psychological phenomenon. Here indeed would be an appropriate topic for a psychoanalytic study!

The most serious incident of this sort was, of course, his claim to be the discoverer of the telescope. Here he really risked his honor and reputation, and allowed himself to be guided by motives that were surely below the dignity of a great man. Not even Emil Wohlwill (*nomen est omen*) is able to acquit him completely in this instance, although after a careful analysis of the documents, he concludes that the fault was not quite as serious as it had appeared to earlier biographers.[2] When Galileo at a later date alleged his superiority to the harmless Dutch inventor, on the grounds that his own rediscovery had sprung from theoretical considerations based on the "secret doctrines of optics", Wohlwill is charitable enough to ascribe this to a sort of self-deception.[3] However this may be, Galileo's unfortunate assertion offered to Father Christopher Scheiner, S.J., later to become one of the leading figures in the hunting party that pursued Galileo, a welcome opportunity to question his trustworthiness. He could easily show that had Galileo really done any systematic experimenting with the two known types of lenses it would inevitably have led him also to the discovery of the much more powerful Kepler telescope.

The wish not to lag behind when important novelties came to his

knowledge seems to have been particularly strong during Galileo's adoles-
cence and early manhood. At the same time, he also displayed a remarkable uneasiness on occasion about the open profession of opinions at variance with the ones commonly accepted, if such opposition was likely to
expose him to public criticism or derision. Giordano had not yet been
burnt at the stake; Galileo himself had as yet encountered none of the
hostility that would later darken his life, so that he could not yet have felt
menaced by any imminent danger. His first letter to Kepler, written on
receipt of the latter's *Mysterium cosmographicum*, clearly illustrates this
sort of hesitation:

> Padua, August 4, 1597
>
> It is not days but only a few hours ago that I received your book, which was
> brought to me by Paul Amberger; as Paul mentioned that he was returning
> to Germany, I thought it would really be taken for ingratitude if I did not by
> this letter express my thanks for your gift. So please accept my thanks and,
> moreover, my gratitude for your having by this means graciously invited me
> to become your friend. So far I have only read the preface to your book,
> from which, however, I got a little insight into what you intend by it; really,
> I congratulate myself with all my heart to have such an ally in searching for
> the truth, such a friend too of this same truth. For it is a sad thing that the
> students of truth are so rare that there are only a few who do not follow the
> perverted way of philosophizing. However, this is not the place to deplore
> the miseries of our century; I should rather congratulate you on all the beau-
> tiful things you presented in support of the truth. I shall only add this and
> promise that I shall study your book patiently, being certain that I will find in
> it marvellous things. This I will do the more joyfully in that I have for many
> years past subscribed to the teaching of Copernicus ("quod in Copernici
> sententiam multis abhinc annis venerim"), and from it I have been able to
> demonstrate causes of many phenomena which without doubt cannot be ex-
> plained by the traditional hypothesis. I have worked out proofs, as well as
> computations of contrary arguments which, however, I thus far did not dare
> to make publicly known, being frightened [*perterritus*] by the fate of our
> master Copernicus who, though having gained immortal fame in the eyes of a
> few, has been ridiculed and exploded by innumerable others—for so great is
> the number of fools. I should indeed venture to disclose my opinion, if there
> were more men like you; since there are none, I shall desist from such a
> task.[4]

A remarkable letter indeed, a moving document of human weakness,
one which gives us something of an insight into Galileo's general attitude,
as well as into his reaction to a book the tenor and the importance of
which he recognized at the first glance. He expresses his joy and his
thanks by return of mail, adding words of gratitude (that have perhaps a
slightly exaggerated ring in our ears) for the author's having thus "admitted him to his friendship". It is an open question whether he really
desires to become acquainted with the book's content (most of which
was completely alien to his own way of thought) or whether we ought to

interpret his words as a variant of the polite but ambiguous phrase, 'I shall lose no time in reading it'. In any event, he almost certainly never read the book, not even superficially—no more than he seems to have read any of Kepler's later books—and he never refers to it in his later writings. But quite evidently, he was deeply impressed by the fact that the much younger German scholar (not yet twenty-five years old at the time he had composed this first book of his) had had the courage to declare himself openly an adherent of Copernicus as well as to make the Copernican theory the basis of his elaborate investigation.

His adoption of Copernicanism

Shall we take for granted what he says about his own attitude toward Copernicanism? Is it true that through many years' occupation with it, he has found new arguments to prove it correct? Or does he claim this only because he does not want Kepler to feel superior to him in that respect? The evidence of his earlier writings hardly supports his assertion, for there is next to nothing relevant to it there, even in the notes not meant for publication. I am afraid that Wohlwill,[5] in trying to trace Galileo's early Copernican tendencies, greatly overrates the importance of the treatise (written while he was still at Pisa) concerning the question: is circular motion natural or violent?[6] This essay, whose external aspect is thoroughly Aristotelian, discusses the nature of circular motion about the center of the universe. With Aristotle, it assumes that any motion by which the center of gravity of the moved object approaches the center of the earth is natural, and that any motion away from that center is violent. This allows Galileo to conclude that the rotation of a marble sphere situated at the center of the earth would be neither natural nor violent, no matter whether the sphere is homogeneous or not; for even where its center of gravity does not coincide with that of the earth (i.e., of the universe), the rotation nevertheless causes no change in the distance between the two points. The question then arises as to whether or not such a sphere, after having received a rotatory impulse from some external mover will continue rotating eternally. Galileo answers evasively: if the sphere is not moved against nature, its rotation should continue indefinitely; otherwise, it would seem that it will have to come to rest. On two other later occasions, he took up the same problem again, but in neither place did he explicitly say that the marble sphere—a metaphor, of course, for the terrestrial globe—will necessarily preserve forever the rotation acquired from the primary impulse.[7]

This "thought experiment" is wholly in the tradition of scholastic natural philosophy; it is no more than a continuation of the age-old discussion of the arguments for and against the diurnal revolution of the earth, a discussion that began at least as early as Ptolemy himself (*Almagest*, I, 7). These discussions, it is seen, lead in one case to a *non liquet*, and in the other to a vague statement that could conceivably be taken as an allusion

to the possibility of a rotating earth. Wohlwill's assertion that they have
to be regarded as pro-Copernican arguments is very hard to justify. For
even if Galileo *had* clearly stated that the earth rotates and that the stars
are at rest, this is still only one—and the lesser—of the claims made for the
motion of the earth by Copernicus. Remember there is not one astronomer
after Ptolemy's time who was not aware that the diurnal revolution of the
fixed stars can be theoretically accounted for quite adequately by having
the earth rotate.

It was in 1597, shortly before he wrote his letter to Kepler, that Galileo
first spoke openly about his attitude toward the two opposing world systems, saying that he regarded the Copernican as the more probable. This
was in a letter of May 30, 1597, to his friend Iacopo Mazzone,[8] written as
a comment upon the latter's treatise *On the comparison of Plato and
Aristotle.*[9] Mazzone tried to prove that the theories of Aristarchus and
Copernicus were untenable, using an argument he believed to be new.
According to Aristotle, he recalled, the rays of the rising sun illuminate the
summit of the Caucasus long before they meet the eye of the observer in
the plain; it is thus obvious, he argues, that more than one-half of the celestial vault can be seen from the summit of a high mountain. Now if this
small difference in altitude (according to the general estimates of the time,
the highest elevations on earth amounted to no more than a mile) is capable
of causing such a change in perspective, how much greater a change ought
to be expected if the earth were to revolve about the sun. Yet no such
effect has ever been observed.

Galileo neatly refuted Mazzone's argument by means of a mathematical
demonstration, pointing out that the phenomenon reported by Aristotle is
due to the difference between the apparent and the true horizons and is
therefore not equivalent to the effect that the anti-Copernicans claimed
should be expected if the earth actually revolved about the sun. What is
surprising in this connection, however, is Galileo's remark that it had cost
him much time and effort to discover the true cause of this paralogism.
Yet the governing principles were evidently anything but new. One of
them can be inferred directly from the last of the arguments adduced by
Ptolemy in the *Almagest* (I, 4) to prove the sphericity of the earth; the
other one derives from the elementary geometrical consideration that the
parallax of a star decreases with distance. The first of these shows that for
an elevation of one mile above sea level the effect would be of the order
of magnitude of 1°; according to the second, as applied to Tycho Brahe's
observational results, the effect would be well below 1′. What this shows
is only that if the Copernican theory is correct, the distances of the
fixed stars are much greater than had been heretofore assumed. In short,
the evidence for saying that Galileo's Copernican convictions were formed
early in his career is scanty. When one looks for "demonstrations of
phenomena otherwise unexplainable", apart from the discussion of the
marble sphere, there is only the horizon argument above, which is not a

proof of Copernicanism but only (in his own words to Kepler) a refutation of a contrary argument.

In point of fact, as late as 1606 he still taught "cosmography" in the traditional, purely Ptolemaic fashion without making the slightest allusion to an alternative way of explaining the celestial phenomena. We can establish this by an analysis of the treatise, *Trattato della sfera* (also called *Cosmografia*),[10] which was composed by him for the purpose of instructing his students in the elements of astronomy. It is preserved in various copies, one of which, below the title on the first page, carries the date, 1606, written by the author's own hand. If the book has a significance, it is of a rather negative kind: it seems indistinguishable from the dozens of similar treatises on the same subject written by known or unknown authors in the course of the preceding three or four centuries. Anyone conversant with this type of text, who opens it up and reads at random, is likely to be able to guess how it will continue. I confess that I have not been patient enough to read it all carefully, but since Wohlwill has done so without making any startling discoveries, one is probably on safe ground in assuming that there are no such to be made.

When Wohlwill claims to discover an "unmistakable irony" in Galileo's remark[11] that the immobility of the earth can be accepted with all the more certainty because nobody so far has asserted the contrary, one can scarcely avoid a feeling of skepticism. Indeed, there is not the slightest irony in this passage, nor could there be any reason for irony there, since it refers only to the possibility of the earth's *rectilinear* motion (a fact which Wohlwill has evidently overlooked): "Adunque, da quanto s'è detto vien esclusa la terra da i moti retti; e ciò si deve ammettere tanto più facilmente, quanto che niuno ha mai detto in contrario." It is true that in the introductory paragraph to the same chapter, Galileo seems to make a promising start by mentioning that there have been "very great philosophers and mathematicians" who, since they consider the earth to be a star, have also thought it to be movable. But to the modern reader's disappointment, he then goes on to reject not only its rectilinear motion but also its rotation about its axis, relying upon the familiar arguments of Aristotle and Ptolemy. The possibility of its revolution, whether about the sun or about any other body or mathematical point, is not taken into consideration at all. Thus, even though he would probably wish to include Copernicus among the "grandissimi filosofi e matematici", he nevertheless does not mention him by name, nor does he deviate in any way from strictly traditional views. In speaking to his students, it seems clear that he deliberately refrained from challenging any major accepted principles.

Most revealing in this respect is that in the last chapter ("De i moti dell' ottava sfera") of the treatise on the sphere, he still presented the theory of "trepidation", in addition to that of precession, despite the fact that Tycho had shown that the apparent irregularities of motion could easily be explained as, and were in all probability due to, errors of observation.[12] It seems obvious that at this time he simply did not yet feel sufficiently sure of himself to undertake the defense of a standpoint totally at variance with the traditional one; his religious convictions as well as his duties as a teacher may well have been additional factors in deterring him from any such radical turn. He apparently preferred, for the moment, at least, to pursue the way of conformism, as he himself says in his letter to Kepler, quoted above.

Galileo, Tycho and the theory of novae

Galileo's reaction to the discovery in 1604 of the nova in Serpentarius (which he, and Italian astronomers generally, called 'Nova Sagittarii') is equally revealing. A similar phenomenon, the Nova Cassiopeiae, had caused Tycho Brahe in 1572 to doubt the truth of Aristotle's doctrine of the invariability of the celestial vault, after he had discovered that the new star had no measurable parallax and was therefore indistinguishable from any other fixed star. His doubt had become certainty when he found the comet of 1577 to have a measurable parallax smaller than the moon's, which allowed him to locate it far beyond our satellite, and even beyond the supposed minimum distance of Venus.[13] Much later, around 1590, Tycho wrote in his *Astronomiae instauratae progymnasmata:*

I now no longer approve of the reality of those spheres the existence of which I had previously admitted, relying on the authority of the ancients rather than driven by the truth of the matter itself. At present I am certain that there are no solid spheres in heaven, no matter if these are believed to make the stars revolve or to be carried about by them. This I am going to prove towards the end of the whole work.[14]

After all this, one would have expected a quite different reaction from Galileo to the nova of 1604. He gave three public lectures before the whole student body at Padua, more than a thousand people, in which he explained the reasons that led astronomers to assign to the nova a place far above the moon's orbit, and even beyond that of Saturn, in the sphere of the fixed stars.[15] So far, so good. Since only fragments of his notes are preserved, it is of course *possible* that by way of improvisation he might have made hidden or even open allusions to the fallaciousness of the Aristotelian doctrine. Yet this seems highly improbable. Even Wohlwill thinks it unlikely in view of the fact that had he done so, an attack would surely have been launched against him, but no record of any such exists.

Concerning the origin and nature of the nova, he agrees with those who refuse to believe that it is actually a new star. Since we do not know the nature of the stars anyway, he argues, how can we be expected to give an adequate explanation of phenomena of this sort? Nevertheless, he does advance a theory of his own. Were it not for the documentary evidence we have, we should never attribute such a fancy to Galileo. Referring to observations of his own on the reflection of light, he suggests that the appearance of the nova is due to the reflection of sunlight upon condensed vapors far out in space. And the vapors themselves (which must, of course, be of gigantic dimensions), he thinks, may have emerged from the earth and risen as far as the vault of the fixed stars.

Here we see with real bewilderment how the greatest physicist of his time, in the decisive years in which he was laying the foundations of a new dynamics, proved a loyal Aristotelian in the field of astronomy. Indeed he did not hesitate to adduce arguments the untenability of which he had himself proved (implicitly, at least) years before. How can vapors ascend from the earth to the fixed stars, whose distance he noted in his earlier letter to Mazzone to be 45,225 terrestrial radii even "according to the ancient astronomers"? [16] How can he account for their becoming condensed when they arrive there? How could they at that enormous distance be capable of producing a perceptible effect by reflecting the light of the sun? Even more significantly, he had already indicated his awareness in the letter to Mazzone that if the Copernican hypothesis were correct, the distance of the fixed stars must be incredibly large, since no perceptible parallax can be observed in the positions of the stars from one season of the year to another. How could a Copernican maintain a theory of terrestrial vapors ascending to the stars? When one reads Tycho's *Apologetica responsio ad Craigum Scotum* (1589), its harsh attack on the Scottish Dr. John Craig would have found an equally vulnerable target in the arguments Galileo uses for his "vapor" theory of *novae*. There is, however, some consolation for the reader of these fragmentary notes: Galileo *does* allude to a motion of the earth (he suggests that such a motion may have diverted the vapors from their vertical path), and he also quotes a passage from Seneca (*Naturales quaestiones*, VII, 2) where the possibility of a rotation of the earth is mentioned.[17]

Even as late as the *Saggiatore* (1623), Galileo was apparently still clinging to some Aristotelian convictions, although he does say on one occasion that the Aristotelian laws of natural vertical motion do not have to be taken "with certainty", whatever this may mean. The whole passage reads as follows:

> Neither Sig. Mario nor I ever wrote that fuming vapors rise from some parts of the earth to the moon and even to the sun, and that having got outside the cone of the terrestrial shadow they are impregnated by solar rays and give birth to the comet, though Sarsi would attribute this to me. What Sig. Mario did write is that he does not consider it impossible that sometimes there may be raised from the earth exhalations and other such things so much subtler than usual that they would ascend even to the moon, and might be material for the formation of a comet; and that sometimes there occur unusual sublimations of the twilight material, as exemplified by the aurora borealis. But he does not say that this is identical with the material of comets, which must necessarily be much rarer and thinner than the twilight mists and the material

of the aurora borealis, since the comet shines much less than the aurora. Thus
if the comet appeared to the east in the whiteness of dawn while the sun was
no more than six or eight degrees from the horizon, no doubt the comet
would not be discerned, for it would be less white than the surrounding field.
Likewise, straight motion upward is attributed to the same material only with
probability and not with certainty. This is said, not to retreat in fear of
Sarsi's objections, but merely to let it be seen that we are not departing from
our custom of declaring nothing as certain except what we know beyond
doubt, as our philosophy and mathematics teach us. Now, it being granted
that we have not said the things with which Sarsi burdens us, let us hear and
examine his objections.

His first objection is founded upon the impossibility of vapors leaving by a
straight line toward the sky when a swift north wind is distorting the air and
everything within it. Such a wind was felt by him for many days after the
appearance of the comet. The objection is really very ingenious, but it loses a
good deal of its force through our having *reliable information* that there was
not the slightest disturbance of the air in either Persia or China during those
days, so I shall believe that the comet's material arose from one of those
regions unless Sarsi proves to me that it came not from thence but from
Rome, where he felt the northerly blast. And even if the vapors had left from
Italy, who knows but that they had set out before those windy days? For
many days would have passed before their arrival at the orb of the comet,
this being some 470,000 miles away according to Sarsi's master. After all, such
a journey takes time, and not a little of it.[18] [Italics mine.]

Leaving aside details other than to note that Sarsi's "master" (Tycho)
had attributed to the comet a "slightly oblate orbit about the *sun*", it must
be stated that Galileo is never at a loss for a subterfuge. While the rejoinder concerning "reliable information about the air not having been in
the slightest disturbed in either Persia or China during those days" could
adorn any funny story placed in the mouth of the Miracle Rabbi of Sa-
dagora, in the bygone days of the Austro-Hungarian Monarchy, it has no
proper place in a scientific polemic. Yet the immediately succeeding section contains, not a joke, but a true spark of genius: the beautiful parable
Galileo tells about the man who is surprised time and again to observe new
ways in which musical tones can be produced, and who eventually is unable to find out what produces the strident sound of a cicada he has cap-
tured in his hand. "The difficulty of understanding how the cicada's song
is formed, even when we have it singing to us right in our hands, is more
than enough to excuse us for not knowing how a comet is formed at such
a distance." And one may add the introductory remark to the parable:
"The less people know and understand about such matters, the more positively the attempt to reason about them, and on the other hand the number of things known and understood renders them more cautious in passing judgment about anything new." Truly, there is profound wisdom in
these two brief phrases. But Galileo himself sometimes fails to heed this
wisdom.

There is, however, no valid excuse for Galileo's not taking sufficient notice, in his public lectures about the nova of 1604, of what he had read —or at least should have read—in Tycho's *Progymnasmata* of 1602. I do not know whether his aversion to the great Danish astronomer can be traced back to this early part of his career, and if so, what was the reason for it. In a letter dated May 4, 1600, Tycho had invited his younger Italian colleague to engage with him in a scientific correspondence, especially stressing in his letter the importance he attributed to his own system of the world.[19] Wohlwill doubts whether an answer to this was ever written, and attributes Galileo's silence to the repugnance he felt for Tycho's system, which he does not even condescend to honor by the name of its propounder. Nevertheless, as we have seen, there is reason to doubt whether Galileo at this time had as yet formed a definitive opinion on the cosmological issue, so his attitude to Tycho in 1600 cannot be known with any assurance. That he knew the *Progymnasmata* by the time the nova appeared (the phenomenon may even have caused him to turn to the book) is evident from his notes and from some of his letters written early in 1605; however, this does not prove that he had by then made a careful study of it. In the latter part of his life, he frequently quoted the work, and never failed to put in words his contempt for its author and his system. In the *Saggiatore* especially, he poured scorn on Tycho, and tried to demonstrate his unreliability, his ignorance of the elements of mathematics, and so forth. Indeed, he went so far beyond limits that Kepler, despite his admiration for Galileo and his notorious opposition to the Tychonic system, felt impelled to defend his former mentor from the unfair attack by composing an appendix to the *Tychonis Brahei Danei hyperaspistes*[20] (*The Shieldbearer to Tycho Brahe, the Dane*). This latter was written in reply to a previous no less violent attack on Tycho from the Aristotelian, Scipio Chiaramonti. This appendix cannot have made pleasant reading for Galileo. Kepler tells him bluntly that "*if* there are spheres, it is necessary that they be eccentric, whence [contrary to what you are claiming] no rays perpendicular to the spheres would reach the earth except at apogee and perigee",[21] and he vigorously refutes Galileo's challenge to Tycho's mathematical abilities.[22] In spite of the politeness of Kepler's style, the appendix contains many arguments that must have deeply hurt Galileo's pride.

It would be interesting to inquire further into the reasons for Galileo's hatred of Tycho, but this is not our concern here. One of his strongest motives in later years, I believe, was that most Jesuit astronomers, and especially his arch-enemy Christopher Scheiner, had gradually passed over to the Tychonic system after having been forced by Galileo's and other contemporary discoveries to abandon their Ptolemaic standpoint. Be this as it may, there is a proverbial German warning against pouring out the baby with the bath water. Though Galileo rejected Tycho's system, he did accept (though to the best of my knowledge without giving Tycho credit for it) his assertion that there are no corporeal spheres. In his sec-

ond letter to Mgr. Piero Dini on March 23, 1615, written in defense of the
Copernican system, he says that the spheres are not real.[23] To do away
with them, he continues, does not imply the abolition of planetary motion
in eccentrics and epicycles. The solid spheres were originally introduced
by the *fabbricatori di teoriche* (i.e., the constructors of the various mechanical instruments that were designed to yield planetary longitudes
without computation) in order to facilitate the understanding of begin-
ners and the computations of the calculators. This last statement is, of
course, erroneous; it was neither for pedagogical nor for practical reasons
of this sort that the conception of the solid spheres was introduced in
astronomy. It originated, in fact, at the latest with Ptolemy himself,
though not in the *Almagest* but in his *Hypotheses*.[24] It would, however,
be unfair to blame Galileo in this context for his lack of historical interest
and knowledge.

It is difficult to say with any assurance when Galileo first came to this
conclusion about the spheres. He quotes freely from Tycho's *Progymnasmata* and his *De mundi aetherei recentioribus phaenomenis* in the
Saggiatore of 1623 and the *Dialogo* of 1632, so he must obviously have
come across the relevant passages about the spheres in these works. But as
we have seen, it is hard to tell when he started to study these works in
detail. Since the *Trattato della sfera* of 1606 was still purely traditionalist
in tone, and since Galileo, during the years immediately following, was
absorbed elsewhere than in astronomy, it seems likely that the necessity of
a total revision of his views did not occur to him until after the great
discoveries made with the telescope. This would be further borne out by
his inveterate tendency—a sound and a modern one, indeed—not to accept any kind of innovation without having himself verified it experimentally; he did not reject traditional views until they had been disproved on
the basis of observation. He was seldom impressed by the accounts given
by others of their findings. His most far-reaching inferences were, in fact,
based almost exclusively on his own experiments and observations.

Galileo and Kepler

This lack of trust in the work of others can be seen not only in his
relations with Tycho, whom he deeply disliked, but also in his attitude
toward Kepler, whom he admired and welcomed as an associate, but from
whose way of thought he was separated by an abyss. Even if he had taken
the trouble to peruse carefully the one thousand or more pages of the
Mysterium cosmographicum and of the *Astronomia nova*, not to speak of
the *Harmonice mundi*, he would probably not have understood what
could have caused a great mathematician and astronomer to drown his
mathematical discoveries in such an ocean of mysticism. And as he never
liked taking such trouble in any event, inevitably those discoveries, which
would have been invaluable to him in support of his later campaign for
Copernicanism, escaped him completely.

Strangely enough, Kepler himself never tried to call Galileo's attention to these crucial discoveries. In his long letter from Prague on April 19, 1610 (an attempt to restore the contact which had been interrupted since 1597), he mentions that he has just finished his great work on the planet Mars, but does not say a word about the revolutionary results of his research.[25] This throws an interesting sidelight on Kepler's own sanguine personality. His letter was occasioned not so much by his own triumph as by the first news about Galileo's discoveries, especially that of Jupiter's four satellites. This fascinated him so much that he seems simply to have forgotten to mention what he himself had been occupied with during those twelve or more years of hard and exhausting labor.

Two further details of some significance may be mentioned from their early correspondence. In his second letter, dated Graz, October 13, 1597 (which was in reply to Galileo's one and only letter to him during the entire period), Kepler enthusiastically thanks Galileo for his friendly reception of his book, and then invites him to work together for the common goal, which is to spread the knowledge of Copernicanism and to win over the indifferent majority (Galileo's "fools"!).[26] He adds the amusing remark that in case this cannot be done by valid arguments, he would not hesitate to use fraudulent ones. It is a pity that nothing is known of Galileo's reaction to this. More important, however, is another point in the same letter. Not having the requisite instrument (a quadrant which would be accurate down to quarters of 1'), he asks Galileo to carry out repeated measurements of altitude of the pole star in upper and lower culmination, and of a certain star in the tail of the Great Bear at different times of the year, in order to find out whether there is a perceptible effect (he avoids using the term, 'parallax'), which he expects to be of the order of 1'–2', or even possibly as large as 10'–15'.

It is not known whether Galileo ever thought of carrying out this task. In his letter to Mazzone, he touches on this crucial question of parallax in rather vague terms. It was only after (and because of) his own great astronomical discoveries that he became keenly interested in it. In the *Dialogo*, he presents a lucid account of the entire subject, and shows that the effect to be expected is much smaller than had been so far believed and that the methods applied by earlier astronomers, especially by Tycho, are not capable of yielding reliable results.[27] This long and very clear discussion of parallax is a masterpiece. What precedes it, however, shows that Galileo is still not aware of (or rather perhaps is not concerned about) what others—even his revered teacher, Copernicus—have discovered. In demonstrating to Simplicio how, if one starts from a "reasonable" assumption, a rough estimate of the distance of the fixed stars can be made, Salviati attempts to relate the period of precession (which according to Ptolemy is 36,000 years) to the periods of revolution of the planets, for whose distances he accepts the Copernican values.[28] He then proceeds by way of simple proportions: since Saturn, being nine times as far from us as the sun, makes one revolution every thirty years, we obtain for the starry heavens a distance of 36,000 x 9/30 or 10,800 times the radius of the earth's orbit. He is thus assuming a simple proportionality between the distances and the times of revolution. But this is a gross oversimplification because it will give a different answer for the distance of the stars, depending on which planet is chosen for purposes of comparison. Galileo himself realizes this. Besides, this method, intrinsically inconsistent, is completely at variance, not only with that of the medieval astronomers, but also with that of Copernicus, and it shows Galileo's unawareness of Kepler's third law.

Ought we to blame him for this? Shall we hold it against him that even in his most mature astronomical work he takes no account of the most important theoretical discoveries, ones that would have furnished a much more adequate basis for the new system he was defending? The answer, I believe, is a matter of taste rather than of absolute standards. If we accept only the most exhaustive, or the best available, argument as a "good" one, our praise of Galileo will have to be severely qualified. But are such rigorous standards acceptable? The answer, it seems to me, has to be "no". A slip of logic may readily occur, if we judge a historical situation on the basis of our own knowledge instead of taking into account only the facts and arguments regarded as incontestable at the period under consideration.

Let us turn back to Kepler for a moment. After having shown that the orbit of Mars could not possibly be circular, he began to experiment with various types of oval curves. Having had to reject them all, he eventually was led to the ellipse and found that it fitted perfectly. However, he tells us explicitly that in dealing with the oval hypothesis, he bore in mind that Erasmus Reinhold, in his commentary on Peurbach's *Theoricae plane-tarum*,[29] had drawn an oval curve for the (geocentric) deferent of the center of Mercury's epicycle.[30] As I have demonstrated in an earlier paper,[31] this oval, resulting from Ptolemy's theory and traceable back to the Muslim astronomer Azarquiel (al-Zarqālī) of Toledo (eleventh century), is a rather complicated algebraic curve, which for an appropriately chosen ratio of its two parameters becomes practically identical with an ellipse. If Kepler, instead of experimenting with other ovals, had tried this "Ptolemaic" curve before a real stroke of genius led him to try the ellipse, he might well have contented himself with it, and it would then have been Newton's task to show that Kepler had succumbed to an unfortunate, though excusable, error. At the time of Kepler and Galileo, there would have been no stringent necessity to reject the Ptolemaic oval in favor of the ellipse, had both been under discussion. The only argument in favor of the elliptic solution would have been its greater simplicity, above all the circumstance that it assigns a "natural", i.e., an easily definable place to the sun, and moreover that the empty focus seems to function as the equant.

Even if Galileo had made a critical study of all of Kepler's findings, he would have been hard-pressed to estimate the validity of Kepler's arguments, where far-reaching neo-Platonic speculations about a universal harmony were combined with an ingenious mathematical analysis of the orbit of the planet Mars resulting in the revolutionary discovery of a new form of planetary motion, which then, by way of simple generalization, was elevated to the rank of a universal law of celestial kinematics. On the contrary, ever since his first telescopic discoveries (though not before then), Galileo had, with an almost fanatic zeal, pursued single-mindedly the goal of justifying Copernicanism. He wanted his demonstrations to be as simple as possible, so as to be understood by everybody willing to listen; he had to base them, therefore, on indisputable evidence. By referring to the revolutionary innovations of his German colleague, he would certainly not have promoted his cause; his arguments would have lost some of their persuasiveness, and another endless debate would inevitably have ensued.

Is it possible that Galileo, by the time he wrote the *Dialogo*, knew more about Kepler's discoveries than he wants us to believe? I hesitate to present this as a serious hypothesis, but am inclined to say that it cannot be wholly excluded. However this may be, the self-imposed limitation characteristic of genius is evident in the composition of his great work on the most fascinating and the most touchy subject of his time. Had this book been his only achievement, he would have been entitled to our highest admiration. But his fame rests on other pillars than this one alone.

NOTES

1. See W. Hartner and M. Schramm, "La notion de l'inertie chez Hipparque et Galilée", 1960*, esp. p. 128.

2. Emil Wohlwill, *Galilei und sein Kampf für die copernicanische Lehre*, Hamburg, 1909, vol. 1, pp. 229ff.

3. *Ibid.*, p. 238. E. Rosen has shown that in sixteenth-century Latin as well as in the vernacular languages of the day, only the term 'primus inventor' indicated absolute chronological priority ("Did Galileo claim he invented the telescope?", 1954*). It is true that Galileo apparently never claimed in clear words, to have been the *primus inventor* of the telescope. But is it thinkable that the Senate of Venice would have raised his salary to 1000 gold florins a year and granted him life tenure in his professorship if they were not convinced that he really was the *primus inventor?* Moreover, in the *Sidereus Nuncius*, he speaks of the *perspicillum a me excogitatum* (*Opere*, *3*, p. 60; Rosen, *op. cit.*, p. 305), which inevitably evokes the impression that he wished to represent himself as the first to have conceived the idea. Yet this expression could be considered appropriate only if he had invented a new type of telescope, different from others already in existence. But this was not the case, of course, nor could it have been intended by him. Thus there remains the question as to why he did not say less ambiguously: "*perspicillum a me confectum*".

4. Translated from the Latin, *Opere, 10*, p. 67f.

5. *Op. cit.*, p. 105ff.

6. *Opere, 1*, p. 304.

7. *Opere, 1*, pp. 299, 373; see Wohlwill, *op. cit.*, p. 106. This problem can be traced back to antiquity; see Simplicius' reference to Xenarchus in his commentary on the *De caelo* (*Simplicii in Aristotelis De caelo commentaria*, ed. by I. L. Heiberg, Berlin, 1894, pp. 50ff.)

8. *Opere, 2*, pp. 193–202. The letter was made accessible to some of his close friends, but was not printed until 1817; see Wohlwill, *op. cit.*, pp. 192ff., and 195n.

9. *Jacobi Mazzonii Caesenatis* . . . *de comparatione Platonis et Aristotelis liber primus*, Venice, 1597.

10. *Opere, 2*, pp. 203–255.

11. In the chapter, "Che la terra stia immobile", *ibid.*, p. 223.

12. *Ibid.*, pp. 253ff. It is true that at the time of composition of the first chapter of the *Astronomiae instauratae progymnasmata* (1588), even Tycho was not yet aware of this. But in the latter part of the work, he says it clearly (*Opera omnia*, ed. by J. L. E. Dreyer, Copenhagen, 1915, vol. 2, p. 253ff.). See Dreyer, *A history of astronomy from Thales to Kepler*, reprinted New York, 1953, p. 371.

13. See W. Hartner, "Tycho Brahe et Albumasar", in *La science au XVIe siècle*, Paris, 1960, pp. 135–150.

14. *Opera omnia, 3*, p. 111; see Hartner, *loc. cit.*, p. 141.

15. Wohlwill, *op. cit.*, vol. 1, p. 215, referring to *Opere, 2*, pp. 277–284.

16. The source of this number seems obscure. Most of the Muslim astronomers assume it to be about 20,000 terrestrial radii; see W. Hartner, "Mediaeval views on cosmic dimensions and Ptolemy's Kitāb al-Manshūrāt" in *Mélanges Alexandre Koyré*, Paris, 1964, vol. 1, pp. 254–282.

17. *Opera omnia, 4*, p. 422; see Hartner, *loc. cit.*, p. 139.

18. *Il saggiatore*, chap. 20. In translation in *The controversy on the comets*, 1960*, p. 233f.

19. *Opere, 10*, p. 79; see Wohlwill, *op. cit.*, p. 202.

20. Frankfurt am Main, 1625. See *Controversy on the comets*, pp. 337–355.

21. Section 14, *loc. cit.*, p. 350.

22. Section 1, *loc. cit.*, p. 339.

23. *Opere, 5*, pp. 297–305; see, in particular, p. 299.

24. Hartner, "Mediaeval views on cosmic dimensions"; see footnote 16. For the term, 'teorica', see O. Pedersen, "Theorica", in *Classica et mediaevalia*, 22, 1961, 151–166; for the instruments, see D. Price, *The equatorie of the planetis*, Cambridge, 1955.

25. *Opere, 10*, pp. 319ff. Printed separately under the title *Dissertatio cum Nuncio Sidereo*, Prague, 1610; see E. Rosen's model translation with commentary, "Kepler's conversation with Galileo's Sidereal Messenger", *The sources of science*, vol. 5, New York, 1965.

26. *Opere, 2*, pp. 69f.

27. *Dialogo*, pp. 369ff.

28. *Ibid.*, p. 365.

29. Peurbach's *Theoricae planetarum*, as well as most of his commentators, have this oval curve for the center of Mercury's deferent.

30. Footnote at end of chapter 46 of *Astronomia nova*, 1609, p. 221: "Figuram

huiusmodi habent libelli sphaerici et commentaria Reinholdi in theorias Pur-
bachii, in theoria Mercurii." Due to a simple slip, Max Caspar's model German
translation (*Neue Astronomie*, München, 1929) in this important passage has
'Mars' instead of 'Mercury': "Eine solche Figur enthalten die Schriften über
die Sphärik und die Kommentare von Reinhold zu Peuerbachs *Theoricae*, bei
der Theorie des Mars", p. 276.

31. W. Hartman, "The Mercury horoscope of Marcantonio Michiel of Venice",
in ed. A. Beer, *Vistas in astronomy*, *1*, 1955, 84–138; see esp. pp. 109–122.

10 ✸ The influence of the early development of optics on science and philosophy

VASCO RONCHI

For about thirty years I have been working on the history of optics, and in this essay I would like to summarize some quite surprising features of this history. We shall see that natural philosophy had a very odd effect on the beginnings of optics, and that the seventeenth-century flowering in optics had, in turn, an equally striking effect on other parts of science and of philosophy. The research in this area is by no means extensive, presumably because it involves a thorough competence in modern optics, an interest in history, and an ability to read the ancient optical texts—traits that rarely coexist in the same person.

The first lenses

When I first began work on my *History of light,*[1] I found that although a great deal of effort had been expended in tracing the elusive individual who built the first telescope (with results even still inconclusive), very little had been done on what one might call the "prehistory" of the telescope, a question of far greater intrinsic interest. And here, right away, a problem insistently presented itself. Although we do not know who first invented spectacle lenses, we *do* know with some exactness when they were first introduced: somewhere between 1280 and 1285. Yet the first telescope did not appear till around 1590. Why did it take three whole centuries to put one spectacle lens in front of another? That was all the first telescope did, using a cardboard tube as mounting. Nothing elaborate, one would say. Why, then, did not someone think it worthwhile long before? This is the *real* problem about the origins of the telescope. Was there something that *prevented* the telescope from being perfected much earlier and thus rather radically altered the "timing" of the history of science in general?

When I tried to discover what "theory" would have been put forward in the thirteenth century to account for the effects produced by lenses, I found an unexpected answer, one that some have refused to accept. But the answer I gave seems to have survived twenty years of criticism. The documentation in support of it I have collected in three volumes.[2] Here I can do no more than summarize the conclusions of that more detailed inquiry.

Around 1280, spectacle lenses were hit upon by some artisan in the course of his work with glass. Possibly a master glassblower noted, as he looked through a glass disc with curved face, that he could see nearby things clearly, as he had done in his youth. The cause of presbyopia was not known at that time, nor had the law of refraction even for a single plane interface been discovered. So that the behavior of a piece of glass with curved surfaces could in nowise have been predicted theoretically; certainly no one could have suspected that such an object could correct presbyopia. The discoverer must almost surely have been an artisan, then, very probably someone who could neither read nor write. So no record of the actual discovery was made.

These miraculous little discs must soon have become known to philosophers and mathematicians. The verdict that the optical science of the day would have led them to pass may seem peculiar to us. The purpose of sight is to discover the truth, they would have begun. These glass "lentils"[3] produce images that are larger or smaller then the real objects perceived by the unaided sense; the objects seem nearer or farther away than they really are; they have a halo of color, and are even upside-down at times. Hence they do not show the truth and cannot be relied on.

Philosophers and the sense of vision

The nature of vision had been discussed for almost fifteen centuries before this time, but it was tacitly admitted that it was not really understood. There were two official theories, neither of them satisfactory. One spoke of "visual rays", the other of "species" or "simulacra" given off by the body. In terms of either of these theories, lenses *altered* sight rather than improving it, so they could only have been considered misleading.

Thus philosophers and mathematicians paid them no heed; and they would have fallen into oblivion were it not for the artisans who, unworried by the quest for truth, saw in them good business.

Since the development of lenses was thus exclusively in the hands of craftsmen, few of them men of education, it is not surprising that over the next three centuries we find virtually no mention of lenses in the surviving literature. After a careful search, Edward Rosen was able to find only three references.[4] Guy de Chauliac, in his medical treatise *Chirurgia magna* (1363) recommended the use of *"ocularia vitri aut berillorum"*. Petrarch notes, in his *Letters to posterity* (c. 1365), that he had to have recourse to spectacles (*ocularia*) after the age of sixty. Franco Sacchetti (c. 1358) wrote a story in which one of the characters, a Prior of the republic of Florence, said that he could not see very well without his spectacles. And that is all. What an extraordinary silence, given the fact that spectacles were actually in use throughout these centuries!

This was no mere chance oversight. It fits in very well with what we know of the general attitude toward the reliability of vision at that time. Medieval philosophers distrusted the sense of vision, and *a fortiori*, optical devices of any sort. This seems strange to us today, but in fact there were good reasons for it in terms of the knowledge of that time. Despite claims to the contrary on the part of natural philosophers, the working of the sense of sight appeared an almost inscrutable mystery. Careful research had been done upon it, especially in order to correlate the data of sight with those of touch. It was discovered that "optical illusions" were quite frequent: the bent stick at a water surface, the mirror image apparently lying behind the mirror, the distorted image quite different from the real object, and so forth. It seemed to follow that the sense of sight could not be trusted and needed a corrective, the sense of touch. To be *sure* of something seen, one had to touch it. "Scientific knowledge [*scientia*] cannot be attained by sight alone" was a common maxim.

The disdain of the philosophers for the artisans' lenses was thus part of a pattern. Touch did not confirm the images presented by lenses, so these are nothing more than deceptive illusions. The repercussions of this negative attitude to visual data were very great in science generally. Vision is by far our most powerful sense, as far as science is concerned. To have rejected it in this way was a philosophic error of enormous proportions, delaying for centuries the development of an adequate empirical method, dependent as this latter would be both upon direct visual observation and upon various optical devices. The correcting of this error was thus a matter of great moment for science. The story of how it happened ought to be crucial to any account of the early development of science, but in point of fact, it is rarely alluded to, and when alluded to, is usually misrepresented. This is mainly due to the fact that the mentality of today is wholly different; it is forgotten that a fundamental change was needed to bring about the acceptance of visual observation.

Della Porta's *Magia naturalis* and Kepler's optics

The first printed book in which lenses were mentioned was the *Magia naturalis* of Giovan Battista Della Porta.[5] This was not a work of science, as such, but rather a collection of "natural magics", that is, odd and interesting physical and chemical effects. The first edition (1558) contained four "books" (really chapters), and was such a success that it ran into many new editions and was translated into the major European languages, as well as Arabic. The author added new "books" to the new editions; by the time the 1589 edition appeared, there were twenty "books" in all. The seventeenth dealt with optical "magics", including lenses. To have discussed lenses in a book of such wide diffusion was enormously effective in ending the long conspiracy of silence. And Della Porta did not hesitate to say of lenses that "such is their effect, they are altogether necessary for human life, though until now no one has discussed their effects or brought reasons to explain them". This was a strong accusation against the world of science. Della Porta could afford to attack this world because he did not belong to it, and did not fear retaliation from academic scientists. His taunt must nevertheless have been noted in many quarters.

Leaving aside the interesting detail on lenses of the *Magia naturalis*, we can turn to a later work by Della Porta, his *De refractione* (1593). The eighth of its nine books is devoted to lenses, and it was the first attempt to provide a theory of their working. The author made use of the "visual rays" and "species" of ancient science; he claimed that he could account in this way for the behavior of lenses. In actual fact, however, it was manifest from his own discussion that the effects produced by lenses could *not* be explained in terms of medieval optics, and that since these effects had been established three centuries before, a new optics would have to be found.

The man responsible for this new optics was Kepler, who in 1604 published his *Paralipomena ad vitellionem* where he provided the first adequate theory of vision, substantially the same as the one we still have. He also laid the foundations of a new geometrical optics, and applied it to explain for the first time the images produced by plane mirrors. This book marked a real turning-point in the history of science. Some of the ideas in it had been proposed before (by Francesco Maurolico, for instance), but on the whole it was an entirely new synthesis and a masterful one. When it first appeared, it was scarcely noticed, so revolutionary were its methods and principles. It took many decades before the new approach to optics it advocated became accepted. Kepler's book demolished the old theories of "visual rays" and "species". But it mentioned lenses only in a brief and accurate account of how converging lenses can correct presbyopia, and diverging lenses, myopia. No general theory of lenses was given; Kepler still did not take them seriously as proper optical systems, presumably influenced by the centuries-old distrust in their regard.

The artisans of Middelburg

But in 1604, something occurred that would in time change all this. Some artisans of Middelburg in Holland began to construct simple optical systems, in which a divergent eyepiece and a convergent object lens combined to produce a modest magnification. They put these telescopes (for telescopes they were, although they were still called simply "spectacles", *ocularia*) on the market as novelties. According to documents discovered by de Waard, these telescopes were modeled on a specimen brought from Italy and dated 1590. It seems likely that the 1590 original was inspired by a phrase in the 1589 *Magia naturalis* which could have been interpreted as a vague direction for the use of divergent eyepieces (although this almost certainly was not what Della Porta meant). And it was quite possibly brought to Middelburg when a number of Italian artisans emigrated there around 1600 to set up a factory for the manufacture of glass. In any event, telescopes came on the market in 1604, but excited very little interest. Scientists regarded them as illusionary devices: if one lens could not be believed, *a fortiori*, the effects of two could give no real knowledge. By 1608, the new *ocularia* were in the show windows of all the optical shops in Paris, and were advertised as bringing distant objects close and magnified. But the public did not regard the devices as anything more than toys, and they did not have any great commercial success.

Apart from the reluctance on the part of philosophers to take such instruments seriously, there was also a technical reason why they did not succeed. Spectacle-makers put their telescopes together by using two standard spectacle lenses; the lens for myopia served as eyepiece and that for presbyopia as objective. But spectacle lenses are simply not good enough to make an adequate telescope; this is still true today. To make a telescope, one must use special optical glass, accurately worked and very carefully annealed, using techniques that are not at all necessary for spectacle lenses. This, of course, was not known in 1604, so that the telescopes produced by the spectacle-makers were of poor quality. The best magnification they could give was by a factor of three; beyond that the images were cloudy and useless. So low a magnification is of very little use, and to make matters worse, the telescopes were carelessly made so that the images were poor. So they had no success either with scientists or the general public.

Galileo

This situation changed radically a few years later when a man of science entered who usually *did* change situations radically. Galileo was at the time teaching astronomy and mechanics in Padua. He had never been interested in optics; the center of his concern was the Copernican question, the great question for all astronomers of his day. During the spring of 1609, he heard a rumor that north of the Alps people were using an instrument with which one could see distant things magnified and clear. At first he paid little attention. But at the beginning of July, a blinding intuition came to him. Just suppose the new instrument could tell more of how things *really* are in the skies! It matters little whether he constructed his first telescope on the basis of a theoretical reasoning (as he was later to claim), or whether he copied it directly from a specimen given to him. By 1609, the telescope had already been in existence for twenty years, and had been on the market for five years. So there can be no question of his having invented it.

The important point is not this, but what Galileo *did* with his telescope. He realized that a telescope was quite useless if the image it produced were not a clear one. But if the image were true, the telescope would be of inestimable importance (as he wrote to the Doge of Venice in August). He was the first man of science to see this. And so he gave himself over entirely to the construction of telescopes, not using the lenses of the spectacle-makers, but rather utilizing his own glass and working the lenses himself with the aid of some "new artifices". Beginning with six magnifications, he soon worked up to thirty or even more. On one occasion, he made a telescope which (as he himself ruefully noted) he was never afterward able to equal. His glassworking and telescope construction were not guided by theory but simply by technical "hunches". He used a method of selection, eliminating all the poorer products. He mentions in passing in a letter that only 6 percent of the telescopes he constructed were usable for his purposes.

A telescope producing good images and magnifying thirty times was in a basic sense a quite different instrument than one which gave a blurred image and magnified only three times. The public was aware of the difference (though not of the cause of it), and called the new instrument a "Galilean telescope", the name it still bears. When Galileo turned this formidable new means of observation on the skies, he was quite sure in advance that he would see things the unaided eye could never reveal. Throughout the autumn of 1609, he worked almost every night, becoming more and more excited about what he was seeing. Finally, in the second week of 1610, he saw the four satellites of Jupiter, the most dramatic disproof that one could wish of the Aristotelian view that the earth is at the center of all astronomical motions. To his mind, this was by far the most important of his telescopic discoveries, which may seem odd to us until we remember that for thousands of years astronomy and even medicine had made much of the axiom that the independently movable heavenly bodies were just seven in number. Now all at once, here were four more!

Realizing the far-reaching significance of what he had seen, Galileo wrote an account of it in the *Sidereus nuncius*, the "heavenly messenger" who comes to tell men some of the wonders of the skies. As soon as the little book appeared (March 10, 1610), a storm broke around Galileo's head. The first reaction of the academic world was to reject his incredible claims, not just because of their altogether unexpected nature but also because they had been made by means of a *telescope!* He was accused of naïveté: did not everyone know that the telescope was no more than an illusionary toy? There was no other evidence for these celestial wonders than the evidence of the telescope. So how could they be believed? Some critics even accused Galileo of bad faith, of a dishonest attempt to gain publicity.

Galileo did not answer these accusations, partly no doubt because he knew very little optics and thus had no direct way of countering his opponents' arguments. But he continued to make telescopes, and to use them to scan the skies for fresh wonders. He was quite sure that he was not being deceived. But how to convince his colleagues? Since one had to have a *good* telescope to see what he had seen, he resolved to send telescopes of his own making to leading astronomers, so that they would not test his words by means of the useless toys of the spectacle-makers. But then a difficulty arose: the majority of the natural philosophers simply did not think it worthwhile even to *look* through his telescopes, since their theoretical *a priori* against its reliability was so strong.

He overcame this obstacle by a clever political move: he named the satellites of Jupiter the "Medicean planets" after his patron, the Grand Duke of Tuscany. This was not the simple play for a patron's favor that at first sight it may seem to be. He intended by it to proclaim to scientists everywhere his absolute conviction of the existence of the four satellites, and thus of the reliability of the telescope, the only means of observing them. Since he was at this time moving to Florence, and accepting an appointment as the Grand Duke's "Mathematician", it would have been the height of folly to commit his patron's name to the satellites unless he was quite certain they would not turn out to be the illusions that everyone else first thought them to be. He also persuaded the Grand Duke to send telescopes as presents to other sovereigns. Most of these rulers had an official "Mathematician" acting as counselor in matters scientific. The "Mathematician" would thus be asked by his master to give an opinion on the new and much-talked-of instrument, and thus he would be forced to test it, whether he wanted to or not.

All through 1610, the battle went on between Galileo, standing at the beginning more or less alone, and the entire learned world: unshakeable faith versus what appeared to be a justified skepticism. Victory ultimately went to Galileo, of course, but it did not come easily or quickly. As always in such cases, the older professors could not be budged: the Galilean novelties ran counter to the habits of thought of a lifetime. It was the young, with no prejudices to be overcome, who became the protagonists of the new astronomy.

The most vociferous of Galileo's opponents was probably Francesco Sizi, a Florentine, whose *Dianoia astronomica, optica, physica* appeared in

1611.[6] He was a second-rate and relatively unknown scholar, but his work echoed the views of the faculties at the Universities of Pisa and Perugia. His book is historically a very interesting one because it contains all the arguments from the older optical science against the serious employment of the telescope, presented in an impressive and logical array. The author ends the work with an expression of his conviction that the ancient science would prevail. But today it is forgotten.

Kepler and Galileo's telescope

Perhaps the most interesting reaction was that of Kepler. As soon as Galileo's sensational pamphlet appeared, scholars from all over Europe wrote to Kepler, already the best-known theoretical optician and astronomer of the day, asking for his opinion of the new discoveries. For a time, he gave no reply; despite his competence in optics, he concurred with the entrenched skepticism of his colleagues concerning the lenses. He tried on his own to make a good telescope for astronomical uses, but without success. Eventually he answered the queries that had been sent him, but in a very noncommittal way, so that Galileo's opponents claimed him in their support.

But in August 1610, five months after the appearance of the *Sidereus nuncius*, the Elector of Cologne received the gift of a telescope from the Grand Duke of Tuscany, and passed it on to Kepler to test it out. Galileo's plan was working. On August 30, Kepler saw the satellites of Jupiter. He then checked the reliability of the telescope in a thorough and critical fashion. On September 11, he wrote a report of his tests, the *Narratio de observatis a se quatuor Jovis satellitibus erronibus* . . . , in which he threw the considerable weight of his prestige and authority unreservedly behind Galileo's claims for the "Medicean planets".

The first effects of this notable conversion to the new faith were seen when Kepler's *Dioptrice* appeared a few months later, in the early part of 1611. Here he extended to lens systems the optical theory developed in his *Paralipomena* of 1604, and gave essentially the same geometrical analysis of the action of lenses upon light that one finds in modern textbooks. The new optics was now safely launched and effectively publicized by the dispute over the *Sidereus nuncius*. Students began to read Kepler on optics instead of turning back to the ancients. The humber "lentils" of the spectacle-maker became the prized "lenses" of the physicist and astronomer. Thus the question posed at the beginning of my essay is answered: a theory of lenses was not only not established until centuries after lenses had come into common use, it was not even available when the telescope had already made some of its most important discoveries in the sky. It is not hard to see, then, why it took three centuries to do what today looks so simple: just to put one lens in front of another and take seriously what happens next. The error of the philosophers was a gross one in today's terms, but it was also a very natural and very human one. It is a pity that it has been so thoroughly forgotten, for it would have its lessons for the scientists of our own day.

The slow start of microscopy

Let us look at one more optical instrument before drawing the moral of our tale. The compound microscope was introduced in the early seventeenth century.[7] Galileo worked on it, as also did the Dutchman, Cornelius Drebbel. Antonius Van Leeuwenhoek made quite a number of them, and published the famous results that earned him the title of "father of microscopy". Yet it has been shown [8] that until G. B. Amici introduced a hemispherical object lens around 1840, the compound microscope was actually inferior to the ordinary "simple microscope", i.e., a single convex lens. So that throughout this entire period of two centuries, 1640–1840, when so much crucial work in microscopy was done, a simple convex lens sufficed to give the results desired. But if this be so, why did someone not use it for this purpose far earlier, since convex lenses were known from 1280 onwards?

But this question can be pushed even farther back. After all, the concave mirror was known in antiquity. It is discussed in the *Catoptrica* attributed to Euclid, and Ptolemy made an accurate study of the images it forms, following the principles of ancient optics.[9] It is quite clear that he had actually worked with such mirrors and had noted the magnification that they produce. Why, then, were these mirrors not used for the purposes of research? After all, they *were* the equivalent of microscopes, and could already have revealed some of the things that would cause a sensation nearly two thousand years later.

One man, Giovanni Rucellai, a Florentine patrician, cousin of Pope Leo X, did use such a mirror to examine the anatomy of a bee, and reported what he saw in a short poem in 1523. But that was almost a century before Galileo, yet no one else followed his lead. Why *did* no one else think this sort of thing worthwhile? The answer by now is familiar to the reader: images formed by lenses or mirrors cannot be confirmed by touch and are thus not worthy of truly "scientific" belief. For two thousand years, man had the microscope at his disposal, and was deterred from using it because his science told him that the knowledge it gave was worthless. So mighty is the *a priori* of prevailing scientific orthodoxy!

The new era

Microscopy could be taken seriously only after faith in optical instruments and, indeed, in observation itself, had been confirmed by Galileo's laborious and difficult victory over the skeptics. The year 1609 marks a quite fundamental turning-point in the history of science. Two leading men of science, first Galileo and then Kepler, declared in that year that truly scientific knowledge could be attained (and in certain areas could *only* be attained) by using an optical instrument. No longer, then, would the sense of touch be regarded as the touchstone—significant term!—of truth and reality. The effect was twofold: first, the sense of sight was rehabilitated after centuries of disrepute among men of science; second, and even more basic, it began to appear that man's senses are quite limited in their range, and that to gain a properly "scientific" knowledge of the world one has to extend the range of the senses by means of complex technical instrumentation. It is hardly necessary to add that both of these were quite fundamental to the seventeenth-century revolution in natural science which has so much changed our world.

But the relationship of the early history of science to the notion of visual observation is more complex than we have so far noted. The ordinary man, now as in prehistoric times, looks to the sense of sight for his most trustworthy evidence. He does not ordinarily question what he sees; his faith in it—of course, he would not call it "faith" since this might suggest a doubt—is unqualified. He is not unaware of optical illusions, but they are thought of as interesting oddities, not affecting the basic validity of our everyday seeing. As long as this attitude was generally shared, it would have been impossible to have any adequate natural science: men were too closely wed to the immediate order of the senses to accept something so contrary to common sense as the heliocentric hypothesis, for example. The sense of sight tells us that the sky is a dome above us and that the earth is at rest beneath us. A geocentric system is the only one admissible at this level of evidence.

The first philosophers of Greece changed all this. They noted that the senses can err, and that none of our sense-knowledge can really be taken for granted. In a very short while, the problem of knowledge became a quite central one for them; some were led to become skeptics about the prospects for human knowing generally; others (like Parmenides) distinguished between senses and reason and placed all their hopes in reason; others (like Plato) distinguished between the "appearances" of sense-knowledge and the reality of which these appearances are but imperfect images. It was only in a climate of opinion such as this that the speculations of a Philolaus (who suggested that the planetary system moves round a center other than the earth) and an Aristarchus (who thought that this center is the sun) were possible.

Once this move away from the commonsense order be countenanced, it becomes a matter of "saving the appearances" in the best way possible, and since the unaided sense cannot provide one with "appearances" stable and accurate enough even to be compared with one another, one must have recourse to measurement. This is already an extension of sense-knowledge, a new sort of knowledge which on the one hand relies on the overall validity of what the senses bring, and yet goes far beyond what sight and touch alone could tell without the aid of material contrivances. Whatever best accounts for the "appearances" is to be adopted as the best theory, even though it may run counter to some of the immediate convictions of sense.

The geocentric system of Aristotle was an attempt to stay as close as possible to the immediate deliverances of sense. Measurement played no role in the justification of its basic principles. As a result, it was almost useless from the point of view of accounting for those special "appearances", the mass of observational data that had been inherited from the Babylonians. It could not predict, and it was difficult to reconcile with even the simplest of heavenly "appearances", the periodic variations in planetary brightnesses. Ptolemy's much more complex geocentric theory with its cycles, epicycles and equants, as well as its complicated methods of computation, had a far greater success, and did actually account for the "appearances" to the degree of accuracy then attainable. Copernicus worked with essentially the same "appearances" and found he could "save" them theoretically in a far more satisfying way than Ptolemy had done. But it was only when Brahe had pushed up the level of accuracy of planetary observations in his powerful observatory at Uraniborg that both Ptolemy's and Copernicus' ways of saving the appearances had to be rejected, and the ellipse substituted for the hallowed circle.

How far we have got here from the simple observation of our ancestors who saw the stars move in great circles around their steady earth! The paradox is that the *beginnings* of astronomical science depended upon a *loss* of faith in the ultimacy of direct visual observation, whereas its successful continuation required some sort of critical rehabilitation of empirical observation in general, and of the sense of sight in particular. That Galileo, aided by Kepler, achieved this, is surely his basic contribution to the development of the powerful science we know. And the achievement itself was a quite crucial intersection between the histories of optics, of empirical science in general, and of philosophy.

NOTES

1. *Storia della luce*, Bologna, 1939. French transl. by Juliette Taton, 1956*.

2. *Galileo e il cannocchiale*, 1942*; *Il cannocchiale di Galileo e la scienza del Seicento*, 1958*; *Storia del cannocchiale*, 1964*.

3. The name 'lentil' was originally based on an analogy with the similarly shaped seed of a food plant popular in Italy. This choice of name again suggests the artisan origin of the "*lentilli*". The more academic term, '*specilli*', was introduced much later when scientists first began to take an interest.

4. See *The naming of the telescope*, 1947*, and the articles by Rosen on the telescope listed in the *Bibliografia Galileiana, 1940–1964*.

5. The anonymous English translation, *Natural magick*, made in 1658, has recently been reproduced (New York, 1957). See also the edition of Della Porta's *De telescopio* made by V. Ronchi and A. M. Naldoni in the *Atti Fondazione Giorgio Ronchi*, 1962*.

6. A translation of this work into Italian by Clelia Pighetti appeared in *Atti Fondazione Giorgio Ronchi* for 1964*.

7. See the essay by S. Bedini elsewhere in this volume.

8. By P. H. Van Cittert, Director of the Museum of the University of Utrecht, on the basis of a careful comparative study of the many early microscopes in the museum.

9. The authorship and date of the *Catoptrica* is debated; it may have been a compilation of earlier writings made by Theon of Alexandria in the fourth century A.D. Archimedes' treatise on mirrors is lost, but we do have Hero of Alexandria's *De speculis*, and a fragment of a work by Anthemius (sixth century A.D.) on "burning" mirrors, in which the properties of parabolic and elliptical reflecting surfaces are discussed. "Catoptrics" (as this part of optics was called) was thus quite well-developed. The basic axiom was that of minimum path for reflected rays, thus implying the equality of the angles of incidence and reflection. See M. R. Cohen and I. E. Drabkin, *A source book in Greek science,* Cambridge (Mass.), 1958, pp. 261ff.

II ☼ Galileo, Newton, and the divine order of the solar system

I. BERNARD COHEN

The divine origin of the order of the solar system

A powerful argument in favor of the Copernican system during the seventeenth century was that this system and no other showed the divine order. As Isaac Newton stated in 1713, in the final General Scholium written for the second edition of the *Principia:* "This most beautiful system of the Sun, planets, and comets, could only proceed from the counsel and dominion of an intelligent and powerful Being." [1] The system was, of course, Copernican, in which the "six primary planets are revolved about the sun" with motions having the same sense "and almost in the same plane", while "ten moons are revolved about the Earth, Jupiter and Saturn" with "the same direction of motion, and nearly in the planes of the orbits of those planets". For Newton, furthermore, the Copernican sys-

NOTE: An earlier version of this essay was published as a companion piece to Alexandre Koyré's "Newton, Galilée, et Platon", 1959*. Professor Koyré's essay has been published in an English translation in his volume of *Newtonian studies,* London, 1965, pp. 201–220. In its present form, my essay has been considerably revised and expanded, chiefly to incorporate new material concerning Newton and the Galileo-Plato problem, uncovered during research supported by a grant from the National Science Foundation.

tem was conceived with Kepler's modifications: these motions, therefore, take place along ellipses that are all but circles, and are such that a line from the sun to a primary planet, or from a primary planet to its secondary or moon, "may describe areas proportional to the times of description" while "the periodic times of the planets may obtain the sesquiplicate proportion of their distances". No wonder that Newton saw fit to exclaim that "it is not to be conceived that mere mechanical causes could give birth to so many regular motions". And he could write in that same General Scholium "concerning God: to discourse of whom from phaenomena does certainly belong to Experimental Philosophy".[2]

At the beginning of the Third (and final) Book of the *Principia*, Newton put a group of Phaenomena, of which the fifth states the regularity and order observable in the heliocentric system, but lacking in the geocentric:

PHAENOMENON V.
Then the primary planets, by radii drawn to the Earth, describe areas no wise proportional to the times; but that the areas which they describe by radii drawn to the Sun are proportional to the times of description.[3]

In the discussion of this statement, Newton directs our attention to yet a further regularity that appears in the heliocentric system but is absent from the geocentric: the fact that the motions of the planets with respect to the sun "are always direct", and "proceed with a motion nearly uniform, that is to say, a little swifter in the perihelion and little slower in the aphelion distances, so as to maintain an equality in the description of the areas". But with respect to the Earth, the planets move far from uniformly, and "they appear sometimes direct, sometimes stationary, nay, and sometimes retrograde".

Johannes Kepler, who discovered the regularities of the Copernican universe, had himself been dedicated to the discovery of a "divine order" in the universe. Thus he wanted to know why there were six planets in the Copernican system rather than the seven required by the Ptolemaic, finding the answer in the existence of only five regular solids which can be placed as separators between six planets but not seven. Just as the Copernican system eliminated the artificiality of retrograde loops by showing them to be merely the effects of observing the planets from a moving earth, so Kepler introduced yet another simplicity by eliminating circles moving on circles, replacing them by elliptical orbits. Furthermore, he reduced the apparently irregular variations in the planets' orbital speeds to the regularity of the Law of Areas. But by far the most significant step Kepler took toward showing a "divine order" in the heavens was his discovery of the Harmonic Law, relating the period of revolution of each planet to its average distance from the Sun. Here was, indeed, the divine plan to which every system of bodies revolving about a central body must conform. How great must have been Kepler's joy to discover that an identical harmonic law obtains for Jupiter's satellite system! [4]

Galileo nowhere referred to Kepler's Law of Areas or to his Harmonic Law, and so cannot be counted among those who saw the signs of a divine order in those particular mathematical relations.[5] In the Third Day of the *Dialogo*, however, he does try to show not only that the Copernican system has advantages over the Ptolemaic (in permitting, for example, a more natural and simpler explanation of apparent retrograde motion), but he is even willing to have Salviati say to Simplicio: "In the Ptolemaic hypothesis there are the diseases, and in the Copernican their cure." [6] Galileo's brief for the Copernican system is too well-known to require any extended discussion here. And so I shall rather concentrate on the "divine order", on Galileo's story of how God created the universe according to number and measure. Curiously enough, Galileo does not put this story directly into the speeches of Sagredo or Salviati, or claim the invention of it for himself; rather he has Salviati attribute it to Plato. In the very paragraph in which the reference to Plato occurs, there is a sentence reading: "A sublime concept and worthy indeed of Plato, which I remember having heard discussed by our friend, the Lincean Academician." [7] Surely Galileo has introduced this particular form of reference to himself so as to declare overtly that he is a Platonist, that he is a member of the Academy of his day just as Plato was in his own. The constant reference to himself in the pages of both the *Dialogo* and *Discorsi* as "our Academician" can only be interpreted, it seems to me, as further evidence of Alexandre Koyré's thesis that Galileo identified himself with what he thought was Platonism, something akin to Pythagoreanism, and that this point of view illuminates Galileo's own concept of the role of experience (or experiment) in scientific thought.[8]

The "Galileo-Plato problem"

The Galileo-Plato problem concerns a mode of creating the solar system introduced by Galileo in the *Dialogo* under the guise of a suggestion by Plato. It shows us how enmeshed he still was in the old dynamics, and to what degree he was under the spell of what Professor Koyré has rightly called "la hantise de circularité". Galileo begins by stating that the planets were "for a certain time set in motion by their maker". Every body, furthermore, "has a natural tendency toward some particular place" and "will be continually accelerating", during the time that it moves toward "its goal". God started the world "at the beginning" by giving to each planet "a straight and accelerated motion", so that starting from rest it would gradually attain the particular velocity he intended to confer upon it. When that velocity had been attained, God converted that straight-line motion into a circular motion at the very same speed: a circular motion "to be kept perpetually uniform forever after"—i.e., a "circular motion whose speed thereafter was naturally uniform". Such a "natural" circular motion of planets exemplifies what has been called Galileo's doctrine of "circular inertia", the view that a circular motion may continue forever without the perpetual agency of a force. Indeed, soon after the first presentation, Galileo returns to this subject, following a discussion of how

> motion in a horizontal line which is tilted neither up nor down is circular
> motion about the center; therefore circular motion is never acquired natu-
> rally without straight motion to precede it; but, being once acquired, it will
> continue perpetually with uniform velocity.[9]

According to Galileo's presentation, not only was each planet put into its orbit by being dropped and then acted upon so as to have its rectilinear motion altered to a circular motion with the same speed, but all of the planets were so dropped from one and the same place! Hence the divine order may be discovered by relating the dimensions of the planetary orbits to the speeds of the planets; this will show the existence of a single place from which the planets can be let fall so as to reach their orbits with linear speeds equal to their respective orbital speeds. And I have called this the Galileo-Plato "problem" because as a matter of fact there is no place in the universe from which the planets, being let fall, will arrive at their orbits with their respective orbital speeds.[10] Furthermore, despite Galileo's attribution to Plato of this mode of creating the solar system, there is no Platonic text in which this story occurs. As a matter of fact, despite rather exhaustive study by scholars for three hundred years, no one has found any text whatever of any author prior to Galileo which contains information about such a dropping of planets.[11]

There are other interesting aspects of this Galileo-Plato problem. For instance, what principles of dynamics did Galileo intend his reader to apply? Clearly that the acceleration of bodies falling over great distances is constant and is the same for all bodies, just as is the case near the surface of the earth. We shall see that Newton's attack on the problem was based on a very different presupposition, that the acceleration (like the force) varies inversely as the square of the distance from the center of the attracting body. Galileo introduced what we have called the Galileo-Plato problem twice during the First Day of the *Dialogo*. But it was not then left aside by its author, for it appears again even more majestically in a discussion of "sublimity" in the Fourth Day of the great *Discorsi*. There, Sagredo points out "the beautiful agreement between this thought of the Author [i.e., of Galileo himself] and the views of Plato concerning the origin of the various uniform speeds with which the heavenly bodies revolve". After a description of the "conception [which] is truly worthy of Plato", Galileo has Salviati remark that "our Author (to whom this idea of Plato was not unknown)" had said "that he had once made the computation and found a satisfactory correspondence with observation". Details of this computation are not given, but the remark is made that "if any one desires such information he can obtain it for himself from the theory set forth in the present treatment".[12]

In the earlier book, the *Dialogo*, Galileo had been a little more positive.

Taking "from the most skilful astronomers the sizes of the orbits in which the planets revolve, and likewise the times of their revolutions", he first used the data concerning Saturn to find "at what altitude and distance from the center of their revolutions must have been the place from which they originally departed". He then tried to see "whether Mars, descending from there to its orbit, is found to agree in size of orbit and velocity of motion with what is found by calculation", and finally did the same for the Earth, Venus and Mercury, "the size of whose orbits and the velocities of whose motions agree so closely with those given by the computations that the matter is truly wonderful".[13]

What shall we make of the above account? Galileo has allowed Salviati to ask how far from the sun would the place have been where these globes were created and let fall, and then whether indeed they could all have been so created in one and the same place. To this purely rhetorical question Salviati replies by sketching out a method of making the computation, but he gives no numerical answer. He does not say, for example, that the planets were all dropped from a point twenty times as far away from the sun as Saturn. Nor does he even give a rough idea of where the point in question may be. Sagredo, however, is permitted to say that "if I did not believe that making these calculations accurately would be a long and painful task, and perhaps one too difficult for me to understand, I should ask to see them." Yes, says Salviati in reply, "the procedure is indeed long and difficult." Even more significant for us in our attempt to understand this myth is Salviati's rather frank admission, ". . . besides, I am not sure I could reconstruct it offhand. Therefore we shall keep it for another time." Are we to infer from this statement that Galileo was actually unable to reconstruct his own previous calculations? It certainly looks like it. Perhaps he had not even made the calculations, but had merely observed that the orbital speeds of planets increase for planets nearer and nearer to the sun and had simply assumed that there must exist some such relation as the one he presented as the invention of Plato. In any event, if he had actually made any such calculations, he must have committed an error; no wonder he could not "reconstruct" the procedure either when writing the *Dialogo* or later when returning to this topic in the *Discorsi*.

It is generally known that the Galileo-Plato problem appears in the correspondence between Isaac Newton and Richard Bentley during the early 1690's, when the latter was putting the finishing touches to his Boyle Lecture.[14] In those letters, Newton refers to certain propositions in Book One of the *Principia*, which had been published some half a dozen years previously.[15] Yet, so far as I know, nobody has pointed out that Newton himself had dealt with problems similar to those raised by Galileo and that in fact Book Three of the *Principia* contains propositions detailing supposed conditions of falling astronomical bodies, including comets and planetary satellites, in relation to their orbital speeds. Furthermore, I shall show that this particular problem so interested Newton that at one time he intended to add a scholium concerning it to the second edition of the *Principia*.[16] It is, furthermore, the subject of a discussion by Newton's friend and disciple, David Gregory, in the preface to his *Elements of astronomy*, which is in good part based on an unpublished essay written by Newton himself.[17]

In what follows, I have analyzed the Galileo-Plato problem from the differing points of view of a number of possible assumptions. The gathering together of this evidence shows that Galileo could not have made the calculations he said he did—unless we are willing to assume that he must have made rather incredible mistakes in arithmetic. Next I have analyzed in modern terms the dynamics both of Galileo's presentation of the fall of the planets and of Newton's rejection of the Galilean argument and his substitution for it of a variation of his own invention. This contrast is of special interest to the historian of ideas insofar as it reveals to us the enormous gulf separating these two great men of science of the seventeenth century.

Invalidity of Galileo's claim

In order to examine the possible validity of the Galilean argument, let us make a translation into modern mathematical language of the conditions he has set forth.[18] Let $a_1, a_2, a_3, \ldots$ be the average distances of the planets from the sun and $T_1, T_2, T_3, \ldots$ the periodic times of revolution of the planets about the sun, so that (considering the planetary orbits as circles) the speed of any planet $V_n = 2\pi a_n / T_n$. Let D be the distance from the sun to P, the point from which all the planets are let fall to their respective orbits. As each planet falls with constant acceleration g from P (starting from rest) through a distance $D - a_n$, it must be the case that

$$V_n^2 = 2g(D - a_n) \tag{1}$$

or

$$\left(\frac{2\pi a_n}{T_n}\right)^2 = 2g(D - a_n) \tag{2}$$

$$\frac{4\pi^2 a_n^2}{T_n^2} = 2g(D - a_n) \tag{3}$$

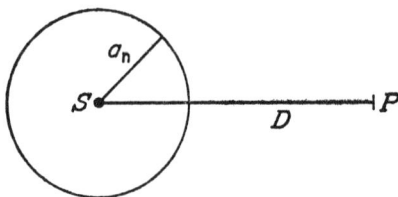

Figure 11–1

But, setting $a_n^3 / T_n^2 = K$, where K is Kepler's constant,

$$4\pi^2 K = 2g a_n(D - a_n) \tag{4}$$

$$D a_n - a_n^2 = \frac{4\pi^2 K}{2g} \tag{5}$$

Thus, Galileo's supposition implies that $D a_n - a_n^2$ is a constant. Consider the case of any two planets, say Mercury and Venus, for which the average distances from the sun are a_1 and a_2; then, according to equation (5),

$$D a_1 - a_1^2 = D a_2 - a_2^2 \tag{6}$$

so that

$$D a_1 - D a_2 = a_1^2 - a_2^2 \tag{7}$$

$$D(a_1 - a_2) = (a_1 + a_2)(a_1 - a_2) \tag{8}$$

and, since $a_1 \neq a_2$ or $a_1 - a_2 \neq 0$,

$$D = a_1 + a_2 \tag{9}$$

Plainly this result is absurd. The average distances of Mercury and Venus from the sun are respectively 0.4 and 0.7 A.U., as was known to Copernicus and to Galileo. Thus equation (9) tells us that the distance from point P to the sun is 1.1 A.U., which is a little more than the radius of the earth's orbit, whereas by definition the point P must lie outside of the orbit of Saturn. Or, a simple computation shows that there are no two pairs of planetary distances from the sun which can be added together to give the same distance D according to the form of equation (9). Thus by a *reductio ad absurdum* we have shown that the original set of assumptions was not true: there is no single point from which all the planets could be let fall from rest toward the sun with the same uniform acceleration so as to arrive at their respective orbits with speeds of the magnitude of their observed orbital speeds.

In this presentation I have, of course, introduced Kepler's third or harmonic law, which seems not to have been known to Galileo.[19] This anachronistic procedure is wholly justifiable, however, since the third law is a quite accurate representation of the relation among planetary data as known to Galileo and other Copernicans. Our use of the third law to simplify the equations does not imply, therefore, any knowledge of this law on the part of Galileo. Going back to equation (3), we see that the Galilean conditions imply that D may have the same value for any pair of planetary values, as a_n, T_n, where

$$D = \frac{2\pi^2 a_n^2}{g T_n^2} + a_n \tag{10}$$

Direct calculation, using the values a_n, T_n for any two planets, shows that for constant g there is no possibility that D is a constant. Since such a calculation was easily within Galileo's powers as a mathematician, one can only conclude that he never really worked out the problem at all. In Galileo's day, the absolute values of the distances of the planets from the sun were not yet known. Nevertheless, Copernicus himself had computed both the relative mean distances (or the distances in terms of the astronomical unit) of planets from the sun and their sidereal periods. It is thus certain, as Dr. Nakayama—author of the most recent study of this topic —points out, "that Galileo, an enthusiastic Copernican, should have been in a position to use these data for his own calculations".

The foregoing argument has been based on the supposition that from one and the same point P all the planets are let fall in a straight line toward the sun, with one and the same constant acceleration g,[20] and that when they reach their respective distances from the sun $(a_1, a_2, a_3, \ldots)$ they have attained their proper orbital speeds. Newton does not indicate in his letters to Bentley how he computed the error of Galileo's argument. He merely says: "there is no common place from whence all the planets being let fall, and descending with uniform and equal gravities (as Galileo supposes) would at their arrival ("to their several orbs") acquire their several velocities, with which they now revolve in them." [21] He also presumably showed the impossibility of Galileo's assumptions by proving that they lead to results incompatible with Kepler's third law.

Other recent analyses of Galileo's position

Two other modern scholars who have studied this presentation of Galileo's have in somewhat different fashions proceeded in the same way. Thus Paul Mansion in 1894 stated that Galileo's assumptions were equivalent to the equation:

$$a_1 + m\frac{a_1^2}{T_1^2} = a_2 + m\frac{a_2^2}{T_2^2} \tag{11}$$

where, as before, a_1 and a_2 are the distances of any pair of planets from the sun and m is a constant greater than zero.[22] Combining this equation with Kepler's third law,

$$\frac{a_1^3}{T_1^2} = \frac{a_2^3}{T_2^2} = K \tag{12}$$

or

$$\frac{a_1^2}{T_1^2} = \frac{K}{a_1} \text{ and } \frac{a_2^2}{T_2^2} = \frac{K}{a_2} \tag{13}$$

gives

$$a_1 + \frac{mK}{a_1} = a_2 + \frac{mK}{a_2} \tag{14}$$

$$a_1 - a_2 = mK\left(\frac{1}{a_2} - \frac{1}{a_1}\right) = mK\left(\frac{a_1 - a_2}{a_1 a_2}\right) \tag{15}$$

$$a_1 a_2 = mK \tag{16}$$

This result, that the product $a_1 a_2$ of any pair of sun-planet distances is equal to one and the same constant mK, is plainly absurd.

More recently, Professor S. Sambursky has examined this question again,[23] and concludes that Galileo's condition is equivalent to the statement that

$$V_n^2 \sim (D - a_n) \qquad (17)$$

This relation is contrasted by Professor Sambursky with "the correct relation following from Kepler's third law":

$$V_n^2 \sim \frac{1}{a_n} \qquad (18)$$

He calls attention to what may be a most significant aspect of his own formulation of the equations: "the fact that the orbital velocities of the planets increase with decreasing radius of the orbit is qualitatively described . . . by the wrong formula of Galileo." Since the relation, given in equation (1), between speed and distance for a body falling from rest with constant acceleration is easy to compute, it is certainly not beyond the bounds of all plausibility that in such a rough qualitative agreement Galileo might have believed he had found confirmation of the proposed mode of creating the world. Yet it is difficult to believe that Galileo would have been satisfied by so crude an approximation when he could easily have computed a more exact set of results by a method such as we have written in equation form (3 and 10).

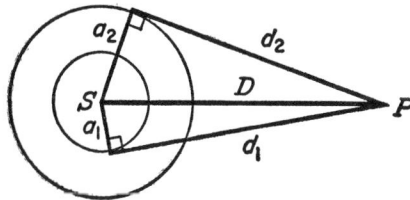

Figure 11-2

In his careful investigation of this problem, Mansion considered two further possibilities. In the first, we may suppose that all the planets do not fall toward the sun, but rather that each one drops along a tangent until it meets its proper orbit. Let d_n be the distance from P to the nth circle along a tangent. Then, since a tangent to a circle is perpendicular to the radius that meets it on the circle:

$$D^2 = a_1^2 + d_1^2 = a_2^2 + d_2^2 = \ldots \qquad (19)$$

If all planets still are assumed to fall with the same uniform acceleration g as before, and if $t_1, t_2 \ldots$ denote the times for planets to fall from P to their respective orbits:

$$d_1 = \tfrac{1}{2} g t_1^2 \quad \text{and} \quad d_2 = \tfrac{1}{2} g t_2^2 \tag{20}$$

$$V_1 = g t_1 \quad \text{and} \quad V_2 = g t_2 \tag{21}$$

$$2\pi a_1 = V_1 T_1 \quad \text{and} \quad 2\pi a_2 = V_2 T_2 \tag{22}$$

Thus, in general,

$$V_n^2 = g^2 t_n^2 \tag{23}$$

$$d_n = \tfrac{1}{2} \cdot \frac{V_n^2}{g} = \frac{2\pi^2 a_n^2}{g T_n^2} \tag{24}$$

and

$$D^2 = a_n^2 + \frac{4\pi^4}{g^2} \left(\frac{a_n^4}{T_n^4} \right) \tag{25}$$

Once again, we use Kepler's third law:

$$\frac{a_n^3}{T_n^2} = K \tag{26}$$

to get

$$D^2 = a_1^2 + \frac{4\pi^4 K^2}{g^2} \left(\frac{1}{a_1^2} \right) = a_2^2 + \frac{4\pi^4 K^2}{g^2} \left(\frac{1}{a_2^2} \right) \tag{27}$$

From this equation, one can get a relation which does not agree with the data of observation, as follows:

$$a_1^2 - a_2^2 = \frac{4\pi^4 K^2}{g^2} \left(\frac{1}{a_2^2} - \frac{1}{a_1^2} \right) \tag{28}$$

$$a_1^2 - a_2^2 = \frac{4\pi^4 K^2}{g^2} \left(\frac{a_1^2 - a_2^2}{a_1^2 \, a_2^2} \right) \tag{29}$$

Since $a_1^2 - a_2^2 \neq 0$, and since all quantities are positive:

$$a_1 a_2 = \frac{2\pi^2 K}{g} \tag{30}$$

There is clearly no single value to be obtained by multiplying by pairs the average distances of the planets from the sun.

Another way of seeing that this result contradicts the data is to substitute from equation (30):

$$a_2 = \frac{2\pi^2 K}{g} \left(\frac{1}{a_1} \right) \tag{31}$$

in equation (27):

$$D^2 = a_1^2 + \frac{4\pi^4 K^2}{g^2} \left(\frac{1}{a_1^2} \right) \tag{32}$$

which gives

$$D^2 = a_1^2 + a_2^2 \tag{33}$$

There can be no single value of D for which this equation is valid and hence no single point from which all the planets may be dropped according to the conditions of the problem.

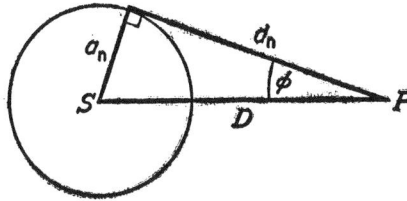

Figure 11-3

Finally, suppose that each planet falls along a tangent from P to its orbit as in the preceding case, but that as a result its acceleration is not g, but the component (along the tangent) of an acceleration g directed from P to the sun S. Then the acceleration of any planet will be $g \cos \varphi = g d_n/D$. The laws of motion now give:

$$d_n = \tfrac{1}{2}g \left(\frac{d_n}{D}\right) t_n^2 \qquad (34)$$

or

$$t_n = \sqrt{\frac{2D}{g}} \qquad (35)$$

which means that all times t_n for planets to fall from the sun to their respective orbits are equal, that is, $t_1 = t_2 = t_3 = \ldots = t$, and the speed V_n of any planet therefore is given by

$$V_n = g \, (\cos \varphi_n)t = g \left(\frac{d_n}{D}\right) t \qquad (36)$$

which is the same as saying that the speed V_n is proportional to the distance of fall along the tangent d_n. Thus, for any two planets:

$$\frac{V_1}{V_2} = \frac{d_1}{d_2} \text{ and } \frac{V_1 T_1}{V_2 T_2} = \frac{d_1 T_1}{d_2 T_2} \qquad (37)$$

But

$$2\pi \, a_1 = V_1 T_1 \text{ and } 2\pi \, a_2 = V_2 T_2 \qquad (38)$$

so that:

$$\frac{a_1}{a_2} = \frac{d_1 T_1}{d_2 T_2} \text{ and } \frac{a_1^2}{a_2^2} = \frac{d_1^2 T_1^2}{d_2^2 T_2^2} \qquad (39)$$

Introducing Kepler's third law in the form $T_1^2/T_2^2 = a_1^3/a_2^3$

$$\frac{a_1^2}{a_2^2} = \frac{d_1^2 a_1^3}{d_2^2 a_2^3} \qquad (40)$$

whence:

$$d_1^2 a_1 = d_2^2 a_2 \qquad (41)$$

But

$$d_1^2 = D^2 - a_1^2 \text{ and } d_2^2 = D^2 - a_2^2 \qquad (42)$$

so that, applying equation (41),

$$(D^2 - a_1^2)a_1 = (D^2 - a_2^2)a_2 \qquad (43)$$

gives:

$$D^2 = a_1^2 + a_1 a_2 + a_2^2 \qquad (44)$$

a relation which once again is incompatible with the data. There is thus no obvious way in which all the planets can fall from some fixed point P to their present orbits, being constantly subjected to a common uniform acceleration g, so as to arrive at those orbits with speeds such as are observed.

Newton's solution

Newton, after rejecting Galileo's results, points out that if each planet were to move in a straight line away from the sun, starting from its own orbit and with its own orbital speed (that is, only the direction being changed), the planet would move against the gravitational force until it came to rest at twice the distance from the sun in which it normally finds itself in its own orbit.

The simplest way to see the validity of Newton's statement is to use modern (post-Newtonian) methods, rather than to follow his own arguments in detail. Assume for the sake of simplicity that planets move in circular orbits, and that the difference between the center of the sun and the center of gravity of the solar system is so small as to be negligible. Then Newton's second law of motion is:

$$F_n = m_n A_n \qquad (45)$$

where $F_1, F_2, F_3, \ldots$ are the forces exerted by the sun on the several planets to produce in each an acceleration $A_1, A_2, A_3, \ldots$ Let $m_1, m_2, m_3, \ldots$ be the respective masses of the planets; $a_1, a_2, a_3, \ldots$ the respective distances of the planets from the sun; and let M be the mass of the sun. Then, equation (45) may be altered by substituting V_n^2 / a_n for A_n, where V_n^2 is the orbital speed, to give:

$$F_n = m_n \frac{4\pi^2 a_n^2}{a_n T_n^2} = \frac{4\pi^2 m_n}{a_n^2} \times \frac{a_n^3}{T_n^2} = 4\pi^2 K \frac{m_n}{a_n^2} \qquad (46)$$

Let us assume that the nth planet is made to stop its circular motion and move away from the sun in a straight line to some distance d_n from the sun. Then the planet will gain in potential energy by:

$$\Delta E = 4\pi^2 K m_n \left(\frac{1}{a_n} - \frac{1}{d_n}\right) \tag{47}$$

since this is the amount of work required to move the planet from its orbit to a new distance d_n from the sun. The conditions of the problem are that at the beginning of the displacement from its orbit the planet will have a linear velocity away from the sun equal in magnitude to its orbital velocity, and that after the planet has suffered a displacement away from the sun of magnitude $d_n - a_n$ its speed will be zero. Hence, in modern language, the gain in potential energy ΔE of equation (47) will be exactly balanced by a loss in kinetic energy $\Delta E'$. Now

$$\Delta E' = \frac{1}{2} m_n V_n^2 = \frac{1}{2} m_n \times \left(\frac{2\pi a_n}{T_n}\right)^2$$

$$= 2\pi^2 K m_n \left(\frac{1}{a_n}\right) \tag{48}$$

Equating the right-hand sides of equations (47) and (48), we obtain:

$$4\pi^2 K m_n \left(\frac{1}{a_n} - \frac{1}{d_n}\right) = 2\pi^2 K m_n \left(\frac{1}{a_n}\right) \tag{49}$$

$$2\left(\frac{1}{a_n} - \frac{1}{d_n}\right) = \frac{1}{a_n} \tag{50}$$

which gives:

$$d_n = 2a_n \tag{51}$$

This result corresponds with Newton's statement that if the "gravity" of each planet toward the sun is "of such a quantity as it really is", and if "the motions of the planets are turned upwards", then every planet "will ascend to twice its height from the sun", to a distance d_n from the sun just twice the radius a_n of its original orbit. Conversely, if the planets fall from rest under the gravitational attraction of the sun from a distance d_n $(= 2a_n)$ to their respective orbits, then the speed each will acquire must be equal to its observed orbital speed. This is a not uninteresting conclusion, but it is not the condition of the Galileo-Plato problem. According to Newton's condition, each planet is dropped from a different point, just twice its normal distance from the sun, whereas Galileo alleged that all planets might be let fall toward the sun from one and the same point.

Suppose next, as Newton suggests, that the "gravitating power" of the sun "be diminished by one half". In this case the gain in potential energy as the planet moves away from the sun from an original distance a_n to a new distance b_n will be just one half of what it was before, or:

$$\Delta E_1 = \frac{1}{2} 4\pi^2 K m_n \left(\frac{1}{a_n} - \frac{1}{b_n}\right) \tag{52}$$

which must once again be equal to the loss in kinetic energy given in equation (48), so that:

$$2\pi^2 Km_n\left(\frac{1}{a_n} - \frac{1}{b_n}\right) = 2\pi^2 Km_n\left(\frac{1}{a_n}\right) \tag{53}$$

an equation which does not hold for any finite value of b_n. To use Newton's words, the planets "will now ascend perpetually".

Consider now the motion of any planet to the next outermost orbit, for
example, planet 2 moving outward to the orbit of planet 3. It is supposed
that during this outward motion the "gravitating power" once again becomes one-half of its actual value. In this case the gain in potential energy
is:

$$\Delta E_1 = \frac{1}{2}4\pi^2 Km_2\left(\frac{1}{a_2} - \frac{1}{a_3}\right) \tag{54}$$

corresponding to a loss in kinetic energy:

$$\Delta E_1' = \frac{1}{2}m_2 V_2^2 - \frac{1}{2}m_2 V^2 \tag{55}$$

where V is the speed of planet 2 when it has reached the orbit normally
occupied by planet 3. Once again, we may equate the gain in potential
energy ΔE_1 and the loss in kinetic energy $\Delta E_1'$, so that:

$$2\pi^2 Km_2\left(\frac{1}{a_2} - \frac{1}{a_3}\right) = \frac{1}{2}m_2 V_2^2 - \frac{1}{2}m_2 V^2 \tag{56}$$

where, as before, the speed V_2 of planet 2 in its normal orbit is $2\pi a_2/T_2$
and the kinetic energy, according to equation (48), is $2\pi^2 Km_2(1/a_2)$; thus:

$$2\pi^2 K\left(\frac{1}{a_2} - \frac{1}{a_3}\right) = 2\pi^2 K\left(\frac{1}{a_2}\right) - \frac{1}{2}V^2 \tag{57}$$

$$\frac{1}{2}V^2 = 2\pi^2 K\left(\frac{1}{a_3}\right) \tag{58}$$

$$V^2 = 4\pi^2 K\left(\frac{1}{a_3}\right) \tag{59}$$

Let us restate this set of equations in words. Planet 2 is moving about
the sun normally in its own orbit at the proper orbital speed. Suddenly
the gravitational attraction of the sun is diminished by one-half, and planet
2 moves out from its orbit along a straight line directed away from the
sun; when it reaches the orbit normally occupied by planet 3, it will then
have a speed V equal to V_3, the speed regularly enjoyed by planet 3 in
its own orbit under normal conditions. To see why this is so, observe that
for the motion of planet 3 in its own orbit, according to equation (48),
the square of its normal orbital speed is:

$$V_3^2 = 4\pi^2 K\left(\frac{1}{a_3}\right) \tag{60}$$

and thus, from equation (59):

$$V = V_3 \tag{61}$$

The right-hand side of equation (59) is merely the expression for V_3, the normal speed of planet 3 as it moves in its own orbit.

In other words, let each planet be instantaneously turned so that it moves out away from the sun in a straight line with its normal orbital speed, but let it be assumed that the sun's gravitational force is exactly one-half of what it actually is. Then, as each planet reaches the orbit of any outer planet, it will have there a linear speed corresponding in magnitude exactly to the normal orbital speed of the planet that usually occupies that orbit. As Newton expressed it: "Mercury when he arrives at the orb of Venus, will be as swift as Venus; and he and Venus, when they arrive at the orb of the Earth, will be as swift as the earth; and so of the rest." Thus we may understand what Newton meant by these words: "if they begin all of them to ascend at once, and ascend in the same line, they will constantly in ascending become nearer and nearer together, and their motions will constantly approach to an equality, and become at length slower than any motion assignable."

The converse statement finally allows Newton to state the conditions under which the Galileo-Plato concept actually applies. Take a distance from the sun so great that the planets, ascending to it along the same line and under the previous conditions, beginning the ascent from their respective orbits "at once", will reach a condition in which they are "almost contiguous" and their motions "inconsiderably little".[24] At one and the same instant, let the motions of all these planets be reversed or, "which comes to the same thing", let the planets be "only deprived of their motions, and let fall at that time". Each planet would then arrive at its own orbit with its proper normal orbital velocity. If, as the planets reached their respective orbits, "their motions were then turned sideways, and at the same time the gravitating power of the sun doubled", so as to return to its usual strength, the planets would then all revolve in their orbits as we find them to do. But if the planets were turned sideways and the gravitational force were not doubled (that is, not converted to its normal strength), then this force would not "be strong enough to retain them in their orbs", and they would move out "into the highest heavens in parabolic lines".

Newton claimed in his letter to Bentley of January 17, 1692/3 that "the divine power is here required in a double respect, namely, to turn the descending motions of the falling planets into a side motion, and at the same time to double the attractive power of the sun". It is clear that the force of gravity alone could not put the planets into their observed motions about the sun, for which reason Newton said he was "compelled to ascribe the frame of this system to an intelligent agent".

As I mentioned earlier, Newton directed Bentley to four propositions of the *Principia*. He had just been describing briefly the conditions under which the planets might fall under the action of a diminished gravity, which would then have to be doubled as each planet would reach its own proper orbit, and he observed to Bentley: "But if the gravitating Power of the Sun was not doubled, they would go away from their Orbs into the highest Heavens in parabolical Lines. These things follow from my *Princ. Math.*, Lib. i., Prop. 33, 34, 36, 37." These four propositions occur in Section VII of Book One of the *Principia*, "Concerning the rectilinear ascent and descent of bodies", in which Newton considers motion in a straight line under various conditions of centripetal force directed to some point fixed in the line.[25] Propositions 32–37 deal with a force varying inversely as the square of the distance, while Proposition 38 deals with a force varying inversely as the distance and the final Proposition 39 deals with any centripetal force. In Propositions 33 and 34, the problem is to find the velocity of the given body at any designated place along the line, and in Propositions 36 and 37 the problem is to find the time of descent. In Proposition 33, Newton proves that the velocity at some point C, at a distance CB from the center of force, bears a specified relation to the motion along a given circle or rectangular hyperbola, and in Proposition 34 the results are extended to include motion along a parabola.[26] The only apparent connection of this pair of propositions with the Galileo-Plato problem, and its discussion by Newton in the correspondence with Bentley, is that the subject is the equivalence in magnitude of a straight-line motion and some motion along a circle (or hyperbola or parabola) under the action of a force inversely proportional to the square of the distance. In the first edition of the *Principia*, Proposition 34 has no corollaries and Proposition 33 has but one, in which a certain proportionality is given when two specified points coincide. But in the second edition (1713), Newton has added a second corollary to Proposition 33: "a body revolving in any circle at a given distance from the centre, by its motion converted upwards, will ascend to double its distance from the centre." This is the result embodied in our equation (57) above, and its introduction into the second edition of the *Principia* is thus one of the direct results of the discussion of the Galileo-Plato problem in the Newton-Bentley correspondence.

In the *Principia* Newton did not use considerations of potential or kinetic energy in dealing with the motion of a body under a variable force. Generally speaking, energy and work are not part of the dynamics of Newton except in certain special cases, e.g., the action of simple machines. Newton, therefore, had need of recourse to a wholly different method than that which I have introduced for heuristic purposes. A single example will show how Newton's application of geometric insights in combination with his doctrine of limits enabled him to solve the problem of a body falling through distances so great that the force cannot be considered constant.

In Proposition 32 of Book One of the *Principia* (Case 1) Newton supposes "that the centripetal force is inversely proportional to the square of the distance of the places from the centre". He states as the problem, "to define the spaces which a body, falling directly, describes in given times". He begins by recalling to the reader that, if the body does not fall in a straight line toward the center of force, it will "describe some conic section whose focus is placed in the centre of force". Let us suppose that S is that focus and center of force, and that the conic section is the ellipse *ARPB*. (See Fig. 11-4.) On the major axis *AB* of the ellipse describe a circle *ADB*, and draw the line *CPD* through the point *P* (the point at which the body may be found on the ellipse at any given time), perpendicular to *AB*; then draw the lines *SP, SD*, and *BD*. According to Kepler's second Law, the area *ASP* will be proportional to the time. But, since an ellipse is an affine transformation of a circle whose diameter is the major axis of the ellipse, the area *ASD* will be proportional to the area *ASP* "and therefore also proportional to the time".

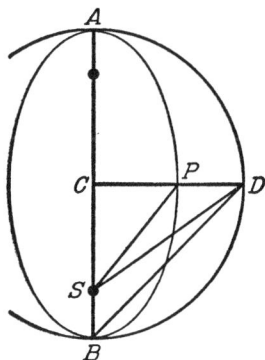

Figure 11-4

Now, keeping the axis *AB* fixed, "let the breadth of the ellipse be continually diminished, and the area *ASD* will always remain proportional to the time". Proceeding to the limit, when that breadth is "diminished *in infinitum*", the orbit *APB* will coincide with the axis *AB*, and the focus *S* with the point *B*; now "the body will descend in the right line *AC*, and the area *ABD* will become proportional to the time". Therefore, the way to find "the space *AC* . . . which the body describes in a given time by its perpendicular fall from the place *A*" (under the action of an inverse-square force centered at *B*) is to take a point *D* (on the circle whose diameter is *AB*) such that the area *ABD* is proportional to the time; then from *D* to draw a perpendicular to *AB*, meeting *AB* at *C*. This is the construction for the ellipse; in Case 2 and Case 3 Newton gives a similar solution for the hyperbola and the parabola.

Newton's ingenious solution has one flaw. For once the body has reached the point *B*, it should then continue to move out along the line *AB* extended to a point *A'*, were *A'B = AB*; then, the body should come to rest, be attracted back again to B and move out to A, and so oscillate between the two points A and A'. But Newton's solution, considering the line AB to be the limit of an ellipse of constantly diminished breadth, would require the body to turn around at B and move out to A rather than following the extension of AB to A', a result which is physically absurd. Hence, we must add a restriction to Newton's solution: it is valid only during the descent from A to B.

There are at least three other places in his *Principia* in which Newton presents problems similar to those we have been discussing. One of these, occurring toward the end of Book Three, is related to the Galileo-Plato problem although it is quite different in appearance. This one occurs in Lemma XI, immediately preceding Proposition 41, on the determination of the orbit of a comet moving in a parabola, from three observations. According to the conditions of this Lemma XI, a "comet void of all motion" is let fall toward the sun from a certain specified height and is "impell'd to the sun by the same force, uniformly continued, by which it was impell'd at first". This problem is essentially the Galilean one because, unlike Corollary 2 to Proposition 33 of Book I, the force is uniform and the acceleration is therefore constant.

Also related to the Galileo-Plato problem is a pair of references at the beginning of Book III to the falling of satellites to planets. One of these occurs in the discussion of Proposition 4. We are to "imagine the Moon, deprived of all motion, to be let go, so as to descend towards the Earth with the impulse of all that force by which . . . it is retained in its orb . . ." Another occurs two theorems later, in Proposition 6: "these satellites, if supposed to fall *toward Jupiter* from equal heights, would describe equal spaces in equal times, in like manner as heavy bodies do on our Earth. And by the same argument, if the circumsolar Planets were supposed to be let fall at equal distances from the Sun, they would, in their descent toward the Sun, describe equal spaces in equal times."

Galileo and Newton

In Newton's own interleaved copy of the first edition of the *Principia*, there are MS notes concerning Plato's supposed method of creating the solar system and of Galileo's presentation of this problem. In the course of these notes, Newton writes: "Galilaeus hoc refert ad gravitatem qua corpora illa primo motu recto accelerato caderent dein flecterentur in gyrum." [27] A set of additional notes on the Plato-Galileo problem are to be found in a collection of MSS in Newton's hand that once belonged to David Gregory, and are now in the library of the Royal Society of London. These are part of a large collection including not merely Newton's discussions of the views of ancient philosophers and scientists, but some planned additions (in the 1690's) to the *Principia*, in which many of the early theorems of Book III were to have new scholia containing rather extensive extracts from Lucretius,[28] and quotations from (or citations of)

Greek and Latin authors. Much of this material had been copied out by
Gregory and a generous portion, partially revised, was printed by Gregory under his own name in the *Praefatio* to his *Astronomiae physicae et
geometricae elementa* (printed at Oxford in 1702).[20] In Newton's MS
pages there occurs a note with a long verbatim extract from the Latin
edition of Galileo's *Dialogo* which is, so far as I know, the only extract
from a book of Galileo's in Newton's hand. It is reprinted below, along-
side the relevant lines from page 17 of Galileo's *Systema cosmicum* in the
London edition of 1663, which was certainly available to Newton during
the 1690's. Newton had in his personal library a copy of the Latin edition
of the *Dialogo* printed in Leyden in 1699, bound up with a uniform Latin
edition of the *Discorsi*, published in the same year, and the first Latin
version of that work to be published.[30]

Newton's MS Note	Extract from Galileo's *Systema cosmicum* (1663).
Quinetiam Plato in eandem sententiam concessisse videtur. Hic enim [Galilaeus in Syst. cosm. sub initio] statuit corpora mundana, etiam tum cum jam fabricata et omnino stabilita essent aliquandiu motu recto agitata fuisse sed postquam ad certa determinataque loca pervenissent paulatim in gyrum revolvi coepisse motu recto commutato cum circulari in quo postea perstiterunt: et Galilaeus hoc refert ad gravitatem qua corpora illa primum motu recto accelerato caderent dein flecterentur in gyrum.[31]	Nisi tamen cum Platone statuere malimus, corpora mundana etiam tum, cum jam fabricata & omnino stabilita essent, aliquandiu, sic ordinante Conditore, motu recto agitata fuisse; sed postquam ad certa determinataque loca pervenissent, paulatim in gyrum revolvi coepisse, motu recto commutato cum jam fabricata & omnino stabilita runt, semperque persistunt.

It will be seen that, except for the omission of the phrase, '*sic ordinante
conditore*', Newton has faithfully copied out that portion of the above
extract beginning with the words, '*corpora mundana*'.

In comparing Galileo's and Newton's approaches to this problem, one
may observe the enormous gulf between the work of these two men.[32] Galileo did not question the assumption that different planets falling from the
same distant point would have the same acceleration *and* that this acceleration would be constant. The situation was thus taken to resemble the falling to the earth of nearby objects of different weight, all having the identical uniform acceleration, as Galileo had shown. But from the point of
view of dynamics, such a simple kinematic model is wholly unsatisfactory.
The gravitational force on the planets varies in direct proportion to the
planetary masses, it is true, a result which may be combined with the
second law of motion to render the acceleration of the planets (as they fall
from some distant point) independent of the individual masses of each
planet. But the acceleration of each planet is not uniform; it varies inversely as the square of the distance of the planet from the sun.

When Newton wrote his letters to Bentley, he changed the conditions of the Galileo-Plato problem by assuming that the acceleration is not uniform, but must vary as the inverse square of the distance. What is the significance of this change of the primary conditions? In an article written in 1959, Professor Koyré—in an aside—explored the significance of Newton's statement to Bentley:

> As for the Passage of Plato, there is no common Place from whence all the Planets being let fall, and descending with uniform and equal Gravities (as Galileo supposes) would at their Arrival to their several orbs acquire their several Velocities, with which they now revolve in them.[33]

Professor Koyré maintained that "Newton had never *studied* Galileo. And that if he had read Galileo's works in his youth, he had in the meanwhile forgotten what is to be found therein." [34] This conclusion was based on the argument that Newton must have used "a later adaptation and actually a misinterpretation" of the authentic "Galilean theory of falling bodies", because in his subsequent analysis of the Galileo-Plato problem, he postulated (contrary to Galileo) that the acceleration of the falling planets is *not* uniform.

But I believe another interpretation is possible. When Newton analyzed the case where the planets move directly outwards from the sun to double their normal distance, it is quite likely that he realized that he was making use in his analysis of a dynamic theory very different from Galileo's, namely one where the attractive force varies with distance from the sun, with a consequent variation in acceleration of free fall toward the sun. Immediately following the sentence just quoted, we find Newton saying:

> If we suppose the Gravity of all the Planets towards the sun to be of such a Quantity as it really is, and that the Motions of the Planets are turned upwards, every Planet will ascend to twice its Height from the Sun . . . and then by falling down again from the Places to which they ascended, they will arrive again at their several Orbs with the same Velocities they had at first, and with which they now revolve.[35]

Does not this sound as if Newton were deliberately juxtaposing two very different theories of falling bodies? The first is that the planets will be "descending with uniform and equal Gravities (as Galileo supposes)"; while the second is that "we suppose the Gravity of all the Planets towards the Sun to be of such a Quantity as it really is", i.e. varying inversely as the square of the distance. I suggest that Newton is dismissing the law of fall that "Galileo supposes", and is doing so not only because Galileo has supposed an incorrect law of nature, but also because this supposition does not lead to the conclusion that Galileo alleges it does. In the 1690's, Newton could have learned the authentic Galilean theory of fall by reading the Latin *Systema cosmicum* from which we have seen him copy out an extract, or from Blondel's *L'Art de jeter les bombes*,[36] which he cited in one of his letters to Bentley and in which he could have found a rather good résumé of Galileo's theory of falling bodies and of projectile motion. We would nevertheless tend to agree with Professor Koyré's general conclusion concerning the lack of importance of Galileo's writings in the development of Newton's thought. For there is only the barest of direct reference to Galileo in Newton's student notes and these appear to be to the *Dialogo*. I have found no evidence that Newton had ever read the *Discorsi* at all, at least prior to 1700.[73]

Newtonian dynamics was based securely on the principle that every accelerated motion requires the continuous action of a force. Hence, the fact that uniform circular motion (and elliptical motion according to Kepler's laws) is accelerated implies the existence of a sun-emanating planetary force. But Galileo, still enmeshed in the older point of view, did not concern himself with celestial dynamics. No better instance could, therefore, be found to illustrate the progress of physical thought in the seventeenth century than the juxtaposition of Newton's dynamical treatment of the solar system and Galileo's simple and unquestioning statement that once the planets were turned into circular orbits at the proper speed they would continue to have a motion in those orbits "perpetually uniform forever after".

NOTES

1. Unless there is a specific indication to the contrary, all of the quotations from Newton's *Principia* are taken from Andrew Motte's translation (London, 1729), rather than the somewhat modernized version of that translation made by Florian Cajori. The latter is now available from the University of California Press as a two-volume paperback, while the pre-Cajori Motte translation has also been printed as a paperback by the Citadel Press (New York, 1964). For a discussion of the differences between these two versions, see I. B. Cohen, "Pemberton's translation of Newton's *Principia*, with notes on Motte's translation", *Isis*, *54*, 1963, 319–351.

2. In the second edition (1713) in which this concluding General Scholium was first published, Newton wrote: "Et haec de Deo; de quo utique ex phaenomenis disserere, ad philosophiam experimentalem pertinet." But in the third and last edition, Newton altered this sentence so that it concluded: ". . . ad philosophiam naturalem pertinet". Although Motte usually used the word 'phenomena' to render the Graeco-Latin '*phaenomena*', in this case he made a rather more literal translation reading: "And thus much concerning God; to discourse of whom from the appearances of things, does certainly belong to Natural Philosophy."

3. In the first edition (1687), these *Phaenomena* and the antecedent *Regulae Philosophandi* were part of a section of *Hypotheses;* and *Phaenomenon V* was *Hypothesis* VIII. The complete details and significance of the changes in this part of the *Principia* are discussed in I. B. Cohen, *Franklin and Newton*, 1956, pp. 131ff., and in A. Koyré, "Les 'Regulae Philosophandi'", *Arch. intern. d'hist. sciences*, *13*, 1960, 3–14, and "L'hypothèse et l'expérience chez Newton",

Bull. Soc. Franç. Philos., *50*, 1956, 59–79, both of which are reprinted in *Newtonian studies* (*op. cit.*).

4. For Kepler's views on order and necessity in the universe see A. Koyré, *La révolution astronomique*, 1961*, pt. II: "Kepler et l'astronomie nouvelle"; I. B. Cohen, *The birth of a new physics*, 1959*, pp. 136–145; Arthur Koestler, *The Watershed*, 1960*; Max Caspar, *Kepler*, 1959*.

5. There seems to be no question about Galileo's ignorance of Kepler's Third or Harmonic Law of planetary motion. Yet it has been shown that Galileo must certainly have known Kepler's first two laws (elliptical orbits, and the law of areas); see Erwin Panofsky, "Galileo as a critic of the arts", 1956*, p. 10.

6. *Dialogo*, p. 341.

7. *Dialogo*, p. 20.

8. On this point see A. Koyré, "Galileo and Plato", 1943*.

9. *Dialogo*, p. 28.

10. At least according to any reasonable interpretation of Galileo's presumed initial conditions, and either by using Galilean principles (that the acceleration of free fall is constant and uniform) or by using Newtonian principles (that the acceleration depends on the inverse square of the distance from the center of the attracting body).

11. Various attempts to find an author of this fable of the creation of the planetary system—all failures—are discussed by A. Koyré in "Galileo, Newton, and Plato", cited above.

12. *Discorsi*, p. 261.

13. *Dialogo*, p. 29.

14. Newton's four letters to Bentley, written at the end of the year 1692 and the early part of 1693 have been printed many times, first as *Four letters from Sir Isaac Newton to Doctor Bentley*, 1756*; this edition, together with the first printing of the two sermons given by Bentley: "A confutation of atheism from the origin and frame of the world", published in 1693, have been reprinted in facsimile, with an introduction by Perry Miller, in *Isaac Newton's papers and letters on natural philosophy*, ed. by I. B. Cohen, Cambridge, 1958. The letters are also available in A. Dyce's edition of the *Works of Bentley*; in S. Horsley's edition of Newton's *Opera*, vol. 4, pp. 427ff.; and have been printed in the *Correspondence of Isaac Newton*, ed. by H. W. Turnbull, vol. 3.

15. The first edition of Newton's *Principia* was published in 1687. A facsimile reprint was published in London in 1954.

16. Actually, as we shall see below, although Newton suppressed the intended scholium when the second edition was printed (1713), he did add a new corollary concerning one aspect of his analysis of the Galileo-Plato problem.

17. This is discussed at the end of the present essay.

18. This topic was explored in my graduate seminar in History of Science. I gladly acknowledge the assistance, insofar as Galileo's presentation is concerned, of my former student, Dr. Shigeru Nakayama. Dr. Nakayama has since published a study of his own on this topic: "Galileo and Newton's problem of world-formation", 1962*.

19. See footnote 5, *supra*.

20. From Galileo's texts, it is plain that in falling to its orbit each planet must have a uniform rectilinear acceleration, as is found to be the case in the motion of freely falling bodies on earth. Thus Galileo describes the motion of the falling planets as having "a natural and rectilinear acceleration such as governs the motion of terrestrial bodies", and also says that they "fall with naturally accelerated motion along a straight line" (*Discorsi*, p. 261), and partake of "the acceleration of natural motion" (*Dialogo*, p. 29).

21. Newton to Bentley, Cambridge, February 25, 1692/3, *Isaac Newton's papers* . . . , p. 306.

22. P. Mansion, "Sur une opinion de Galilée relative à l'origine commune des planètes", *Ann. Soc. Scient. Bruxelles*, *18*, 1893–1894, 46–49; 90–92. In a circular orbit of radius a_n with period T_n, a planet would have a velocity $V_n = 2\pi a_n / T_n$. If it falls to its orbit with constant acceleration g through a distance $D - a_n$, the equation of the motion is:

$$V^2 = 2g \ (D - a_n) \text{ which on substitution for } V_n \text{ gives}$$
$$a_n + (2\pi^2/g)(a_n^2/T_n^2) = D$$

Letting m stand for $2\pi^2/g$, we get:
$$a_1 + m \ (a_1^2/T_1^2) = a_2 + m \ (a_2^2/T_2^2.)$$

23. S. Sambursky, "Galileo's attempt at a cosmogony", 1962*.

24. The situation here is not identical with that assumed by Galileo: the planets are not considered to be at rest, nor to be at the same place, but rather moving as slowly, and being as near to each other as one wants. If they were at rest and let fall from the same place, at a *finite* distance from the sun, they would not arrive at their orbits at the same time.

25. The best summary available of the *Principia* is still that of W. W. Rouse Ball, *An essay on Newton's Principia*, London, 1893, chap. 6.

26. The other two propositions mentioned by Newton to Bentley (Props. 36 and 37) are associated with the Galileo-Plato problem only insofar as they deal with falling bodies, starting from rest, or bodies starting with a motion of projection upward or downward, and an associated motion along a circle or conic section. But since these two propositions are concerned with times of descent (or ascent), they are not really as closely related to the Galileo-Plato problem as is the first pair of propositions.

27. This copy of the *Principia* is at present in the Cambridge University Library, pressmarked: Adv. b. 39. 1. The full text of Newton's MS annotations will be printed in the critical edition of the *Principia* by the writer and Professor Koyré. The above-mentioned notes appear between pp. 112 and 113, toward the beginning of Book III.

28. Newton's use of Lucretius in planning a revised edition of the *Principia* is discussed by me in an article entitled "Quantum in se est—Newton's concept of inertia in relation to Descartes and Lucretius", *Notes . . . Royal Soc.*, *19*, 1964, 131–155.

29. In Gregory's English translation, *The elements of astronomy, physical and geometrical* (London, 1715, vol. 1, p. vii), the passage about Galileo and Plato reads as follows: "From some things mention'd by Diogenes Laertius, concerning Plato, which also are obscurely hinted at in his *Timaeus*, I am apt to

believe with Galileo, that the divine Philosopher suppos'd the Mundane Bodies, when they were first formed, were moved with a Rectilinear motion (by the means of Gravity), but after that they had arrived to some determined places, they began to revolve by degrees in a Curve, the Rectilinear Motion being chang'd into a Curvilinear one." There are three footnotes accompanying this sentence, of which the first is: "These at first were mov'd in a confus'd and irregular manner, but when they were duly adjusted and rightly settled, then the World was establish'd by God in just order and proportion. [*Diog. Laert. in Plat.*]" The second is: "He gave it a Motion altogether agreeable to its nature as a Body (that is a direct one) and a little further. Therefore he afterwards made it continue its course in a Circle. [*Plat. in Timaeus*]" The third is merely a reference to Galileo's statement, "in his Cosmical System". The possibility that Galileo might have been referring to Plato's *Timaeus* is discussed at the conclusion of Koyré's article cited earlier.

30. Since Newton copied out extracts from the *Dialogo* in Latin during the early 1690's, he must have used one of the three Latin editions printed before 1699. For a catalogue of Newton's library, see R. de Villami, *Newton the man*, London, 1931.

31. In Newton's interleaved copy of the *Principia* (see footnote 27 above), the paragraph referring to Plato begins: "Statuit Plato corpora mundana . . ." and is thereafter identical to the extract quoted above save for the use of *primo* for *primum* (". . . corpora illa primo motu recto . . .").

32. Lest the falling of planets appear to be only an idle historical curiosity, it should be pointed out that the Galileo-Plato problem is still part of the literature of modern mathematico-physical science. Thus, in a currently used manual of celestial mechanics (F. R. Moulton, *An introduction to celestial mechanics*, London, 1914, p. 150), the problem appears in the following new guise: Let an object move in an elliptical orbit under the action of an attractive force (varying as the inverse square of the distance) emanating from O, a focus of the ellipse. About O as center draw a circle of radius $2a$, the length of the major axis of the ellipse. Through any point P of the ellipse draw a line from O to the circle, meeting it at P'. Then the speed of the body at P is equal to the speed it would acquire in falling from P' along a straight line to P.

33. Letter III (according to the dates, it should be Letter IV), Horsley, *Opera omnia*, vol. 4, pp. 440ff.; Cohen, *Newton's papers*, pp. 306ff.; Newton, *Correspondence*, vol. 3, pp. 253ff.

34. *Newtonian studies*, p. 212.

35. For a more concise mathematical discussion than ours, see Newton, *Correspondence*, vol. 3, p. 256, nn. 5–8.

36. Newton, in his first mention of the Galileo-Plato problem, wrote to Bentley, "Blondel tells us some where in his book of Bombs that Plato affirms that ye motion of ye planets is such as if they had all of them been created by God in some region very remote from our systeme & let fall from thence towards ye Sun. . . ." Blondel, in his *L'Art de jetter les bombes* (Amsterdam, 1685, p. 199) presents this Platonic conceit as part of his summary of Galilean dynamics. Newton's failure to mention Galileo could, of course, have merely been an oversight, but it also can be taken as an indication that he had not read about the Galileo-Plato problem in either the *Dialogo* or the *Discorsi*, or that if he had done so he had by that time forgotten all about it.

37. Newton's youthful acquaintance with Galileo's *Dialogo* was established by John Herivel's identification of a reference to Galileo in one of Newton's college notebooks (C.U.L. Add. 3996, f. 121v). It is a reference to Thomas Salusbury's 1661 translation of the *Dialogo*. (See Newton, *Correspondence*, vol. 3, p. 52.) Two other sources of Galilean ideas available to the youthful Newton were identified by R. S. Westfall ("The foundations of Newton's philosophy of nature", *Brit. journ. hist. science, 1*, 1962, 171–182) as Walter Charleton's *Physiologia Epicuro-Gassendo-Charletoniana* (London, 1654), and Kenelm Digby's *Two treatises* (Paris, 1644). Of course, after 1673, Newton was in possession of Huygens' *Horologium oscillatorium* (Paris, 1673), of which "Pars secunda: De descensu Gravium & motu eorum in cycloide" was in part devoted to a rigorous and systematic presentation of certain major aspects of Galilean dynamics, in which Galileo is mentioned by name; see *Oeuvres complètes de Christiaan Huygens*, vol. 18, pp. 124ff., esp. p. 136n., and p. 141n.

I have explored Newton's knowledge of Galileo in three articles now in press: one for *Intern. Galileo Symp.* (Florence, 1964); one for *Saggi Galileiana* (Rome); and one for *Physis*. The conclusion to which I have been led is that prior to writing the *Principia* (1687), and apparently up to 1699 (when Galileo's *Discorsi* appeared for the first time in Latin), Newton seems never to have read Galileo's famous *Discorsi*, and thus must have learned what he did concerning Galilean dynamics from the English and later the Latin version of the *Dialogo*, and from various secondary sources (a term intended to include publications he had read, lectures to which he had listened, and conversations).

12 ❋ Galileo's place in the history of mathematics

CARL B. BOYER

The two "histories of mathematics"

George Sarton a generation ago wrote that: "the history of mathematics should be the kernel of the history of culture." Nevertheless, he realized that a history of culture with the history of science at its center, and with the history of mathematics as the core of the history of science, was virtually an unattainable ideal. He recognized that "mathematics, being far more esoteric then the other sciences, its history can only be told to a select group of initiates. . . . If the history of science is a secret history, then the history of mathematics is doubly secret, a secret within a secret." [1] There is in addition a difficulty not always recognized by historians: mathematics is not a science—at least not in the sense that it is based upon evidence derived through experience. The recognition of this fact was regarded by Bertrand Russell as one of the greatest discoveries of the nineteenth century. Nevertheless, it remains true, as Sarton wrote: "Take the mathematical developments out of the history of science, and you suppress the skeleton which supported and kept together all the rest." [2]

Sarton was not alone in realizing that "the history of mathematics is essentially different from the history of other sciences in its relationship with the history of science." Charles Singer also wrote: "in the history of scientific development, mathematics and the mathematical sciences stand somewhat apart from the other departments of knowledge." [3] Just as there has been a traditional distinction between those who create science and those who utilize the results of science, so too there must be a distinction between those who create mathematics and those who use the results of mathematics in the natural and social sciences. In the former case, we distinguish the two classes by calling one activity "science" and the other "technology"; in the latter case the best that current terminology has done for us is to label one activity "pure mathematics" and the other "applied mathematics". To the mathematician, the word 'mathematics' invariably implies the former, whereas to the nonmathematician it more often suggests the latter. In view of this semantic problem, we shall touch upon both aspects, although generally we shall have the former sense uppermost in mind.

Pure and applied mathematics obviously did not develop in isolation from each other, any more than did science and technology; but emphases have differed from age to age. Pre-Hellenic civilizations put the main stress on the utilization of mathematics, whereas the ancient Greeks emphasized theory and form, developing mathematics largely to satisfy the yearnings of the mind. Archimedes, the man whom Galileo admired above all others, did indeed make contributions to applied mathematics; but his best works, including the one on the spiral, in particular, concerned pure mathematics—and these were the ones he himself most valued. The mathematics of Archimedes was rigorous in the extreme, but it was difficult to follow because of the dependence of the Greeks on a geometrical algebra. Today a magnitude is thought of as something to which a real number can be assigned, but in Greek antiquity it was thought of as something which can be represented by a line segment, a view which may have been suggested by the discovery of incommensurable lines. Numbers were magnitudes, but magnitudes (it seemed) were not necessarily representable by numbers. During the long interval between Archimedes and Galileo, however, thinkers less careful than the Greeks developed a numerical algebra to replace geometrical algebra; and in Renaissance Europe, this took on an increasingly symbolic form, with special notations for operations and relationships. Even as early as the time of Regiomontanus, there had been some application of the new algebra to the solution of problems in geometry; and the application of algebra to geometry culminated in Descartes' work on analytic geometry, which appeared one year before Galileo's *Two new sciences*.

Concomitant with the development of algebraic geometry, coordinates came to be used in Latin Europe in a primitive graphical representation of variable magnitudes. These latter were known as "forms" and later as "functions". This use of coordinates, stemming from the late medieval period, seems not to have been influential in the rise of Cartesian geometry, but it did have an important place in the dynamics of Galileo. A student of mathematics today thinks of analytic geometry and the function concept as almost inseparable, but historically their origins were scarcely related, as a study of Galileo's work clearly shows. Descartes' geometry was essentially an outgrowth of pure mathematics, through a study of questions concerning geometrical constructibility, whereas the function concept was more directly related to problems in dynamics which first crystallized in medieval discussions of the "latitude of forms", concerning the application of geometry to the study of change. Galileo was involved only in the latter evolution, as we shall see.

Galileo's introduction to mathematics

When Galileo was a young man there were conflicting currents in mathematics, as in other fields. For one thing, there had been a revival of interest in all of the ancient classics, including those of the Greek geometers. The young Galileo was tremendously impressed by two ancient writers in particular: Euclid and Archimedes. The recovery of ancient works might be referred to as the "conservative" current in mathematics, and Italy took an active role in it. Early in the sixteenth century, however, Italy had also taken the lead in the introduction of Arabic algebra, a newer and more radical current in mathematics. This latter branch became increasingly symbolic throughout the later Renaissance and early modern period, and by the time Descartes' *Geometry* appeared, algebraic notations had become virtually those in use today. During this time, leadership in algebra passed from Italy to other countries, notably France and England; these were, indeed, the very years when Galileo was teaching at Pisa and Padua and writing at Florence. The nation which had more or less given birth to symbolic algebra thus abandoned the infant subject under Galileo's very eyes, as it were. Yet had they but known it, the future of mathematics was to belong to those who espoused the newer algebraic method, renamed "analysis" by Galileo's slightly older contemporary, François Viète.

Galileo's own apparent myopia in this regard may perhaps be explained by the circumstances surrounding his early education. He was preparing for medicine when he enrolled at the University of Pisa, and perhaps the new and barbarous algebra did not appeal to the curriculum-makers at his university, where little mathematics seems to have been taught. Yet elsewhere the sixteenth century produced a remarkably large number of physicians who made striking contributions to mathematics in general, and to algebra in particular—from Cardan in Italy to Recorde in England.[4] It appears that in any case Galileo learned his mathematics not so much through his university courses as through his own efforts, guided at times by a friend, Ostilio Ricci. It is said[5] that Ricci had once studied under Tartaglia, celebrated for his algebraic solution of the cubic equation; but if there is truth in this, any algebra which Ricci learned from Tartaglia evidently failed to reach Galileo. Ricci himself seems to have been attracted less to algebra than to practical geometry, his literary remains indicating special interest in applications to architecture and mechanics.[6] For some time he taught at a sort of polytechnic institute in Florence, one with required instruction in mathematics. Whether or not it was Ricci's fault, it is clear that Galileo was attracted less to pure than to applied mathematics. It has often been claimed that mathematics advances most rapidly when it is related to the world's work,[7] but history scarcely bears this out, and Galileo's case confirms the argument against such a thesis.

We are told that Galileo's father refused at first to have his son learn mathematics for fear of distraction, and that when he discovered that Ricci had been giving Galileo lessons in mathematics, he ordered the lessons discontinued.[8] The elder Galilei may have been correct about the distraction, for the son continued reading Euclid on his own, and he did not take a degree after completing his medical studies.[9] Upon returning home to Florence, Galileo evidently dropped the thought of medicine and took up reading Archimedes. Perhaps it was his unbounded enthusiasm for Euclid and Archimedes that blinded him to the possibilities in the algebraic techniques of his day; possibly it was the close relationship between algebra and computational devices which repelled him. Algebra already had been applied to problems in commerce, but it would—had Galileo but realized it—have been equally applicable in his "two new sciences".

It is of interest to note that Blaise Pascal, like Galileo, was at first prevented by his father from pursuing a mathematical bent, and that he, too, later hit upon and greatly admired Euclid; Pascal likewise had a blind spot when it came to algebra. However, he was obviously a mathematical prodigy, whereas Galileo was a "late-bloomer". Pascal had no mathematical disciples, but Galileo had two protégés, Evangelista Torricelli and Bonaventura Cavalieri, and they too showed a strong predilection for the methods of classical geometry. In science, Galileo was to a large extent responsible for a new spirit,[10] but when it came to mathematics he was a faithful follower of the tried and true, as found in Euclid and Archimedes.[11] His hesitancy to strike out in new paths may have been due to his late start in the field. He was almost twenty before he had had any substantial introduction to the subject—one in which it is notorious that the great discoveries are primarily the work of young men.[12]

Galileo has been hailed as "the greatest physicist, astronomer, and mathematician of Italy in his time, and one of the greatest in the world".[13] As physicist and astronomer, such a judgment is justified without difficulty; as a *mathematician*, at least in the modern sense of the word, one wonders if Galileo's reputation has been borrowed in part from his success in the other two fields. Here one runs into a semantic problem, for the word 'mathematics' has not been uniformly used throughout its history. When, for example, Galileo held the chair of "mathematics", first at Pisa from 1589 until 1592 and then at Padua from 1592 to 1610, his teaching duties presumably included much less of what we think of today as mathematics, and far more of practical applications. To Renaissance scholars, as to the ancient Greeks, the word 'mathematics' included *all* sciences related to number and magnitude. And where the ancient Greeks had thought primarily of the liberal arts, men of the sixteenth century looked with a far more favorable eye on the practical arts. John Dee in 1570 listed almost a score of practical subjects which might be part of "mathematics"—from anthropography to thaumaturgy, and from astronomy to trochilic (the study of combinations of circular motions).[14] Histories of mathematics written in the eighteenth century[15] devote about as much space to such subjects as mechanics, optics, and astronomy as to what today is thought of as mathematics. If, then, we interpret our title, 'Galileo's place in the history of mathematics', in the narrower sense, we are in a way being unfair to Galileo. Today we give him the threefold title, 'Astronomer, Physicist, Mathematician', but Galileo would have thought of the last as comprehending the first two as well. To cut off the first two from the last, as we are now doing, is to leave out of consideration the two branches in which he felt most at home and in which he was particularly eminent. Nevertheless, an analysis of Galileo as a mathematician in the narrower modern sense is not inappropriate for a commemorative volume. Galileo himself would indeed have frowned upon simple unbounded eulogy.

Compasses and computations

Had Galileo died before the age of forty—as did Regiomontanus before him and Torricelli after him—his name would today be but little remembered, for he had published nothing before the year 1606. Evidently he had been a successful teacher at Padua, for he was able to attract private students, even from foreign countries, and this augmented his income from his university salary. But it is likely that much of the teaching was on a relatively elementary level, and perhaps largely practical. His first publication in 1606, though it brought him publicity through controversy, was scarcely such as to establish a niche for him in the history of mathematics. It was a pamphlet entitled *Le operazioni del compasso geometrico et militare*.[16] This little work, his closest approach to a strictly mathematical book, represents an elementary contribution of limited originality; but (perhaps in virtue of Galileo's subsequent reputation) it sometimes is highly praised, a portion of it being the only piece by Galileo to be included in the *Source book in mathematics*.[17] The English translation is introduced with the remark: "Before the slide rule was invented or logarithms were known, he [Galileo] devised the simple but ingenious proportional compasses, or as he called them, the geometric and military compasses." [18] Such a statement leaves two unfortunate impressions: (1) that the device was an original invention by Galileo; and (2) that the device was comparable, in use and significance, with logarithms.

In reality, the proportional compasses were not strictly new. In particular, a description of such an instrument used by Jobst Bürgi was published in 1605, a year before Galileo's work. Another edition of the description of Bürgi's compasses appeared in 1607, the year after Galileo's book.[19] Galileo seems to have thought of his instrument by 1597, whereas Bürgi's version may date only from 1603; but then both men had been anticipated by Commandino, who thought of the device as early as 1568.[20] That Galileo was to some extent aware of the existence of rival instruments is indicated by his statement in the preface that he had striven for, and achieved, results which others, projecting similar instruments, had not thought of.[21] The mathematics behind the instrument is nothing more elaborate than the proportionality of the sides of similar triangles and rules for proportional parts in linear interpolation. Galileo's contribution to the instrument lay in the use of additional and more elaborate scales on the two arms of the instrument. His role was less that of a pure mathematician than that of a mathematical practitioner and entrepreneur concerned with the manufacture and sale of the instrument. There was no new theoretical element involved either in its construction or its application. The last sections of the book on the *compasso* are the routine methods for finding heights and distances of inaccessible towers familiar to students in trigonometry courses. The instrument could be used, of course, only where very crude approximations sufficed, quite unlike logarithms, which could attain any desired degree of accuracy. Artisans evidently did find use for the proportional compasses, inasmuch as Galileo seems to have sold them widely and to have been rather jealous of his rights in connection with the instrument. This is quite unlike his attitude toward copies of his early lectures on mechanics, for these apparently circulated rather freely among his associates.[22]

The *Compasso geometrico* cannot be said to have noticeably influenced the course of mathematical development; but neither can the work be regarded as a just indication of its author's level of achievement in mathematics. The book was largely a commercial venture appealing to practitioners who had need for simple computations. Yet Galileo himself seems to have been little attracted to the computational side of mathematics, and he was not *au courant* with new contributions in this field. Decimal fractional notations were being used by Viète, Stevin and Bürgi; but Galileo evidently took no interest in these. He was in general more concerned with accuracy in thought than with precision in measurement or computation, whether in physics or astronomy or mathematics. He did not have the temperament to commit himself to a life of computational drudgery, such as Kepler endured. But it was on the astronomy of Kepler that Newton later built his *Principia*.

During Galileo's life, there were striking developments in trigonometry, yet he seems to have been unaware of them. Trigonometry was becoming a branch of mathematics in its own right, instead of being merely a handmaid to astronomy. Galileo made no contribution to this development; he was satisfied with a few routine applications of those trigonometric functions which were needed in terrestrial and celestial mensuration. Sixteenth-century mathematicians had devised an effective trigonometric means of converting products and quotients to sums and differences, thus greatly easing the burdens of astronomers who were working with multiplace numbers. This method, known as "*prosthaphae-resis*", inspired both Napier and Bürgi in their independent invention of logarithms; but Galileo paid no attention, so far as we know, to this, the most striking mathematical discovery of the first part of the seventeenth century. Nevertheless, it was a protégé of his, Cavalieri, who is said to have introduced logarithms into Italy.[23] Today, logarithmic and trigono-metric functions are regarded as indispensable for the physicist; they are part of that mathematical language in which Galileo said so memorably that the Book of Nature is written. In his day, however, logarithms and the prosthaphaeretic formulas were thought of chiefly as clever means of easing the burden of computation, and with this Galileo had little to do. His disregard of the publications of Napier and Bürgi in the years from 1614 to 1620—years during which he was at the height of his reputation—may indicate that mathematics was but a poor third to astronomy and physics in his interests. The inner development of mathematics interested him far less than the thesis of its external applicability as the language of science; and it is possible that he might have left it aside entirely, as he had medicine, had it not been for this extrinsic interest.

Galileo as a "pure" mathematician

Galileo seems to have had but few books and to have read but little.[24] Even in the case of his favorite authors, Euclid and Archimedes, he was conspicuously eclectic. Those parts of the *Elements* which are concerned with the construction of roots of equations, the classification of incom-mensurable magnitudes, the derivation of theorems in number theory, the inscribing of regular solids within a sphere these attracted him little. When Kepler sent Galileo a copy of his *Mysterium cosmographicum*, in which planetary distances were related to the relative dimensions of the Platonic bodies, the latter was politely noncommittal about the scheme.[25] Much has been written about whether or not Galileo was a Platonist. It is perhaps of interest in this connection that Galileo showed least interest in those portions of Euclid's *Elements* which one thinks of as especially "Pla-tonic" in character. With respect to the works of Archimedes the distinc-tion is less clear, for the Syracusan's geometry comes closer to what one thinks of as applied—or better, *applicable*—mathematics. Nevertheless, some of Archimedes' most brilliant results were concerned with such im-practical things as angle-trisections and circle quadratures, and these did not interest Galileo. Nothing is easier, of course, than for an engineer to trisect an angle or to square a circle to any degree of accuracy desired. To limit the problems to the use of certain instruments only is, after all, a purely mathematical conceit; and with such purist attitudes Galileo seems to have had but little sympathy.

There is in Galileo's early work on motion, written perhaps during his days as a teacher of mathematics at Pisa, a chapter which clearly betrays the author's lack of close attention to the finer points of pure mathematics.[26] In the works of Aristotle, it is asserted that a circular motion can have no ratio to a rectilinear motion inasmuch as a straight line does not bear any ratio to a curve. Commentators had repeated the assertion that straight and curved are not comparable, until with Averroes it had become a dogma. Galileo castigated them as "far more inept in geometry even than Aristotle". Yet he himself thought to demolish the Aristotelian view simply by reference to *Elements*, Book V, definition 3: "Those magnitudes are said to have a ratio to one another which are capable, when multiplied, of exceeding one another",[27] and to Archimedes' theorem in the work *On spirals*,[28] in which a straight line is found which is equal in length to the circumference of a circle. As every physicist knows, Aristotle was in a sense correct: circular motion *is* different from rectilinear. And as every mathematician knows, Galileo was essentially correct in holding that a straight line *does* have a ratio to a curved line.

Yet both men miss the finer points in the comparisons of straight and curved which their contemporaries were worrying about. In the first place, there was as yet no definition of what is meant by the *length* of a curve—nor even of a prime prerequisite for that definition, *real number*. More importantly, in the ancient comparisons of straight and curved, the problem had been to construct with Euclidean tools alone a straight line equal to the circumference of a circle (or other given curve). If this is what Aristotle originally had in mind, he was right and Galileo was wrong. At all events, the Aristotelian statement had been taken by mathematicians of Galileo's time to mean that no algebraic curve could be rectified by Euclidean methods; Descartes went further and presumed that such a curve could not be rectified even in a broader algebraic sense. In the *Geometry* of 1637, he wrote:

> Geometry should not include lines that are like strings, in that they are sometimes straight and sometimes curved, since the ratios between straight and curved lines are not known, and I believe cannot be discovered by human minds, and therefore no conclusion based upon such ratios can be accepted as rigorous and exact.[29]

Descartes had explained earlier that by 'exact' he meant expressible through what we should call algebraic functions. Essentially, then, Descartes believed that the length of an algebraic curve is never expressible algebraically. This constituted at the time, then, a nice unsolved problem; but Galileo would clumsily cut the Gordian knot with a simple appeal to common sense:

> Who is so blind as not to see that, if there are two equal straight lines, one of which is then bent into a curve, that curve will be equal to the straight line?

Or if a circle moves over a straight line, who will doubt that in one revolution it traverses a straight line equal to its circumference?[30]

These statements would lead a mathematician of today to say that Descartes, while wrong, was a pure mathematician, whereas Galileo, although technically correct, lacked the finesse essential to the mathematical point of view. Descartes did not live to see his error, but at least he had stated the problem clearly. The question was taken up by many others; between 1657 and 1660 at least three mathematicians independently discovered that a segment of a semicubical parabola can indeed be rectified, not only in the Cartesian sense, but even with Euclidean instruments. Galileo was right—but only in part and for the wrong reasons, as Lindemann in 1882 showed when he proved that the circle cannot be rectified in either the Cartesian or the Euclidean sense. (The Archimedean rectification to which Galileo had referred was accomplished through the use of the spiral, a transcendental curve.)

The egregiously ingenuous phoronomic argument which the young Galileo had used against the Aristotelian tenet on rectifiability may have had unanticipated results. It may have been responsible for the fact that his protégé, Torricelli, many years after, discovered that a new spiral he was investigating—the logarithmic or equiangular spiral—could easily be rectified with compasses and straight-edge alone. From such results Pascal and others went on to generalizations of the ordinary spiral, studies which were influential in the rise of the calculus. Just how much inspiration the remarks of Galileo may have provided cannot be known with certainty, but it is clear that Galileo was not adequately aware of the importance of generalization in mathematics.

Be this as it may, it can still be plausibly argued that "if pure mathematics had attracted Galileo as strongly as its application to physics, he would have . . . founded the Fluxional Calculus".[31] But it did not, and the reason lies as much in Galileo's temperament, his restless energy and his gregarious habits, as anywhere else. He had no desire to shut himself up in the ivory tower of the research mathematician, he wanted a hand in the making of the world. Indeed, this may very well have been a factor in inducing him to forsake the relative academic calm of Padua for the marketplace of ideas that was Florence.

The rise of algebra

The increasing importance of algebra in the sixteenth century has already been noted. It was through this subject that the most striking generalizations developed. The spectacular mathematical triumphs of the sixteenth century were the algebraic solutions of the cubic and quartic by Tartaglia and Ferrari, published by Cardan in the *Ars magna* of 1545. Seeing that when all the roots of a cubic equation are real numbers, the formula of Tartaglia and Cardan involves square roots of negative num-

bers, Bombelli and others began toying with a generalization of the number
concept to include what became known, quite unjustifiably, as "imaginary" numbers. However, Bombelli had no followers in Italy; it was in
France that Viète, the leading mathematician of the time, through the use
of appropriate notations for parameters and for what we now call variables,
developed algebra into the study of magnitudes in general, a striking instance of the way in which mathematics has moved ever since in a process
of successive generalization. Viète also showed his ability for effective generalization in trigonometry. He saw that it could become far more than a
triangle-solving device; his union of trigonometry and analysis may be
taken as the inauguration of the goniometric or analytic approach which
today is emphasized in the teaching of mathematics. He was not a mathematician either by training or by profession, whereas Galileo was one at
least by profession; and yet it was Viète who, because of his emphasis upon
general formulations rather than special cases, was described by E. T. Bell
as "the first mathematician of his day to think occasionally as mathematicians habitually think today".[32]

Galileo appears to have lived through the stirring mathematical developments of his day without paying much attention to them. Part of the
explanation may lie in the fact that he was, as we have seen, largely self-
taught, a handicap that was accentuated by his limited acquaintance with
contemporary literature. Possibly he shared to some extent the humanist
aversion to Arabic algebra, for it is apparent that the then recent publications of the "classical" works of Euclid and Archimedes gave him a one-
sided view of mathematics. Even in his latest and most significant work,
the *Two new sciences* of 1638, Galileo adhered to a geometrical pattern
in mathematical reasoning, representing magnitudes as line segments
rather than as numbers. Where we today think of an arbitrary rational
ratio as a number m/n, Euclid and Galileo drew two line segments to
represent this ratio. It is customary to say of Newton's *Principia* that it
was composed in the language of synthetic geometry. But such an assertion is true only to a very limited extent, for there are many places in the
Principia where algebra and an analysis by infinite series are employed.
Galileo's *Two chief systems* and *Two new sciences*, however, were written in the manner of synthetic geometry, for they lack algebraic notations
and analytic methods.[33]

In astronomy and physics, Galileo's views were imaginative and transcended all national barriers; in mathematics, his ideas were conservative
and bound by local prejudices. Indeed, he was not always even aware of
local developments. Leibniz was later to assert that notation is half of
mathematics, and there are today those who hold that symbols are the
very essence of good thought. Galileo's mathematics, however, had not
progressed beyond Euclid's in its use of symbols, even though all around
him new notations were blossoming in Italy, like flowers in springtime.
That he did not contribute to the development of notations is all the more

striking in view of his complaint that the colloquial language of his time failed to contain the words needed in mathematics.[34]

Galileo had exceptional mathematical ability, but it showed itself episodically rather than in a treatise on some branch of mathematics. In this respect he differed from Viète, who laid out a program of books he planned to write. Galileo's relationship with mathematics was somewhat like that of Leonardo da Vinci: both were acutely aware of the importance of mathematics for physical science, but they rose only occasionally to flashes of brilliance in mathematical research itself. Like Leonardo, in his early years Galileo began a number of things, but finished little. In 1585 he was prompted by his reading of Archimedes and by correspondence with Guidobaldo del Monte to work on a treatise on centers of gravity, the results of which apparently contributed to his appointment to the chair of mathematics at Pisa a few years later; but the project was not completed and it was not published during his lifetime. At the very close of the *Two new sciences,* published more than fifty years later, Galileo attributed the nonappearance of this work to the fact that Luca Valerio had achieved more extensive results. Whether or not this was the real reason may be questioned, since Valerio's *De centro gravitatis* appeared only in 1604. It may once again be recalled that for the first forty years of his life—those years when "pure" mathematicians are wont to make their name—Galileo had published nothing.

Cycloids and calculus

In many ways, Galileo was typically a Renaissance man, and for him as for the humanists it was true that *nihil humanum mihi alienum est.* Whatever he saw interested him, frequently from a mathematical point of view. Greek mathematics had been a product of the mind, not of the hand and the eye, and hence the ancients saw no curve in nature beyond the circle and the straight line. Galileo, however, noticed in 1589 that the path traced out by a point on the rim of a wheel as the wheel rolls along a horizontal straight line is a curve with very special properties. This curve, later known as the roulette or the cycloid, played a fundamental role in the mathematics of the seventeenth century, perhaps in part because of Galileo's observation. Yet we cannot be sure that Galileo was either the first to note the curve or responsible for later investigations of it. His own study of the curve was very limited. Through cutting out and weighing a model cycloid, Galileo concluded that the area under one arch of a cycloid is a little less than three times the area of the generating circle—a result more reminiscent of the engineer than of the mathematician. Instead of making further intensive mathematical study of the curve, he was satisfied to make the aesthetic observation that its beautiful form made it appropriate for the arch of a bridge. (It was used for this purpose long years afterward in the construction of the Ponte di Mezzo across the Arno.)

Galileo's lack of success in the measurement of the cycloid may have stemmed from his mathematical conservatism in disregarding algebra and goniometry, the most appropriate tools for such study; but his protégé, Torricelli, using much the same weak tools as Galileo, later found the area of an arch of the cycloid to be exactly three times the area of the generating circle. When this result was announced, a bitter controversy ensued between French and Italian mathematicians, for Roberval had also squared the cycloid, and the French suspected Torricelli of plagiarism. The polemic raged throughout the seventeenth century, and it continues to some extent even today. Pascal's *Histoire de la roulette* (1658–1659) was grossly unfair to Torricelli, and the *Tractatus duo, prior de cycloide . . . posterior . . . de cissoide* by John Wallis (1659) was excessively partial to Torricelli. Roberval's discovery seems to have been made first, but Torricelli's evidently was independent. The attention of Roberval had been drawn to the cycloid in 1628 by Mersenne, who had noticed the curve in 1615. Galileo may well have been responsible for Torricelli's interest in the cycloid in the early 1640's, but that he had any role in Mersenne's observation is doubtful. It is true that Mersenne was virtually Galileo's representative in France;[35] but there is no record of correspondence between them concerning the cycloid. An examination made by Loria shows that the cycloid is mentioned only once in Galileo's entire extant correspondence, in a letter to Cavalieri of February 24, 1640, in which Galileo says that he had noticed the curve more than fifty years before.[36]

Torricelli was a brilliant mathematicain who died five years after Galileo at half Galileo's age; and one is tempted to say of Galileo what had been said of Plato—that he was the maker of mathematicians, rather than the author of mathematical treatises. At one time, Galileo had intended to write a volume on an aspect of mathematics which had strong appeal for him and which afforded him scope for speculation and argument without tedious computation—the nature and use of the infinite. This was the part of mathematics in which Archimedes, Galileo's idol, had achieved fame, and it was natural for Galileo to have thought of following in the same path. One wishes in this connection that the *Method* of Archimedes (long lost, but rediscovered in 1906) had been available to Galileo, for the mechanical balancing device, by which many Archimedean theorems had been discovered, would have appealed immensely to him. In the absence of the *Method*, mathematicians of the early seventeenth century—notably Stevin, Valerio, Kepler, Galileo, Torricelli, and Cavalieri—developed a geometry of indivisibles which achieved much the same results as did the Archimedean integral calculus. Had Galileo been a single-minded mathematician, he might have become known as the one primarily responsible for the method of indivisibles, now attributed to Cavalieri. In fact, some historians, moved perhaps by Galileo's impressive and well-deserved reputation in physical science, have assumed that much of Cavalieri's *Geometria indivisibilibus continuorum nova quadam ratione promota* (1635) really is due to Galileo,[37] but such a judgment appears to be unfair to the author of the book. When earlier, Cavalieri had made a *faux pas* in publishing, without the prior approval of Galileo, the first account of the parabolic trajectory of a projectile, Galileo made his own claims known; and had he had a significant hand in Cavalieri's *Geometria*, Galileo undoubtedly would have announced this fact.[38] Cavalieri had hoped to see Galileo's projected work on the infinite appear, and when it became apparent that this was unlikely to happen, the author went ahead with his *Geometria*.

Mathematician and philosopher to the Grand Duke

For just about his whole adult life prior to 1610 Galileo had borne a title equivalent to that of professor of mathematics,[39] and in this role he had achieved only a limited recognition, for he had, as we have seen, published almost nothing. Then with dramatic suddenness he acquired international fame, not through pure mathematics, but through his astronomical observations made with a telesocpe of his own construction. Some idea of the magnitude of the change can be gained from the fact that the correspondence for the three-year period from 1611 through 1613 occupies a whole volume of the *Opere*, whereas the volume before contains the entire correspondence for 1574–1610, a span about a dozen times as long! Padua tried in vain to hold its now distinguished professor by doubling his salary to 1000 florins and giving him life tenure.[40] It is of some significance that it was Galileo himself who requested that he be given the title of philosopher as well as of mathematician in his new post with the Grand Duke of Tuscany. In explaining what may have seemed a rather odd request, Galileo asserted that he had worked for as many years in "philosophy" (i.e. natural philosophy or physics) as he had months in pure mathematics. Here he is confirming what we have noted earlier—that he was at heart a physicist and astronomer, rather than a mathematician in our sense of the word, despite the title he bore at Pisa and Padua. Moreover, the list of projected works (over and above the practical inventions he anticipated) which Galileo supplied in his application for the position at Florence verifies the direction of his interests.[41] The chief works which occupied him or which he planned to write included two books on the system of the world ("full of philosophy, astronomy and geometry"), three books on local motion ("an entirely new science")[42] and three books on mechanics. Then Galileo mentioned opuscula on natural subjects, including sound and voice, sight and colors, the tides, the composition of continua, on the motions of animals, *et altri ancora*. Finally, he intended also to write some books for soldiers containing applications of mathematics. Only one item in the list would attract a mathematician of today—the composition of continua—and even that perhaps belongs more in the realm of philosophy! Moreover, the adulation which his telescopic discoveries brought him could not but turn his attention more and more from pure mathematics, and hence it is not surprising that he should wish to be known as a "philosopher".

Belisario Vinta, with whom Galileo corresponded in connection with the desired position, wrote in reply (June 5, 1610) that Galileo would receive 1000 scudi per annum and that he would be given two titles: 'Matematico primario dello studio di Pisa' and 'Filosofo del Serenissimo Gran Duca'. Moreover, he would be under no obligation to teach, but could pursue his studies and finish his compositions.[43] In his reply (June 18, 1610) Galileo accepted the position, with the important proviso that it be for life; and then he made an odd request. The titles of First Mathematician at Pisa and Philosopher to the Grand Duke somehow didn't quite satisfy him. He wrote that he would like to have the title not only of "Filosofo del Ser. G. D., ma di Matematico ancora".[44] The significance of the request is not clear, but evidently there was for Galileo some magic in the word 'mathematician'.

"Horn angles" and infinitesimals

The change in Galileo's titles and position brought no great change in the nature of his research, although it did greatly increase his rate of publication. As before, he turned to mathematics not for its own sake, but when it supplied him, as it did not infrequently, with arguments to bolster a point in astronomy or mechanics. In the *Two chief systems*, there is very little mathematical astronomy; and when during the discussion of the Third Day, some questions arise concerning stellar parallax, the exposition is quite elementary.[45] The modern reader will perhaps be more struck by the avoidance of decimal fractional notations than by the felicity of the exposition. Galileo was at his best not in computation, but when he needed an argument involving infinitesimals to clinch a scientific point, and a very appropriate occasion arose in the course of the

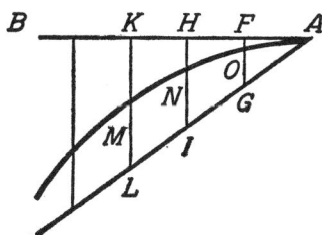

Figure 12-1

Second Day's dialogue. Here Simplicio had argued that on a rapidly rotating earth objects would be thrown off tangentially, for the initial downward tendency is indefinitely small as compared with the rapid horizontal motion. To answer this cogent objection, Salviati cleverly introduces what mathematicians later were to call infinitesimals of higher order. Galileo imagines the uniform tendency to horizontal or tangential motion to be represented by equal distances *AF* and *FH* and *HK* along a line *AB* which is tangent to the circle of the earth at *A*, the distances corresponding to the equal increments in time. (See Fig. 12–1.) At each of the points F and H and K, he erects line segments FG and HN and KM proportional to the distances AF and AH and AK; and inasmuch as the degrees of speed acquired by a falling body are proportional to the times elapsed, the points G and I and L will lie on a straight line through A. Salviati points out that as one proceeds backward from K toward A along the line BA, the lines KM and HN and FG, which represent the tendencies toward downward motion, become smaller *ad infinitum*, just as the lines KA and HA and FA become smaller *ad infinitum*.

Salviati accepts hypothetically Simplicio's argument that if one lets the weight of the body diminish indefinitely, the downward tendency to motion will diminish indefinitely too, so that the line of speeds $AGIL$ will tend toward the horizontal line AB, for the angle BAL tends indefinitely toward zero. Hence there would appear to be a combined diminution *ad infinitum* in the downward tendency of light objects, apparently confirming Simplicio's argument that a very light object must be thrown off by a rotation of the earth. But now Salviati counters with an ingenious argument from the geometry of the "horn" angle—the angle formed by the arc of the circle and the tangent at A. He points out that if the circle (representing the surface of the earth) cuts the lines KL and HI and FG in points M and N and O respectively, then the lengths of KM and HN and FO decrease *ad infinitum* far more rapidly than do the lengths of KL and HI and FG, as one approaches A, no matter how small the rectilinear angle BAL may be—that is, no matter how light the object under consideration may be.[46] But the distances KM and HN and FO are the distances the object must fall to remain on the earth while it rotates, and hence the lightest object will not be thrown off—that is, not unless one argues that the downward tendency increases in a proportion greater even than the weight. And this possibility can be excluded by an appeal to experience: Salviati notes that a ball of lead, the weight of which is thirty or forty times that of cork, "will scarcely move more than twice as fast". Sagredo, delighted with Salviati's argument, expresses one of Galileo's favorite theses: "trying to deal with physical problems without geometry is attempting the impossible". Simplicio, of course, falls back on the argument that mathematical explanations may be all right in theory, "but when it comes to matter, things happen otherwise".

In the above portion of the *Two chief systems*, we see clearly Galileo's principal role in the history of mathematics: his unbounded faith that the operations of nature are to be understood through a combination of experience and mathematical reasoning. In the demonstration above, he was on the verge of discovering an important mathematical concept—the order of an infinitesimal—but he did not carry the matter far enough. He did not give careful proof of his statements, nor did he even define clearly the terms involved in the argument. He was satisfied to apply a bit of plausible geometry to dispose of an opponent's scientific position. A mathematician cannot help but regret that Galileo did not pursue his thesis further; it was, in fact, equivalent to saying that the function exsecant x (that is, sec $x - 1$) is an infinitesimal of higher order with respect to the angle x. At the same time, one must admire the cleverness with which he made use of this relatively abstruse notion in support of his scientific position.

Galileo was fascinated by infinitesimals, and a somewhat similar argument about horn angles appears in a slightly different context elsewhere in the same work. Toward the middle of the discussion on the Second Day, Salviati is considering the trajectory of an object dropped from the top of a high tower on a rotating earth. Were the downward motion of the freely falling body uniform, he asserted, the body would reach the center of the earth (assuming unimpeded motion) along an approximate Archimedean spiral. More accurately, the orbit would be a semicircle whose endpoints are the starting point and the center of the earth. Galileo was almost as devoted to circular motions in physics as the ancients had been in astronomy, and this may be why he here proposed the semicircular trajectory in the very year in which his protégé, Cavalieri, published (in his *Speccio ustorio*) the more correct parabolic trajectory—an idea which he had, in fact, got from Galileo himself.

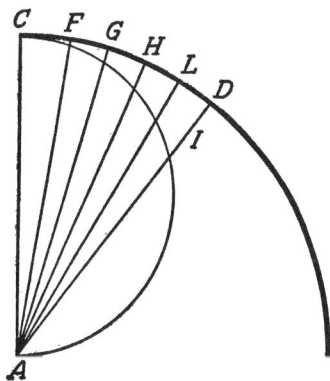

Figure 12–2

The hypothesis of a circular motion had the *ad hominem* advantage of refuting the Aristotelian dichotomy between circular celestial motions and rectilinear terrestrial motions. Besides, it enabled Galileo to use his "horn angle" analysis in describing the increasing speed of falling bodies. If the arcs CF and FG and GH and HL and LD along the circle, with center at A, through which the top of the tower moves, are taken as equal (Fig. 12–2), and if the semicircle CIA is that along which the falling body moves toward the center of the earth, it is at once apparent that the portions of the radii AD and AL and AH and AG and AF intercepted between the two circular arcs which form the sides of the horn angle DCI

decrease *ad infinitum* far more rapidly than do the arcs *CD* and *CL* and *CH* and *CG* and *CF*. Galileo had a good feeling for orders of infinitesimals, but the physical phenomena he is describing are not in good agreement with his formulation, and the mathematical exposition lacks precision. He frequently presents plausible arguments whose mathematical basis he has not fully worked out. In this respect, he differed *toto coelo* from his hero, Archimedes, whose spirit he shared only in part. In all fairness, it must be pointed out that Galileo later admitted that he was here in error (he claimed indeed that he had been only joking). Moreover, the problem of the orbit of projectiles was a complex one in which Newton himself at first committed an error. His first suggestion for the trajectory was some sort of spiral, and only later did he arrive at the ellipse as the correct answer.[47]

Transcendental curves

Galileo's error concerning the semicircular trajectory may possibly have been of significance for the history of mathematics. Mersenne noted the mistake, and in 1635 passed the problem on to Fermat, who under different assumptions concluded that the path was a certain spiral. When Galileo was told of Fermat's conclusion, he wrote that he had had a similar idea—that of generalizing the Archimedean spiral to one in which the radius vector rotates uniformly while the point on the radius vector moves so that distances are as the squares of the times. (Note that his generalizations are limited in scope and suggested by natural phenomena rather than by the inner logic of mathematics itself.) He mistakenly assumed that this spiral was the one which Fermat had suggested. One outcome of this confusion seems to have been an increased interest, especially in Italy and France, in spirals of various sorts. The study of spirals, cycloids, and other transcendental curves had been excluded by Descartes from the study of geometry,[48] and Galileo played at least a modest role in calling attention to their importance. Descartes was a far better mathematician than Galileo, and it is of course mathematically important to distinguish between algebraic and transcendental curves; but Newton and Leibniz might not have invented their general analytic methods if the Cartesian point of view had prevailed. Galileo's mathematics was at times naive, but it was frequently suggestive; and his attention to such curves as the cycloid and the spiral helped to make respectable a class of curves, the transcendental, which have far outdistanced the algebraic in scientific applicability.

Among the transcendental curves which Galileo noticed, but misunderstood, was the catenary. In the *Two new sciences*, Galileo had a much greater opportunity to introduce various types of curves than he had had in the *Two chief systems*. It may have been his respect for circular motion which continued to prevent his appreciating Kepler's application of the ellipse in astronomy,[49] but he made up for this by utilizing the parabola in both of his "new sciences". In the discussion during the Second Day on the strength of materials, Salviati explains the superiority of beams with parabolic cross sections: they have greater strength for their weight than do beams with rectangular cross section. Salviati then tells Sagredo that he has two ways of quickly tracing parabolas. One is to project a brass ball so that it will trace a curve on a metallic mirror placed in a very nearly vertical position; the other is to suspend a light chain over two nails driven into a wall at the same height. The proof that the first curve is a parabola is not given until the Fourth Day when the second of the "new sciences", dynamics, is being developed. Here, however, Salviati is less categorical about the shape of the catenary, saying this time merely that a cord stretched more or less tightly assumes a curve which closely *approximates* the parabola. Unlike the modern mathematician, Galileo is less concerned about the exact equation or properties of the two curves than he is about a plausible physical analogy he thinks he sees between the forces forming them:

> The curvature of the path of the shot fired horizontally appears to result from two forces, one (that of the weapon) drives it horizontally and the other (its weight) draws it vertically downward. So in stretching the rope you have the force which pulls it horizontally and its own weight which acts downward. The circumstances in these two cases are, therefore, very similar.[50]

Here again one notices the plausibility characteristic of physics rather than the precision of much pure mathematics. It is true that the parabola and the catenary *do* look much alike, as observation of the cables of a suspension bridge, before and after the roadbed is added, will confirm—and yet mathematically the properties of the two curves are very different indeed, for the one is an algebraic curve of second degree, the other is a transcendental curve and has no degree (or, as Newton expressed it, has infinite degree). Galileo could not reasonably have been expected to derive the properties of the catenary, given his conservative mathematical background; but his hero, Archimedes, would never have reasoned so loosely about the similarity of two curves.

But then neither did Archimedes attempt a science of dynamics. Had Galileo been the cautious type, we should not have had his *Two new sciences* in the first place, and the world would be the poorer for it both mathematically and scientifically. It is not enough merely to encourage the study of mathematics. Ramus, another Renaissance scholar, had wished to revive the teaching of mathematics because of its importance in the quantitative practical arts; but he thought that purely theoretical mathematics was useless, and his influence on the history of mathematics was very slight.[51] Galileo, too, was much concerned about the practical arts; but he went further. He is remembered in the history of mathematics for encouraging his contemporaries to apply mathematics with a more philosophical motive: the revealing of plausible relationships between mathematics and natural phenomena. In his day, Galileo played somewhat the role that George Polya would play in ours, calling attention to the importance that induction and analogy and the search for patterns of plausible reasoning have in mathematical discovery. It was in this respect that the spirit of Galileo was important in the mathematics of the Century of Genius.

The infinite

Although Galileo made no great mathematical discovery, he came closest to this in his study of the infinitely large and small. His use of infinitesimals in the *Two chief systems* has been noted; but it is in the *Two new sciences* that he uses the notion of the infinite most extensively in both mathematical and physical contexts.[52] His chief difficulty was his tendency to let analogy play too large a part in his reasoning. Occasionally the analogy was carried to the point of whimsy, as when Salviati assures Simplicio that it is as easy to resolve a line segment into an infinite number of parts as it is to divide the line into its finite parts. First he gets Simplicio to admit that one need not separate the parts, but merely mark the points of division. If for example, a line segment is bent into the form of a square or a regular octagon, one has resolved it into four or eight equal parts. Salviati then concludes that by bending the line segment into the shape of a circle he has "reduced to actuality that infinite number of parts which you claimed, while it was straight, were contained in it only potentially", for the circle is a polygon of an infinite number of sides.[53]

There are occasions in the *Two new sciences* on which Galileo's statements on infinity recall Pascal's view that the infinitely large and small are mysteries which nature has proposed to man, not to understand, but to admire.[54] Salviati, for example, says that infinites and indivisibles:

> transcend our finite understanding, the former on account of their magnitude, the latter because of their smallness. In spite of this, men cannot refrain from discussing them, even though it must be done in a roundabout way.[55]

A little later, after a demonstration involving the use of indivisibles and the so-called "theorem of Cavalieri", Salviati again says that "infinity and indivisibility are in their very nature incomprehensible to us; imagine what they are when combined".[56] Yet Galileo toyed for a while with analogies between problems of the indivisible in geometry and problems of cohesion and strength of materials in physics.

He took particular delight in paradoxes such as the "wheel of Aristotle" and a "proof" that the circumferences of all circles, however large or small, are equal to a point. Beginning with a discussion of the infinite in geometry, Salviati leads Simplicio and Sagredo to admit that a one-to-one correspondence can be set up between all the integers and the perfect squares, despite the fact that the further one proceeds in the sequence of integers, the scarcer the perfect squares become.[57] The correspondence is established by the simple expedient of counting the perfect squares, a process in which each integer is matched against a perfect square, and vice versa. Despite the fact that there are many whole numbers which are not perfect squares, and that the proportion of these increases as we consider larger and larger numbers, "we must say that there are as many squares as there are numbers".

Galileo here was face to face with the fundamental property of an infinite set—that a part of the set can be equal to the whole set (in the sense that the part and the whole can be put into one-to-one correspondence). This is the property which was rediscovered a couple of centuries later by Bolzano and Dedekind, and which became the foundation of the arithmetic of transfinite numbers established by Cantor; but Galileo did not draw what we now think of as the obvious conclusions. It is not even likely that Galileo's observations were influential in later developments concerning infinity.[58] An admirer of Euclid, he was unable to break with the statement in the *Elements* that the whole is greater than a part—whatever this vague phraseology may mean. While he correctly concluded that the number of perfect squares is not less than the number of integers, he could not bring himself to make the statement that the sets are equal. Instead, he simply concluded that: "the attributes *equal, greater*, and *less* are not applicable to infinite, but only to finite, quantities". Because of his failure to distinguish adequately between classes and magnitudes, he wrongly concluded that one could not say that one infinite number is greater than another, or even that an infinite number is greater than a finite number— points cleared up later by Cantor. Here Galileo's role was that of a Moses who led his readers within sight of the promised land, but who could not himself enter it. Hilbert was later to write: "no one shall expel us from the paradise which Cantor has created for us".[59]

There are reasons for the differences in achievement between Galileo and Cantor, not the least of which is the fact that Cantor was born more than two hundred years after Galileo died. Besides, Cantor had been university-trained in mathematics and physics, whereas Galileo was largely self-taught. Above all, however, was the difference in attitude on the part of the two men. Both called themselves "mathematicians", but one was a product of the Renaissance, the other of the age of rigor, and the word 'mathematics' had changed meaning in the interval. It has been said that the mathematician worships at the shrine dedicated to rigor, but the physicist worships at the lesser shrine dedicated to plausibility. In this sense, Cantor was a mathematician, Galileo a physicist.[60] It was Galileo's great contribution to science to replace the older teleological view of nature with that of a universe subject to mathematical law.[61] Where his predecessors had at best applied mathematics to certain aspects of the natural sciences, Galileo had faith that the subject was related to all aspects of life.[62] That we have honored him four hundred years after his birth is ample proof that his faith was not vain. Pure mathematicians nevertheless will regret that Galileo's faith was not bolstered by their golden rule (and here I parody the words of one of our great presidents): "ask not what mathematics can do for you, but ask rather what you can do for mathematics".

NOTES

1. George Sarton, *The study of the history of mathematics*, New York, 1936; reprinted 1957, pp. 4–7.

2. *Ibid.*, p. 4.

3. Charles Singer, "Greek biology and its relation to the rise of modern biology", *Studies in the history and method of science*, 2, 1921, 7.

4. David E. Smith, "Medicine and mathematics in the sixteenth century", *Annals of medical history*, Summer 1917, pp. 125–140.

5. See the preface to the Drake edition of the *Discourse on bodies in water*, 1960*.

6. See Leonardo Olschki, *Galileo und seine Zeit*, Halle, 1927, p. 141ff.

7. See Lancelot Hogben, *Mathematics for the million*, New York, 1937, p. 36.

8. Gino Loria, *Galileo Galilei nella vita e nelle opere*, Pavia, 1936.

9. In a letter from his sister in 1593, he is addressed as "Dotore Galileo Galilei" (*Opere, 10*, p. 60); but at that time the title could be taken as somewhat synonymous with "learned". John Dee was addressed as Dr. Dee, the term evidently being used in this general sense.

10. See Ernst Cassirer, "Galileo: a new science and a new spirit", 1942*.

11. Only a few days after I had written these words I ran across an article in which a celebrated mathematician of our day describes two essentially different ways in which mathematics progresses, one of which is in a sense applicable to Galileo: "The mathematicians whom I might call the tacticians pounce head on at a problem, using only old and well-tested tools, and they rely on their cleverness to give some new twist to traditional arguments, and thus reach the solution which had eluded previous attempts. The strategists, on the other hand, will never be satisfied until the concepts involved in a problem have been so thoroughly analyzed, and their connections put in such a clear light, that the final solution almost appears as a triviality." See p. 239 of Jean Dieudonné, "Recent developments in mathematics", *American mathematical monthly, 71*, 1964, 239–248.

12. See Paul Tannery, "Sur la date des principales découvertes de Fermat", *Bulletin des sciences mathématiques, 18*, 1883, 116–128.

13. See David E. Smith, *Source book in mathematics*, New York, 1929, p. 186.

14. See Marie Boas, *The scientific renaissance: 1450–1630*, 1962*, p. 197.

15. See, for example, A. G. Kaestner, *Geschichte der Mathematik*, Gottingen, 1796–1800, and Etienne Montucla, *Histoire des mathématiques*, rev. edn., Paris, 1799–1802.

16. Two copies of this work are listed in the card catalogue of the New York Library, but these are reported as missing. I have therefore used the version in the *Opere*, 2, pp. 335–424.

17. See Smith, *op. cit.*, pp. 186–191.

18. Smith, *op. cit.*, p. 186.

19. The Bürgi instrument was described by Philip Horcher in a work with the title: *Libri tres in quibus primo constructio circini proportionum edocetur*, Moguntiae, 1605, and a German translation of this by Levinus Hulsius was published by Hulsius' widow in 1607. See Kaestner, *Geschichte der Mathematik*, vol. 3, pp. 336ff.; 382ff. For other details see A. Favaro, "Per la storia del compasso di proporzione", *Atti R. Istit. Veneto*, 67, 1908, 723–739.

20. See Cortes Pla, *Galileo Galilei: su vida—su obra*, 1943*.

21. Moritz Cantor, *Vorlesungen über Geschichte der Mathematik*, Leipzig, 1892, vol. 2, p. 631.

22. An account will be found in S. Bedini's essay elsewhere in this volume of the bitter quarrel between Galileo and the Capras over their plagiarization of his work on the "geometric compass". His polemic against them, the *Difesa* (1607), which Cantor (*Vorlesungen über Geschichte der Mathematik*, vol. 2, p. 632) describes as perhaps the most biting polemic in the history of mathematics since the Ferrari-Tartaglia controversy, was very widely distributed, thus perhaps giving Galileo's compasses an exaggerated reputation.

23. It has been pointed out that Galileo in his dynamics and Napier in his theory of logarithms both began from a consideration of a motion in which speed is proportional to distance (see Jean Itard, "Sur une prétendue erreur mathématique de Galilée", 1946*) but there is little likelihood that there was any influence of one upon the other.

24. An article by Jean Pelseneer, "Gilbert, Bacon, Galilée, Kepler, Harvey et Descartes: leurs relations", *Isis*, 17, 1932, 171–208, brings out clearly with what surprisingly little patience Galileo and his contemporaries read each other's works.

25. See *Opere*, 10, p. 68, for Galileo's letter of 1597 to Kepler at Prague.

26. Chapter 15 of the *De motu*. See *On motion and On mechanics*, 1960*, pp. 70–71.

27. *Elements*, Book 5, definition 3.

28. *The works of Archimedes*, 1897*, p. 171.

29. *The geometry of René Descartes*, ed. by D. E. Smith and Marcia L. Latham, reprinted New York, 1954, p. 91.

30. *On motion and On mechanics*, p. 71. The interesting suggestion has been made by Marshall Clagett that Galileo may have misunderstood Aristotle's intention in the passage under consideration. Perhaps Aristotle had in mind a distinction between rectilinear and curvilinear motion similar to the physicist's distinction between scalar and vector quantities. See Marshall Clagett, *The science of mechanics in the Middle Ages*, 1959*, p. 181.

31. William Jack, "Galileo and the application of mathematics to physics", *Nature*, 21, 1879, 40–43; 58–61.

32. *The development of mathematics*, 1945*, p. 99.

33. The same thing can be said of Galileo's other works. See, for example, *On motion and On mechanics*.

34. See *On motion and On mechanics*, p. 145.

35. Galileo's *Mechanics*, for example, was first published by Mersenne in 1635 in French.

36. See Gino Loria, "Le pretendu 'larcin' de Torricelli", *Archeion, 21*, 1938, 62–68. A good and impartial account of these matters is found in Evelyn Walker, *A study of the Traité des indivisibles of Gilles Persone de Roberval*, New York, 1932, pp. 55–65. The comments on the controversy made by Aldo Mieli, "Il tricentenario dei *Discorsi e dimostrazioni matematiche di Galileo Galilei*", *Archeion, 21*, 1938, 193–297, appear to be biased in favor of Torricelli. It should perhaps be pointed out that Paul Tannery believes that the cycloid had been noticed by the ancient Greeks (see his *Mémoires scientifiques, 2*, 1912, 1–47), but even if it was, it is very unlikely that Galileo or any of his contemporaries were aware of this.

37. See, for example, the judgment by Gino Loria in *Storia delle matematiche*, 1950*, p. 410.

38. Mr. Stillman Drake has kindly called my attention to the thoroughness with which Cavalieri was willing to make amends to Galileo for his not acknowledging more explicitly his indebtedness to Galileo concerning the parabolic trajectory. See Galileo, *Opere, 14*, pp. 394–395.

39. In letters while at Padua he gave his title as "Lettor publico delle matematiche nello Studio di Padova". See *Opere, 10*, p. 171.

40. One reason he gave for leaving was that his teaching left him insufficient time for research. Nostalgia for the city he always counted as "home" no doubt played a role too. In connection with formal letters and titles, he frequently added '*fiorentino*' after his name. See, e. g., *Opere, 10*, p. 171.

41. *Opere, 10*, pp. 348–353.

42. It should be remembered that Galileo's exaggerated claims with respect to the novelty of his work were prompted by the fact that he was applying for a position which he very much wished to fill. His results in dynamics were indeed of the greatest significance to his day, but one should not overlook his indebtedness to medieval speculations. It is easy to find accounts which tend to overemphasize the novelty in Galileo's dynamics. See, for example, Ernst Cassirer, "Galileo's Platonism", 1944*; Raymond Seeger, "On the role of Galileo in physics", 1963*. In G. Govi, "Galileo e i matematichi del Collegio Romano nel 1611", *Accademia Nazionale dei Lincei, Atti* (2), *2*, 1875, 230–240, Galileo's mechanics is described as "entirely original—even audacious". A contrary view will be found in Clagett's *Science of mechanics in the Middle Ages*, especially on pp. 346, 666.

43. *Opere, 10*, p. 369.

44. *Opere, 10*, pp. 372–375.

45. *Dialogo*, pp. 293–315.

46. For purposes of exposition we have modified slightly the Galilean diagram. See the *Dialogo*, p. 199.

47. See Alexandre Koyré, "A documentary history of the problem of fall from Kepler to Newton", 1955*. Cf. also E. J. Dijksterhuis, *The mechanization of the world picture*, 1961*, p. 351.

48. *The geometry of René Descartes*, p. 44.

49. See Samuel I. Mintz, "Galileo, Hobbes, and the circle of perfection", 1952*.

50. *Two new sciences*, p. 290.

51. See R. Hooykaas, *Humanisme, science et reforme: Pierre della Ramée (1515–1572)*, Leyden, 1958.

52. For an extensive analysis of the *Discorsi*, including reference to work on infinitesimals, see Mieli's article referred to above.

53. *Discorsi*, p. 47.

54. See Blaise Pascal, *Oeuvres*, ed. by Leon Brunschvicg and Pierre Boutroux, Paris, 1908–1914, vol. 9, p. 268.

55. *Discorsi*, p. 26.

56. *Discorsi*, p. 30.

57. *Discorsi*, pp. 32–33.

58. See Paul Schrecker, "On the infinite number of infinite orders", *Studies and essays in the history of science and learning*, ed. by M. F. Ashley Montagu, New York, 1944, pp. 359–373; also Edward Kasner, "Galileo and the modern concept of infinity", *Bulletin of the American Mathematical Society*, 11, 1905, 499–501. For an excellent acount of the mathematical development, see P. E. B. Jourdain, "The development of the theory of transfinite numbers", *Archiv der Mathematik und Physik*, 10, 1906, 254–281; 14, 1908–1909, 287–311.

59. E. T. Bell, *Men of mathematics*, New York, 1937, p. 577.

60. So fascinated was Galileo by plausible applications of mathematics to physics that he concluded, from his views on the geometrical continuum, that "physical bodies are composed of infinitely small indivisible particles". This view he said was supported by "striking and conclusive examples". See *Discorsi*, p. 55.

61. See I. B. Cohen, "The heritage of Galileo", 1942*; E. A. Burtt, *The metaphysical foundations of modern physical science*, 1955*, p. 64; J. W. Herivel, "Galileo's achievements", 1962*, 4–5.

62. See Gino Loria, *Storia delle matematiche*, p. 411. Galileo was not alone in this view, however. A recent article by Dudley Shapere, "Descartes and Plato", 1963*, argues that "the new conception of the role of mathematics in the study of nature, the view that nature is amenable to exact and complete mathematical treatment, is for the most part implicit or incidental or at best peripheral in his [Galileo's] work. It is Descartes who first makes this view the explicit focal point of a developed world-system oriented toward the new science." Shapere here appears to attribute to Descartes an unwarranted degree of the credit due to Galileo and Descartes jointly; this contribution is of such magnitude that it may easily be shared by two men, rather than given to one alone.

13 ❋ The instruments of Galileo Galilei

SILVIO A. BEDINI

The name and fame of Galileo Galilei are inextricably interwoven with the invention and development of eight scientific instruments which made their first appearance on the scientific scene during the late sixteenth and early seventeenth centuries. Much useless effort has been expended by scholars in controversies about whether Galileo was in fact the inventor of each, or whether he merely improved or developed them. In most instances the answer is still uncertain, for the relevant facts have been obscured by the mists of time. It has been established beyond doubt, however, that most of the instruments in question did exist, in some rudimentary form at least, before Galileo expressed an interest in them.

The historical origin of the instruments attributed to Galileo is not, in the final analysis, of crucial importance in assessing Galileo's own achievement in their regard. The important, and apparent, fact is that it was Galileo who developed and improved them and first applied them scientifically to make observations that were crucial in their effects on the Scientific Revolution he helped to shape. He was indeed one of the very first true scientists; he pursued investigations according to principles and practices which he was forced to formulate and establish for himself. His role in the evolution of the scientific instruments associated with him is best expressed in the words in which Galileo had Salviati praise William Gilbert:

> To apply oneself to great inventions, starting from the smallest beginnings, is no task for ordinary minds. To divine that wonderful arts lie hidden behind trivial and childish things is a conception for superhuman talents.[1]

The *pulsilogium* (1582–1583)

The first scientific instrument with which Galileo's name was associated is the *pulsilogium*, which he produced shortly after his alleged observation of the isochronism of the pendulum in 1582 in the cathedral at Pisa. At this time Galileo was a medical student, and it is entirely logical that in his mind he would associate the phenomenon of the pendulum with his studies in medicine. There is an obvious similarity between the beat of a pendulum and a patient's pulse, and it is easy enough to understand how Galileo would have seen the relationship and visualized how the pendulum could serve as a measurer for the pulse rate. He constructed a small pendulum suspended from a string, the upper end of which was attached to a scale marked with diagnostic terms. By swinging the pendulum at the same time that he was counting the patient's pulse rate, he was able to obtain a direct reading for the patient's pulse-beats per minute by stopping the string with his thumb at the point of the scale which coincided with the patient's pulse rate. The device was later greatly elaborated, perhaps by Galileo and certainly by others, into several more complex forms.[2] The basic source for Galileo's work with the *pulsilogium* is Viviani's letter of August 20, 1659, to Prince Leopold de'Medici, in which he described the history of the pendulum-regulated clockwork (*19*, pp. 647–659).[3]

However, Galileo never claimed the invention of the *pulsilogium* for himself. Although he referred to his experiments with suspended heavy objects in a letter to Guidobaldo del Monte, he did not specifically mention the *pulsilogium* (*10*, pp. 97–100). Meanwhile, the instrument appears to have been further exploited by Santorio Santorio (1561–1636), a member of the faculty of the University of Padua. The first description of the invention in published form appeared in 1620 in a work by him,[4] and again in another work published in 1625.[5] Santorio developed it in several forms for a variety of purposes, including the regulation of the time for breathing on his air thermometer, and the measurement of the rate of breathing of a patient. An advanced version was, in fact, a crude form of watch to measure the systole and diastole of the heart. With Santorio's death in 1636, interest in the *pulsilogium* and its application ceased, until Sir John Floyer evolved his pulse watch around 1685.

Galileo's invention of the *pulsilogium* is of significance for two reasons. The instrument was the first actual application made of the discovery of the pendulum, and as such became a milestone in the history of measurement. At the same time, it was a pioneering effort in the new tendency toward the achievement of accuracy in the field of medicine.

The thermoscope (c. 1593)

The source for the attribution to Galileo of the thermoscope (which was, in effect, a thermometer without a scale) is Viviani's biography, but there is a serious discrepancy of date. In a discussion of the work on which Galileo was engaged in 1593, Viviani notes that:

> In this same time he discovered thermometers, that is, those instruments of glass with water and air, used for distinguishing the variations of temperatures of places from the alterations of heat and cold [*19*, pp. 597–632].

Viviani's account placed Galileo's development of the thermoscope between 1593 and 1597, while he was teaching mathematics at the University of Padua. In a survey of Galileo's correspondence and papers, however, references to his work with the thermoscope are limited to the period between 1604 and 1606.

The principle of the thermoscope was not, of course, a new discovery. It had been noted much earlier in the works of Heron of Alexandria (end of first century A.D.), in which the nature of the vacuum and the elasticity of air were discussed. Heron's work was well-known, or at least available, in Italy by the end of the sixteenth century. The *Spiritali* had been translated into Latin in 1575,[6] and into Italian in 1592.[7] Galileo was certainly familiar with this work and had studied it, as is evident in his letter of January 11, 1594, to Alviso Mocenigo (*10*, pp. 64–65). The experiment exemplified by the thermoscope was already well-known in Italy even before this time; it formed part of G. B. Della Porta's *Magia naturalis*, published in 1589.[8]

Several letters in Galileo's correspondence refer to the instrument and clarify his role in its development. On June 30, 1612, Giovanfrancesco Sagredo wrote to Galileo that:

> Sig. da Mula was at the Santo and he told me that he had seen an instrument of Sig. Santorio with which it was possible to measure cold and heat with a compass, and finally he told me that this consisted of a large flask of glass with a long neck. I immediately began to make some which were beautiful and exquisite. The ordinary ones cost me 4 lire each, that is, a flask, a small ampule and a glass hose; and my production was such that in an hour I made as many as ten. The best one that I produced was finely worked, and was of such a size and design that it included within it all the arts . . . [*11*, pp. 349–351].

In this letter, Sagredo made no mention of the experiments which Galileo had presumably made six or more years earlier with this instrument. In fact, the equipment observed by da Mula at Santorio's home appears to have been new to him, which is difficult to explain. The exchange of letters after this date, including Galileo's reply to Sagredo, has not been preserved, and would presumably explain a great deal. However, in another letter from Sagredo to Galileo, almost a year later, acknowledgment of Galileo's role in the development of the thermoscope is clearly made:

> The instrument for measuring heat invented by you has been by me reduced to diverse forms which are quite convenient yet exquisite, and so much so that the difference of the temperature from one room to another can be discerned to 100 degrees [11, pp. 505–506].

The "difference of temperature to 100 degrees" is rather puzzling in this statement. It implies that Sagredo had devised a scale of gradations which measured to one hundred degrees, but he provided no details of the construction or division of such a scale. In another letter of March 15, 1615, he provided Galileo with additional data about his thermoscope:

> Concerning the instrument for measuring temperatures, I have continued daily to add and change in such a manner that . . . I could, beginning from the beginning, easily recount all the history of my inventions, or more accurately, improvements. But because, as you write to me, and as I certainly believe, you were the first author and inventor, and because I believe that the instruments made by you, or by your excellent artisans, are much better than my own, I therefore beg you to write to me at the first opportunity about what sort of works you have until now had done, and I will in turn inform you of what has been done here; and touching in each of our letters upon various things in this connection, I shall write to you my own imperfect speculations [12, pp. 156–158].

Sagredo unquestionably pursued his study of the thermoscope far beyond the degree to which Galileo had developed it, for in a reply to a letter from Galileo, he noted:

> As for the glass instruments for measuring temperatures, the first which I made were of the manner in which you had had your own made; but afterwards I multiplied the invention in various forms, about all of which I am unable to write at present [12, pp. 167–171].

Some explanation of Sagredo's lack of knowledge of Galileo's experimentation with the thermoscope may be found in Favaro's suggestion that Galileo's pioneer work took place while Sagredo was serving as Consul for the Venetian Republic at Aleppo (20, p. 528). Confirmation is found in a letter dated September 20, 1638, from Benedetto Castelli to Monsignor F. Cesarini informing the latter that:

> I remember an experience which I was allowed to see more than thirty-five years ago by our Signor Galileo, which involved taking a glass flask of the size of a small hen's egg with a neck about two palms in length, and as thin as the stalk of a plant of grain; after the flask was well warmed by the palms of the hands and its mouth turned into a vase below it, in which there was a little water, when the heat of the hands was removed from the flask, the water immediately began to rise in the neck, and surpassed the level of the water in the base more than a palm. Sig. Galileo utilized this effect for the construc-

tion of an instrument for examining the degrees of heat and cold [*17*, pp. 377–380].

This account provides a clear description of the character and details of Galileo's experiment. However, the date of the experiment does not coincide with that given by Viviani (1593–1597), since a period of thirty-five years prior to the date of the letter, 1638, would place the incident not later than 1604. The date can be further established by a letter from Galileo of April 25, 1626, in reply to one from Cesare Marsigli at Bologna. Marsili reported that an engineer visiting Bologna had claimed that the motion of the tides of the sea could be shown, with the aid of salt water in a flask, to be due to celestial causes. Galileo replied:

> I do not believe that this effect, according to my understanding, can depend on any celestial reason or cause other than the reheating of air during the day and the cooling of it at night, and the selection of salt water is, I believe, a cover employed by the artisan; sweet water could do as well. Such a prank I did myself twenty years ago in Padua, but it had nothing to do with the movement of the tides [*13*, pp. 319–320].

This statement limits the incident to about 1606, placing the period during which the thermoscopic experiments took place between 1604 and 1606.

The invention of the thermoscope and the thermometer has been claimed by, and for, many but rarely with supporting evidence. In addition to Galileo, claims have been made for Fra Paolo Sarpi, Della Porta and Santorio in Italy, while in England the invention was attributed to Cornelius Drebbel, Francis Bacon and Robert Fludd. Other than Galileo, the strongest contender for the honor is Santorio, already mentioned in connection with the *pulsilogium*. He received an appointment to teach theoretical medicine at the University of Padua a little more than a year after Galileo's departure. It must be noted, however, that Santorio did not mention thermoscopic instruments in his chapter on "De instrumentis medicis non amplius visis" which appeared in 1603.[9] It may thus be assumed that he did not become interested in the instrument until after Galileo's development of it. He first described it in his *Commentariorum*, which was published in 1612.[10] There he states that he had inscribed a scale of degrees on the tube so that the increase and decrease of heat could be measured by means of the compass (*compasso*). He may have first learned of the thermoscope at the University of Padua during the period 1604–1606 when his colleague, Galileo, was working with it, and conceived the notion of using it for the examination of feverish patients. The instrument as visualized by Galileo would not have been suitable for such a purpose, so that Santorio would have had to adapt and simplify it for his medical requirements.

It is just as likely, of course, that Santorio was inspired by the writings of Heron of Alexandria, as Galileo presumably had been. This is supported to some extent by Santorio's references to Heron in his commentaries on Avicenna.[11] The instrument developed by Santorio was a large glass bubble into which was passed a straight tube somewhat longer than the one used by Heron. Consequently it was a measure-instrument quite different from Galileo's, not only because of the manner of its use, but also because of the variable applications that could be made with it. In the Galilean instrument, as the heat expanded the air in the bubble, the liquid in the tube dropped and ascended with the cold upon contraction of the air. In Santorio's instrument, as the air in the bubble expanded with heat, the liquid rose in the tube, and descended with the cold as the air contracted.

The first published illustration of an Italian thermoscopic instrument was of Santorio's thermoscope. It appeared in Giuseppe Biancani's *Sphaera mundi*,[12] the manuscript of which was completed in 1617, but which was not published until 1620. It was Biancani who suggested that the instrument be named a *"thermoscopium"*. The name *'termometro'* was not applied until four years later when it was used for the first time by Giovanni Leurechon to describe Galileo's thermo-baroscopic instrument.[13]

The transformation of the thermoscope into a thermometer is generally claimed to have been the accomplishment of Evangelista Torricelli. The claim is made not only by Viviani in his life of Galileo but by Urbino Davisi in his *Trattato della sfera*, as well as by Francesco Terzi in his *Prodromo: vero saggio di alcuni inventioni nuove . . .* Meanwhile, the first published illustrations of a thermometric instrument appeared in 1617 in England. Ironically enough, these illustrations represented neither the instruments of Galileo nor of Santorio, but those of Robert Fludd (1574–1637), who independently of both Italian inventors, had developed an instrument called a *Speculum calendarium* some years earlier.[14]

Some relationship may possibly be established between Galileo's work and the contributions made by Cornelius Drebbel (1572–1634) in England, which are described in a series of letters from Daniello Antonini to Galileo. In a letter of February 4, 1612, Antonini wrote from Brussels:

Some days ago, I heard that the King of England had a perpetual motion device, in which water moves in a glass tube, sometimes rising, sometimes falling in the manner of, it is said, the tides of the sea. As far as I can determine, this is not the ebb and flow of tides—this is said in order to cover the true cause—the truth is that the motion derives from the changes of atmosphere, that is, of heat and cold. I assume this from the speculations upon that experience of the *bellicone* which you know; and thus I was tempted to make myself one of these devices. I made it, not in the manner of the one designed in England, which has a tube [*canale*] made round like a ring, but with a straight tube, as you can see from the sketch which I enclose, in which the tube is to be of glass and the rest of metal, well enclosed. In the vase is enclosed the liquid, which as a result of the compression of air within the large closed vessel is attracted, and rises within the glass tube, and when the air becomes rarefied, descends. Behind the tube I have placed a tablet, divided

with frequent equidistant lines, with their numbers marked, so that it is possible to note the movement. . . . I have discovered a means of applying this
irregular motion to a regulator, to operate a clock. I am now at the point of
beginning to put it into operation; it will be an artful machine, and I hope
that it will be successful; if it does succeed, I shall then send you the design
[*11*, pp. 269–270].

A week later, Antonini wrote again with fuller details of the English
thermoscope (*11*, p. 275). The date of these letters, 1612, is significant,
because it coincides with the period of Sagredo's experimentation with the
thermoscope.

Galileo's thermoscope was undoubtedly the very first of the new developments in the science of heat. Although he never applied it for more
sensitive purposes than as an indicator to determine whether temperatures
were rising or falling, he was, nevertheless, the first man of science to
employ the expansion of air for the measurement of temperature.

The geometrical and military compass (c. 1597)

One of the most disputed inventions of the late sixteenth and early seventeenth century was that of the geometrical and military compass, attributed to Galileo. This invention was claimed by many, and priority of
claim was disputed even by nations. The controversy developed from a
confusion of terminology, and, in fact, involved not one instrument, but
several which, though similar, were not identical. The instrument was well-
known during the second half of the sixteenth century in various forms.
The most comprehensive early work on the subject was entitled *Fabrica
et uso del compasso polimetro* by Muzio Oddi d'Urbino.[15] Oddi reported
that prior to 1568, Federigo Commandino, the well-known engineer of
Urbino, had designed a compass with four points, having a movable pivot;
a series of numerical designations inscribed along its sides allowed one to
divide a straight line into a specific number of equal divisions. This instrument, which Commandino called a *compasso di riduzione* or "proportional compass", was constructed for him by a mechanic of his native city,
named Simone Baroccio. Copies of it were produced by Baroccio for various people who visited Commandino. Oddi noted that, in 1586, such an
instrument was made for Bartolomeo d'Eustachio, and that when Guidobaldo, Marchese del Monte, visited Commandino, he saw and examined
the compass and presumably even used it during his sojourn at Urbino.
After studying the compass, Guidobaldo decided that he could produce a
more efficient form of it at reduced cost. He accordingly ordered an instrument of his own design to be made by the same Baroccio in 1570.
Guidobaldo specified that it was to have flat legs formed by two rulers of
a width greater than the thickness, to be inscribed on each side with
straight lines from the center of the joint to the points, and with each side
marked in the same manner as in Commandino's compass. The other side
was to be inscribed with the sizes of the sides of various equilateral figures,
while equal angles were to be shown on the circle. Guidobaldo's instru-

ment was unquestionably a revised form of the proportional compass, although no name was assigned to it.

Other variations of the compass were produced in Italy and elsewhere prior to Galileo's preoccupation with the instrument. Among the most important of these was the *Pantometra*, a form of the proportional compass devised by Michel Coignet (1549–1623), of Antwerp.[16] Coignet was a schoolteacher who wrote on geography and navigation and established a workshop for making mathematical instruments, where he employed a number of artists and craftsmen. Associated with the Coignet instrument was another of similar characteristics devised by Fabrizio Mordente of Salerno, Mathematician to Emperor Rudolph II. He described it in his *La quadratura del cerchio*[17] and again in his *Le propositioni*.[18] Examples of Mordente's compass have survived in some of the major collections.[19] Other versions of the proportional compass, produced elsewhere during the same period, include an instrument in the Museo di Storia della Scienza in Florence which is inscribed *Jacobus Kynuyn fecit 1595 London*, and another compass, which is unsigned but dated 1596, in the collection of the Istituto di Fisica at the University of Padua.

During the period that Galileo began to work on the improvement of the compass, an instrument of the same category was produced by Justus Burgius (1552–1632), the famed clock and instrument-maker of the Landgrave of Hesse at Kassel. An example of the Burgius instrument is displayed in the Heimatsmuseum at Lichtensteig. It was described at considerable length in a work by Levinus Hulsius published in 1605.[20] It featured a mobile pivot, as did the compass of Commandino, but it also included the divisions which made it adaptable for other variable and analogous applications, ones that could be accomplished by giving Galileo's instrument a fixed point.

In all probability, Galileo first learned of the proportional compass, as Favaro has suggested, from Guidobaldo del Monte himself.[21] He and Galileo were close friends and Galileo visited his home at Pesaro often. It was to del Monte that he owed his appointment at the University of Padua. There can be little doubt that Galileo saw the compass there, and became interested in trying to improve it. It is immediately apparent from a study of the literature of this instrument and from a consideration of the many individuals who produced versions of the proportional compass independently of each other, that the invention of the proportional compass as such cannot be attributed to Galileo. He did, however, improve and develop the instrument by combining two separate instruments into one to form what was virtually a new instrument, which he called a "geometrical and military compass". It consisted of a pointed sector which could be converted to an observation instrument by the addition of a quadrant to its arms. The sector consisted of a pair of pivoted arms, which formed a calculating instrument when used alone. The proportional compass, which is an instrument of older origin, also consisted of two arms, which, however, were pointed at both ends and joined by a movable pivot. The two arms of the sector of Galileo were engraved symmetrically, each containing a set of scales radiating from a central point. The primary scales, which were inscribed on the inner edge of the front face and graduated in 250 equal divisions, were the "lines of numbers".

The pointed sector opens to make the distance between one pair of such divisions equal to a given length which has been transferred from an auxiliary scale by means of a pair of dividers. The distance between some other pair of divisions on the line of numbers is then taken with the dividers, maintaining the opening of the sector constant, and then by applying the dividers to their auxiliary scale, the result of any arithmetical multiplication or division may be derived. With such an instrument, working by the setting out of similar triangles, it is fairly simple to obtain an accuracy of 1/4 division in 250 or .1 percent, which is quite adequate for the purpose for which it was devised. Other radial scales were divided proportionally to the various functions, squares, cubes, roots, etc., and an additional scale was marked with the densities of metals and stones. The many scales made the sector a very widely used calculating instrument for gunnery, surveying, navigation and dialing. Contrary to the claim which is occasionally made, it was not displaced by the slide rule until the middle of the nineteenth century.[22]

By screwing an engraved quadrant to its arms, when opened to an angle of exactly 90°, the sector was easily converted into an observing instrument. By holding the instrument in a vertical plane, angles could be measured by sighting along one arm of the sector and reading the quadrant scale by means of a plumb-bob suspended from a tiny hole in the pivot boss. Scales for measuring scarps and laying out polygonal battlements were also provided. A foot support, which was detachable, enabled the instrument to be steadied on a flat surface while readings were being taken. The quadrant was already a well-known instrument by Galileo's time, having made its first appearance in London in about 1575. The earliest maker appears to have been Humphrey Cole. Similar instruments were produced by other English makers of about the same period, notably James Kynvyn and Charles Whitwell, and examples of their work were introduced into Italy late in the sixteenth century.[23]

Galileo first became interested in the development of the geometrical and military compass in about 1597. In the preface to his short treatise on the compass, published at his own expense in 1606, he stated: "my geometrical and military compass was first conceived by me only ten years ago, found again and perfected; in it, no others had any participation." Additional verification is to be found in Galileo's correspondence, in references made to gifts of these instruments which he gave to his associates, students and friends. Early in 1598, Sagredo received an instrument and an illustrated description of it from Galileo (2, p. 534), and in the same year an instrument and description were acknowledged by Iacopo Badovere (2, pp. 534–535).

A statement made by Fra Paolo Sarpi on April 20, 1607, gives further support. He reported that "in Padua already about ten years ago the aforementioned Galileo demonstrated to me the instrument . . . together with its application" (*2*, pp. 534–544). Finally, and even more conclusively, there is the evidence of Marcantonio Mazzoleni. According to a statement he made in 1607, he moved into Galileo's home at Padua on July 5, 1599, to become his maker of mathematical instruments (*2*, p. 535; p. 601). He continued to work for Galileo for the next ten years, producing a great number of "geometrical and military compasses" from the designs with which Galileo had furnished him at the beginning of his employment. The autograph records of payments made by Galileo to Mazzoleni throughout this period have survived, as well as accounts of payments received for instruments distributed (*19*, pp. 130–206).

Mazzoleni constructed a variety of other instruments for Galileo for commercial distribution. Noted among the records were parts of instruments, such as "a foot for an instrument", the four-pointed compass, "a compass with twisted points", squares, magnetic compasses, and drafting instruments. An item noted was a "*nocella*" or joint for a pair of compasses. The same word is used to mean a ball-and-socket joint, and it is interesting to contemplate the nature of the instrument in question.

According to Galileo's own statement, Mazzoleni produced for him in brass at least one hundred specimens of the geometrical and military compass, in addition to several examples made of gold and silver for the Archduke of Tuscany and the Landgrave Philipp of Hesse (*10*, pp. 297–298). In all, he claimed to have distributed at least three hundred of these instruments. In addition to those produced by Mazzoleni, he noted that on account of the great demand other instruments had to be constructed for him outside Padua by instrument-makers in Urbino, Florence, and in some of the German centers. Verification of the claim that he consigned some of his work to other instrument makers is to be found in a letter of November 11, 1605, to the Grandduchess Christina of Lorraine in which he informed her that "I am waiting to have sent to me the two instruments in silver so that I may sign [inscribe?] them and forward them in perfected condition . . ." (*10*, p. 149).

Whether the number of instruments produced really did total the number that Galileo claimed is somewhat dubious when account is taken of the output of other instrument makers of the fifteenth and sixteenth centuries. The instruments produced in Galileo's shop at Padua were apparently unsigned, either by Galileo himself or by Mazzoleni, since no signed examples have survived in any of the world's private or public collections. And the examples which we can attribute with some certainty to Mazzoleni, such as the one in the Museo di Storia della Scienza,[24] and another owned by Mr. David P. Wheatland, to mention only isolated examples, bear no signature.

Galileo made an equally large distribution of the printed description of the compass and its use, copies of which seem to have accompanied almost every instrument which he distributed. It was in this work that he made his strongest claim to the invention of the compass with his statement that he was ". . . the true, legitimate and only inventor, in that no others had any part whatsoever in the instrument . . ." Writing in the following year, he again reasserted his claim:

> It is already ten years since I perfected one of my instruments, which I called a "geometrical and military compass", and began to allow it to be seen by various gentlemen, demonstrating to them its use and publicizing the instrument and its operation in writings [*10,* pp. 171–172].

It was inevitable that the great diffusion that the instrument and its published description received would lead others to contemplate its duplicaion. The first incident resulted from the arrival in Padua in 1602 or 1603 of a well-known Flemish instrument-maker, Johann Zugmesser, who brought with him a proportional compass of which he claimed to be the inventor.[25] Galileo, in his own account of the incident, stated that, although Zugmesser's instrument did have some of the lines which appeared on his own, each of the instruments had features that marked it off from the other (*2,* p. 545). Incensed by the fact that some question arose about the originality and priority of his own invention, Galileo brought about a meeting with Zugmesser at the home of Iacopo Cornaro. A discussion brought out the fact that the two instruments were not copied in part or in whole from the other but were independent productions. Following this confrontation, Galileo obtained a dated statement of the proceedings and decisions signed by Cornaro, and by another witness (*10,* pp. 173–176).

The next incident, which became a notorious controversy, related to a Milanese, Aurelio Capra, who had settled in Padua soon after Galileo moved there. At this time Capra's son, Baldassare, was a young man of about twenty-seven who was engaged in studies of medicine and astronomy. Having first observed the use of Galileo's compass in Cornaro's home, the Capras, father and son, managed to borrow it and kept it for several months (*2,* pp. 536–537). It was later noted also that during this period Baldassare spent considerable time in the shop of Mazzoleni, and consequently observed the details of construction of the compasses again and again.

The next development was the publication of a treatise by Baldassare entitled *Usus et fabrica circini cujusdam proportionis.*[26] According to Favaro, this work was little more than a rephrasing of Galileo's published work on the compass which had appeared a year earlier.[27] In it, Capra not only appropriated the compass as his own invention, but he included uncomplimentary remarks about Galileo, whom he accused of plagiarism although not mentioning him by name. When the elder Capra presented a complimentary copy of the work to Cornaro, the latter was so shocked by its contents that he not only returned the copy but informed Galileo in a

letter dated April 4, 1607 (*10*, pp. 174–175). Galileo took action immediately. He went to Venice where he presented a statement to the magistrate of the Riformatori of the Studio at Padua. This statement or *memo-
riale* was published later in the same year as the celebrated *Difesa*.[28] Capra
was summoned to Venice and on April 19, both accuser and accused appeared before the magistrate. After a prolonged trial, the Riformatori
pronounced sentence on May 4. Galileo was completely vindicated, and
all copies of Capra's book were to be delivered to Venice and suppressed.
Galileo then proceded to publish his *Difesa* which was widely distributed. Many writers have felt that the incident did not merit the heated
reaction manifested by Galileo, and that he employed the occasion to
bring his own name to wider publicity. There is some basis for this belief,
because Galileo later expressed regret for his extreme action.

Sixteen years after the event, Galileo referred to the controversy with
Capra in his great polemic, *Il saggiatore*, in which he placed the blame for
the incident squarely on Simon Mayr of Guntzanhausen who was at the
University of Padua during the period of Galileo's residence.[29] According
to Galileo:

> He it was in Padua, where I resided at the time, who set forth the uses of
> my compass in Latin and had one of his pupils [Baldassare Capra] publish
> this and sign it. Then, perhaps to escape punishment, he departed immedi-
> ately for his native land and left his pupil in the lurch. In Simon Mayr's
> absence I was forced to proceed against his pupil, in the manner described
> in the *Difesa* which I published at this time.[30]

One cannot help but be somewhat skeptical of Galileo's explanation, inasmuch as the name of Simon Mayr did not appear in his *Difesa*, nor in the
legal proceedings against Capra. It must be admitted, however, that Mayr
was mentioned with praise in Capra's preface to his *Usus et fabrica*. Galileo's dislike of Mayr is clear:

> Now four years after my *Starry messenger* appeared, the same fellow (in
> the habit of trying to ornament himself with other people's works) unblush-
> ingly made himself the author of the things I had discovered and printed in
> that book. Publishing under the title of *The world of Jupiter*, he had the
> gall to claim that he had observed the Medicean planets which revolve about
> Jupiter before I had   But note his sly way of attempting to establish his
> priority. I had written of making my first observation on the seventh of
> January, 1610. Along comes Mayr, and, appropriating my very observa-
> tions, he prints on the title page of his book that he had made his observa-
> tions in the year 1609. But he neglects to warn the reader that he is a Protes-
> tant, and hence had not accepted the Gregorian calendar. Now the seventh
> day of January, 1610, for us Catholics, is the same as the twenty-eighth day
> of December, 1609, for those heretics. And so much for his pretended prior-
> ity of observation.

The Capras, father and son, returned to Milan shortly after this incident, and their name did not appear again in the annals of science. Galileo

continued to produce compasses and treatises regarding their use at least
until 1610. Writing to Belisario Vinta in March of that year, he noted:

> I am forced to reprint also *The use of the geometrical compass*, since there
> are no more copies, and we continue to construct continually these com-
> passes of mine, of which until now more than three hundred have passed
> through my hands, and for which I have requests from various groups . . .
> [*10*, p. 299].

The treatise on the use of the compass was reprinted several times during
Galileo's lifetime; it was translated into Latin by Matteo Bernegger with
additions and explanations. This version was in turn retranslated into Italian.

Galileo thus continued to produce the compass until the advent of the
telescope diverted him to astronomical observation. It is worth asking
what the reaction of Galileo's sponsor, the Marchese del Monte, was to
the notoriety which the mathematician had achieved with the compass for
which he had himself provided the inspiration. Happily, documentation of
del Monte's reaction has survived. During the period of the controversy,
Orazio, Marchese del Monte, Guidobaldo's son, was in Padua visiting Galileo (*2*, p. 531; *10*, p. 71, p. 143). Clearly, no difficulties had arisen between
the two older men over the attribution of the compass, since Guidobaldo
had sent his son to Padua to study with Galileo. When Orazio returned
home, he brought with him an example of Galileo's compass, which he
undoubtedly showed to his father, who was still alive. Guidobaldo gave
no indication that he was the first inventor of the instrument, nor was any
perturbation noted. Several years later (June 16, 1610), Orazio del Monte
wrote to Galileo that "we are expecting something relating to your geometric instrument, because in your little books you promise some day to
reveal something more . . ." (*10*, p. 372). And in the same letter Orazio
noted that he planned to bring to light various unpublished works by his
father, describing "the construction of several instruments discovered by
him", among which was undoubtedly the proportional compass he had
designed.

The combination which Galileo made of the sector and the quadrant
resulted in probably the most useful mathematical instrument of that
period, not only to the mathematician but to the engineer, the navigator,
and others. It is consequently not surprising that the instrument and
his description of its construction and use enjoyed such wide distribution
and popularity throughout Europe, not only in his own time, but in the
decades that followed. It was developed into still other versions with improvements, and it led to the publication of numerous writings on its description and use, including those by Ottavio Revesi Bruti,[31] Domenico
Lusuerg,[32] Paolo Casati,[33] Giovanni Pagnini,[34] and D. Henrion,[35] to mention only the most outstanding.

The lodestone (c. 1601)

The publication of William Gilbert's *De Magnete* in 1600 aroused considerable interest everywhere in the new science of magnetism. It was inevitable that this new field would come to the attention of Galileo and incite him to pursue the subject. He was vastly impressed by Gilbert's work:

> I have the highest praise, admiration and envy for this author, who framed such a stupendous concept concerning an object which innumerable men of splendid intellect had handled without paying any attention to it . . . [7, p. 432].

One of the earliest references to Galileo's preoccupation with the study of magnetism occurs in a letter from Fra Paolo Sarpi at Venice (September 2, 1602), in which the writer reported his attempts to construct the apparatus described by Gilbert, in order to pursue further experiments of his own:

> I had no difficulty whatsoever with the spring; it is a fine type of helical generated from two circular motions. I beg you to have some consideration concerning my difficulties, and I plead with you because of the lack of my author [Gilbert], who has left the causes to the most obscure parts of his book. If he had only stated how he arrived at them! Therefore, because I wish to experiment with this declination, it would save me much work if you would write to me the manner in which the electroscope [*versorio*] is made, with what the pivots are applied, whether with fire or with glue, and how and of what material they are made, and on what they are placed, and in fact every detail, because I do not want to waste time experimenting with many things, since you have already done this work [*10*, pp. 91–93].

This statement shows that Galileo had already been experimenting with magnetism, to Sarpi's knowledge.

Without formally replying to Sarpi's letter, Galileo sent him instead a magnetic compass (*bussola de diclinazione*) which he had already had constructed. It was delivered by Sagredo, whom Galileo had instructed in its details, so that he could provide Sarpi with any additional data he required. The instrument was Galileo's interpretation of Gilbert's somewhat obscure description, and presumably it included improvements.

On October 18, 1602, after his arrival in Venice, Sagredo wrote to Galileo:

> I thank you for the irons [*ferri*]. I shall give to P. M. Paolo the *declinatorio* [dip needle], and I shall serve as ambassador for that which you require. I have tried out the *declinatorio* in the manner in which you showed me. The effect of remaining perpendicular, when it is placed exactly upon the meridian, worked out very well for me, and when situated under the parallel, I have seen the declination, but regarding the (degree of) more or less it seems to me to be a matter for philosophizing . . . [*10*, pp. 96–97].

Galileo's interest in the new magnetic science was hampered by other projects on which he was engaged at the time, but he planned to make new observations, and to continue his studies as opportunity presented itself. It was probably not until five years later, in 1607, that Galileo resumed his studies of magnetism. This was brought about by the desire expressed by Prince Cosimo de'Medici, one of his pupils, to acquire a lodestone for himself. According to Favaro, the lodestone was probably first brought to the Prince's attention by Galileo himself on one of his sojourns in Florence during academic vacation at Padua, and his account of its properties may have inspired a desire in the Prince to own one.[36]

This led to a long correspondence between Galileo at Padua with the Prince's secretary, Curzio Picchena, and with Belisario Vinta, the Tuscan Secretary of State. On November 16, 1607, Galileo informed Picchena that he had acquired a small lodestone which, however, was "of an inelegant shape" (*10*, pp. 184–186). He added that a friend (who later proved to be Sagredo) owned a fine, large lodestone having a good shape, and which weighed about 5 *libre*.[37] Sagredo was willing to sell it for a suitable price, which he estimated to be about 400 gold *scudi*. The Prince's emissaries considered the price to be exorbitant and refused the offer. Galileo then managed to convince Sagredo to reduce the price, and he purchased the lodestone for himself without obtaining a commitment from Florence beforehand. He informed Vinta that the stone weighed 53 Venetian ounces and that it might possibly total five ounces less in Florence but that such a small reduction in weight was inconsequential (*10*, pp. 194–195).

Galileo experimented with armoring the lodestone, and succeeded in having it sustain 5½ *libre* of iron, and expressed the hope that he could increase the amount of suspended weight even more. He reported the results of new experiments with the lodestone to Vinta (February 8, 1608), noting that:

> first of all, the points in the stone where the strength is greatest, are two poles only, and it is necessary to exercise diligence to locate them. Furthermore, the virtue of the suspension is not less in the iron than in the lodestone, inasmuch as it is not all iron nor of any shape or size that is sustained equally, but the most elaborate steel of a particular shape and size is that which attaches most strongly. Furthermore the armoring of the poles, whether attached a little more this way or that, can result in considerable variation, and during these four days during which I have been preoccupied with it, I have caused it to sustain almost a *libra* more than that which the owner of the stone had ever seen it sustain, and I have hopes that I can construct some pieces of steel most fine which will result in its sustaining even more weight [*10*, pp. 188–191].

A few months later (May 3, 1608), Galileo wrote to Vinta that he had succeeded in having the lodestone sustain more than twice its own weight, and that he had constructed an armature in the form of a small anchor (*anchorette*). The name 'anchor' (*ancora*) he said was:

given always to the iron which fits closely within the poles of the lodestone. I have had these two irons constructed in the form of two small anchors, partly in order to give it some form, and also for the purpose of being able to say, when alluding to it, that a lodestone has been found so large and strong that it upheld a ship's anchor, as well as for the convenience of these branches from which may be suspended other diverse pieces (of iron) to the final limit of its strength [*10*, pp. 205–209].

The price of the lodestone was finally fixed at 100 *dobles* (doubloons). Payment for it was made to Galileo after April 20, 1608 (*10*, pp. 200–201), and Galileo accordingly forwarded the lodestone to Picchena at Florence on May 3. In an accompanying letter, Galileo noted that he had armored the lodestone in such a manner that it sustained a weight two and a half times its own weight. He added that, in his opinion, the strength of the lodestone would be increased or diminished in proportion to its distance from the Arctic and Antarctic Poles. He informed Picchena that the longer the lodestone sustained the iron weight, the greater would be its subsequent strength, and that, in effect, the attachment of the weight reinvigorated the lodestone. The high-priced lodestone which Galileo furnished to Prince Cosimo was subsequently lost, according to letters from G. W. Leibniz to Antonio Magliabecchi, dated January 17,[38] and June 13, 1698.[39] The loss was greatly deplored by Leibniz, who apparently attributed some importance to Galileo's work with magnetism.

Galileo was subsequently distracted from his study of magnetism by the development of the telescope and his astronomical observations, which occupied almost all of his time during the years that followed. He did not return to the subject of magnetism, it seems, until almost ten years later. In a file relating to the Medici family, there is an entry marked '1618?', noting that Galileo had delivered "a squared piece of magnetite [lodestone] without decoration, inside a small walnut case enclosed in a small sack of blue parchment".[40] This lodestone, which appears to have been small in size and without armature, did not occur in subsequent records.

Magnetism is not mentioned again in his correspondence until eight years later (June 27, 1626), when he informed Cesare Marsigli about his efforts to improve and increase the strength of a lodestone by means of an armature:

For the past three months I have been on an admirable project which is the extreme multiplication of the strength of a lodestone for the suspension of iron by artificial means. I have already succeeded in having a lodestone of six ounces, which by its natural force alone did not sustain more than one ounce of iron, succeed in sustaining 150 ounces by means of artifice, and hope to have it soon exceeded even more . . . [*13*, pp. 327–328].

Galileo probably made these tests with a lodestone which he subsequently presented to Archduke Ferdinand II. This was a smaller example than the one he had purchased for Prince Cosimo. The gift was described by Benedetto Castelli in a discussion of the lodestone, based on Gilbert's theory, which he addressed to Monsignor Cesarini:

> I have seen a lodestone of weight of six ounces only, which was armored in iron with exquisite diligence by Galileo, and presented to the Most Serene Archduke Ferdinand, which was able to hold suspended fifteen *libre* of iron and which was constructed in the shape of a sepulchre . . .[41]

It seems quite certain that this lodestone is in fact the example now preserved in the collection of the Museo di Storia della Scienza in Florence, since all details coincide as to the size of the lodestone and the form of the suspended iron.[42] Although numerous payments for the construction of instruments are itemized in the autograph records of the expenses of Galileo's workshop from 1599 and 1634 there does not appear to be any mention of lodestones or armatures (*19*, pp. 130–149). Mariner's compasses are, however, mentioned now and then, a fact of some interest in this context. The earliest of these compasses was produced for Galileo by Mazzoleni in 1599. The accounts for October 25 of that year listed "a mariner's compass pierced with fretwork and engraved by him". In the following year, five such mariner's compasses are mentioned in the records, all of which were made for an unidentified German noted as "S". On January 25, 1601, Galileo paid Mazzoleni 30 *lire* for "a mariner's compass pierced but not engraved"; while on June 28, 1603, Mazzoleni was paid 20 *lire* for "a mariner's compass divided only, and for having pierced its card". On September 9 of the same year, Galileo noted that Mazzoleni had agreed to complete for him two pierced mariner's compasses. The last entry for these items appeared under the date of December 9, 1606, when Mazzoleni was paid 18 *lire* for a mariner's compass.

From a study of Galileo's correspondence relating to his experiments with magnetism, it is obvious that he was early aware of the inadequacy of the armature prescribed by Gilbert, and that he proceeded to improve it in a variety of ways. It is interesting to speculate what Galileo might have achieved in his study of magnetism and electricity had he not been diverted by his astronomical observations. Although his experiments with armatures were unquestionably successful, he does not appear to have added anything of notable significance either to the understanding or to the development of the field.

The telescope (1609)

It has been established with a fair degree of certainty that the first telescopes made in Italy were produced by Galileo. He learned of the instrument for the first time in Padua around June 1609, and constructed, or had constructed for him, his own first telescope before July 25 of the same year. The advent of the telescope in Italy was recorded in the correspondence of Galileo's contemporaries, as well as in his own. The instrument was first viewed and mentioned in Italy by Fra Paolo Sarpi late in 1608 at

Venice. According to his anonymous biographer, when a telescope "was presented to the Serene Signoria, with a request for a thousand zecchini, it was Sarpi who was assigned to make tests to determine who could use it and give judgment; and he conferred with Sig. Galileo, who found that Sarpi had given the sign . . ." [43]

It was specified that Sarpi was not permitted to dismantle the instrument, and consequently he knew nothing of the details of its construction. Although scholars have questioned the account because of lack of supporting evidence, there is no doubt that Sarpi was, in fact, involved with the first telescopic instruments brought into Italy. He seemed to assign little importance to the instrument at that time, however, as is clear from his letter of January 6, 1609, to De l'Isle Groslot, in which he noted that "I have already had the notice about the new telescopes more than a month ago, and I believe that it is not necessary to search any further, nor to philosophize over it, Socrates having prohibited philosophizing over things not personally observed . . ." [44]

Meanwhile the telescope had already made its appearance in other parts of Europe, particularly in Paris, as noted in *La Mercure François:*

In this same month of April (1609) in Paris may be seen in the shops of the lens-makers a new fashion of lenses. On the two ends of a round tube of white iron and one foot in length, there are two glasses, each of them disassemblable; to observe that which one wishes to see, one closes one eye and places the *lunette* at the other eye, and with it one can recognize a person of half *lieue;* there are craftsmen who make these better than others . . .[45]

Galileo made it clear in his own writings that the telescope first came to his attention sometime in June 1609. He described the circumstances in a letter to his brother-in-law, dated August 29:

About two months ago a rumor spread here that in Flanders a gift had been made to Count Maurice of a telescope, constructed with such skill that it made very distant objects look as if they were close by, so that a man two miles away could be seen distinctly [*10*, p. 253].

Although the editors of the National Edition of Galileo's collected works have questioned the authenticity of this letter, it has since been substantiated by E. Rosen.[46]

The incident was noted again in the early part of his *Sidereus nuncius* (1610). After announcing his discovery of the satellites of Jupiter, he noted that "about ten months ago a report reached my ears that a certain Fleming had constructed a spyglass by means of which visual objects, though very distant from the eye of the observer, were seen distinctly as if nearby . . ." [47] The phrase 'eight months ago' in the original manuscript was changed to 'ten months ago' in the published version, again coinciding with the date of June 1609 (*3*, p. 18).

How Galileo became involved is related in the continuation of the passage quoted from the *Sidereus nuncius:*

A few days later the report was confirmed to me in a letter from a noble
Frenchman at Paris, Jacques Badovere, which caused me to apply myself
wholeheartedly to inquire into the means by which I might arrive at the
invention of a similar instrument. This I did shortly afterwards, my basis
being the theory of refractions.

According to his account in *Il saggiatore*, he reacted much more
quickly than is to be assumed from the foregoing, in which he seems to
indicate that several days had passed before he did so:

> The part that I had in the invention of this instrument, and whether I can
> reasonably call it my own offspring, I made clear long ago in my *Sidereus
> nuncius*, in which I stated that while I happened to be in Venice, the news
> came that a Dutchman had presented to Count Maurice an eyeglass with
> which it was possible to see distant objects as clearly as if they were quite
> close. Nothing further was added. At this report I returned to Padua, where I
> was then living, and began to think over this problem. I solved it the first
> night following my return. The next day I made the instrument, and gave an
> account of it at Venice to the same friends with whom I had discussed the
> project the day before. . . . Then I applied myself to making a better one,
> which I brought to Venice six days later. It was seen there with great aston-
> ishment by almost all the leading gentlemen of that republic for more than an
> entire month, but I was very weary. Finally, upon the advice of one of my
> sympathetic supporters, I presented it to the Doge before the full Collegio
> . . . [*6*, pp. 257–258].

The full story of Galileo's first two telescopes is summarized in that passage. As a recompense, the Doge rewarded Galileo with a renewal and
confirmation of his professorship at the university of Padua for the remainder of his life, at a salary of one thousand florins a year. Galileo stated
that he planned to make his presentation of the telescope to the Doge and
the Collegio on July 25, and the resolution confirming Galileo's appointment was made on the same date. Since Galileo noted that the telescope
was being observed by the Venetian gentlemen for more than a month, it is
clear that his second instrument was completed and presented in Venice
before June 25, and that his first instrument had been constructed a few
days earlier. A comprehensive study made by Rosen of the contemporary
evidence has established these dates with a fair degree of certainty.[48]
   Although the telescope presented by Galileo to the Doge and the Signoria of Venice has not survived, an indication of its focal power was
noted by Galileo, who described his instrument as:

> a new artifice of a telescope [*occhiale*] constructed by means of the most
> recondite speculations of perspective, which conducts visible objects close to
> the eye; so large and distinct are they represented, that that which is distant,
> say, nine miles, appears to be at a distance of only one mile [*10*, p. 250].

A complete description of the instrument's appearance was recorded in
the *Cronaca* of Antonio di Girolamo Priuli.[49] He had personally taken part

The Scientific Instruments of Galileo Galilei

The scientific instruments which Galileo redesigned or modified and used for scientific purposes were constructed for him by artisans in Florence and other Italian cities. Extremely few of these have survived, and almost all of the instruments personally associated with Galileo are in the Medici collections in the Istituto e Museo di Storia della Scienza in Florence.

The cooperation of the Director of the Istituto, Prof.ssa Dott.ssa Maria Luisa Righini-Bonelli, in making photographs of these instruments available for this work is gratefully acknowledged.

Figure 1. Large astrolabe in contemporary table mounting attributed to Egnazio Danti 1584 and claimed to have been owned and used by Galileo, and owned in seventeenth-century Medici collections. *Courtesy of the Istituto e Museo di Storia della Scienza, Florence.*

Figure 2. Early Italian sliding tube compound microscope attributed to Galileo, but probably constructed circa 1660. *Courtesy of the Istituto e Museo di Storia della Scienza, Florence.*

Figure 3. Armored lodestone in the Medici collection, believed to have been made for Galileo for presentation to Archduke Ferdinand II. *Courtesy of the Istituto e Museo di Storia della Scienza, Florence.*

Figure 4. Two telescopes and an object lens used by Galileo. The instruments consist of wooden tubes covered with cloth or leather, with biconvex objectives and biconcave ocular lenses. Also shown is a biconcave objective of Galileo, mounted in an ornate ivory and ebony frame. *Courtesy of the Istituto e Museo di Storia della Scienza, Florence.*

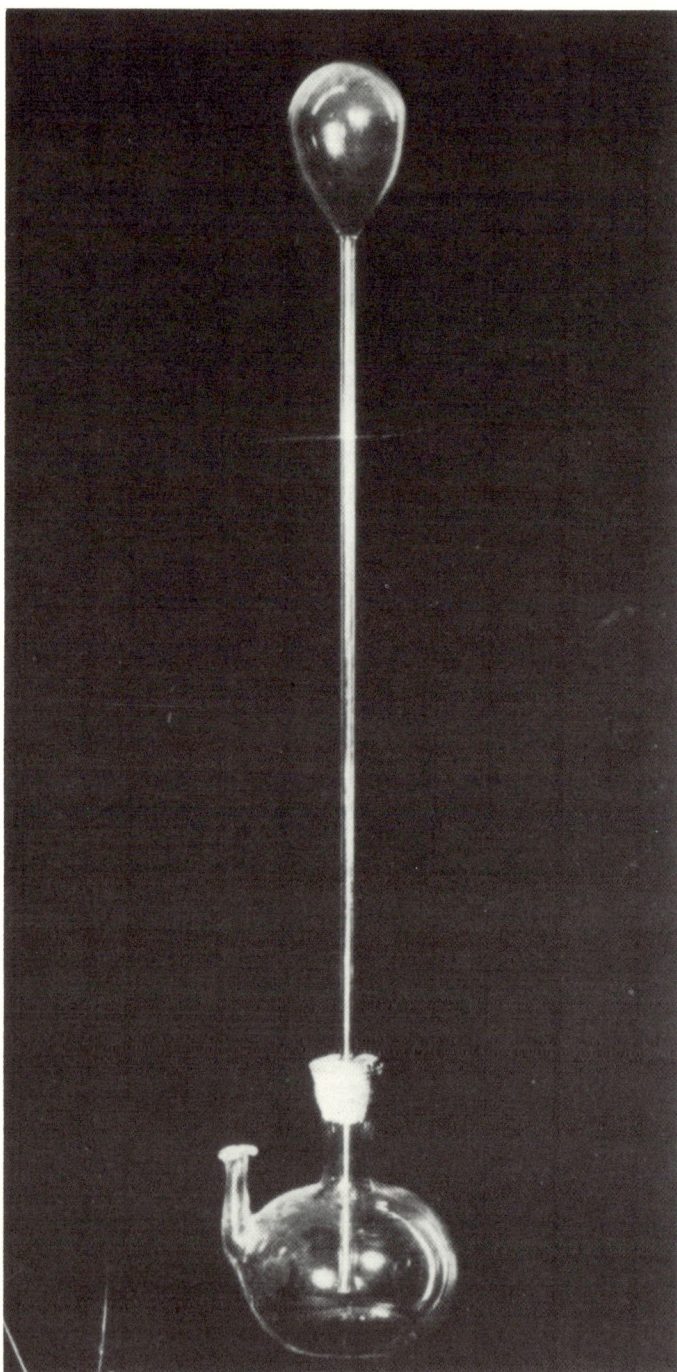

Figure 5. Model of Galileo's thermoscope. No contemporary model is known to have survived. *Courtesy of the Istituto e Museo di Storia della Scienza, Florence.*

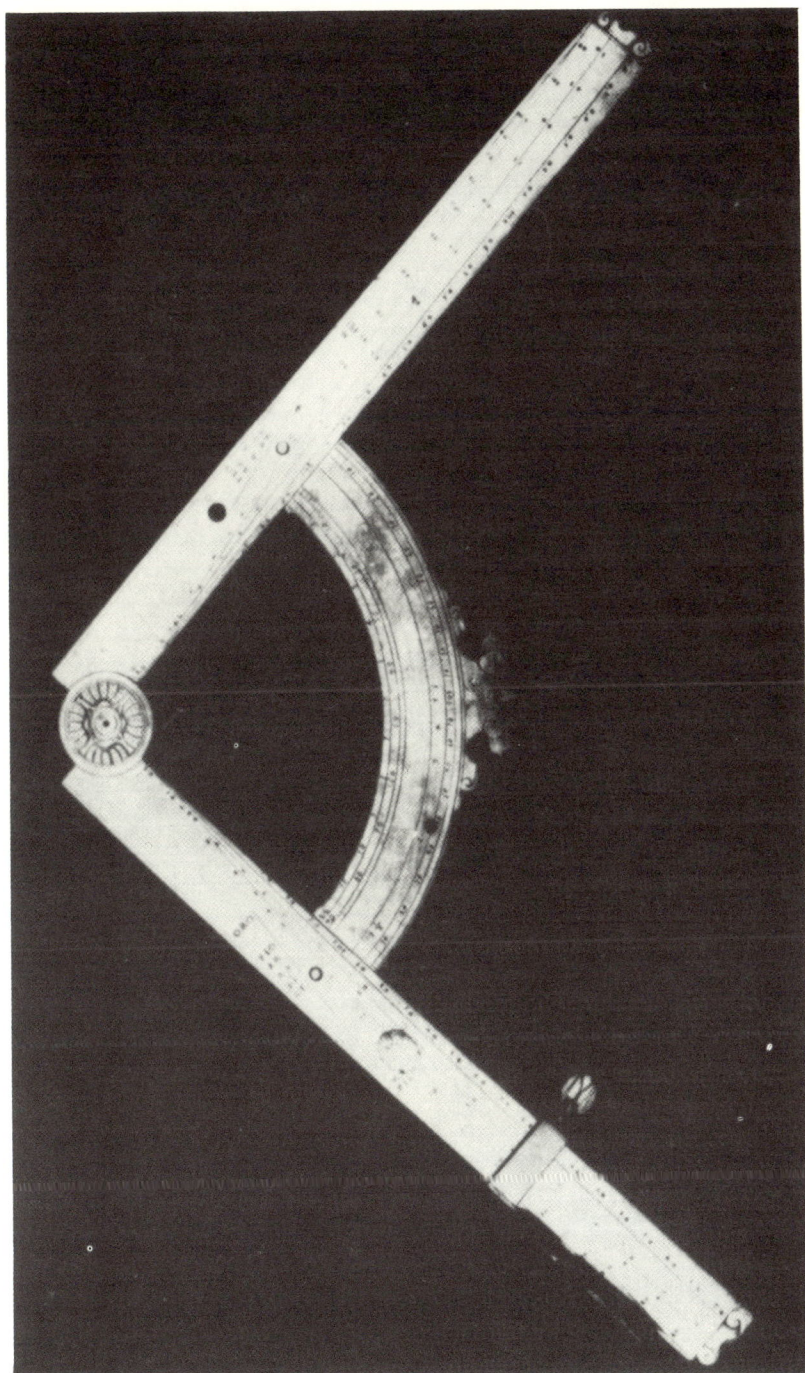

Figure 6. Galileo's geometrical and military compass. None of the instruments produced for Galileo are known to have been signed with the name of either Galileo or the craftsman. *Courtesy of the Istituto e Museo di Storia della Scienza, Florence.*

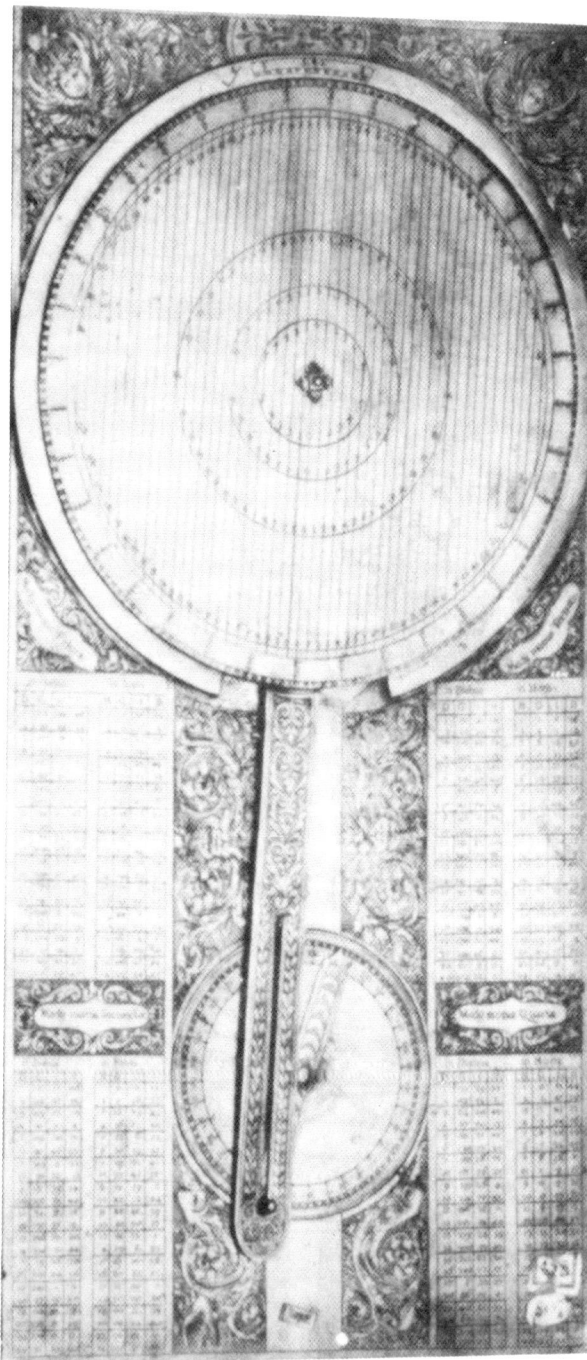

Figure 7. Galileo's 'Giovilabio', formerly the property of Prince Leopold de Medici. Based on Galileo's
design, the instrument was probably made after his
death. *Courtesy of the Istituto e Museo di Storia
della Scienza, Florence.*

in the tests of Galileo's instrument, and he related that he had climbed to the campanile of Saint Mark's with Galileo and the gentlemen of Venice on August 21, 1609:

> to see the marvellous and effective singularity of the telescope [*cannocchiale*] of the aforesaid Galileo, which consisted of *banda* [50] covered on the outside with a variety of crimson cotton material, of a length of about three quarters and a half,[51] and of the diameter of a *scudo*,[52] with two glasses, one . . . [*sic*] concave, and the other not, on either end, with which, when raised to one eye and the other eye closed, any one of us were able to see distinctly as far as Liza Fusina and Marghera, even Chioza, Treviso and as far as Conegliano and the campanile and cupola with the facade of the church of Saint Giustina of Padua.[53] It was possible to distinguish those who entered and departed from the church of Saint Giacomo of Murano, and one could see persons entering and dismounting from the gondolas at the ferry at the Collona at the beginning of the Canal of the Glass-workers, with many other details in the lagoon and the city which were truly admirable . . . multiplying the vision with it more than nine times.

Meanwhile, Giovanni Bartoli, a Tuscan agent in Venice, could not resist the temptation to report some additional details and conjectures about the telescope's introduction to Venice, in the course of his correspondence with Belisario Vinta, Secretary of State of the Florentine court. On August 22, 1609, he reported that:

> there has arrived here a certain person who wishes to give to the Signoria the secret of a telescope [*occhiale o cannone*] or other instrument with which can be seen a distance of 25 to 30 miles very clearly, which (it is said) appears as if it is present at hand; and many have seen and made trials with it from the Campanile of St. Mark's. But it is said that in France and elsewhere this secret is already common, and that it can be purchased for little money; and many are said to have had it and seen it . . . [*10*, p. 255].

A week later, on August 29, Bartoli again wrote to Vinta that:

> almost more than anyone else, Sig. Galileo Galilei, Mathematician of Padua, has caused talk this week with the invention of the telescope or tube to observe at a distance. And it is recounted that this certain stranger who had come here with this secret, having heard from I do not know whom (it is said from Fra Paolo, Servitan Theologian) that he would have no success whatsoever here, in his claim for 1000 zecchini, departed without attempting anything else; so that, since Fra Paolo and Galileo are friends, he told him of the secret he had seen; it is said that this Galilei, with his mind and the help of another similar instrument, but not of such a good quality, which had come from France, investigated and discovered the secret; and putting it into action, with the prestige and favor of various senators, he acquired from these gentlemen an augmentation to his own provision to the amount of 1000 florins a year, with the obligation, however, it seems to me, to serve perpetually in his lectureship [*10*, p. 255].

A useful picture of the events of the next few months emerges from Bartoli's mixture of news and gossip. On September 5, 1609, he wrote Vinta that:

> the secret or "tube of the long view" of Sig. Galileo is now being sold publicly by a certain Frenchman, who is constructing them here as a secret from France, not of Galilei's; it is possible that they might not be the same, and that the (instrument of the Frenchman) truly is worth few zecchini . . . [*10*, p. 257].

It was inevitable that local competition in the production of telescopes would develop immediately. Once more the circumstances are reported by Bartoli to Vinta on September 26, 1609:

> Of the secret or "tube of long vision", it must be said that truly they are being sold in many places, and every spectacle-maker pretends to have found it, and they make and sell them. A Frenchman in particular, who makes them secretly, sells them for three or four zecchini and even for two or less, according to the degree of perfection. Some are of rock crystal, which costs a great deal, ten or twelve scudi for the glasses alone, others of crystal from Murano, and of ordinary glass; and this person pretends that his is the true "secret", and that it is equal to or better than those of Galilei. But as for me, who have seen several and in particular one which (the Frenchman) sold for three zecchini to the Master of the Post at Prague, I must confess that they do not give satisfaction, because, being longer than a *braccio*, it is necessary to struggle for a while to find with the eye the object that one wishes to see, and when found, it is necessary to keep the instrument very steady, because if it moves a little, the object will be lost. Those of Galilei are said not to suffer as much from imperfection (although even those a little). He has given it as his "secret", and having made twelve of them for the Signoria, has orders not to instruct others in making them; and I have been unable to talk to him about it, because he is in Padua. Believe me, however, it will soon be discovered by others with ease that the secret lies in the good quality of the material of the lenses and in their adjustment in the tube [*10*, pp. 259–260].

It is quite clear from the writings of Galileo himself, as well as from the accounts of his contemporaries on the scene, that the first two telescopes which Galileo produced were terrestrial telescopes designed for viewing objects at a distance. They were inspired by, and based upon, the instruments produced in Flanders and France, which were admittedly designed for military purposes, to observe ships at sea and enemy action in wartime.

It was not until late in 1609 that Galileo was first inspired to turn his instrument skywards and apply it to celestial observations. In a letter dated January 7, 1610, to Antonio de'Medici, he described his first astronomical observations:

> I shall briefly relate that which I have observed with one of my telescopes looking at the face of the moon. I was able to observe it as though at a distance of less than three diameters of the earth . . . (and) of a diameter twenty times larger than it appeared with a naked eye; its surface appeared

400 times larger, and its body 8000 times larger, than it ordinarily does [*10*, p. 273].

It was with this instrument that Galileo made his first observations of the planet Jupiter. In the same letter, he provided some basic instructions on the use of the telescope for this purpose, and described some of the problems in its employment. He emphasized that it was necessary:

> that the instrument remain steady and therefore, in order to avoid the wavering of the hand which proceeds from the motion of the arteries and of the respiration itself, it would be wise to attach the tube to some stable place. The lenses must be kept very bright and clean with a cloth, and free of mist [54] from the breath, the humid air and fog, and the steam from the eye itself, as well as from excessive heating and evaporation.[55] It would be well if the tube could be capable of being elongated or shortened a little (about 3 or 4 inches),[56] because I have found that in order to see objects close by distinctly, the tube must be longer, and for distant objects shorter. It would be well if the convex lens, which is the furthest from the eye, were in part covered, and that the opening which is left open be of an oval shape, because in this manner it would be possible to see objects much more distinctly.

Galileo's reference to the oval shape of his object lens is of considerable interest. Further details on the subject are found in a letter to him (December 17, 1610) from Cristoforo Clavio, in which the latter inquired why the objective was covered (*10*, p. 485). He remarked that it was thought that the object-lenses were made in this manner so that they could be uncovered at night for observing the stars. Galileo replied to him that:

> I have made some lenses much larger, although I then covered a large part of them, and this is for two reasons: the first is so that I can grind them more accurately, since on a more spacious surface it is possible to maintain the shape much better than on a small one, the other is if one wished to have a wider field of vision for an observation, it is possible to uncover the lens; but at the eye-piece it is necessary to have a lens less acute and to shorten the tube, otherwise the object will be seen very clouded [*10*, pp. 501–502].

During this period, Galileo established a workshop for the construction of telescopes, for which requests came to him from all parts. In order to fill an order for twelve instruments for the Signoria of Venice, he had to order lenses from Florence; the Murano supply apparently could not suffice for such a large order (*10*, pp. 259–360). In August 1609, Enea Piccolomini wrote to Galileo that he had been asked by His Highness (de'Medici) to say that he would be grateful if Galileo would make a telescope for him and forward it (*10*, pp. 254–255).

Galileo obtained some of his early lenses from Florence as well as from Venice. In another letter on June 19, Piccolomini congratulated Galileo on the telescope and the honors it had brought to him. He went on to say that lenses (*cristalli*) conforming to your specifications are being forwarded to you, and if you would wish to do something pleasing to His Highness, manage that the telescope is made at the first opportunity, because it is by him much desired [*10*, pp. 258–259].

Galileo must have kept a large number of lenses on hand at home during this period. His mother, who had recently departed from Padua, on one occasion suggested to Alessandro Piersanti, Galileo's servant, that he should take three or four without the owner becoming aware of it, but not those for short-sightedness which are concave, that is, the ocular lenses (*10*, p. 279). Instead he was to take them "from those which are plane and which go into the tube, that is those which are at the end, and which when one observes from that end, one can see distant things"; they were thus object-lenses.

There is no way to determine how many telescopes Galileo produced, but it is certain that they were numerous, as attested by a draft of a letter to Vinta (March 19, 1610): "I still have ten telescopes, which alone, of a hundred and more which I have constructed at great expense and effort, are suitable for making the observations of the new planets and of the fixed stars" (*10*, p. 298).

In the copy of the letter which he mailed from Padua, he added that:

> the most exquisite telescopes suitable to demonstrate the observations are extremely rare, and from among more than sixty which had been constructed with great expense and effort, I have been able to select only the smallest number, for these few I had planned to send to great princes and in particular to the relatives of the Most Serene Archduke; and already I have requests from the Most Serene Duke of Bavaria and the Elector of Cologne as well as the Most Illustrious and Most Reverend Cardinal Del Monte; to whom I shall send them at the first opportunity together with the treatise [*10*, p. 301].

Galileo wrote again to Vinta on May 7, 1610, referring to telescopes and stated that he would: "try to bring myself to finish a pair or two, although for me it is considerable work. Yet I do not wish to have to demonstrate to others the true method of making them." [57]

Upon his arrival in Florence, Galileo informed Giuliano di'Medici that:

> I have not yet been settled into a house, and I will not be settled until All Saints' Day, conforming to the usage in Florence. For this reason, I have not been able to provide accommodations for my equipment for making telescopes, of which some parts have to be cemented in, and they cannot be transported: so do not be surprised if I delay in sending Your Highness your telescope, but I shall do my best to see that the delay will be compensated for by the excellence of the instrument. It is necessary to delay the work also because of the lack of glass; four days ago Niccolo Sisti, upon the commission of the Archduke, was to have put a pan of glass into the furnace, and promised me to make some most pure and excellent for these artefacts [*10*, pp. 440–441].

Galileo continued to produce telescopes for a considerable period of time, even while negotiating with the States General of the Netherlands, as evidenced in a letter from Dino Peri dated February 18, 1637 (*17*, pp. 30–31). Meanwhile, other craftsmen during the same period had begun to make telescopes in Italy, including such artisans as Giovanni Lodovico Ramponi, Antonio Santini, P. Paolo Lembo and Daniello Antonini.

Another invention ascribed to Galileo by Giovanbattista Clemente de Nelli was the binocular telescope.[58] Nelli claimed that, although binoculars were first mentioned in print in 1645,[59] the instrument had actually been constructed in 1618, twenty-seven years earlier, by Galileo. Galileo named the instrument a *"celatone"* or "large helmet" because of its form. He devised the instrument for making astronomical observations on board ship, in order to determine longitude at sea in any location. As far as can be ascertained from Galileo's letters, the instrument consisted of two telescopic tubes attached to a type of helmet or morion, which, when placed on the head, held firm before the eyes of the person wearing it the *"celata"* or binocular telescope. By means of this instrument, it was possible to see at its proper elevation any object immediately and without delay, which was not possible otherwise on shipboard. The motion of the ship would not permit a tripod-mounted instrument to remain fixed on the object to be observed. This alleged invention of Galileo is mentioned also in Viviani's life of Galileo:

> His Highness desired that this invention . . . (for determining longitude at sea) should be immediately undertaken and wished that Sig. Galileo should facilitate the means for bringing it to successful completion, and confer on His Majesty another of his new discoveries which was also of considerable use in navigation, highly esteemed by His Highness, and treated with great secrecy. This consisted of a different type of telescope, by means of which it was possible from the top of a tree or from the mast-head of a galley, to recognize in the distance the quality, number and force of enemy vessels [*19*, pp. 614–615].

Galileo made his first field tests of his binocular instrument in March 1617 on the *Molo* at the harbor of Leghorn. The vessel on which he was testing his equipment was struck by a heavy wind which caused the vessel to roll excessively. This inspired Galileo to design a special "machine" in which the observer could be seated and completely disassociated from the movement of the vessel. Galileo had this "machine", or special chair, constructed at the Arsenal at Pisa (*12*, pp. 311–312). It was installed in a small boat which floated on a body of water apparently contained on shipboard. Galileo's theory was that this arrangement of "a vessel within a vessel" would eliminate the effect of the motion of the galley on the observer. This arrangement was mentioned some years later in a letter from Giovanni Pierucci to Galileo (September 6, 1641), in which he remarked:

> I for one did not plan to say anything to anyone of the means of putting it into practice, nor of the thoughts or discoveries I learned from you many

times verbally, and particularly of that equilibrium with water to be made in the middle of a vessel, in which was to remain the man with a telescope [*18*, pp. 348–350].

Galileo, working together with Castelli, made further field tests of his binocular helmet aboard Tuscan galleys in the harbor at Leghorn during the month of September 1617. He subsequently developed a special harness into which the observer with the binocular helmet was strapped. This harness was then suspended within a framework which in turn was attached to another framework upon the boat on board the galley.[60] It was Castelli who brought the helmet to the attention of Giovanni de'Medici at Pisa during this period (*12*, pp. 373–374). Castelli also informed Archduke Leopold of Austria of Galileo's new instrument when the latter passed through Pisa, and he expressed an interest in it. Galileo presented him with one of his binocular helmets and in an accompanying letter dated May 23, 1618, he mentioned that:

> I am sending you also another smaller telescope [*cannoncino*], made with a head-strap (or hat block) of brass. It is made without any adornment, because it would not be useful to your Highness except as a model and sample from which another could be constructed which would fit the shape and size of your own head, or the head of the person who will be using it. This instrument and its attachment cannot possibly be fitted for use without some knowledge of the head and the eyes of the person who is to use it. The adjustment consists in a difference of position, higher or lower, inclined a little more to the left or to the right, almost indivisibly. Since your Highness does not lack for artisans who from this model can serve you exquisitely, I beg you to keep it as secret as possible for my various personal interests [*12*, pp. 389–392].

Archduke Leopold acknowledged receipt of

> the little telescope with a helmet about which instrument I was informed while passing through Pisa by Don Benedetto [Castelli], the memory of which gives me great pleasure. All of these items arrived safely, and have been found to be in good order [*12*, pp. 397–398].

A short time later Galileo took an opportunity to present one of his binocular helmets also to the Spanish Ambassador to the Tuscan court, offering at the same time his method for determining longitude at sea (*17*, p. 12).

Galileo's experiments with the binocular telescope have been little noted by historians, since it did not achieve success in the application for which it had been designed. Although it never emerged beyond the experimental stage, the binocular instrument was a most interesting example of Galileo's versatile mind and tenacious enterprise.

The *giovilabio* (1612)

The least known of the instruments associated with Galileo is probably the *giovilabio*, a calculating device for the computation of the periods and distances of the satellites of Jupiter. The instrument derived from Galileo's observations of the four satellites of Jupiter between 1610 and 1616. He devised a series of schematic drawings describing the orbits of the satellites, measured in terms of the apparent diameter of Jupiter (*3*, pt. 2, pp. 403–424). After each observation, he made a note in his table of *Ephemerides* that the satellite appeared on a certain day at a certain hour at a point so many diameters in distance from the planet.

He mentioned at the beginning of his work on hydrostatics in 1612 (*4*, p. 64) that these schematic drawings were used in drawing up the first *Ephemerides* of Jupiter, described in the *Sidereus nuncius*.[61] In this work, Galileo described for the first time in print the periods and positions of the satellites of Jupiter, with the comment that they would have to be corrected eventually, and noted his resolve to bring the tables to perfection in the future. He called these tables "*giovilabii*". He added that:

> the first observations are not adequate, not even for the briefest intervals of time, but since I have not yet found a means of measuring with any instrument the distance of the positions between these planets, I have noted such interstices with their simple relations to the diameter of the body of Jupiter, estimated by eye; which, being accurate only to the first minute of arc are not sufficient, however, for the determination of the precise sizes of the spheres of its stars. But since I have now found a means of taking such measurements without the error of even the most minute seconds, I will continue the observations [*3*, pt. 2, p. 446].

Galileo made use of this "instrument" for the first time on January 31, 1612, according to a note inserted in his *Ephemerides;* he added that the instrument was not yet fully ready. He went on to note a simple method for determining whether the satellites moved in planes parallel to the ecliptic. Later in the same year, on June 23, 1612, Galileo sent a complimentary copy of his *Discorso* to the Tuscan Ambassador at Prague, Giuliano de'Medici, with a note:

> Kepler will, I believe, be pleased to learn how I have finally discovered the periods of the Medicean stars, and have constructed exact tables, so that I can calculate their past and future constitutions without the error of a single second . . . [*11*, p. 335].

He continued to make new observations for the purpose of revising his tables. Finally, around the end of 1612, he produced a new table (his "good table"), in which the positions and periods of the second and four satellites of Jupiter were especially carefully listed; he apparently continued to use this for reference until at least July 16, 1616.

Considerable confusion has developed concerning the nature of this "instrument". R. Caverni argued that the instrument could not have been the telescope with perforated bracts or pinhole sights, since Galileo had found this inconvenient and unsatisfactory for his observation of the satellites of Jupiter.[62] He also noted that Galileo never stated the nature of his instrument, except in letters to Castelli and to Renieri which have not survived. Caverni assumed that Galileo's mysterious instrument was that described in 1666 by Borelli in his *Theoricae medicaeorum planetarum.*[63] Borelli himself, however, was not convinced that this was the case; it seemed to him that Galileo's telescope was not sufficiently powerful, and that the amount of illumination necessary for the micrometric lines to be visible would interfere with observation of the satellites. Galileo appears to have utilized his "instrument" for a period of only twenty-one nights, from January 31 to February 20; on February 21, he noted that his observations had been made without its aid.[64]

Favaro likewise assumed that these observations had involved the use of a micrometer.[65] Yet it is apparent that such could not have been the case, since a micrometer could not have been adapted to the Galilean type of telescope. It could have been used only with the Keplerian type of instrument, the first of which was produced probably between 1613 and 1617 by Christopher Scheiner.[66] The micrometer was invented by William Gascoigne in about 1638, and developed by others during the following several decades.[67]

Of considerable interest in connection with Galileo's *giovilabio* is a mechanical instrument, apparently devised for the calculation of the periods and distances of the satellites of Jupiter. Its existence was first noted in the catalogue of instruments at the Museo di Storia della Scienze. It is described as a parallelogrammic brass plate inscribed with various horary tables and having two movable parts. It measures about 40 cm. in length and 19 cm. in width. A large revolving disk, divided into 360°, is encased in a fixed ring, and its rotation is limited to angular intervals of 12°–0°–12° to the left and right. The rest of the instrument consists of a long arm, through an elongated slit of which appears the stud of a revolving smaller circle, inscribed with the divisions of the zodiac. This instrument can be immediately identified as a mechanical form of the *giovilabio* described and illustrated in the Galilean papers. The large disk is divided in 24 equal parallel chords, the distance between each of which represents a semidiameter of the body of the planet Jupiter. It is inscribed with four concentric rings for the orbits of the satellites. The surface of the instrument is elaborately decorated and engraved, but it is neither signed nor dated. According to the catalogue (3178), this instrument appears to be unique. It was first listed in the Medicean inventories among the household goods of Prince Leopold de'Medici.[68] Discernible on the instrument are several inventory labels, one of which bears the number ('807') of the seventeenth-century Medici inventory.

The instrument was mentioned in a recent article by G. Righini.[69] He describes it as a type of calculating device which permitted Galileo "to derive the positions of the satellites of Jupiter, corrected for the motion of the earth around the sun". It is possible that it was constructed under Galileo's direction, as Righini claims, but it seems much more likely that it was produced under the supervision of one of his immediate disciples for a

Medici prince. All we can be certain of is that it dates from the mid-seventeenth century. Further research may tell us more of the origins of this interesting instrument and of the *giovilabio* from which it derived.

The microscope (1610)

Galileo's role in the development of the microscope has never been definitely ascertained because of a confusion of claims and counterclaims, a paucity of contemporary documentary evidence, and a total absence of surviving artifacts. It was not until fifteen years after Galileo first worked with the instrument that he called an *"occhiale"* or an *"occhialino"* that the term 'microscope' was invented, yet it seems clear that Galileo's instrument was, in fact, a microscope.

One of the most important bits of evidence relating to Galileo's microscope is an account of how he transformed a telescope into a microscope. His former student, John Wodderborn, described the incident in a work published in Padua in 1610:

> I will not now attempt to explain all the perfections of this wonderful *occhiale;* our sense alone is a safe judge of the things which concern it. But what more can I say of it, than that by pointing a glass to an object more than a thousand paces off, which does not even seem alive, immediately recognize it to be Socrates, son of Sophronicus, who is approaching! . . . I heard a few days back the author himself [Galileo] narrate to the Most Excellent Signor Cremonius various things most desirable to be known, and amongst others, in what manner he perfectly distinguishes with his telescope the organs of motion and of the senses in the smaller animals; and especially in a certain insect which has each eye covered by a rather thick membrane, which is, however, perforated with seven holes, like the visor of a warrior, and allows it sight. Here hast thou a new proof that the glass concentrating its rays enlarges the object . . .[70]

Another important report relating to Galileo's microscope occurs in the account of the travels of Giovanni du Pont, who visited Galileo, then sick in bed, on November 12, 1614. After a discussion of astronomical discoveries, du Pont related that Galileo told him:

> that the tube of a telescope for looking at the stars is no more than two feet in length, but to see objects which are very near, but which we cannot see on account of their small size, the tube must have two or three lengths. He tells me that with this long tube he has seen flies which look as big as a lamb, and has learned that they are all covered over with hair, and have very pointed nails, by means of which they keep themselves up and walk on glass, although hanging feet upwards, by inserting the point of their nail into the pores of the glass.[71]

Although no mention of the microscope is found in Galileo's correspondence during the same period, he spoke of it as follows in *Il saggiatore,* written between 1619 and 1622.

I might tell Sarsi something new if anything new could be told him. Let him take any substance whatever, be it stone, or wood, or metal, and holding it in the sun, examine it attentively, and he will see all the colours distributed in the most minute particles, and if he will make use of a telescope arranged so that one can see very near objects, he will see far more distinctly what I say [*4*, p. 248].

The next evidence forms a part of an extensive correspondence between Gerolamo Aleandro at Rome and Nicole de Peiresc at Aix, ranging over a period from 1622 to 1624. A number of the letters relate to two microscopes made by either Kuffler of Cologne or his kinsman, Cornelius Drebbel, which had been sent to Scipione Cobellucci, Cardinal of Santa Susanna. The Cardinal did not know how to use one of the two instruments, and he showed it to Galileo, who happened to be in Rome at the time. As soon as Galileo saw the microscope, he was able to explain its use, according to Aleandro's letter to Peiresc on May 24, 1624. He added that "Galileo told me that he had developed an *occhiale* which magnified these minute objects as much as fifty thousand times, in a way that a fly is seen as large as a hen." [72] G. Govi has argued that this magnification was one of volume, thus giving a linear enlargement of about 36 times.[73]

No details of the construction of the microscope developed by Galileo have survived. If it was the same type as the ones obtained by the Cardinal from Drebbel or Kuffler, some idea of its optical structure may be derived from Peiresc's earlier letter of March 3, 1624 to Aleandro, in which he noted that the major problem with the Cardinal's instrument involved:

the direction of the mobile plate upon which the object is placed, in order to make it remain firmly under the point upon which is terminated the line of sight, which passes from the eye through the center of the two lenses. . . . The effect of the lens is to show the object upside down . . . so that the natural motion of the animalcule, when, for example, it goes from east to west, seems to be contrariwise.[74]

Peiresc reported to Aleandro on July 1, 1624, that:

the *occhiale* mentioned by Galileo, which makes flies as large as hens, is of the same invention as this one (the Cardinal's), of which the author made a copy for the Archduke Albert, of pious memory. When it was placed on the ground, a fly was seen the size of a hen, yet the instrument was no higher than an ordinary dining-table.[75]

Another mention of Galileo's *occhialino* occurs in a letter of May 11 from Giovanni Faber to Federico Cesi:

I was last night with our Signor Galileo . . . he gave a most beautiful *occhialino* to Cardinal de Zoller for the Duke of Bavaria. I examined a fly which Signor Galileo himself had me observe. I was astonished and I said to Signor Galileo that this was truly another creator, since it makes visible objects which until now it was not known had been created.[76]

Galileo called his instrument an *"occhialino"*, as attested in his correspondence in 1624 with various patrons for whom he produced it. Bartolomeo Imperiali, for instance, in a letter of September 5, thanked Galileo
for having given him such a perfect instrument (*9*, pp. 64–65).

Another document, written by Agnolo Medici, secretary to Archduke
Ferdinand II, probably in July 1624, described the acquisition by the
Archduke of three *"occhiali detto di moltiplicatione"* from foreign
lands.[77] The writer admits that he was unable to describe how the *occhiali*
were made, because he had been forbidden to do so "since they wish to
see whether Galileo will be able to discover it. He has been working at it
over a month now, and so far nothing has resulted."

During these weeks, Galileo wrote (July 24) that he had sent an *occhialino* to Imperiali. Its arrival was acknowledged by A. Santini on August 9
(*13*, pp. 197–198), and Imperiali later (September 5) thanked Galileo for
it (*13*, pp. 201–202). But at the same time, Galileo was having difficulties
with another *occhialino* for Cesi:

> I am sending your Excellency an *occhialino* to see minute objects close up.
> . . . I have delayed in sending it, because . . . I have had difficulty in dis-
> covering a means of producing perfect lenses. The object is to be attached
> upon the movable band, which is in the base, and it must be moved in order
> to see it completely . . . that which can be seen at a glance is only a small
> part. And for this reason, the distance between the lenses and the object must
> be extremely accurate. In observing objects which have relief, it is necessary
> to be able to move the glass closer or further away, depending on whether
> one observes this or that part. For this reason, the little tube [*cannoncino*] is
> made movable on its base or guide. . . . It is [best used] in the sun itself, in
> order that the object be sufficiently illuminated. I have observed a great many
> animals with infinite admiration, among which the flea was most horrible, the
> mosquito and the moth were most beautiful. It was with considerable content
> that I observed how flies and other little animals were able to walk attached
> to mirrors, as well as upside down. But your Excellency has opportunity to
> observe thousands and thousands of details, of which I request that you will
> inform me of the most curious . . . P.S. The *cannoncino* is in two pieces,
> and can be elongated or shortened at pleasure [*13*, pp. 208–209].

Cesi acknowledged receipt of the instrument on October 26. (*13*, pp.
219–220). During the same period, Bartolomeo Balbi informed Galileo
(October 25) of his desire to own "the little *occhiale* of new invention"
(*13*, pp. 218–219). Finally on December 17, Galileo advised Cesare Marsigli at Bologna that "I would have sent you an *occhialino* for observing
minute objects closely, but the jeweller who makes the tube [*cannone*]
has not yet completed it" (*13*, pp. 239–240).

Galileo apparently abandoned the microscope after 1624, and proceeded
to devote himself exclusively to astronomical observations. The fact that
the *occhialino* no longer figured in Galileo's papers after 1624 has been
taken by Govi to be evidence that the instrument had been nothing more

than a small Dutch telescope fitted with a concave and a convex lens, and not a miniaturized Keplerian instrument of the type constructed by Drebbel in 1621.[78]

Ironically enough, the term 'microscope' was not applied to the instrument until after Galileo apparently abandoned its construction, yet the name was first applied to one of Galileo's own instruments. It occurred for the first time in a letter from Faber to Cesi on April 13, 1625:

> Glance at what I have written concerning the new inventions of Sig. Galileo; if I have not put in everything, or if anything ought to be left unsaid, do as best you think. I also mention his new *occhiale* to look at small things and call it a "microscope". Let your Excellency see if you would like to add that, as the Lyceum gave to the first the name of "telescope", so they have wished to give a convenient name to this also, and rightly so because they are the first in Rome who had one.[79]

The only surviving artifacts associated with Galileo's development of the microscope are a sliding-tube compound microscope, and a pair of screw-barrel compound microscopes in the Medici collection of the Museo di Storia della Scienza.[80] The screw-barrel instruments have been traditionally attributed to Galileo, primarily because they originally formed part of the collection of instruments of the Accademia del Cimento (1657–1667). A careful examination of their construction, however, leaves no doubt that the instruments were not constructed until at least several decades after Galileo's death.

The sliding-tube microscope has bi-convex ocular and object lenses, and is of a type which antedates the screw-barrel instrument. However, the inclusion of a field lens indicates that the instrument must be of a later date, since the field lens was unknown prior to 1660, when it was noted by Balthasar de Monconys in his visit to Augsburg. In his study of these so-called "Galilean" microscopes, Allodi has asserted that this instrument was produced by Galileo himself.[81] Yet the features it incorporates did not come into being until more than a quarter of a century after the date to which he attributes the instrument.

On the basis of the present incomplete knowledge of the microscope's history, it is impossible to evaluate Galileo's contributions to the development of this instrument. Although published histories of the microscope are numerous, none have adequately explored the early history of the simple microscope in the Netherlands, nor the evolution of the compound microscope in Italy prior to the second half of the seventeenth century. The documentation of the later seventeenth-century development of this instrument in Italy has recently been compiled,[82] but much remains unstudied in this period also. Until much fuller research has been carried out, it will be impossible to ascertain whether Galileo was, in fact, the inventor of the compound microscope, as various scholars have claimed, or whether his *occhialino* was no more than another version of the simple microscope.

Vibration-counters (1637)

The last of the instruments with which Galileo was preoccupied was a pendulum-regulator for clockwork, as well as vibration-counters derived from the pendulum. Because the subject has been covered comprehensively elsewhere,[83] only the salient features need be included here.

The traditional account of Galileo's discovery of the isochronism of the pendulum from a swinging lamp in the Duomo at Pisa around 1582 is a familiar one (*19*, pp. 647–659). The first application which he made of the pendulum was the *pulsilogium* already discussed, but throughout his life he continued to be concerned with the pendulum as a means of measurement. From 1612 onwards, he was vitally interested in developing some means for the determination of longitude at sea. It was his conviction that the pendulum could be employed for this purpose, with or without clockwork. On June 6, 1637, for instance, he informed Admiral Reael of the States General of the Netherlands that he had constructed a time measurer utilizing the pendulum's oscillation, without the addition of clockwork (*17*, pp. 96–105). This pendulum was shaped like a sector, and was made of copper or bronze. It was thickest at the center, terminating in a knife edge to reduce air resistance. The center was perforated to permit the insertion of a small iron, which terminated at its lowest extremity in an angle, and had two bronze supports at its upper end.

Galileo specified that the pendulum's oscillations during the course of a day were measured by some form of dial which he called a "fixed star", and which made it possible to record the number of oscillations per hour, minute or second. The mechanism included a toothed wheel rotated by means of an elastic bristle attached at the end of the solid pendulum, so that each swing of the latter moved a horizontal crown wheel one tooth at a time. The instrument was described in sufficient detail to leave no doubt that Galileo contemplated the application of the pendulum as a regulator for clockwork as early as 1637, the year in which he was overtaken by blindness. This instrument was quite similar in general concept to the *cotyla* devised by Santorio, although the latter has left us no details of the construction of the interior mechanism.

Galileo was convinced of the suitability of the pendulum for time-measurement, as he reiterated in a letter to G. B. Baliani on September 1, 1639 (*18*, pp. 93–95), explained also in his little work, *L'Usage du cadran ou de l'horloge physique universel*, published in Paris in the same year.[84] In 1641, he attempted to produce a clock with a pendulum regulator (*19*, pp. 647–659). Because he was unable to carry through his plans due to his blindness, he communicated his ideas to his son, Vincenzio, and after several discussions, the details were worked out. For fear of having the idea pirated, Vincenzio repeatedly postponed construction of the clockwork and meanwhile Galileo's death intervened. It was not until 1649 that Vincenzio returned to the project and hired a locksmith, Domenico Balestri, to construct an iron framework, blanks for the wheels and the arbors and pinions. Vincenzio decided to cut the teeth in the wheels himself but while engaged in doing this, he succumbed to a fever, and the model remained unfinished. Although several other models appear to have existed, they were subsequently lost and the only record that remained were three copies of a sketch made by or for Viviani in about 1659.[85] This was drawn directly from the incomplete model that Vincenzio had been working on when he died, and it showed the main wheel left incomplete. From these sketches, several operating models of the clockwork have been produced during the past century for museum displays.

Several features of the Galilean clockwork are of considerable significance. First of all, the use of the pendulum as regulator in place of a balance wheel, although later patented by Huygens in 1657, can be attributed to Galileo without qualification, even though an operating model was not completed within the lifetime of the father or son. Of equal importance is the pin-wheel escapement embodied in Vincenzio's clockwork model, which remained neglected for almost a hundred years until reinvented by (Jean?) Amant of Paris and reworked by Jean-André Lepaute in 1753. This escapement was widely popularized, and remains in use in regulator clocks for precision timetelling to the present time.

Meanwhile, Galileo's vibration-counter was used in various experiments at the Accademia del Cimento. According to Viviani, a counter was constructed by J. P. Treffler, clockmaker to Archduke Ferdinand II, which appears to have been almost identical with the instrument described by Galileo in his letter to Reael in 1637 (*19*, pp. 647–659). It was made prior to 1659, probably at the request of Prince Leopold for use in experiments of the Accademia. Later on, several other forms of vibration-counter were produced for the Accademia to record the variation in amounts of moisture collecting on a cooling glass under varying conditions. These instruments were noted in the *Minutes* of the Accademia for 1662, and illustrated in the *Saggi*.[86]

Conclusion

Galileo's contributions to scientific instrumentation were many and significant. He had an uncanny ability for ferreting out instruments which already existed in rudimentary form and for recognizing their hitherto unrealized potentialities. By improving them and finding revolutionary applications for them, he transformed them into the versatile tools of the new sciences. He was truly a pioneer in his grasp of the importance of quantified measurement: five of the instruments listed above are instruments of measure that brought whole new ranges of parameter, or a new dimension of accuracy, to the descriptive groundwork of scientific inquiry. His famous claim that the Book of Nature is written in the language of mathematics would have remained only a promise if he had not so clearly seen the need to develop a technology of instruments, the findings of which would be quantitative. His unceasing labor on instruments can thus be regarded as complementary to, and vitally interconnected with, his mathematical metaphysics.

NOTES

1. *Dialogo*, Drake transl., pp. 406–407.

2. S. W. Mitchell, "The early history of instrumental precision in medicine", 1892*, pp. 159–198.

3. To conserve space, references to the *Edizione Nazionale* of Galileo's work, will be given in this abbreviated form within the text.

4. *Methodus vitandorum errorum omnium qui in arte medica continguit*, Venice, cols. 76B, 219C.

5. *Commentaria in primam Fen primi libri canonis Avicenna*, Venice, 1625, col. 365; Appendix D.

6. *Heronis Alexandrini spiritalium liber a Federico Commandino conversus*, Urbino, 1575, 1v–8r. See also R. Caverni, "Intorno all'invenzione del termometro", *Boll. Bibliog. Storia Scien. Mat. Fis.* (Rome), *11*, 1878.

7. *Spirituali di Herone Alessandrino*, transl. by A. G. da Urbino, Urbino, 1592.

8. Naples, p. 288.

9. *Methodus . . .* , p. 190.

10. *Commentariorum in artem medicinalem Galeni*, Venice, pt. III, col. 229.

11. *Commentaria . . . Avicennae*, cols. 22–24.

12. *Sphaera mundi seu cosmographia demonstrativa*, Bologna, 1620, p. 111. See also A. Favaro, *Galileo Galilei e lo Studio di Padova*, Florence, 1883, vol. 1, pp. 249–275.

13. *Récreation mathématique*, under pseud. A. von Etten, 1624.

14. Robert Fludd, *Utriusque cosmi . . . metaphysica physica atque technica historia*, Oppenheim, 1617, vol. 1, pp. 30–31; 203–204.

15. Milan, 1633. See also G. P. Gallucci, *Della fabrica et uso di diversi strumenti di astronomia et cosmografia*, Venice, 1598, cols. 192–196.

16. *La géometrie reduite en une facile et briéfe pratique par deux excellents instruments*, trans. into French by P. G. S., Paris, 1626.

17. Antwerp, 1584.

18. Rome, 1598.

19. A drawing instrument for angles of gilt brass inscribed *Excogitatore Fabrico Mordente* is in the Mensing collection of the Adler Planetarium and Astronomical Museum in Chicago (Cat. M-69). A brass sector, very similar to the one described in *La quadratura del cerchio*, although undated and unsigned, is in the collection of the Museum of the History of Science at Oxford University, while another of similar construction forms part of the collection of the Museo di Storia della Scienza in Florence. See M. L. Bonelli, "Di una bellissima edizione di Fabrizio Mordente Salernitano . . ." *Physis*, *1*, 1959, 127–148, and "Su di un

compasso appartenente al Museo di Storia della Scienza di Oxford", *Physis, 1*, 1959, 244–245.

20. *Beschreibung und Unterricht des Jobst Bürgi proportional Circhels*, Frankfurt, 1605.

21. "Per la storia del compasso di proporzione", *Atti Istit. Veneto*, 67(2), 1908, 728.

22. I am indebted to Prof. Derek de Solla Price of Yale University for this description of Galileo's compass. For a comprehensive study of the artisans who produced Galileo's instruments, see Silvio A. Bedini, "The makers of Galileo's scientific instruments", *Galileo Galilei nella storia e nella filosofia della scienza*, Florence, 1967, pp. 89–115.

23. James Kynvyn (or Kynfin) (fl. 1569–1610) made instruments for Thomas Digges and John Blagrave and probably for Robert Dudley as well. Charles Whitwell flourished during the same period and was an engraver and maker of mathematical instruments and may have been apprenticed to Humphrey Cole. Instruments by both of these makers in the Museo di Storia della Scienza suggest that they worked also for Robert Dudley (1573–1649), son of the Earl of Leicester, who moved to Florence in 1606. He was the author of *Arcano del Mare* (Florence, 1606), which is illustrated with a number of instruments of his own design.

24. M. L. Bonelli, *Catalogo degli strumenti nel Museo di Storia della Scienza*, 1954*, pp. 23–24.

25. Zugmesser (or Zieckmesser) was born in Speyer. He was listed as belonging to the Arts Faculty in Padua in 1600. He was earlier "mechanic" to the rulers of Cologne.

26. Padua, 1607. *Opere*, 2, pp. 424–511.

27. *Galileo Galilei e lo Studio di Padova*, vol. 1, pp. 237–238.

28. *Difesa di Galileo Galilei contro alle calunnie ed imposture di Baldassar Capra*, Venice, 1607. *Opere*, 2, pp. 512–601.

29. Simon Mayr (or Simon Marius) (1573–1624), was court astronomer at Ansbach to the Elector Christian from 1606 to 1624. He made observations of Venus and the satellites of Jupiter and discovered the nebula in Andromeda. Earlier he served as German representative to the faculty at Padua from 1603 to 1605. See G. Boffito, *Gli strumenti della scienza e la scienza degli strumenti*, Florence, 1929, pp. 81–85.

30. Drake, *Discoveries and opinions of Galileo*, 1957*, p. 233.

31. *A new and accurate method of delineating all the parts of the different orders of architecture . . .* , London, 1737.

32. *Di G. Galilei ed il compasso geometrico*, Rome, 1698.

33. *Fabrica et uso del compasso di proportione . . .* , Bologna, 1664.

34. *Saggio sopra il giusto pregio delle cose* (Rome?), 1803.

35. *Les récreations mathématiques . . .* , Paris, 1661.

36. *Galileo Galilei e lo Studio di Padova*, vol. 1, pp. 306–307.

37. A Paduan *libbra* is equal to .7984 pounds. A Venetian or Paduan *oncia*

equals 3.527 of our ounces, while a Florentine *oncia* is equivalent to 0.9982 ounces.

38. *Clarorum Germanorum ad Ant. Magliabechium* . . . *epistolae* . . . , Florence, 1746, vol. 1, p. 87.

39. *Ibid.*, p. 90.

40. Filza 365, "Debitori e creditori della Guardaroba", c. 73.

41. *Discorso sopra la calamità di Don Benedetto Castelli Abbate* . . . Manuscript filed in *Mss. discepoli galileiana* (I, c. 303v), Florence. See also *Dialogo*, Drake transl., p. 405.

42. M. L. Bonelli, *Catalogo* . . . , p. 24. See also M. L. Bonelli, *Cimeli galileiani*, 1962*, pp. 7–8.

43. *Vita di Paolo Sarpi teologo* . . . , Milan, 1824, p. 177; See also A. Bianchi-Giovini, *Biografia di Fra Paolo Sarpi* . . . , Zurich, 1836, p. 79.

44. *Lettere di Fra Paolo Sarpi*, ed. by F. L. Polidori, Florence, 1863, vol. 1, p. 181.

45. Paris, 1609, c. 244. See also the *Journal di Pierre l'Estoile* for April 30, 1609, cited in Arago's *Oeuvres complètes*, Paris, 1855, vol. 3, pp. 264–265.

46. "The authenticity of Galileo's letter to Landucci", 1951*.

47. Drake, *Discoveries and opinions of Galileo*, pp. 28–29.

48. "When did Galileo make his first telescope?", 1951*.

49. *19*, pp. 587–588. See also A. Favaro, "Galileo Galilei e la presentazione del cannochiale alla Repubblica Venetà", *Nuovo Archivio Veneto*, *1*(1), 1891, 55–75.

50. 'Banda' is a Venetian colloquialism for a metal plate of tinned iron. Galileo himself noted elsewhere, however, that it was made of lead; see *Opere*, *10*, p. 60.

51. This measure referred to is probably the *braccio* of wool, .683 meters.

52. The Venetian *scudo* of the period was about 42 mm. in diameter.

53. About 35 kilometers.

54. 'Nuola' is an unusual term, perhaps belonging to a Venetian dialect. The translation here is conjectural.

55. Particularly true in Galilean-type telescopes, where the eye had to be placed almost in contact with the ocular lens.

56. 'Dita', meaning finger, is a measure of about one inch.

57. He apparently experienced considerable difficulty in making object-lenses, whereas ocular lenses were comparatively easy to produce (*10*, p. 507).

58. *Vita e commercio letterario di Galileo Galilei*, Lausanne, 1793, vol. 1, pp. 280–283; vol. 2, pp. 680–683. See also Nelli, *Saggio di storia letteraria fiorentina del secolo XVII* . . . , Lucca, 1759, pp. 70–72.

59. A. M. Schyrlaeus de Rheita, *Oculus Enoch et Eliae* . . . , Antwerp, 1645, pt. 1, p. 337.

60. *17*, p. 12. Letter from D. Peri, dated 1636, but probably January 21, 1637.

61. Drake transl., pp. 51–58.

62. *Storia del metodo sperimentale in Italia*, Florence, 1891, vol. 1, pp. 412–414.

63. Florence, 1666, pp. 141–149.

64. Caverni, *op. cit.*, vol. 2, p. 421.

65. "Intorno alle opere scientifiche di Galileo Galilei nella Edizione Nazionale", *Atti R. Istit. Veneto Scien. Lett. Arti, 58*, 1899, 154–158.

66. Described in his *Rosa Ursina*, Bracciani, 1630.

67. S. J. Rigaud, *Correspondence of scientific men of the seventeenth century*, Oxford, 1841, letters 19 and 20.

68. *Guardaroba Mediceo*, no. 826, c. 420.

69. "Galileo Galilei astronomo", 1962*.

70. *Quatuor problematum quae Martinus Horky contra Nuntium Sidereum . . . proposuit*, col. 7r.

71. *Relations des Voyages*, Paris, *Ms. Fonds Perigords, 106*, c. 20 seq.

72. Fonds Français, Codice 9541, Bibliothèque Nationale, Paris, letter of May 24, 1624.

73. "Il microscopio composto inventato da Galileo", *Atti R. Accad. Scien. Fis. Mat.* (Naples), *2*(1), 1888, 3–4. See also G. Govi, "The compound microscope invented by Galileo", *Journ. Royal Micros. Society*, 1889, 574–598.

74. Codice N. A. 1975, Barberini Library, Bibliothèque National, Paris, letter of March 3, 1624.

75. *Ibid.*, letter of July 1, 1624.

76. *Lettere di molti accademici Lyncei . . .* , letter of May 11, 1624, quoted by Govi, *op. cit.*

77. Codice viii, F. 2. Undated letter quoted by Govi, *op. cit.*, p. 33.

78. Govi, *op. cit.*, pp. 13–16.

79. *Lettere di molti accademici Lyncei*, letter of April 13, 1625.

80. *Catalogo*, nos. 3245–3246.

81. F. Allodi in *Studi e ricerche sui microscopi galileiani . . .* , 1957*, pp. 10–19.

82. S. A. Bedini, "Seventeenth century Italian compound microscopes", 1963*.

83. S. A. Bedini, "Galileo Galilei and time measurement", 1963*; "Galileo Galilei and the measurement of time", *Saggi su Galileo Galilei*, Rome, to appear.

84. Dom Jacques Allexandre, *Traité general des horloges*, Paris, 1734, p. 298.

85. The original is filed in *Mss galileiani, 4*, part 6, c. 50. A second (sent by Prince Leopold to Ismael Boulliau) is in *Fonds Français*, no. 13039, Bibliothèque National, Paris. A third (made from the second) is among the Huygens papers, *Hug. 45^II*, Bibliothek der Rijksuniversiteit, Leyden.

86. *Saggi di naturali esperienze fatte nell'Accademia del Cimento*, Florence, 1666, pp. 19–22; plate 2.

Part IV

Galileo as a philosopher of science

14 ❋ Galileo's methodology of natural science

DOMINIQUE DUBARLE

Introduction

The extent to which Galileo made use of "scientific method" and the conception of science that underlay his work have given rise, since the beginning of this century, to surprisingly wide disagreements, disagreements that recent advances in our knowledge of the history of science may perhaps allow us to resolve. In the nineteenth century, Galileo was not difficult to visualize as the pioneer of positivism. According to this view, he would have brought to science, right from its origins, the essentials of what positivism assumed to be its proper method.[1] This would be by way of contrast with Descartes, whose *a priori* ideas and "metaphysical" approach excluded (so it was supposed) the scientific attitude necessary for the study of physical reality.

In recent years, a reaction against this positivist interpretation of Galileo has made itself strongly felt. No one, perhaps, has done more than Professor Alexandre Koyré to give us an idea of Galileo markedly different from the earlier one.[2] The Galileo revealed to us in the *Études Galiléennes* is no positivist; he is above all a man who seeks to grasp the physical universe by mathematizing it. He is, across the gap of centuries, the heir of Archimedes; his thought, like that of his master, is impregnated with Pla-

NOTE: Translated from the French by Ernan McMullin.

tonism. Galileo calls upon experience, of course, and even insists upon the experimental confirmations that theories and theoretical deductions require. But despite this emphasis on experience, the physics of Galileo, like any good physics, is constructed *a priori*, that is, on the basis of ideal conceptions posited by the mind.[3] Besides, in Galileo's work, experimentation remains almost always at the imaginary level, ingeniously conceived by its author but never actually carried through. It is a "thought-experiment", as Mach called those schematic representations of phenomena to which physical theories, in the early stages of development, often have recourse.[4] In all this, Galileo is much nearer to Descartes than one would formerly have been inclined to admit. Between these two founders of modern science, the difference of intellectual climate is obviously quite marked. Nevertheless, in many respects their modes of procedure were quite similar, even to the extent of their making the same mistakes on occasion, for example in their researches on free fall.[5]

Thus far Professor Koyré. Based on a precise study of the key texts of Galileo as well as on a wide knowledge of the predecessors and the scientific background of the great Florentine, the claims of Professor Koyré seem fairly generally accepted today, though with reservations in some important respects, particularly concerning the role of experience in Galileo's thought. So little, indeed, is Galileo an empiricist, according to Koyré, that the defender of "experience" in his *Dialogo* turns out, significantly, to be the Aristotelian, Simplicio, and not Galileo's own spokesmen, Sagredo, the "honest man" without prejudices or Salviati, master of scientific reasoning. Professor Koyré likewise supposes that all, or almost all, the experiments proposed by Galileo in support of his theories were no more (at the time that Galileo proposed them, at least) than imaginary experiments which he himself had never performed and which if he *had* performed with the means at his disposal would by no means have made evident the correctness of his theoretical views.

On this point, Professor Koyré is not followed by all. Professor René Dugas, author of the well-known *Histoire de la mécanique*, thinks that the principal experiments alleged by Galileo in favor of his mechanical theories really *were* performed, and supports this claim by a criticism of M. Koyré's case.[6] The arguments he brings forward seem worth consideration. One finds in the works of Galileo descriptions of quite a large number of experiments which are "scientific" in their principle, if not in every detail of their execution, and many of these he seems quite clearly to have carried out himself. Later on, we shall look at some of these in more detail.

These questions concerning experiential warrant and experimental practice show themselves to be quite crucial if one is to grasp at all accurately, not only Galileo's own scientific achievement, but on a wider plane that unique focusing of self-awareness that characterized the first stirrings of the spirit that would in the course of the seventeenth century lay the groundwork for modern natural science. Supported by the precise and penetrating studies of Professor Koyré, we may reconsider the whole problem of Galileo's teaching on scientific method, a teaching which—it must at once be admitted—was one of practice rather than precept. We may see better by means of this scrutiny of the lessons of history how the mind comes to adopt the attitude which characterizes modern physics. For that which lies behind what we have called "Galileo's scientific method" is in fact a pedagogical concern with orienting the human mind in a decidedly new way toward physical reality, as well as toward what had until then been said about this reality. It is not without interest, even today, to meditate on the motives that underlay this concern.

Galileo never provided a systematic treatment of his views on scientific method. The tentative fitting and trying that went on throughout his life led him ultimately to crystallize a new view of physical reality. This view had been long in shaping by many predecessors; with him, it first attained to some sort of viable consistency. What we see first in all this is the way in which the mind of Galileo "lived" this view, so to speak, followed a certain method of approach, before being able to formulate its rules with any sort of exactness. What strikes us is the way in which he becomes steadily more conscious of the essential axes of his "own" thought—of the "scientific" way of thinking, if you prefer—as soon as he first finds himself constrained to enter the lists against the Aristotelians and against their conception of a philosophical physics, to his mind almost entirely foreign to true "science". It is in polemic, in the constant attempt to break the hold on people's minds of scholastic prejudices, that Galileo usually discovers the need for a sharp formulation of some point of practice or theory hitherto implicit in the actual exercise of his scientific work. In this way, he is led to elaborate on points of methodology, while leaving to the reader, and ultimately to posterity, the task of unifying these multiple explications of that which he bore in him.

The philosophical situation of mechanics and of Galileo's research

Galileo was responsible for a beginning of scientific mechanics, of a discipline that far surpassed the stage of anticipatory intuitions and unanchored claims that preceded him. It is true that his basic discoveries in mechanics were relatively few. And it might well seem, with mechanics now established for us as only one in a whole roster of natural sciences, that the volume of his concrete achievement was thus small indeed. Yet, to understand Galileo and the inspiration of his method, one must push farther than this. Because for him mechanics was the science of the entire natural universe, and the choice of a mechanics involved a kind of decision about the proper intellectual *attitude* to adopt toward that universe.

Nevertheless, in Galileo's mind this decision had to rest upon a careful review of the attitude earlier adopted not only by the unlearned but even by the greatest scholars. In the West, these latter had been formed in the

Aristotelian tradition and in the cosmology that went with it. Galileo himself never doubted that the scrutiny which his own generation was being forced to make would lead to the abandonment of an entire world-view. He also believed himself qualified to replace it with something sounder, something to his mind of a quite general import. What Galileo urged amounted implicitly—and often explicitly—to the adoption of a *philosophical* position concerning the reality and nature of the universe, and in consequence concerning the teachings of the scholastic cosmology of the day, now at one bound to be definitively susperseded.

Already Copernican astronomy had sounded the knell of the geocentric world-view. Furthermore, the perceptive inquirer was being forced to concede that the Aristotelian fashion of understanding the simplest of all changes, namely local motion, was inadequate and erroneous. This latter point had no less cosmological import for Galileo than the first. For he well knew that Aristotle had linked the fortunes of his natural philosophy with that of an accurate understanding of change. It was Aristotle himself who had emphasized the fundamental significance of everything dealing with local motion, that form of change which he affirmed to be most characteristic of the simplest elements of the physical world, the change which was involved in all other changes. On these points, Galileo was in entire agreement with Aristotelian philosophy, though he would draw very different consequences from these same first principles. For him, the exact understanding of motion would play a far larger role than it had for Aristotle and the scholastics; it would become the first and indispensable kind of knowledge of the physical universe. Galileo and Descartes were both in accord with the doctrine that can rather easily be inferred (if one wishes to press the matter) from that which Aristotle himself said about the universal role of local motion. Mechanics, the science of motion, was thus recognized to be the first of those sciences which have something to say of the cosmos as a whole.

From the beginning, Galileo saw the study of movement almost as the study of the universe itself. And in this study it seemed that he could not count on Aristotle's help. It was no longer possible to look upon the universe with the eyes of a biologist, as Aristotle had done, and seek to understand physical reality by analogies with life and moving intelligences, instead of with simple motion. The universe which Galileo and Descartes envisaged was one which would be everywhere in motion but *not* everywhere in living motion. It is thus to the science of motion, not of life, that one must turn for the most basic truths about the world. Once this be admitted, and once Aristotle's analysis of local motion be rejected, Aristotelian natural philosophy is no longer relevant to the issue. It only remains to be seen what sort of science of the universe is to be sought; Galileo and Descartes sought it by means of an application of a *mathesis universalis* to the whole of physical reality. Galileo stood firm in his belief in the possibility of a mathematical understanding of motion, a possibility until his time largely underestimated, and almost entirely neglected in ancient natural philosophy.

It is true that some mathematical description of movement *had* been recognized in antiquity in the domain of descriptive astronomy, and in the construction of kinematic models of planetary motions in the manner of Eudoxus and Ptolemy. But this knowledge remained at best external to philosophy, whether that of Plato, who made of it a preliminary *mathema*,[7] or that of Aristotle, who was content simply to borrow from it some results for his natural philosophy. In particular, it was not—indeed, *could* not yet be—a science of the universe; it could be a science only for celestial beings, whose far-off reality (according to both Plato's *Timaeus* and Aristotle's *Physics*) was quite other than that of the terrestrial objects familiar to us, and which, though observable, admitted of no kind of experimental manipulation. The Epicureans of earlier times had tended to question the existence of any fundamental distinction between celestial and terrestrial realities; but it was Copernican astronomy, far more than the mild revival of Epicureanism by Renaissance scholars, that now led to an outright denial of this distinction. It still remained to extend the mathematical mode of analysis to the terrestrial order. Or more accurately, what had to be done was to set the mathematical analysis of motion on a basis firm enough and broad enough that it would for the first time be capable of being extended, in principle at least, anywhere in the universe.

Galileo was one of the first to grasp the broader implications in natural philosophy of a commitment to Copernicus' revolutionary astronomy. He realized that it was necessary to begin with a mathematical analysis of the motions of the terrestrial realm, which despite their familiarity had until then never been properly untangled, as the failure of Aristotelian physics in this regard only too clearly showed. After that, it would be necessary to unify this knowledge with what had already been put in mathematical form for the celestial regularities. This task (which he clearly foresaw) was carried out, not by him, but by Newton who, fifty years after the publication of Galileo's *Discorsi*, brought about the definitive union in mathematical form of the celestial and terrestrial motions. But Galileo already knew that he was tending toward the sort of synthesis that would be so admirably expressed by the title of Newton's great work: *The mathematical principles of natural philosophy.*

The "mathematicism" of Galileo

Galileo's approach to the physical universe was, therefore, governed from the beginning by Copernican astronomy and its intellectual implications, which he worked so hard to have accepted by the learned world of his day. He envisaged the universe under the aspect of motion, of motion as encountered in a terrestrial context. Despite the difficulties which had defeated earlier natural philosophers, this motion would have to be analyzed mathematically in order to wrest from it a properly mathematical sort of understanding. Mathematics thus is to become the principle of a knowledge of the universe as a whole, the preamble of valid cosmological thought. It is the flat opposition on this point to the whole spirit of Aristotelian natural philosophy that constituted probably the most basic feature of Galileo's method, and indeed of all the physical science to come after him. Galileo was well aware of this right from the beginning. One recalls the well-known passage in the *Assayer:*

> Signor Sarsi, things are quite otherwise. Philosophy is written in a great book which is constantly held open before our eyes—i.e. the universe—but it cannot be grasped unless one knows the characters in which it is written. . . . These characters are triangles, circles and other geometric figures, without the aid of which man cannot grasp a word of the language, and without which one would simply wander vainly in a dark labyrinth.[8]

It is in this context, and only in this context, that the issue of Platonism becomes relevant. Professor Koyré sees in Galileo's work a sort of "Archimedean" spirit, and behind it the spirit of Plato as he discusses the *mathemata* and especially the astronomy in the *Republic*.[9] The question at issue here is the mathematical understanding of motion. But how *is* motion to be understood mathematically, or more exactly *what* motion can be understood this way? Galileo was fully conversant with the distinction already clearly drawn in earlier discussions of mathematics, between that which is perceived and that which is imagined or represented. Pure mathematics is the science of the representation, not of that which is perceived. This latter can never suggest, in any other than a distant and inexact way, an object of true mathematical knowledge. Galileo, like Archimedes, extended this doctrine to any object whose characteristics in any way lent themselves to mathematical treatment, such as weight (Archimedes) or movement and mechanical action (Galileo).

Mechanics is not, then, to be taken to be a direct mathematization of perceived phenomena. It is a knowledge having to do with these phenomena, but gained by means of a mathematical grasp of the pure representations that in some fashion correspond with them. These representations are geometrical and also kinematical; they become properly mechanical when the physicist begins to treat, in mathematical fashion, physical magnitudes which he can both intuitively represent and at the same time relate to what he perceives. Mass, impulsion and force would fall in this category. It is absolutely essential to the constitution of physical knowledge, as Galileo saw it, to have the representation as intermediary. It is in one way identical with the phenomenon perceived, but in another way it is altogether distinct from anything perceived. Galileo's lively sense of the *necessity* of such an intermediary is probably the most essential, as well as the most "anti-positivist", facet of his scientific temper. The science of motion that he had in mind is a mathematical science, of the sort Plato and Archimedes sought after; it is like geometry in being a science of thought-objects.

Transcending the ancient mathematicism

But it seems that once this initial epistemological community with Plato and Archimedes be admitted, Galileo soon began to diverge from them. Plato saw in the perceived object the occasion of pure intuitions which make up the ground of science. As soon as this latter has found its subject-matter, one restricted to abstract problems, the perceived object loses interest, indeed comes to be regarded as a source of aberrations which work against pure thought and threaten the soul of the free man. Archimedes, though an engineer, does not seem—in his written work at least—to have diverged very much from the Platonic approach in this regard. Once his thought reaches the level of theorems in statics, it seems to manifest a sort of indifference to the perceived object and to the instrumental and experimental extensions that might easily enough have been conceived. But this was no longer true of Galileo, who in this regard was not simply a geometer in the Greek tradition, faced with a new problem.

For Galileo, it was a question henceforward of considering systematically, as something essential to physical science, a relation between that which holds at the level of mathematical representation and that which holds at the level of the perceived object. That which is represented is an image of the perceived, i.e., of the very reality of the universe in Galileo's view. This image is something derived, an ideal for the mind, but it is concerned primarily with the perceived real. Infused with intelligibility by the very act of science itself, it must return to the perceived order in some fashion. Knowledge of the universe in its reality, of the universe presented to us first and foremost in perception, is the primary goal of the science of those objects that lend themselves to simple geometrical representation. The distance between the two levels of knowledge was clearly recognized by Galileo, who inherited this insight from traditional geometry and its attendant Platonism. But the appreciation that Galileo had for this distance was dominated by his acceptance of a positive orientation of formal "image" science to perceptive knowledge of the real order. This order is recognized to be regulative of the whole functioning of scientific knowledge.

Ancient science, that of Plato, Euclid and even of Archimedes, did not recognize, in any explicit fashion at least, this regulative relation between the two orders. By incorporating it as he did in his method, Galileo was reverting to the tradition (which had never been lost) of the practitioners of ancient astronomy. But he was transferring this tradition to the level of a mathematical physics, not only of the heavens, but of the entire universe. Into this universe, man is assumed to have some real insight, however little that be. Thus he would introduce (and this will be the great innovation) experimentation as the vital link in the achieving of this regulation of the theoretical order by the perceived real.

But experimentation is not as yet emphasized in any obvious way. Later on we shall see its role in the physics of Galileo. For the moment, it is necessary to ask how Galileo regarded the universe, the concrete universe of movements, and how, more clearly than anyone before him, he managed to disengage a factor which lends itself to mathematical analysis and at the same time is in agreement with the *perceived* realities of motion.

From the object simply represented to the object constituted by thought

It is at this point in the analysis of motion that things become more difficult for human intelligence. The empirical perception of movement, unlike that of extension, does not suggest directly to the mind the elements of intuition and representation sufficient for an assured science. If, indeed, perception had been capable of this, the consideration which Aristotle and the scholastics had already given to the question of what is immediately evident in perceived motion would have succeeded in furnishing an adequate basis for an abstract science of mechanics, just as the consideration of plane figures and a rather primitive philosophy of the continuum were sufficient to make geometry possible for the Greek intelligence. But in fact, after some initial promise of success, the Aristotelian conception did not work out. Perception does not provide, when it passes directly from the level of pure representation, proper intellectual elements for a workable theory of motion. This was well known by the time of Galileo among those working on problems of mechanics.

The immediate perception of movement suggests at first the geocentric point of view. Copernicus realized that this point of view is not an accurate one. He insisted that movement involves a relativity which no longer allows one to take empirical appearances for granted. One is forced, not only to *represent* movement, but also to situate this representation explicitly at the level of *thought* and relate it to a particular frame of reference. This is necessary if one is to grasp the true object of science, to which it will henceforward be assumed one has access. Before this, no matter what level of ideality a simple representation reached, it was not as yet an object, properly speaking, for science.

In the same way, the immediate perception of mechanical facts leads one to an immediate representation of force or of mechanical energy, of a sort which is incapable of being generalized. At first sight, it seems to fit many cases. The dynamics of Aristotle *is*, as has often been pointed out, quite close to the everyday experience we have, ever since our very first mechanical relationships with reality. Nevertheless, a whole multitude of facts cannot be brought under it. Throughout the three centuries that separate us from Galileo, scientists have reflected about this point more and more seriously. By now it has become quite clear that to transpose into abstract representations even the most obvious features of mechanical experience will not furnish us with a schema which is at the same time simple and general. It is necessary, therefore, to make an analysis of the fact of perception itself, before being able to grasp that in it which the

representation will retain, not any more in a simple fashion, but by evok-
ing different factors such as, on the one hand, the interplay of kinetic
impulses, and on the other hand, that of dynamic forces and resistances of
the environment. Abstract thought will therefore crystallize in intuition
the true elements of science. It will no longer be sufficient to construct
pure representations of movement. It will be necessary to know how to
think in this way and to do that one will have to *learn* to think that which
is to be represented. This is the point which perhaps gives us the key to
those discussions in Galileo's *Dialogo* which today seem to us so long and
so prolix.

It has often been remarked that these discussions had a pedagogical aim.
They did indeed have this aim; but at the time of Galileo—for Galileo himself, at least—it was because one had to learn from the beginning what it
was to "think" movement in an abstract way. Pure representation, already
foreshadowed by Plato and Archimedes, had to be united with an element
of objectivity in a way that was truly new, and one that brought thought
and representation together. From the moment that Galileo left aside discussion of the brute fact of perception, he was pursuing the method which
we now associate with him. He resolved an epistemological problem, not
hitherto encountered, of elevating the perceived to the ideal order, not just
to the simple ideal of pure representation but to the ideal where objectivity
has been realized in a truly universal way. And these latter are by no means
the same thing, especially in the case of motion.

Where does the mathematical rationalism of Galileo lead?

The behavior of Galileo was thus rather remarkable. At the beginning
of his work he hesitated, tried different directions. He chose, on the
basis of the work of his predecessors, that which seemed to him valid
in the study of empirical facts, something that could give him the truth in
simple form about the fall of heavy bodies, the movement of projectiles,
the pendulum and so on. The scientist's research will thus consist of a long
series of attempts to disengage, as it were from "behind" the immediate
evidence, the components of representation or more exactly of rational
objectivity. Each of these components is to be envisaged only as a supposition which must subsequently be put to the test. But even more centrally,
it is to be envisaged as an element of objectivity which one must know
how to associate with other similar elements, whose association with one
another one must be able to exploit, but deductively and constructively,
by reasoning, in order to allow thought to *reconstruct*, as it were, the
original brute evidences of perception.

Ordinarily, Galileo was careful not to overstress these postulated elements of representation, taken in isolation by themselves. As such, they are
only hypotheses. But their synthesis is quite another thing: the development of their deductive fertility and the possibility this gives of reconstructing the facts gives the ensemble a new solidity. Coming back to the

facts of perception, and realizing that they square with ideas constructed at the level of pure representation and of rational objectivity, the mind of the scientist recognizes a strengthening within itself of the presentiment it had formed as to the true nature of things. It is possible, therefore, that by returning constantly to its first efforts, thought will succeed in becoming ever clearer, in reducing itself ever more exactly to the basic elements of science, in a simpler, more powerful, and more convincing way. Galileo needed a whole lifetime to acquire the scientific style of those key passages in the *Discorsi* on which the science of mechanics is based. But from this time on, it must be emphasized, this science took on its first really universal objectivity.

In this respect Galileo was very different from Descartes, perhaps the only one of his contemporaries who may have surpassed him in intellectual power. Confronted with the universe in motion, Descartes, even as early as the *Traité du monde*, felt that he possessed a knowledge both absolutely fundamental and absolutely elementary in its objectivity. The knowledge in question is that which assimilates extension to body and motion to a quantity which is conserved. It can, then, be constructed, and must be deduced, starting from these first and fundamental truths. From the beginning, therefore, Descartes took up an attitude toward the universe of bodies in motion exactly like that of Archimedes toward the universe in which bodies have weight. One may say that, for him, it needed only a transition from perception to the ideal to allow the constructing of a kinetics as though it were a geometry of the universe, just as the statics of Archimedes had been a geometry of masses.

The situation was quite different in Galileo's work. Confronted with the universe in motion, he had not the calm assurance of Descartes. He was not really sure that he knew reality as it ought to be known. On the contrary, his scientific mind was aware of facing a difficult complexity in which, of course, scientific thought would ultimately find its way, but would do this only after having patiently tried to isolate insights far removed from sense evidence. These insights would not immediately be corroborated by the senses in some simple fashion. Perception would indeed confirm them only by coinciding with the reconstructions they permit, as when a motion is regarded as slowed down by the resistance of the medium, for example.

One might say that, confronted with the problem of constructing a universal science of motion, Descartes fell back too quickly on the familiar epistemology of Archimedes and the traditional geometricians. Galileo hesitated, then made long efforts to put straight whatever he was able to put straight, thus adopting a far less categorical attitude than that displayed by Descartes. Nevertheless, in his view too the theorist will, at the proper moment, display a confident rational certitude, once sure of his basic facts. He will then feel no further dependence upon experience, or rather, he will tranquilly expect agreement between it and his views. In his initial hesitation, however, Galileo gave to the scientists an important methodological counsel: that the human intelligence is not immediately in contact with the elementary intelligibles of reality. The access of science to the level of theory is still by no means the definitive conquest of the cosmos by the intelligence, even though it might seem that science has fully grasped the objectivity of some aspect of the universe, or has stated some universal law. Galileo's physics was a rational physics in a more radical sense than that of any of his contemporaries. But, at least as far as *research* is concerned, it remained a hypothetico-rational physics, far more so than was the case with Descartes.

From familiar experience to instructed experience

But what of the appeal to experience? We are now ready to approach this controversial question. There will always be disagreement as to what experiments Galileo performed, as to experiments he did not perform, and as to experiments he said he performed but apparently didn't, except by anticipation. An experiment such as that of the fall of bodies of unequal weight from the Tower of Pisa belongs to the realm of Galilean legend.[10] Other experiments were proposed explicitly by him, but he equally explicitly says he has not performed them, though he is quite sure in advance what results they would give.[11] According to the most recent researches of historians of science, many of the experiments which he proposed and claimed to have successfully carried out seem impracticable or inconclusive, given the means at his disposal.[12] Most of these have, therefore, been interpreted as no more than "thought-experiments". This does not mean, of course, that the proposing of them was without value, because they could easily serve as useful indicators of the plausibility of the theory with which they are associated. They might also suggest ideas about the shape of possible experiments for the future. For my part, however, I think that at least the *principal* experiments recounted in the *Discorsi* (such as the inclined-plane experiment,[13] considered by Koyré to be only a thought-experiment, or that of the pendulum stopped in its swing by an obstacle of variable distance from the support[14]) were really performed by Galileo. But before making this point, some preliminary discussion will be necessary. It is clear that the *experience* on which the scientific method of Galileo rests is far from being some sort of uniform thing. The word has for him, as for others, a multiple significance which has to be carefully explored.

Galileo spent much of his effort in opposing Aristotelian physics and its scholastic prolongation. Against it he appealed to experience. This could easily cause misunderstanding. The situation in which he was placed was in this respect extremely complex, as a close reading of his two major works shows. He appealed to experience against Aristotelians who themselves were busy appealing to experience against him. As Koyré has stressed, Simplicio comes out rather more the empiricist than does Galileo, in some respects at least.[15] It is essential to see that the differences here were rooted in a distinction between two successive "moments" or levels of experience. Galileo was appealing to a sort of second, more elaborated "moment" of experience, and opposing, therefore, an approach which resolutely fixed itself at an earlier, more primitive, level.

Aristotelianism does, it is true, integrate in its natural philosophy a "moment" in human experience which is already quite far from primitivity. But this moment is just short of the point from which a general science of motion could be constructed. For convenience, I shall describe the sort of experience on which Aristotle's world-view rests as "pre-scientific". It must also be remembered that the doctrinal systematization of this experience later became the basis for a school-teaching by way of received authority. Galileo contrasted his way of calling on experience with that of his opponents, not only because they had recourse to a different "moment" but also because they relied on an appeal to an authority which served as its own ground. Experience versus authority, careful scrutiny versus a hasty glance that drew its warrant ultimately from an ancient tradition: it is not hard to see how a quick reading of the texts could easily lead the modern reader into serious errors of interpretation.

But what then is the *"experience"* that Galileo chose to emphasize? It is certainly not a series of personally conducted experiments, providing a basis for new inductions which would run counter to the erroneous opinions of Aristotelianism. Such an interpretation of Galileo's approach, reducing it to the abstract methodology with which later empiricism tried to characterize all scientific thought, would be a serious misunderstanding of his position. The experience he relied on was, first of all, the *collective* experience of a considerable number of competent inquirers spread through the three centuries before his own day. These men were perfectly familiar with the details of Aristotelian physics. They had frequently established the fact that the Aristotelian conception of movement was inadequate. True, they were not always sure what they should put in its place; but they had made new, and not entirely unsuccessful, efforts to work toward a solution. Galileo did not hesitate to avail himself of their results for his own purposes. He singled out their central features, well realizing that what he had was not yet science. But he was also aware that, in its very opposition to the Aristotelian doctrine of movement, a beginning might be found of true science. And he intended to carry it through to that goal.

We might state this in terms of Aristotelian methodology by saying that the experience first invoked by Galileo was that of a fairly extensive body of *warranted opinion*, of *doxa*, in Aristotle's sense of that term. Their warranting required a closer study, involving observations that were, in fact, relatively technical and precise. This novel precising of experience and validating of what had been but opinion was needed in order to effectively oppose a body of long-received opinion, one which usually claimed for itself the status of valid, indeed definitive, knowledge. Thus Galileo was appealing to an "experience" which implicitly included a good number of observations actually made; he called in his support the most important and the most striking of these, ones, however, that he himself may well not have troubled to repeat. It must be noted that these observations were not mere recordings of fact. The part played in them by interpretation, often a rather free interpretation, was quite considerable. What counted, however, was the questioning and the deliberate testing of accepted habits of thought, procedures which Aristotle had relegated to what he called "dialectic", an auxiliary knowledge which was intended to facilitate the winnowing-out of true science.

There was much that was new in Galileo's methodology, compared with that of Aristotle. It was aimed at a *mathematical* rather than a *philosophical* knowledge of nature. Besides, the new body of acquired experience and of warranted opinion was epistemologically and historically posterior to the acceptance of the earlier rival system as a properly philosophical doctrine. Consequently, it had to do battle with the older view, and take account of the orientation it gave, with a view to re-educating minds for whom that orientation had become inveterate. Nevertheless, the experience which was requisite for going beyond Aristotle in this way was not yet enough to constitute "scientific experience" in the proper sense. It was still at the level immediately *preceding* science, much nearer to science, however, than the pre-scientific experience on which Aristotle's doctrine of motion (and consequent vision of the world) rested. And it contained within itself the seeds of the transition to truly scientific knowledge.

This explains why we today, trained as we are in a well-established scientific tradition, find find ourselves rather at a loss when we come to inquire as to what sort of experiences Galileo and the other scientific pioneers of his day were really calling upon. The account of these "experiences" contains so many obscurities, so many imprecisions, so many downright errors of interpretation, that it seems impossible that such material could have been legitimately brought to the support of truly scientific knowledge. Indeed, the very first principles of scientific method seem to be violated: no exact measurements, no specification of the circumstances of observation. And still, it was through this means that the mind, questing for science, first saw the truth, saw how to validate a truth of natural knowledge, or more exactly decide between it and another thesis. One must not, therefore, judge this fund of experience to which Galileo appeals, nor the "observations" and "experiments" it is said to yield, by the standards one would invoke today in judging experiments instituted specifically with a view to testing scientific theory, or to providing observations meant to serve as an inductive basis for research in a specialized and well-defined domain.

An appeal to "experience" in this broad sense does not at all conform, then, to the narrowly positivist account of science. But it was just such an appeal, nevertheless, that triggered a new phase in the developments that led to science as we know it. Of course, it is still necessary for the historian of science to analyze in detail the exact epistemological significance of each historical instance where "experience" was cited. Galileo's great achievement was to discern in the amorphous body of experience amassed subsequently to the establishment of Aristotelian physics what was vital to the needs of science, and then to bring this in decisive fashion to the requisite stage of clarity. The inertial continuation of motion, the fall of bodies, the effects of force, the motion of projectiles, the behavior of pendulums —generations of observation were put to work, and put to work so effectively that the first foundation was laid for an adequate mechanics of the isolated body, and a first glimpse given of the wide universe of which physics was soon to take possession.

Experiments that are specifically generative of science

Observational and experimental data on the topics just mentioned became at this point privileged, as it were. Galileo realized this very clearly, and accordingly he paid special attention to them, though not, of course, in the fashion of the modern experimental scientist. What was important for him was not so much the obtaining of exact quantitative data as it was the thinking through of the facts in a new way. Bodies fall with increasing speed. Here he was faced with a simple fact, and the whole experience of the profession of which he was a member assured him that there was in this something relatively simple and essential. His goal was not so much to *comprehend* a thing in its ultimate essence as to *represent* it correctly. This led him to the typically modern procedure of separating the question of the "cause", or ultimate explanation, of free fall—a question which he left aside—from that of the specifically mathematical description of the experimental fact. This distinction between two sorts of intellectual approach to the natural world turned out to be of crucial importance. Once it was drawn, Galileo was led quite naturally to suppose that he could define the simplest form of motion in terms of mathematics: it would come out as rectilinear and uniform. He tried, therefore, to think through in experimental fashion the motion of free fall, assuming it to be uniformly accelerated. Others had already done this, up to a point, but he attempted a more ambitious though still crude dynamics by linking together different sorts of instance of fall, especially of fall on a (controllable) inclined plane. In each case, he tried to reconstruct the diverse facts in the light of his principle that fall ought ideally to be thought of as uniformly accelerated.

This was the first seed, and from it grew a whole living tissue, as it were, in terms of which more and more phenomena could be comprehended and further experimental questions designed. This was the core of the scientific endeavor to which Galileo would henceforth devote himself. To the extent that he succeeded in it, he transformed the initial datum of experience into a sort of elementary yet fundamental system of basic experiments, which would henceforward continue to underlie all scientific thought. These were the experiments that a d'Alembert or a Lagrange will later propose as the basis for the development of mechanics, emphasizing their altogether primitive and indispensable character as principles of that science. But it is hardly necessary to emphasize that experience taken in this sense is never *truly* experimental. It is idealized and transformed by thought; it is a privileged perception, a proposition become axiomatic. In the last analysis, it is to Galileo that modern mechanics is indebted for the original choice of those fundamental experience-experiments, as well as for their first quasi-axiomatic presentation.

Experiment in the proper sense

But this by no means says all that has to be said about the role of experiment in Galileo's scientific methodology. In a sense yet to be touched on, he was a true "experimenter", constantly aiming to confirm by specially designed experiments one or another feature of his theories. As an experimenter, he also endeavored to plan experiments that would reveal previously hidden aspects of nature; we shall see an example of this at the end of this essay. What, then, was the doctrine and the practice of Galileo in this matter?

His clear and constant lesson is that good scientific theories must return naturally to reality, and in this way allow the data to be reconstructed in a reasonably satisfactory, if approximate, way. It is indeed in this reconstruction that the quality of the theories is tested. When, then, is a theory truly valid, and how are we to know when it is? If the very conditions of its origin contain a sort of intrinsic guarantee of its soundness, the mind which can appreciate this guarantee will often have no further need of confirmation by new experiments. On the contrary, the scientist in such a case may feel able to say with confidence what would happen if an experiment *were* to be performed. As we have already seen, Galileo sometimes felt he had arrived at such a point. And the same principles were at work in the far-out and speculative predictions which good theories often bring forth. This does not betray some sort of distrust of experience on his part; rather, he is relying upon that feeling of success which accompanies a work of the intellect well performed, a feeling that is surely inherent in the skillful deployment of every truly "scientific" method.

But even when in possession of a theory of which he was already confident, Galileo nevertheless did not disdain all recourse to experimentation. Among the many reasons for this recourse, the most immediate was that one had in the long run to verify the assumptions made in the original setting-up of the theoretical process. In addition, one had to obtain whatever quantitative data the theory involved. Galileo was particularly aware of the first of these reasons. He assumed, for instance, that free fall was uniformly accelerated *in vacuo*. But it was impossible for him to test the

truth of this directly: free fall could be observed only in a resistant medium, such as air, and in any event it was too rapid for his means of timing. By planning an indirect attack on the problem through the use of an
inclined plane, he was, however, able to test the accuracy of the assumption he had made. The action of the inclined plane was conceptualized as a
purely mechanical one; the combination of this with the original assumption about uniform acceleration *in vacuo* easily lent itself to the formulation of a prediction about the behavior of heavy bodies on inclined planes
—allowance being made for frictional and other disturbing factors—a
prediction which could readily be tested experimentally. This was the test
which Galileo proposed in the Third Day of the *Discorsi;* he describes in
a detailed manner the way in which he carried it through.

But did he *really* carry it through? Professor Koyré thinks not, because
the means at his disposal could not have provided conclusive results. Professor Dugas, on the other hand, thinks he did, as we have seen; to his
mind, Galileo's words are too explicit to be taken as describing an imaginary experiment. The latter view seems to me the better-founded, provided that it be properly understood. Galileo quite certainly observed the
behavior of objects on inclined planes in as careful a way as he could, and
with a view to grasping as clearly as possible the effect of gravity upon
movement. What he saw led him to believe that he had theorized accurately. In this sense, experiment yielded him the results that he expected
of it.

It is true that on occasion he reports measurements of times of descent
over relatively long distances, using methods that were casual even though
ingenious. The results of such measurements could not but have been
marked by large uncertainties, leaving the overall implications of the experimental study in doubt. On this point, Koyré is, I believe, correct. If Galileo did, in fact, perform measurements of this sort in the way he said he
did, their results would not have contributed very much to his quest,
other than a somewhat vague assurance of the general compatibility between his thinking and his observing. But that would seem to have been all
that he really expected from the kind of experiment he performed.

It is necessary to make an effort to understand the precise state of mind
in which Galileo approached his experimental work. He had already carried out a rational analysis of the fall of heavy bodies, as well as of the
mechanics of the inclined plane. He felt that he could estimate the disturbing effects of subsidiary factors such as air resistance and rolling friction.
The whole progression of the *Discorsi* shows this rational progress in action, leading to a synthetic reconstruction of the phenomenon of motion
on an inclined plane. Galileo could almost have said what he said about the
stone dropped from the masthead of a moving ship: "without making the
experiment, I am sure of what will happen". His turning to experiment,
when it occurred, had something of an instinctive character; the requirements a reasonably exact measure would have imposed never so much as

crossed his mind. The determination of the numerical constants appearing in the equations of fall interested him even less. All he wanted to know was whether he had given a good overall analysis of accelerated fall. And what he could see, without taking any elaborate experimental precautions, sufficed to reassure him on that point.

To put this in another way; if there was one approach to experiment that would never have occurred to Galileo, it was the one that empiricists and positivists are wont to extol: deploy all the available techniques of measurement, gather all the facts one can, and wring from these, via induction, a new "law" of which one was, up to that moment, entirely ignorant. If he had had to obtain his inclined-plane law in *that* way, the experimentation he carried out would have been entirely inadequate for the purpose. Indeed, this was just what the empiricists of the day reproached him with. And this was quite understandable if one agreed with their notion of scientific discovery—but then Galileo did not. Because as he saw it, the inclined-plane experiment represented a *return* of the scientist's thought to the facts and not at all a risky venturing forth from the facts by the thought in search of unknown forms.

It is entirely possible that Galileo had his empiricist colleagues in mind as he composed the *Discorsi*, and that in consequence he embellished the experimental accounts with a show of details and impressive precautions. They would, in this case, be a clue to his style of rhetoric—always an effective one—rather than to his actual modes of experimental procedure. It must always be remembered that experiment had *not*, in his day, taken on the aspect of a strict scientific protocol, well-tested and modified in the light of centuries of growingly self-conscious employment. On the contrary, it was just beginning, still only partially realized, the ideal and the actual not quite disentangled; it was as yet easy to mistake what had been at best only half-seen for something already achieved before ever the moment for describing it came around.

This was almost certainly what happened with the inclined plane and the pendulum experiments described in the *Discorsi*. Galileo, it would seem, really did attempt them. But he was able to carry them through only in the most approximate way, while at the same time re-creating them in his own mind in a much finer detail. This sufficed, as we have seen, for his purpose. And it must be noted that by representing these experimental procedures as being more carefully wrought and more exact than they could in the nature of the case have been, he did in fact lay down for his successors a better set of experimental protocols than were available to himself. Whether or not imagination added to the experimental description does not matter so much; what matters is that the scientific mind would not forget the model here held up to it. As soon as it could fully live up to this model, it would do so. In this sense, at least, Galileo undoubtedly anticipated later scientific canons of experimental procedure. And this very anticipation was of vital importance.

Now let us look at an experiment described in the dialogue: *On the force of percussion*, one which can certainly not be regarded as in the least imaginary. It proves that Galileo did, on occasion, see in experiment a point of departure for new research, and not just a verification of a theory already partly drafted. He was struggling with the problem of percussion, to no avail as it turned out. (Huygens was the first to give a satisfactory treatment of it.) To this end, he was led to ask what would happen if water was allowed to fall from one container into another, where both are suspended from the same point on the arm of a balance, initially in equilibrium.[16] In the *Dialogo*, he admits that he had no idea in advance as to the outcome, and that he was, in fact, quite surprised by it. He did this experiment "just to see what would happen", as Claude Bernard liked to put it. He describes what he saw, unexpected as it was, with great care and precision: the slight impulse given the container-system at the beginning of the experiment, at the exact moment when the upper orifice is opened, then the rapid return to equilibrium once the jet of water hits the lower container, and the subsequent maintenance of this equilibrium. This could not have been described in his day unless it had really been *seen*.

The experiment must, then, have been performed, and performed in a perspective very different from that of the theorist already confident of what he would find. It was, of course, still at a qualitative level; measurement played little part in it. Indeed, the unexpected null result gave no opportunity for measurement. This was, in fact, why Galileo was disappointed in the results, which in turn gives us some insight into what he hoped for from experiments of this sort. He wanted some measurable consequence of the impact of the water, a numerical law of some kind. The balance was there both to indicate the departure from equilibrium and to provide a measure of the weight needed to restore it. Galileo already had grasped the technique of posing questions that would not only decide an issue in a yes-or-no way, but would also provide some numerically expressible data.

Conclusion

There is here something of the spirit of modern experimental method. One can see the beginnings of the dialogue, at once instrumental and mathematical in its techniques, between the human mind and the natural universe. Thanks to these techniques, it is possible to assert that the universe behaves in a uniform way, both qualitatively and quantitatively, under similar circumstances. Experimentation in *this* sense, Galileo grasped very well. He practiced it and preached it, thus giving to the new science of physics a basic lesson in methodology, one barely hinted at elsewhere in the works of his contemporaries.

Nineteenth-century historians of science were not wrong when they judged Galileo far the superior of Descartes on this point. The latter, at first sight at least, gives the impression of one who simply continues, with

no apparent discomfort, along the familiar path of the geometrization of
the perceived world, after the fashion of Archimedes. He seems to move
at a level of abstraction that dispenses him from consulting experiment
except where the multitude of abstract possibilities summoned up by the
mathematician makes a recourse to the order of experience mandatory if
he is to decide which possibility, among the multitude, is in fact actualized
in the real world. The Galileo who describes experiment in the terms we
have seen has adopted a very different intellectual approach, whether or
not the experiments he describes were in all instances carried out or not.
He knew, with a certitude as well as a precision born of a lifetime of test,
what characteristics one might expect in a type of knowledge which issued from a network of humanly conceived instrumentation stretching in
a sort of linkage between human thought and physical reality. And this
was the altogether crucial epistemological point at issue.

The error of the nineteenth century, on the other hand, was to see in
Galileo no more than an anticipation of the good positivist, and to contrast
him on that score with a Descartes equally erroneously presented as a
dogmatist, lost in the abstractions of metaphysics and entirely unable to
cope with mechanics. Galileo was very far from being anything of the
sort; in his day, procedures in the new mechanics were necessarily a far
cry from the limited positivist routines which are possible within the confines of a science already well-established.

The rather faded thesis of nineteenth-century positivism, which looked
so bright in those last decades of classical physics before 1880, tended to
obscure what is in the last analysis the most profound and the most penetrating aspect of the scientific mind, faced with a universe that it does not
yet know, in the sense in which 'know' will henceforward come to be
taken. Since then, science and specifically mechanics has had an unlooked-
for reopening of questions then thought to be closed. In this century, a
new horizon has opened up; the confident certitude of the mid-nine-
teenth-century physicist and the natural philosophy that underlay it, have
both suffered a very similar shipwreck to that suffered by the Aristotelian
world-view three centuries earlier. In this situation, the most valuable part
of Galileo's legacy to the methodology of physical science could still serve
as a useful reminder, no longer for Aristotle's Simplicio, but for other
Simplicios, if some there be, among the theorists of contemporary science.

NOTES

1. This thesis is implicit in the exposition of Galileo's work given by E. Mach
in his *Science of mechanics*, chap. 2, sect. 1.
2. A. Koyré, *Études Galiléennes*, Paris, 1939. The author presents what is to
his mind Galileo's basic attitude toward science, as exemplified in his work in
mechanics. See also: "Le *De Motu Gravium* de Galilée: de l'experience imagi-

naire et de ses abus", 1960*, *Galilée et la revolution scientifique du XVIIe siècle*, 1955*.

3. *Études Galiléennes, 3*, p. 67.

4. *Ibid.*, *2*, pp. 71–73.

5. *Ibid.*, *2*, pp. 1–2.

6. For example in: *La mécanique au XVIIe siècle*, Paris, 1954, pp. 81–83, esp. n. 1, p. 83.

7. *Republic*, VII, 527d–528a.

8. *Opere, 6*, p. 232.

9. *Republic*, VII, 529b–530c.

10. See Lane Cooper: *Aristotle, Galileo and the Tower of Pisa*, Ithaca (N.Y.), 1935.

11. The stone, for instance, allowed to fall from the masthead of a moving ship, which would, according to Galileo, fall in exactly the same point of the deck as it would if the boat were not moving (*Dialogo, Opere*, 7, p. 171).

12. See, for example, the observation mentioned in the *De Motu* (*Opere, 1*, p. 334) where light bodies are said to fall initially more quickly than heavy ones (Koyré, *Études, 1*, p. 62); also experiments with inclined planes (*op. cit., 2*, pp. 71–72); "Le *De Motu gravium* . . ." 1960*.

13. *Discorsi, Opere, 8*, pp. 212–214.

14. *Ibid.*, pp. 206–208.

15. *Études, 3*, p. 67.

16. See Mach, *Science of mechanics*, chap. 3, sect. 4.

15 ⚬ Galileo's use of experiment as a tool of investigation

THOMAS B. SETTLE

What part did experiment play in Galileo's investigations? In one form or another this question is involved in all the literature on Galilean science, and it has received various answers. Some scholars, for instance, portray Galileo as a pure theorist, a deviser of doctrine, with little real need or use for experiment, while others show him as a modern empiricist *par excellence*. Unfortunately for the advocates of the several positions, there has been little detailed scrutiny of the cases in which Galileo seems to have been very much concerned with the empirical fit of his propositions. Those who have tended to accept the "theorist" view have either ignored, devalued or discredited outright the face value of Galileo's own testimony.[1] And those more sympathetic to the "empiricist" view, e.g., the late F. Sherwood Taylor,[2] have generally accepted the testimony at its face value alone without providing a critical analysis of any instance in which an experiment might have played a crucial role in the progress of Galileo's work. Thus far, in other words, there exists no systematic discussion of the exact historical role of any of Galileo's alleged experimental activity. What is required is a minute examination of the historical sequence of changes in Galileo's scientific conclusions, paying particular attention to those factors which may have *forced* him to alter his opinions along the way. Here I shall present a survey of the genesis of one of his major achievements, the enunciation of the so-called law of free fall. We shall find, in fact, that an excellent case can be made for saying that Galileo began his empirical investigations into this problem as early as the time of his Pisan professorship, 1589–1592, that these led him to perfect the inclined plane as a research tool, and that this in turn provided the data from which he constructed part of the Second Science of the *Discorsi*. My immediate purpose is only to establish some general assertions about this one strand of Galileo's work. Although I have been investigating for some time several other interesting and ultimately related facets of his science, still more work will be needed before a more ambitious portrait could be undertaken. It did seem worthwhile, however, to make even these limited results available.[3]

The sequence suggested by the *Discorsi*

Most accounts of the discovery of the properties of natural acceleration have relied fairly exclusively on Galileo's own exposition of the subject in the Third Day of the *Discorsi*. With minor variations, the common interpretation has Galileo following the "hypothetico-deductive" model, performing the inclined-plane experiment, if at all, only to test deductions from a theoretical presupposition, postulated in advance as the true definition of natural acceleration. Very little attempt is ever made to find the order in which Galileo discovered the various propositions or how he may have come upon them. We are often left with the conclusion that by and large the sequence of exposition of the Third Day follows the same order as that in which Galileo originally gained his knowledge, almost that the text is a transcription of a daily research journal. Ernst Mach, for instance, provides a typical summary of this version of the chronology of the work.

The modern spirit that Galileo discovers is evidenced here, at the very outset, by the fact that he does not ask *why* heavy bodies fall, but propounds the question: *How* do heavy bodies fall? In agreement with what *law* do freely falling bodies move? The method he employs to ascertain this law is this. He makes certain assumptions. He does not, however, like Aristotle rest there, but endeavors to ascertain by trial whether they are correct or not.

The first theory on which he lights is the following. It seems in his eyes plausible that a freely falling body, inasmuch as it is plain that its velocity is constantly on the increase, so moves . . . that the velocities acquired in descent increase proportionally to the distances descended through. Before he proceeds to test experimentally this hypothesis, he reasons on it logically.

After Galileo fancied he had discovered this assumption to be untenable, he made a second one, according to which the velocity acquired is proportional to the time of descent. That is, if a body fall once, and then fall again during as long an interval of time as it first fell, it will attain in the second instance double the velocity it acquired in the first. He found no self-contradiction in this theory, and he accordingly proceeded to investigate by experiment whether the assumption accorded to the facts. It was difficult to prove by any direct means that the velocity acquired was proportional to the time of de-

scent. It was easier, however, to investigate by what law the distance increased with the time; and he consequently deduced from his assumption the
relation which obtained between the distance and the time, and tested this by
experiment . . .[4]

Indeed, this follows the path seemingly outlined by Galileo himself.

Galileo opened the discussion of natural acceleration by proposing the
"correct" definition of it: "A motion is said to be uniformly accelerated,
when starting from rest, it acquires, during equal time-intervals, equal increments of speed." [5] He then went on to elucidate informally certain of
its features, first showing by an easy observational reference that acceleration does take place, then explaining that he conceived this acceleration to
be "continuous" and not "jumpy", and finally clearly indicating what his
criterion of uniformity entailed. It was during the discussion of the latter
that he mentioned that he once tried an alternative definition according to
which velocity would be directly proportional to the distance covered.
He immediately rejects this alternative, though his argument against it is
inconclusive; it seems clear that these passages are the basis for Mach's
reference to Galileo's initial wrong asumption. But having rejected this,
the other logically possible definition, Galileo was then in a position to
proceed with the formal demonstration of his theorems.[6] The first of
these was the average speed rule: a body in uniform acceleration from
rest will cover the same distance in the same time as a body in uniform
motion, traveling with a velocity of one-half that of the final velocity of
the accelerated body. From this in turn, Galileo deduced a second theorem, relating distance covered to the square of the time taken, as well as its
corollary, the odd-number rule: for bodies in natural acceleration, the
successive increments of distance are related in the ratio of the odd numbers beginning from unity.[7] Then reverting to informal discussion, Galileo described the famous inclined-plane experiment by means of which he
claimed to have confirmed the propositions empirically. Thus, in Mach's
view (as in that of many others), he picked an ultimately successful definition, deduced testable consequences from it, and then experimented.

This is a plausible interpretation; there is nothing in the *Discorsi* against
it. On the other hand neither is there anything there to confirm it. We
shall see that Galileo had at one time considered the incorrect definition,
but the mention of it in the *Discorsi* is more likely to have been a rhetorical device for underscoring by contrast the precise meaning of the correct
definition.[8] Nor are there any other historical markers. There is no indication that Galileo had any intention in the Third Day of describing the
actual sequence of steps he had followed, no indication that he had any
other purpose in mind than providing a systematic and convincing exposition of his *finished* work, with the scaffolding removed and the debris of
construction discarded. The two criteria of deductive rigor and clarity of
exposition govern the sequence and these are in nowise dependent upon
the chronology of discovery. We know better today than to expect a

Euclid or a Newton to give the history of his thought in his final polished treatise. Any interpretation of the evolution of Galileo's conclusions based on the *Discorsi* alone can at best lead to a verdict of "not proven".

The letter to Sarpi of 1604

In an important document of 1604, we shall find both that Galileo had considered the wrong velocity-distance definition, and that he knew of the substance of the second theorem above before he knew the correct definition. It is a letter of October 16, 1604, written in answer to one from Fra Paolo Sarpi posing some questions in natural philosophy. In it, Galileo outlined, in brief, the current state of his ideas on natural motion:

> Thinking about the matter of motion, for which, in order to demonstrate the accidents there observed by me, I was in need of a principle completely indubitable that I could pose as an axiom, I came upon a proposition which was very natural and evident; and this supposed, I then demonstrated the rest, namely that the spaces passed in natural motion are in proportion to the squares of the time taken, and consequently that the spaces traversed in equal successive time intervals are as to the odd numbers *ab unitate*, and other things. And the principle is this: that the natural mobile will go on increasing its velocity with the proportion by which it is removed from the start of its motion. Take, for example, a body falling from the terminus *a* along the line *abcd*. I suppose that the ratio between its velocity at *c* and its velocity at *b* is as the distance *ca* to the distance *ba*. Consequently, at *d* it would have a degree of velocity greater than at *c* according as the distance *da* is greater than *ca*.[9]

If we take this at its face value, it would appear that Galileo had been observing examples of natural acceleration, and had discovered that certain "accidents" obtained, such as distance of fall varying as the square of the time and incremental distance varying as the odd numbers. With these generalizations in mind, he was in the midst of trying to elaborate a rational scheme based on a single principle from which he could deduce these, as well as other "accidents" not mentioned. The first principle that occurred to him to try was the direct velocity-distance proportionality, the one we find him rejecting later in the *Discorsi*. If this is so, it is clear that the first step in acquiring the knowledge displayed in the *Discorsi* was the observational discovery of the time-squared and the odd-number laws, perhaps as the result of some sort of experimental work, rather than the postulation of a definition of natural acceleration. It seems that only after he had observed these regularities did he begin to look for definitions. First he tried the velocity-distance version. Presumably sometime later he rejected that and tried the velocity-time one, and this ultimately proved successful. If this picture is generally correct, we have arranged the chronology of some of the important components of the *Discorsi*, and have isolated one of the crucial steps in the discovery of the "new science", the step that led him to the two laws. It is to the problem of how Galileo came to take this step that I wish to devote the remainder of this essay.

Where are we to look? In the letter cited above, observations are mentioned. Is it possible that the two "accidents" were arrived at by generalization from experimental inquiry? Admittedly, the reference in the letter is not entirely unambiguous. However, it is certainly reasonable to interpret it such that the "accidents there observed" include the two laws. Unfortunately Galileo did not indicate what sort of "observing" he conducted. Nor did he give any hint of what might have led him to construct an experiment in such a way that this particular type of information could have been elicited. Happily, we can find all the information needed to construct a plausible answer to both of these questions in one of Galileo's early scientific efforts, the *De motu*.[10]

The theory of motion in the *De motu*

It was in the *De motu* that Galileo first attempted to set down a systematic treatment of the theory of motion. He began its composition during the period 1589–1592, while teaching at the University of Pisa. During his last year or two as a student at Pisa and during the four years before his return on the faculty, he had delved deeply into mathematics and physics and had conceived an admiration that was to be lifelong for Archimedes and Archimedean method. Out of these studies grew two papers which circulated in manuscript, and which earned him a reputation in natural philosophy, as well as a lectureship at Pisa. One was a hypothetical reconstruction of Archimedes' discovery of the hydrostatic principle, including detailed directions for making an appropriate instrument, *La bilancetta*;[11] the other was a treatise concerning mathematical methods for determining the centers of gravity of certain regular solids, *Theoremata circa centrum gravitatis solidorum*. Whether he was working already on the theory of motion in this period is not certain; one senses that he must have been, but establishing this is not crucial to the ideas presented here. On being appointed to the university, he had to teach the theory of motion, and this seems to have given him the immediate occasion for beginning the composition of the *De motu*. In the process, he produced two texts embodying roughly the same material, one an essay and the other a dialogue. It is not clear that one of these versions distinctly preceded the other. The phraseology of particular discussions is often the same in both.[12] In any event, it is obvious that Galileo composed both to give expression to very much the same body of information and thought, an elaborated science of motion often referred to as his "Pisan dynamics".

The theoretical structure of this dynamics is built on two postulates: (1) the central feature of natural motion is that it possesses a uniform speed, proportional to the specific gravity of the moving object; (2) non-natural motions are a result of a *virtus impressa*, an impressed force. The first and more important of these propositions assumes that a body has a natural tendency which guides it to its natural place. This power is directly related to the specific gravity of the body, and is an absolute property. And associated with a given specific gravity is a specific uniform speed, which is the speed with which the body would move were it in a vacuum. And as the *effective* specific gravity of a body is diminished by an amount corresponding to the specific gravity of the medium in which .it is immersed, so the "natural" speed of a body is modified in the same way. In a vacuum, the body would move as its true speed; in a medium of the same density as the object, there would be no motion. The overtone of Archimedes is unmistakable: the relative density of an object and a fluid determines the hydrostatic equilibrium state of the system. In the *De motu*, the relative density determines the hydrodynamic equilibrium, the "equilibrium" being realized here in terms of a definite uniform speed. And this limiting speed, it should be noticed, is not conceived as imposed by frictional resistance, since it holds true of fall *in vacuo*. The medium is assumed to act only by altering the effective density, not at all in terms of friction.

The second proposition accounts for the obvious fact that bodies do not just jump from rest to their proper speeds. *Per accidens*, they must undergo a period of acceleration. To account for this, one supplements the first assumption with the notion of a *virtus impressa*, a power that can be imposed on the body from the outside and which decays steadily after the external force ceases. Thus when a body sits on a table, the support communicates to it the *virtus impressa*, which is just sufficient to counteract its natural tendency downward. When the body is released, this impressed power cannot vanish immediately; it only slowly leaks away. As this happens, the innate power of the body gradually asserts itself, and the speed of the body steadily increases until finally all the impressed power is gone and the body assumes the speed proper to its own density in conjunction with that of the medium.

Galileo, then, had a comprehensive theory of motion at hand. He could account for a wide variety of phenomena, even in a quasi-quantitative way, as we shall see. Yet as he experimented within its framework, he was sowing the seeds of its own destruction. The obvious flaw was that he could not find one good experimental example illustrating the major premise, the uniform specific speed. There was no clear experimental instance in which a freely moving body had lost its retarding impressed power, and was proceeding at a uniform speed. How do we know he was experimenting? To establish this, we shall proceed with an analysis of the essay version of the *De motu*.[13]

The hydrostatic analogy

The essay consists of twenty-three short chapters; rather, one should say, that in the National Edition, Favaro grouped together twenty-three short essays which he considered to have constituted the original essay. And he also included different versions of the chapters, showing textual variants of Galileo's thought. In his recent translation, the late Professor Drabkin included the original twenty-three, and also included some of the more significant reworkings.

The essay begins with a definition of 'heavy' and 'light'. We are given to understand that these terms will be used only in a relative sense; in effect, all bodies have heaviness, and we only call those "light" which are less heavy. He also made it clear that the terms were meant to be taken per unit volume. This he underscored by explaining why a stone sinks in the sea. One could argue, he said, that since the total weight of the sea is greater than that of the small stone, one should expect the stone to be cast out. Not so:

> The stone is, in fact, heavier than the water of the sea, if we take a quantity of water equal in volume to that of the stone; and so the stone being heavier than the water will move downwards in the water.[14]

Along with the definition of heavy and light, then, was the correlated idea that a "natural" motion is one caused by heaviness or lightness. In the early version, Galileo called both the falling of a stone and the rising of a bubble in water "natural" motions. Later he would restrict that term to falling only, emphasizing that heaviness was the essential property of all matter and lightness only accidental.[15] We note that at the very outset the study of motion is based on a hydrostatic analogy.

Thus far Galileo had spoken only qualitatively. So that there would be no ambiguity in the ensuing discussions, he set out formal proofs that: (1) "bodies of the same heaviness as the medium move neither upward nor downward"; (2) "bodies lighter than water cannot be completely submerged".[16] Having demonstrated these, he thought it should be clear why bodies heavier than water should continue to move downwards: the cause of downward motion and the extrusive upward motion lies in the relative densities of the object and the medium. He then goes on, by way of support, to give an analogy from the behavior of an equal-arm balance.[17] When comparing weights in fluids, one compares quantities of matter having equal volumes. Likewise when comparing weights on a balance, one assumes equal arm lengths. The cause of relative upward and downward motion in fluids can be understood by analogy with the cause of the various motions of the arms due to the weights in the pans. If this seems a trivial exercise at this point, we shall find that Galileo uses the balance analogy in a very crucial demonstration later on.

So much for motions in terms of their directions. It was now time to introduce speed into the discussion. First, speaking qualitatively, he related the speed of a falling object to its weight in a given medium. There followed a discussion leading to a hypothetical quantitative illustration. The speed of fall in a given medium can be estimated by finding the difference between the density of the object and that of the medium. And this holds whether we are considering the sinking of a relatively heavy object or the rise of a relatively light one.

> For example, if there are two bodies equal in volume but unequal in weight, the weight of one being 8, and the other being 6, and if the weight of a

volume of the medium equal to the volume of either body is 4, the speed of the first will be 4 and of the second 2.[18]

The general line of argument is clear enough. A body's speed is determined by its density, and its speed in a medium by its net density in that medium. But there is not as yet any clear evidence that would tie what he is claiming to any particular experimental work. We would wonder perhaps whether the theory actually works. So apparently did Galileo:

> But note that a great difficulty arises at this point, because those ratios will not be observable by one who makes the experiment. For if one takes two different bodies, which have properties such that the first should fall twice as fast as the second, and if one lets them fall from a tower, the first will not reach the ground appreciably faster or twice as fast. Indeed, if an observation is made, the lighter body will, at the beginning of the motion, move ahead of the heavier and will be swifter. This is not the place to consider how these contradictions and, so to speak, unnatural accidents come about (for they are accidents). In fact, certain things must be considered first which have not yet been examined. For we must first consider why natural motion is slower at the beginning.[19]

By the first postulate, the only one explicitly mentioned by him so far, the body having twice the density should arrive at the foot of the tower in half the time. But when the experiment was tried, the two reached the ground almost simultaneously. Moreover (he says) the lighter one actually preceded the heavier for a while. Galileo did not, however, believe that this upset his postulate; something else, he suggested, had arisen here as an "accident" to be explained later. The results of the experiment were not wanted, and thus had to be explained away. This he would do shortly in terms of the second postulate concerning impressed power. Had Galileo actually dropped things from a tower? Or had he read about someone else doing it? Or did he simply see that it "had to be so"? There is evidence that there might have been a written source for this particular experiment, as we shall see in a moment. Perhaps the greatest objection to supposing that he carried it out himself is that it seems hard to believe that he could have actually seen a light body lead a heavy one for a while. To this difficulty also we shall return.

Impressed force

Galileo took up the topic of impressed force in a chapter entitled: "By what agency projectiles are moved". Impressed force is compared with impressed heat. The terms of the analogy tell us something about the way he viewed both motion and heat:

> The body, then, is moved upward by the thrower so long as it is in his hand and is deprived of its weight; in the same way the iron is moved, in an alternative motion, towards heat, so long as the iron is in the fire and is deprived of its coldness. Motive force, that is to say lightness, is preserved in

the stone, when the mover is no longer in contact; heat is preserved in the iron after the iron is removed from the fire. The impressed force gradually diminishes in the projectile when it is no longer in contact with the thrower; the heat diminishes in the iron, when the fire is not present. The stone finally comes to rest; the iron similarly returns to its natural coldness. Motion is more strongly impressed by the same given force in a body that is more resistant than in one that is less resistant, e.g., in the stone, more than the light pumice; and, similarly, heat is more strongly impressed by the same fire upon very hard, cold iron, than upon weak and less cold wood.[20]

The impressed force, then, is something that can be put into an object by an external mover, and can modify the action of the innate power of the object. When we project a body upwards, we have impressed upon it a power which overcomes its natural heaviness. It becomes temporarily light; and thus will continue to move upwards until the extrinsic lightness has departed.

In the following chapter, Galileo argued from the observed fact that upward projectile motion always ceases, to the conclusion that it must decrease *continuously*, and not by steps.[21] For should the motion remain constant over any one finite segment, there is no reason why it should not remain constant over the next segment, and so on. If this were to happen, the motion would continue upwards forever. But this does not happen; therefore, the motion must decrease continuously. And we can further conclude that the impressed force must also decrease continuously. He uses the term, 'continuous', here in its mathematical sense. If one were to omit reference to the impressed force, the argument is very similar to the one already alluded to in the *Discorsi*, where Galileo was arguing for the continuity of acceleration. Both are based on a principle of sufficient reason, and neither is altogether valid or convincing.

There must be a reason why a body is less heavy at the beginning of a fall than later. In a given case, at the beginning:

> The natural and intrinsic weight of a body has surely not been diminished, since neither its volume nor its density has been diminished. We are left with the conclusion that the diminution of weight is contrary to nature and accidental. If, then, we have found that the weight of the body is diminished unnaturally and from without, we will then surely have found what we seek.[22]

The impressed power seemed to explain the diminution perfectly. Galileo could now go on to describe the whole cycle of events in projectile motion: the initial preponderance of the impressed force, its gradual diminution, and the growing dominance of the intrinsic weight. Since the impressed force gradually decreases, it follows that the body can only be at the peak of its trajectory for an instant:

> Local motion upward and downward is a consequence of that alternative motion of change from light *per accidens* to heavy *per se*, in such a way that upward motion flows from an excess of impressed force, downward from a

deficiency thereof, and rest from equality, and since this equality does not persist over an interval of time, it follows that neither does the state of rest persist.[23]

This gives a fair theoretical account of why there should be an initial period of acceleration in heavy bodies, and even of why projectiles move as they do.

Dropping things from towers

Getting closer to actual experimental problems, Galileo turned next to the tower observations. First, as to why the heavy objects from a tower should land almost together:

> For in the case of heavier bodies, since a great deal of contrary force must be used up in the course of fall, more time will be required to use it up. Now in the course of this time, since they move more quickly, they will fall a great distance. And since we cannot avail ourselves of such large distances from which to let heavy bodies fall, it is not strange that a stone let fall merely from the height of a tower will be observed to be accelerated all the way to the ground. For this short distance and short time of motion are insufficient for the destruction of the whole contrary force.[24]

He presumes that the falling bodies would not yet have completed the phase of acceleration before they hit the ground. And even if a lighter one were to do so, it would not have been moving at its proper uniform speed long enough for large differences to appear between its motion and that of a heavier body.

He next tackled the difficulty arising from the alleged fact that the lighter object moves ahead of the heavier at the beginning of the acceleration. One might suppose that heavy and light bodies would pace each other exactly as they fell, "for though heavier bodies have more of the opposite quality to destroy than do lighter bodies, still they also have greater weight with which to destroy it".[25] And this would be reasonable, he surmised, except for the fact that it is not the intrinsic weight which destroys the impressed weight. The two are independent.[26] The impressed weight is a self-destroying quality. Some materials appear to lose impressed force more quickly than others, e.g., a lead bob on a string will continue to swing longer than a wooden one will. (He did not use the word, 'pendulum', but this seems to be the first reference to pendulum motion in his writings.) From this and other examples, he inferred—the validity of the inference is questionable—that the rate of decay of the impressed force is different for different materials. If lighter objects lose their impressed force at a higher rate:

> in the time in which one unit of the quality departs from the lead, more than one unit has left the wood; and as a consequence, while the lead has recovered only one unit of weight, the wood has recovered more than one. It is because of this that the wood moves more swiftly during that time. Again,

in the time in which two units of the quality depart from the wood, less than two depart from the lead. And it is because of this that the lead moves more slowly during that time. On the other hand, because the lead finally reacquires more weight than the wood, it follows that by that time the lead is moving much more swiftly.[27]

A neat explanation, indeed. This theory of an impressed force, which decays steadily when left to itself, allowed him to account for everything quite well.

We might well ask ourselves again: *had* Galileo actually experimented with heavy objects from towers? On the one hand, there is the part of the passage quoted already in which he said that "if one lets [two bodies of different weights] fall from a tower, the first will not reach the ground appreciably faster". Now the fact reported here is *not* one which would have been expected or appreciated by Galileo; this would lead us to assume that he must have actually seen it for himself. On the other hand, in the passage immediately following, he adds that "if an observation is made, the lighter body will, at the beginning of the motion, move ahead of the heavier and will be swifter". Since this *could* not (it would seem) have been observed, we are tempted to conclude that he must have been talking in terms of a thought-experiment, or else relying on some piece of contemporary hearsay. Yet if this be so, we must ask ourselves why Galileo would spend an entire chapter on a thought-experiment or a piece of hearsay which clearly did not fit his original theory. Would he not have made some kind of experimental check?

Drabkin noted that one Jerome Borri had mentioned a similar experiment in his *De motu gravium et levium*, published in Florence in 1576:

> Borri (who taught at Pisa while Galileo was a student there) describes an experiment of throwing two equal weights of lead and wood simultaneously from his window. Seeing the wood fall faster (in repeated trials), he reasons as Galileo relates. Borri does not limit his statement to the start of the fall; his reasoning is refuted by Galileo, who asserts that the wood falls faster *only at the beginning*.[28]

Galileo had seen this text. It might, then, be supposed that he had derived his "fact" from this source, although he apparently asserted more than had Borri; he claimed that the wood fell faster than the lead only for a while. Borri worked from his window; Galileo said that he had himself worked from a tower. Had he started working from lower elevations, found the same thing as Borri did, and then gone to higher ones in order to try to disprove his teacher? It seems pretty clear that the explanation he gives of the wood's preceding the lead is "after the fact". It can be made to follow (after a fashion) from his basic assumptions, yet these latter would never have sufficed to predict such an unexpected outcome. It seems unlikely, then, that Galileo would have accepted the alleged fact on hearsay from Borri without testing it for himself. Admittedly, the arguments on both sides of the case are inconclusive. Yet on the whole, those in favor of Galileo's having performed the experiments he mentioned are somewhat stronger.

If we admit that Borri did what he apparently claimed, why not say that his work was the stimulus to Galileo's own, that Galileo undertook similar experiments in order to establish whether the facts were as Borri had claimed, or whether they were not closer to his own Archimedean style of argument. Finding, for some reason, that the wooden ball seemed to out-strip the leaden one from low elevations, Galileo then took the balls to relatively high towers, perhaps even to the Leaning Tower.[29] There seems to be enough evidence for us to conclude that Galileo was carrying out experiments with falling bodies at this time. If we wonder why he did not emphasize them more in his writings, the answer, of course, is that accord-ing to the theoretical background against which they were being per-formed, they were relatively unsuccessful. What he would presumably have wanted to investigate was the uniform velocity proper to each kind of body in free fall, as prescribed in his first postulate, and especially the proportionality between it and the density of the body. But the accelera-tion of fall simply refused to diminish to zero as his postulate said it should.

Theoretical determination of the speed of fall on the inclined plane

The scope of the essay kept extending. The chapter entitled: "Contain-ing a discussion of the ratios of the motions of the same body moving over various inclined planes" opened with a statement of his general aims:

> The problem we are now going to discuss has not been taken up by any philosopher, so far as I know. Yet, since it has to do with motion, it seems to be a necessary subject for examination by those who claim to give a treat-ment of motion that is not incomplete. And it is a problem no less necessary than neat and elegant. The problem is why the same heavy body, moving downward in natural motion over various planes inclined to the plane of the horizon, moves more readily and swiftly on those planes that make angles nearer a right angle with the horizon. In addition, the problem requires us to determine the ratio of the motions that take place at the various inclinations.[30]

The tone of this opening recalls both the introduction and the conclu-sion to the Third Day of the *Discorsi:* "There is, in nature, perhaps noth-ing older than motion, concerning which the books written by philosophers are neither few nor small, nevertheless I have discovered by experi-ment . . ." And: "I think we may concede to our Academician, without flattery, his claim that in the principle laid down in this treatise he has established a new science dealing with a very old subject." [31] Galileo was proud of his accomplishments in both cases, though the *De motu* only marked a first step toward the treatment given to motion in the *Discorsi*.

However his interest in inclined planes had first come about, he was now asking himself how the differences in speed on differently inclined planes should be explained and perhaps predicted. He had in mind here the uniform motion of his theory rather than the accelerated motion of experimental fact, and his problem was to discover how the downward motion would be modified by the angle of the inclined plane. The first step was to state the problem more precisely. He noted that he had already shown that a "body tends to move downward with as much force as is necessary to lift it up".[32] The total force downwards he took to be the index of the body's natural speed of fall. If one could find the ratio of that force to the vertical weight of the body, the ratio of speeds (he reasoned) would be the same as the ratio of forces. Knowing the ratio of the speed on any plane to that in the vertical, one could then find the ratios relating the speeds proper to any two angles of inclination.

To calculate the desired ratio, he started with an equal arm balance.[33] Initially, it would balance with equal weights at each end; the weight at D would tend to move along EF. He argued that if we allow AD to pivot around A towards B, the initial tendency at S would be along GH. But the tendency to motion is a consequence of the effective weight; what we need to find, then, is this weight at any given point in the direction of the tangent line. If, then, we could discover the ratio of the effective weight at S to that at D, we would have solved our problem. At D, a given weight would balance with an equal weight at C. But at S, the same weight would

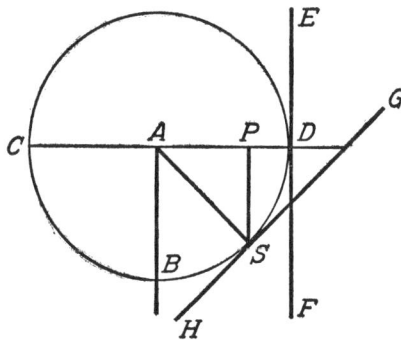

Figure 15-1

exert less force because it acts through point P, and AP is shorter than AC. The ratio of the force that the weight exerts at S to that which it exerts at D is measured by the ratio AP to AD. If AD be extended to Q, this ratio is equal to that of SP to SQ, i.e., the ratio of the vertical distance to the oblique distance between AD and S. Thus, the ratio between the speed of descent along GH and that along EF will be as the ratio of the vertical height to the oblique intercept of the tangent plane.

This is a neat proof. Galileo had no difficulty with the theory of bent levers. The only gap in the argument lies in the effect of the change in the direction of action of the weight as it moves from *D* to *S*. But it probably seemed clear enough to Galileo that if the weight were at *S* a real balance would move counterclockwise. By reducing the amount of the weight at *C* by the ratio *AP* to *AD*, it could once again be brought to balance. The ratio is the same as before, so that we have a direct way of estimating the effect of the weight at *S*, and indirectly a way of finding the speed of a body on an inclined plane for any angle of inclination.

This led to a far-reaching consequence:

> A body subject to no external resistance on a plane sloping no matter how little below the horizon will move down in natural motion, without the application of any external force. This can be seen in the case of water. And the same body on a plane sloping upward, no matter how little, above the horizon, does not move up except by force. And so the conclusion remains that on the horizontal plane itself the motion of the body is neither natural nor forced.[34]

At this point, Galileo was not ready to take the further step he did later take in the *Discorsi*, i.e., to conclude that such a body would go on moving forever.[35] If it were moving, presumably it would be moving by virtue of an impressed force at a speed determined by that force. But such a force in his view (as we have seen) steadily diminished, once left to itself; thus motion on a horizontal plane would, presumably, come to a halt. He did not say this explicitly, but this seems to have been the train of thought that led him to his next demonstration. If motion on such a horizontal plane is neither natural nor forced, one could move an object by "the smallest of all possible forces". His reasoning presumably was that since the motion is not natural, it would require some impressed force, yet since it is not forced either, there would be no finite inherent resistance to overcome. Therefore the required force could be less than any assigned value. It follows that "a body subject to no external resistance can be moved on a plane which slopes neither up nor down by a force smaller than any given force whatever". His proof of this is ingenious. Suppose we choose a force of arbitrarily small magnitude, and let it act upon a body; there would be a definite ratio between the force and the downward weight. But such a ratio would define a particular inclined plane, the force being proportional to the height, and the weight being proportional to the intercept (or "slope") length. Now since the slope of a *horizontal* plane is zero, the force to move the body on *it* would be less than the arbitrarily small force originally chosen.

Did he experiment with inclined planes?

So much for his theory. Experimentally, he continued to have trouble finding the results that his theories predicted. In order that his method of deriving of the ratios should work, one must assume that:

there is no accidental resistance (occasioned by roughness of the moving body or of the inclined plane, or by the shape of the body). We must assume that the plane is, so to speak, incorporeal or, at least, that it is very carefully smoothed and perfectly hard, so that, as the body exerts its pressure on the plane, it may not cause a bending of the plane and somehow come to rest on it, as in a trap. And the moving body must be perfectly smooth, of a shape that does not resist motion, e.g., a perfectly spherical shape, and of the hardest material or else a fluid like water.[36]

The plane has to be hard; for unless it is, the sphere resting on it for a while would cause a small hollow to form; to be moved, it would then have to be raised, i.e., "forced", out of the hollow. The friction of the normal plane surface would, of course, have much the same effect.

This seems to suggest experimentation. Admittedly it might only represent the results of a thought-experiment. But there follows a more explicit statement:

And our demonstrations, as we have said above, must be understood of bodies free from all external resistance. But since it is impossible to find such bodies in the realm of matter, one who performs an experiment on the subject should not be surprised if the experiment fails, that is, if a large sphere, even though it is on a horizontal plane, cannot be moved with a minimal force.[37]

This suggests that he had tried to move bodies on inclines with very small forces, perhaps by putting a sphere on a horizontal plane and then raising one end of the plane very slightly, or perhaps by pushing the sphere with a straw or the like. In any case, there seems to have been some observation here. He added a second theoretical reason to account for the observation. On a plane supposedly parallel to the horizon of the earth, one point is nearer than any other to the center. If the experimental sphere is placed at that point, any attempt to move it away from there would have to move it uphill, he argued, and therefore would require more than the arbitrary minimal force.

In the next illustrative problem, his basic theoretical assumptions are immediately evident. The problem posed was this:

Given two bodies of different material but equal size, to construct a plane so inclined, that the body which, in a vertical fall, moves more swiftly than the other will descend on this plane with the same speed with which the other would fall vertically.[38]

He assumes that two bodies of different material will fall with different speeds. It is *density* rather than total weight that counts; the denser body falls faster. The problem he poses is easily answered by the method of "*ratios*" he had already outlined: the slope of the required plane is determined by the ratio of the densities of the two bodies. But once again, this assumes that the bodies will rapidly attain uniform speeds, characteristic both of their densities and the angle of the planes on which they move. And

Galileo once more had to report, here quite clearly calling upon the results of observation, that:

> just as was said before of vertical motion, so also in the case of motions on inclined planes, the ratios we have set down are not observed. This happens not only for the reasons just now given, but also—and this is accidental—because a lighter body descends more quickly than a heavier one at the beginning of its motion. How this comes about we shall make clear in its proper place: for this question depends on the question why natural motion is accelerated. But, as we have often said, these proofs of ours assume that there are no external interferences with the motion resulting from the shape of the body, or the roughness of the plane or body, or motion of the medium in the opposite or in the same direction, or the force of an external mover that promotes or retards the motion, and the like. Rules cannot be given for these accidental factors since they can occur in countless ways.[39]

The "reasons just now given" probably refer to the denting of the plane, and accidental roughness of plane and ball. Another reason why uniform ratios would not be observed (he noted) is that the light initially goes more quickly than the heavy. It is not clear whether he is claiming to have observed this as a feature of motion on an inclined plane, or whether he has just transferred the argument from the case of vertical motion. But he does seem to have noted that acceleration occurs on the inclined plane as well as in vertical movement; the explanation once again is in terms of an impressed power which takes time to decay away completely. And he also reminds the reader that his proofs assume that there is no external interference. He appears unshaken in his basic assumption that density determines specific speed, even though motion on the inclined plane has not produced any more support for this claim than vertical motion had done.

The answer to a problem posed earlier now becomes obvious. How did Galileo come to devise an experiment which would yield the law of free fall in the first place? In particular, why would he use an inclined plane, unless he knew what to look for? The answer is that he began work with the inclined plane having a completely different set of purposes in mind than those with which he finished. More than ten years before he mentioned the odd-number rule to Sarpi, Galileo had already begun to take an interest in inclined-plane motions. His interest was not only theoretical, but very likely experimental also. If one can accept that he had been dropping objects from towers, there is no reason not to accept equivalent testimony to the effect that he had been rolling balls down inclines. It is not clear just how far his work progressed at this time, in terms of the measurements he took or the instruments he used. To discover the effects described in the passages quoted above would have required nowhere near the refinement of technique that was later to characterize the work reported in the *Discorsi*. He probably tried an ordinary board and ball, and just watched the ball roll. But this is still the experimental germ of his later researches; it seems safe to conclude that he used some sort of inclined plane as an experimental tool as early as the *De motu* period of his career, i.e., before he left Pisa in 1592.

Explaining away the observed acceleration

If my account is correct, then, Galileo was attempting to substantiate his postulate of uniform specific speed of fall. He began with direct fall, and then moved on to inclined-plane observations. Yet he could never get the results he was looking for, and had to keep invoking a hypothetical "impressed force" in order to explain why. There are indications that this was bothering him considerably. In the dialogue version of *De motu*, for instance, there is a section in which he attempted to explain away apparent observed acceleration in the fall of an object from a tower by calling attention to the perspective of the viewer. The two characters in the dialogue are Dominicus, representing the intelligent inquirer, and Alexander, espousing Galileo's own views. Dominicus poses a problem:

> If the slowness of natural motion at the beginning comes about from the resistance of the impressed force, that force will ultimately be consumed, since you assert that it is continuously diminished. And, therefore, once that force has become nil, the natural motion will not be further accelerated. But this is contrary to the view of many.[40]

Alexander acknowledges this. Sometimes we do not find what we expect in experience: "if a stone fall from a high tower, its speed is observed always to be increasing." He explains, however, that:

> this happens because the stone is very heavy in comparison with the medium through which it moves, i.e., the air. Since it starts with an impressed force equal to its own weight, it starts, of course, with much impressed force; and the motion from the height of the tower is insufficient for the using up of all this impressed force. Thus it happens that the speed continues to increase all through the distance of the single tower.

Galileo is using two explanatory concepts: the basic one is that of a uniform specific speed of fall, and the auxiliary one is that of a *virtus impressa* (to account for the nonuniform motions actually observed). The main reason, then, why the uniform specific motions have not yet been found in nature, is the lack of sufficiently high towers.

Now he tries a new way of accounting for this troublesome discrepancy, one that indicates his sensitivity to the requirements of critical observation. An observer's position affects what he perceives. If, for instance, a body moving uniformly from B to E were observed from A, it would appear to travel the segment EF faster than the segment BC. The times to traverse each segment are the same, and the times taken to fall through angles BAC and EAF are also the same. But EAF is larger than BAC and on that account it could seem to the observer at A that the motion from E to F is the quicker. Hence, Alexander concludes:

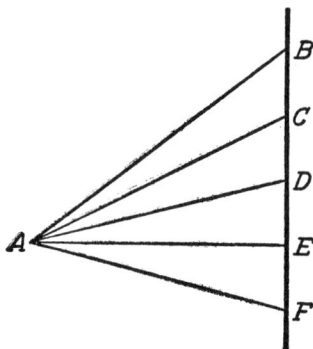

Figure 15–2

in order to distinguish between accelerated motion and uniform motion, the distance must be great enough for the body to be able in the course of it to use up the entire (impressed) force that resists (the downward motion), and the observer's eye must be so placed as not to be deceived by the disparity of angles.

So far we have found Galileo in the paradoxical situation of holding, on *a priori* grounds, for a theory of uniform speed of fall for which he can find no direct observational support at all. All of his energies have gone to the explaining away of the acceleration he has found in all motions of fall, as an "accidental" feature, not part of the basic nature of fall. Toward the end of the *De motu*, however, there was a slight but very significant shift of emphasis. For the first time, he began to accept the possibility that acceleration may be an "interesting" feature of fall. His theory was a very ingenious attempt to combine this admission with his original basic postulate about uniform specific speed as characterizing the "natural" motion of fall. He set out to prove that: "if natural motion could be extended without limit, it would not [necessarily] become swifter without limit." He had to demonstrate that a body could continue to accelerate, and still never pass a certain characteristic terminal velocity. Such a thing would seem impossible but:

> it is like the proposition that seems impossible to virtually all who are incapable of following the demonstration, i.e., that two lines can be found which when indefinitely produced, always approach each other but never meet, so that the distance between them always becomes smaller and smaller without end, yet is never entirely consumed.[41]

Galileo referred the reader to the classical geometrical treatment of asymptotes. It is possible, likewise, he suggested, to construct a hypothetical acceleration in which the speed would increase forever, yet never exceed a given value. Let two lines *AB* and *CD* represent the speeds of the bodies and let *AB* equal 2/3 *CD*. Then:

starting from rest [let a body acquire] by the end of the first mile, a speed *AB*, which is two-thirds of *CD;* and if by the end of the second mile, its speed were increased by one-third of speed *AB*, by the end of the third mile by one-third of one-third of *AB* . . . [and so on]. Surely the speed will always increase, and yet will never equal *CD*, but will always be less than *CD* by one-half the last increment. . . . Let us conclude, therefore, that in the case of a body, for the reasons previously given, the speed does not grow indefinitely great, but that there is a certain speed beyond which its fixed weight does not permit it to move naturally. But even if it were conceded that the velocity of the body underwent continuous increase forever, the velocity still would not necessarily become indefinitely great.[42]

He is still not sure how basic a feature of motion acceleration is, as his "even if it were to be conceded" shows. But his observations have apparently convinced him, against his will, that he must be prepared to accommodate a continued acceleration to his original assumption of uniform speed. He was not yet willing to commit himself as to whether bodies actually *did* accelerate forever. But *if* they do, their speed will still have a natural limit. It looks as though he was beginning to be impressed with the fact that acceleration kept cropping up everywhere. And it is not without interest that he here for the first time gave it a hypothetical mathematical representation. Already, then, in the *De motu*, one can find hints of two basic aspects of his later conclusions: acceleration as a feature of natural motion, and the use of mathematical models to describe it.

Experiment and the discovery of the law of free fall

If I have dwelt at length on the *De motu*, it has been to follow two main themes. First, I wanted to show what Galileo's theory of motion was at this period, and to emphasize how deeply he was committed to it. Second, I tried to ascertain the types of experiment he may have been performing, what he may have looked for and why.

Let us put ourselves in his place for a moment. Having adopted the "uniform-speed" dynamics, perhaps because of its strong analogy with Archimedean hydrostatics, he was led to perform various experiments in order to test it. His knowledge of Borri's work may possibly have suggested the lines the experiments might take. Not finding the steady velocity his theory postulated at low altitudes may have led him to try high towers. The argument from optical illusion was a last attempt to read uniform motion into the observations. This argument was not given in the essay version; perhaps Galileo was coming to realize that he was confronted with real and permanent acceleration, however much he might wish he were not. The analogy from asymptotic approach would, then, represent a transition, since it accepts continued acceleration—hesitantly, it is true. It is not clear whether he had begun with inclined planes before he devised these two arguments. But it is quite possible that he was led to use planes simply because the observations he had made of vertical fall did not support his original theory.

He may have reasoned thus: the entire impressed force does not have time to decay in the short time taken by a body to fall from a tower; on a slightly-sloping plane, the component of the force initially holding the ball from horizontal motion would be small; it might therefore disappear quickly enough to allow us actually to observe a natural uniform speed. He had said that the decay of the impressed force was independent of effective weight; perhaps he might have inferred from this test that the decay would occur as fast on the inclined plane as it would for the same body in free fall. In any event, at the time he wrote the sections of the *De motu* that deal with the inclined plane, he was still looking for support for the uniform-speed postulate. But (to his great chagrin, one senses) he had to fall back on the unsatisfactory: "rules cannot be given for these accidental factors . . ." This was the state which his investigations had reached in 1592.

Twelve years later, in his letter to Sarpi, he wrote of the distance-time squared rule of acceleration; one may surmise that during this time he had continued to work with the inclined plane, refining his techniques, especially that of measuring small intervals of time. There is some independent evidence for claiming this. In a letter to Guidobaldo del Monte in 1602, he described some experimental work with the pendulum. He seemed as much interested in it for the help it could give in formulating a theory of motion as in its properties as a timer;[43] it would be of some value to know which interest came first. In a passage written for the *Discorsi*, he described an attempt to "weigh" the thrust of a jet of water flowing out of a small hole in the bottom of a pan.[44] This pan might very well have been the timer associated with the experiment on planes described in the *Discorsi*.[45] These tantalizing glimpses into those early years at Padua are unfortunately not conclusive one way or the other.

It is certain, however, that by 1604 Galileo had formulated an entirely different theory of natural motion. In the *De motu*, he was committed to holding that the two central features of free motion were the uniform speed it ultimately attained, and the dependence of this speed on the density of the object. It was admitted that fall was accelerated, but acceleration was treated as an "accident" for which rules could not be given. By 1604, he had become convinced that acceleration was the key *fact* of free motion; it is not clear whether he still believed that the speed of fall depended upon the density of the body. And by 1604, he could describe acceleration accurately in terms of distance and time. What had brought about this change? The earlier theory was a reasonably consistent and complete one; it seems safe to say that the only thing which could have induced him to give it up was his continued inability to find experimental illustrations of its major assumption, as well as a growing realization (grounded in experimental results) that acceleration *could* in fact be reduced to rule. He discovered that no matter how slight the incline, balls still accelerated; when they stop accelerating, it seems rather to be for reasons of friction, than because they have reached a specific uniform speed.

It had already occurred to Galileo that the acceleration of fall might be represented by a convergent mathematical series in which the terms represent successive increments of the speed. Suppose he decided to see if he could find the actual series for successive equal time intervals (rather than the equal space intervals of his *De motu* example). This could have led him to the odd-number rule relating distances covered in successive equal time intervals. He may have tried to lengthen the incline, yet could still find no unambiguous evidence of any slackening of the rate of acceleration other than the slackening due to friction. The conclusion would have been that acceleration follows a rule given by the odd-number series of the Sarpi letter; though the latter does not mention this, it was a simple inference from this series that the acceleration of free fall is uniform and permanent. This would then be the step Galileo had reached in 1604.

It would seem, then, that two things had to occur in this period before dynamics could progress as a science, before a Galileo could establish the foundations of a new science: a shift in primary focus from uniform motion to acceleration as the essential mode of natural motion, and the discovery of a mathematical description of that acceleration. And it would seem that we must credit systematic experimentation by Galileo with a key role in both of these discoveries.

NOTES

1. For instance: E. A. Burtt, *The metaphysical foundations of modern physical science*, 1953*, Alexandre Koyré, *Études galiléennes*, Paris, 1939*; "An experiment in measurement", 1953*; "Galileo and Plato", 1943*; E. J. Dijksterhuis, *The mechanization of the world picture*, 1961*.

2. *Galileo and the freedom of thought*, London, 1938. See also René Dugas, *Mechanics in the seventeenth century*, 1958*.

3. This paper is a sequel to one by the author entitled "*An experiment in the history of science*", 1961*. There it was argued that the inclined-plane experiment described by Galileo on the Third Day of the *Discorsi* was a perfectly good one, and that there were no empirical reasons to suppose Galileo had not performed it. Here I shall take the next step, by trying to establish the role this experiment may have played in the course of his later investigations.

4. *The science of mechanics*, Chicago, 1919, pp. 130–131; 522–523. In the ninth German edition (English edn., 1960), the parts quoted here have been revised in the light of new information, some of which we present below.

5. *Discorsi*, p. 162.

6. Actually there intervenes a discussion of a second assumption: "That speeds acquired by one and the same body moving down planes of different inclinations are equal when the heights of these planes are equal" (*Discorsi*, p. 169).

However, this and the pendulum observations related to it can be treated independently, and will not concern us here.

7. *Ibid.*, pp. 173–178.

8. For further discussion of the problem of the false definition, see I. B. Cohen, "Galileo's rejection of the possibility of velocity changing uniformly with respect to distance", 1956*, and E. Mach, *op. cit.*, pp. 247–248. Cohen suggests that Galileo's "refutation" indicates an awareness on his part of the "mean speed theorem" of the fourteenth-century kinematicists. While it is possible that Galileo did know of it, I do not believe that it influenced him here. Some reasons for claiming this will become clear in the development of this essay; I plan on another occasion to address the problem more directly.

9. *Opere, 10*, pp. 115–116. The author's translation.

10. *On motion*, transl. by I. E. Drabkin, 1960*. It is widely believed that Galileo derived his knowledge of the properties of natural accelerations from fourteenth-century sources. He is supposed to have used these earlier arguments and diagrams when writing the *Discorsi;* his first theorem is equated with the Mertonian mean speed theorem. Leaving aside the question of what Galileo may have read *after* this letter to Sarpi, it would seem that if he had knowledge of the Mertonians or Parisians before it, he had not been notably impressed by them. The axiom he chooses is in sharp conflict with their theories. If his point in the letter had been derived from his reading, he should surely have restated the whole earlier speculation. It is hard to see how he could have appropriated only half of it, if he were actually "influenced" by it. See Marshall Clagett, *The science of mechanics in the middle ages*, 1959*, esp. chaps. 5, 6, 9; see also pp. 218–249, 252–253.

11. Translated in L. Fermi and G. Bernardini, *Galileo and the scientific revolution*, 1961*, pp. 134–140.

12. I. E. Drabkin, "A note on Galileo's *De motu*", 1960*. Also see his introductory remarks to his edition of the work.

13. That it corresponds substantially with the dialogue version can be checked in E. A. Moody, "Galileo and Avempace: the dynamics of the Leaning Tower experiment", 1951*, esp. pp. 163–183.

14. *De motu*, p. 17.

15. *Ibid.*, pp. 115–116.

16. *Ibid.*, chaps. 4 and 5.

17. *Ibid.*, chap. 6.

18. *Ibid.*, p. 37.

19. *Ibid.*, pp. 37–38.

20. *Ibid.*, p. 79.

21. *Ibid.*, chap. 18.

22. *Ibid.*, p. 88.

23. *Ibid.*, pp. 99–100.

24. *Ibid.*, p. 101.

25. *Ibid.*, p. 107.

26. *Ibid.*, pp. 107–110.

27. *Ibid.*, p. 110.

28. *On motion*, p. 106 and note. I have not been able to check Borri's book directly.

29. Since the wood and the lead would *have* to fall side by side (leaving aside slight differences in air resistance due to the greater volume of the wooden ball), how could Borri or Galileo have got these results? The balls may not have been released simultaneously in Galileo's case, or they may not have had equal pushes to begin with in Borri's experiment. And there is unlikely to have been extensive testing in either case. But there is a problem here that is likely to remain insoluble.

30. *De motu*, p. 63.

31. *Discorsi*, pp. 153, 242.

32. *De motu*, p. 64.

33. I have already noted a previous use of an analogy from balances. In the paraphrase of the argument of pp. 64–65 that follows, the order of the text is somewhat altered, but much of the original phraseology is retained.

34. *De motu*, p. 66.

35. *Discorsi*, pp. 212–218.

36. *De motu*, p. 65.

37. *Ibid.*, p. 68.

38. *Ibid.*, p. 69.

39. *Ibid.*, p. 69.

40. *Ibid.*, p. 127.

41. *Ibid.*, pp. 102–103.

42. *Ibid.*, pp. 104–105.

43. *Opere, 10*, pp. 97–100.

44. *Opere*, "Della forza della percossa", *8*, pp. 319–346. This is discussed in Mach, *op. cit.*, pp. 309–313. See also the essays by Bedini and Moscovici elsewhere in this volume.

45. *Discorsi*, p. 179.

16 ❀ Mathematical mysticism and mathematical science

ERNST CASSIRER

Of all the problems posed for us by the history of ideas, the question of the historical origin of the exact sciences is surely the one that most concerns the philosopher. For here one is not concerned with an isolated fragment of the history of knowledge, such as one can sometimes validly separate off. As a preliminary—even an indispensable one—the historian can describe the development of knowledge as though it were simply a matter of an ever-broadening *scope*. But it is only the particular *form* by which the raw data of knowledge are characterized that raises them to the level of genuine knowledge. And this form does not evolve mechanically from a particular set of facts. To grasp it, we must look not so much at the elements to be chronicled as at the basic functions of our knowledge itself.

It thus becomes apparent that the techniques ordinarily employed in the service of the historian will not suffice when we come to the history of knowledge. The strictly philological method of investigation and interpretation of sources here betrays very definite limitations. While this method may help us to know the material as it is, to find and order it, it

NOTE: This essay first appeared in *Lychnos* as "Mathematische Mystik und Mathematische Naturwissenschaft: Betrachtungen zur Entstehungsgeschichte der exacten Wissenschaft", 1940*. The translation was provided by the courtesy of Dr. E. W. Strong, and was edited for publication by Ernan McMullin.

fails to provide an answer when the problem is one of *understanding* the material. Such an understanding cannot be gained directly from the simple facts of the history of science, even if we could succeed in recovering these facts in their entirety, without any of the gaps that so trouble the historian. Extensions in our factual knowledge of the past do not bring us nearer to answering the really crucial questions. The history of human thought shows us that in certain significant periods, knowledge seems not so much to increase in quantity as to change its entire conceptual framework. In place of a simple quantitative growth, all of a sudden there is a qualitative change. Instead of evolution, we witness a sudden revolution.

It was within just such a revolution that the ideal of an exact scientific knowledge of nature first appeared. It took a leap of thought, an entirely new intuitive perception. But it should not be supposed that it was without antecedents. As historians of thought, we can never point our finger to the spot where the old vanished and something quite new appeared. Every dividing of history into epochs would be arbitrary if this is what it would signify. The modern ideal of an exact natural science certainly introduced a new epoch, but not in the sense of something with a definable beginning. Every time that someone has tried to claim such a sharp cut, the facts have risen up against him. In any temporal becoming, we never witness a really sharp break in continuity. Indeed, this continuity is so self-evident that one can easily lose confidence in one's ability to make any sharply delineated divisions at all. It comes to seem a steady flow. But does this mean that we must, as historians of ideas, resign ourselves to a Heraclitean stream in which there is nothing definite, no patterns that can be sharply distinguished from one another?

If one glances at the best histories of science, this dilemma of methodology becomes apparent. For a long time, it was a dogma that modern science made a radical break with scholastic thought. Here for once it seemed as though strictly factual boundaries could be distinguished, sharp enough in outline to make a clear cut between the Middle Ages and the Renaissance. As more and more intensive efforts were made to confirm this distinction by reference to historical sources, the boundaries that had seemed so clear became blurred once again. As Duhem's historical researches progressed, it began to appear that modern physics possessed scholastic antecedents after all. As early as the fourteenth century, new theories of motion began to challenge the Aristotelian physics and cosmology in a serious way. But it was admittedly venturesome of Duhem to claim that the pioneers of the new "impetus" theory, Buridan, Albert of Saxony and Oresme, also laid down the *theoretical* bases of modern mechanics.[1]

The sources of Galileo's science

Galileo's *"nuove scienze"* of mechanics still deserves its title if it be judged not just by the results it achieved but even more by the philosophical spirit which permeates even the most minute particulars in its con-struction. His accomplishment can be justly appreciated only if this be the main criterion used. His work was not simply that of a great experimental-ist or of a mathematical genius. In the *Dialogo*, he quite consciously made use of the language of philosophy in many places. He liked to compare himself in this respect with Simplicio, the defender of scholastic natural philosophy, and to strike at him with his own sort of weapon. But his command of philosophy was not just a formal one; it was not just a matter of scoring dialectical points against philosophically inclined opponents. Rather, his approach to nature was governed by definite and characteristic philosophical assumptions. He *could* conceivably have formulated his sci-ence of nature in a purely empirical way, making use of empirical meth-ods only. But the method of justification that he chose for his science, and which he regarded as basic to it, was of a quite different sort. He felt it necessary to rely upon a universal theory of knowledge, and to use a "logic" quite different from that of Aristotle or the scholastics. His philo-sophical greatness can, perhaps, best be discerned in the fact that he con-structed this "logic", not in a vacuum, but by means of, and in the midst of his scientific work.

In a series of earlier works,[2] I have tried to analyze the interpenetration of philosophical and empirical motifs in Galileo's work, and noted, in par-ticular, the decisive influence upon him of Platonism. This last point has been confirmed by more recent researches. In a number of interesting and penetrating writings (1939*), Koyré has argued that Platonism must be considered the central factor in the formation of Galileo's world-view. He asserts that the Galilean ideal of science was formed within a Platonic-Archimedean context, and that even those features of it that were novel can be understood historically only by reference to this context. A simi-lar view has been upheld by E. A. Burtt in his classic work, *The Metaphys-ical foundations of modern science* (1924); indeed, he extends the thesis to cover not only Galileo but the other pioneers of the "scientific revolu-tion" as well. In the rebirth of Pythagoreanism, he sees one of the main sources for the mathematical-scientific Renaissance; he asserts that only from such a starting point could the quantitative approach to Nature, characteristic of modern science, have been developed.

But opponents of this thesis have not been wanting. Burtt's argument has been critically analyzed by Edward B. Strong in his *Procedures and metaphysics* (1936*). Strong concedes that Pythagorean and neo-Platonic influences affected Kepler and even to some extent Galileo. But he feels that it is wrong to see in these the major source of the new view of nature. In his view, the Pythagorean speculations of the sixteenth and seventeenth centuries were so explicitly mystical in character that it would be difficult to construct any genuine historical connection between them and the ideals of an exact empirical science. Galileo's law of motion could not simply have grown out of metaphysical speculation. Its origins must be sought much closer to concrete experience. More specifically, it was in the new *technical* experience, in the technological problems under whose guise the ancient mystery of nature began ever more insistently to present itself at this time, that the new approach to theoretical natural science was formed.

In his *Galilei und seine Zeit*, L. Olschki had already made this same point.[3] Galileo's mechanics cannot, in his view, be analyzed as though it were a wholly abstract creation. Its principles were not reached deductively, nor by any simple generalization from experiment. Galileo arrived at them within the context of specific technical problems. He was indeed one of the first to be a great technician as well as a great theoretical scientist. He had to create the very tools by which he would observe Nature; without this prior material accomplishment there would have been no later theoretical one.

Strong accepts this thesis, and develops it further. The true forerunners of the new science of nature were, to his mind, not philosophers but men who approached nature with concrete problems to solve. Da Vinci was the first great example of the practical mathematical genius. As a builder of military fortresses, a technician of the art of war, he was constantly involved in difficult problems of statics and dynamics, problems that he clearly realized to be capable of solution in terms of a more general theory. Mechanics seemed to Leonardo to be "the paradise of the mathematical sciences", because only there could the seeds of mathematical thought receive the nourishment they require; only there "can the fruit be reached".[4] This gradual shift of approach is represented in the century before Galileo by the thought of great mathematicians like Tartaglia and Cardano, and practical geometricians like Benedetti, Valla, Veglia, Cataneo, Clavius, Stevin.

Strong concludes that it is here that one must search for the true roots of Galileo's scientific thinking. It was a direct contact with the exigencies of *things* that shaped Galileo's concepts; it was the pressure of definite technical problems that led him to construct the aids that a solution to these problems would require. Strong summarizes the various intellectual and practical techniques evoked by these problems under the term, 'procedures'. His thesis can then be stated in brief: the real source of Galileo's science must be sought in the "procedures" which he brought to a new level of precision and reliability, rather than in any speculative metaphysical themes inherited from his predecessors.

Procedures and metaphysics

Strong supports his claim with an extensive survey of historical materials, whose validity and relevance I would in nowise challenge. The reservation I wish to express is about his conclusion, not about the material brought in support of it. If one wishes to situate Galileo's thought, one cannot sufficiently emphasize the fact that it derives so constantly and directly from concrete sources. Goethe once characterized his own approach by saying that for him: "thought does not separate itself from material objects; the elements of the material objects penetrate the concepts and are penetrated by them to the fullest extent." [5] Next to Goethe, Galileo is surely one of the foremost representatives of this sort of "objectivist" thought. That Goethe would concur in this judgment is clear:

> Galileo showed already in his early youth, by developing for himself the laws of the pendulum and of the fall of bodies from the observation of swinging church lamps, that for the genius one example is worth a thousand. In science, everything depends on what is called an "insight", on a perception of the particular factor that is really basic to a phenomenon. Such a perception can be infinitely fruitful.[6]

Here we see a typical example of the interpenetration of the specific and the general, of the concrete material thing and the conceptual. Out of such fruitful "insights" came the decisive impulses for Galileo's entire research. But there was much more to it than isolated flashes of insight. For he was the first true *theoretician* of physics; he could not be satisfied with disconnected observations. What he demanded was a clear-cut conceptual framework, an inner consistency to science. Any time that he moved away from the facts, it was to inquire after principles from which the facts would follow, and which would, in his view, thus provide the only true justification for the facts; thus and only thus was a true science possible. From this view of what constituted knowledge Galileo never strayed; it served as the starting-point and goal of all his inquiries.

Any attempt to characterize Galileo's scientific achievement must be inadequate if it does not keep these two poles constantly in view. An artificial "either-or" will not serve; the two poles are complementary, not contradictory. Thus the problem of the relation of "experience" and "metaphysics" in Galileo's work becomes much more complicated than Strong makes it appear. His book is limited by the polemical context in which it was conceived, the context of Burtt's thesis which Strong attempts to disprove, or at least to qualify very substantially. Strong argues that the basic ideas of Kepler and Galileo grew in an immanent way out of the empirical observation of nature and out of the progressive evolution of new mathematical concepts. He denies that any other factors, especially "transcendent" ones of metaphysical origin, had any decisive influence on this growth.

In this regard he is, in my opinion, quite correct, in comparison at least with the position taken by Burtt. One cannot, as the latter tried to do, directly relate the concepts of modern science with the metaphysics of neo-Platonism or with Pythagorean number mysticism. Close as they may have been in time, and difficult as it may be to draw a sharp line between them, yet the transition from one to the other meant that the concepts of mathematics underwent a complete change of meaning. And only because of this change could they function as they did in the construction of a new natural science. There is no evidence that during the productive period of his research Galileo was influenced by the peculiar "meta-mathematics" one finds in Ficino, Pico della Mirandola, or Reuchlin, even though this had, in fact, some effect on "true" mathematics later on. For him, number had no magic or secrecy; it was first and foremost a workaday tool of discovery.

This does not mean that Galileo dismissed any observation that did not lend itself to being quantified. Nor does it mean that he took a formalist approach to mathematics itself. No seventeenth-century thinker could ever have gone in this direction. Descartes, Malebranche and Leibniz were all concerned with the necessity of explaining and justifying the sort of certitude given by mathematics; formalism would not have appeared to them a valid solution to this problem. They did not seek a metaphysics which would be cut off from mathematics; rather, they tried to devise a metaphysics from mathematics itself.[7]

In principle, Galileo does not differ on this issue from these founders of "modern" philosophy; it is crucial to an understanding of his work to see that this is the case. It is doubtless true that he began from concrete problems and devoted his life to their solution. But this in no way stamps him as a mere "practical mathematician". For he was concerned not only with the elaboration of mathematical procedures for the practical investigation of nature; he also wished to understand these procedures and to ask why they functioned as they did. To accomplish this, he had to take the decisive step that Plato demanded of his philosopher-mathematician, the step from the geometrician who utilizes the techniques successfully to the dialectician who grasps why the techniques must be what they are.

It is clear from the historical sources that Galileo did not take this step haltingly or against his will; he fully believed in its necessity. So far as I can see, Strong's book contains no argument, no reference to sources, that could lead on to hesitate on this point. He examines all those passages where Galileo goes beyond the immediate empirical issue to develop a general theory of knowledge. Yet his own response is to deny, equivalently, that the views expressed in these passages are really significant; he regards them as incidental to the really basic factors affecting Galileo's science. This is evidently a subjective judgment on Strong's part, one deriving largely from his own methodological assumptions, and lacking adequate support in the historical material.

It is true that Galileo himself in his *Saggiatore* dilated upon the "subjectivism of intellectual procedures". Yet this was an incidental inspiration on his part, as was the inspiration for the piece as a whole. There is no evidence to indicate that the intellectual conception at the back of his procedures was equally incidental. There is a kernel, a central insight, here which cannot be ignored without endangering the integrity of his entire enterprise. He had a very definite concept of truth, one that pretty well defined his idea of what a scientific theory should be. If one decides to characterize such issues as "metaphysical", then without doubt Galileo's laws rest in some sense on a metaphysical basis. But their significance for science ought in no way be diminished by such a statement. For the "metaphysics" here is no longer of transcendence, but of immanence. In Kantian terms, the emphasis is on the metaphysical sources of natural science itself. Strong is correct, in my opinion, when he seeks to distinguish Galileo's laws from neo-Platonic speculation or Pythagorean number mysticism. But these laws did not develop from the exigencies of practical geometry either. Rather, they owe their origin to a new relationship between experience and thought which they attempt to define, and which they helped to form. And in this relationship the distinctive methodological autonomy of each of the poles is maintained.

From Plato and Augustine

Only when this point has been grasped can the relationship of Galileo to Plato be understood. Galileo's deep admiration for Plato shows itself frequently and explicitly in the *Dialogo* and the *Discorsi*. Strong is not unaware of this; indeed, he comments on these passages in detail. But his conclusion is that while a historical connection between Platonism and exact science cannot be denied, the connection has on the whole been harmful to science. Whatever modern science has accomplished, has been accomplished not with Plato's aid but in spite of him.[8] This rather sweeping judgment cannot, for want of space, be discussed here; it would involve a detailed analysis of the concepts and methods and goals of modern natural science. But if we restrict ourselves to the historical point at issue, and leave the value judgment aside, a precise answer can be given.

To reach this answer, it is important that we distinguish between Plato and Platonists. As a Florentine, Galileo could scarcely have avoided being influenced by the great Platonic tradition of the Florentine Academy; the traces that this tradition left on his intellectual development are readily seen. Yet in many ways, he manifested a striking independence of this tradition. It might be said that he succeeded in penetrating the veils with which the Florentine School had surrounded Plato. He did not go to the Plato of the medieval pseudo-Dionysian writings, nor to the Plato of the neo-Platonic Academy, nor even to the Plato of the *Timaeus*. It was the Plato of the *Meno* and the *Phaedo* and the *Theaetetus* that captivated him; it was the Platonic concept of knowledge, not the philosophy of nature of the *Timaeus*, that made him a Platonist.

Even *this* concept, though, was modified and expanded by him. Plato's dialectic was modeled on mathematics, and never strayed far from the realm of mathematical Forms. Dialectical knowledge was possible only about that which exists always and which always behaves in the same manner. Knowledge loses its power as soon as it turns to the domain of becoming, to the ephemeral. But this was just the restriction that Galileo dared to challenge. In his theories of mechanics, he made the explicit claim that the mastery over truth provided by number and line is not restricted to the fields of arithmetic and geometry, but extends also to the inner essence of things empirically existing and constantly changing. In the sphere of the changeable, knowledge loses nothing of its power; indeed, it is only here that its strength is fully realized. This is still Platonism, but it is Platonism which has changed its course, so to speak. It now contains no restriction on the tasks and ideals of scientific knowledge, but rather serves as a motivating factor in the attainment of this knowledge.

It is only from this new vantage-point, perhaps, that the line between Middle Ages and Renaissance can be drawn with any precision. Of the many changes that occurred during the Renaissance, one of those that best characterizes the Renaissance itself involved a shift in men's thinking about the purpose and value of mathematics. But it is much more difficult to grasp and define this shift than it might appear at first sight. It would be quite wrong to assume (as some have assumed) that medieval thinkers were blind to the value of mathematics, so that the task of the Renaissance was to rediscover this value after centuries of neglect.

No one had a greater influence on medieval thought than did Augustine. And in his writings on the nature of knowledge, the significance of mathematics is in no way undervalued; on the contrary, an exalted place is given it. In his view, mathematical and religious certainties are complementary to one another, united by a curious and intimate bond. Mathematics is a step, an indispensable one at that, in the progress of humanity to God. In support of this, he quotes the words of *Ecclesiastes:* "I have gone about, my heart and I, that I may know and consider, and that I may seek wisdom and number . . ." Number is the visible symbol of wisdom, and is placed on a level with it. Wisdom comes forth from God, and is manifested in the corporeal order in terms of number, weight, and the like. Even in the human body, it is in such quantitative terms that the spiritual order is reflected. What wisdom is for souls, number is for bodies. As one and the same fire warms nearby bodies and also illuminates bodies that are too distant to be warmed, so one and the same source fills spirits with the warmth of wisdom and also illuminates, with the light of number, bodies that are too distant from spirit in their corporeal natures to be warmed.[9] Despite the dualism that Augustine sees between the realms of spirit and matter, then, he maintains that they are linked by a single Reality which manifests itself on the one hand as wisdom and on the other as number.

These views had an enormous influence throughout the medieval period, and were commented upon, over and over again. They provided a definite "philosophy of mathematics" which led to mathematics being allotted one of the highest places in the hierarchy of intellectual values. From the early thirteenth century onwards, this even suggested to some that mathematics ought to be fruitful in the solution of problems in natural philosophy. Grosseteste, for example, wrote: "To consider lines, angles and figures is of the greatest utility, because it is impossible to understand natural philosophy without their help . . ." [10] According to him, geometry provides the only way of grasping the interconnections of cause and effect; this was the premise from which his extraordinary work in optics began.

But there was yet one decisive obstacle in the way of any genuine mathematicization of natural science. The number to which the medievals turned and in which they saw a reflection of Divine Wisdom was *intelligible*, not bodily, number. To the extent that number is incarnated in body, its true form tends to be lost. Contemplation of the bodily world can lead us to *scientia*, but such *scientia* is still far removed from *sapientia*. *Scientia* and *sapientia* can never be on the same level; there is a gulf between them because of the difference in their objects. *Sapientia* is directed to intelligible form; the *scientia* of nature remains tied to the material visible world.

The gulf was an impassable one for Augustine, and for his medieval followers. The distinction was not just a theoretical one. It involved a profound ethical separation: *sapientia* turns to God; *scientia* turns to things. One leads to the creator; the other tends to hold us to the world of created things:

> If, therefore, the correct way to distinguish wisdom (*sapientia*) from knowledge (*scientia*) is to say that to wisdom belongs the intellectual cognition of eternal things whereas to knowledge belongs the rational cognition of temporal things, it is not very difficult to decide which of these ought to be put ahead of the other.[11]

From such an unassailable distinction as that between the eternal and the temporal, it seemed to follow that the mathematical knowledge of nature had to belong to a lower level.

Augustine's maxim about the dependence of all forms of knowledge upon theology cannot be effectively called in question unless the criterion of what constitutes knowledge be itself modified. And this is what one notices happening in Renaissance thought from the fifteenth century onwards. It came increasingly to be said that the value of knowledge depends not on the object but on the way it was attained and the level of certainty reached. Da Vinci's famous aphorism about the small truth being worth more than the big lie expresses something of the change.[12] It is justifiable, as we have seen, to place Galileo on the side of Leonardo and the "practical mathematicians", as Strong does. Yet if one does this, one must not forget that Galileo was never the simple pragmatist; when he had recourse to mathematics, as he so frequently did, it was not just because of its technical utility. For him, mathematics was the expression of truth itself; it had for him not only a theoretical but also a religious dimension. He saw in it a revelation of God which cannot be excelled or qualified by any other, not even by the "verbal inspiration" of the Bible.[13]

Only if one penetrates to this basic layer in Galileo's thinking can one understand what is distinctive not only in his science but also in his character and personality. When Bonaventure wished to prove the subordination of all worldly knowledge (such as mathematics and natural science) to the knowledge of God, he gave an interesting argument from experience. While true believers are able to sacrifice everything else to their faith in God, he said, worldly knowledge cannot command such a sacrifice. No human being is willing to suffer for a truth which is only speculative. A geometrician who would choose death rather than deny a geometrical truth would, Bonaventure adds, be thought little more than a fool. One can here plumb the depths that separate the medieval from Galileo. With him there emerges not only a new way of thinking but also a new way of living. He was a new sort of man, in fact, one for whom theory and practice, life and thought, are no longer held separate but are taken to be mutually interpenetrating.

From mathematical mysticism to mathematical science

To see more clearly the relationship between mathematical science and mathematical mysticism, we may turn now to a work by Dietrich Mahnke, *Beitrage zur Genealogie der mathematischen Mystik*.[14] It forms an interesting contrast with Strong's book, starting as it does from quite different assumptions and making use of different source material. In one chapter, Mahnke traces the history of the metaphor which compares God to an infinite sphere without center. He begins with its most recent version in the geometric symbolism of German Romanticism (Nomalis, Baader, Schelling, Oken); further back lies the geometric mysticism of the Baroque (More, Pascal, Boehme, Comenius); thence to the Renaissance (Cusa, Bruno, Ficino, Bovillus); before that, the mysticism of Eckhart and of the *Book of the twenty-four philosophers* (a pseudo-scientific work, probably twelfth century). This last had it sources in Dionysius the Areopagite, Scotus Erigena, Boethius and Augustine; ultimately, we are led back to the main source of Hellenistic geometrical mysticism, Plotinus. Mahnke rounds off his study by tracing his topic back to the very beginnings of Greek philosophy in Parmenides, Empedocles, Anaxagoras and Anaximander.

From this extraordinarily rich survey, I would like to pick out only one moment, the decisive one when the centuries-old tradition of mathematical mysticism and the new spirit of mathematical science met in one man, Kepler. In his first work, the *Mysterium cosmographicum*, the two lines cross. And at this point, Kepler had not chosen which of the paths he would follow. The symbolism of numbers and of solids still had him in their sway. He felt that to understand the structure of the universe, he had to immerse himself in a sort of cryptography. His inquiry fused physics and theology into one. The sphere, for example, is the symbol of cosmological relationships as well as of the threefold nature of God. The

Father is the center and point of departure; the Son is "the universal manifestation of the simplicity of the point in the symmetrical bending of the upper surface"; the Holy Spirit is "the constancy of the space between center and sphere".[15] Mahnke relies on passages such as these to make his overall thesis about Kepler, and he insists that they are not just characteristic of the great astronomer's earlier writings, but are equally present in his later works.[16]

According to him, Kepler held fast all his life to the "cosmographic intuition" of his youth; as time went on, all he did was to relate it better to results being achieved by the new science, and to formulate it in an ever more exact manner. The guiding thread of his researches from beginning to end was his belief that "God himself plays with the signatures of things", and thus that the beauty of the heavens and of Nature generally is geometry made visible.[17] Mahnke concludes:

> There can be no doubt that geometrical mysticism provided the speculative metaphysical basis on which rested, not only Kepler's philosophical worldview, but also his specific scientific achievements. We can even specify in a precise way the very sources from which he drew his "cosmosophy". He had repeated recourse to Plato, Proclus and the later Neo-Platonists for his views on the perfection of God and creation, on the pervading World Spirit, on the basic meaning of mathematics, and on the nature of truth itself. And he referred to the Pythagoreans for his notion that geometry gives the archetype of the world and that the five "perfect" solids consequently provide an indispensable clue to the natures of things. . . . It was, however, on Nicholas of Cusa, perhaps, that Kepler most leaned. Nicholas attributed both logical and cosmological significance to geometric figures and even to the difference between curved and straight lines. If the evidence in its favor were not so overwhelming, it would surely be hard to believe the statement that Kepler's discovery of the [planetary] laws . . . was heavily dependent upon Cusa's mystical theological symbol of the sphere . . .[18]

When Strong discusses Kepler, he arrives at conclusions that are, predictably, just the reverse of Mahnke's. He sees no reason to qualify his general theme about "procedures" even in the case of Kepler. He concedes the influence of the "metamathematical tradition", as he calls it, in this instance, but maintains that Kepler's fundamental discoveries were made in spite of this influence, rather than because of it. According to him, the development of methodological insight in Kepler's work up to the *Epitome* (1618) was based on "operational considerations", and did not require "subsequent metaphysical arguments, distinctions and sanctions".[19]

That two authors could draw such diametrically opposite conclusions about Kepler's work shows how difficult it would be to settle this problem according to purely historical criteria. It might seem that the only thing to do would be to leave it to each to judge according to his own metaphysical predisposition. Yet I do not think such pessimism to be warranted here. To be sure, Kepler prevents a far more complex problem in this regard than does Galileo. His physics is still Janus-faced: it looks to the future, and yet it does not break with the past in the emphatic way in which Galileo's physics does. It is, however, just this struggle between old and new which makes Kepler's astronomical discoveries so extraordinarily significant for the history of ideas. Only very gradually do the new forms of thought make their appearance in his writings, and only gradually does he grasp their significance. I have treated this topic extensively elsewhere,[20] and wish to remark here only that the analyses of Kepler given by Strong and Mahnke do not lead me to modify my earlier position. Both writers confirm the peculiar intermingling of motifs in Kepler's thinking, even though their appraisals of the value of these motifs differ so widely.

Kepler's early *Mysterium cosmographicum* (1596) is a typical representative of the ancient Pythagorean number mysticism. Yet in his *Harmonice mundi* (1619), one of his last major works, and the one where his entire empirical astronomy is reviewed, the tie to the older tradition is by no means broken; in fact, it is in this work that in many ways it appears most obvious. Yet he could never have become the founder of the new astronomy if he not been able to remove magic from his path, a slow and steady effort which we can follow in his writings. The culmination of this effort is to be found in his *Pro suo opere Harmonices mundi apologia*, a polemic against the mathematical mysticism of Robert Fludd.[21] From the point of view of methodology, this work is a crucial one. In it we find Kepler, though still speculating in the mystical vein, now restricting these speculations within very definite limits. Once this was done, his mysticism no longer endangered his empirical cosmology. The Pythagorean mysticism never lost its aesthetic attraction for him. But he became the creator of mathematical astronomy by ultimately refusing to use pseudo-science as a *basis* for his work, even though he still continued to derive *inspiration* from it. It did not mislead him or lessen his achievement as an empirical researcher, because more and more he learned to discipline himself in a logical manner.

Just how far this discipline went, and how much he was himself conscious of its importance can be seen from a letter he wrote to Joachim Tanck while engaged on the composition of the *Astronomia nova* (1609). These lines hold the key to his entire life's work:

> I play, indeed, with symbols, and I have started a book called *The geometric Cabbala*, which is concerned with reaching the forms of natural objects by means of geometry. But when I play, I never forget that I *am* playing. For nothing is proved in symbols alone; nothing hidden is arrived at in natural philosophy by geometrical symbols . . . unless it is shown by conclusive reasons to be not only symbolic but to be an account of the connections between things and their causes.[22]

Here, for the first time perhaps in the history of human thought, a line is drawn between the merely analogical and the exact mathematical-empirical. In all likelihood, Kepler did not wish to cut them off entirely from one another. Just how flexible the boundaries between them were, even down to the nineteenth century, has been fully documented in Mahnke's study. Yet Mahnke has drawn too one-sided a conclusion from his materials. He has not shown how Kepler's astronomy *really* originated, because he omits one decisive factor. And it was only this factor that enabled Kepler to go beyond the limitations of a "cosmosophy" to construct a true "cosmophysics". That such a "cosmophysics" *could* have grown out of other sources we can concede to Strong. But that in point of fact it *did* not, must be insisted upon.

Kepler himself quite clearly realized that his work, inseparably inter-twined with neo-Platonic and Pythagorean mysticism though it was, yet stood at a great turning-point in time and was destined to lead to a new ideal of knowledge. In his epoch-making and laborious discovery of the true orbit of Mars, he no longer sought a theology and a metaphysics of the heavens, as Aristotle had done. Instead, to quote his own words, he sought a "philosophy and physics of the heavens", which would at the same time be a "new arithmetic." [23]

NOTES

1. P. Duhem, *Études sur Léonard de Vinci*, Paris, 1913, p. *xi*.

2. *Das Erkenntnisproblem in der Philosophie und Wissenschaft der Neuren Zeit*, Berlin, 1922, vol. 1, pp. 377–418; *The individual and the cosmos in Renaissance philosophy*, transl. by Mario Domandi, New York, 1963, pp. 155ff.; "Wahrheitsbegriff und Wahrheitsproblem bei Galilei", *Scientia*, 62, 1937, 121–130; 185–193 (French transl. in *62* suppl., 41–48; 69–76). [For titles subsequent to 1940, see the Bibliography at the end of this volume. See also the interesting comment by Walter Solmitz, "Cassirer on Galileo: an example of Cassirer's way of thought", 1949*.]

3. *Geschichte der neusprachlichen wissenschaftlichen Literatur*, Halle, 1927, vol. 3. [A chapter of Olschki's book appears in translation in this volume.]

4. *Scritti*, ed. by J. P. Richter, London, 1883, vol. 2, p. 289, n. 1155.

5. *Naturwissenschaftliche Schriften*, Weimar edn., vol. 11, p. 58.

6. *History of chromatology, Farbenlehre*, Weimar edn., vol. 3, p. 246.

7. This has been clearly shown in the case of Malebranche by Paul Schrecker in his essay: "Le parallélisme théologo-mathématique chez Malebranche", *Revue Philosophique*, *63*, 1938, 87–124.

8. *Op. cit.*, pp. 217ff.

9. *De libero arbitrio*, Book 2, c. 11, art. 32.

10. See E. Gilson: *La philosophie au Moyen Age*, Paris, 1930, "Le Moyen Age et la nature", pp. 205ff. [This is more fully discussed by A. C. Crombie in his *Robert Grosseteste and the origins of experimental science*, 1953*.]

11. *De Trinitate*, Book 12, chaps. 15, 25.

12. *Scritti*, vol. 2, p. 296, n. 1184. On Leonardo's concept of truth, see *The individual and the cosmos*, pp. 153ff.

13. See my "Wahrheitsbegriff und Wahrheitsproblem bei Galilei".

14. Halle, 1937. See especially the chapter on: "Unendliche Sphäre und Allmittelpunkt".

15. *Opera omnia*, Frisch edn., vol. 1, p. 122.

16. *Op. cit.*, p. 134.

17. *Tertius interveniens*, 1610; *Opera omnia*, vol. 1, p. 639; see Mahnke, pp. 139ff.

18. *Op. cit.*, p. 140.

19. *Op. cit.*, p. 183.

20. *Das Erkenntnisproblem*, vol. 1, pp. 329–377.

21. [This controversy is discussed at length by W. Pauli, "The influence of archetypal ideas on the scientific theories of Kepler", in *The interpretation of nature and the psyche*, Bollingen: New York, 1955, pp. 190–208. Editor's note.]

22. *Opera omnia*, vol. 1, p. 378; see also *Das Erkenntnisproblem*, vol. 1, p. 348.

23. Letter to Brengger, October 4, 1607; *Opera omnia*, vol. 3, p. 31.

17 ❋ The relationship between metaphysics and scientific method in Galileo's work

EDWARD W. STRONG

The whole history of science perhaps cannot point to a single figure about whom opinions differ so widely as about Galileo. No one indeed is prepared to challenge his scientific greatness or to deny that he was perhaps the man who made the greatest contribution to the growth of classical science. But on the question of what precisely his contribution was, and wherein his greatness essentially lay, there seems to be no unanimity at all. . . . He was, on the one hand, rooted in a past to which he was tied none the less securely because he disowned it vehemently, and on the other hand he was preparing a future in which his ideas were to lead to conclusions that went far beyond what he could ever have foreseen. Thus, there is no better method for gaining some insight into this transition [from ancient and medieval to classical science] than to follow his development as a link between the old and the new.[1]

Dijksterhuis' mention of the "past" in which Galileo was "rooted" raises perhaps the most crucial question in the entire range of Galileo scholarship. The past that he "disowned" by his experimental and mathematical treatment of the problems of motion was surely that of Aristotle's *Physics*. And here he was continuing a tradition of critical analysis of Aristotelian natural philosophy going back to the fourteenth century and beyond. The past to which he alluded with respect was that of Euclid and Archimedes. His first published work in physics, the *Discourse on bodies in water* of 1612, is concerned with that which "was subtly demonstrated by Archimedes", he himself notes, though he adds that it will be "with a different method and by other means" that he "will endeavor to demonstrate the same, by reducing the causes of such effects to more intrinsic and immediate principles". But the world he built was still a world in which Euclid and Archimedes would have felt at home:

> The world of Galileo's imagination in mechanics was in fact Euclid's geometrical space with the addition of mass (later defined precisely by Newton), motion and gravity. The secret of science, in Galileo's outlook, was to transfer a problem, properly defined, to this abstracted physical universe of science which, as ever greater complexities are added to it, approximates more and more closely to the actual universe. For the architecture of the real world is no less mathematical than that of Euclidean space, the book of nature being written in "mathematical language". . . . On this account, he has been called a Platonist, whereas perhaps he was rather a Euclidean in mechanics, never cultivating the mathematical mysticism that distinguished Kepler. Galileo recognized that while mathematical logic is infallible, it may rest on false assumptions . . .[2]
> Galileo no sooner arrives at a general relationship of a mathematical sort than he deduces all sorts of particular cases. . . . In this way, by a succession of propositions and theorems, he builds up his book in a way resembling Euclid's books of geometry.[3]

Galileo and Plato

But how about Plato? Cassirer in his essay, "Mathematical mysticism and mathematical science"[4] maintains that Galileo was equally indebted to the doctrines of Plato. There can be no question about Galileo's esteem for Plato, nor of his preference for Plato over Aristotle. The crucial question is really this: in what respects was Galileo's scientific thought derived from, and shaped by, predecessors and contemporaries identifiable as Platonic in their philosophy of nature? If, as Cassirer agrees, the Pythagorean speculations extant in Galileo's time have a strongly mystical character and conceive of mathematical objects in a transcendental role, and with an efficacy alien to the logic and method of the exact sciences, surely the conclusion follows that the tradition of number mysticism could not be the metaphysical *basis* for the significant scientific contributions of Galileo and Kepler. Cassirer remarks that Kepler's aesthetic sense drove him to return again and again to Pythagorean number mysticism. But such an impulse toward pseudo-science and the "inspiration" provided by pseudo-scientific doctrines do not supply either criteria or foundations for a mathematical-physical science.

In my book, *Procedures and metaphysics*, I examined Pythagorean and Platonic doctrines—doctrines which cast numbers and geometrical figures in a cosmological role—in order to show that these doctrines (drawn mainly during the Renaissance from Theon, Nicomachus and Proclus) do not qualify as a foundation for Galileo's mathematical-physical science. These mathematical mystics asserted that, to attain divine wisdom, the cave of the sensible and material must be escaped by mounting through the superior, incorporeal Numbers, the principles of all things, to the mystery of Supreme Unity. Their doctrine I summarized as follows:

> True number is incorruptible and independent, superior to the natural number that depends upon it. In the natural world, and in experience, number is entangled in multiplicity and change. Philosophy therefore turns from experience to incorporeal number; and, in knowing the latter, it gains real knowledge. By incorruptible number, man is enabled to penetrate into the numbered nature of each thing, since each is created in number (and as a number) from the exemplary number. Metaphysical arithmetic is the means and prelude to understanding the mysterious efficacy of divine number. . . . The metaphysical numbers engendered in the animal are the immutable forms of species, the creative numbers which produced the created numbers of existent things. Each existent thing is therefore numbered into existence from its appropriate archetypal number. Knowledge of divine arithmetic is the key to the original or first number from which all else is numbered . . .[5]

It will be noted that these neo-Platonists conceive of numbers as efficient causes. A conception of a world of things as thus "composed through number" is alien to Plato.[6] For on this view (but not on Plato's), generated and corruptible things in their kinds of being receive their proper forms from such efficient making:

> He, who is the necessary and glorious source from which all goods proceed has made all things in number, in weight, and in measure, and so great is the profundity and subtlety of the intention of these words that rare intellects of men understand them to be the root and principal foundation of all these knowledges (music, architecture, arithmetic, geometry); that things composed through number, weight, and measure of the elements that enter therein, for those reasons are distinct in various kinds of being. The giver and founder of forms gives and distributes them according to the disposition and capacity of matter . . . and this is the efficient and material cause of why one thing is a tree, and another an animal . . . If the matter of a frog does not hold the numerated, proportioned, and weighted elements of certain number understood in nature, it would never receive the proper form: and so of other things generated and corruptible.[7]

Galileo does not embrace this bastardized "Platonism" in which the root and foundation of knowledge in the sciences consists of number cast in an efficient role of this sort. If, then, as Koyré and Cassirer claim, there is a continuity between Galileo and the "Platonic tradition", where is there a tradition to be found, other than the unsuitable one just noted, which can in some proper sense be identified as "Platonic"?

Both Koyré and Cassirer are well aware that Galileo departed from Plato by attributing an intrinsic mathematical structure to the sensible world. Such a break with Plato points up, however, the crucial question faced by those who argue (as they do) for a continuity: did some identifiable Platonic (or neo-Platonic) tradition exert a decisive influence on him in his construction of a "new view of nature"? For example, was Galileo's faith in the mathematical ordering of nature influenced by Plato's argument that the "likely stories" of mathematical-physical science demand an ultimate justification in the dialectic whereby the searcher after truth penetrates a realm of eternal Forms? By what Platonic tradition known to Galileo could his reasoning have been shaped in a clear, unequivocal way, so that he might be correctly and meaningfully called a "Platonist"?

Cassirer asserts that Galileo viewed Plato in a very different way than did the Florentine neo-Platonists. The difference is said to lie in the emphasis placed by Galileo on the Platonic concept of knowledge. Yet Galileo is also asserted to have set aside Plato's restriction on the power of mathematics in the "sphere of the changeable", the domain that is empirically observable by an investigator of nature. The old Platonic emphasis on mathematics is altogether reoriented, however, by extending mathematics to nature in this way, as an immanent principle of exact knowledge of things "empirically existing". Cassirer maintains that the scientific laws developed by Galileo owe their discovery to a new interpenetration of experience and thought (i.e., of experiments and of mathematical demonstrations) in which the methodological autonomy peculiar to each remains. Yet such a relationship is altogether antithetical to the Plato of the divided line. And as far as methodological autonomy is concerned, the quantification essential to exact physical sciences in the formulation and application of laws cannot be obtained without measurement. The central role played by time-measurement in Galileo's inclined-plane experiment shows how essential it is for an experimenter to know what to measure and how to measure it.[8] Cassirer maintains that Galileo penetrated the veil of pseudo-scientific (mystical and magical) speculations in such a way that the basic concepts of mathematics underwent a complete change of meaning. Number had for him lost all magic and secretiveness; it had become "primarily an instrument of research". If one examines how Galileo employed mathematics as an instrument of research, does it seem that he sought from Plato, or from a Platonic tradition, a metaphysics based on mathematics, which would serve as a *justification* for his employment of mathematical methods and concepts? Or is it not rather evident that the revolutionary character of his scientific thought consisted in so combining mathematics and experimentation as to establish the autonomy of kinematics by a direct appeal to the very methods of discovery and proof employed, rather than to some prior metaphysics?

What motivated Cassirer to make his search was his major theme: that it was necessary for Galileo to justify his "new sciences" in opposition to Aristotelian physics, and hence to return to a universal theory of knowledge and a "logic" of a kind that could not be found in Aristotle or the scholastics. By a "logic of science", Cassirer may mean no more than the procedures followed by Galileo in the course of discovery or demonstration. If, however, he includes in it also the philosophical attempt to *justify* the initial working assumption Galileo made (that nature is so ordered in its regularities that it can and indeed *must* be mathematically investigated), this would be a further and very difficult task that Galileo would have set himself. The movement to the order of "dialectic" that Plato requires of the "philosophical mathematician" would in this instance require the justification of a mathematical ontologism of a kind far transcending anything that Galileo could have constructed in and through an exact empirical science. Pure mathematics, considered simply as a system of consistent reasoning from postulates, requires no extramathematical justification. When it comes to employing mathematical concepts to provide testable theories of physical phenomena, however, a Simplicio can rightfully demand an answer to his question: how do mathematical demonstrations, true in the abstract, hold good when applied to sensible and physical matter?

> After all, Salviati, these mathematical subtleties do very well in the abstract, but they do not work out when applied to sensible and physical matters. For instance, mathematicians may prove well enough in theory that a sphere touches a plane at a point . . . but when it comes to matter, these things happen otherwise. What I mean about angles of contact and ratios is that they all go by the board for material and sensible things.[9]

Galileo's methodology of science

In reply to this difficulty, Galileo does not have recourse to a counter-metaphysical position (as Cassirer's thesis might seem to indicate that he should). Instead, he speaks of *procedures* of abstraction and approximation. By an imaginative abstraction which eliminates material impediments, while retaining all the essential elements, he claims to be able to reach a generalized solution which can then be corrected for imperfections, complexities and variations encountered empirically:

> The mathematical scientist, when he wants to recognize in the concrete the effects which he has proved in the abstract, must deduct the material hindrances. And if he is able to do so, I assure you that things are no less in agreement than are mathematical computations. The errors lie, then, not in the abstractness or concreteness, not in geometry or physics, but in a calculator who does not know how to make a true accounting. Hence, if one were to have a perfect sphere and a perfect plane, they would touch one another in one point, even if they were material . . .[10]

Or as he will later put it in the *Discorsi:*

> Of these accidents of weight, of velocity, of figure, infinite in number, it is not possible to give any exact description. Hence, in order to handle this matter in a scientific way, it is necessary to cut loose from these difficulties; having discovered and demonstrated the theorems in the case of no resistance,

one must apply them with such limitations as experience will teach. The advantage of this method will not be small. For the material and shape of the projectile, for instance, may be chosen as dense and as round as possible so that it will encounter the least resistance in the medium.[11]

Ideal definitions may, of course, unknowingly incorporate elements that are incompatible with the physical situation. Galileo is perfectly aware of this danger, which is never absent when mathematics is employed as an instrument in a physical science. He notes:

> These conclusions, proved in the abstract, will be different when applied to the concrete and will be fallacious to the extent that neither will the horizontal motion be uniform, nor the natural acceleration be in the ratio assumed, nor the path of the projectile a parabola, and so forth . . . When we wish to apply our proven conclusions to distances which, though finite, are very large, we must find out, on the basis of demonstrated truth, what correction is to be made for the fact that our distance from the center of the earth is not really infinite, but merely very great in comparison with the small dimensions of the apparatus.[12]

What the physicist has to do, then, is to stay as close to the empirical as he can. He must:

> find a definition best fitting natural phenomena. For anyone may invent an arbitrary type of motion and discuss its properties. . . . But we have decided to consider the phenomena of bodies falling with an acceleration such as actually occurs in nature, and to make this definition of accelerated motion exhibit the essential features of observed accelerated motions.[13]

It is quite clear from these passages that the *verification* of a principle of physics involved, for Galileo, its testing in the empirical order. To know that it was a true physical law, it was not enough to recognize its purely mathematical properties. *A fortiori*, the applicability to a physical context of a particular proposition whose mathematical necessity has already been demonstrated in the abstract is in nowise aided by the belief that God knows infinitely more true propositions than does the human intellect, or by the doctrine that the human mind is divinely imprinted with mathematical ideas which it can recollect clearly and distinctly, or by the conviction that the Word of God, creative of Nature, was uttered in mathematical language. Such Platonic beliefs may have inspired Galileo, indeed, but even if they did, would he have contended that his contributions to the exact sciences needed a foundation and a justification in such beliefs?

It is too simple to say that Galileo's contribution to mechanics was to apply mathematics to it. Many before him had attempted to do just this. Upholders of the *impetus* theory, Cardano, Tartaglia, Benedetti and Galileo's own teacher Buonamici, had for a century been trying to set down the theory in mathematical terms. Hall has noted that after Tartaglia (d. 1557), who was the first to try to compute the ranges of cannon by means of tables derived from a dynamical theory, if not before him, it became clear that:

a dynamical theory ought to be quantitative; it should be capable of making exact numerical predictions. Many writers on gunnery, with varying degrees of imagination, continued to search for this desideratum within the framework of impetus theory until well after Galileo had offered a better one. This essential sterility of the impetus theory in the sixteenth century is the important point. Able men failed to derive from it a mathematical description of the phenomena of motion, yet failed also to develop the concepts which could take its place. It is not, therefore, the case either that Galileo's ambition to mathematize dynamics was something unusual in the contemporary scientific milieu or that, once this ambition had been framed, it was easy to mould the necessary modern dynamical concepts out of the crude impetus forebears. Modern dynamics did not spring from a modified version of the impetus theory: Galileo was compelled to return once more to the fundamental concepts of motion.[14]

It did not require any new impulse from neo-Platonism, then, any new declaration that God had made all things "in number in weight and in measure", to set Galileo on the road to a mathematical dynamics. What was needed, rather, was a fresh attack on the conceptual basis of mechanics itself (where the impetus theory had proved ineffective), allied with a means of verification based on exact measurement.

Plato and Archimedes

Koyré has charged me with the "mortal sin" of failing to recognize the existence of *two* "Platonic" traditions, one of mystical arithmology and the other of mathematical science.[15] Galileo more than once rejected the numerical speculations of the Pythagoreans as meaningless, but also explicitly remarks:

> I know perfectly well that the Pythagoreans had the highest esteem for the science of numbers and that Plato himself admired the human intellect and believed that it participates in divinity solely because it is able to understand the nature of numbers. And I myself am well inclined to make the same judgement.[16]

Here, we have, in my view, the only possible grounds in Galileo's work for calling him a "Platonist", namely that he agreed with Plato in holding that the ability to discover and understand mathematical truth linked the human mind with the Divine. But this is surely a slender thread on which to hang such a weighty label, especially if the metaphysical differences be as profound as they were between Galileo and Plato.

Koyré himself has a somewhat more restricted view of what constitutes a "Platonist". According to him, anyone who attributes to mathematics "a real and commanding value, and a commanding position in physics" is, *eo ipso*, a "Platonist". There are just two sorts of philosopher for him, and the division between them is precisely on the issue of mathematics. But on this, of course, other things will depend: "What is in question in this discussion is not certainty—no Aristotelian has ever denied our right to measure what is measurable and to count what is numerable—but the structure of science and therefore the structure of Being." [17]

One might just as readily and just as meaningfully claim Galileo for the "Aristotelian" camp by noting that he believed physics to be capable of certainty (like Aristotle, but unlike Plato), and correlatively that he thought the formal structure of sensible Being to be entirely intelligible (again with Aristotle and against Plato). Or one could put him in a camp over against both the great Greek thinkers (perhaps with Pythagoras?) because he insisted that the structure of the physical world is completely expressible in mathematical terms, a thesis which (for quite different reasons) neither Plato nor Aristotle would ever concede. In the light of all this, one wonders about the utility of this incessant effort to label Galileo a "Platonist".

But then we note that Koyré himself is more impressed by the credentials of Archimedes as Galileo's forerunner than he is even by those of Plato. If this be so, was Archimedes influenced by Plato in his own scientific investigations? He was often called a "*philosophus platonicus*" by later writers because of his emphasis on mathematics. But references such as these do not indicate any real direct intellectual influence; in particular, there is no reason to assert that Archimedes was indebted to Plato for the assumptions that formed the basis of his science. In his discussion of Archimedes' work on hydrostatics and the theory of levers, L. W. H. Hull remarks:

> The proper function of mathematics in the scientific scheme is to reveal the hidden consequences of observed facts. . . . The conventional Greek methods were not particularly apt weapons of discovery at the stage geometry had now reached. Archimedes first obtained some of his results in mensuration by experimental methods such as weighing. He had a shrewd notion of the answer before he began to construct mathematical proofs. Two solids of the same material have volumes proportional to their weights, so that an unknown volume of one can be estimated from the known volume by weighing. Such a method of discovery would have been anathema to Plato, but Archimedes had assumed a modern freedom.[18]

Another who has noted that Archimedes "shows himself quite indifferent to the Platonic anathema", and derives his intellectual heritage more from the Ionian tradition, is G. de Santillana. He asserts that Archimedes "felt no guilt" even when he used methods which "involved endowing geometric figures with the properties of matter".[19] In support of this, he can quote Archimedes' own words from his little treatise *On method*:[20]

> Certain things first became clear to me by a mechanical method, although they had to be demonstrated by geometry afterwards, because their investigation by the [mechanical] method did not furnish an actual demonstration. But it is, of course, easier to supply the proof when we have previously acquired by the [mechanical] method some knowledge of the questions, than it is without any previous knowledge. This is the reason why, in the case of

the theorems that the volumes of a cone and a pyramid are one-third of the volumes of the cylinder and prism respectively having the same base and height, the proofs of which Eudoxus was the first to discover, no small share of the credit should be given to Democritus, who was the first to state the fact, though without proof.[21]

Presumably Democritus had discovered these truths by a purely empirical method of weighing; Archimedes finds this a valuable initial approach to the problem. But he believes that a proper demonstration of the theorem can be given only by "geometry". Here he would rejoin Plato. And Galileo, too, although one would have to broaden the scope of "geometry" to include concepts like *velocity* and *weight*. With this broadening, Archimedes, who had done something similar in his statics, would surely have sympathized. But it is to be doubted whether Plato would have, since these concepts involve the "changeable" in a direct way, and thus are irrevocably bound to the shifting and uncertain domain of image.

Grosseteste as a precursor

Cassirer and Koyré both recognize that Galileo set himself over against the number mysticism of the Renaissance neo-Platonists: Ficino, Pico della Mirandola, Reuchlin, Bungus, Zamberti, John Dee, etc. These writers extolled the magical and mysterious powers of numbers and figures in the creation of the world. They believed that the incorporeality of mathematical entities give them a special causal efficacy. According to John Dee, the "ravishing perswasion" of numbers lies in the threefold role they possess: "one, in the mind of the Creator; another in every Creature, in respect of his complete constitution; and the third, in Spiritual and Angelical Minds, and in the Soul of Man." [22] His central cosmological theme is that in God's "continual Numbering of all things is the conservation of them in being. And when and where he will lack a Unit, there and then that particular thing shall be Discreated".

Cassirer suggests that a better clue to Galileo's lineage can be found in the Augustine-Grosseteste tradition, which extolled the central importance of mathematics for physics, but without investing mathematics with the sort of magical efficacy that the more flamboyant neo-Platonists hankered after. Augustine and Proclus made mathematics an indispensable step in the journey of the soul to God. Mathematical forms can be recollected by us because divinely implanted in our souls, and they bring us "to similitude of that Divinity who presides over every science, who manifests intellectual gifts, and fills the universe with divine reasons".[23] The practical effect of this teaching was to ensure that throughout the Middle Ages, mathematics would be regarded as one of the highest forms of knowledge. The physicists of the thirteenth century were the beneficiaries of this tradition. Roger Bacon, for instance, will say that "nothing within the range of reason can be known without the power of geometry".[24]

Crombie argues a much stronger thesis regarding the credentials of

Grosseteste and Bacon to be precursors of Galileo. He quite disagrees with Cassirer's thesis that Galileo had to find a new "logic of science" to justify his work against the physics of Aristotle. Crombie, by contrast, asserts that Galileo ". . . made the great advance of combining the scholastic logic of science systematically with mathematics and with accurate systematic measurements so as to express the regularities observable in quantitative terms." [25]

Grosseteste not only exalted mathematics as a means of physical insight (here Crombie and Cassirer agree), but also foreshadowed (according to Crombie) the very methodology that Galileo would later follow:

> Instead of searching for the essence, Galileo proposed to correlate accidents. He proposed, moreover, to . . . correlate them by means of a mathematical function. This last was fundamental. . . . Like Newton's, his approach was to establish the descriptive mathematical laws before considering their causes, but the mechanical causes remained his ultimate objective in science. . . . The success of seventeenth century physics depended on the adaptation to each other of a "mechanical" philosophy of nature, a methodology of experimental science with functional correlation as its aim, and effective algebraic and geometrical techniques . . . [One sees the] beginning of this combination in the conception of science presented by Grosseteste and Roger Bacon: a conception of nature in which the essence or "form" itself is mathematically determined, and a conception of the immediate objective of enquiry as mathematical and predictive laws instead of the Aristotelian essential definition . . . [Grosseteste through his neo-Platonically inspired "metaphysics of light"] made his fundamental move toward the mathematization of the concept of nature, and the shift from the "form" to the "law" as the object of scientific enquiry.[26]

To this one cannot help objecting that the resemblances between Grosseteste and Galileo are surely outweighed by the differences. Grosseteste and Bacon are certainly not propounders of a mechanical philosophy. In their view, the utility of mathematics for optics is based on the fact that light radiates instantaneously from God himself, and thus follows perfectly geometrical patterns. The mode of causality is generative and exemplary, not at all mechanical, as the seventeenth century would view it. Furthermore, as Crombie himself goes on to remark, the thirteenth-century physicists made no attempt "at precise mathematical definition, at expressing amounts quantitatively in numbers, or at measurements". This was equally true in the fourteenth century. Crombie writes of the scholars who discussed the remission and intension of forms, in an attempt to find laws of motion, that they displayed:

> an apparent lack of interest in finding means to apply their results to actual motions. They went through the whole discussion without making a single measurement, although certainly leading scholars like Bradwardine and Albert of Saxony were looking for true laws of motion and although they formulated their problems mathematically in such a way that they could find

the answer only by measuring the concomitant variations in the parameters involved.[27]

The alleged continuity of method and aim between Grosseteste and Galileo rests on a rather precarious basis, it would seem. Hall has argued that Galileo was faced with two separate problems:

> On what foundations was the intellectual structure of science to be built, and what criteria of a satisfactory explanation were to replace those of Aristotle? With Galileo these questions were not answered in prolonged metaphysical or logical analyses—though it seems clear that his ideas were shaped by just such analyses carried out by his predecessors—but the answers were given as they became necessary in the progress of his attack on the prevailing ideas of nature. As a scientist, Galileo's aim might be to attack Aristotle's errors in fact or reason, while as philosopher he demonstrated more fundamentally how these errors had arisen from weaknesses in method that were to be avoided by taking a different course.[28]

What had to be done, then, was to bring all of the previous discussions in mechanics to the level of measurement and trial. Had Galileo not done this, of what avail would his high esteem for the science of numbers have been? He would have got no further than had the host of neo-Platonists in the two centuries before his birth. Had he simply held that mechanics had its foundations in geometry, he would have been no further forward than the fourteenth-century scholastic physicists of Merton, who attempted to find geometrical solutions to physical problems. Galileo went beyond these last. When asked: how does a geometrical demonstration hold for the effects of a machine, for the acceleration of a body on an inclined plane, for a beam that breaks under pressure? he answered by making various assumptions. If these assumptions could then be brought approximately into accord with the observed phenomena by means of ideal functional correlations, they were regarded as acceptable, and the mathematical demonstrations could then be considered "conclusive", i.e., properly applicable to this sort of physical instance.

One may or may not wish to call this an entirely new method, as Bell does:

> We must credit Galileo with the development of what is in effect an entirely new method. . . . His method was in fact a mathematical and experimental one. He saw how important it was to make one quantity vary so as to trace concomitant variations in another, or how to eliminate disturbing factors which would otherwise obscure the real facts.[29]

But it is quite clear that the nerve of the properly Galilean contribution did not lie in neo-Platonism nor in scholastic method. It lay in the new procedures which he himself devised and perfected, procedures that provided an empirical base for physics that it had never before possessed.

Conclusion

Cassirer professes disagreement with the theme of my book. Yet the exact grounds of his disagreement become more and more difficult to grasp as his essay progresses. In the final section on Kepler, he repudiates Mahnke's thesis that neo-Platonic geometrical mysticism formed the speculative basis of Kepler's science. He concedes the hold that this sort of "pseudo-science" (his own term) had over Kepler, but judges that Kepler's achievement was precisely to *limit* this factor in his thinking, so that it could no longer endanger his empirical cosmology. But this was exactly my own conclusion concerning Kepler.[30] Like Cassirer, I grant that neo-Platonism provided Kepler with inspiration. Like him, I argue that the methodological criteria laid down by Kepler for the astronomer (in his *Epitome astronomiae copernicanae*, for example) imposed far more stringent criteria of evidence than any that the neo-Platonists had ever conceived. My own conclusion is that in gaining inspiration from mathematical mysticism, Kepler cannot be said in any sense to have acquired a metaphysical foundation for modern physical science. I cannot see that Cassirer, in the last analysis, is saying anything different from this.

When I undertook the research on which *Procedures and metaphysics* was based, I did so in the expectation of confirming Burtt's thesis. But I rapidly found it to be untenable, and my conclusion was (and still is) that "the achievements of Galileo and his predecessors were in spite of, rather than because of, prior and contemporary metaphysical theories of mathematics".[31] Galileo was very clearly aware that the logical necessity of an abstract mathematical demonstration does not of itself constitute an *a priori* necessity in the physical order. Had he supposed that it did, he would certainly not have concerned himself with a careful relating of abstract to concrete by measurement, by the use of approximations, and by the experimental elimination of variable parameters other than the one under examination. His final great work, the *Discorsi*, shows all of these techniques at work, and is an eloquent plea for the autonomy of physics, an autonomy he defends against theological and metaphysical arguments to the contrary. Galileo commends Plato as a philosopher who realizes the importance of mathematics to the understanding of Nature, but his own mode of employment of mathematics, as a consequence of his insistence upon measurement as the ground of physical evidence, does not support the claim that he is properly to be labeled a "Platonist".[32]

NOTES

1. E. J. Dijksterhuis, *The mechanization of the world picture*, 1961*, pp. 333–334.
2. A. R. Hall, *The scientific revolution, 1500–1800*, 1954*, p. 168.
3. A. E. Bell, *Newtonian science*, 1961*, p. 85.

4. Reprinted in this volume.

5. *Procedures and metaphysics*, 1936*, p. 196.

6. [T. McTighe in his essay elsewhere in this collection shows that for Plato himself there could be no question of seeing mathematical forms (or any other sort of forms) perfectly incarnated in the image-world of the senses. The sensible world is defective and partially lacking in intelligibility. Editor's note.]

7. Gabriel Giolito de Ferrari, *Summario di tutte le scientie del magnifico M. Domenico*, Vinegia, 1556; quoted in *Procedures*, p. 202.

8. See Thomas B. Settle, "An experiment in the history of science", 1961*.

9. *Dialogo*, p. 203.

10. *Dialogo*, pp. 207–208.

11. *Discorsi*, pp. 252–253.

12. *Op. cit.*, pp. 251–253.

13. *Op. cit.*, p. 160.

14. *The scientific revolution*, pp. 78–79.

15. "Galileo and Plato", 1957*, p. 172.

16. *Opere*, 7, p. 35; quoted and translated by Koyré, "Galileo and Plato", 1957*, p. 172.

17. *Op. cit.*, p. 168.

18. *History and philosophy of science*, London, 1959, pp. 78–84.

19. *The origins of scientific thought*, Chicago, 1961, p. 239.

20. This treatise was lost for centuries, and was dramatically rediscovered as recently as 1906 by Heiberg on a palimpsest in Constantinople.

21. Quoted by de Santillana, *op. cit.*, p. 240.

22. Quoted in *Procedures and metaphysics*, where Dee's doctrine of forms and numbers as the causes of created things is expounded (pp. 204–211).

23. *The philosophical and mathematical commentaries of Proclus on the First Book of Euclid's Elements*, ed. by T. Taylor, London, 1788, vol. 1, end of Book 1.

24. *Opus Maius*, chap. 3.

25. *Medieval and early modern science*, 1961*, vol. 2, p. 293.

26. "The significance of medieval discussions of method for the scientific revolution", 1959*, pp. 86–88. See also his *Robert Grosseteste and the origins of experimental science*, 1953*, esp. chap. 5: "Mathematical physics".

27. *Op. cit.*, p. 92.

28. *The scientific revolution*, p. 168.

29. A. E. Bell, *Newtonian science*, p. 82.

30. *Procedures and metaphysics*, chap. 7: "Scientific method and metaphysics in Kepler".

31. *Op. cit.*, p. 11.

32. I am indebted to Professor Ernan McMullin for his help in revising my essay to fit the format of this book, and in so doing, improving the essay's organization.

18 ❋ Galileo's "Platonism": a reconsideration

THOMAS P. McTIGHE

Sense of the question

Is Galileo a Platonist? I am not concerned to prove that some aspect of Galileo's properly scientific contributions had a Platonic origin, in the way, for example, a recent article in *Isis* did; the author showed that a text in the *Timaeus* influenced Galileo's cosmogony.[1] Rather the issue is Galileo's supposed Platonism as it relates to his conception of the nature of science; i.e., Galileo's theory *about* physics and not his theories *in* physics. In the discussion of Galileo's Platonism, this important distinction has not always been made.[2]

Is Galileo a Platonist, then, in his philosophy of science? The key issue is, of course, Galileo's justification of the applicability of mathematics to what he calls the "things of nature". Alexander Koyré does not, I think, exaggerate when he claims that the real subject of the *Two chief systems* is not so much the opposition between two astronomies as it is the justification of a mathematical over a nonmathematical physics.[3] The Simplicio of the *Two chief systems*, is, no doubt, a buffoon, yet the frequency and the insistence with which Galileo has him make the Aristotelian objection to a mathematical physics indicates that Galileo takes this objection quite seriously.[4] The Aristotelian claim that the science of mathematics and the science of nature move on two quite different planes of abstraction, and that natural science must therefore seek an appropriately *physical* explanation of nature, had to be met head on. Galileo was, in other words, forced to construct a philosophy of science which would provide a theoretical justification for the fusion of mathematics and experience in the new science.

Does his theoretical justification take a Platonic form? Many, though not all commentators, claim that it does. Thus Alexandre Koyré,[5] Ernst Cassirer,[6] A. C. Crombie,[7] and E. A. Burtt,[8] to name but a few, would agree with Professor A. R. Hall's remark that "the lesson of Galileo's Platonism [is] that nature's language is mathematical".[9] My own view is that Galileo is not a Platonist, and that the efforts to classify him as one turn out to be simplistic or inconsistent. Either the definition of Platonism is too loose to be of any real help in identifying the special genius of Galileo's philosophy of science, or else the various elements of his philosophy are made to exhibit an unacceptable lack of coherence when forced into a Platonic mold. Galileo's conception of the nature of the new physics involved a blending of Aristotelian and Pythagorean strains. However, rather than characterize his efforts with an "ism", it is, I think, best to see it for what it is in itself, neither Platonic, nor Aristotelian, nor Pythagorean, but a personal effort to establish on theoretical grounds the applicability of mathematics to the phenomena of nature. This cautionary note is not superfluous, because Galileo has too often been the object of a philosophical tug-of-war with Kantians, rationalists and idealists on one end of the rope and empiricists on the other.[10]

Defenders of Galileo's "Platonism"

Let me first review two well-known Platonic interpretations of Galileo, those of Koyré and Crombie. I leave the more qualified position of Cassirer until later. After that, I shall contrast what I take to be the authentically "Platonic" and "Galilean" conceptions of science to try to show that they are, in fact, polar opposites. First, Koyré's position as it is stated in his now classic discussion of Galileo's Platonism:

> If you claim for mathematics a superior status, if more than that you attribute to it a real value and a commanding position in Physics, you are a Platonist. If, on the contrary, you see in mathematics an abstract science, which is of lesser value than those which deal with real being (physics and metaphysics), if in particular you pretend that physics needs no other basis than experiences . . . you are an Aristotelian.[11]

Now if this be the principle of interpretation, Koyré is clearly correct in seeing Galileo as a Platonist. Galileo's philosophy of science together with its metaphysical and epistemological substructure is unmistakably a pan-mathematicism. Moreover, Galileo *says* of himself that he is a Platonist, in this sense of the term. In reply to an Aristotelian critic, Antonio Rocco, Galileo leaves no doubt about his sympathy for what he takes to be the mathematical method of Plato in physics, as against the purely physical method of Aristotle.[12] Other texts reinforce Koyré's thesis, to the extent at least of showing that Galileo thought of himself as a Platonist. In the *Two chief systems*, Galileo alludes approvingly to Plato's theories of reminiscence[13] and participation.[14] Hence, if "Platonism" in science simply means the alliance of mathematics and experience, then Galileo is a Platonist. But is this sufficient evidence? I think not. For it leaves unanswered the crucial question: Why *is* mathematics applicable to the things of nature, according to Galileo? Is it because nature is an intrinsically intelligible mathematical structure? Or is it because natural phenomena are of themselves devoid of intelligibility and so have to be supplied with a measure of intelligibility via the imposition of mathematical schemata? The former is, I think, true of Galileo while the latter is the more authentically Platonic position.

At one point in his well-known study on Robert Grosseteste, Crombie attributes to Plato the notion that "in natural science, theories are tentative and at best only probable",[15] and that the best physics can do is "save the appearances" (*salvare apparentia*).[16] This "saving the appearances" approach, as is well-known, originated in Greek astronomy with the problem that Plato is supposed to have set for the Academy:[17] assuming that celestial bodies in their movements describe circular orbits, what combination of circular motions can be hypothetically constructed to reduce to rationality the apparent chaos observed in the heavens by the senses?[18] Koyré claims that "saving the appearances" has as its purpose "the revelation of the permanent stability of the real behind the seeming irregularity of the apparent".[19] But this is simply not true. No account, either Greek or medieval, of this method of inquiry ever claimed that it could attain to the intrinsic essential structure of things. On the contrary, as Crombie among others shows, it was regarded as essentially hypothetical and constructural. Yet Crombie in the work already cited goes on to attribute to Galileo, whom he characterizes as a "Platonizing scientist", an objectivist conception of science; that is, one which suggests that the aim of physical theory is to uncover the intrinsic essential structures of nature and to state them in necessary propositions.[20]

I think Crombie is quite correct in his account both of Plato's and Galileo's notion of science. The Platonic view of physics *does* make it a "saving of the appearances". He is correct, too, in attributing an objectivist theory of science to Galileo, though perhaps he does not concede it to be quite as objectivist as in fact it was. But if all this be true, it would seem that Galileo cannot, without serious ambiguity, be described as a "Platonizing" scientist. He cannot consistently hold *both* that mathematical physics is hypothetical and constructural *and* that it produces true and necessary demonstrations,[21] the conclusions of which reveal the necessity of nature.[22] The inconsistency lies here not with Galileo but with this way of classifying him. Crombie, like so many other historians, subscribes without qualification to the thesis that in physics, *"ubi mathematica, ibi Plato"*. Indeed, even among those who reject the label of 'Platonist' for Galileo, some implicitly agree that "Platonism" in science amounts to holding that the order of nature is essentially constituted by mathematical structures.[23]

This is the heart of the issue. The source of the entire ambiguity is the implicit assumption that mathematical realism is a characteristically Platonic position. Since such a realism is unquestionably present in Galileo's work, he is thus labeled a "Platonizing" scientist. In common with Koyré and many others, Crombie quotes as evidence for Galileo's "Platonism" the famous assertion made in the *Assayer* that the great Book of Nature is "written in the language of mathematics" and that "its characters are triangles, circles, and other geometrical figures".[24] This and other similar passages unquestionably give grounds for attributing to Galileo a mathematical realism. Geymonat, it is true, thinks that these texts are simply metaphorical and that they are simply intended as a polemic against those who would philosophize out of written books.[25] Nevertheless, the reasons for taking Galileo to have opted for a mathematical ontology appear overwhelming. But they do not support a *Platonic* interpretation of Galileo, in any strict sense of that term. On the contrary they prove just the opposite.

Plato's account of the world of sense

Dudley Shapere has recently emphasized in an excellent essay that an analysis of the *Timaeus* reveals a great divergence between Plato's and Galileo's conception of why mathematics is applicable to the sensible order.[26] According to the *Timaeus*, the phenomena of nature are fundamentally irrational.[27] *Ananké* or necessity (which for Plato means the essential irrationality of "multipliability") is never fully persuaded by reason.[28] Hence a mathematical description of nature can never achieve an *exact* account. There is a kind of recalcitrance or intractability in the sensible order that refuses to allow a complete transformation of nature into rationality. In Leibnizian terms, it is impossible to transform truths of fact into truths of reason.[29]

But for Galileo, says Shapere, the contrary is true. Nature is amenable to an exact and complete mathematical treatment. In fact, Galileo comes very close to a Leibnizian position and precisely at that point where Simplicio raises his usual Aristotelian objection that the abstractions of mathematics never obtain in the concrete. Rejecting this thesis, Salviati (Galileo's spokesman) claims that "what occurs in the concrete occurs in the same fashion in the abstract".[30] Therefore, he continues:

> when the geometrical philosopher would observe in the concrete the effects demonstrated in the abstract, he must transcend the impediments of matter; and if he knows how to do that, I assure you, the things shall jump no less

exactly than arithmetical computations. The errors therefore lie neither in the abstract nor in the concrete, nor in geometry, nor in physics, but in the calculator, who does not know how to adjust his accounts.[31]

There is, therefore, for Galileo no intractable surd in the things of nature which defies rationalization. At least, there is no ontological or noetic surd, no intrinsic failure in the real or in the scientific mode of knowing the real. Failure is purely personal, a matter of lack of mathematical competence. As we shall see, it is just such a defect in competence or education and not the exigencies of scientific method that (in Galileo's view) makes the technique of experimental confirmation necessary.

Shapere, therefore, explains the contrast between the ideals that Galileo and Plato set for their mathematical physics as that between a complete and exact and an incomplete and inevitably inexact mathematization of nature. His analysis is exceedingly helpful, but to demonstrate the sharp cleavage between the two positions, perhaps we can adduce still more evidence. The account in the *Timaeus* is really about the Demiurge's efforts to persuade necessity with reason, and not about mathematical physics as such, so that we must press a little further if we are to piece together Plato's answer to the question: Why is it necessary to utilize mathematics in the first place in understanding nature?

For Plato the answer lies in the exigencies of the physical object. The sensible order, in fact, every order of multiplicity, even that of the Forms, is devoid of any intrinsic intelligibility. There cannot be plural Forms, each a center of essential density, as natures are for Aristotle. Determination, differentiation is negation. Each thing is what it is by not being all else.[32] For Plato as for Bradley, plurality and reality are simply contradictory. They cannot live together in harmony. By reality, Plato means that which is *to kath' auto*, and there cannot be a plurality of such radical "inseities". Every member of a multiplicity is by its very membership in multiplicity not an inseity but an entity internally constituted by an inexhaustible series of relations.[33] Only in the transcendent One is an essence truly identical with itself, but then it is also identical with everything else, and consequently is ineffable.[34] The kind of endlessness that the relational character of the various orders of multiplicity entails can only be coerced from without. If there is to be a science of the plural it must involve the construction and not the discovery of intelligibility. In the case of the sensibles, an intelligibility can be supplied from without by mathematical schemata.

The assertion that orders of multiplicity lack intelligibility does not mean that for Plato the natural order is featureless, totally devoid of character.[35] Rather it is a question of understanding in what sense there are in the natural order only imperfect copies of triangles, circles, spheres and the like. The Platonic image-thing certainly cannot be regarded as a kind of weakened Aristotelian form inexplicably united to a substrate. Just as the Forms regarded as Being are defective images of the One, so the *eidola* or image-things are defective images of the Form-Beings which are never truly received in the material substrate which Plato calls *chora*. This substrate, variously described as "the other", "nonbeing", the "infinite", "indeterminate dyad" (Aristotle's term), is pure relationality.[36] It is utterly unintelligible, since it exists neither in-itself nor in-relation-to. Imagine the relationship, *taller-shorter* with the *tall* and the *short* withdrawn. The resulting *er-er* conveys some idea of the purely unintelligible, featureless relationality that is Plato's material substrate. Its apparent substantiality is spurious and so is our knowledge of it.[37] The sensible order, however, is something more than the pure relationality of its substrate. Yet its members are still essentially relational and hence indefinite. For Plato, then, in contrast with Galileo, the sensible order—indeed, *every* order of plurality —is incapable of being known as it is in itself, because nothing short of the One *is* in itself.

These remarks allow us to appreciate the traditional affinity between Platonic philosophy and the view of physical theory that would restrict it to "saving the appearances". For Aristotle, physical natures are centers of intelligible necessity. Hence, it is possible to have a physics which aims at knowing things as they are—that is, in terms of their proper natures. Hence, Aristotelians, even in astronomy, will regard theory as a set of necessary propositions responsive to centers of objective, natural necessity. For Plato, there are no such centers of intelligible necessity. Hence theory is regarded as symbolic. It supplies through intelligible constructions the intrinsic intelligibility lacking in things themselves.[38]

Plato's methodology of physics

If Galileo is to be accurately classified as a Platonist, one would expect a similarity between his and Plato's conception of method. Ernst Cassirer, in fact, did attempt a rapprochement of the two on this score. A brief account of Plato's method of analysis will help us understand his account of hypothesis. Analysis succeeds to the extent that it can terminate in unanalyzables that are simultaneously ultimate and rational. But as the *Theatetus* shows,[39] no such analysis is possible in the case of things as they are in themselves. Either the analytic process is endless when it works upon composite wholes or it terminates in undifferentiated, simple ultimates which are so utterly discrete as to be incapable of being bonded in intelligible ratios. A second-best form of analysis is necessary, therefore, if one wishes to reach rationally constructed wholes. But these are, at best, substitutes. Plato uses a simple paradigm in making this point: the problem of correlating side and diagonal in a square. Incommensurable as lines, the side and the diagonal can be commensurated in terms of the areas generated by each line.[40] Commensuration, that is to say, rationality, cannot be had at the level of the original integrity of the objects. Rationally constructed surrogates are always other than things in themselves. The latter may be approached as to an asymptotic limit but never attained. The ana-

lytic enterprise cannot, therefore, succeed in uncovering a nonhypothetical principle of dialectic.

Ernst Cassirer claims as evidence of "Platonism" that Galileo adopted
Plato's method of hypothesis as expressed in the *Meno*, but gave it a new
ontological status by discarding Plato's *chorismos* between the physical
and mathematical orders.[41] It is, of course, true that for Galileo there is
no separation between the physical and mathematical orders. But it is not
true that Galileo adopted Plato's "hypothetical" method, as a brief consideration of that method will show. The famous metaphor of the Divided
Line in the *Republic* distinguishes two dialectics, a hypothetical dialectic
appropriate to *dianoia* (postulatory mathematical reasoning) and a nonhypothetical dialectic of *noesis* which leads to a knowledge of the Good
and the other Forms.[42] In the literal sense of "steps placed under something", the dialectic of *noesis* makes use of hypothesis. But the soul as it
mounts up discards its "stepping-stones" until it reaches the Good, the nonhypothetical principle of all. There dialectic formally begins. The Good
known through itself generates a dialectical progress culminating in a
complete knowledge of all the Forms. By contrast, the method of *dianoia*
is, in the modern sense, genuinely hypothetical; its starting points never
shed their postulatory status. However systematic the deduction of consequents, the starting point of such a deduction can never be transformed
into a proposition whose truth is independent of verification through its
deduced consequents. This method is, therefore, essentially defective, for
in Platonic language it involves an eristic confusion of principles and consequents, or to put it in the familiar language of logic, the fallacy of the
consequent.[43] Hypothesis, therefore, is incapable of grasping real being,
but must always deal in substitutes. In the *Meno*, that which is sought—
virtue in its true being, that is, in its radical inseity—fails to manifest itself
as the dialogue develops.[44] Socrates is thus forced back on the method of
hypothesis—"let us suppose that virtue *is* knowledge"—instead. But at
that point, his own advice to begin with "essence", the real as it is in itself
and not "property", the surrogate of the real, is disregarded.[45]

The method of hypothesis described in the Platonic dialogues bears a
close resemblance to the method of "saving the appearances". The random
celestial motions evident to the naked eye can be reduced to rationality by
deducing them from a set of hypothetical propositions. But the principles
of this hypothetico-deductive effort can never shed their status as assumptions. The demonstrative process, as the *Republic* states, "passes not to a
new beginning, a first principle, but an end". "Passing to an end", that is,
deducing (and verifying) conclusions, cannot in principle transform an
hypothesis into a nonhypothetical truth.

Galileo: science as a necessary truth

Now, as we have already noted, Galileo emphasizes that the aim of natural science is true and certain demonstrations. Therefore he must reject,
and in point of fact does reject, a pure "*salvare apparentia*" conception of

physical theory. Cassirer's thesis, then, that Galileo's notion of method is heavily indebted to the *Meno's* account of hypothesis cannot, it would seem, be sustained.

But need Galileo's rejection of "saving the appearances" have entailed the opposite view, namely, that physical theory is capable of immediately penetrating the intrinsic necessary structures of things? Why not opt for a middle-of-the-road position? Let us say that the hypothetico-deductive method provides an *approximation* to actual states of affairs, or in other words, that physical theory in some qualified realist sense is capable of converging toward real structures. Actually the speculation of some of Galileo's immediate predecessors provided something like this alternative. As Duhem [46] and Blake [47] have shown, in the century before Galileo there was a shift in attitude concerning the realist implications of astronomical hypotheses. Christopher Clavius, S.J., George Horst, Luis Coronel and finally Kepler himself opposed the view that scientific hypothesis is a pure fiction, the view expressed in Osiander's famous preface to the *De revolutionibus*. Clavius, for example, regarded hypotheses as capable of generating probable knowledge of the real order. But a theory's realist implications must be tested, according to Clavius, against all available evidence from sources extrinsic to the theory itself, and especially from the principles of "higher" sciences, such as natural philosophy or Sacred Scripture; which is why, despite a certain sympathy for the Copernican hypothesis, he rejected it.[48] Kepler, like Galileo, maintained the homogeneity of physics and astronomy, but held that an astronomical theory can be at the same time both hypothetical and "true", that is, in conformity with actual celestial motions. He tried to overcome the fallacy of the consequent apparently inherent in this claim by means of various logical maneuvers. In addition, he claimed that an *a priori* demonstration on metaphysical grounds of such a theory ought in principle to be available.

Neither of these alternative ways of describing the realist implication of the method of hypothesis appealed to Galileo. He is as disdainful of the possibility of relevant extrinsic evidence as he is of the fictionalist approach itself. There are not, in his eyes, two "physics", one philosophical and true, the other, mathematical and constructural and dependent on the former. There is but one physics of both terrestrial and celestial phenomena. As to the other possible extrinsic source of evidence, he asserts in his *Letter to the Grand Duchess* that Sacred Scripture cannot in his view provide evidence for the truth of a scientific theory.[49] Neither is there any evidence that he was satisfied, as Kepler was, with the logical claim that alternative astronomical hypotheses either have different consequences or else must in principle be reducible to one another.[50] In the *Two chief systems*, he says:

> For one of the two positions being of necessity true and the other of necessity false, it is impossible that . . . the reasons alleged for the true hypotheses

should not manifest themselves as conclusive, as those for the contrary vain and ineffectual.[51]

Again in the *Assayer*, he affirms that:

> just as there is no middle ground between truth and falsity in physical things, so in rigorous demonstrations one must either establish his point beyond any doubt or else beg the question inexcusably.[52]

Steps in Galileo's method of science

Now, if Galileo means what he says when he identifies science with true and necessary demonstrations, two important consequences bearing on the nature of method in physics would seem to follow. It would appear that neither hypothesis nor experience as a means of verifying conclusions drawn from hypothesis are integral parts of his method. For it is clear that the conclusion of a necessary demonstration need not wait upon sensible verification as the final assurance of its truth and necessity. It is also clear that the principles of true and necessary demonstrations are more than merely hypothetical. The starting-points of such demonstrations must be firmly grounded in the intrinsic necessary structure of things, and their truth value must be apprehended independently of the consequences which can be deduced from them. But is this an accurate description of Galileo's theory of physics? And if it is, what justification does he offer for implying that mathematical physics attains to the necessary structures of the things of nature? In response to these questions, I shall try to show that Galileo's metaphysics, his theory of knowledge, and notably, his theory of God make it possible for him to regard physics as a "necessary" knowledge whose demonstrative principles must be nonhypothetical and whose deduced conclusions, in principle, at least, need no experimental verification. Once these dimensions of his philosophy of science are exposed, there will, I believe, be sufficient evidence that Galileo's theoretical justification for seeking a mathematical physics cannot be characterized as Platonic.

It will be helpful first to have a brief general outline of Galileo's method. According to him, the termini of method are the *an sit?* and the *quomodo sit?*,[53] the fact revealed in sensible observation and the mathematical truth of that fact. Since the passage between the termini is difficult, doubt is needed to facilitate discovery.[54] Doubt prepares for the application of the positive instruments of discovery to the experienced effects of nature.

The positive instruments of discovery are the methods of resolution and composition.[55] Resolution involves the analysis of the experiential datum into its geometrical structure. Once this structure is revealed, it is possible to describe it in terms of a principle, either one *per se notum* (i.e., carrying its own intrinsic warrant), or one which has already been demonstrated. This principle then becomes a basis for further deductions. The compositive or synthetic phase of method involves the actual geometrical derivation of such deductions or theorems. The two phases of method are thus linked together in a strict relationship. Composition, which is mathematical deduction, proceeds from principles which the resolutive method guarantees to be grounded in nature.

Galileo's treatment of accelerated motion in the Third Day of the *Two new sciences* is a good example of the relationship between the resolutive and compositive phases of method.

> And first of all it seems desirable to find and explain a definition of accelerated motion best fitting natural phenomena. For anyone may invent an arbitrary type of motion and discuss its properties; thus, for example, some have imagined helices and conchoids as described by certain motions which are not met with in nature, and have very commendably established the properties which these curves possess in virtue of their definitions; but we have decided to consider the phenomena of nature falling with an acceleration such as actually occurs in nature, and to make this definition of accelerated motion exhibit the essential features of observed accelerated motions.[56]

The question now to be asked is: do the conclusions demonstrated in the compositive phase require experimental verification? It appears not. In a letter to his friend Carcavi, Galileo clearly indicates that the properties of accelerated motion that can be mathematically deduced from its definition are automatically verified in nature; it is not necessary to go on to test them empirically:

> From such a consideration of motion, I demonstrate conclusively many properties. I add further that if experience should show that such properties could be found to be verified in the natural motion of bodies, we could without error affirm this to be the same motion which I defined and supposed. Even if that is not the case, my demonstrations founded on my supposition lose nothing of their force and conclusiveness. . . . But in the case of the motion which I imagined, it happened that all the properties which I demonstrated are verified.[57]

The wording of this passage is instructive. Galileo is saying that the conclusions about the many properties of accelerated motion are "demonstrated" in the compositive phase of method. If, in addition, experience should verify the conclusions in the actual motion of freely falling bodies, so much the better. But the presence or absence of sensible verification makes no intrinsic difference with regard to the force and conclusiveness, that is to say, the truth and necessity of the demonstrations.

Another letter on the same matter, this time to Baliani, expresses the same notion in even stronger terms. It is of "little importance", he says, that the conclusions which express the properties of accelerated motion should themselves be susceptible of experimental verification.[58] Finally, in a letter to Ingoli, he says of a certain experiment that previous to it "natural reason had most firmly persuaded me that the effect had to come off as it actually did".[59]

The language of the Book of Nature

Galileo's famous metaphor of the "Book of Nature" will help us understand his approach to demonstration and evidence.[60] By means of it, he expresses his fundamental metaphysical intuition that nature is essentially geometrical and that its intelligibility is consequent upon its geometrical structure. Nature, so to speak, writes itself in mathematical language. Its alphabet consists of the figures of Euclidean geometry. Unless one understands the natural language of its concrete geometrical structure, it will not be possible to understand the "Book".

Following out the implications of this mathematical ontology, Galileo assigns to nature the properties of immutability and rigorous necessity.[61] In the *Two chief systems*, Salviati speaks of natural effects as following "with necessity, so that it is impossible that it should happen otherwise, for such is the property of . . . natural and true things".[62] The link between the necessity and immutability of nature and that of God is most evident in Galileo's contrasting of Scriptural interpretation and scientific investigation. In his *Letter to the Grand Duchess*, Galileo distinguishes between Nature and Holy Scripture. Both proceed from the Divine Word, but Nature is "the most observant executrix" of the Divine order, while Scripture often departs from absolute truth since it is accommodated to everyone. Nature, on the contrary, never transgresses its duly constituted laws.[63] Again, in a letter to Diodati, Galileo reaffirms that nature is the "inexorable and immutable minister of God".[64]

In the light of these remarks, it is not hard to see why God became for Galileo the guarantor of scientific knowledge. Such knowledge had always been assumed to require a stable and necessary object, a requirement all the more stringent when scientific knowledge is held to be exclusively mathematical. The nagging voice of Simplicio was, as we have noted, always ready to counter Salviati's mathematical demonstrations of the properties of nature with the Aristotelian objection that since mathematics and physics are distinct sciences, they do not communicate in their objects. Mathematics is abstract, necessary, and immutable knowledge. Physics deals with the concrete, the mutable and contingent.[65] To meet this objection, Galileo assigned to the "things of nature" the same necessity and immutability that geometrical knowledge itself exhibited. In that way he could be confident of complete correspondence between a geometrical physics and the order of nature.

By claiming this rigorous and absolute necessity for nature, Galileo could not avoid the implication that God Himself was necessitated to create the order which He did create. For if God were absolutely free, there would be no guarantee that the object of scientific knowledge would maintain its permanence and necessity. As Malebranche was to put it: "if God does not follow the laws of motion, there would be nothing certain in physics. . . . The result would be a chaos in which nothing could be comprehended".[66] Galileo's way of putting this is to say that nature does not transgress its laws. God is therefore a guarantor of the object of physics inasmuch as He creates and conserves necessarily the unique, stable, necessary, geometrically structured order of nature. But apparently Galileo was not altogether easy in his mind about the demands made by a necessary object of physics, and its consequence, a necessitated Creator of that object. In one place, his hesitation shows: "the deliberations of nature are the best, one, and perhaps [*forse*] necessary".[67]

God is, however, not only a guarantor of scientific knowledge *ex parte rei*. He is also in Galileo's system the guarantor of knowledge *ex parte subiecti*. In this system, as we have seen, true and necessary demonstrations are the stuff of genuine science and they are achieved only with the aid of mathematics.[68] Truth is, in fact, identified with geometrical truth.[69] Consequently the natural sciences become true and certain only when they are formally geometrical. Nor does geometry function simply as a kind of paradigm of intelligibility as it does for Descartes. In Galileo's mind, the natural sciences *are* the mathematical sciences brought to bear upon the things of nature.[70]

Here again, God must supply the ultimate ground for the validity of man's mathematical reasoning when applied to nature. Following what he takes to be a Platonic position, Galileo claims that the human intellect "participates in the Divinity",[71] and in a famous passage of the *Two chief systems*, he explores the nature of that participation.[72] To this end, he distinguishes between the extensive and intensive consideration of knowledge. Extensively, understanding is defined by the range of the intelligibles to which it extends. Here the difference between divine and human knowledge is an infinite one. Intensively, one looks to the perfection of the act of knowing, that is, the degree of necessity and consequently the degree of certitude with which the understanding grasps its object. Such necessity and objective certitude are to be found in mathematics. Galileo goes on to say that when the human intellect knows its objects mathematically, the perfection of its act "equals the Divine in objective certitude because it succeeds in understanding their necessity, beyond which there can be no greater assurance".[73] Thus, when the human intellect knows the things of nature through geometrical demonstration, it has the strongest possible guarantee—the univocal community of perfection of its knowing with the Divine knowing. Galileo's geometrizing God underwrites, therefore, both the object and the mode of knowing of mathematical physics at once.

We are now in a position to see how the Divine guarantee functions within the methodic enterprise of physics, and in particular how it affects the role of experience. Unquestionably, the latter remains an absolute necessity at the outset of physical inquiry. The sensible effects of nature must be the starting point of physics, and experience is necessary to determine what these effects are. This point needs to be stressed, for some commentators tend to read Galileo's mathematical realism as a form of *a priorism*.[74] But he is no rationalist locating the origins of physics in a set of principles whose validity is prior to experience. Yet does experience function in any way as a terminus of method for him?

Mathematical knowledge is perfect knowledge because it reaches the necessity of things. Its object is the true object and its truth is the perfect truth, since it is the very same truth that God possesses in His intuitive geometrical knowledge. There is a point-for-point correspondence between mathematical knowledge and the geometrical structure of things.[75] There is but one order of nature: it is what it is and cannot be otherwise. When one has arrived at a system of theorems, by that very fact one's knowledge is conformed to the actual intrinsic structure of nature, or in Galileo's words, to "the Book of Nature where things are written in one way only . . ."[76] The termination here is the *"quomodo sit?"*, the "how" or mathematical account of the effects of nature. We can now equate this stage of scientific method with mathematical and thus quasi-divine truth. Its terminus, then, is the mathematical grasp of the objective necessity of things.

Sensible verification is, therefore, superfluous. A geometrically demonstrated conclusion of physics is guaranteed with respect to factors lying on the side both of the knower and the known. By knowing geometrically, we attain to the necessity of things and thus participate on terms of equality in the perfection of God's knowledge. It makes little difference whether or not one gives experimental confirmation. And the ultimate reason why experimental verification is not intrinsic to the structure of scientific method is the geometrizing God who guarantees it independently.

Yet Galileo does seem at times to make use of experimental verification. For example, the well-known experiment of the inclined plane in the *Two new sciences* is a means of verifying one of the conclusions about the properties of accelerated motion. Yet a careful examination of this passage reveals, I think, that the experiment is introduced for nonmethodic reasons. It is the Aristotelian, Simplicio, and not Salviati who requires the experimental confirmation. Simplicio is the typical Aristotelian, unschooled in mathematics. He is a much less tendentious fellow here than he was in the *Two chief systems;* he is more ready to admit the importance of mathematics in physical demonstrations. He is even willing to recognize the validity of the analysis Salviati gives of accelerated motion. What he doubts is the conformity between the mathematically formulated conclusion and the accelerated motions one actually finds in nature. His doubt is not the methodic doubt which prepares the way for the resolutive phase of method. It is, in reality, a doubt raised by one who cannot follow complicated mathematical reasoning, and who therefore cannot read the Book of Nature. For the benefit of Simplicio and "others like him",[77] Galileo offers an experiment which will remove the doubt by revealing the conformity between knowledge and nature. Methodologically speaking, however, experiments of this sort are superfluous.

Here then is the point of the "great Book of Nature" texts. The mathematical realism which they profess provides a ground for physics as a science of the necessary structures of nature. Because nature is itself geometrically constituted, a mathematical physics is not only possible, but is the only way that the physical world can be known with truth. Nor is mathematics to be regarded merely as a formalism which imparts deductive rigor to physical demonstrations. Rather it makes possible a full conformity of deduced theorems to the order of nature. No contingency remains except perhaps "in the calculator who does not know how to adjust his accounts". For "the order of the world is one only, nor can it ever be otherwise; hence he who seeks what is other than that which is, seeks the false and the impossible".[78] The Platonic method of using hypothesis to save appearances *does* seek to know that which is other than what is.

For Galileo, then, method in physics is nonhypothetical. Analysis or, as he calls it, "resolution", can terminate, as Plato's analysis cannot, in ultimate unanalyzables that are intrinsically intelligible. Once a mathematical structure is uncovered, it can be stated in the form of a deductively fertile principle of demonstration, whose truth-value, however, need not wait upon the sensible verification of the propositions deduced from it. Galileo, in other words, does not have to fret over that annoying feature of the hypothetico-deductive method, the fallacy of the consequent.[79]

Galileo and Descartes

It might be useful to interpose here a brief comparison between Galileo's philosophy of science and that of Descartes. It is often said that Descartes, too, regards physics as a science of necessary truth. Duhem, for example, claims to find in Descartes the "audacious" assertion that the properties of matter can be derived from its essence, extension, by a linear *a priori* deduction ultimately grounded in the *Cogito* itself.[80]

Descartes' method in physics in essentially hypothetico-deductive. True, the ultimate principles of physics—*extension, motion* and *figure*—are grounded in an *a priori* deduction from metaphysical principles. But this deduction cannot be prolonged so as to reveal the actual structures of the phenomena of nature. The sixth part of the *Discourse* clearly indicates the necessity for a recourse to experience at the outset of the methodic enterprise in physics proper.[81] Experience at this point provides the data which may suggest an hypothesis. The conclusions deduced from the hypothesis then require experimental verification. Method in physics proper is, therefore, hypothetico-deductive. The third book of Descartes' *Principles of philosophy* contains a very revealing passage which is worth quoting in full:

> We have noted that all the bodies which make up the universe are constituted of the same matter which can be divided into parts which are diversely moved, and whose movements are in some fashion circular; and finally that

there is always an equal quantity of these motions in the universe. But we have not been able to determine in the same fashion how many are the parts into which this matter is divided, nor what the velocities are with which they are moved, nor what circles they describe. For, since these could have been ordained by God in an infinity of different ways, *it is experience alone and not the force of reasoning* which allows us to know which of all these God has chosen. That is why we are now free to suppose what we wish, provided that all the things which are deduced from those suppositions are fully in accord with experience.[82]

Descartes could not have stated more unequivocally the thesis that physics is not a science of the necessary. It is interesting to note, too, that the hypothetical character of physics and the contingency of natural phenomena are grounded in a totally free and omnipotent God. The contrast between Descartes' God and the geometrizing God of Galileo is striking.

Indeed, Descartes' physics is not at all a mathematical physics in the way in which Galileo's is. Nowhere in the last two books of the *Principia*, the mature statement of his physics, does there erupt the cascade of equations which Poincaré regards as the mark of a genuine mathematical physics. For Galileo, mathematics is not merely a formalism or an instrument for predicting experimental results. Rather, it is substantive to physics itself. Descartes, on the other hand, conceives of mathematics not as constitutive of physical demonstrations, but as providing a paradigm of intelligibility.[83]

In a letter to Mersenne, he clearly indicates that physical demonstrations cannot be formally mathematical:

> But to demand of me geometrical demonstrations in a subject which depends upon physics is to require of me the impossible. If you wish to call demonstrations only the proofs of geometers, you are then obliged to say that Archimedes has demonstrated nothing in mechanics, nor Witelo in optics, nor Ptolemy in astronomy, etc., which is not the case. For one is satisfied that in such matters the authors having presupposed certain things, which are clearly not contrary to experience, have in all other respects spoken consistently and without fallacy, even though their suppositions may not have been exactly true.[84]

The reason for Descartes' sharp distinction between physics and mathematics lies in the difference of their objects. The object of mathematics is the possible, whereas physics deals with that which is *actu et qua tale existens*, i.e., with actually existing, spatially located concrete things.[85]

As a consequence, the certitude proper to physics is only "moral", the kind of certitude proper to a coherent systematic explanation sufficient for "the conduct of life".[86] Physics does not achieve the absolute certitude where it would be "impossible for a thing to be otherwise than as we judge it".[87] Doing physics is akin to solving a cipher. If by techniques of substitution a coherent and meaningful set of words are discovered, we are assured that the solution is correct, though it is still remotely possible that the maker of the cipher really intended a quite different message. Similarly, if physics produces a coherent account of the disparate phenomena of nature, this account is morally certain even though God could in fact have made things quite differently from the way the physicist postulates.[88]

Thus, contrary to what is often supposed, it is Galileo and not Descartes who opts for physics as a "science of the necessary". Moreover, it is Galileo and not Descartes who conceives the object of physics as an order possessing the fullness of reality and truth. Descartes never misses an opportunity to distinguish sharply between the derealized world of scientific objects and the plane of authentic being. Nature is not "some goddess".[89] It is not an object of "admiration".[90] Nature is figured mobile extension; it is inert, spread out in space and time. It is complete exteriority, being moved entirely from without. Like the automata of the royal gardens, it presents a specious interiority capable of exciting the infantile mind. But a properly conducted reflection reveals that authentic being is elsewhere—in the finite interiority of the self and the sovereign interiority of God. Surely, then, one cannot agree with Crombie that "the most extreme form of mathematical ontology was that advanced by Descartes".[91] We must attribute this rather to Galileo.

Physics: science of the necessary

In summary, then, the use of mathematics in physics is not by itself an adequate criterion to determine whether or not Galileo is a Platonist. What needs to be pinpointed are the theoretical grounds for the applicability of mathematics to nature. For Plato, there are no essential structures, whether mathematical or otherwise, embodied in sensible things. Instead, mathematical structures are *imposed;* hence astronomy, for example, appears as a saving of the appearances, a constructural and hypothetical enterprise whose task it is to rationalize the essentially irrational.

For Galileo, on the other hand, nature is essentially intelligible independently of the mind's constructive effort. And it is so because mathematical entities constitute its essential structure and confer upon it a rigid necessity. Hence a mathematical physics is the only possible way to describe nature. Moreoever, the mathematical physicist is assured of being able to reach conformity with nature not only by reason of the constitution of the object but also by reason of the mode of knowing proper to mathematics. Once one knows mathematically, one attains to the perfection of Divine knowledge, in terms of cognitive necessity, at least. For Plato, it goes without saying that no participation can ever entail the equality of participant with that in which he participates.

Paradoxical as it may sound, Galileo's conception of physical science is not too distant from that of Aristotle. Aristotle thinks it is possible for physics to achieve necessary demonstrations. In his view, the physical world is essentially intelligible because it contains natures which are centers of positivity and necessity. True, the physical character of these natures calls for properly "physical" demonstrations, a notion which Galileo sets aside, yet the ideal of a nonhypothetical physics capable of generating necessary demonstrations is the same for both Galileo and Aristotle. Not so for Plato, or for neo-Platonists such as Nicholas of Cusa.[92]

Galileo, therefore, is no Platonist.[93] He is his own man, struggling not only to overthrow Aristotelian qualitative physics, but also to overthrow the increasingly fashionable conception of natural science as a "saving of the appearances". Fusing the Aristotelian conception of science as a knowledge of the necessary with a neo-Pythagorean mathematical ontology, he endeavored quite consciously to fashion mathematical physics as an apodictic discipline. To my mind, no other of the great seventeenth-century pioneers in science ever attempted so ambitious a theoretical justification of mathematical physics as a "science of the necessary".

NOTES

1. S. Sambursky, "Galileo's attempt at a cosmogony", 1962*. Sambursky shows that Galileo relied on certain passages from the *Timaeus* (esp. 38c–39a) to develop a theory of the common origin of the planets.

2. See, for example, E. A. Moody, "Galileo and Avempace", 1951*. Moody maintains that Galileo's Pisan dynamics was influenced by Avempace's law of motion and his theory of impressed force, both of which are out of the neo-Platonic tradition of Alexandria. Therefore, "there would seem to be not merely theoretical, but historical grounds, for the claims of Cassirer and Koyré that Galileo's science—at least, in its Pisan phase—was in the Platonist and Alexandrian tradition" (p. 206). But the fact that Galileo rejects Aristotle's formula for the velocity of natural motion neither proves nor disproves the Koyré-Cassirer thesis that Galileo is Platonist in his philosophy of science.

3. A. Koyré, "Galileo and Plato", 1963*.

4. Almost at the very outset of the First Day, Simplicio maintains "with Aristotle that natural things do not always behave with the necessity of a mathematical demonstration" (*Opere*, 7, p. 38; see also pp. 231–233, 256). Though he is eventually won over to the mathematical approach to nature, the Simplicio of the *Discorsi* originally makes the same objection: "Le considerazioni e dimonstrazioni sin qui fatte da voi, come che son cose matematiche astratte e separate dalla materia sensibile, credo che applicate alle materia fisiche . . . non caminerebbo" (*Opere, 8*, p. 96). Shapere maintains that Galileo's development of "the new conception of the role of mathematics in the study of nature . . . is for the most part implicit or incidental or at best peripheral in his work" ("Descartes and Plato", 1963*). Certainly this new conception is peripheral to his work, if by that is meant his work in physics and astronomy. It is by no means peripheral to his efforts as a philosopher of science. To be sure, Galileo (unlike Descartes) wrote no treatise on the method and nature of science. Yet scattered though they are throughout his corpus, his remarks are sufficiently explicit, as we hope to show, to indicate the presence of a coherent account of the nature of the new science.

5. *Op. cit.* See also his *Études galiléennes*, 1939*, vol. 3, pp. 117–131.

6. "Galileo's Platonism", 1946*.

7. *Robert Grosseteste and the origins of experimental science*, 1953*. See also his "Galileo's *Dialogues concerning the two principal systems of the world*", 1950*.

8. *The metaphysical foundations of modern science*, New York, 1925, pp. 61–95.

9. *From Galileo to Newton, 1630–1720*, 1963*, p. 71.

10. See A. C. Crombie "Galileo Galilei, a philosophical symbol", 1956*. A case in point is Koyré's note: "Traddutore-Traditore", 1943*, accusing the Crew-de Salvio translation of the *Discorsi* of an *a priori* commitment to empiricism, when it translates the 'comperio' of "symptomatum [motus] . . . adhuc inobservata necdum indemonstrata comperio" (*Opere, 8*, p. 190) by "I have discovered by experiment". Koyré is quite right, as the terms 'inobservata' and 'indemonstrata' clearly indicate. But his objection is weakened by his lament over the empiricist predilections of American historians of science. For it allows Philip P. Wiener in his rejoinder (1943*) to accuse Koyré—with some justification—of an equally *a priori* Platonic reading of the text.

11. Koyré, "Galileo and Plato", p. 168.

12. "Esercitazioni filosofiche di Antonio Rocco con postille di G. G.", *Opere, 8*, p. 144. See also *Discorsi, 8*, p. 64.

13. *Opere, 7*, p. 218. Simplicio's claim that Salviati leans to the Platonic view ("nostrum scire sit quoddam reminisci") receives a rather noncommittal response. See *Opere, 8*, p. 596 for a more forthright statement.

14. "Che Platone stesso ammirasse l'intelletto umano e lo stimasse partecipe di divinità solo per l'intender egli la natura de'numeri, io benissimo lo so, ne sarei lontano dal farne l'istesso giudizio." (*Opere, 7*, p. 35.)

15. *Op. cit.*, p. 291.

16. *Ibid.*, pp. 5–8.

17. See P. Duhem, *Le système du monde*, vol. 1, pp. 102–106.

18. The classic Greek version of "saving the appearances" is that of Geminus which Simplicius reproduced. (*In Aristotelis Physicorum Libros . . . Commentaria*, ed. by H. Diels, Berlin, 1892, pp. 291–292.) Duhem traced the development of the theory of "saving the appearances" in "Sozein ta phainomena: Essai sur la notion de théorie physique de Platon à Galilée", *Annales de philosophie chrétienne, 6*, 1908, 113–139; 277–302; 352–377; 561–592.

19. *From closed world to infinite universe*, 1957*, p. 16.

20. "Whereas in practice Galileo decided upon the truth of a 'hypothetical assumption' by the familiar criteria of experimental verification and simplicity, it is plain that he was aiming at something more than merely . . . 'saving the appearances' . . . The momentous change that Galileo, along with other platonizing mathematicians like Kepler introduced into scientific ontology was to identify the substance of the real world with mathematical entities . . ." (*op. cit.*, pp. 309–310).

21. "Ma nelle scienze naturali, le conclusioni delle quali sono vere e necessarie." (*Dialogo, 7*, p. 78; see also pp. 75, 387, and *6*, p. 296; *8*, p. 296.)

22. *Considerazioni circa l'opinione copernica, 5*, p. 369. Referring to Coper-

nicus' astronomical theory he states that "non è dunque introdotta questa posizione per satisfare al puro astronomo, ma per satisfare alla necessità della natura".

23. See L. Geymonat, *Galileo Galilei*, 1957*, pp. 63–66, 195–197.

24. *Il saggiatore*, 6, p. 232; translated by Stillman Drake in *The controversy on the comets of 1618*, 1960*. See pp. 183–184.

25. L. Geymonat, *op. cit.*, pp. 199–202.

26. "Descartes and Plato", 1963*.

27. "We must speak of both kinds of causes, but distinguish causes that work with intelligence to produce what is good and desirable [soul and intelligent nature] from those which being destitute of reason, produce their sundry effects at random and without order [necessity or the errant cause]." *Timaeus*, 46E, translated by F. M. Cornford in *Plato's cosmology*, London, 1937, p. 157. See Shapere, *op. cit.*, p. 573.

28. *Timaeus*, 56C. See Cornford, *op. cit.*, pp. 171–177.

29. A. E. Taylor in his *Commentary on Plato's Timaeus*, Oxford, 1928, pp. 300–301, seems to hold for just such a Leibnizian interpretation of "necessity", though he modifies this position considerably in the later editions of his *Plato*. See Cornford's critique of Taylor's position, *op. cit.*, pp. 164–165.

30. "Quello che accade in concreto, accade nell' istesso modo in astratto." (*Dialogo*, 7, p. 233.)

31. Adapted from the de Santillana translation of the *Dialogo*, p. 172.

32. *Sophist*, 255E.

33. *Ibid.*, 258C–259B.

34. See L. Eslick, "The Platonic dialectic of non-being", *New scholasticism*, 29, 1955, 33–49. See also his "The material substrate in Plato" in *The concept of matter*, ed. by E. McMullin, Notre Dame, 1963, pp. 59–74. My description of Plato's thought is heavily indebted to these and other articles cited in the latter essay.

35. See L. Eslick, "The material substrate in Plato", pp. 67–69.

36. *Ibid.*, p. 67.

37. *Timaeus*, 52B.

38. See P. Duhem, *Le système du monde*, vol. 1, pp. 141–150, 173–177.

39. *Theatetus*, 201D–208B.

40. The opening conversation in the *Theatetus* (146A–148D; Cornford, *op. cit.*, pp. 22–24) describes the incommensurability of side and diagonal and the efforts to subsume all cases of incommensurability under "a single collective term". How profoundly ironic it is, then, that Socrates should counsel the use of the same "model" in the search after the radical inseity in question, viz., knowledge itself. "Take as a model your answer about the roots [the incommensurable sides]: just as you found a single character to embrace all that multitude, so now try to find a *single formula* that applies to the many kinds of knowledge." Such a single formula cannot possibly exhibit what the thing itself—knowledge—is.

41. *Op. cit.*, pp. 285–292.

42. *Republic*, 509–511.

43. *Ibid.*, 510B–510D.

44. *Meno*, 86E–87C.

45. *Ibid.*, 71C. See also *Epistle* 7, 342.

46. "Essai sur la théorie physique", *supra*, pp. 561–577.

47. "Theories of hypothesis among Renaissance astronomers" in *Theories of scientific method*, 1960*, pp. 23–49.

48. *Ibid.*, pp. 38–43.

49. Translated by S. Drake, *Discoveries and opinions of Galileo*, 1957*, pp. 174–216.

50. See Blake, *op. cit.*, pp. 41–42.

51. *Dialogo*, 7, p. 282; de Santillana translation, p. 366. See also 7, pp. 287, 350; 5, pp. 354, 369.

52. *Il saggiatore*, 6, p. 296; Drake, *op. cit.*, p. 252.

53. *Letter to Liceti:* "Qui non vorrei che mi venisse detto che io acquietassi sulla verità del fatto, poiche mi mostra succedere l'esperienza. Questa potrei dire in tutti gli effetti di natura, per mi ammirandi, mi assicura dell' *an sit*, ma guadagno nessuno mi arreca del *quomodo*." *Opere*, *18*, p. 248. See also *4*, p. 160.

54. *Letter to Liceti:* "E manifesto anche troppo . . . che il dubitare in filosofia e padre del invenzione, facendo strada alla scoprimento del vero." *Opere*, *18*, pp. 125–126.

55. "Riposta all opposizioni di L. delle Colombe", *Opere*, *4*, 521. See also *Dialogo*, 7, p. 75; de Santillana translation, p. 60.

56. *Discorsi*, *8*, p. 197; *Two new sciences*, p. 160.

57. *Opere*, *17*, pp. 90–91.

58. "Sicchè quando bene le conseguenze non rispondessero alli accidenti del moto naturale de'gravi descendenti, poco a me importerebbe." *Opere 18*, pp. 12–13.

59. *Opere*, *6*, p. 545; de Santillana translation, p. 140, n. 26.

60. The best-known text occurs in *Il saggiatore*, *6*, p. 232; Drake translation, pp. 183–184. See also *18*, p. 295 and *11*, pp. 107–108. Msgr. Francesco Olgiati has a good summary of Galileo's philosophical texts in his "La metafisica di Galileo Galilei", 1942*. His thesis is that Galileo developed a metaphysics to supplant the "Aristotelico-Thomist" conception of the real, just as his physics dethroned Aristotelian physics. This Galilean metaphysics Olgiati characterizes as a "metaphysical phenomenism". The former point, however, is questionable. There is no evidence in the text that Galileo is trying to construct a substitute for a metaphysics of "being as being". Olgiati's special meaning for "phenomenalist" (reality is determined "not in function of the actuated essence of being but of the content of experience affirmed as real") seems farfetched when applied to Galileo.

61. "Ma l'ordine del mondo è un solo, ne mai è stato altrimenti." *Opere*, 7, p. 700.

62. *Opere*, 7, p. 450. See also: "Le vere, cioe quelle che sono impossibile ad essere altrimenti", p. 183.

63. *Opere, 5*, pp. 282–283. See also Drake, *Discoveries and opinions*, p. 182.

64. *Opere, 11*, p. 149. See also "Ella [la natura] non muterebbe un iota delle legge e statuti suoi", *6*, p. 538, and "Natura . . . veridica ed immutabile in tutte le cose sue", *8*, p. 640.

65. See note 4.

66. *Recherche de la verité*, ed. by G. Lewis, Paris, 1946, vol. 2, p. 193.

67. *Opere, 4*, p. 24.

68. *Dialogo*, 7, p. 229.

69. *Il saggiatore:* "Che 'l contradire alla geometria è un negare scopertamente la verità", *6*, p. 24.

70. *Dialogo*, 7, p. 356. In this passage Galileo, though he admired Gilbert, criticizes him because his demonstrations are not geometrical and, hence, do not conduce to "*conclusioni naturali, necessarie ed eterne*".

71. See note 14.

72. *Opere, 7*, pp. 128–129.

73. *Ibid.*, p. 129. Kepler also developed a mathematical epistemology which stressed the *equality* of human and divine mathematics. In a letter to Herwart (April 9/10, 1599) he states: "Our knowledge [of numbers and quantities] is the same kind as God's, at least insofar as we can understand something of it in this mortal life". In the *Harmonice mundi* (Bk. 4, ch. 1), he says of the archetype of harmony that the soul possesses "not an image of the true pattern [paradigma] but the true pattern itself. . . . Thus finally the harmony itself becomes entirely soul, nay even God." These two passages are quoted in Gerald Holton's excellent study, "Johannes Kepler's universe: its physics and metaphysics", 1956*. Apparently, however, the rigorous geometrization of physics and the physical object did not suggest to Kepler the methodological consequences which it did to Galileo. Precisely because of this geometrization of nature and knowledge, Galileo is able to bypass Kepler's problem of how a scientific demonstration can be both hypothetical and true.

   Both Galileo and Kepler are very much in the Renaissance tradition of the "humanization" of truth. So also, of course, is Descartes. But where Galileo and Kepler accomplish the humanization of truth by elevating man's cognitive powers to the status of the divine, Descartes does just the reverse. For him, the grounds of intelligibility—the eternal truths and mathematical essences—are created by God in the human mind in a condition of primitive diversity. Scientific truth is, therefore, *only* human. There is no equality whatsoever between the divine and human modes of cognition. On this point see F. Alquié, *La découverte métaphysique de l'homme chez Descartes*, Paris, 1948, ch. 5.

74. See A. C. Crombie, "Galileo's *Dialogues* . . .", p. 178.

75. See note 30. Karl Popper interprets Galileo as a scientific realist, an "essentialist", as opposed to an "instrumentalist" for whom theories are only instruments for predicting observations. See his *Conjectures and Refutations*, 1963*. But aside from alluding to the issues raised by Osiander's preface, he offers no evidence for his view, though his description of Galileo's scientific realism is accurate enough.

76. "Errori de Giorgio Coresio", *Opere, 4*, p. 248.

77. "Ma se tale sia poi l'accelerazione della quale si serve la natura del moto de

i suoi gravi descendenti, io per ancora ne resto dubbioso, e pero, per intelligenza mia e di altri simili a me, parmi che sarebbe stato opportuno in questo luogo arrecar qualche esperienza." *Opere, 8*, p. 212.

78. *Opere*, 7, p. 700.

79. Duhem held that Galileo regarded physical principles as hypotheses which could be transformed into apodictic truths by the Baconian method of crucial experiments. "Galilée a, de la valeur de la méthode experimentale et de l'art d'en user, à peu près l'opinion que va formuler François Bacon; il conçoit la preuve d'une hypothèse à l'imitation de la démonstration par l'absurde usitée en géometrie; l'experience, en convainquant d'erreur un système, confère la certitude au système opposé; la science positive progresse par une suite de dilemmes dont chacun est resolu à l'aide d'un *experimentum crucis*." "Essai sur la notion de théorie physique", *supra*, p. 584. The evidence for this interpretation simply does not exist. The one text which Duhem cites (see Drake, *Discoveries and opinions*, p. 169) does not sustain his thesis. It merely claims that for the true position (Copernicanism) a host of proofs can be adduced. There is no mention of anything resembling a crucial experiment. Duhem is correct in attributing to Galileo a nonhypothetical physics, but he failed to see that such a physics is *ab initio* nonhypothetical. Hence there is no need for a "transformation" via crucial experiments.

80. See Pierre Duhem, *The aim and structure of physical theory*, transl. by P. P. Wiener, New York, 1962, p. 44.

81. *Oeuvres de Descartes*, ed. by C. Adam and P. Tannery, Paris, 1895–1913, vol. 6, pp. 63–65.

82. *Oeuvres*, vol. 9, pp. 124–125 (Italics mine). See G. Buchdahl, "Descartes' anticipation of a 'logic of scientific discovery' ", in *Scientific change*, ed. by A. C. Crombie, 1963*, pp. 405–406.

83. *Oeuvres*, vol. 8, p. 79. In physics, demonstrations are to be so made "*ut pro mathematica demonstratione sit habendum*".

84. *Oeuvres*, vol. 2, pp. 141–142.

85. *Oeuvres*, vol. 5, p. 160.

86. *Principia, Oeuvres*, vol. 8, p. 327.

87. This definition of absolute certitude is added in the French version of the *Principia, Oeuvres*, vol. 9(2), p. 324.

88. *Principia, Oeuvres*, vol. 8, pp. 327–328.

89. *Le monde, Oeuvres*, vol. 11, pp. 36–37.

90. For a discussion of the role of *admiratio* and the distinction between the plane of object and the plane of being see the remarkable study of Alquié, already cited. A decisive evidence that Descartes is concerned to maintain the distinction between the two is the distinction he is constantly at pains to make between *comprendre* and *connaître* or *savoir*. *Comprendre* is to "embrace" the object as one embraces a tree. Such an object is completely intelligible; no corner of it remains opaque. *Connaître* (and its various synonyms) is to attain the object, to "touch" it as one touches the immensity of a mountain. See his letter to Mersenne, April 15, 1630, *Oeuvres*, vol. 1, p. 145.

91. See A. C. Crombie, *Robert Grosseteste*, p. 310.

THOMAS P. MCTIGHE 387

92. Cusa's metaphysics of the One entails a Platonic reduction of essence to otherness or relation. Since there are no quidditative densities, there can be for him no philosophy of nature in the Aristotelian sense. The only science of nature is a kind of mathematical physics in which finite things are compared with one another in terms of relations of number and weight. See my "Nicholas of Cusa as a forerunner of modern science" in *Proceedings X Intern. Congress History Science*, Paris, 1966, pp. 619–622.

93. G. de Santillana puts it accurately: "Matter is always and everywhere absolutely exact, down to the shape of any bit of stone; mathematics is present in substance as well as in motion. If this is anti-Aristotelian, it is certainly not Platonic, or Platonic only in so far as Plato had once been himself a Pythagorean" (*op. cit.*, p. 221, n. 76).

19 | ⊙ Galilean physics in the light of Husserl's phenomenology

ARON GURWITSCH

Husserl's analysis of Galilean physics, on which I am to comment, is contained in his book *Die Krisis der Europäischen Wissenschaften und die Transzendentale Phänomenologie*. A translation true to the spirit rather than the letter might render the title as *The crisis of Western sciences and transcendental phenomenology*. 'European' was not meant by Husserl to be taken geographically; rather, he took it to have an historical sense as referring to the Occidental world, understood as the scene of an unfolding and a unified intellectual development. To this, his last work, Husserl devoted the closing years of his life, but he was unable to bring it to completion.[1] In Husserl's lifetime, the first third of what was later to become the book appeared in the form of an article under the same title.[2] The discussion of Galileo occupies the center of this article.

Both the article and the book have the subtitle: "An introduction to phenomenological philosophy". The subtitle indicates the general perspective in which Husserl places his analysis of modern science or, as Husserl calls it, the "science of Galilean style". His intention was to open up a new avenue of approach to phenomenological philosophy. The novelty of this approach consisted in the fact that, in contradistinction to his earlier writings, he takes his departure from certain basic problems that beset modern science or, more accurately, from the very existence of this science of "modern style" itself. It appears legitimate to isolate, or at least to concentrate upon, his analysis of Galileo, and this is what I shall try to do. When read in this light, Husserl's book acquires a significance of the first order for the philosophy of science. It marks a turning-point in the development of this discipline and inaugurates a new phase in its history.

Three phases in the philosophy of science

Roughly speaking, one can distinguish two phases in the philosophy of science prior to the appearance of Husserl's work. The first phase extends approximately from the middle of the seventeenth century to the middle of the eighteenth century. Descartes' *Meditations on first philosophy* may be considered as a representative document of this first period. Descartes sets out to provide a foundation for, and a validation of, the new science. It is to rest upon and be guided by the following thesis: The universe is not as it appears in common experience; its nature and structure do not lay themselves open to perception; on the contrary, they have to be uncovered by means of mathematical notions. In reality, then, the universe is not as it seems to be, but as it is conceived and constructed by the mathematical physicist.

We children of the twentieth century may find it difficult to realize the boldness of this thesis because we are heirs to a tradition of science which we have come to take for granted as something definitively possessed, rather than as something to be acquired and justified. We hardly see any necessity, therefore, for a justification of the thesis upon which modern science rests. In the seventeenth century, the situation was quite different. The men of that day were not heirs but inaugurators, to whom the legitimacy of their endeavor presented a real problem. Descartes' solution to this problem was to have recourse to the Divine veracity in order to guarantee the validity of the principle that whatever is clearly and distinctly perceived is true. It was on the basis of this principle that mathematical knowledge and the geometrical conception of the external world seemed to him to be justified. Along similar lines, though in some respects differently from Descartes, Malebranche conceived of the intellectual life of man, insofar as he engages himself in genuinely cognitive endeavors, as some kind of participation in the intellectual life of the Deity. Galileo in a famous passage speaks in the same vein.

The second period in the development of the philosophy of science began in the year 1748, when Leonhard Euler, the great Swiss mathematician, submitted to the Royal Prussian Academy of Berlin a memoir entitled *Reflexions sur l'espace et le temps*. This memoir, which concerns itself with the problems of absolute motion, absolute space, and absolute time, is Euler's contribution to the discussion regarding the nature of space, which had been going on for over a century, and in which Descartes, Malebranche, the Cambridge neo-Platonists, Newton and his followers, Leibniz, Berkeley, and others had taken part. Euler grants that philosophy must concern itself with the fundamental concepts of the sciences, especially of physics. However, the decision as to whether or not a given concept should be admitted among these falls under the competence of physics rather than of philosophy. If it appears that the laws of dynamics, especially the law of inertia, require for their formulation the notions of absolute space and absolute time, then these notions (as well as that of absolute motion which they immediately imply) must be admitted as valid. They derive their right of citizenship from the part they play within the theoretical context of physics. Against such a decision, which is based upon the theoretical exigencies of physics, no appeal is possible. Consequently, philosophy must accept this decision, and accommodate its constructions and theories accordingly.

Euler's memoir contains a "declaration of independence" on the part of physics with regard to philosophy. Such a claim to autonomy was made possible by the accomplishments of the science of physics during the preceding century and a half, and it expresses a self-confidence rooted in those accomplishments. Euler's memoir opened up the second phase of the philosophy of science, a phase in which science is no longer considered as in need of justification and validation, but on the contrary, as a given fact simply to be accepted. The phrase 'science as a fact' is, as a rule, associated with the name of Kant. But what Kant did was to provide an elaborate realization of the program which Euler had not only anticipated but conceived in a rather concrete fashion. Husserl's *Crisis of Western sciences* thus marks the beginning of a third phase in the philosophy of science. Whereas in the second phase science was accepted as a fact, in the third phase it appears as a *problem*. It is under this historical perspective, I suggest, that Husserl's discussion of Galileo can best be understood.

Two preliminary remarks are worth making. In the first place, this attribution of a problematic status to science must not be mistaken for the expression of an "anti-scientific spirit". Awareness of problems which beset the very existence of modern science is something quite different from hostility toward science itself. I feel impelled to apologize for this truism. Yet judging by what one reads, it seems necessary to insist upon it. Hostility to science was totally alien to Husserl, whose own scholarly career had begun in mathematics. It was, in fact, because of his training in, and first-hand acquaintance with, modern mathematical science that Husserl was not prepared to listen in an attitude of superstitious awe to slogans about "Science" or "Scientific Method".

In the second place, Husserl was not an historian of science and never made any claim to be one, even though he presented his views on "science as a problem" in the form of an analysis of Galileo's work. One may doubt whether he ever gave to the study of Galileo's writings that time and attention which a professional historian would devote to them as a matter of course. Cassirer's discussion of Galileo in *Das Erkenntnisproblem in der Philosophie und Wissenschaft der neueren Zeit* may well have been one of Husserl's main sources of information. He remarks himself that he does not distinguish between Galileo's own contributions and those made by his predecessors (nor those made by his successors, one might add). As a matter of fact, he ascribes some ideas to Galileo with which Descartes or Huygens should have been credited instead. In the face of such historical inaccuracies of fact, it may not be out of place to recall the judgment of an authority in the history of science, the late Alexandre Koyré, who once remarked to me that even though Husserl was not a historian either by training or by temperament, or by direction of interest, his analysis provides the key for a profound and radical understanding of Galileo's work. At any rate, we can assume that when Husserl speaks of "Galileo," he does not really mean the historical figure bearing that name. Rather, as he says himself, he uses the name as a symbol. It symbolizes for him the "spirit of modern physics", a spirit of which the real Galileo was, of course, a pioneer. This is what he means by a "physics of Galilean style". He submits this physics to a critique, not (once again be it said) a criticism.

Galilean physics as a problem

Let us approach this topic from different angles, since it has many facets. Husserl compares scientific activity, as it has developed during the last three centuries, to the functioning of a machine. He has in mind not so much the machines of industry as the "machines" of the logician or mathematician, i.e., the symbolic procedures which have proved of such paramount importance for the development and formalization of mathematics. Such algorithmic procedures can be applied in a purely mechanical fashion, their use demanding no more than the observance of formal rules of operation. Methods of science, once invented, tend to become formalized and to undergo a process of "technization" of this sort, in the course of which their application becomes a matter of routine. We possesss scientific methods; we operate and manipulate, and we invent new and better— that is, more effective—methods. In this way, results of the highest importance from both the theoretical and the practical points of view are obtained. If by an "understanding" of science no more is meant than the successful application of methodical procedures, there seems to be no difficulty. In fact, the "technician of science"—a term not meant in any pejorative sense, but simply to denote someone whose exclusive interest lies in practical achievement—might simply rest his case on the successful operation of the scientific "machine", since it yields results of the kind he wishes to obtain.

Not so the philosopher, whose very *raison d'être* is to raise radical questions, radical in the etymological sense of going to the roots. The philosopher cannot be satisfied with the actual working of the machine, he must wonder why and how it functions. From the machine as a fact here and now, he will go back to the mechanism which makes it work, to the principles involved in its construction, to the conditions upon which this construction depends. To express this less metaphorically, we have to inquire into the presuppositions which underlie the elaboration of science of the Galilean style, presuppositions from which that science derives its sense and which defines, in consequence, its limitations. They are well-concealed, and remain so as long as one adopts what I have called the attitude of the scientific technician. Since they determine the sense of scientific activity, to make them explicit is to elucidate the meaning of science itself. What is in question is not the meaning of particular scientific conceptions and theories, like quantum physics or the theory of relativity, but rather the meaning of modern science in its entirety, the meaning in particular, of that progressive mathematization of nature which Galileo first conceived.

A question that must occur to anyone who has to deal with science in its historic aspect is: why did the mathematization of nature start around 1600 and in Italy? Why did it not start before then, or in another civilization? Why not in Greece, or in Rome, where the engineers were of a remarkably high level of competence? Why did it not start during the Middle Ages? It would obviously be silly to try to explain this in terms of some sort of intellectual inferiority during those periods. To answer the question, one would have to turn to a historically oriented sociology of knowledge. But I am raising the question merely for the purpose of emphasizing that the existence of science of the modern style must not be taken for granted. For many centuries, a highly civilized mankind got along without the mathematical conception of nature. To be sure, there were the Pythagoreans and there was Archimedes. But these thinkers left no enduring imprint upon the intellectual development that immediately followed them.

Physics and the *Lebenswelt*

The mathematical conception of nature is, therefore, not essential to the human mind. In direct experience, nature does not present itself as a mathematical system. There has been a discrepancy from the beginning between the universe constructed by physical science and the world given to us in immediate (mainly perceptual) experience. This latter is the world into which we are born, within which we find ourselves at every moment of our lives, no matter what activities we are engaged in, and no matter what goals and aims we are pursuing. Within that world, we encounter our fellow men, to whom we stand in relations of the most diverse kinds. With the ways of this world—the "life-world" (*Lebenswelt*) as Husserl calls it—we have acquired, both through education and through personal experience, a familiarity of a very special sort. The objects which we encounter in this world have human significance; they present themselves as tools, as utensils to be handled in specific ways in order that desired results may be obtained. Moreover, they exhibit certain intrinsic properties of their own. For instance, over there is a blue chair. In the *Lebenswelt* we take our bearings from perceptual experience and thus unhesitatingly consider the blue color to be a property intrinsic to the chair. Unless we have studied physics or are indirectly influenced by it, it would not occur to us to regard the color as a subjective phenomenon, a content of our consciousness, on the same footing as, say, a feeling of joy, a desire, or the like. What is at issue here is not merely the substitution for the color of processes that are completely describable in mathematical terms, like wave-length, frequency, velocity of propagation, and the consequent replacement of qualitative differences by quantitative ones. Of equal importance is the ever-growing alienation of the universe of physics from the world of perceptual experience. The physics of the nineteenth century, even the field theories of Faraday and Maxwell, still made use of models that had intuitive content and lent themselves to visualization. Lines of force were conceived by analogy with rubber bands which stretch and contract. Contemporary physics, however, relies on constructs of a totally abstract nature which have to be treated according to algorithmic rules of operation alone. They no longer have a visualizable content, and no intuitive significance is claimed for them. What in the beginning appeared as a discrepancy has grown into an ever-widening gulf.

In an earlier phase of the modern period, the constructions of mathematical physics were not simply regarded as models, meant for convenience of systematization, prediction or even explanation. On the contrary, they were thought to express the true state of affairs, the real nature of the external world. By means of his mathematically expressed theories, the physicist was believed to pierce through the veil of perceptual appearance and thus to describe nature as it really is. This realistic interpretation of physics finds few defenders today, yet so recent and so great a physicist as Max Planck still adhered to it.

We seem somehow to be confronted with two realms. One is the realm of reality, of nature as mathematically conceived and constructed; the other is the world of appearances. Malebranche speaks of *"illusions naturelles"*. They are natural, because they are grounded in the real condition of things, on the basis of which they occur in regular fashion. (The explanation of this regularity is, incidentally, one of the principal tasks of the science of psychology in the specific modern sense.) But they *are* illusions, since they do not correspond to the true state of affairs. Nevertheless, the persistence of these illusions is most remarkable. Despite the rapid development of science, the perceptual world continues to be its familiar self. To the physicist and layman alike, things continue to exhibit chromatic qualities as though they were intrinsic to the things themselves. On a summer evening by the seashore, we still see the sun dipping into the ocean, all our knowledge of astronomy notwithstanding. Such facts point to some sort of priority on the part of the *Lebenswelt*. After all, scientific theories must be verified by means of observations, which, even if reduced to mere pointer readings, are still perceptual experiences. One might object that this priority holds good only *quoad nos:* to arrive at the universe as it really is, we naturally have to take our departure from the world as it appears to us. Even if this objection were to be granted, the original point is still strong enough to make it worthwhile to inquire into those general features of the world of common experience which provide the initial motivation for constructing a mathematical conception of nature. Then we shall have to ask further what else, in addition to that motivation, is required for the actual elaboration of a mathematical physics.

Three features of the *Lebenswelt*

Fortunately for us, it is not necessary to present a full analytic description of the general structure of the *Lebenswelt*. This would be a very arduous task indeed, the more so as no complete and exhaustive analysis of it has yet been made, though many authors in recent decades have made valuable additions to Husserl's pioneer work. For our purposes, a few major points from Husserl's analysis will suffice. In the first place, the world of everyday experience is extended in space and time; these constitute a comprehensive frame, in which all the existents of our experience can be related in spatial and in temporal terms with one another. Furthermore, things exhibit spatial forms. Trees, for instance, present a cylindrical shape. The phrase 'cylindrical shape' is, of course, not meant to be understood in a strictly geometrical sense, but rather as indicating a physiognomic aspect of spatial form. It does not denote a determinate figure, but rather a generic type of spatial configuration, one that within limits not precisely defined allows variation and deviation. Going beyond Husserl's analysis, it may be noted that psychologists, especially of the Gestalt school, have long used terms like 'circularity' or 'rectangularity' in this physiognomic sense, when they speak, for instance, of a circle as "bad" or of one right angle as "better than another". From a strictly geometrical point of view, such phrases would be nonsense; they make good sense, however, when applied to the phenomenal aspects of perceptual experience. This experience is always affected by some vagueness and indefiniteness; its determinations only hold by and large. (For reasons to be made clear in a moment, I avoid speaking of "approximation".) One might, perhaps, characterize perceptual experience by saying that it is determinate as to type, but that there will ordinarily be some latitude about the manner in which the type is particularized.

In the second place, the "life-world" exhibits various regularities. As far back as we can remember, we have been familiar with the alternation of day and night and with the change of the seasons. Living in the northern hemisphere, we have always known that in July it is hotter than in February and we act accordingly in choosing our clothing. Things, as Husserl expressed it, have their habits of behavior. It is not from science, either Aristotelian or Galilean, that we learn that stones, when lifted and released, fall down. It is a matter of everyday experience in the life-world that water can be boiled and that, when further heated, it evaporates. Generally speaking, the life-world exhibits universal causality of a certain style. Events hang together with each other; occurrences of one type are regularly followed by occurrences of another type. Familiarity with such regularities, that is, with the "style" of the universal causality, is of paramount importance for our existence and the practical conduct of our lives. It, and it alone, permits anticipations. Because of this familiarity, we know fairly well what to be prepared for in the near future; we can often influence the course of affairs to bring something about. As the late Alfred Schutz has shown in his penetrating analyses, all activities within the life-world are dominated throughout by the pragmatic motive. Since causal connections come to our attention originally on account of their pragmatic significance, it is natural that this same significance should determine the degree of accuracy with which these connections will be established and described. That is to say, our familiarity with particular causal connections as well as with the universal style of causality in the life-world is affected by the kind of indefiniteness and vagueness already commented upon, which thus appears to be a general feature of perceptual experience.

Finally, things in the life-world present themselves, as Husserl expresses it, in a certain relativity with respect to the experiencing subjects. All of us perceive the same objects in this room, but each one of us sees them from his own point of observation. The same things appear under a variety of changing aspects. The exigencies of social life make adjustment of these differences absolutely necessary. Some are considered to be irrelevant and are therefore ignored; others are handled by what Schutz calls the "interchangeability of the standpoints", or the "reciprocity of perspectives". Intersubjective agreement is brought about in a number of different ways, into the details of which we have not time to enter. All of us find ourselves living, therefore, in one and the same life-world. The pragmatic motive still retains its predominance here, since it is essentially related to the concrete conditions under which a certain social group exists. Hence the intersubjective life world remains subject to a degree of relativity, no longer, to be sure, with regard to this or that individual, but with respect to the social group in question, however small or large.

Geometry and dualism in Greek thought

Greek philosophy claimed to discover an opposition between the multifarious appearances involved in perpetual change and an immutable realm of existence, forever persisting in strictest self-identity. This latter was called "Being-as-it-is-in-itself", *ontos on*. To this distinction there corresponded one between *epistémé* and *doxa*. *Doxa* covers our beliefs about appearances, and is thus changeable. *Doxa* is necessary (and also sufficient) for the practical conduct of affairs in the realm of appearances. It depends upon the situation in which the subject finds himself, on his interests and plans. The Greek term, '*doxa*', thus conveys something of the relativity and indeterminateness that we have seen to characterize our relation with the life-world. *Epistémé*, on the other hand, is knowledge in the genuine and emphatic sense. Since it is concerned with Being-as-it-is-in-itself, it is free from all relativity with regard to subjects, their standpoints, and the vicissitudes of their lives. Because of the persistent self-identity of this Being, genuine knowledge is perpetually true, under all circumstances and for everyone. Whereas the domain of opinion is that of persuasion and plausibility (i.e., of rhetoric in the classical sense of that term), these qualifications have no place in the domain of *epistémé*, where only cogent argument and conclusive demonstration count. Either a thesis can be fully demonstrated, e.g., by proving that its negation leads to contradictions and absurdities, or it has no right to be advanced at all. If any disagreement appears, it can, at least in principle, be definitely resolved. Otherwise the argument would not have the permanent and universal binding force claimed for it.

These correlated notions of Being-as-it-is-in-itself and *epistémé* are important to us on account of their bearing upon Greek geometry and its consequent philosophical significance. In view of the importance of geometry for Galileo's work we must try to trace its far-off origins in the practices of the life-world. Every society, however primitive, possesses an art of measurement. The degree of accuracy obtainable in measurement will depend, of course, upon the techniques available. Furthermore, like every other activity in the life-world, measuring is dominated by the pragmatic motive. The degree of accuracy desired depends upon the purpose at hand, which is always of a practical nature. This leads to more skillful uses of a particular technique, as well as to the invention of new techniques. All these improvements are made in view of practical purposes; they are carried out within a horizon of practicality or, as Husserl calls it, a horizon of finiteness.

While this is going on, a jump may occur by means of which the power of the pragmatic motive is broken and the horizon of finiteness transcended. Husserl gives the example of a craftsman working on wooden planks, so as to make them planer and smoother. In the course of this, the idea may arise of perfect planeness, of planeness as an ideal of perfection. The notions of straightness, circularity, and the rest can be reached in the same way. But then the corresponding terms gradually come to denote geometrical figures in the strict sense, now understood as ideal entities located at infinity, ideal "limit-poles". Spatial shapes and configurations encountered or deliberately produced in perceptual experience may then be compared with the ideal limit-poles. Naturally, they fall short of the ideal. No perceived spatial shape can ever coincide with the strict geometrical figure with which we may correlate it. Here it is appropriate to speak of *approximation*. We have a series of perceptual spatial configurations and a term totally outside the series, to which they can be said to approximate to a greater or lesser degree. (This is in marked contrast with what we saw of the merely typical determinations of the spatial shapes given in perceptual experience, where no ideal limit-pole is involved.) Not surprisingly, the perceptual configurations are now given the ontological status of imitations. The ideal geometrical figures are conceived as originals, which the perceived entities (in Plato's metaphor) strive unsuccessfully to attain. In a beautiful passage in the *Republic*, Plato compares the relation between outlines drawn in the sand and the geometrical figures of the mathematician, with the relation between shadows thrown on water and the objects throwing the shadows.

Geometrical figures conceived as ideal entities may well pass for beings-in-themselves. Free from every ambiguity, exempt from all change and variation, they persist in self-identity, irrespective of knowing subjects. Whereas measurements in the life-world admit of varying degrees of accuracy, geometrical determinations are made with exactness. Exactness implies the absence both of fluctuation and of any restriction in terms of practical purpose. In Euclid's axiomatization of geometry a small number of fundamental propositions, as well as some elementary methods of construction, were explicitly specified. From them, various properties of plane figures can be cogently demonstrated. Thus an infinity of exact spatial forms are situated relatively to one another by means of a single coherent theory, coherent because deductively developed. Geometry thus perfectly exemplifies the ideal of *epistémé*. Mastery of the methods of geometrical reasoning allows one to reach results that are permanently and universally valid. All relativity with regard to subjects and their situations is overcome.

The Platonism of Galilean physics

Galileo inherited not only geometry as a body of technical knowledge, but also the Platonic interpretation of geometry as embodying the ideal of true knowledge. Here I must touch upon a topic frequently treated elsewhere in these essays, namely the Platonism of Galileo. I was greatly interested in the views of my colleagues on this issue, even though I tended to disagree with them. Following Cassirer, Koyré and Crombie, I still persist in considering Galileo as a "Platonist" and, going even further, I maintain that the whole of modern physics—the "physics of Galilean style" —is of Platonic inspiration. This involves a wider sense of the term 'Platonism' to be sure, but one I think to be preferable. Galileo, it is true, did not espouse the mathematical speculations of the *Timaeus*. Platonism, however, need not necessarily be construed in the narrow sense of endorsing all the doctrines found in the writings of Plato. I will take it to signify the defense of a two-world theory, of a distinction between two realms of unequal ontological status. One domain is assumed to be subordinated to the other and to lead a merely borrowed existence; it has to be explained in terms of the domain of higher order. Galileo's work may be said to mark a turning-point in the historical development of "Platonism" in this sense of the term; it was thoroughly transformed and renewed by him.

Galileo's acceptance of geometry as the model of knowledge is in Husserl's view his fundamental presupposition. One might even speak of a "prejudice", since Galileo makes use of a Platonic conception of genuine knowledge and a corresponding conception of true Being, without attempting in any way to justify them, without apparently even noticing that they required justification. The sort of reflection we made in the last section on the origins of geometrical concepts was very far indeed from Galileo's mind. Once geometry be accepted as the standard of knowledge, it follows that if a science of nature is to be possible at all, it will somehow *have* to be conceived after the model of geometry. Galileo's Platonism appears in the distinction between the perceptual appearance of nature and its true, that is its mathematical, structure. The disclosure of this structure is the task of the new science of physics which proceeds to a thoroughgoing mathematization of nature. Spatio-temporal occurrences must, in consequence, be idealized, that is, referred to exact mathematical relationships. If motion be simply considered as change of spatial position in time, an exhaustive mathematical treatment of mechanics becomes possible, though this will require the redefinition of the concepts of velocity and acceleration. This is necessary because these concepts already had roles in describing the life-world, where, however, they denote quantities only roughly estimated, just as in the case already noted, of spatial configurations. The mathematization of motion leads to the study of the different possible forms of motion, among which uniformly accelerated motion proves to be of special interest. Mathematically expressed hypotheses are developed and tested against observation in order to ascertain which hypothesis applies to a given case, e.g., that of freely falling bodies.

Testing the consequences of such hypotheses against experiential data requires measurement, eventually under laboratory conditions. The accuracy of the measurement once again depends upon the available techniques, with improved techniques yielding results of increasing accuracy. It seems very like the situation we have already seen regarding measurement in the life-world, independently of geometrical idealization. This idealization bestows, however, a radically new sense upon the results of measurement. No longer do the increasingly accurate results obtained by means of improving techniques stand side by side with one another, each fully justified by the practical purpose for which it is intended. By being referred to an ideal limit-pole, the results of measurement come to be interpreted as *approximations*, in the strict sense of forming a sequence which converges toward a true and exact value. Technically speaking, measurement is still carried on under the conditions prevailing in the life-world; its interpretation, however, is placed—as Husserl puts it—under a "horizon of infinity".

For this reason, the perfectibility of measuring techniques now begins to acquire the overtone of an *unlimited* perfectibility. We have already seen that the art of measurement in the life-world prepared the way for geometrical idealization. Now the relationship is in a sense reversed. Geometrical (and more generally, mathematical) idealization comes to inspire the application of measuring techniques, in that the idea of mathematical exactness yields incentives not only for the obtaining of increasingly closer approximations, but also for the contrivance of "better" techniques. Mathematical idealization thus provides a built-in method for improving upon itself, as it were, without direct reference to any practical purposes, hence with the sense of a possibly unlimited, i.e., an infinite, progress.

Thus far the idealization and mathematization of only the spatial and temporal aspects of the life-world have been considered. Things encountered in perceptual experience exhibit, in addition to these aspects, qualitative properties—color, temperature, and so forth—which fill the spatial forms. These properties do not lend themselves to quantification. A certain red may be said to be "brighter" than another, but it is not possible to go beyond rough estimates of this sort and to ask "how much brighter?", expecting an answer in numerical terms. There is only one geometry, and it is related to space, not to qualities. This becomes clear if one notes that any spatial shape can be conceived as a limited portion of the one, unique, all-encompassing space, whereas there is no universal qualitative form into which all qualitative configurations might be inserted in an analogous manner. Hence if a mathematization of qualities is possible at all, it can, at best, only be contrived in an indirect way. It is to this indirect mathematization that we must now turn. Husserl associates it too with Galileo, though it would be historically more correct to mention Descartes and, especially, Huygens. As we have already seen, Galileo's name is for Husserl a symbol.

Indirect mathematization of the qualities requires that they be correlated with occurrences which, because they are describable in spatiotemporal terms, are capable of direct mathematization. Take, for instance, the Pythagorean discovery of the dependence of the pitch of a musical note upon the length of the vibrating cord. This dependence by itself does not warrant the conclusion that the note heard is a mere subjective datum and that all that exists in reality are the vibrations of the cord. Rather we have here the regular correlation of one occurrence with a different one, an instance of the "universal causality" found in the life-world. As far as our experience of that causality goes, events of one kind are known to depend upon events of a different kind; changes in one respect are accompanied by changes in other respects. This, however, gives us no reason to assume that qualitative phenomena are causally dependent upon spatiotemporal occurrences in some simple unilateral way.

But this is just what *has* been assumed as physics has continued to progress. It has become more or less taken for granted that qualitative phenomena are produced by processes that interact with our sense-organs and are definable in spatio-temporal terms exclusively. Qualitative phenomena and their changes are thought both to reveal and to conceal the true state of affairs. They reveal it, because as effects of quantitative processes, they point to these processes, and can be read as their symptoms, at least by the physicist who has learned to decipher the language. They conceal the true state of affairs (so it is said) because of the utter heterogeneity between the symptom itself and that of which it is a symptom. Nature as it *really* is (by contrast with its perceptual appearance) is mathematical structure, perhaps a plurality of such structures, and it matters but little whether the structures are comparatively simple, as in the early phases of modern science, or extremely complex and abstract, as in contemporary physics.

Mathematics and Nature

What logical status should be assigned to the thesis that nature is mathematical throughout? Obviously, it is not a formulation of empirical findings, nor is it arrived at by generalization from experience. On account of its generality, it cannot pass for a law of nature; in fact, every determinate law of nature is one of its particular specifications. Because of its generality, it cannot be considered as an hypothesis in the usual sense. If, as Husserl does, one calls it an "hypothesis", one must, following him, underline its peculiar nature. One might speak of it as the "hypothesis underlying hypotheses", as a "regulative idea" in the sense of Kant, as a methodological norm which directs the formulation of scientific hypotheses and guides all scientific activities, theoretical and experimental alike. An "hypothesis" of this kind cannot be defended by direct argument, but can only be substantiated by the continuing success of the methodological norm itself. And this means on-going, never-ending work. The thesis that nature is mathematical throughout can be confirmed only by the entire historical process of the development of science, a steady process in which nature comes to be mathematized progressively. No matter how far the process has advanced, that is, no matter what confirmation the thesis has already received, it still remains an hypothesis in the sense of being in need of further substantiation. The distinction between nature as it is conceived by science at a moment of its history, and nature as it actually is in scientific truth must never be overlooked. This last phrase does not denote a concealed reality lying behind the appearances in the life-world and waiting to be discovered, but rather a goal to be reached, or more correctly, to be approximated to asymptotically.

Instead of stating that nature is mathematical, it is more appropriate to say that nature lends itself to mathematization. This is not just a matter of words. The latter formulation brings out the point that mathematization does not necessarily mean the disclosure of a pre-given, though yet hidden, reality. On the contrary, it suggests an accomplishment yet to be achieved, a universe yet to be constructed. Science takes on this task and, under the guidance of its own methodological norms, constructs its universe by means of a complex continuing process of idealization and mathematization. The resulting universe is the product of a methodological procedure, a "tissue of ideas" (*Ideenkleid*), which must never be mistaken for reality itself. Reality is, and always remains, the life-world, no matter how vast the possibilities of systematization and prediction that have been opened up by the development of science of the Galilean style.

This science is certainly one of the greatest accomplishments of the human mind. Coming from Husserl's pen, this phrase is no pious declamation, but rather suggests a problem for future research. It is at this point that the analysis of Galilean physics flows into the mainstream of phenomenology. As a product of the mind, science of the Galilean style requires phenomenological clarification. Because of the role of the life-world as the presupposition of scientific construction, the problems which (if one is to be systematic) have to be attacked first, are those related to the life-world itself and the experience through which it presents itself, i.e., perceptual experience. Subsequently, a phenomenological account must be given of the higher intellectual processes which, like idealization, formalization, and so on, are basic to the construction of pure mathematics and the mathematization of nature.

I hope you will forgive me for not going beyond these sketchy hints for a phenomenological philosophy of science. And you must forgive me also for saying, in conclusion, that notwithstanding the voluminous recent literature on the philosophy of science (whose value I do not in the least belittle), we do not yet possess a philosophy of science in a truly radical sense. Husserl's analysis of Galileo's physics indicates the direction in which a "radical" (i.e. a properly rooted) philosophy of science must develop. Ten years after the appearance of Husserl's work, I can just begin to see something of its outlines. As always in the case of Husserl's writings, at the end of work accomplished, more work is looming on the horizon. The work will be long and hard but—I am convinced—most rewarding.

NOTES

1. It was edited in 1954 by Walter Biemel of the Husserl Archives, and appears as volume 6 of the *Husserliana* series.
2. In the little-known and long-extinct periodical, *Philosophia* (Belgrade), *1*, 1936.

Part V

Postscript

20 ❋ Galileo's influence on seventeenth-century English scientists

MARIE BOAS HALL

Until lately, scientists have been far more negligent than literary men in naming their sources, and the task of tracing scientific influence is made even more difficult for the historian by the fact that scientists (inevitably) read more science than their literary contemporaries do. It is decidedly easier to trace the influence of a particular scientific discovery upon poets than upon scientists; for the limited scientific knowledge—and interest— of poets makes every reference gleam brightly, conspicuous for the historian. Besides, there are no layers of influence among poets: either a Milton has heard of a Galileo and his discoveries or he has not. But a scientist may know of and even mention a scientist's work without being influenced by it, and, conversely, he may be profoundly influenced by a scientist whose work he mentions but rarely.

In the case of Galileo there is a further complication. By and large the poet's imagination was caught by Galileo, the searcher of the heavens, the astronomical genius whose telescope discovered things unimaginable in the heavens. These discoveries were both spectacular and comprehensible to the layman. They were, paradoxically, of lesser importance to scientists in some respects: though all telescopic astronomy stems ultimately from

Galileo's work of 1609 and 1610, yet astronomers were not wholly converted to the telescope until the end of the seventeenth century (Hevelius,
for example, refused to use telescopic sights), and there was little important advance over the discoveries contained in the *Sidereal messenger* for
some thirty years. And observational astronomers perhaps apart, scientists
generally found the *Sidereal messenger* the least profound of Galileo's
works though the most obviously novel; their warmest praise was re-
served for the *Dialogo,* the *Discorsi* and *Le meccaniche.*

Translations

Mention of this last may well cause surprise, even to readers who have
spent much time in the study of Galileo; for is it not a very minor work?
Among even scholarly readers of the *Dialogo* or the *Discorsi* how many
ever looked at *Le meccaniche* before Mr. Drake's admirable translation
appeared in 1960? [1] And even since then, how many have read *Le meccaniche* as carefully as they have the associated translation of *De motu?*
Yet *Le meccaniche* was widely read in the seventeenth century, circulat-
ing probably in three forms: in Italian manuscript (comprehensible to
few among English scientists); in Mersenne's French translation (published at Paris in 1634); and in an unpublished English translation hastily,
as the inscription proclaims, done from the Italian by Robert Payne in
1636.[2] This translation is headed: "A Tract by Sigr. Galileo Galilei,
Florentine. Of the Profit wch is drawn from the Art Mechanique & it's
Instruments". It was made for Payne's patrons, William Cavendish, Earl
of Newcastle, and his brother, Sir Charles Cavendish; the latter endorsed
the manuscript with Payne's name and the date. The text itself is probably
in the hand of Hobbes, who returned to England from a journey to Italy
and France in the fall of 1636; perhaps he brought an Italian manuscript
with him.[3] Payne is a mysterious figure, evidently a linguist, certainly
skilled in optics, a clergyman with a living from which he was usually
absent, and a dependent of the Earl of Newcastle.[4] But he appears only
during the early and middle 1630's, and then vanishes as mysteriously as he
appeared. It is not clear whether anyone outside the Cavendish circle
knew of Payne's translation, but as it is unlikely that the mathematician,
John Wallis, read Italian there is an intriguing possibility that the manuscript copy of the *Mechanics* he possessed in 1666 was Payne's translation.
It is worth noting that John Collins, whose queries elicited Wallis' mention of the manuscript, was familiar with the work.[5]

One cannot but wonder whether Hobbes's great interest in Galileo did
not stem from the Cavendish brothers. The earliest reference to Galileo in
their correspondence is to be found in a letter from Hobbes to the Earl of
Newcastle of January 26, 1633/4; Hobbes had just accompanied "My
Lady and her family" to London. He wrote:

> My first business in London, was to seeke for Galileo's *Dialogues;* I thought it
> a very good bargain, when at my taking leave of your Lordship I undertooke

to buy it for you, but if your Lordship should bind me to performance it would be bad enough, for it is not possible to get it for money. There were but few brought over at first, and they that buy such books are not such men as to part with them againe . . . I doubt not but the translation of it here will be publiquely embraced, and therefore wish extremely that Dr. Webbe would hasten it.[6]

The reference to a translation, potentially so welcome to lovers of science, is puzzling. Did Hobbes mean to imply that Webbe had begun such a translation? If so, what copy was he using? Had this Webbe (whoever he was) any connection with the Cavendishes? If there were truly no copies to be had, it is unlikely that Webbe was then in fact engaged in translation. It is tempting to guess that the copy of the *Dialogo* that Hobbes failed to secure in London was to be used at Welbeck for making a translation. If so, perhaps he had sent a copy back from Italy for this purpose, though whether Payne, Webbe or some other was to be the translator cannot be determined. Possibly that English translation of the *Dialogo* beautifully and lavishly bound, carefully translated, dating from about 1635 and now preserved in the British Museum [7] was made for the Cavendishes. (This assignment of date is partly based on the argument that it is unlikely that an English translation would be undertaken immediately after the appearance of the Latin translation of 1635.) That the translator had some connection with the Cavendish circle, and that its date is really 1635 is the conclusion best supported by Galileo's own statement (in a letter dated December 1, 1635) that Hobbes had visited him a few days previously and had told him that the *Dialogo* had been translated into English.[8] But the facts are too shadowy to permit further concrete speculation.

Once the *Dialogo* had been published in Latin, it was completely accessible to English scientists; they did not need to wait for Salusbury's English translation, warmly though they welcomed it when it appeared. The *Dialogo* was received with immense respect, and had the effect of introducing not only Galileo's discoveries and cosmological views, but also his theory of the tides,[9] often discussed, and, most important, his discoveries about falling bodies, projectile motion, and much else. Witness, for example, William Gascoigne, who in 1640 spoke of the:

> choicest foreign wits within these thirty years as Galileus, Scheiner, Kepler, Hortensius, and Monsieur des Cartes who have so diligently pried into perspectives, that it may credibly be thought, that their rarest use is already known.[10]

But these, as he charmingly explained, had "stumbled at" what he had "stumbled on", namely his method of measuring the angular distances between stars. Gascoigne had read the *Discorsi* (which he calls "*mecan*"), for in another letter he cited from thence Galileo's figures for the specific gravity of air in relation to water.[11] Presumably therefore he read Italian, unless indeed he had read Mersenne's French version, *Les nouvelles pensées de Galilée*, published in 1639. That Gascoigne had studied the *Dialogo* attentively is indicated by a reference in the same letter to a work he called "*Syst. Mund.*" for Galileo's discussion of refraction and parallax.

Hobbes and Digby

It is hardly surprising that among the earliest Englishmen to deal with the material of the *Dialogo* and the *Discorsi* in great detail were those who had traveled abroad and had moved in Mersenne's circle in Paris. Hobbes, obviously, was already predisposed to an interest in Galileo, and probably was able to read the original Italian. He was also stimulated by the work of many Continental writers who concerned themselves with problems raised by Galileo: for example, by such diverse figures as Mersenne (who eagerly accepted Galileo's new scientific and philosophic ideas) and Thomas White, an English Catholic who meditated long on the *Dialogo* before writing an Aristotelian and orthodox reply.[12] Hobbes had no doubt of the importance of Galileo's work on motion; indeed in the "Epistle dedicatory" to *De corpore*, dated April 23, 1655, he named Galileo as "the first that opened to us the gate of natural philosophy universal, which is the knowledge of the nature of *motion*",[13] and when he came in Part IV to discuss such things, he cited Galileo's "*Dialogues of motion*" (i.e., the *Discorsi*) for the law of falling bodies. No doubt it was this view which led him to lay such stress on motion when he came to consider human sensation, human psychology and human passions, as he did in *Leviathan*. Whether he had read the famous passage on primary and secondary qualities in the *Saggiatore* or no, his discussions read as if he had—as indeed his appreciation of the fundamental position of the concept of *motion* in philosophy necessitated.

Kenelm Digby is another example of the Englishman abroad who was intimately aware of the work of Galileo, and appreciated the great importance of the science of motion. Again, it is difficult to judge whether Digby discovered Galileo for himself, or was led to his works through the writings of Mersenne, Thomas White and Descartes. Certainly the *Two treatises* of 1644 are filled with references to both the *Discorsi* and the *Dialogo*, as Mr. Drake has shown. Even though Digby only partially accepted Galileo's views on motion, he set them out in some detail, and the *Two treatises* must have been a useful source for those who did not read Italian. That such sources were of interest at least until a Latin version was available is suggested by a letter from Henry Oldenburg, then in Paris, in the spring of 1659: he wrote to Boyle enthusiastically about Honoré Fabri's *Tractatus physicus de motu locali* (first published in 1646 and being discussed in scientific circles in Paris in 1659), in which the third book dealt "wth Galilaei his demonstration" of the law of falling bodies.[14] As Fabri's book was certainly well known in Paris, it provided a further (Latin) source for knowledge of Galileo.

The Royal Society

Gascoigne, a royalist, died in his early thirties at the battle of Marston Moor in 1644; his more pacific and parliamentary contemporaries, many of them (like him) associated with the mathematician William Oughtred, were equally interested in the work of Galileo. Mr. Drake has already ably discussed the influence of the Galilean astronomy upon John Wilkins. Now Wilkins was one of the prime movers of that group of later eminent English scientists who "about the year 1645" began to meet weekly at Gresham College to discuss "particularly . . . what hath been called the 'New Philosophy' or Experimental Philosophy".[15] Among the topics for discussion (as John Wallis later remembered them) were:

> the Copernican hypothesis, the nature of comets and new stars, the satellites of Jupiter, the oval shape (as it then appeared) of Saturn, the spots in the sun, and its turning on its own axis, the inequalities and selenography of the Moon, the several phases of Venus and Mercury, the improvement of telescopes, and grinding of glasses for that purpose, the weight of air, the possibility, or impossibility of vacuities, and nature's abhorrence thereof, the Torricellian experiment in quicksilver, the descent of heavy bodies, and the degrees of acceleration therein.

Galileo's own Italian pupils could not have followed the work of their master any more faithfully. And that this Galilean influence was one of which its proponents were well aware is indicated by Wallis' further designation of these scientific problems as being:

> some . . . then but new discoveries, and others not so generally known and imbraced, as now they are, with other things appertaining to what hath been called the "New Philosophy", which from the times of Galileo at Florence, and Sir Francis Bacon (Lord Verulam) in England, hath been much cultivated in Italy, France, Germany, and other parts abroad, as well as with us in England.

And as it was these men who promoted and kept alive the spirit of this new philosophy during the Commonwealth years, in London and Oxford, until it could culminate in the foundation of the Royal Society, their Galilean bent is of great importance. It is significant that by no means all of these young scientists were mathematicians and astronomers: the spirit and content of Galileo's work was spread among medical men as well. And when the chemist Robert Boyle joined the group at Oxford about 1653 he proved to be also well versed in Galilean matters. Educated abroad, he had actually been in Florence at the time of Galileo's death and there he read in Italian what he called "the new paradoxes of the great stargazer Galileo, whose ingenious books, perhaps because they could not be so otherwise, were confuted by a decree from Rome".[16] Boyle was also a constant reader of Mersenne, and, fluent in French, unlike most of his English contemporaries, made many references to Mersenne's *Nouvelles pensées*, particularly in regard to specific gravities,[17] though he may well have referred to the First Day of the *Discorsi* in Italian or (later) Latin. Boyle was also keenly appreciative of Galileo's telescopic discoveries and well aware of the importance of Galileo's study of motion.

Indeed, the Royal Society was throughout its early years much devoted to the study of motion, as well as to other Galilean matters. At the meeting of September 10, 1662, "Mersennus's account of the tenacity of cylindrical bodies was read by Mr. Croune, to whom the prosecution of that matter by consulting Galileo was referred, when the translation of that Italian treatise, wherein Galileo treats of that subject, shall be printed." [18] Evidently Mersenne's version of the *Discorsi* (the *Nouvelles pensées*) was not taken to represent Galileo accurately enough, and evidently, too, Salusbury's second tome was awaited impatiently by the Royal Society. Soon after this began a series of experiments on falling bodies, in which Hooke, the Curator of the Society, and Brouncker, its President, were especially concerned. Hooke devised an instrument for measuring the force of impact of falling bodies which was discussed at the meeting of February 18, 1662/3,[19] but though the intention of pursuing such experiments was expressed, nothing was done for a year and a half, when the whole question was raised again. This time Hooke and several other members of the Society ("Sir Robert Moray, Dr. Wilkins, Dr. Goddard, Mr. Palmer, Mr. Hill and Mr. Hooke", as Oldenburg reported to Boyle on September 1) tried an experiment with a 200-foot pendulum from the top of old St. Paul's.[20] During September, experiments of weighing bodies at the foot and on top of St. Paul's were tried.[21] No more experiments of this kind were attempted in that year, and soon plague and fire rendered such experiments impossible. The whole matter was, rather curiously, brought up again on April 4, 1678, when Hooke cited the data from these experiments made fourteen years earlier, and some of them were repeated from the Monument by Hooke and others; this was specifically referred to as an extension and confirmation of Galileo's work.[22]

Wallis

Meanwhile, other Galilean interests were occupying John Wallis. He had for some time been interested in the problem of tides and on April 25, 1666, he wrote an account, in the form of a letter to Boyle, for publication in the *Philosophical Transactions*.[23] Wallis showed himself here thoroughly familiar with Galileo's discussion of the problem in the *Dialogo;* but perhaps more significant is the importance he attached to following what he took to be Galileo's scientific method. So he wrote:

> since that *Galilaeo*, and (after him) *Torricellio*, and others, have applied *Mechanick* Principles to the solving of *Philosophical* Difficulties; *Natural Philosophy* is well known to have been rendered more intelligible, and to have made a much greater progress in less than an hundred years, than before for many ages.

Wallis continued his interest in the tides, elaborating his hypothesis and gathering data from all over England; although he fiercely combated all who disagreed with his hypothesis, he never ceased to praise Galileo for suggesting the importance of the Earth's motion for the production of tides, though Wallis, unlike Galileo, took into account the Moon's influence as well.[24]

Even before he published his speculations upon tides, Wallis had been concerned with problems of motion. This interest was acute in 1668 and 1669 when Wallis, Huygens and Wren all published on the subject, stimulated by Oldenburg's sending them copies of William Neile's hypothesis of motion. For Oldenburg reckoned it to be part of the Secretary's job to urge Fellows of the Society to publication and public debate, which could only be done by communicating one man's work to another and his in turn to a third, until finally the protagonists might be willing to publish in *Phil. Trans.* As early as March 1666/7, Oldenburg had sent Wallis a copy of Neile's hypothesis, without telling him whose it was. Wallis dismissed it at this stage somewhat cavalierly. He wrote:

> The Hypothesis in Philosophy, wch you were pleased to send, . . . is, as to many parts of it, rationall inough; though I will not promise to comply with it in all. The main thing in it; That a Body at Rest, will so continue till some positive cause put it in motion; And, a Body in Motion, will continue in motion, & with ye same celerity, and the same way, till some positive cause do either stop or alter it: I take to bee very true. And I think I have sufficiently demonstrated it from its proper cause; in some papers of myne which Mr Boyle was pleased to have transcribed for him some years ago. I think it is, a notion taken for granted by Galilaeo, Toricellio, & others of later times; but I do not know that any of them have gone about to prove it: but rather (as ye proposer of what you now send) take it for a Postulate.[25]

Wallis finally developed his laws and hypotheses into *Mechanica, sive de Motu Tractatus Geometrius* (London, 1670), which is conveniently summarized in the *Philosophical Transactions* for December 13, 1669;[26] from consideration of the laws of motion and of falling bodies, he proceeded to the principles of statics and simple machines. Although Galileo's name does not appear frequently, there can be no doubt of his influence. Perhaps, indeed, Wallis is the source for Newton's belief that Galileo thoroughly understood the law of inertia.

Newton

Newton, of course, read others besides Wallis who admired Galileo. His principal instructor in the mathematical sciences when he was an undergraduate was Isaac Barrow, first Lucasian Professor in mathematics at Cambridge. In his prefatory Oration of 1664 Barrow cited Galileo (together with Gassendi, Gilbert, Mersenne and Descartes) as among "those Moderns resembling and nearly equalling the Ancients in Sagacity" who "were famous for having extended the Circuits of Natural Science beyond its ancient Bounds".[27] Barrow's mathematical lectures range over the whole of mathematics, especially its more philosophical aspects, thus including such topics as "of the Nature of First Principles". He revealed throughout a knowledge of Galileo's work (though he did not always accept his conclusions) and had evidently read the *Discorsi* as well as the *Dialogo*.

Very possibly it was Barrow who directed Newton's attention to the *Dialogo*, which he seems to have read in Salusbury's translation. There are at least two revealing references from Newton's early years. One is the citation of Galileo's value for the apparent diameter of stars of the first and sixth magnitudes, to be found in discussion of the Third Day; this reference dates from 1665 or 1666.[28] And in some calculations of 1666, Newton again used Galilean data, this time on falling bodies, contained in the Second Day.[29] Newton thus early discovered in Galileo's work a source of information; more important, even, was that he found a source of inspiration. It cannot have been only because he opposed Descartes that in the *Principia* he ascribed his own first two laws to Galileo rather than to Descartes (though Descartes understood inertia better than Galileo did); it was perhaps rather because his admiration of Galileo convinced him that Galileo *must* have used these laws in discovering the law of free fall.[30] It is indeed singularly appropriate that Newton should have derived so much from Galileo and felt so warmly towards his predecessor, whose work he did so much to complete. And it is no accident that Newton, coming fresh to the scientific scene in the mid-1660's, should have taken so avidly to the study of Galileo's work. For Salusbury by his translations and the Fellows of the Royal Society by their interest in the laws of motion had created, just over a hundred years after Galileo's birth and just over twenty since his death, a scientific atmosphere which recognized Galileo as one of the supreme exponents of the New Philosophy.

I have here discussed only the first three quarters of the century; needless to say, I do not mean to imply that Galileo's influence ceased to be important in the last quarter. But Galileo's creative stimulus to English science necessarily diminished as his magisterial eminence increased; by 1687 he was already assuming the position of the great man of the past whose contributions to modern science were known with certainty. For all who read the *Principia*, Galileo was firmly placed as a prime originator of modern mechanics.

NOTES

1. Galileo, *On motion* and *On mechanics*, 1960*.
2. British Museum, Harleian MS. 6796, no. 28, ff. 317–339. The preceding number (also translated by Payne but in the previous year) is Castelli's treatise on rivers.

3. See Jean Jacquot, "Sir Charles Cavendish and his learned friends", *Annals of science, 8*, 1952, 13–27, and "The manuscripts of His Grace the Duke of Portland, preserved at Welbeck Abbey", *Historical Manuscripts Commission*, vol. 2, p. 129.

4. See the letters exchanged between Walter Warner, Payne and Cavendish in the years 1634–1636, printed in J. O. Halliwell, *A Collection of letters illustrative of the progress of science in England*, London, 1841, pp. 65–69, printed from British Museum Birch MSS. 4279, 4444 and 4458, and the letters from Hobbes to Newcastle in H.M.C. Portland MSS., vol. 2, pp. 124–130. A letter from Payne to Newcastle, March 22, 1631/2, summarized in the Portland volume, p. 122, shows that his living was in Gloucestershire.

5. See S. J. Rigaud, *Correspondence of scientific men of the seventeenth century* (Oxford, 1841), vol. 2, pp. 463, 466 for Collins' letter to Wallis of August 1, 1666, and Wallis' reply of August 7.

6. H.M.C. Portland MSS., vol. 2, p. 124.

7. Harleian MS. 6320.

8. *Opere, 17*, p. 355.

9. Some MS. copies of Galileo's preliminary work "On the flux and reflux of the sea" many have reached England earlier. Thus Bacon knew of Galileo's theory of the tides when he wrote *Novum organum* (see Book 2, Aphorism 46), but possibly only by report through his friend Tobie Matthew, then in Italy.

10. Rigaud, vol. 1, p. 33, Gascoigne to Oughtred, December 2, 1640.

11. Rigaud, vol. 1, pp. 37 and 48, respectively, the same to the same, undated; Rigaud assigned it to February, 1641. Gascoigne's reference to the *Dialogo* is to a passage in the Third Day, pp. 315–317 in Drake's translation; that to the *Discorsi* is at p. 124 of that volume of the *Opere*.

12. Jacquot in an article in *Notes and records of the Royal Society (9*, 1952, 188–195), has extensively discussed an early version of *De corpore*, written before 1645, and its connection with Thomas White's *De mundo dialogi tres . . .* , 1642. Mersenne and Hobbes were on the friendliest intellectual terms, and Mersenne published Hobbes' *Tractatus opticus* in 1644 as part of *Cogitata physico mathematica*.

13. *The English works of Thomas Hobbes*, ed. by William Molesworth, London, 1839, vol. 1, p. viii.; see further, p. 514.

14. Letter of April 11, 1659; see T. Birch, *The life and works of the Honourable Robert Boyle*, London, 1772, vol. 6, p. 144.

15. Our knowledge of these events, and what was there discussed, depends on two accounts by John Wallis, one in the pamphlets: *A defence of the Royal Society, and answer to the cavils of Dr. William Holder* of 1678, the other from Wallis' brief autobiography published first in the Preface to Thomas Hearne's edition of Peter Langstoft's *Chronicle*, which was written in 1696–1697. They are in substantial agreement. The relevant passages are conveniently available in vol. 1 of C. R. Weld, *A history of the Royal Society*, London, 1848, pp. 36–37 and 30–33, respectively, from which I have quoted here.

16. "An account of Philaretus during his minority", written soon after Boyle's return to England in 1645. Printed in Birch, *Life of Boyle*, prefixed to vol. 1 of Boyle's *Works*.

17. Most of Boyle's references, whether to specific gravity (e.g., Birch, *Boyle*, vol. 1, p. 83) or to falling bodies and projectiles (e.g, vol. 3, pp. 428, 431) are cited in conjunction with references to Mersenne. Besides the *Nouvelles pensées*, Boyle used Mersenne's *Harmonie universelle*, though it is not clear in what version.

18. Thomas Birch, *History of the Royal Society*, London, 1756, vol. 1, p. 109.

19. *Ibid.*, pp. 195–197; reprinted in R. T. Gunther, *Early science in Oxford*, 1930, vol. 6, pp. 107–110.

20. Birch, *History*, vol. 1, pp. 460, 461 and 464 (August 17, August 24, and August 31, 1664); reproduced in Gunther, pp. 187–192.

21. Birch, *History*, under September 14, 21 and 28; on the last occasions Boyle offered some comments.

22. *Ibid.*, April 4, April 18, and May 30, 1678; reproduced in Gunther, vol. 7, 482, 484, 487–488. Hooke had bought "Galileo's dialogues of motion" on May 29, 1673.

23. *Phil. Trans.*, 2, no. 16 (August 6, 1666), 264–289, including the Appendix containing answers to criticism. The passage quoted below is from p. 264.

24. See, for example, Wallis' letter to Oldenburg of June 8, 1666, in Royal Society MS. W 1, no. 24.

25. Wallis to Oldenburg, March 21, 1666/7, in Royal Society MS. W 1, no. 32. Wallis' brief account of the "laws of motion" was published in *Phil. Trans.*, 3, no. 43 (January 11, 1668/9), 864–866; Wren's is in the same volume, 867–868; and Huygens' in 4, no. 46, 925–928.

26. *Op. cit.*, 4, no. 54, 1086–1089.

27. Isaac Barrow, *Mathematical lectures*, transl. by John Kirkby, London, 1734, p. *xxvii*.

28. This is Cambridge University Library MS., Add. 3996 (f), f.51. It is followed by a note on Auzout's estimate from *Phil. Trans.*, 1, no. 4 (June 4, 1665), 63. Galileo's data are given on p. 359 in Drake's translation.

29. MS., Add. 3958 (2), printed in *Correspondence of Isaac Newton*, ed. by H. Turnbull, Cambridge, 1963, vol. 3, pp. 45–50; the source was noticed by the editor.

30. Scholium to "Axioms, or laws of motion", *Principia*, ed. by F. Cajori, Berkeley (Calif.), 1934, p. 21.

21 ❋ Galileo in English literature of the seventeenth century

STILLMAN DRAKE

Several years ago Professor Marjorie Nicolson discussed vividly the literary impact of the telescope, of Galileo's first astronomical observations, and of the new cosmogony that rapidly gained acceptance after those events.[1] It is not my intention to describe the purely literary effect of Galileo's work in seventeenth-century England, when that has been set forth so admirably by Professor Nicolson and elaborated by others. Rather, I wish to show that seventeenth-century English literature, giving that term a rather liberal interpretation, provides evidence that the English public was more responsive to the discoveries and opinions of Galileo during that period than is generally realized. In my exposition, I shall exclude from the domain of English literature only those works which are of a technical-scientific nature. I shall include, however, in addition to books which belong to literature in the ordinary sense of the word, others of a philosophical, didactic, controversial or popular-scientific character which were written by Englishmen, whether published in England or abroad. And having stretched the concept of English literature that far, I shall go farther and include some books written in Latin by Englishmen for the purpose of expounding, defending, or criticizing the views of Galileo.

The Carli-Favaro bibliography of Galileana lists 390 items published in the seventeenth century. The great majority of these were of course printed in Italy. England's representation is numerically meager, at least in comparison with that of France or Germany. Yet it is my considered opinion that, far from his having been neglected by English authors of his time and throughout the balance of the seventeenth century, Galileo was on the whole more favorably received, and his ideas more widely expounded and circulated, by Englishmen than by men of any other nation outside Italy. Two facts contribute to the misleading impression of a relative neglect of Galileo in England that one might form after a quick perusal of the Carli-Favaro bibliography. The first is that a number of important English works dealing with Galileo remained unnoticed by his Italian bibliographers, and the second is that a large proportion of the French and German works listed by them were written in opposition to the ideas of Galileo, whereas nearly all the British writers of the period who dealt with the subject spoke in their favor.

You may be interested in some very rough statistics concerning Galilean publication in the seventeenth century, classifying these by place of publication and by attitude toward Galileo and his ideas. These were compiled using the Carli-Favaro bibliography as a basis, with additions to the English section from my own notes. Of 405 books included, 234 were Italian, 56 French, 43 German, 22 English, and 50 from other places of publication. Of the same group, 160 were generally favorable to Galileo or his ideas, 114 unfavorable, and 131 neutral; in the neutral category were included Galileo's own works or translations of them, biographical works, compilations of letters, and the like. France, which contributed the largest number of books printed outside Italy, was the only country in which books falling in the unfavorable category outnumbered those in the favorable; while England, though it contributed the fewest books, was the only country in which the favorable category outnumbered the total of the other two. The proportion of favorable books was almost precisely 40 percent in Italy, in Germany, and in the miscellaneous countries, whereas it ran under 30 percent in France and over 60 percent in England. These figures are admittedly highly subjective, depending on my own judgment as to classification and including as they do some duplications of titles because of reprintings, while doubtless omitting many books that have thus far escaped census.

I shall now proceed to mention in chronological order all the works (other than purely scientific ones) known to me which were published by Englishmen in the seventeenth century in which Galileo is named or his ideas are discussed, and to say something about each of these and its author. I do not pretend that this listing will be complete, but it represents a substantial advance over that of the Carli-Favaro bibliography with respect to English books. It seems to me fitting that we should also recall and honor those men, some of them famous and some whose names have been long forgotten, who put England in the early ranks of Galileo's ultramontane supporters.

The very broad concept of English literature which I have adopted enables us to begin with 1610, the very year in which Galileo first made known to the world his revolutionary astronomical observations made with the telescope. The *Starry messenger*, published at Venice in March of that year, became at once the object of attacks by other astronomers and philosophers, in which the observed phenomena were questioned, the telescope was denounced as a fraud, and Galileo was derided. He did not attempt to answer these attacks in print, though he commented on them and defended his discoveries and his views in personal letters. By the same means he disclosed additional telescopic discoveries with which he had been occupying the time he might have devoted to the writing of polemics. Other men, however, sprang to his defense. The first attack to be published was licensed on June 18, 1610, scarcely three months after the *Starry messenger* appeared and about the time Galileo left Padua for Florence. It was called *A brief excursion against the Starry messenger*,[2] and was written by Martin Horky, a Bohemian protégé of Galileo's rival Giovanni Antonio Magini, professor of astronomy at Bologna. The first of two replies to Horky's attack was published at Padua in November 1610, and was entitled *Confutation of four problems proposed by Martin Horky in his Disputation against the Starry messenger*.[3] The author was John Wedderburn, a Scottish student at Padua and friend of Galileo's. (I trust that the inclusion of the Scottish, even at this period of British history, does not put too great an additional strain on the concept of English literature.) Wedderburn's book was dedicated to Sir Henry Wotton, then British ambassador to the Venetian government, and one of the first men to communicate news of Galileo's discoveries to England by letter. It was a witty and effective refutation of Horky. I shall mention one example of its sprightly style. Horky had argued against the existence of Jupiter's satellites by saying, among other things, that since astrologers had already taken into account everything in the heavens that could have any influence on the earth and on mankind, and they did not reckon with these stars, the satellites had no purpose. And since nature does nothing in vain, these pointless planets could not exist. But they did have a purpose, retorted Wedderburn; it was to torment Horky, confuse the astrologers, and alarm the superstitious. Wedderburn's book, besides being amusing, is significant in the history of science because it mentions some observations that had been made at Padua of insects and other small objects as magnified by the telescope. This was a full fourteen years before the time at which Galileo is known to have modified his lens-system to perfect a usable compound microscope.

John Wedderburn was born at Dundee in 1583; his younger brother, James, was tutor to the children of Isaac Casaubon. John is mentioned by William Lithgow, a celebrated traveler, as having befriended him and taught him Italian at Padua in 1609, from which fact it may be presumed that Wedderburn had already been in Italy for some time. In August 1609, he was elected Counsellor to the Scottish "Nation" at the University of Padua. It is likely that he received a medical degree there, as he was practicing medicine in Moravia in 1628.[4] Little more is known of him except that he revisited Scotland occasionally, the last time being in 1637, when he founded a school there. He died before 1651, and it is reported by Antonio Favaro that a Moravian family still bearing his name in slightly modified form are his descendants.

Another Scot, Thomas Seggeth, who was born at Edinburgh around 1580, had gone to Padua in 1597 after studying at Louvain under Justus Lipsius. He became acquainted with Galileo, since both moved in the illustrious circle of Italian and foreign scholars and literati who frequented the home of Giovanni Vincenzio Pinelli. Seggeth ran afoul of the Venetian authorities in 1603, served a prison term, and was banished from the Venetian state for twenty years, despite a plea by Sir Henry Wotton on his behalf. At the time of publication of the *Starry messenger*, Seggeth was at Prague, where he was a friend of Kepler's. To the *Narration of observations of Jupiter's four satellites*, published at Frankfort in 1611, in which Kepler confirmed Galileo's discoveries, there was added a set of epigrams in honor of Galileo composed by Seggeth. One of those epigrams included the punning use of the famous expression, '*vicisti Galilaee*', which has often been mistakenly attributed to Kepler by reason of the place of its first appearance. Seggeth and Kepler made some observations of Jupiter's satellites together, and when Kepler cited him as a witness, he called him a man noted for his books, which however were chiefly poetical and did not concern science. It was Seggeth who first put into Kepler's hands a copy of the *Starry messenger*, sent by Galileo for that purpose to the Tuscan ambassador at Prague. Kepler in his acknowledgment of this fact, in the preface to his *Conversation with the Starry messenger* (1611), spoke of Seggeth as a man of wide erudition. Several letters of Seggeth to Galileo survive, as does his *Album amicorum*, which contains the signatures of Galileo and a host of his friends and pupils.

While this Scottish poet was extolling Galileo to the Germans at Frankfort, a truly great English poet was introducing him at London to a far wider audience. In 1611, John Donne published anonymously a satire against the Jesuits entitled: *Ignatius his Conclave, or his inthronisation in a late election in Hell: wherein many things are mingled by way of satyr; concerning the disposition of Jesuits, the creation of a new Hell, the establishing of a Church in the moone* . . . and so on. This book appeared both in English and in Latin in London in 1611, and was frequently reprinted in England and abroad. In the second sentence of the book, Galileo's name appears for the first time in an English work; he is said to have ". . . of late summoned the other worlds, the Stars, to come nearer to him and give him an account of themselves",[5] while in another passage,

Galileo's telescope and his observations of the moon are described.[6] Donne's *Conclave* also contains a curiously prophetic passage in which he makes Loyola say to Lucifer, with regard to the candidacy of Copernicus:

> And if hereafter the fathers of our Order can draw a Cathedral Decree from the Pope, by which it may be defined as a matter of faith: *That the earth doth not move*, and an Anathema inflicted upon all that hold the contrary; then perchance both the Pope which shall decree that, and Copernicus his followers (if they be Papists) may have the dignity of this place.[7]

I hasten to add that when I said "prophetic", I meant only with regard to the decree against the earth's motion, and not with regard to the present whereabouts of any popes or Copernicans; also to add that when the decree came, it was not *ex cathedra*. Elsewhere in Donne's writings, there are other references to the new astronomical discoveries and to the new philosophy that came in their train, though none to Galileo by name.[8]

In 1619, Sir Francis Bacon had an opportunity to see copies of Galileo's important published books and manuscript copies of his essays on the hydrostatic balance and on the theory of the tides, brought to England by Richard White. It is perhaps significant that Bacon withheld from publication in the *Instauratio magna* of 1620 his essay on the tides, written about 1616 probably for inclusion there, presumably because his essay had concluded against any motion of the earth, whereas Galileo's treatise supported a double motion. Galileo too had written on this subject in 1616, though he had formulated his theory long before, and there is a contemporary suggestion that he may have known of Bacon's theory when he wrote out his own.[9] Bacon mentioned Galileo, though only in passing in two other essays, *Descriptio globi intellectualis* and *Thema coeli*, similarly written in preparation for the *Instauratio magna*. These also remained unpublished during Bacon's lifetime, though they were probably known to literary men of the period.

About the same time, the telescope was mentioned by Ben Jonson in several of his plays, but, as Professor Nicolson remarks, references to the telescope in the seventeenth century are too numerous to warrant listing.[10] Galileo was, however, mentioned by name in Jonson's *Staple of news*, performed early in 1626, in which he was credited with the possession of a powerful burning glass, capable of setting fire to ships at sea. This curious story, reminiscent of the well-known legend about Archimedes, is perhaps to be explained by a fanciful conversation composed by another English author, George Fortescue, whose *Feriae academicae* was published at Douay in 1630. This book is now rare, and I have not personally consulted it. A summary of its contents was published about a century ago,[11] and from this I learn that Galileo enters as an interlocutor together with the Jesuit Fathers, Christopher Clavius and Christopher Grienberger, in a discussion *De lumine*, where Galileo is made to speak of the telescope and of the discoveries made with it. Clavius describes a powerful burning

glass, which may account for Jonson's attribution of this to Galileo. Fortescue was born in Kent about 1587. He was educated at Douay and went
to Rome in 1609, where he was entered in the English College, presumably of the Jesuit Collegio Romano. Possibly he saw Galileo there in person
at the time of the celebration held at the Collegio for Galileo in 1611, at
which Clavius and Grienberger were present. Fortescue returned to England in 1616, where he soon became so distinguished in the literary world
that his name was included in a list of proposed members of a Royal Academy, plans for which were drawn up by Edward Bolton. The Academy
was never realized because of the Civil War, but the lists proposed in 1617
and 1624 included the names of such men as Ben Jonson, Michael Dray-
ton, George Chapman, Inigo Jones and Kenelm Digby, indicating the circles in which Fortescue moved and the respect in which his work was
held. Letters between Fortescue and Galileo in 1630 have survived; Galileo requested several copies of the *Feriae* and described to Fortescue the
Dialogo on which he was then at work.

Although Galileo wrote principally in Italian, his books were eagerly
sought after in England. Evidence of this is contained in a letter written in
January 1634, by Thomas Hobbes to William Cavendish, later Duke of
Newcastle.[12] Hobbes had undertaken to buy for him a copy of the *Dialogo*, but found that none could be had in London for any money. Few
copies had been brought over, he said, and men who buy such books do
not part with them again. A few months later, Hobbes left for an extended stay in Europe. In November 1635, he visited Galileo at Arcetri
and informed him that the *Dialogo* had already been translated into English. Apparently the work had been completed before he left England in
1634, and there is little doubt that the translation in question is that which
is now preserved in manuscript at the British Museum. The translator
was in all probability Dr. Joseph Webbe, who had received a medical
degree at the University of Padua in 1612, and who may have known
Galileo there before 1610. Webbe conducted a language school in London
for several years, and was the author of two books on methods of instruction in language, one in English in 1622 and one in Latin in 1626.[13] The
translation of the *Dialogo* which I ascribe to him was never published,
perhaps because of the appearance of a Latin translation at Strasbourg in
1635. It was, however, probably known to other British men of letters as it
was to Hobbes.

In 1638, while Galileo was still living, a book appeared anonymously in
London with the title, *The discovery of a new world in the moone*, of
which there were two editions in the same year. The third (1640) bore
an engraved title page on which Galileo, Kepler and Copernicus were
depicted, together with a diagram of the Copernican system. Galileo holds
a telescope in his hand, and this appears to be the first printed picture in
England of either the man or the instrument. The likeness is good having
apparently been taken from the 1624 portrait by Ottavio Leoni as re-
engraved for the 1635 Latin translation of the *Dialogo*. The book sets

forth in popularized form the principal discoveries and opinions of Galileo
from his *Starry messenger* and *Dialogo*, with many lively additions by the
author, who was in fact John Wilkins. Wilkins was born in 1614, and in
1648 became Warden of Wadham College, Oxford. In 1659, he was made
Master of Trinity College, Cambridge, and in 1668 became Bishop of
Chester. He has been called the true father of the Royal Society because
of the role he played in organizing the informal meetings of the so-called
"Invisible College", a group of people interested in natural science. These
meetings began in London in 1645, and continued at Oxford after 1648.
Wilkins was a man of great wisdom and infinite tact, virtues that were
much needed during the political upheavals of the Civil War, Commonwealth and Restoration periods in maintaining the traditions of scholarship
in the English universities.

In 1640, Wilkins' *Discovery of a new world* was again reprinted, this
time with a supplemental section on the possibility of travel to the moon,
and with the addition of a second book called *Discourse concerning a
new planet, tending to prove that 'tis probable that our earth is one of the
planets.* The principal concern of the author in this second book, apart
from astronomy, was the reconciliation of the earth's motion with Biblical
passages. Wilkins drew heavily on Galileo's concepts for his argument,
and reproduced numerous diagrams and textual passages from the *Dialogo.* It is difficult to say whether Wilkins had seen Galileo's *Letter to
Christina*, published in 1636 at Strasbourg, though he cites many of the
same arguments and authorities relating to Scriptural interpretation that
had been employed by Galileo in that document.

These two works are of great interest as Galileana, because they set out
to do in English precisely what Galileo had tried to accomplish in Italian.
Wilkins wanted to bring the new astronomical discoveries and their interpretation within the reach of every intelligent reader. I do not know of
any book of the period written in any other language which had the same
objective. Generally those who wrote about Galileo's ideas, whether to
support them or combat them, approached the subject with a particular
group of professionals in mind—astronomers, philosophers, or theologians
—and composed all arguments within the technical framework of one of
those subjects. Wilkins, on the other hand, conducted a popular crusade
for Galileo's ideas much as Galileo had done for the ideas of Copernicus.
To this campaign he brought some new arguments in the style and spirit
of Galileo's own work, of which I shall mention only a single example. In
discussing the interpretation of the light and dark areas on the moon, he
repeated the arguments Galileo had given to show that the light areas are
rougher than the dark spots, and that if there were bodies of water on the
moon, they would appear dark rather than bright. To these he added the
observation, which I do not believe is to be found in Galileo's own writings, that from a high mountain, lakes and ponds appear much darker than
the surrounding land areas.

Wilkins' second book, the *Discourse concerning a new planet*, is of further Galilean interest because it was directed against the arguments of Libertus Fromondus, a Belgian Jesuit opponent of Galileo's, and because it also included arguments against a book that had been published at London in 1634 by Alexander Ross, entitled: *Commentary on the earth's circular motion in two books . . . refuting . . . Lansberg and Carpentarius.*[14] Here I shall depart slightly from the chronological sequence I have been following, in order to describe the response occasioned by Wilkins' rebuttal of Ross.

Alexander Ross was born at Aberdeen in 1591; in 1616 he became master of the Southampton Grammar School, and later served as chaplain to Charles I. He was a prolific writer, chiefly of polemics, who was endowed with a mentality very similar to that of Simplicio in Galileo's *Dialogo*. Although Ross gave witty titles to his books, his arguments were childish and his mind was completely closed to anything that disputed the authority of Aristotle or the literal interpretation of the Bible. In 1645, he published a book called *Medicus medicatus* in refutation of Sir Thomas Browne's *Religio medici*, and another called *The philosophical touchstone*, attacking two treatises by Sir Kenelm Digby of which I shall speak presently. In 1651, Ross disposed of Thomas Browne's *Pseudodoxia epidemica* in his *Arcana microcosmi*; in the following year he refuted Sir Francis Bacon's *Natural history* and William Harvey's *De generatione* in a revised edition of the *Arcana*; in 1653, he published his *Leviathan drawn out with a hook*, which took care of Thomas Hobbes. Ross was very fortunate, considering his gifts, to live at a time when so many ridiculous new ideas were being proposed in opposition to Aristotle, the refutation of which kept him quite busy and presumably happy. To read all of his books was such a task that Samuel Butler opened the second canto of *Hudibras* with the lines:

> There was an ancient sage philosopher
> That had read Alexander Ross over.

I have mentioned only a few of Ross's titles to prepare you for the title of his reply to Wilkins, which was published in 1646.[15] It reads, in part: *The new planet no planet, or the earth no wandring star except in the wandring heads of the Galileans. In answer to a discourse, that the earth may be a planet . . .* This title is not only amusing, but is historically revealing in one respect. It appears that Ross had not yet got hold of Galileo's *Dialogo* in 1634, or he surely would not have neglected to include Galileo with Lansberg and Carpentarius in his refutation of the earth's motion published in that year. Yet by 1646 he had come to regard Galileo's name as synonymous with support of that doctrine, and relegated the name of Copernicus to mere mention. If Ross is at all representative, one may deduce that John Wilkins had been as effective in bringing Galileo's cosmological ideas to the attention of the English as others had been in telling them of his telescope and his early discoveries.

To resume my chronological listing: in 1642, there was published at Paris a book called *De mundo dialogi tres*, inspired by the reading of Galileo's *Dialogo*. The author was Thomas White, an English Catholic theologian who could not publish in England at that time. He was a friend of Thomas Hobbes, Sir Kenelm Digby, and other prominent British intellectuals of both parties and various religions. He was the younger brother of Richard White, who had brought many of Galileo's works to Francis Bacon in 1619. Thomas White was born to a prominent Catholic family in Essex in 1593; his mother was the daughter of the celebrated jurist, Edmund Plowden. He was educated at the English Jesuit college of St. Omer, in Belgium, and then at Valladolid and Douay. He was ordained priest in 1617. White was a noted controversialist in religion and politics. Many of his published propositions were officially condemned by the college at Douay, where the priests especially repudiated his advocacy of passive obedience on the part of English Catholics, a policy which he hoped would gain tolerance toward them from Cromwell. His denial of papal infallibility ultimately got him into trouble with the Inquisition.

White's dialogues *De mundo* are three in number. The first deals with the material of the universe, the second with questions of motion, and the last with problems of cause. Galileo's views play a part in the first dialogue, particularly with regard to the nature of comets, and his ideas on motion occupy most of the second dialogue. Although White repudiated the circular motion of the earth in this book, he took pains to set forth Galileo's arguments at length and with care, giving special attention to his theory of the tides. Since Galileo's *Dialogo*, in which these arguments had originally appeared, was a rigorously banned book, one may well wonder whether White was entirely opposed to Galileo, or whether he had in mind the purpose of keeping his ideas in circulation as much as that of criticizing them. Not a few Catholic writers of the seventeenth century appear to me to have written with such an ulterior purpose, a ruse which had a long and distinguished tradition behind it.

In 1644, Galileo was mentioned by yet another of England's truly great literary figures, the peer of John Donne. In that year, John Milton published his *Areopagitica* in defiance of the Parliament. In this celebrated defense of a free press, Milton recalled his visit to Florence a few years earlier, saying: "There it was that I found and visited the famous Galileo, grown old, a prisoner to the Inquisition for thinking in Astronomy otherwise than the Franciscan and Dominican licensers of thought."

In the same year, Sir Kenelm Digby published at Paris the first edition of his *Two treatises, in the one of which the nature of bodies; in the other, the nature of man's soule, is looked into*. Another edition of this book appeared at London in 1645. Digby, also a Catholic, was born at Gadhurst in 1603. He was an extraordinarily brilliant, courageous and courtly gentleman who distinguished himself as a naval commander, served as envoy of the Queen of France to the Pope, whom he dared to contradict and by whom he was styled mad, and ultimately retired to Gresham College for scientific studies. His influence on the intellectuals of his time, both in England and abroad, was considerable. He had read White's dialogues and referred to them often in his treatise on bodies. Digby was deeply impressed by the learning and discoveries of Galileo, "unto whom we owe the greatest part of what is known concerning motion".[16] Although he did not always agree with Galileo's physics, he called him "that miracle of our age, whose wit was able to discover whatsoever he had a mind to employ it about".[17] Digby did not believe that the speed of fall could be entirely independent of weight, and he also thought that Galileo's inertial principle was incorrect because of certain experiments performed by Mersenne, whom he knew at Paris. Although he scrupulously presented Galileo's arguments to his readers, Digby was unable to overcome his fundamental respect for Aristotle's principle that every moving body requires an external mover, and was willing to accept the medium as a source of motion for projectiles. His attempts to answer Galileo's arguments on this point furnish an interesting sidelight on the evolution of physical thought during the period which immediately followed Galileo's death.

I have previously mentioned Richard White, the older brother of Thomas White. Richard was born at Essex in 1590. He became a pupil of Benedetto Castelli's at Pisa, was personally acquainted with Galileo, and was a good mathematician. He resided most of his life in Italy. In 1648, he published at Rome the *Hemisphaerium dissectum*, an original if largely inconsequential mathematical work. In the preface to this book he inserted a specific tribute to Galileo, though it was published at Rome under license during a period in which many Italian writers found it prudent to forgo any favorable reference to Galileo in their published works. White also conducted some elaborate experiments concerning specific gravities and made accurate observations of Halley's comet.

In 1648, John Wilkins published at London a book called *Mathematicall magick, or the wonders that may be performed by mechanicall geometry*. In the first chapter of this book, citing ancient and modern writers on the subject of mechanics, he mentioned Galileo, but in the text generally he followed Guidobaldo del Monte, Galileo's patron and friend. Galileo's treatise on mechanics was not published until the following year, and though there was a manuscript English translation and a printed French translation, Wilkins may not have been able to consult them directly. He did, however, acquaint British readers with the fact that Galileo had written on this topic also.

In 1651, Digby's *Two treatises* were translated into Latin and published at Paris with a preface by Thomas White.

In 1655, Thomas Hobbes published his book *De corpore*, and in the following year a revised English translation of the same work appeared. The book entangled him in a series of disputes with eminent English mathematicians such as John Wallis and Seth Ward because of his conviction that he had succeeded in squaring the circle. In the preface, Hobbes included Galileo in his list of men who had contributed to knowledge in important ways during the seventeenth century. It is interesting to note that the only Englishman included in the list was William Harvey. Francis Bacon was conspicuously absent, which is surprising in view of the fact that Hobbes in his youth had been intimately acquainted with him and had been employed to put into Latin many of his *Essays*. In view of Hobbes's importance as a founder of the British empiricist tradition, it is significant that he repudiated Bacon's concept of experimental physics, while at the same time regarding Galileo as a leader in the new critical philosophy to which Hobbes himself contributed so much.

Hobbes was in Europe in 1610, and says in his autobiography that it was then that he first became aware of the general European neglect of the scholastic philosophy he had learned at Oxford, and the growing favor toward the critical methods of Galileo, Kepler and Montaigne. After his visit to Galileo in 1635, mentioned previously,[18] Hobbes had spent several months in the circle of Mersenne at Paris, and rejoined him in 1640 when he fled England in fear of reprisals from the Long Parliament because of his political writings. Hobbes vigorously disputed many of the scientific and philosophical tenets of Descartes, to whom his attention had been drawn by Mersenne. He told John Aubrey that if Descartes had confined himself to geometry, he would have been the best geometer in the world, but that he had no head for philosophy.[19] Thus to the extent that Hobbes influenced the origins of British empiricism, it was in the direction of Galileo rather than in that of Bacon or Descartes.

In its later development at the hands of John Locke, the central empiricist distinction between primary and secondary qualities may have been derived from Galileo's suggestion of such a distinction in *Il saggiatore*, though Galileo's name is not in fact mentioned. A somewhat similar analysis of the action of the senses is also to be found in Kenelm Digby's *Two treatises* and in Hobbes's *Human nature*. In the latter work, Hobbes remarked in passing on Galileo's physical analysis of musical sounds. That crucial problem of language, the relation of words to things, was stressed by Hobbes in the opening sections of the *Leviathan* in 1651, and later became a central preoccupation for Locke also. Sir Kenelm Digby had dwelt on this problem at the beginning of his *Two treatises*. Their concern with this problem may well have been inspired by Galileo's remarks on the word-thing relation in the *Sunspot letters*, the *Assayer*, and the *Dialogue*, remarks that had much influence on the origins of scientific analysis. The writers of the article on Hobbes in the eleventh edition of the *Encyclopaedia Britannica* concluded that:

> his relations backwards are with Galileo and those others, who, from the beginning of the seventeenth century, occupied themselves with the physical world in the manner that has since become distinguished by the name of science in opposition to philosophy.

With the founding of the Royal Society shortly after the Restoration, a new era in British science began. At this time, many of Galileo's books were published in English translation for the first time through the monumental labors of the mysterious Thomas Salusbury. The first volume of Salusbury's *Mathematical collections and translations* was published at London in 1661. It contained complete English translations of Galileo's *Dialogo* and his *Letter to Christina*, as well as English versions of works by Galileo's pupil Benedetto Castelli relating to hydraulics. The *Dialogo* and the *Letter* had already appeared in Latin translations, but neither had been printed in any colloquial language other than the original Italian. Indeed, no other translation of the *Dialogo* into a modern language was undertaken until 1892, when a German translation by Emil Strauss was published. Salusbury's in reality was the second English translation of the *Dialogo* to have been made, though he knew nothing of the unpublished manuscript which I have attributed to Joseph Webbe. There are now translations of the *Dialogo* into Spanish, Polish, Russian, Japanese and Rumanian, but these are products of our own century, inspired by a growing interest in the history of science. So far as I know, there is still no French translation of the complete work.

The second volume of Salusbury's *Mathematical collections* was printed at London in 1665, though technically one might say it was never published. Both volumes had been undertaken on a subscription basis, and most copies of the second volume were destroyed in the printer's shop by the Great Fire of London in September 1666. The second volume, like the first, was divided into two parts. Eight copies are known to survive today, all lacking the second part. The first part contains complete English translations of Galileo's *Discorsi*, his *Intorno alle cose, che stanno in sù l'acqua* and his *Le meccaniche*, in addition to works by Tartaglia and Descartes. Once again, Salusbury scored for our language the priority of translation for all but *Le meccaniche*, which Mersenne had published in French in 1634. German was again the second colloquial language to have a complete translation of the *Discorsi*, but this also came more than two centuries after Salusbury. It should be mentioned in passing that a second English translation of the *Discorsi* was published by Thomas Weston in 1730, prompted no doubt by the extreme scarcity of copies of the Salusbury version after the Great Fire.

The extraordinary labor applied by Salusbury to the translation of Galileo's books is difficult to explain in the absence of concrete information about the man himself. Despite much industrious research, no one has yet been able to determine his date or place of birth, nor the place of his education. Salusbury died in London about August, 1666, just before the stock of his second Galileo volume was destroyed. He left a widow and two infant daughters. He was probably born in the 1620's and was connected in some way with the prominent Welsh families of the name. He was certainly a Royalist, and appears to have spent some nine years on the

Continent during the Civil War. After the Restoration, he was for a time in favor at the London court, having perhaps met members of the royal family abroad during their exile. He says in the preface to the first volume of his *Collections* that he had emptied his purse in the service of the king, and he certainly appears to have had small means after the Restoration. He was engaged as London correspondent and mentor to the young Earl of Huntingdon, and as a sort of librarian by the Marquis of Dorchester. Considering his other occupations, Salusbury's literary output is impressive, even if (as his printer asserted after his death) he did not actually compose everything that was printed over his name. In addition to the *Mathematical collections*, Salusbury published a translation of a romance called *Arnaldo*, and of *The learned man defended and reformed* by the Italian Jesuit, Daniel Bartoli. Other elaborate works had been announced by him as ready for the press in 1660, but were never published.

The second part of the second volume of the *Collections* contained three things: a translation of Evangelista Torricelli's work on the motion of projectiles, a treatise on bodies in water composed by Salusbury himself, and—most important of all—the first extensive biography of Galileo to be published in any language. This second part of the second volume, of which no copies are now known, is often regarded as a bibliographical "ghost", that is, a work reported as published which never actually appeared. It was certainly printed, however, and was consulted by the author of the article on Galileo in the great English translation and continuation of Bayle's biographical dictionary (1737),[20] and a few passages from it were cited directly by John Elliot Drinkwater-Bethune in his anonymous biography of Galileo, published at London in 1829.[21] Both these writers had seen the unique copy known to have survived the fire, which was then in the library of the Earl of Macclesfield. It has since disappeared, and all subsequent efforts to trace it have failed. One passage quoted by Drinkwater is worth repeating as an indication of Salusbury's opinion of Galileo and Descartes: "Where or when did any one appear that durst enter the lists with our Galileus? save only one bold and unfortunate Frenchman, who yet no sooner came within the ring but he was hissed out again." [22] This is a curious remark, coming two decades before the publication of Newton's *Principia*, at a time when Descartes still had many followers in England.

The plan of Salusbury's biography of Galileo was set forth in the prospectus for his entire work, and it shows that a very detailed life was contemplated. Unfortunately those who saw the printed work did not describe its length, so there is no way to tell how much of the plan was in fact carried out. But it is fascinating to ask what sort of Englishman could ever hope to obtain sufficient information in London in the 1660's to write a full biography of Galileo. The only notices of his life that had then been published were extremely brief, and because of Galileo's status in Italy at the time and the long period that had elapsed since his death, little could have been expected from Italian correspondents. The printer of the volume, William Leybourn, told John Collins after the fire that the life was not actually written by Salusbury, but by an Oxford scholar named Bargett on the basis of letters from Vincenzio Viviani.[23] Now, the records of Oxford mention no one of that name, nor of any name reasonably resembling it, and the extensive surviving correspondence of Viviani includes no letters or references to Salusbury, Bargett, or anyone in England who could have been connected with the project. It is true that Viviani, at the request of Prince Leopold de'Medici, had compiled in 1654 a biographical sketch of Galileo, and though this was not published until 1717, Salusbury may have got hold of a copy of it in manuscript. On the other hand, neither the sketch nor the outline of the more elaborate biography, which Viviani had planned to write for a collected edition of Galileo's works, bears any resemblance to the plan of Salusbury's work printed in his prospectus. Whatever the circumstances were, and whoever was the true author of the life printed by Leybourn, England may claim priority of publication for the first detailed published biography of Galileo as well as for vernacular translations of his principal works.

It is a curious fact that in 1663, with Salusbury's English translation of the *Dialogo* already in circulation, the first printing in England of the Latin translation (originally published in 1635) was brought out at London. The printer was Thomas Dicas. It would appear likely that Salusbury's extensive labors to popularize the works of Galileo in England had partly resulted from, and partly succeeded in creating, a demand for his original works; and that Dicas, being aware of this demand, attempted to satisfy it. Since Salusbury's work was costly and was limited in supply, this explanation is plausible, though no more than conjectural.

Next in this recital of Galileo's literary fortunes in England comes the most celebrated poem of the age, Milton's *Paradise lost*, of which the first edition appeared at London in 1667. Galileo is mentioned in it by name, and there is at least one other clear reference to him personally:

> . . . as when by night the glass
> Of Galileo, less assured, observes
> Imagined lands and regions in the Moon.
> (V, 261–263)
> . . . the moon, whose orb
> Through optic glass the Tuscan artist views
> At evening, from the top of Fiesole
> Or in Valdarno, to descry new lands,
> Rivers, or mountains, in her spotty globe.
> (I, 287–291)

In addition, there are many references in this and other works of Milton to the new discoveries and ideas. The relations of Milton and Galileo have been extensively discussed by Professor Nicolson, Kester Svendsen and others.[24] Whatever influence Galileo's astronomical work had on Milton —and authorities differ widely in their appraisals of it—that influence passed on to a wide English literary audience through this poem.

A third edition of Digby's *Two treatises* was published at London in 1669. In 1672, Captain Thomas Venn published his *Military and maritime discipline*, to which was added *The doctrine of projects applied to gunnery by Galilaeus and Torricellio . . . now rendered in English*. Venn appears to have been unacquainted with Salusbury's translations of these works, and translated anew the passages which concerned him. In addition to the reprinting of Galileo's tables of parabolic trajectories, Venn discussed the contributions of Tartaglia to gunnery, which had not been included in the Salusbury translations.

A still more striking instance of the widespread lack of knowledge of Salusbury's volumes is found in *The sphere of Marcus Manilius made an English poem*, published by Edward Sherbourne at London in 1675. This work included a biographical sketch of Galileo, and referred to Viviani's biography, though Sherbourne had not seen it. He deplored the lack of patronage in England for serious books, and rather unexpectedly attributed to this the absence of English versions of Galileo's books, even though Salusbury's translations had been printed in the same city only a decade before.

The final item I wish to mention is a new joint edition of John Wilkins' *Discovery of a new world* and his *Discourse of a new planet*, which was printed in London in 1684.[25] These two works had been translated into French in 1655, and were translated into German in 1713, suggesting that they constituted the best popularization of Galileo's views and discoveries that appeared up to the beginning of the eighteenth century.

Here I shall conclude. By the end of the seventeenth century, Galileo's science was going out of date. Once Newton's works had been published, there was little point in an Englishman's consulting those of Galileo except out of curiosity. But I think it is sufficiently clear that from the year of his first world-shaking discoveries up to the time of Newton, Galileo's work was widely appreciated by Englishmen at home and abroad, and that his admirers in Britain included some of the most distinguished philosophers and men of letters of the century.

NOTES

1. Marjorie Nicolson, *Science and the imagination*, Ithaca, 1956.

2. *Martini Horky . . . brevissima peregrinatio contra Nuncium sidereum nuper ad omnes philosophos et mathematicos emissum . . .* Mutina, 1610.

3. *Quatuor problematum quae Martinus Horky contra Nuntium sidereum de quatuor planetis novis disputanda proposuit. Confutatio per Ioannem Wodderbornium scotobritannum.* Padua, 1610.

4. William Lithgow, *The rare adventures and painful peregrinations* . . . London, 1632.

5. *The complete poetry and selected prose of John Donne*, ed. by Charles M. Coffin, New York, 1952, p. 319.

6. *Ibid.*, p. 349.

7. *Ibid.*, p. 324.

8. Nicolson, *op. cit.*, pp. 48–55.

9. *Opere, 19*, p. 450.

10. Nicolson, *op. cit.*, p. 38.

11. *Gentlemen's Magazine, 28*, 1847, p. 382.

12. *Opere, 20*, pp. 606–607. See M. B. Hall's essay for further discussion of this question.

13. *Appeal to truth . . . about the most expedient course in languages*, and *Usus et authoritas, id est liber loquens.*

14. *Commentum de terrae motu circulari, duobus libris refutatum, quorum prior Lansbergii, posterior Carpentari argumenta, vel nugamenta potius, refellit. (Opera Alexandri Rossaei, aberdonensis.)* London, 1634.

15. The *Bibliografia Galileiana* shows, as item *156, a purported Latin edition of 1636. No such edition is known, and since the English edition of 1646 was written in reply to Wilkins' *Discourse* of 1640, a 1636 date is impossible. It may also be noted that item 160 in the *Bibliografia* is incorrect; the Wilkins book of 1638 was the *Discovery of a new world in the moone*, and not the *Discourse*. Finally, the *Bibliografia* omits under the year 1640 the reprint of the *Discovery* supplemented by the first edition of the *Discourse*. The starred items in the *Bibliografia* represent books which the compilers had not personally examined, but accepted on derivative reports.

16. Kenelm Digby, *Two treatises* . . . , *London*, 1645, p. 85.

17. *Ibid.*, p. 87.

18. "When he was in Florence, . . . [Hobbes] contracted a friendship with the famous Galileo, whom he extremely venerated and magnified; and not only as he was a prodigious witt, but for his sweetness of nature and manners." *Aubrey's Brief Lives*, ed. by O. L. Dick, London, 1950, p. 157. This remark has been overlooked, and Hobbes's only visit to Galileo has been supposed to have occurred in 1635. Had Hobbes met him in 1610, during his earlier European tour? This seems not unlikely, as it would help to account for the inclusion of the name of Galileo (whose then published works did not criticize Aristotle's philosophy) with those of Kepler and Montaigne in the autobiographical passage mentioned above.

19. *Ibid.*, pp. 94–95.

20. *A general dictionary, historical and critical* . . . , London, vol. 5.

21. *The life of Galileo Galilei with illustrations of the advancement of experimental philosophy.*

22. *Op. cit.*, p. 87.

23. *Correspondence of scientific men of the seventeenth century*, Oxford, 1841, vol. 1, p. 120.

24. Nicolson, *op. cit.*; Kester Svendsen, *Milton and science*, 1956*.

25. The *Bibliografia* lists this as item 362, appending a note questioning the words 'the fourth edition' on the title page. This is, in fact, the second edition of the work as a whole, the first being that of 1640, which was not known to Carli and Favaro (cf. note 17, above.) It was, however, the fourth edition of the *Discovery of a new world in the moone*, of which the first and second editions appeared in 1638 and the third in 1640, when the supplementary *Discourse* was first added.

22 ❋ Torricelli's *Lezioni Accademiche* and Galileo's theory of percussion

SERGE MOSCOVICI

Torricelli's *Lezioni Accademiche* was published in Florence in 1715.[1] Three years later, Tommaso Bonaventuri brought out Galileo's dialogue on percussion under the title: *Giornata Sesta del Galileo, della forza della percosse da aggiungersi alli Discorsi e alle Dimostrazioni matematiche intorno a due nuove scienze*.[2] The order of appearance of the two books was an unusual one, the commentary before the work commented on. It suggests that by the time they appeared, both were of historical interest only, echoes of a scientific debate whose details had by then been forgotten. Let us recall some of those details.

At the time he was preparing to make known his discoveries in mechanics in a definitive form, Galileo thought of adding a "science" of percussion to the other two "new sciences" he was announcing. He never succeeded, however, in formulating this third science. The *Discorsi* of 1638 alluded to it, but no more. He did manage an outline of what it was to

NOTE: This article was written during a stay at the Princeton Institute for Advanced Study. I would like to take this occasion to thank Professor J. R. Oppenheimer for the welcome he extended, and for the numerous aids to research so freely extended me by the Institute. The article was written in French; the translation is by Ernan McMullin.

contain, in a dialogue which was supposed to be set on the fifth or sixth "day" of the famous meetings, where Salviati and Sagredo discussed the laws of movement. The "Sixth Day", *On the force of percussion*, remained unpublished for nearly a century. Its central theme was the autonomy and infinity of the "force of percussion". These views were probably being spread by word of mouth among scientists at the time the dialogue was being written. They must have evoked a fairly lively opposition to call forth in their defense a treatise as detailed as that of Torricelli. As someone who had been closely associated with Galileo's final efforts to bring clarity to this difficult problem, Torricelli was in a good position to undertake such a defense. An occasion was provided by his election to the Accademia della Crusca, before whom the *Lezioni accademiche* were first presented. Their composition must be dated within two or three years of the death of Galileo, thus somewhere around 1644–1645.

A direct witness, Torricelli was also a priveleged one. As he in his turn tried to grasp the nature of the force of percussion, his efforts help us to understand the sources of the Galilean theory better. He marshals together the themes of the great physicist, themes that never became explicit in the text of the *Sixth Day*. Though lacking in original solutions, the *Lezioni accademiche* incorporate a general approach whose importance was very great in the history of mechanics. Even if the results were not spectacular, they yet merit the closest scrutiny.

Galileo's experiments with the "force of percussion"

One of the most striking features of both Torricelli's and Galileo's accounts of percussion is undoubtedly the enthusiasm with which the existence of forces of percussion was asserted. It was exciting to hit upon a force whose effects are much greater than those of ordinary forces, a force so difficult to explain that any effort of the scientist in this regard, however great, was evidently worthwhile.

> The force of percussion . . . is first among the marvels before us. That is because it is the most striking of the discoveries made in mechanics, besides being perhaps the most hidden and most abstruse of the secrets of nature [p. 5].[3]

To penetrate the "secrets" of this force, Torricelli tells us that Galileo worked hard, both in performing experiments and in elaborating theoretical analyses of the nature of percussion. This research provided the starting-point for Torricelli's treatise:

> If fortune had not grudged the glory of this demonstration to our century, the illustrious Galileo would certainly have worked this jewel to enrich with it the necklace of Tuscan philosophy. Nevertheless, in his writings and in his familiar converse, one could still gather two clues about the force of percussion: one was the experiment involving bent bows by which he tried to demonstrate the immensity of the force, and the other was the emphatic way in

which he stressed his assurance that the force of percussion would turn out to be infinite [pp. 5–6].

One can see that Torricelli had been a party to that "familiar converse", where Galileo had unburdened himself of his reflections on matters scientific to those nearest him.[4] Foremost among the topics discussed was assuredly the series of experiments by which he had tried to show that the force of percussion is incommensurate with the force of gravity, and also that the effects of the former are much greater than those of the latter. We have no reason to reject either the possibility or the actual occurrence of these experiments, which must have been performed in Padua. They were inspired by a relatively simple principle, but were not (so it would seem) very well adapted to accomplish their end. In most cases, there was nothing more than a transposition of a simple observation from everyday experience, one which would be used to support a philosophical thesis rather than to establish an exact empirical fact.

Let us look more closely at these observations. Galileo chose bows of different tensions:

> Then he took the weakest, and at the middle of the bow-string suspended a leaden ball of about two ounces from a long cord, about a fathom in length, perhaps. The bow was fixed securely in a clamp. He lifted the ball and then letting it fall, noted (by means of a sounding vessel placed underneath) how far the *impetus* of the ball bent the bow and to what extent the bow-string was pulled down. Let us suppose it was pulled about four fingers-width. Then he would attach to the string of the same bow a weight which at rest would bend the bow and draw down the cord by the same four fingers-width. He noted that this weight was about ten pounds [pp. 22–23].

The guiding idea behind this experiment is not hard to grasp: the intention was to compare the effect of a weight in movement with that of a weight at rest. The measures used were rather indefinite, and the "sounding vessel" cannot have helped very much to sharpen them. Galileo was reaching for the definition of the force of percussion as a dynamic form of a static force, and was trying to understand the nature of gravity in the context of a dynamic concept of the action of bodies. After working with the "weakest" bow, he took a stronger one and repeated the experiment, using the same leaden ball on the same cord, noting the new deflection:

> Then he attached to the cord the quantity of lead which at rest produced the same effect, and noted that ten pounds was no longer enough, but that twenty was needed. Trying stronger and stronger bows, he found that to equal the force of that same leaden ball falling through the same distance, he had to take larger and larger weights [at rest]. He argued, therefore: if I take a strong enough bow, this leaden ball whose weight is no more than two ounces will have an effect on it equivalent to that of a thousand pounds of lead. Then if I take a bow a thousand times as strong again, the same little ball will have an effect equivalent to that of a million pounds of lead—which

clearly indicates that the force of this little weight falling through this distance is infinite [p. 23].

It is striking that Galileo should have reasoned thus, because his experiments really only showed one thing, something presumably familiar to all physicists of his day: that a weight suspended at rest produces less effect than the same weight in motion. Galileo's claim went, however, beyond this fact, and was not strictly derivable from it. Not that his observation was a useless one, but since it was not planned in order to verify some relation previously arrived at in a theoretical way, it did not constitute a true experiment. When one knows the law of falling bodies, the use of a pendulum to verify the law is an experiment in the proper sense. But in the instance we have been studying, what we have is rather the systematic observation of a common fact under various different forms. The bowstring observations are supposed to illustrate the infinity of the force of percussion, because a "percussive" body (here a falling weight) produces in the limit an effect equivalent to that of an infinitely heavy weight. We can say that the first form of the alleged "infinity" of percussion is of mechanical origin, and that it does no more than express a particular aspect of the force, a dimension added to that of gravity. Note that Galileo always refers in this context to *weight*. In all later theories of percussion, this reference to weight will disappear. For the moment, however, it allowed Galileo to treat the theory of percussion as part of his mechanics. But it also turned out to be the very element that prevented his thought from developing further.[5]

Pressure and percussion

By these experiments with bent bows, Galileo thought he had clarified the distinction between percussion and gravity. To establish this distinction more securely, Torricelli went on to analyze the phenomenon of *pressure*. Suppose one wishes to snap a table in the middle without using percussive forces. Suppose further that a weight of 1000 pounds placed on it be just sufficient to do this. A smaller weight, say 100 pounds, would produce no result. Torricelli asks how this would be described in a temporal perspective:

> At any instant one chooses, there will be an unequal contrast between the force of 100 pounds and the resistance of 1000. Thus, even though the lighter weight presses eternally on the marble, it will never succeed in breaking it; its effect will never be any more than it was in the very first moment it was placed there. Again, imagine that thirty of us hold the end of a pole with all our force. Not all the peoples of Europe, not even all those who have ever lived can budge us, if we hold our ground. The reason for this is clear: as long as the others apply their force one by one, we shall always be thirty to one . . . [p. 7].

The metaphor is an eloquent one: the effect of a weight at rest is exhausted in an instant. No matter how long it lies upon a table, its effect will be the same. With a *moving* body, however, it is altogether different; its elementary "actions" accumulate and make a difference to its final impact. The force of percussion derives from the summation of these *momenti*[6] which would otherwise perish were they to be engendered separately. Thus, while for gravity time is something external and indifferent, for percussion it is an essential condition of its existence. This is what marks it off; Torricelli was very sure of this point, whereas Descartes, for instance, had wavered on it. He provides for us a "model" of how percussion is supposed to be generated, a model whose details Galileo had left almost entirely vague. We know today what the origin of this model was; the earlier exponents of *impetus* theory had used it many times. And does it not correspond to common sense?

Let us look a little more closely at this accumulation of *momenti*. The *momento* of a weight at rest is zero. As it moves, its elementary *momenti* accumulate. Contrary to the opinion of the Aristotelians, Torricelli, following Galileo, asserts that percussion is not linked with increase of weight but rather with the aggregation of *momenti*. Time is here the differentiating factor. Percussion originates in time, and has an extension in time. This axiom, in many ways an evident one, is the basis of Torricelli's development of the Galilean view of percussion. It expresses both the continuity of the movement of fall and its relation to acceleration. The *momento* of a body let fall from any height is greater than any finite force or *momento*. Take, for example, a falling body whose *momento* is 100 pounds, 100 times greater than the *momento* of the same body at rest:

> Suppose one imagines the time of fall divided into more than 100 equal parts, into 110 finite divisible intervals, for example. According to Galileo's (and our own) definition of accelerated motion, it is clear that the falling body will produce in each of the 110 intervals of time a *momento* equal to one pound at least, and will in addition conserve these *momenti* and accumulate them together. Thus the body which at rest had a *momento* of one pound, will have a *momento* of two pounds after only the second small interval of time [p. 10].

By the last interval, the *momento* will exceed 100 pounds. Instead of dividing the time by 100, one could just as easily divide it by a thousand or a million. So that: "in proving that a falling body exerts a force greater than any finite force, one shows this force to be infinite".

The reasoning is an elegant one. But does it illuminate anything other than the nature of accelerated motion?[7] Is it at all appropriate to the analysis of percussion? One might well doubt this. In a sense, it appears to concern only the "finite" and the "infinite" aspects of the action of bodies, the "infinite" here revealing itself through a change in the number of dimensions. Nevertheless, one can see behind these kinematic constructs what it was that led Galileo to assert the existence of a new force. The essential mechanism of percussion-force is thought to be the way in which it is generated by an accumulation of *momenti* over time intervals that can be made as small as one wishes. The accelerated motion of a falling body exemplifies this process, because a *momento* is added at each instant, and the force increases. By the accumulation and conservation of *momenti*, an infinite force of percussion is formed.

This model helps in distinguishing pressure from percussion; it corroborates their incommensurability; and it accords with the presupposition of an infinite force. But this last is not without its difficulties.

Infinite effects

Let us begin with a paradox. If the force of percussion is infinite, each percussion, no matter how small, must have an infinite effect. The objection was an inevitable one, and Torricelli had to attempt a response. Yes, he said, if the percussion were to be instantaneous, its effect would indeed be infinite. Thus:

> the body will apply the entire accumulation of *momenti*, which it has gathered within itself, and which are truly infinite; in a single instant of time, it will bring them to bear on whatever resists its motion [pp. 10–11].

But this is impossible: impact requires a finite time. Hence, the effect of percussion need not be infinitely great after all. From the infinitely great, we must return to the infinitely small: if the force of percussion "be applied over a time interval, it is no longer necessary that its effect should be infinite; on the contrary, it can be as small as one wishes, though never zero" (p. 11).

We encounter here another principle of Galilean percussion theory, namely, that any body no matter how small can move any other, no matter how large. In other words, there is percussion if the time during which the moving body meets with the resisting body allows it to produce an effect. The finite time taken by the encounter is able to transform an infinitely great percussion into an infinitely small one. Because of considerations of continuity the effect cannot, however, become a zero one; the great and the small are *quantitative* variations of the same force. Beyond this, it is a different force that intervenes, that of weight, and here we move out of the context of dynamics. What is the rule governing this quantitative variation in the encounter of a percussive body with a resistance? It must be admitted that Torricelli's rule, though professedly a scientific one, is somewhat disappointing. It is not a law, nor even a statement capable of being tested by measurement. It expresses, at best, something that is not essential: "To annul a given impetus, times will be inversely proportional to resistances".

Torricelli goes on to explain his rule and the consequences to which it leads:

> Suppose a body multiplies its *momento* 100 times as it falls. If in the interaction of percussion, it applied the entire multiplication of its forces in a single

instant, the resisting body would register an impact equal to 100. But if the body distributes these forces in 10 instants, for example, the resisting body will register not 100 but 10 *momenti*. Thus, for the percussion to have its fullest effect, the opposing body must not yield. The act of percussion is then instantaneous, and the forces are released in a single instant [p. 12].

The different ways in which the resistance manifests itself serve, therefore, to modify the form under which the accumulated *momenti* are released, and to determine the length of time during which the release occurs. The process of resistance is in a certain sense the inverse of that by which the force of percussion is built up. The latter accumulates, the former dissipates. Resisting bodies may be soft or rigid or elastic, and thus differ in that they impose different rhythms of release upon the accumulated *momenti*. Bags of wool hung upon the walls of a fortress "choke" the impetus of the bodies that strike them. The force of percussion would have infinite effects, "if one could find materials that would in no way yield", that is, materials such that percussion would be an instantaneous contact. But infinitely hard materials of this sort do not exist: "we will stop, then, philosophizing upon the impossible". In other words, as though one had not known it already, the infinity of percussion is itself an abstraction, an ideal limit, impossible of active attainment. Regarding this latter impossibility, however, one is obliged to do some philosophizing on one's own. Without it, the entire structure of the theory would collapse; it constitutes an indispensable limiting case in terms of which real percussions are to be ordered:

> But we should not be astonished if percussion, even though it disposes of infinite forces, has in fact only limited and small effects. All materials yield to some extent; during the time interval in which they yield, they provide the infinity of forces with an opportunity to dissipate the infinity of *momenti*, which having accumulated one by one can also be dissipated in the same fashion, when the time is available. The force of percussion can, therefore, be infinite just as reason persuades us; yet it is not necessary that an infinite effect follow [p. 14].

The notion that the percussion-force is infinite was strongly affirmed by Galileo.[8] But it must be admitted that the notion was an awkward one. Torricelli was well aware of the difficulties to which it gave rise, and it is to his credit that he faced them. But what could he do? The accumulation of *momenti* (or of elements of impetus) was apparently regarded as a real accumulation. This would have some plausibility, and might even be acceptable, if the total impetus were finite. But this was not the case. Furthermore, if the force and the resistance were both infinite in magnitude, to establish a finite relation between them was a task beyond the mathematical resources of the day. In this situation, the process of summation was no longer valid, and the entire model of percussion in which this summation had been so central appeared to be threatened. For those who had adopted this model, therefore, everything hinged around a notion that even to them must have seemed quite dubious.

Arguments in favor of the infinity of percussion

There is no need to search for texts to prove that the sources of the notion of an infinite percussion-force were two: the theory of accelerated motion in mechanics and the theory of indivisibles in mathematics. Galileo's *Discorsi* already suggests as much. Nevertheless, neither the *Discorsi* nor his posthumous *Sixth Day* say so directly. But Torricelli quite explicitly presents his theories of accelerated motion and of indivisibles as the basis for his own treatise on percussion. The arguments he uses to try to establish the properties of the force of percussion are not very convincing, and in particular they do not succeed in proving anything really new. But the reader has already been warned: Torricelli noted at the beginning that he is undertaking this quest "more through curiosity than because of any hope of profit" (p. 6). Yet we ought not to underestimate the value of his arguments; they prove to be most suggestive.

Let us recall the example with which we began. If one places a weight on a table, its *momento* is annulled by the resistance of the table. If the operation is repeated, the second *momento* is annulled in the same way, without adding to the first. But if we were to let them be added together, these *momenti* would produce a definite effect. Cutting short the series of illustrative instances, Torricelli counsels a return to the Galilean "definition" of accelerated motion. This will be enough of itself (he says) to reveal the secrets of the mysterious force of percussion:

> The source of gravity can be understood in this way. Let us lift a ball to such a height that it will, on falling, remain in the air ten instants of time, and thus gain ten *momenti* of force. I say that these ten *momenti* are conserved, and are accumulated together [p. 8].

This is just what we would have expected him to say. But the difficulties in the way of this approach are very grave. It soon involved its authors in criticism.

It would seem that Galileo's views on the nature of percussion were, despite what one might have expected, widely known and discussed. In effect, Torricelli's treatise was intended as a response to the objections which Galileo's theory had encountered. These objections had centered around the supposition of a continuous accelerated motion, divisible into an infinite number of time "intervals". If one admits this infinity of intervals and thus of *momenti*, how can one say that the number of *momenti* that a body at rest possesses is to be multiplied by a *finite* number in order to compute its *momento* when falling?

Up to this point, Torricelli made use of arguments from mechanics. But the reader had been warned from the beginning about the provisional character of the route to be taken: "I will prove it demonstratively first without mentioning those 'instants', since they could be contested by those who do not admit the doctrine of indivisibles" (p. 9). The contested doctrine could not, however, be kept indefinitely in the background. It might help to make a bridge between the accumulating of an infinity of instants and their apprehension in a finite relation:

> Here the objections are clear. First, it is never possible for a falling body to sustain itself in the air for 10 or 30 or 100 instants, because the time of even the smallest fall necessarily contains an infinity of instants, so to speak. Thus, according to this supposition, it will never be the case that a falling body will multiply, by a factor of 10 or 30 or 100, the *momento* it had while at rest. It follows that if it is to multiply [its *momento* at rest], it must multiply it an infinite number of times. In the time of even the shortest fall, there is an infinity of instants. As a result of this, the force of each small fall, of each small weight, must be infinite, which is contrary to all observation. I respond to this objection by simply conceding it, and going on to agree that the force of each percussion is indeed infinite. . . . Then I shall say why I think percussions do not in practice have an infinite effect, but rather a very small one each time [p. 9].

The danger here is obvious: if infinity is recognized as a property of *every* force, the autonomy and distinctive character of the force of percussion can no longer be maintained. Torricelli insists so often on the necessity of avoiding any direct recourse to the "doctrine of indivisibles" that it is clear it must have been at the center of his thinking. From it his notion of infinity was surely derived. And, as we shall see, the "doctrine of indivisibles" provided the occasion for applying this notion of infinity to the concept of force, if it did not indeed actually give rise to this latter concept.

There is, as we have seen, one case where the effect of the percussion force would theoretically have to be infinite, namely, where the contact is instantaneous. But such a contact is, in actual practice, impossible. Every percussion, as Torricelli noted, must take a finite time both for the bodies to come into full contact and for them to disengage. If the force is infinite, the speed it produces must be infinite too. How will Torricelli handle a conclusion at once so logical and so clearly contrary to the facts? Surprisingly, he simply accepts it, but with some transformation of the terms used:

> If someone were to say: "when the internal *momento* of a falling body has increased by a factor of infinity, the speed also must have increased infinitely", I would say that his reasoning is sound. Because if a body had as its *momento* one pound weight when at rest, which after a period of fall would have multiplied by a factor of infinity, the speed would have had to increase by the same factor. When it had a *momento* of one pound at rest, its speed was zero; once it begins to fall, it has picked up some speed, and this, it seems to me, can be called an infinite increase. The passage from nothing to something is generally considered an infinite leap [pp. 15–16].

We now have the clue we needed. "The passage from nothing to something", that is, a change in the number of dimensions, is the element which for Torricelli defines the infinite.[9] The doctrine of indivisibles helped to make this view an accepted one in his day. Before Cavalieri's work appeared, the theory of the infinite suggested that a geometrical object, no matter how small, would have the same number of dimensions if divided up indefinitely. But the indivisible was not only infinitely small; it also had one dimension less than the original object.[10] Torricelli continued to defend this view. In the context of percussion theory, he maintained that "infinity" is not in itself a question of size, but rather of a transition from one number of dimensions to another:

> Note that when one reasons thus, and concludes that it must have an infinite speed, the critic will immediately jump to the conclusion that a speed greater by a factor of infinity than any given finite speed, is intended. But I have never said that the *momento* after a long period of fall is an infinity of times greater than that after a shorter one; on the contrary, I believe this to be false [p. 16].

Torricelli here challenges the Aristotelian position. His opponent was unlikely to be convinced, however, especially if he realized where he was being led. Discussions in which the notion of infinity figured tended to be extremely complicated in writings of those days; where they were not purely mathematical, they by no means necessarily helped the reader to comprehend the physical real. How, for example, could one reconcile these infinite *momenti* with the diversity of percussion forces one discovers in interactions that are empirically observed? Could one hold that when the force of impact in one collision is observed to be greater than that in another, the infinite *momenti* are somehow "more" in the first case, or are, at least, produced by a greater force?

To respond to this difficulty, it was no longer permissible to evade the "contested doctrine" of indivisibles. Torricelli invoked the authority of Cavalieri: mathematical reasoning must be properly applied to mechanical phenomena, he says. His motive is clear: he wishes to show that the contradiction the critic claimed to find in the consequence that one infinite would have to exceed another, is in fact no contradiction:

> I will have to appeal this case to the tribunal of the great Fra Bonaventura, before whom it would not only not be absurd that one infinite should exceed another, but would in fact be necessarily true. That all the lines of a large parallelogram should have the same relation to one another even if they are infinite; that all the circles of a large cylinder and those of a small cylinder should have the same relation to one another as do the cylinders, even if they are infinite—these are indeed among the very premises of his doctrine [p. 20].

It would be easy to show today that the problem is more complex than Torricelli realized, and that his response was subject to the inevitable hazards of such an analogy. But the value of analogies ought not be underestimated. Even though they may not be demonstrative in their force, they nevertheless provide a foothold for a truth that is still hesitating. The analogy from indivisibles relieved the strain of contradiction for Torricelli. One could respectably defend the view that the force of percussion involves infinite *momenti* without being committed to holding that all forces of percussion had to be equal, or that their effects had to be infinitely great. And these latter were the two "scandals" about the notion of a percussion-force. The first of them follows from the application to a mechanical process of modes of analysis appropriate to the geometry of indivisibles. The other had to be explained away while describing the deceleration or acceleration of bodies during impact. It is clear that Torricelli in a sense was simply transferring the difficulty from mechanics to mathematics. The doctrine of indivisibles did not provide a satisfactory method of summing infinitesimal quantities. And the description given by Torricelli of the relation between bodies at impact was not much help either. It may seem to tell us why a blow has a finite effect, but it does not permit any quantitative estimate of the interactions involved. The reason is that the indivisibles are here elements of a "model", an instrument of analysis, not a calculus. Torricelli may make his thesis about the infinity of the percussion-force seem acceptable, but he cannot calculate any consequences for specific instances. And this alone was enough to greatly reduce the significance of his theory.

The historical importance of the notion of a percussion-force

We have by now seen the two sources of the Galileo-Torricelli theory of percussion: the doctrines of accelerated motion and of indivisibles. Mathematics and mechanics were thus interwoven in its development. Why was the study of this force so important at the time?[11] One of the strongest motives was the hope of solving certain problems arising from the discussion of falling bodies. Galileo had correctly formulated the law of fall. However, the force which is responsible for falling motion is, rather paradoxically, a constant force whose effects appear to be variable. Galileo could not admit the Aristotelian doctrine of the gradual increase of weight as the speed of fall increases. He did admit, *sit venia verbo*, the increase of weight with increase of acceleration, but here a different force appeared to intervene, the force of percussion. This allowed him to regard the force of gravity as constant and to relegate all variations to the other force, that of percussion. Thus the weight of a body, its internal resistance or heaviness, could remain the same, even though the body might bring about reactions of varying intensity by its fall. Nevertheless, the elimination at one point of various difficulties, notably that of providing a causal theory of fall, did not prevent these difficulties from reappearing elsewhere. Torricelli emphasizes that the constancy of weight can be maintained if his views on percussion are conceded:

That the same body must constantly differ insofar as it is constituted by different *momenti* of force, depending on whether the fall is greater or smaller, I believe to be one of the most evident truths of the mechanical philosophy. I once marvelled at the steelyard balance where by merely moving nearer to or further from the fulcrum, equilibrium can be maintained for 4, 20, 100 pounds. The constancy of repeated experience has by now accustomed me to this marvel, which the explanatory powers of mathematics in nowise diminish. It is enough that the absolute weight of natural bodies should be invariable and that in commerce when one weighs merchandise, one weighs it, not in motion but at rest. I believe that one must concede that in the same body there may be different *momenti*, which vary in different ways, depending on the distance from the fulcrum, or the inclination of the plane or the time through which the body has fallen [pp. 20–21].

What is lacking in this text, and in the entire discussion is the notion of *mass*. The illustration of the balance, suggestive as it may be, is not altogether a happy choice. It indicates that gravity is being envisaged in a relatively static way. Its invariance is confused with passivity. Percussion by contrast is regarded as active, dynamic, varying, in a word: *causal*.

I will ask: what is the cause of downward motion of heavy bodies? It clearly cannot be other than internal gravity; and if this latter were to be invariable, the speed also would have to remain constant. But we observe the manifest increase in speed of fall. Thus it must be allowed that its cause also increases [p. 21].

In the course of fall, as the *momenti* accumulate and the time of fall increases, internal gravity becomes percussion. The conceptual apparatus which served for the study of falling bodies is put to work again for percussion. The application of the theory of indivisibles to accelerated motion is the origin of the different "infinities" of the force of percussion. But the function of this latter is to resolve the various paradoxes (especially that of the relation between gravity and speed) which appear in the description of fall, by furnishing a dynamic account to complement the kinematic one. Not only is the conceptual apparatus retained, the dimensions also remain the same. Time is important in the theory of percussion for the obvious reason that if these "conserved and multiplied" *momenti* are related to speed, they must, according to Galileo's law, be put in comparison with it.

The appearance of the dynamic and causal point of view was accompanied by a refurbishing of the conceptual framework that had been associated with the older theory of impetus. Torricelli set about this task methodically, and one can admire the mathematics that allowed him to employ notions like *indivisible, divisible momento, infinite dimension,* all of them revolutionary in their inroads on the scholastic ideas of the day, making possible the establishing of entirely new truths. But on the other hand, these new truths were not used either to pose the old problems in a new way or to state new problems. The *Lezioni accademiche* did no more than systematize a conceptual impasse; it helped to reveal the sources of this impasse but did not bring about the clarification that the learned world sought.

Percussion and impact

In his treatise, Torricelli discussed the percussion which arose during the fall of a heavy body. This he thought of as "natural" percussion, because the cause of the action is internal. From this he passed on to "the second sort of percussion which we will study under the name of 'impact' ". He treats us to some seductive metaphors:

> Impact seems properly to be the brother of percussion, and could become the father of numerous speculations. Up to this point, it has been assumed that percussion is the mutual encounter of two bodies, where one of the two is accelerated by intrinsic gravity. By *impact*, however, we mean the encounter of two bodies where one receives its movement from an *external* cause, such as the wind, animal force, fire, the archer's bow, or the like. Under this category of "artificial" percussion are included impacts due to artillery or other forms of projectile, hammer-blows (especially when they strike with a horizontal or upward motion, so that internal gravity does not operate as a cause) [p. 25].

"Impact" is defined as occurring when the accelerating force is not that of gravity. The problem of impact is conceived to be that of transmitting the force which moved the original body to the body struck. Torricelli knew—who did not?—the elements traditionally thought to play a role in impact: "quantity of matter, the species of gravity, and the shape". He set out, however, to show that this "artificial" percussion depends neither on the matter nor on the speed, but on the force and on the fashion in which it had been generated. This is the example he invites us to scrutinize:

> Suppose an immense galleon lie ten paces from the shore of a pond or quiet harbor, and that a man haul it to the shore with all his might. I am pretty sure that when it strikes the shore, no matter how slowly it has been moving, it will cause a tremor that could make a tower shake. If the same man were to drag a small skiff or a wooden table over the same distance, with the same force, through the same calm water, it would strike the bank at higher speed than did the galleon, but I do not think it would have a thousandth of the effect that the larger vessel did [p. 27].

Let us follow him in his search for the cause of this difference. It does not lie in the matter (he claims), but in the inequality between the times taken for the effort to transfer itself to the galleon and the skiff respectively. It took half an hour for the force to accumulate sufficiently in the galleon, whereas less than "four bars of music" sufficed for a fraction of the same force to accumulate in the skiff and bring it to shore. The theory is astonishing and inappropriate. The relation between the mass of the galleon and the terrestrial mass it collides with is left out of account. Torricelli considers the way in which the force accumulates instead of the action of the force. In effect, it is as though impact were not really responsible for the transmission of the force. It is interesting to see how his demonstration runs:

> The remaining possibility would be to make quantity of matter the cause. But in my view, the matter has nothing to do with this. Matter of itself is quite certainly inert, and can do no more than limit or resist operative power. Matter is nothing other than an enchanted Circean urn, serving as the receptacle of forces and moments of impetus. Force and impetus are entities so subtle, are quintessences so spiritual, that one cannot collect them in vials other than the intimate corporeal recesses of natural solids.
>
> My opinion, therefore, is that the force of the man pulling is that which causes motion and impact alike. I do not mean by this the force that he was exerting at the precise instant where the timber struck the bank; I mean all the force that had been accumulating from the beginning to the end of the motion. If someone were to ask us for how long had the man to endure the fatigue of pulling the galleon, our answer would be that to move this great structure a distance of twenty paces would require a good half-hour of continuous effort. But to drag the little wooden skiff would take no longer than the duration of four bars of music. The force which proceeds from the arms and nerves of the man who hauls steadily for half an hour, does not vanish in smoke or disappear in the air . . . it is lodged in the innermost parts of the timber and iron. There it is conserved; there it increases except for the little that is lost to the resistance of the water. It is not surprising, then, that an impact which bears in itself *momenti* of force that have been accumulated over half-an-hour, has a far greater effect than one bearing only the *momenti* that accumulate during four bars of music [pp. 27–28].

Torricelli applies to the impact produced by an external mover the principle that time is the sole measure of the force of percussion. He is not interested in mass or speed. The former is passive; the latter is only a resultant of the time. It is not because Torricelli is unaware of the concept of mass that he is misled here. He is misled because of his way of thinking of inertia and his manner of estimating force. It is clear also that in his study of artificial percussion, he does not treat of the communication of movement. What he wants to do is to show that an external force follows the same laws as does the internal force of gravity. What we have in this study of impact is not, as one would expect, a many-body analysis; only one body is thought to be relevant. His own words are interesting here:

> We have said that gravity in natural bodies never sleeps, but works continually, and that in every brief time-interval an impetus is generated which is equal to the absolute weight of the body. We have also said that these same bodies falling in air conserve these *momenti*, provided that there be no resistant solid by whose opposition they would be destroyed. The multiplication of forces in every falling body as it strikes must therefore be infinite. We have given many reasons for saying that the operation itself is a finite one, even though the power be infinite. Finally, we noted that besides the impetus

engendered in bodies by their intrinsic gravity, there is also the impetus due to external agencies. The force of impact does not depend simply upon the speed nor the quantity of matter; it depends only upon the quantity of force which has been impressed upon the body which strikes.

In discussing artificial percussion, we noted that here too the force of impact does not depend upon the quantity of matter; if it did, a 60-pound ball would have the same effect whether thrown by a man or propelled by a cannon. Nor does it depend upon the speed: a wooden table drawn by a man over calm water is moving faster, as it hits shore, than is the great galleon. Yet the slower of the two brings about a far greater impact.

We have, therefore, reason to assert that when a body is set in motion by a percussion from outside, the agency which is effective in the impact is the power imparted by the force which moved the body. One can see, then, that the force of impact will not depend upon the matter or the speed or the gravity, but only on the body's resistance to being moved. For the greater this is, the longer it takes to move the body, and thus the greater the opportunity for the motive power to give the body a continually increasing accumulation of force. That the force of impact too must be infinite is shown by the reasons already given for this in the case of natural percussion [pp. 31–32].

The audience at the Accademia della Crusca must have felt some surprise. If the same reasons held for artificial as for natural percussion, why had the distinction between them been thought so important in the first place? Is the summation of impetus, so plausible in the case of the falling body, equally plausible when the acceleration is horizontal? Are the "paradoxes of infinity" found in the analysis of percussion equally important in the exchange of "forces" between two bodies that strike one another "artificially"? The purpose of Torricelli's conferences had not been to put an end to these and similar uncertainties. They were intended to bring to completion Galileo's theory of the nature of percussion, and present it to the world as something remarkable. In this aim, they were undeniably successful.

The end of an era

The force of percussion, the communication of movement, the transformation of forces, are themes that, each of them in turn, define a phase in the historical development of the analysis of impact phenomena. Galileo is identified with the first of them, at the earliest stage of this analysis. He devoted himself to the study of the force of percussion for two reasons: on the one hand, he wished to complete his theory of fall, and on the other he wished to supplement his kinematics with a dynamics. Problems of ballistics had already rendered such a study necessary, although not much profit of this practical sort was to result for a long time yet to come.

Torricelli followed Galileo along the same road. He did not simply repeat what his master had said, but gave it more precision, more depth, and a wider relevance. The key concept of the entire theoretical structure was that of the infinity of percussion. To justify it, Torricelli adopted a model of "*momenti*" that accumulated, of mechanical "indivisibles" of impetus that are added one to another in the course of time. The summation of these produces a first infinite magnitude; it then becomes a matter of great difficulty to show how this can have a finite relation with the second infinite magnitude, the resistance of the perfectly hard body.

The obstacles in the way of Torricelli's program appear at first sight to be basically mathematical ones. But in reality, it was the notion of the force of percussion from which the whole analysis began that was the real problem. In the context of Galilean mechanics, this force is a primitive given, an unanalyzed physical entity. If one begins with such a force, one is led to a certain view of how speed or acceleration is generated. The percussion-force responsible is not a quantified entity; only its effects or its manifestations can be treated in quantitative fashion. Time is then introduced as the dimension which permits quantification of the various measures involved.

The advance which later opened the way to a properly scientific analysis of impact involved a breakdown of the primitive notion of *momento* into a complex quantity, the product of mass (or "quantity of matter" as it would still be called) and velocity. One can then bring the varying velocities into the picture, and also begin to treat the various relevant impact-properties of the bodies (hardness, elasticity . . .) as irreducible physical attributes. This radical change of view regarding the nature of percussion-force sounded the knell for the old impetus model of mechanical causality. With the abolition of the intrinsic causal quality of impetus regarded as a primitive force, one has no longer to explain by its means the generation of speed, of acceleration and of various other dynamic effects. Percussion in the new view will be nothing more than the communication of movement, and it will be manifested only by a certain sort of selection between two or more bodies. The accumulation of *momenti* over time will no longer be treated as its distinctive feature.

The revolution is a thoroughgoing one. From what did it begin? One might say that it began when artificial percussions were "naturalized", and natural percussions came to seem artificial.[12] These latter were originally linked with gravity, considered as a privileged force, one that is somehow given, not produced. To take it as privileged in this way prevented Galileo and Torricelli from generalizing the phenomena of motion properly. The unification of the facts of motion brought about by the study of impact ultimately rendered void both the distinction between "natural" and "artifical" percussions and the special attention accorded to gravity in this context. The "force" that appears in the analysis of impact is no longer a special entity, but a generalized "force" defined not by such qualities as infinity, but by the velocity and the mass of the bodies involved in the impact. The unification that resulted from this approach ruined the premises from which Galileo had tried to construct a theory of a percussion-force analogous with gravity.

The *Lezioni accademiche* may impress us today as a series of attempts to justify a useless conceptual system. The problems to which the work was directed were, in effect, abolished at the moment when percussion came to be regarded as nothing more than the communication of movement. Torricelli's demonstrations retain something of the grandeur of one of those great baroque mansions, now empty and moldering, of which one cannot help asking whether it was ever really habitable. We see them as pertaining to a definite stage in the history of the mechanics of impact; they proudly announce an advance, while mutely signaling their own demise. We cannot properly judge their influence today, because the traces of it are hard to uncover. But as an effort of the spirit, they have much to say to us; they reveal the inner working, the "conceptual laboratory" of the great school of Galileo.

NOTES

1. *Opere*, Faenza, 1919, vol. 2, pp. 3–99.

2. *Opere, 8.*

3. Page references will be given directly from *Opere*, vol. 2.

4. R. Caverni, *Storia del metodo sperimentale in Italia*, Florence, 1898, vol. 5, pp. 111–194.

5. See S. Moscovici, "Remarques sur le dialogue de Galileo: *De la force de la percussion*", 1963*.

6. ['*Momento*' is going to be a key term in this entire discussion. But its use was as yet quite imprecise. To avoid confusion with the temporal sense of the term, we shall use the Italian form throughout. *Momento* was closely linked with notions of weight and impetus in the mechanics of Galileo's day, and was the direct ancestor of four quite different concepts of later science: force (ma); momentum (mv) of a moving body; turning moment of a static force (Fd); action of a moving body (product of momentum and the distance through which it acts: mvd). The reader will notice that in Torricelli's use of the term in the various passages quoted below, all four of the later senses are foreshadowed. This introduces a distressing ambiguity into the dimensions of the quantities he is talking about. Translator's note.]

7. A. Koyré, *Études galiléennes*, 1939*.

8. See the Carugo-Geymonat edition of the *Discorsi* (1958*), pp. 810ff.

9. D. T. Whiteside, "Patterns of mathematical thought in the later 17th century", 1961*.

10. A. Koyré, "Bonaventura Cavalieri et la géométrie des continus", 1953*.

11. I have discussed this also in my "Remarques sur le dialogue . . .", *supra*.

12. See S. Moscovici, "Recherches de G. B. Baliani sur le choc des corps elastiques", *Actes II Congr. Intern. Hist. Sciences*, Florence, 1961, pp. 98–115.

23 ✻ A note on the disciples of Galileo

ANGIOLO PROCISSI

One could liken the doctrines of Galileo in natural philosophy to a "tree planted near running water, that yields its fruit in due season, and whose leaves never fade".[1] The tree struck deep roots during Galileo's own lifetime, and it was to be tended by a numerous and active group of disciples.

Galileo's two major published contributions were the *Dialogo* of 1632, which destroyed many of the central theses of Aristotelian physics, and the *Discorsi* of 1638, which became the foundation of classical mechanics. Among those who continued the work thus begun, the most important were Benedetto Castelli, Bonaventura Cavalieri, Evangelista Torricelli and Giovanni Borelli. These men extended the "Galilean" approach to many fields the master had not touched upon. In a more formal way, the same thing was done by the Accademia del Cimento in the decade from 1657 to 1667. The group associated with the Accademia can legitimately be called the "Galilean School", and the Accademia became a center from which Galilean ideas radiated far outside the bounds of Italy or the Italian language. The *Saggi di naturali esperienze fatte nell'Accademia del Cimento* of 1667 was, perhaps, the first formal treatise on experimental physics as we know it.[2] It brought to a close, and summarized, sixty of the most significant years in the development of experimental science.

The quite central significance of the achievements of the "school of

Galileo" has long been realized. Consequently, attempts were made to gather together as much as possible of the manuscript remains of the school. The *Collezione Galileiana* was begun by the last Grand Duke of Tuscany; today it consists of 347 folios of manuscripts, and is preserved in the *Biblioteca Nazionale* in Florence. The collection is divided into five parts and an Appendix. Part I (9 folios) is devoted to Vincenzo, Galileo's father. Part II (89 folios) contains the works and correspondence of Galileo himself. Part III (11 folios) covers the *"Contemporanei"* of Galileo. Six of these are devoted to the first Accademia dei Lincei, founded by Prince Federico Cesi, of which Galileo was a proud and enthusiastic member; five more contain works of Luca Valerio, Sigismondo Coccapani, Giovanni Doni and Marino Ghetaldi. Part IV (148 folios) is concerned with the *"Discepoli"*. No less than 101 of these are needed for the works of Vincenzo Viviani, Galileo's "last pupil" and literary executor; 24 folios are concerned with Torricelli, and the remainder cover: Cavalieri, Castelli, Arrighetti, V. Ranieri, C. Noferi, D. Peri, F. Michelini, N. Aggiunti and A. Nardi. Part V (49 folios) contains all available material from the Accademia del Cimento. And the collection is brought to a close by an Appendix (40 folios) with an assortment of other relevant material, and duplicates of manuscripts already in the main collection. Nearly a century of the history of science is represented in this collection, one of the world's greatest. Though all of Galileo's own works have already been published in the magnificent Edizione Nazionale, many of the others still await an editor, or have been published in poor editions.

Benedetto Castelli, 1577–1644

The first in time of Galileo's major pupils was Benedetto Castelli. Born in Brescia, he was a Benedictine monk of the Cassino community. Galileo introduces him to us in a memorable phrase: "a pupil of mine, an intelligent man, free from prejudice, as one should be".[3] It is in this same context that Galileo describes the method recommended by Castelli for the sketching of sunspots; it would seem that Castelli was the first to make use of the real image produced by a telescope on a piece of white paper.

Castelli had studied under Galileo in Padua, and moved to Florence in 1611, just after Galileo did. Two years later, he was appointed to a chair of mathematics at Pisa, where Galileo himself had begun his university career. In 1623, he left for Rome on the invitation of Pope Urban VIII, who wanted him to tutor his nephew, Taddeo Barberini. Later he became a professor of mathematics in the University of Rome, a post he retained until his death. His name appears very frequently in Galileo's correspondence; he was his close friend and frequent collaborator.

In 1613, Castelli was invited to a dinner at the home of the Grand Duke, Cosimo II. In the course of the evening, a discussion arose about the new telescopic discoveries, in particular the satellites of Jupiter, which Galileo had named after the Grand Duke the "Medicean planets". The talk moved on to Copernicanism, and one of those present asserted that it was contrary to Scripture. This led Castelli to argue that this was not the case; he convinced most of those there, except the mother of the Grand Duke, Cristina of Lorraine. When Galileo heard of the incident, he wrote just a week later a long letter to Castelli about the proper interpretation of Scripture in matters pertaining to the nature of the physical world. This letter he later amplified in a pamphlet sent as a "letter" to Cristina in order to ensure its publication. The famous *Letter to the Grand Duchess* was one of the main sparks that set off the explosive controversy in 1615, which in turn led to the banning of Copernicus' work by the Congregation of the Index, and the beginning of Galileo's woes. Through all the later years, Castelli remained Galileo's loyal supporter. On October 20, 1632, just after the fateful publication of the *Dialogo*, he wrote to Galileo from Rome: "I did my best to prevent a hasty decision from being taken against your useful and noble work . . . I said that if they deliver a hasty judgment upon an author who has written in such a modest, respectful and prudent manner, it will later become an excuse to reject them in turn, scornfully and resolutely".[4] Whatever about the "prudent manner", these were surely prophetic words.

Castelli cooperated with Galileo directly on several works. He published some notes on Galileo's early writing, the *Bilancetta* (which was not published during Galileo's lifetime), which made its contents available to the public in *Annotazioni alla Bilancetta di Galileo*.[5] The book was popular, and was often republished. He also produced a pamphlet in which the various observations made by Galileo and himself on the "Medicean planets" were organized and summarized. In several instances, he defended Galileo's work on floating bodies (1612). In the *Errori di Giorgio Coresio nella sua operetta sul galleggiare della figura*, for instance, he refuted Coresio's Aristotelian views about the relevance of shape to the buoyancy of bodies. While in the *Riposta alla opposizioni di Lodovico della Colombe e di Vincenzo di Grazia . . .* of 1615, he allowed his own name to stand on a defense of the 1612 treatise, although this defense was actually written for the most part by Galileo himself.

Castelli wrote two very important works of his own. The best-remembered of them is his *Della misura delle acque correnti* (Rome, 1628), which has often been described as the first work on hydrodynamics. He gives a formula for the flow of liquid in a pipe. No critical edition of this work is as yet available. In his posthumous *Opusculi filosofici* (Bologna, 1669), an assortment of physical problems is discussed. Among them, one finds a very ingenious study (the *Mattonata*) of the effect of color on absorption of radiant energy. He painted one part of a brick white and another black, and noted the difference in temperature gradients when the brick was placed in the sun. In a letter to Galileo (June 27, 1637), he tells him of the experiment, and relates an amusing anecdote about the reaction of an Aristotelian colleague. A selection of Castelli's writings was published by Antonio Favaro; his correspondence has unfortunately not been preserved.[6] A one- or two-volume complete edition of his works would be of great value.

Bonaventura Cavalieri, 1598–1647

The most spectacular result of Castelli's years of teaching in Pisa was assuredly his great pupil, Cavalieri, who belonged to the order of the *Gesuati.*[7] The order was later suppressed in 1668 by Pope Clement IX, which partly explains why many documents pertaining to Cavalieri have perished. Cardinal Federico Borromeo, founder of the *Biblioteca Ambrosiana* in Milan, recommended Cavalieri to Galileo, who subsequently wrote of him: "I think sincerely that few men (perhaps, indeed, no one) from the time of Archimedes on have attained a greater knowledge of geometry. . . . He has discovered a new method for the study of mathematical truths; by it, he proves in a shorter manner many of the theorems of Archimedes and of other mathematicians." At the time Galileo said these words Cavalieri was, in fact, preparing his great work, the *Geometria indivisibilium continuorum nova quadam ratione promota*, which was published in 1635 in Bologna, where Cavalieri taught mathematics.[8] The work was a crucial one in the early development of the notion of "indivisibles", which ultimately led to the construction of the infinitesimal calculus of Newton and Leibniz.[9] His *Exercitationes geometricae sex* (1647) was a continuation of the same topic. A theorem first proved by Cavalieri is still found in today's textbooks: "If two solids have equal altitudes, and if the cross-sections made by planes parallel to the bases and at equal distances from them have a certain ratio, then the volumes of the solids have the same ratio." He also developed a formula for the area of a spherical triangle. Other works of his include a treatise on plane and spherical trigonometry, the *Directorium generale uranometricum* (1632), and another on conic sections, *Specchio ustorio* (1632), as well as some pamphlets on astronomy and on trigonometry. As it happens, the most important of his mathematical ideas appear rather in his correspondence. His letters to Galileo are easily available in the Edizione Nazionale, but his much more important correspondence with Giannantonio Rocca (1607–1656) can be found only in an edition of 1785 which is nowadays very hard to find.[10]

Evangelista Torricelli, 1608–1647

Surprisingly little is known of Torricelli. We do not know where he was born. He died at thirty-nine, like Pascal and Leopardi. He is buried somewhere in the basilica of San Lorenzo in Florence, but no inscription identifies his grave. He studied under Castelli in Rome, and was fortunate enough to work with Galileo during the latter's last years. He succeeded to Galileo's post as Mathematician to the Grand Duke. During his lifetime, only one of his works appeared, his *Opera geometrica* (1644). In a letter the following year to G. B. Doni, we find Marin Mersenne saying: "To us his incredible genius seems near miraculous".[11] After his death, his manuscript remains were taken over by Viviani, but they were published only in 1919, and in a poor edition.[12] He had probably the best mathematical mind of all Galileo's disciples. Despite his early death, he treated brilliantly of such crucial topics as curved indivisibles, and the extension of integration to functions which include infinite values within the range to be integrated. His best-remembered achievement is, of course, the *esperienza dell'argento vivo*, the barometer experiment he suggested to Viviani; he was much interested in the crucial problem of the possibility of producing vacua, and also wrote much on the causes of winds.

Vincenzo Viviani, 1622–1703

Viviani liked to describe himself as "Galileo's last pupil". He spent much time in Arcetri, and was of much service to the old scientist in the last few years of his life. He inherited from him his vast collection of unpublished materials and letters. Viviani followed Torricelli as Mathematician to the Grand Duke, and also taught mathematics at the Accademia delle Arti del Disegno in Florence.

His voluminous works fall into four categories: mathematics, history of mathematics, matters concerning Galileo, and practical hydraulics. (It will be noted how well the range of interests of the pupils reflected the versatility of the master.) His principal works in mathematics were the following. In 1674, he published *Quinto libro degli Elementi d'Euclide* (subtitled: "A general theory of proportions, developed along Galilean lines"). In it, there were some brief previously unpublished pieces by Galileo, originally intended to form the Fifth Day of the *Discorsi*. They appear in modern editions of this latter. In 1676, he brought out a book of mathematical recreations: *Disporto geometrico;* there followed: *Enodatio problematum universis geometris praepositorum a D. Claudio Comiers; Elementi piani e solide d'Euclide* (1690), an excellent textbook, containing Books I–VI, XI, XII of the *Elements*, which went through many editions; *Aenigma geometricum* (1692); *Formazione e misura di tutti i cieli* (1692). His knowledge of Euclidean geometry was very wide, and many of his shorter pieces on it still remain unpublished.

He was very interested in the early history of mathematics, and made an ingenious attempt to re-create the lost Book V of the *Conics* of Apollonius (concerning maxima and minima) in his *De maximis et minimis geometrica divinatio* (1659). (Books V–VII are known even still only through an Arabic translation.) More than forty years later, he did the same sort of thing for a lost text by Aristaeus in *De locis solidis secunda divinatio geometrica* (1701). He did a translation into Italian of Archimedes' works, which was never published.[13]

Viviani had in his possession the entire Galileo manuscript collection, and had determined to do a major biography of his master based on this and on his own recollections. But he never succeeded in carrying through this project (which would have so greatly helped later historians); he contented himself with a brief and not always reliable biographical sketch, which was not published until after his death (in the 1718 edition of Galileo's *Opere*). In addition he, like Castelli, did a commentary on Galileo's unpublished *Bilancetta* (the hydrostatic balance). And he wrote an addition to the second part of the *Discorsi* of Galileo, called *Trattato delle resistenze*. Like Castelli also, he wrote on hydraulic engineering: *Discorso intorno al difendersi da' riempimenti e dalle corrosioni de fiumi* (on erosion); an essay on the protection of Pisa against flooding from the river and many other similar works. A volume of his correspondence, containing 680 letters, is due soon for publication.[14]

Other important writers influenced by Galileo may also be listed: Vincenzo Ranieri (1606–1648), who carried on Galileo's observations on the satellites of Jupiter; Orazio Ricasoli Rucellai (1604–1674), who wrote more than seventy philosophical dialogues of Platonic inspiration; Francesco Redi (1626–1696), the great biologist, who extended Galilean methods into medicine and biology; Giovanni Alfonso Borelli (1608–1679), an important mathematician, who urged the use of mathematics in biological research.[15] All in all, they were a group worthy of their great teacher, and the best testimony to the enduring quality of his genius.

NOTES

1. Psalms, *1*, 3.

2. This was reprinted in Pisa (1957*) in honor of the third centenary of the foundation of the Accademia.

3. *Opere, 5,* p. 136.

4. *Opere, 14,* p. 401.

5. It may be found, for instance, in the Alberi edition of Galileo's works, 1855, *14*, pp. 209–210.

6. I found five letters in the *Archivio di Stato* at Siena, but they are of no scientific importance.

7. Founded by Giovanni Colombini in Siena three centuries before, and not to be confused with the Jesuits.

8. Reprinted 1653. It has recently (1940) been translated into Russian.

9. See the article by M. G. Sittignani: "Sulla geometria degli indivisibili di Cavalieri", *Periodica Matem., 13*(4), 1933, 266–288. [See Boyer's essay elsewhere in this volume.]

10. I have recently found some unpublished letters which are now being made available in print.

11. In an unpublished letter I came across recently in the *Biblioteca Marucelliana* in Florence. The whole passage reads: "Numquid etiam urgebit vestra dominatio magnum vestrum Torricellium, ut varia qua mente gerit, et forte scripsit, tandem promat? Nobis certe propemodum miraculo est stupendum illius ingenium."

12. Ettore Bortolotti (1866–1947) has been the leading commentator on Torricelli's writings in recent times.

13. See my note on these in *Boll. Unione Matem. Ital.*, 8, 1953, 74–82.

14. G. de Santillana, E. Torelli and I have worked on this edition. Ten thousand other letters connected with the early Accademia del Cimento still await publication.

15. In 1964, a Committee was formed to further the publication of the writings of Galileo's disciples, on a scale comparable with that of Galileo's own Edizione Nazionale.

NAME INDEX

Abelé, Jean, 89
Abu'l-Barakat, 43
Aggiunti, N., 450
Albert of Saxony, 9, 11, 87, 339, 361
Albertus Magnus, 91
Alexander of Aphrodisias, 8, 123
Allexandre, Jacques, 292
Allodi, F., 286, 292
Alquié, F., 385–386
Amant, (Jean?), 288
Amici, G. B., 203
Ammanati, Giulia, 52
Ammannati, Bartolomeo, 120, 148
Anthemius, 206
Antonini, Daniello, 261–262, 279
Apollonius, 150, 453
Archimedes, 48, 53, 75–76, 78–79, 93, 96–97, 108, 110, 118, 121, 171, 206, 233, 234–235, 238–239, 241–243, 248–249, 253, 295, 300–301, 303–304, 313, 319, 352–353, 358–360, 379, 392, 419, 452
Arentino, Pietro, 148
Ariosto, Lodovico, 128, 145, 147–150, 152–153, 156, 158
Aristarchus, 183, 204
Aristotle, 5, 7–9, 13–15, 18, 20, 24–25, 32, 36, 44, 54–55, 59, 70, 75–76, 79, 87–89, 92–99, 102–105, 108, 110–115, 120, 122–123, 127–129, 131, 136–137, 144, 155, 165–173, 177, 182–185, 205, 239, 250, 298–299, 302, 306–307, 313–314, 316, 340, 350, 352–

353, 355, 359, 361–362, 367, 369–370, 380–382, 422, 431
Arrighetti, Niccolo, 133, 450
Aubrey, John, 425, 430
Augustine, Saint, 33, 344–347, 360
Avempace, 8, 46, 92, 336, 381
Averroes, 91–92, 123, 127, 239
Avicenna, 43, 88, 123, 261, 289
Azarquiel (al-Zarqālī), 191

Bacon, Francis, 5, 168, 253, 260, 386, 409, 413, 419, 422–423, 425
Bacon, Roger, 94, 360–361
Badovere, Jacques (Giovanni Badoer), 57, 264, 274
Balbi, Bartolomeo, 285
Balestri, Domenico, 287
Baliani, Giovan Battista, 174–175, 287, 374, 448
Banfi, Antonio, 132
Barberini, Maffeo (Urban VIII), 59, 62
Bargett, 428
Baroccio, Simone, 262
Baron, Hans, 125, 136
Barrow, Isaac, 411–412, 414
Bartoli, Giovanni, 275–276
Battista, Giovanni, see Benedetti, Giambatista
Bedini, Silvio A., 206, 253, 290, 292, 337
Beeckman, Isaac, 74, 86
Bell, A. E., 362, 364

SUBJECT INDEX

acceleration, 8, 14, 28, 44, 74, 116–117, 164, 171, 226, 317, 330–336, 357, 436–439, 442
antiquarianism in Florence, 125–127
Aristotelianism, 13–14, 20, 24–25, 31, 32, 69–70, 80, 108–114, 123, 127–128, 160–170, 298, 302, 306, 362, 380–381
Augustine: hermeneutics, 33–34; philosophy of mathematics, 345–347
authority, Florentine attitude to, 123–129

balance, 327–328
Bible and natural science, 33–35, 60
Bilancetta, La, 53, 319

Calculationes, 9, 11, 17–18, 95
Christina, Letter to the Grand Duchess, 33–35, 60
comets, theory of, 61, 186–187
color and heat absorption, 80
comic stylist, Galileo as, 150–153
compass, military and geometric, 56, 236–238, 253, 262–268
conceptual analysis, 11–15, 342
Copernican astronomy, Galileo's adoption of, 20–24, 165–173, 182–189
cosmogony: Galileo's, 209–227; Newton's, 218–224
curve, rectification of, 239–240
cycloid, 242, 254

De motu, 7, 9–11, 14, 24, 30, 54–55, 171, 182, 319–335
De motu locali, 22, 164–169
demonstration, science as, 31–35, 371–378, 380–381, 386
Descartes: theory of knowledge, 304, 312–313, 386, 389; theory of science, 378–380
Dialogo, 24–36, 41, 62, 70, 74, 165–166, 169, 192, 227, 407–408, 412, 422–423, 428
Discorsi, 28–31, 63–64, 74, 76, 163–166, 227, 311, 316–320, 326

education, Galileo's, 142–145, 234–235, 241
experiment, role of, in Galileo's work, 11–15, 18–19, 26, 32, 37, 47, 50, 54–56, 65, 69, 72, 80, 170–171, 209, 304–312, 315–338, 357, 362–363, 369, 373–374, 377, 398–399, 434–435

falling bodies, law of, 8, 9, 15, 18, 22, 26, 46, 72–74, 99–102, 108–111, 226–228, 296, 308–310, 316–326, 331–333, 411, 442; time-squared law of, 11–12, 18–19, 22, 46, 174, 316–317
Floating bodies, Discourse on, 59–60, 80, 353
force, nature of, 12, 27, 30–31, 50, 169, 173, 447
Florence, 119–132
forms, latitude of, 233–234, 361–362